AFRICAN HISTORY

AFRICAN HISTORY

Philip Curtin
THE JOHNS HOPKINS UNIVERSITY

Steven Feierman
THE UNIVERSITY OF WISCONSIN, MADISON

Leonard Thompson
YALE UNIVERSITY

Jan Vansina
THE UNIVERSITY OF WISCONSIN, MADISON

LONGMAN
London and New York

Longman Group UK Limited
Longman House, Burnt Mill, Harlow,
Essex, CM20 2JE, England
and Associated Companies throughout the world

*Published in the United States of America
by Longman Inc., New York*

First published 1978
Tenth impression 1992

ISBN 0-582-64663-4

Printed in Malaysia by PJB

ACKNOWLEDGMENTS

We wish to thank the following for permission to use their material in preparation
of the maps:

Page 40: From R. J. Harrison Church, *Africa and the Islands* (London: Longman, 1964),
p. 120. © Longman Group Ltd.

Pages 46, 59, 69: Adapted from *A World History*, Second Edition, by William H. McNeill.
Copyright © 1971 by Oxford University Press, Inc. Reprinted by permission.

Page 56: From William H. McNeill, *The Rise of the West: A History of the Human
Community* (London and Chicago: University of Chicago Press, 1963), p. 334. ©
1963 by The University of Chicago. All rights reserved.

Pages 64, 104, 105, 184, 196: From J. D. Fage, *An Atlas of African History* (London:
Edward Arnold, 1958), pp. 10, 13, 14, 16, 19.

Page 109: From Margaret Shinnie, *Ancient African Kingdoms* (London: Edward Arnold,
1965), pp. 44, 52, 57, 69.

Pages 236 and 241: From J. F. Ade Ajayi and Ian Espie, *A Thousand Years of West
African History* (London and Ibadan: Ibadan University Press, 1965), pp. 164–165,
310. By permission of the Ibadan University Press, Ibadan, Nigeria.

Page 245: From J. F. Ajayi and Michael Crowder, *History of West Africa* (London:
Longman, 1972–74), vol. 1, p. 272. © Longman Group Ltd.

Pages 279, 280, 420: From Roland Oliver, ed. *The Cambridge History of Africa, vols. 3
and 4. c. 1050–1600,* (Cambridge: Cambridge University Press, 1977 and 1975), pp.
600, 387, 326.

Pages 307, 314: From John E. Flint, ed., *The Cambridge History of Africa, vol. 5,
c. 1790–1870* (Cambridge: Cambridge University Press, 1976), pages 320, 354.

Page 334: From Bernard Lewis, *The Emergence of Turkey* (London: Oxford University
Press, 1961). By permission of Oxford University and the Royal Institute of International Affairs.

Page 412: From Czeslaw Jesman, *The Ethiopian Paradox* (London: Oxford University
Press, 1963), p. 50.

Page 415: From *Histoire de Madagascar,* Fourth Edition, by Hubert Deschamps, 1972, p.
155. © Berger-Levrault.

Page 515: From L. H. Gann and Peter Duignan, *Colonialism in Africa* (Cambridge:
Cambridge University Press, 1975), vol. 4, p. 326.

Preface

AFRICAN HISTORY has come of age, thanks to a quarter century of detailed, innovative, and laborious research by a new generation of historians. Some were Africans pioneering in the effort to write new and unbiased history of their own countries. Others were foreigners trying to shake off the ethnocentric attitudes that were all too common when European and American historians tried to write the history of other peoples. Both Africans and foreigners tried very consciously to reconsider the history of a continent that was only then beginning to emerge into independence after a period of alien rule.

The growing maturity of African history is again reflected in the fact that two multivolume, multiauthored reference works are beginning to appear: the *General History of Africa,* under the auspices of UNESCO, and the *Cambridge History of Africa.* When these series have been completed, we shall have two extensive syntheses of the subject, the former embodying an essentially African viewpoint, the latter reflecting the views of mainly British scholars.

We hope that this book will help to mark African history's coming of age in another way. It, too, is a general history of Africa, though much shorter in scope. We have designed it as a textbook for courses in African history, but even more we have set out to create a new synthesis, different from the main lines of African history as they were understood in the past. And we have aimed for a broader conception of the content appropriate to a general history of any continent — a broader understanding of the nature of history, for example, than is customarily found in textbooks of American or European history. We are less interested in events and more interested in patterns of historical change. We are less interested in the deeds of the great than we are in the culture and behavior of ordinary people. With this in mind, we intentionally give less than the usual emphasis to political history and more to social, economic, and intellectual trends. Because we would like to say something significant about peoples' changing ways

of life, we have introduced more than the usual concern for the kinds of problems and solutions dealt with by anthropologists.

We are also consciously seeking to look at African history from an African
point of view, a tendency found in most African historiography of the past
twenty years. But an African point of view is not easy to come by, even for
historians of Africa who were born and raised there. In fact, there are many
different African points of view toward African history. Most of the existing
text books written by Africans for African schools and universities are, as perhaps they should be, centered on a particular country or region. The African
history normally taught in Egypt barely extends beyond the Sudan and Ethiopia.
African history of South Africa only just takes in Zimbabwe. The African history
taught in francophone and anglophone tropical Africa carries strong vestiges of
the educational system that formed the intellectual elite. Each of these "African
histories" is different because each asks the implicit question, "how did our particular African society come to be as it is today?" That is a proper question. As
historians from outside Africa, our implicit question is somewhat different. It is,
"how did the societies on the African continent come to be as they are today?"
We hope that our perspective of distance may help our perspective in understanding, and that our respect for and sympathy with Africans from many parts
of the continent may help to overcome the fact that none of us is African in
birth or education. This implies a conscious effort on our parts to rise, if possible,
above all ethnocentrism — African or Western — to look at African history in
a way that may help us to see what — even at our present and still-incomplete
degree of understanding — the African experience over time can tell us about
the human experience at large.

The first three quarters of this book are organized by regions — North
Africa including the Nilotic Sudan, East Africa from Ethiopia to Madagascar,
Africa south of the Zambezi, Equatorial Africa (essentially Angola north through
Zaïre to the edge of the Sahara in Chad), and the conventional West Africa between the Sahara and the Gulf of Guinea. These regions are far from equal in
either size or importance. The recorded data for North Africa exceed those for
the rest of the continent several times over, especially for early millennia. West
Africa is far more populous than any of the other four regions. Southern Africa
has had the most rapid economic development recently, hence the greatest weight
of wealth and power; and contemporary challenges to the gross economic and
political inequities in the region might warrant more emphasis on South Africa's
recent past. We have nevertheless given these regions approximately equal attention in most time periods, to increase the variety of historical circumstances
examined. A lightly populated and comparatively poor region like Equatorial
Africa, for example, contains many different societies whose historical experiences were markedly different from those elsewhere. Our use of a regional organization, however, may suggest that the regions were internally more homogeneous and more sharply divided from one another than they were in fact. This is

one reason why precise regional boundaries are not always carried over from one chapter to the next.

North Africa is a special case and a long-standing problem for the organization of historical knowledge. Since the ninth century A.D., it has been part of Islamic civilization, whose main centers lay in western Asia. But it is also part of the African continent, illuminating similarities and contrasts among African countries, especially in the period of the colonial impact. Other aspects of sub-Saharan history — like the rise and penetration of Islam — require knowledge of North Africa and even of Arabia before they can be clearly understood. The problem, quite simply, is that North Africa belongs to two cultural worlds, one related to the Sudanic belt across the Sahara, the other reaching out to the broader world of Islam (which incidentally included more of sub-Saharan Africa as well after the twelfth century or so). Our effort here is an admitted compromise. Space limitations make it impossible to treat North Africa within the full context of Muslim civilization. Yet we have included North Africa as an essential stepping-stone toward understanding Africa's place in world history. To put it in another way, we have tried to deal with North Africa's part in the African world, realizing that we may well have slighted the perspective of North Africa within the world of Islam.

Periodization is another organizational problem without consensual guidelines. One part of the periodization problem is a search for the real watersheds of history, where the style of change seems to alter sharply — as it did with the beginning of agriculture, the coming of the iron age, or of industrialization. Historians of Europe and Africa alike sometimes spend a good deal of effort locating such dividing lines, and quarreling about whose lines are most significant. We have divided our book at about 1500, 1780, and 1880, but these are chosen purely for convenience — we do not claim them as true watersheds. Even where they may appear validly to mark off historical periods for some part of the continent, they will not be accurate for all.

Periodization raises another kind of conscious decision, ratios of time to printed words. Starting with an index of 1 for the period before 1500, the index of pages to centuries raises to about 10 for 1500–1780, 25 for the precolonial century, and 30 for the colonial and postcolonial period. The general pattern of greater detail for the more recent past is common and understandable. Some may wonder, however, why the treatment of the precolonial century is nearly as detailed as that of the colonial period itself. This decision is based on the fact that Africa was so overshadowed by Europe in the colonial period that the internal dynamics of recent change in Africa might have been lost unless we gave special emphasis to the period just before the European impact became overwhelming.

The colonial and postcolonial period is treated in a series of topical chapters, each dealing with the whole continent, rather than according to the regional pattern set in the first three-quarters of the book. This decision followed from our original intention to look for patterns rather than detailed events; these patterns became Africa-wide with colonial rule. We have written a general, analytic overview of this very complex period in African history, recognizing that readers who want more political detail can find it elsewhere.

Although all authors contributed something to most chapters, Jan Vansina was broadly responsible for Equatorial Africa and for chapters 1 and 18, Leonard Thompson for southern Africa in all periods, Steven Feierman for East Africa and chapter 19, and Philip Curtin for North and West Africa and for chapters 15, 16, 17, and 20. Curtin also served as general editor. As to the assistance we have had from others, the cliché about our debts being too numerous to mention is literally true. We have avoided detailed recognition of our authorities in footnotes, but insofar as this book moves out in new directions, it is because of the heritage we have all received from the painstaking research of the numerous scholars in Africa and abroad who have created a new African history in the past quarter-century.

Contents

8
EQUATORIAL AFRICA
BEFORE THE NINETEENTH CENTURY   249

9
SOUTHERN AFRICA TO 1795   277

10
SOUTHERN AFRICA (1795–1870)   304

11
NORTH AFRICA IN THE SHADOW OF EUROPE
(c. 1780–1880)   332

Maps

Chapter 1
The Roots
of African Cultures

VEILED FIGURES on the glistening terraces of a *kasbah* in Tunisia, a forlorn little group in the eternity of the Kalahari, chatting away around a smoldering fire. These two ways of spending an evening in very different surroundings are symbolic of the great variety of cultures that flourished in Africa until recent times — hundreds of cultures in endless variations, like so many different flowers in the same bed. Yet despite the differences, all have grown from humble and very similar origins, and underneath all the variation common themes can still be discerned, themes and patterns that go back to the hallowed past. The unity, then, derives from the roots, for these African cultures have grown up in the surroundings where they flourished for thousands and thousands of years. Ever since the first pebble tools were invented, Africa has been inhabited. For a million years — perhaps two — cultures have developed there, growing slowly in complexity, very slowly at first as the societies of which they were an expression slowly increased in size.

Yet the *history* of Africa does not go back through the uncounted ages of the first developments. The time scales involved are so immense that the chronology of Stone Age archaeology is not really the chronology of historians. Change in these early times was so slow that even a small deviation in the pattern of shaping a hand axe could take many generations to become accepted. Because history deals with change, it is not at ease with the story of human infancy. In practice, African historians seem to have agreed that their best starting point is the food-producing revolution, the period when agriculture, stock raising, and, later, ironworking were introduced. These changes in people's livelihood made them much more independent from their environment than before. Earlier, when the population merely hunted or gathered, the nomadic way of life and the need to keep each community down to a size related to the availability of game and wild plants had stunted the possibilities for further growth. Still, it has been proven that these gatherers and hunters found their food without strenuous effort, so that the desire to augment the food supply cannot have been a major reason for the switch to agriculture. Only the desire to stop roaming about, and later the wish to live in larger communities, can explain the switch from the relatively easy life of the gatherer and hunter to the more arduous existence of the cultivator.

Once people became sedentary in large numbers, the communities grew and food had to be produced rather than gathered. As environment gradually became less of a dictating agency, cultural and social change could increase, leading to greater and greater variety in cultures. A history of society and a history of culture now become meaningful.

We shall begin with the tale of how the major varieties of African ways of life unfolded. Here is a sketch of the gatherers' roaming life and how people made the shift to agriculture and husbandry, how metallurgy was introduced, how the Bantu-speaking peoples came as a tide that swept over almost half the continent, and how the first states arose. The story runs from 6000 B.C. to 1000 A.D., a period seven times longer than that covered in all the other chapters of this book.

THE LATE STONE AGE WAY OF LIFE:
HUNTERS AND GATHERERS

By 6000 B.C., all Africa still lived in the Stone Age, but most of the continent had entered the most refined period of that age, the Late Stone Age. Hunters and gatherers had adapted to the environments in which they lived, producing basically two ways of life, one an adaptation to the forest, such as pygmy hunters still show, and the other an adaptation to the open grasslands, a tradition to which the Bushmen or San in southern Africa still bear witness.

Direct evidence about life in the savanna during this period can still be found. One example is the remains of a camp that flourished around 2300 B.C. at Gwisho near the Kafue River in Zambia. The inhabitants belonged to the so-called Wilton stone culture. Like the other Late Stone Age cultures, the Wilton is characterized by a greater number of tool types than its predecessors. This variety indicates that artifacts were increasingly specialized for particular uses. In addition, the Wilton people had a developed bone industry with items such as awls, rubbing tools, spoonlike instruments, ornaments, and composite arrows. The dog had been domesticated, bows and arrows were used for the chase, and large bone points may have served as spearheads. These people also made wooden tools, such as digging sticks to uproot edible roots, and they used shells as implements. They worked skins and used natural pigments. Gwisho does not show it, but the Wilton people were responsible for the magnificent rock art of southern Africa. Their descendants today are the San.

The living on the Kafue flats was good. Wildlife seems to have thrived as it did in the nineteenth century, when the environment was exactly the same. This we know from pollen analysis. The Gwisho hunters supplemented their meat diet by foraging for roots, seeds, nuts, and berries as they came into season. At the site some of these vegetable remains were not easily recognized by archaeologists. But it is a remarkable comment on the unchanging character of Late Stone Age life that a twentieth-century San or Bushman, brought up from the south, was able to recognize all these without exception, to describe their uses and the seasons when they could be found, and to explain the function of all the tools found in situ! The people of this camp used basketry, built wind screens for housing, and may have used mats for bedding. Evidence of lean-tos or houses was not found there, but because the seasonal rains were (and still are) heavy at times, shelters must have been available.

It seems fair to assume that Gwisho was the focal point of a corporately owned hunting territory of relatively large size. There are in fact four sites at Gwisho that may reflect individual family lodgings of the same band at the same time. The evidence shows a truth that was already assumed: hunting bands have to remain small to exist. Although they sometimes numbered as many as 100 in wetter areas and even 300 in some wet season camps, usually the band would not include more than 50 (or nowadays in the Kalahari, 20) people. With such small numbers, leadership posed a problem. Obviously there could be no organized role of chieftainship, for the chief would soon have quarreled with all his followers in turn. Face to face relationships of so few people for a whole lifetime simply mean that people know each other too well to obey the same person always. In addition, a leader could not arbitrate because his decision would first hurt one member, then another, and soon he would find himself isolated and ostracized. It is likely therefore that then, as now with almost all hunting and gathering peoples of the world, decisions were communal, offenders were punished by banishment or by beating, and mutual help was the cardinal value of the camp.

The people in a camp would belong to a single *kinship group,* a collection of persons related to each other by descent, which was calculated in a variety of ways, a group called a kindred or bilateral group by anthropologists. They would find wives to marry by a straight exchange of one of their girls for a girl of another group. All of these consequences in social and political structure may seem to be speculative, but they are not. The small size of the community leads by necessity to this organization of life.

At Gwisho the hunting itself may have been communal, because the animals were all big mammals such as zebra, buffalo, antelope, and occasionally even a rhinoceros. Fully grown elephants, however, seem to have been avoided and smaller animals were not very important in the diet. Despite the proximity of an excellent river and marshes, few fish or marsh antelopes were eaten and then only in one of the four sites. But big game must have been plentiful and close to the camps, because the hunters carried the whole carcasses of the animals home for butchering. From the tools that remain we can see that these hunters must have been a little bit bigger and stronger than the San of today, perhaps because their diet was so much richer. Yet despite their success in hunting, most of the food supply may have come from gathering edible vegetable matter.

In the forest no sites have survived and we can only extrapolate from the present-day life of the pygmies. This, however, is especially difficult because pygmies have adapted themselves quite well to the presence of Negro farmers, changing their way of life as a result. Still, we can see once again that the food quest determined the size of the band and its nomadic character. Today there are minimum and maximum numbers per settlement for hunters. As with the hunters of the grasslands, edible roots, leaves, stems, and fruits now form 75 percent of the diet, and the whole pattern — a social structure based on the bilateral kinship group, marriage by exchange, absence of leadership, communal decisions, and sanctions in social life — is present here as well. So too is the supreme value given to sharing, because only mutual help could equalize the difference between successful and unsuccessful days for the individual hunter and preserve the ill from starvation.

A more efficient technique of hunting may lead to less social flexibility. An illustration is the practice of hunting with nets. Bands that hunt with nets need at least thirty members but cannot exceed fifty. Bands that hunt with bow and arrow also have an upper limit of fifty members, but they can exploit their environment successfully with fewer than thirty members. The technical efficiency of the net is offset by the need to keep community size within narrow limits. Bow and arrow hunters can split up a camp to meet unforeseen circumstances, such as a major quarrel or simply a scarcity of game. The different forms of hunting and gathering all over Africa in the Late Stone Age must have been limited in similar ways, by conflicts between relative social flexibility and the inflexible requirement for food.

By the nineteenth century A.D., very few hunters and gatherers were left in Africa. The equatorial forest sheltered pygmies, and San were still found in many parts of southern Africa. These people had once covered the whole southern part of the continent as far north as the mouth of the river Zaïre and at least central Tanzania (just as the pygmies seem to have occupied southern margins of the forest, where they mixed with San — and possibly further north as well, since the dwarf brought back for Pharaoh Pepi II (c. 2600 B.C.) may well have been a pygmy!). They were also the aboriginal population of at least the western fringes of the East African lake region. Elsewhere in East Africa, the hunting populations probably looked more like the Ndorobo of Kenya, who were still roaming the plains and hills by 1900 A.D. Though larger than the San or pygmies, they were still of slender build, reminding one of the Ethiopian Amhara on a smaller scale. Other hunters, collectively called *mahalbi* after their Hausa name, or known as *daramde* in the lands between Chad and Nile, were spread as outcast populations among the other peoples from the big bend of the Niger eastwards into Ethiopia.

In the nineteenth century A.D. all of these had adapted to a symbiosis with their agricultural or pastoral neighbors, with the possible exception of some *gorane* (Teda-Daza) hunters in northern Chad. And their way of life had no doubt changed considerably with the major changes in flora and fauna in and around the Sahara. The Late Stone Age hunters there lived in a relatively lush environment and hunted the big mammals in the same way as the Gwisho people did. They too left colorful records of their way of life in rock paintings and rock engravings dating from 7000 years ago and more.

FISHERMEN IN THE LATE STONE AGE

A picture of Africa as peopled only by hunters and gatherers by 6000 B.C. would not be quite correct. There were already some sedentary populations of fishermen as early as 7000 B.C. The excavations at Ishango on Lake Mobutu (formerly Lake Albert) and at Baringo on Lake Turkana have uncovered beautiful and efficient barbed harpoons for catching fish, and also net weights, showing that no doubt nets too were used. And along with nets one may surmise that dugouts, paddles, weirs, and most of the other later fishing gear had been developed or were being developed. With all this equipment and the resources of lakes, oceans, and rivers, settled life became possible and desirable. Nevertheless, some fishermen would eventually have to move out for two or three months in a dry season to make the most of favorable conditions for fishing, especially on broad, flat rivers such as the Congo and many of its effluents, or the upper Zambezi or parts of the Niger.

The fishing settlements could grow much larger than those of the hunters without danger of falling short of food and could have permanent houses, to be improved as the generations went by. So sedentary villages grouping from 100 to 1000 people came into being, and with them village life. Obviously a social structure based on the informal kindred was no longer suited to such settlements. Specialization of social roles became necessary and fishermen began experimenting with other formulas. Time and again unilineal principles of descent must have been discovered. By counting only certain *actual* relatives as *legal* relatives in matters of inheritance, succession, marriage, and other arrangements, it became possible to found groups that were based on kinship but could endure for a long time. These kin groups could then be used as building blocks to provide a structure for social and political relations. It was found that by tracing common descent only through males or only through females such permanent groups resulted. These are called *unilineal descent groups,* because only one line of descent counts. When only descent through men was recognized the group was *patrilineal,* and when only through women, *matrilineal.* Now obviously this system did not mean that people would no longer recognize other relatives as kin, but only that it excluded other categories from legal consideration in some matters.

Along with the discovery of the unilineal lineage, or clan, came the realization that one man could represent the whole descent group in dealings with other groups, and such men were invested with specialized social and political roles. The distribution of labor and status that had formerly been restricted to a division by sex now became more elaborate. Associated with the development of specialized leaders was an evolution in cultural values and in religious outlook. Religious specialists may have emerged. The development of kinship structures provoked a parallel development of supernatural sanctions based on ancestor worship. The need to maintain a balance between esprit de corps within a group and peaceful relations between groups found expression in beliefs and rituals that sanctioned group cohesion. Fear of sanctions for noncooperation may well have been the crucial element in the group's solidarity. Thus, belief in witchcraft developed. People could conceive of the power of witches as a quality possessed by antisocial elements within their group that allowed them to kill other members without having to use any visible artifact to do so. Accusations of witchcraft usually signal intragroup pressures and competition for leadership, but the fear of being accused, and perhaps killed as a consequence, contributed also to group solidarity.

Sorcery was tied more to intergroup relations than witchcraft was. A sorcerer was a person believed to kill enemies by using a magical charm or even an actual poison. By and large it was thought that this behavior went on between members of different groups rather than within a group. The status of a sorcerer was therefore much more ambivalent than that of the witch, for he could protect his group by attacking outsiders. On the other hand most sorcerers disrupted intergroup relations and harmed peaceful collaboration.

All of this must have taken generations and generations to develop. No one has recorded the many trials and errors that preceded the evolution of the successful patterns of social structure that finally emerged. Fishing communities between 7000 and 2000 B.C., however, must have been a major laboratory where social patterns for sedentary life could be tested and elaborated. When sedentary life became common as people turned to agriculture, the models were there. Only in this way can we explain how the immense diversity and the amazing efficacy of the different African sociopolitical systems came into being.

Later, when most people had become agricultural, the fishermen of the rivers still played a major role in African history. They moved up and down the streams and rivers according to the seasons and they traded with inland groups, exchanging fish and pottery for cereals or root crops. Later they began buying products from one group and selling them to another. As commercial intermediaries they also carried news of the outside world to each of their customers, breaking down cultural isolation. They carried the information and goods that led to much diffusion of ideas, behavior, and artifacts and stimulated the growth of the different civilizations.

By the nineteenth century A.D. many fishermen were still plying the waters that had been navigated since the Late Stone Age. But the most crucial groups had vanished. Those were the communities that had lived along the mighty lakes and the huge rivers of the Sahara, especially in its southern half. They had been responsible for introducing agriculture to sub-Saharan Africa. Only sedentary populations could really become involved with the growing of cereal crops, and they were the only sedentary populations in this area by the sixth millennium, when this innovation occurred.

THE SPREAD OF FOOD PRODUCTION
TO 2000 B.C.

The domestication of cereals and of animals such as sheep, goats, and cattle was first achieved in the Middle East. From there, the new way of life spread into Africa, first into lower Egypt and then along the coast to the Atlantic Ocean, as well as into the then lush Sahara. By 5500 B.C. cattle were kept in Fezzan (see map), in southern Libya, and presumably all over northeastern Africa. And cereals were cultivated in the same area at similar dates. The Middle Eastern cereals were barley and wheat. These and the domestic animals could spread without difficulty to the west, to Morocco and Mauritania, and to the southern half of the Sahara. Characteristic of the early phase of diffusion is the overall cultural similarity from the Nile to northwestern Africa during the fourth millennium, a similarity attested to by finds of pottery and tools and depicted in rock paintings and engravings.

But even this early, local developments in Egypt were heralding the rise of the Pharaonic civilizations (after about 3200 B.C.). These further Egyptian changes were quite rapid, as can be seen in relics recovered at Fayum. The rate of technical improvement in pottery making, stone carving, leatherwork, basketry, and the weaving of linen is astonishing. Constant communication with the older centers of the Middle East account for it in part. But the extraordinary fertility of the Nile valley played a role too. It allowed specialization of tasks to proceed quickly, with rapid growth of local communities and political entities.

Meanwhile, life in the Sahara and northwestern Africa during the fourth millennium retained some nomadic features. Even though the populations grew cereals, husbandry of cattle was their major pursuit. A great many polychrome scenes on rock paintings show herding, milking, and social life. Cattle are often shown in huge herds and this period of rock art has therefore been called the Bovidian Pastoral style. The style lasted from 5500 B.C. to 3000 B.C. at least. Hunting scenes were rare now, and human figures including the face were frequently portrayed with absolute realism. Pottery was also used. The most typical manifestations of this civilization were found in the central Sahara at Tassili, Fezzan, and Ennedi, but traces were also left in Algeria. It is now believed that some of the artistic techniques of the Saharan paintings were acquired by Egyptians, perhaps before the time of the pharaohs, from Saharan populations. The most ambiguous feature about this period in Saharan art, unfortunately, deals with the evidence for cultivation of domesticated plants. Some authors interpret a few rare scenes as the reaping of a harvest, but others are inclined to dismiss this reading and see only the gathering of wild grasses.

Along the northwest coast of Africa and in the mountainous Maghrib

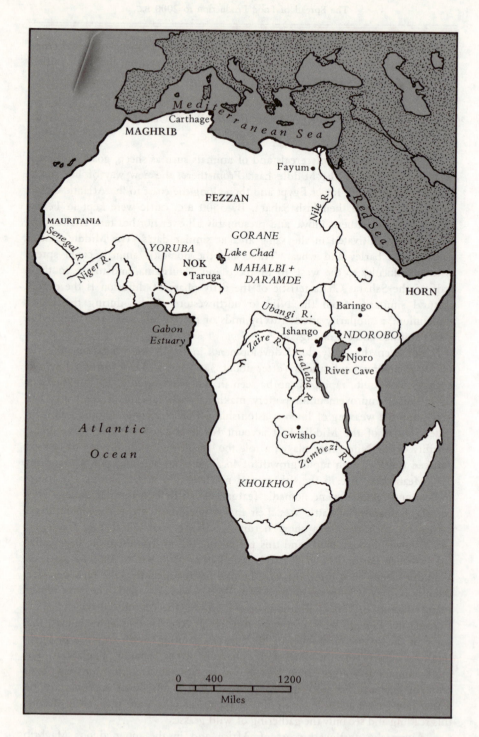

Late Stone Age and Early Food Production in Africa

developments already diverged in this millennium from the basic pattern in the Sahara. Agriculture may well have been far more important there and connections with Spain may be responsible for a different development. Certainly this was true in the succeeding millennia. But very little is known of the archaeology of this area between the arrival of agriculture and the beginning of the Bronze Age, around 2000 B.C.

Barley and wheat will not grow in the humid tropics near sea level. Cereal cultivation was thus stopped at the *sahel,* or southern "shore," of the Sahara, inexorably barred by the environment. Yet this barrier was overcome by human ingenuity. African groups — they must have been sedentary fishing communities living at the limit where wheat and barley cultivation was still possible — began to experiment with local grasses and succeeded in domesticating the millets, sorghums, pennisetum, and eleusine, which were to become the cereals of sub-Saharan Africa. The experimentation involved a very long time, since domestication was achieved probably no earlier than the third millennium. After that time, some of the crops spread back to the Middle East. Thus, sesame was developed in Africa on the southern fringes of the Sahara and reached Sumer by diffusion before 2350 B.C.

Botanists know that sorghums and millets were domesticated somewhere along the sahel, or desert-savanna boundary, between the Atlantic near Cape Verde and Ethiopia, or else from Ethiopia southward into East Africa. This is the region where the wild ancestors of those plants grew. It is known as Burkill's *L* after the shape of the region, the long branch of the *L* representing the stretch from the Atlantic to Ethiopia. From the diffusion of wheat and barley it is clear that domestication actually occurred in the sahel and perhaps in Ethiopia as well. In addition to the cereals, many other plants were domesticated in two centers: the Ethiopian highlands and the upper Niger-Senegal rivers area.

The use of new cereals south of the Sahara was a first break with major cultural patterns of northeastern Africa, but the simultaneous deterioration of the climate in the Sahara was much more momentous. Between 2500 B.C. and 2300 B.C. the great rivers stopped flowing, the lakes gradually dried up, and the desert smothered many forms of life. Most Saharans were slowly driven out of the emerging desert, but not without a struggle, and some clung to life there and adapted completely to the new conditions. At first the populations came to rely more and more on cattle husbandry, ultimately abandoning agriculture almost completely except around the oases that began to form. To survive the rigors of the drier environment, it was now necessary to spread the cattle and the men out over every last square mile of the huge expanses of land during the short periods when there was rain, because after each rainfall grasses would sprout up quickly (but dry out almost as quickly). But at the heights of the droughts hundreds of people and all their herds had to be concentrated around a waterhole. These necessities required a principle of social organization that would function equally well to govern the people when they were spread out in small groups of ten or fewer and when they were crowding around the wells.

To cope with this dual way of life, a *deep segmentary kinship* system was developed. Whole "tribes" — that is, very large groups who believed that they were descended from one ancestor — were linked by a commonly accepted official genealogy. This system codified to an extent the groups to which a person was to belong at different times of the year. All pastoral nomads of Africa and Asia developed the same type of social organization, which may have been invented over and over again as the need arose.

Thus pastoral nomadism became a new way of life, a distinctly original adaptation to environment. Its very success, however, limited the ability of these societies to introduce further innovations to meet new challenges. In Africa, two further major innovations in some cases were to complement the basic segmentary kinship system. In the Sahara, nomads gradually dominated the sedentary populations of the oases and evolved a "casted" society, which later came to be widespread in the sahel. In East Africa, age-grade systems complementary to segmentary organization emerged later.

While this new type of social organization was taking shape, cattle herders also began to leave the Sahara after 2500 B.C. A large group went to the Nile valley, south of Egypt, and onwards to the horn of Africa, where they were settled by 2000 B.C. Others moved south, following the retreating pastures to settle ultimately in the sahel of West Africa, from the Niger bend to Lake Chad and north of the *sudd* region, a permanent papyrus marsh in the shallow Nile of the southern Sudan. None seem to have migrated into Egypt proper, probably because, even when the central Sahara was good pastureland, the Libyan Desert was already one of the more forbidding landscapes of the world. Many went west to Mauritania where the desiccation proceeded much more slowly than elsewhere, and a great number followed the grasslands to the north into North Africa. By 2000 B.C., the desert itself had become an almost empty area, eventually covering almost one third of the continent and isolating northwestern Africa and Egypt from Africa south of the Sahara. Or rather, the desert acted as a sieve allowing certain influences to trickle through while blocking others, although the isolation was great enough for northwestern Africa, Egypt, and West Africa to begin to acquire their markedly divergent civilizations. Different adaptations to problems posed by the ecology and the confrontation of different populations led to even greater differentiation.

With progressive desiccation, the quality of life in the Sahara itself gradually changed. The predominance of cattle in the flocks was exchanged gradually for sheep and goats. These animals could eke out a subsistence long after increasing aridity had made the land unsuitable for cattle, but their activity also increased erosion. The nomads came to rely more and more for part of their food supply on cereals and other domesticated plants from the oases. Even here, changes in the patterns of food production had to adapt to dry conditions and gradually irrigation techniques, including underground channels for distributing water to the fields, were invented. Necessity also prompted the farmers to live close together in larger settlements and to accept a fairly strong communal authority to supervise an equitable distribution of water.

The needs of the nomads were such that an accommodation between oasis dwellers and pastoralists had to be worked out. This led gradually to a dominance of the nomads over the farmers, probably because with their mobility the nomads could attack the farmers by surprise. It is possible that this complex evolution was a beginning for a "caste" system in which farmers came to be "protected" by some nomads in return for a pay-off in fixed amounts of cereals and a supply of water.

In their push southward, following the retreating grazing grounds, the cattle pastoralists met and mixed with communities of fishermen, hunters, and gatherers, first in what is now the southern Sahara and later in what is now the sahel. From this contact flourishing communities arose, based on farming sorghum and millet and relying as well on fishing, hunting, and gathering. Their social organizations were probably evolved from the preexisting fishermen's settlements. These sedentary villagers took to keeping sheep and goats, but they raised few cattle, mainly because cattle required too much care. Here, then, a specialization of labor developed. Some groups clung to the nomadic way of life and the raising of large cattle herds, while buying their vegetal food from the farmers, who in turn bought the milk and meat they needed from the herders. Thus a steady trade based on ecological symbiosis developed gradually.

In North Africa similar developments may have occurred, although here cattle seem to have been even less important than in the sahel. Sheep and goats formed the nomads' flocks.

Food production had also diffused up the Nile in the Sudan and into Ethiopia at an unknown time, but probably long before 2000 B.C. In the highlands of Ethiopia, special conditions of the environment once again forced an adaptation. New crops were evolved, among them especially the cow pea and the *ensete,* a relative of the banana that became a staple food for many peoples. By 2000 B.C., settled communities of farmers existed in the highlands, and they may have begun to integrate cattle into their farming activities more than elsewhere. A farm would keep a few head of cattle, using the milk and the meat for food and spreading the manure as fertilizer on the fields. Once the grain was harvested the cattle could eat the stubble. Of all this, however, we have no direct record. Perhaps linguistic work may one day clarify the picture further.

LANGUAGES

Languages, and groups of languages, are said to belong to a single *family* when their resemblance to one another is so strong that it cannot be ascribed to chance, but must be a result of common origin. When languages are grouped in a family, it means that at some distant time in the past the ancestor of them all — a protolanguage — existed as a living, changing language, spoken by people with a culture and a history of their own. Language changes over time as it is passed on from parents to children. As groups speaking the protolanguage separate from one another their languages diverge. Successive divergences of the groups descended from a protogroup can lead to large numbers of languages within a family, with the pattern of descent and the sum of their relationships looking like a family tree.

According to Joseph H. Greenberg, the leading specialist in African language classification, there are only five independent language families in Africa. The whole of North Africa, the Horn, and the area around Lake Chad speak *Afro-Asiatic* languages. This family has five coordinate branches: Semitic in Asia, Ancient Egyptian, Berber in northwestern Africa, Cushitic in Ethiopia, and Chadic in parts of present-day Chad and Nigeria. Recently it has been suggested that West Cushitic would form a separate and sixth branch. The ancestral language from which all these branches are descended was spoken long before 3000 B.C., for Egyptian and some Semitic languages can be traced that far back. From the distribution of the branches of the family it is evident that Berber-speakers must have made up much of the nomad population of the Sahara when it was good pastureland. By 2000 B.C., the farmers of Ethiopia spoke Cushitic languages and West Cushitic.

The hunters and gatherers of southern Africa and similar populations in East Africa, such as the Sandawe and Hadze of Tanzania, spoke the *Khoisan* languages, a language family whose name comes from those of the Khoikhoi and San of South Africa and which is a stock of very great but unknown antiquity. By 2000 B.C., they were spoken by all the hunters of East Africa and Africa south of the equatorial forest, perhaps even by populations in the forest. Some authorities believe that there are several San families totally unrelated to Khoikhoi or to each other.

The third major stock is *Congo-Kordofanian* with two families: *Niger-Congo* and *Kordofanian*. If Greenberg's classification is confirmed, the ancestral language was spoken in the lands between Chad and Kordofan at a very remote time. Niger-Congo itself is subdivided into six branches, of which five cover West Africa and one the grasslands of Cameroons and the Central African Republic, while a single offshoot of the West African branches covers most of Africa south of the Equator. The five West African branches are the oldest, and one of them, the Mande group, may eventually have to be recognized as a separate family. (The Mande live in the upper Niger area where African rice was developed and it seems probable that the farmers who first domesticated that crop spoke Mande.) Although there is no way of dating Niger-Congo securely, the languages that make it up are as different as are the various Indo-European languages whose ancestral tongue was spoken, it is believed, around 2700 B.C. Mande would be even older.

The last family is *Nilo-Saharan*. It is divided into six branches of which one, Chari-Nile, comprises a great many languages; the five others are isolated

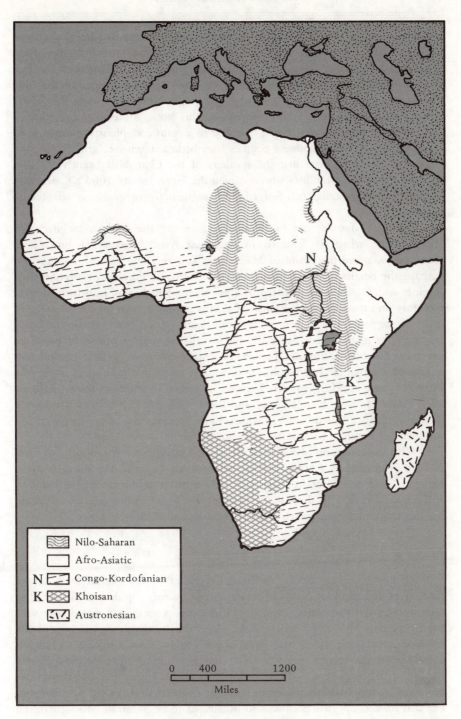

The Languages of Africa

tongues found in small regions south of the Sahara or in the desert northeast of Lake Chad. There can be no doubt that the ancestral tongue of this stock, too, was spoken many thousands of years ago, and the distribution of the languages indicates that the eastern Sahara or sahel between Chad and the Nile was its original home. The people who fled to the Nile valley from the Sahara when it dried up were probably speakers of this stock. More than any other in Africa, the speech of these people is linked to a culture emphasizing cattle, even though many of the component peoples later became intensive farmers. Circumstantial evidence suggests that the speakers of the Chari-Nile branch of Nilo-Saharan were the pastoralists who occupied the Horn around 2000 B.C. and that they developed first the full-fledged deep segmentary organization adapted to pastoral life.

One more family, not to be reckoned among the African languages, is *Austronesian,* which is centered in Southeast Asia. Speakers of one of its languages occupied the island of Madagascar at a very late date (for linguists), perhaps the beginning of the Christian Era. Intrusive European settlers carried English and Dutch into southern Africa, where Dutch was transformed over a century and more into Afrikaans. Afrikaans is well known as the language of many of the overseas-European minority in South Africa, but it is also the home language for many others, especially the so-called Coloured people of the Cape province. Elsewhere, English, French, or Portuguese have become general languages of international communication, so that many Africans speak and write in one of these as a fully mastered second language. In addition, these originally alien languages have blended here and there with African tongues to produce mixed languages called *creoles,* which have become the home language for scattered but significant elements of the population.

With the exception of Khoisan, all of the indigenous African families seem to have originated in a fairly narrow belt between 10° and 16° north latitude, between Chad and Ethiopia. They did not originate at the same time but it is still remarkable that the three major families developed in that one area. Perhaps one day archaeological research will tell us the explanation.

RACE

All human beings belong to the same species — they can all mate among themselves and produce fertile offspring — but human populations lived for so long in comparative isolation that a particular group sometimes mated only with nearby people who had similar genes. As a result, that group drew from a common gene pool, which may have lacked certain genes available to humans elsewhere or had genes that were not common among other peoples. People sharing a particular gene pool are properly labeled a *population* and should not be called a race. Each recognizably different population is constantly changing. For that matter, no gene pool was so isolated as to be unmixed with others. To talk about different races at all is only a convenient inaccuracy.

In ancient sub-Saharan Africa, the various gene pools were so blended together and merging at the edges that it is not even convenient to distinguish different "races," but rather to consider that all Africans belonged to a single large and diverse race. An exception might be made for bands of Khoikhoi or San hunters, who met infrequently with other bands and did not mate with them, but even this distinction can be doubted. When agriculture and husbandry were introduced, contacts between populations increased, the overall density increased, and relative genetic barriers weakened. Africans came to share more and more in one genetic pool. In addition, many observable physical characteristics, such as muscular strength, stature, and forms of nose or lips, may be the result of differing patterns of nutrition or slow genetic adaptation to an environment. The sturdy size of fishermen comes from a better diet in protein, and the large stature and black skin of the Nilotes may be an adaptation to the great heat and dry climate in which they live. Human biology is only beginning to explore such questions. Today's classifications of race cannot be trusted because they are based on crude phenotypical, or outwardly visible, characteristics.

On appearance alone, the peoples of Africa were classified in six major groups: (1) Caucasian, (2) Khoisan, (3) pygmies, (4) Negroes, (5) Erythriotes, (6) Mongoloids. North Africa was supposedly Caucasian. South Africa was the home of the Khoisan, a people of small stature with peppercorn hair, a yellowish skin, the mongoloid fold, the mongoloid spot, and steatopygia. The Khoisan's small stature is like that of the pygmies, who also have a yellowish skin, but pygmies also show a large flat nose, a wide mouth, and very thin lips. Both pygmies and Khoisan can be recognized as regional variations of the Negro, whose morphology, apart from a dark skin color, is quite variable. Negroes are traditionally distinguished from Erythriotes or Ethiopids by the fact that the latter are often taller (but not taller than the Negro Nilotes!), have a long, straight, narrow nose, more reddish skin, and a spindle-shaped body. Finally, the Malay type of Mongoloids of Madagascar, who had interbred with others for centuries, also illustrate the axiom that there are no distinct races in Africa.

In fact all the characteristics of pygmies and Erythriotes can be explained by genetic adaptation to their environments, and this may be the case for most of the Khoisan attributes. The whole classification, then, is virtually worthless. The one modern attempt to cope with the physical anthropology of populations south of the Sahara, established by Jean Hiernaux, emphasizes human diversity and abandons the concept of race. He speaks of a population defined as a partially closed gene pool, often comparable with a distinct linguistic or ethnic group. For each of the populations he studied he examined more than twenty different features, described by measurement and characteristics of the blood. He concluded that to reduce the diversity of African populations to a restricted number of units, as is done in a racial classification, is not only unwarranted but flatly contradicts known facts and leads only to confusion. The influence of the environment on the selection of genetic characteristics, and thus on the hereditary evolution of a population, is much greater than was assumed. In fact this process, along with intermixture of adjacent gene pools, and in some cases common origin of later differentiated gene pools, explains most of the results found. Human biology no longer pretends to be able to prove a common origin for populations in a very remote past. The whole impact of recent work is to limit the time involved in somatic human differentiation, or race formation.

Historians must therefore learn to reject all summary classifications and conclusions drawn from them. They should be suspicious of statements concerned with somatic appearance made for a long gone past, such as the statement that agriculture and husbandry were first brought to East Africa by Caucasoid populations. Evidence of a few skeletons cannot be trusted because the somatic characteristics of a population can be established only if measurements can be made on the full range of the people participating in one gene pool. Valid statements must therefore be expressed in statistical terms and take into account the whole *range* of appearances within a population. The study of just one skull or a couple of skeletons cannot achieve this.

In contrast with linguistics, little can be said about the appearance of people in Africa around 2000 B.C., and almost nothing about their physical makeup. The only known elements are that paintings in the Sahara frequently depict brown, tall people as well as white people and that contemporaneous data from southern Africa suggest that populations there may have looked rather like the San, but taller and stronger.

THE SPREAD OF FOOD PRODUCTION
AFTER 2000 B.C.

By 2000 B.C., the desiccation of the Sahara was complete and its former populations had been integrated into the various areas where they had sought refuge. But this did not mean the end of the spread of food-producing economies in Africa.

From the Atlantic Ocean in the west to the Nile in the east, the southward expansion of agriculture proceeded without great hindrance until the margins of the equatorial forest were reached. There the diffusion stalled for a while, confronting a new environment. The forests were then inhabited by gatherers and hunters and also perhaps by more or less sedentary fishermen. Some of these gatherers had gradually evolved a technique of producing food called *vege-culture*. Without really domesticating a plant to begin with, they found that certain roots and fruits and trees would grow again in the same spots, provided slips were put into the ground and a little weeding was done afterwards. In this way, they gradually domesticated several types of yams, all sorts of gourds and calabashes, as well as the oil and raphia palms. These did not become the mainstay of their food supply, however, and most food was still collected from wild leaves, roots, and berries or came from hunting both large and small animals. Because there is no archaeological evidence for the practice of vegeculture, it cannot be dated, but it may have existed for thousands of years. Its major advantage was to make the supply of food more secure and above all to allow people to stay a little longer in each camp. Incipient sedentarization was the motive for vegeculture, rather than better nutrition.

When the growers of cereals met with these populations, stimulus diffusion began to take place. The forest people began to pay more and more attention to planting root crops and may have taken the notion of regular fields from their new neighbors. Slowly they also learned to clear some bush by burning and found that some cereals could be cultivated there as well. But they were never able to rely on them as staple crops. They took over the sheep and the goats and found that goats in particular could be kept in a forest environment. Cattle were not at all suited to the new conditions; only very gradually would a breed develop in southern Dahomey (in West Africa, near Nigeria) that could be useful at the forest margins, and it never penetrated deeply into the forest. But this whole evolution finally led some forest people to a fairly sedentary way of life. They began to live in villages, cleared fields, and relied on root crops, tree crops, and fishing as their major activities. Hunting persisted, and the social values attached to hunting proved to be almost impervious to the economic changes. But hunting gradually declined in importance, and with it the need for migration disappeared and made village life possible. What evidence we have shows that this evolution took place all along the northern margin of the forest from the upper Ubangi River to the Gambia.

Meanwhile food production spread from Ethiopia southward, especially all along the Rift Valley of Kenya and Tanzania and in the highlands on both sides. This spread can be dated to 1500 B.C., perhaps, and certainly before 1000 B.C. Several cultures in East Africa, of which the best known is the Njoro River cave culture, date from this period. These people kept cattle and grew cereals. Finds at the site included basketry, cords, gourds, and a well-carved wooden vessel, presumably a milk container. Njoro River people loved to adorn themselves and many different forms of beads were found, all made of locally available materials. The common tools were of wood or stone, principally obsidian, which provided very sharp edges. Pottery was used, but stone bowls turn up in so many sites of this culture that it is often referred to as the stone bowl culture. Evidence from grindstones and pestles indicates that cereals were grown. Cattle bones are found, and goats or sheep were also kept.

This culture was founded by Cushitic people, probably by South Cushitic speakers. It was a true farming economy in which cattle had been integrated, not a pastoral economy. These people may already have started the irrigation works that are found all over East Africa. If so, it is an indication of the pains they took to insure a good yield for their fields.

Gradually the art of keeping cattle and farming spread from Tanzania to Zambia and hence to southwestern and southeastern Africa. Unfortunately we have no chronological data for this movement. It seems that the keeping of cattle traveled faster than the practice of agriculture; the Khoikhoi and

Herero learned about cattle, but not agriculture. It also appears that cattle raising spread faster than the knowledge of how to milk them, because ethnographic distribution maps show a small area in Angola where cattle are still kept but not milked. These data imply that cattle husbandry was spread to southern Africa by mobile pastoralists, rather than by the South Cushitic speakers. If so, these pastoralists were probably Chari-Nile speakers, who also introduced the deep segmentary kinship system later adopted by the Southwestern Bantu-speakers and brought the cultural syndrome known as the cattle complex to the whole of eastern and southern Africa. The syndrome may have been introduced, according to Christopher Ehret, by speakers of the larger Central Sudanic language family of the Chari-Nile branch of Nilo-Saharan, but the evidence remains quite tenuous.

The cattle complex grew out of placing an extremely high value on cattle. They were looked on not as sacred animals but as jewelry, man's most prized possession, or as pets, man's closest friends. Transactions in cattle came to be the foundation of all relations between groups or persons: marriage, dependence, subservience, exchange, alliance. This cattle ethos and perhaps the slower spread of agriculture explains why in southern Africa cattle keeping and agriculture were never integrated in a single farming operation. Manure was little used, if at all; cattle were not used for transportation, except among the Khoikhoi; pastures and fields were not meshed into a single comprehensive use of the land. All of this contrasts sharply with the practices of the southern Cushites in East Africa and even more with Ethiopian farming.

It is possible that agriculture spread out from southern Tanzania, westward around Lake Tanganyika into the savanna south of the equatorial forest. It may well have been taken up by some of the original inhabitants there after about 1000 B.C. This is at least suggested by the botanical evidence about cereals, but without archaeological proof. However, archaeological excavations are still rare in that region, and it remains possible that agriculture may have come instead with the first Bantu-speakers.

At a later but uncertain date, new Southeast Asian root and tree crops reached Africa, including taro (cocoyams), sugarcane, and banana and coconut trees. The domestic fowl, the use of the bark of fig (or *Ficus*) trees for cloth, and perhaps the xylophone also came from Southeast Asia. The Malagasy themselves stem from Indonesia. All these did not of necessity arrive at the same time, and the evidence is rather against such a possibility. Still, the banana arrived early enough to diffuse to Buganda and produce there twenty-one original somatic mutants — mutations in the body cell, not from cross-fertilization. N. W. Simmonds estimated that this must have taken about two thousand years. The banana was therefore introduced before our era. If, as is generally believed, it was carried up the Zambezi River and then along the great lakes to Buganda, it may have come much earlier.

Bananas and taro apparently spread very fast throughout the forest. They were the ideal food crops in these conditions, so rewarding, in fact, that to grow them was easier than planting cereals in the grasslands. Domestic fowl may have been introduced along with them. The linguistic evidence in the Bantu languages for both banana and fowl is quite similar.

While this diffusion was happening in the interior of Africa, further domestication went on in northern Africa. The most important new animals introduced were the horse, the donkey, the domestic fowl, the pig, and new breeds of cattle. The donkey, pig, goose, and duck were all reared in dynastic Egypt (after 3200 B.C.), and the horse was introduced there during the Hyksos period around 1650 B.C. When the donkey was domesticated remains unknown, but it was used as a beast of burden; cows were used for ploughing about 2300 B.C. Donkeys and onagers were used in Mesopotamia for drawing chariots before the horse became available. The first domestic fowl appears about 1300 B.C., but the animal was reared on a larger scale only after the Persian invasion of 525 B.C. It is interesting to note that during the Old Kingdom from 3000 to 2300 B.C. or so, Egyptians tried to domesticate other species such as cranes, gazelles, and hyenas. After this period the spirit of experimentation died out. Another curious development is linked with the domestication of the pig. Domestic swine were reared from predynastic times onwards and were a major source of meat until some time between 1000 B.C. and 500 B.C., when people came to have a strong avoidance of pork. Its diffusion into other parts of Africa took place before the taboo developed, along routes from Egypt to the upper Nile area and perhaps from North Africa to West and Equatorial Africa.

Ponies, and later horses, came to the Sahara, Ethiopia, and the sahel in the first millennium B.C. and may have followed donkeys in all these areas, but they could not spread further south, mainly because of the tsetse fly, which induces a disease called *nagana* that kills horses and cattle. Horse-drawn chariots were the means of transportation throughout the Sahara from perhaps 1000 B.C. to the coming of the camel. By the eighth century B.C., zebu cattle were introduced into northeastern Africa from India, perhaps by Semitic peoples who at that time crossed the Red Sea into northern Ethiopia. The crossing of the zebu with the East African longhorn produced (several times and apparently in several places in East and South Africa) the sturdy strains of cattle known as Sanga. Later crossings produced breeds such as the Afrikander, which are fairly resistant to the tsetse fly. The last domestic animal to be introduced was the camel. Earlier known and used in the desert between the Nile and the Red Sea, it spread to the Sahara only in Roman times.

Meanwhile, agricultural change continued to influence the farming civilizations to the south of the desert. Agriculture made for sedentary life; better crops made larger, more compact villages possible; these in turn adapted the social organizations pioneered by the Stone Age fishermen. The unilineal principles of descent formed a backbone for social organization. The emergence of specialization in labor and differentiation in status was pregnant with potentialities for further development. Above all, farming implied relative freedom from the yoke of the environment, just the contrary of the adaptation the nomad had made to his environment. Out of this freedom grew a great diversity of local cultures. Sometimes the strengthening of positions of authority led to the development of a notion of authority based on common residence rather than on common kinship. This type of authority was chieftainship. It emerged necessarily wherever descent was matrilineal, but marriage was virilocal (that is, the wife followed her husband to his place of residence) because the village could not provide a common residence for all the males of a matrilineage. So authority had to be based on common residence. But a similar evolution could and did occur in some patrilineal societies. With a stronger central authority, expansion beyond the village level was possible, and thus chiefdoms consisting of several villages emerged. The last step was the creation of kingdoms, something which may have happened in West Africa near the beginning of the Christian Era. A kingdom was more complex than a chiefdom in two ways: its ideology of authority was more developed, and this was reflected in the courts, etiquette, and legal and financial organizations; and it consisted of chiefdoms, adding, therefore, one more layer of territorial organization to the structures based on residence.

In other farming societies shallow lineage structures were developed and a strong sense of ownership of the land led to the creation of patron-client relationships, providing the basis for a larger community. Elsewhere, the single village or a dispersed settlement linked with shallow lineage organization was felt to be adequate, and participation in common rituals often provided a focus for coordination between individual settlements. Still elsewhere, most notably in East Africa, age-grade organizations evolved. In short, then, the settled agricultural life was accompanied by a social organization that remained very malleable and thus open to further innovation and change. Through the interaction of different farming societies, each with its own way of life, cultures found more stimuli for improving their style. In the process they grew more complex. The later introduction of metal tools would only hasten this trend, since it gave a still greater degree of freedom from the environment. With the advent of ironworking, the notion of economic, as opposed to political or religious, specialization gained great prestige. This accentuated even more the overall division of labor.

In short, sedentary life on a large scale was made possible by new ways of producing food. It led, in turn, to the efflorescence of stable, yet flexible, societies whose cultures show astonishing continuity. These cultures also had a potential for growth and change, so that civilizations of that early period are directly linked to those which flourished in the recent past.

THE IRON AGE

Most of Africa never knew the Bronze Age. North Africa did. Bronze was worked in Egypt since early Pharaonic times and metallurgy reached the Maghrib (northwestern Africa) around 2000 B.C. The technique seems not to have spread south except along the Atlantic coast, so that a limited use of bronze objects was made in Mauritania and Senegal around 500 B.C. It is possible that metallurgy itself came to be known in these areas.

By the Bronze Age, the Mediterranean was becoming a well-traveled sea, and eastern influences continued to spread west. Eventually settlers from Phoenicia arrived in the western Mediterranean and founded colonies in North Africa after 1000 B.C. These activities culminated with the rise of Carthage. Thus, northwestern Africa found itself heavily influenced by the technologies and some social patterns and religious ideas of the Middle East, and gradually entered the classical world. Among the new techniques brought by the Phoenicians was knowledge for smelting iron.

Ironworking is complex and it may have been invented only once in eastern Anatolia around 1500 B.C. In spite of considerable local differences in furnace types and other techniques, the basic process of iron smelting was similar everywhere until the fourteenth century A.D., when Europeans developed mechanical means for forcing a blast of air into the fire and started down the road toward the technology for comparatively cheap cast iron. Before that time, and long afterward in most of Africa, no furnaces were hot enough to produce molten iron as they did molten copper.

The secret of all early ironmaking was a chemical change. When charcoal was mixed with iron and burned in an enclosed space, one combustion product was carbon monoxide, which picked up an oxygen molecule from the hot ore. The ore turned from ferrous oxide into iron, while the gas turned from carbon monoxide to carbon dioxide. At the end of the smelting period, hot slag was drawn off and the product in the bottom of the furnace was bloom, or a mass of iron or steel mixed with some slag and other impurities. The bloom had to be reheated and hammered to remove slag and create a usable piece of iron. This product could be highly variable, depending on the mixture of other elements, which depended in turn on the ore, the type of furnace, and the temperature maintained during smelting. Carbon content was crucial. If too little carbon had been absorbed by the hot iron, the iron might be soft, malleable, and not likely to hold an edge. Just a little more carbon yielded steel, which was malleable and yet could be tempered by heating and sudden cooling. Still more carbon, and the product became brittle cast iron, impossible to shape on an anvil.

Most of Africa used the shaft furnace, perhaps of Graeco-Roman origin. This was a much more efficient device than the bowl furnace, which had been used in the Nile valley since the Bronze Age and was still reported in Kordofan in the early nineteenth century. It is still in use today in the northern part of East Africa. Smelting ore in a shaft furnace means placing alternating layers of carefully dried ore and charcoal in the furnace. Oxygen is then admitted during the firing either by means of bellows (pot bellows for most of sub-Saharan Africa, bag bellows in North Africa, and pump bellows of Indonesian origin in southeastern Africa), or by natural draft through a series of terra cotta tubes that lead outside air to the base of the fire. The crucial skill was proper control of the air admitted, but further ramifications of African iron technology were highly varied responses to local conditions of ore or charcoal supply. A shaft furnace would yield about five kilograms of iron in one smelting, while a bowl furnace would yield only one kilogram or so at best.

Iron ore was available in most parts of Africa, although the iron content of usable ore might run as low as 25 percent to as high as 75 percent. Most of it was dug from surface deposits, but extensive mines have been found in a few places, the best example being the mine of Télénougar in southern Chad, where shafts and galleries were dug. Mining and smelting involved considerable labor that had to be directed by a master founder, who had all the knowledge and all the responsibility. No wonder that the "masters of the fire" held such a special status — either prestigious, or (as in Ethiopia, the eastern and western Sudan, and generally in North Africa) as despised persons living in a small caste, marginals to the society.

A few years ago it was assumed that iron had spread into sub-Saharan Africa from Meroë, where it would have been imported by the Assyrians who conquered Egypt in around 600 B.C. But this theory has had to be modified, because Meroë started producing iron on a fairly large scale only in about 500 B.C. It now seems more likely that West Africa learned metallurgy indirectly from the Phoenicians, the great ironworkers of the Middle East, who had introduced it to some of their Mediterranean colonies, such as Carthage. Indeed, by 400 B.C. the southernmost Phoenician outpost at Cerne in southern Morocco was not so far from the Senegal River and much of the intervening land was still good grazing ground, allowing easy communication to the north. In addition, these areas were precisely those to which the craft of copper melting and bronze making had already spread from southern Morocco. Thus, the technique in northern Nigeria (where it is attested to in sites of the Nok culture by 280–180 B.C. at Taruga) may have come from Carthage, and across the Sahara. From Senegal and Nigeria ironworking spread rapidly all over West Africa, and even though exact data are still lacking, the diffusion may be taken to have been complete by the beginning of our era.

The engravings and paintings of the eastern Sahara show that ironworking spread from Meroë to Lake Chad and then probably southward toward the equatorial forest. In East Africa iron was introduced by about 250 B.C., first to the region of the great lakes, then to the coast, where it was smelted by about 200 A.D. This early ironwork was associated with two kinds of related pottery styles, and the whole is subsumed under the name *Early Iron Age Industrial Complex*. This Early Iron Age Industrial Complex reached central and southern Africa in two streams, an eastern stream spreading southward between about 300 and 400 A.D., and a western stream that reached present-day Zambia a century or so later. Evidence of the movement of this stream across Zaïre is very spotty, but it certainly reached as far west as the Kasai River. Even though many different cultures were involved, all their pottery shows a collateral relationship. They are "in the same tradition."

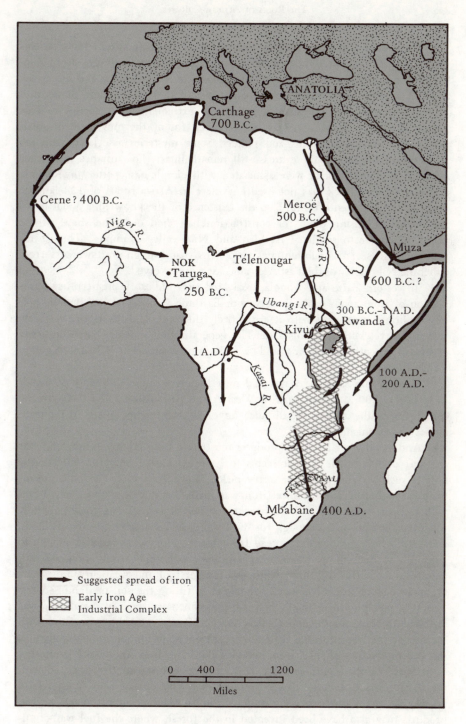

The Diffusion of Iron in Africa

The data thus indicate that the knowledge of smelting spread fast over this whole area and was brought by one general type of pottery culture. From Zimbabwe (or Rhodesia) the craft reached Ngwane in Swaziland by 410 A.D. ± 60, and a Transvaal site dates from the early part of that millennium. Similarities in the potteries raise the suspicion that the extremely rapid spread in East Africa, Zambia, and Malawi may be accounted for by the movement of small bands of professional smiths and potters. Some mysteries associated with the introduction of iron in these areas still remain intact. For instance, numerous kilns made of burnt brick were associated with dimple-base pottery in Rwanda and Kivu. Burnt brick was not used anywhere in Africa south of 12° latitude north in the nineteenth century, so the existence of the knowledge about burning bricks and using them for construction had died out. The shape of the bricks is similar to southern Arabian and Nile valley examples. Thus, brick making in these areas substantiates suspicions that foreign craftsworkers from either the Nile valley or the East African coast were involved.

In western Zaïre and Angola, excavated sites indicaté a first-century introduction of iron, again contemporary with East and Central Africa. But the pottery traditions associated with it are entirely different. Unfortunately, very few sites are as yet known in this area. The generalization is really based on a site excavated recently at Luanda and a fifth-century site near Mbanza Ngungu (Thysville) in Zaïre.

Most of sub-Saharan Africa had nevertheless acquired the craft of metallurgy before 500 A.D., and most of West Africa perhaps by 250 B.C. Given the complexity of the art and the distances involved, the further spread of the techniques was astonishingly rapid.

And yet the earliest iron products must have been clumsy. The metal was too soft or too brittle, and it seems to have been used only for small bulky objects such as arrowpoints or heavy picks. However, a Nok terra cotta seems to indicate that at Taruga, sheet iron was made, because it shows a small bell with clapper, presumed to have been made out of iron. If so, the technology was even then advanced enough for the forging of serviceable spearheads, hoes, and axes. The technique that spread from Meroë, also, was advanced enough to allow for such smithing, for large spearheads are the major indications on rock paintings about this diffusion. With this type of tool and weaponry, iron users began to have a true advantage over others in tilling the soil or fighting wars.

It is possible, then, that a first, early rudimentary stage of metallurgy was confined to East, South, and Central Africa. It was probably associated with the use of the bowl furnace. Later, more advanced techniques, including welding and production of sheet iron, heralded the Later Iron Age, which is attested to in Shaba by the eighth century. This advance was apparently associated with the shaft furnace, and the new techniques may have spread from West Africa by way of the Cameroons. Innovations and substantial improvement in iron products may also have been invented in the forest, where the fuel was of superior quality. By the eleventh century, the Later Iron Age was well established in eastern, central, and southern Africa, but probably still earlier in Shaba. Along with it came new pottery styles, and they constitute a sharp break with earlier traditions. The Later Iron Age also shows greater variation among local styles, and these local variants are everywhere directly ancestral to present-day pottery styles. By the eleventh century, then, the technological level everywhere south of the Sahara was similar to the one that still existed at the end of the nineteenth century, so that all the achievements in other sectors of society have been at least potentially present since then.

Some authors have argued that Bantu language–speakers brought iron to East, Equatorial, Central, and South Africa. The evidence is a common Bantu root, "to pound" or "to hammer," now mostly applied to smithing. But in older times it may have been used to describe the manufacture of stone tools, and this evidence is inconclusive.

THE COMING OF THE BANTU

The Kongo on the Atlantic Ocean call a person *muntu,* with a plural *bantu.* On the Indian Ocean the Swahili say *mtu* (singular), *watu* (pl.). In the equatorial forest the Mongo say *bonto* (sg.), *banto* (pl.), while the Duala in Cameroons say *moto* (sg.), *bato* (pl.), and the Xhosa of the Eastern Cape *umntu* (sg.), *bantu* (pl.). The similarity in all these words is clear. Linguists recognized this similarity very early and called this group of languages *Bantu* after the term the ancestral language used to designate "people." The ancestral language is called Proto-Bantu.

Bantu languages are spoken in Africa south of a line running roughly from the Bight of Biafra to the Indian Ocean near the Kenya-Somali border. The group includes more than four hundred languages, all as closely related to each other as are the Germanic languages. The Bantu-speakers occupy a huge area, for the only non-Bantu languages in the subcontinent are the Khoisan tongues, which are now restricted to parts of South and southwestern Africa.

This linguistic discovery raises a major question. How did the Bantu languages spread? From where, and when? Were any movements of people associated with the spread of the languages? The answer to these questions is still taxing the ingenuity of historians today.

First, it has been shown by linguists, especially by Joseph H. Greenberg, that the Proto-Bantu language itself formed part of a larger group in the Benue-Cross River area, and that group was itself a branch of Niger-Congo. The closest relatives of the Proto-Bantu language within the Benue-Cross branch all lie in the Cameroons and adjacent parts of Nigeria. Now this situation can only be explained by assuming that the ancestral language of all the Bantu-speakers originated in that area of Nigeria in close proximity to the others. How else could one account for the presence of all the languages closely related to

Proto-Bantu in such a small area? For any other hypothesis we would have to invent complicated schemes to explain this situation. So linguistic evidence again shows where the Bantu languages came from.

The other questions are not answered so easily, although all linguists accept the idea that population movement was associated with the spread of the Bantu languages, not only because they extend over such a huge area, but mainly because that seems to be the simplest explanation. Bantu languages are no more attractive than any other, so they could not spread by themselves. Comparable and well-known cases indicate that languages have been spread either by the migration of large numbers of people who imposed their language on the minority they overran, or by migration of a small number of people who imposed

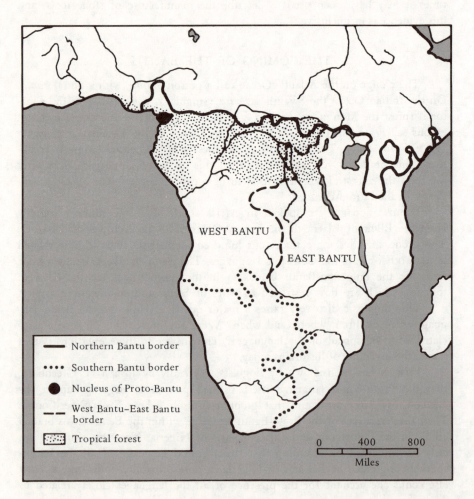

WEST BANTU

EAST BANTU

—— Northern Bantu border

•••• Southern Bantu border

● Nucleus of Proto-Bantu

–– West Bantu–East Bantu border

▦ Tropical forest

0   400   800
Miles

Bantu Language Diffusion

their language because they either conquered the area or were considered by both the local people and themselves as vastly superior in civilization. Most of the Germanic languages spread in the first way; the Romance languages (for example French) diffused in the second fashion.

But how did so many come to speak the Bantu languages? The lead again should come from the linguists, who have hoped for almost a century to show that within all Bantu languages certain groups could be distinguished and proven to be much more closely related to each other than to the rest of the language family. Only very recently has this effort begun to yield results. It is becoming clear that the migration of Bantu-speakers began somewhere in Nigeria and brought them first to Cameroon and Gabon. Gradually they spread eastward north of the forest and southward to the forest's edge near the lower Congo or Zaïre and lower Kasai. The occupation of the northwestern quadrant (Cameroon-Gabon) was fairly slow, to judge by the degree of differentiation between languages. Elsewhere, and especially in eastern and southern Africa, beginning at the edge of the forest, the spread must have moved very fast, since the languages remain so closely related. This close relationship also indicates that these Bantu-speakers were not isolated and must have influenced one another over a long period by mutual borrowing, so that the genetic sub-divisions in eastern and southern (including central) Bantu languages are hazy and very hard to detect. An image of eastern Africa or southern Africa as a region where people lived in isolation is completely wrong. Even within the forest there is evidence of continuing contacts, though they were less frequent than elsewhere. For the moment no more can be said, because linguistic studies happen to be in flux, and perhaps even on the verge of a breakthrough.

Nor can linguists tell when the migrations and the spread of languages occurred. It was hoped at one time that a technique called glottochronology might do just that. The technique was based on the premise that words are replaced in languages at a constant rate, at least in the basic vocabulary. By tabulating lists of basic words for related languages and comparing them, one could calculate when the languages had split apart by counting the differences in the basic vocabulary. Linguists today either discount the technique entirely because the basic assumption is arbitrary, or else hold that the result will only indicate a "relative distance" between languages with an uncertain implication for chronology. Hence they speak of *lexicostatistics* instead of glottochronology.

In order to know when the Bantu spread, one has to rely on other sources. The only certain early date is that of the eighth century A.D., when a Bantu lan-guage was in use on Zanzibar and the coast opposite; Bantu words were re-corded by Arab geographers and travelers of that century. We can only guess when the language may have arrived there, or when the Bantu expansion may have begun.

But linguists can tell us other things about the speakers of early Bantu languages through their reconstruction of Proto-Bantu vocabulary. If the languages from which later Bantu languages are derived had words like *canoe,*

fishhook, goat, leader, witch, or *religious specialist,* it is fair to assume that
the culture of the people who spoke that language also included those features. Present reconstructions are in practice largely derived from Malcolm
Guthrie's massive *Comparative Bantu.* They refer to speakers of a Proto-Bantu
in the Cameroons, although some of the reconstructions are not valid because
insufficient attention has been paid to the northwestern quadrant of the Bantu-
language area.

From this Central African protovocabulary the following picture can be
reconstructed. The Proto-Bantu were fishermen. They used canoes, nets, lines,
and fishhooks. They also hunted big and small game and cultivated African
yams and palm trees as well as some cereals, probably millets or sorghums. The
grains were crushed into flour and consumed as porridge after cooking. The
people made pottery, used barkcloth, and perhaps already wove fibers of the
raphia tree on a wide loom. They bred goats, perhaps sheep, and had some
cattle. But they did not take the cattle with them during their migrations. They
did not work iron, so tools must have been fashioned of wood or stone. Data
about weaving is only partly derived from the protovocabulary. It rests partly
on the distribution of looms in the nineteenth century A.D., and the fact that
cloth was woven on a wide loom is attested by some Nok sculptures that date
from the first centuries B.C. The fishermen were sedentary and lived in compact
villages of unknown size.

Social organization was partly based on kinship; polygyny was common.
Village organization was not based entirely on kinship. Perhaps the settlement
was governed by a council of elders, perhaps by a headman. Certainly there is a
term which meant "leader," and it was linked to territorial power. In eastern
Bantu the same term later came to mean "diviner." The ancestral Bantu-speakers feared witches and blamed them for most evil. They employed religious
specialists who were often both medicine men and diviners at the same time.
It is probable, but less clear, that they believed in nature spirits as well as in
the power of ancestors. From distribution studies, one can postulate that they
were good sculptors in wood (at the least they could make dugouts!) and
that they believed in a First Cause of all things.

The exceptionally large Proto-Bantu vocabulary gives even more detail
about some other aspects of culture. The Proto-Bantu kept dogs, for instance,
but no fowl, pigs, ducks, or pigeons. The argument here is based on the absence of certain words, combined with knowledge about their presence in other
languages and the distribution of this language. From the mention of plants
and animals we can conclude that the Proto-Bantu lived on the margins of the
forest. The vocabulary can be exploited further by simple biological knowledge
about species of animals and plants.

All of the preceding linguistic data have been a launching pad for historians and anthropologists. Some have maintained that it was because the Bantu
knew how to smelt iron that they could enter deep into the forest, cut the
trees, and also overcome their Stone Age enemies. Their superiority in tech-

nology allowed them to dominate all peoples they met and thus their language diffused. But the forest can be burned more efficiently than it can be cut, and there is no clear evidence that any word for iron or the technology associated with it is Proto-Bantu. Others have thought that the Proto-Bantu adopted the cultivation of plantains, bananas, and the Asiatic yam, allowing them to live comfortably in the forest. But again the evidence from the protovocabulary does not bear this out.

In fact the reconstructions for words involving iron as well as banana-plantain suggest that these items came to be known to Bantu-speakers after they had already differentiated into various languages, and that the items and the associated techniques spread rapidly from one language to another. The reconstructed words point more to early borrowing than to original Proto-Bantu.

Why the Bantu-speakers could impose their language on other people has raised further speculation. Here, the answers are more like a hypothesis bolstered by analogy to known processes elsewhere than a deduction from known evidence. One possible explanation, for example, comes from analogy to the alien settlement of the Americas: European and African newcomers from the much more diverse disease environment of Afro-Eurasia brought diseases with them to which they themselves had childhood-acquired immunities, but against which the Amerindians in their comparative isolation had no defenses. For the Americas, the result was a population decline of 50 to 100 percent in the first century after Columbus. Something similar might have happened to the relatively isolated peoples of the African forest zone and the southern savanna, just as the Khoikhoi of the far south were to suffer once more from the impact of sea-borne smallpox in the eighteenth century.

Because Bantu-speaking people settled in compact villages in the midst of scattered non-Bantu-speakers, hypothetically the village would act as a center for a region and in time set standards of value. This and intermarriage would lead to a gradual predominance of Bantu speech, even if the absolute number of Bantu-speaking migrants had been smaller at first than that of the native-born inhabitants.

Still, no available hypothesis can yet explain the full complexity of reality over such a long time so far in the past. Ecological readaptations to forest, then savanna again, must have been extremely complex and varied. In theory, something could be made of archaeological materials, but artifacts that have survived tell nothing about the language of those who made or used them. Archaeologists are still quarreling as to what they have to contribute to the search for the location of Proto-Indo-European communities. In India, correlations between archaeological "cultures" and the Aryan invasion are certain only because myths and epics have survived about this invasion and their clues correlate completely with the archaeological evidence. In Africa there may have been too hasty a correlation between Bantu-speaking settlements and the Early Iron Age Industrial Complex. The whole question certainly merits reexamination. It would also be unwise to believe that Bantu-speakers were wedded to just one style of pottery that would betray their origin as certainly as a postage stamp does that of a letter. On the contrary, there is every reason to believe that during their expansion these communities were strongly influenced by the cultures of the local people whom they found, and they may often have taken over the local pottery.

Most, if not all, scholars agree that the last areas into which Bantu languages moved were eastern Africa and a little of southern and southwestern Africa. Here the evidence is not merely geographical (South Africa being the farthest away), but is based on the distribution of the languages itself. The linguistic map of East Africa (page 26) clearly shows that a seesaw effect had been underway for centuries, with Bantu making no progress or only slow advance in the Rift Valley. In southern Africa the large influence from languages spoken before the Bantu arrived suggests that Bantu speech did not have as much time to assimilate all of these borrowings as it had in Central Africa, where one can scarcely detect traces of the aboriginal languages. In southwestern Africa, the arid and difficult environment suggests that the southernmost extension of Bantu speech, that of the Herero, is recent. The Herero had to adopt most of Khoikhoi culture before they could move into the areas they occupy today. A close examination of the grammar and vocabulary of each of the Bantu languages will add much to the possibility of finding traces of aboriginal languages, and will certainly add to our knowledge of how the Bantu-speakers accommodated themselves to the aboriginal inhabitants.

Fortunately, in many parts of the Bantu-speaking area there still are remnants of the aboriginal groups, such as the pygmies of the forest or the hunters of East and South Africa. The situation allows for ethnographic studies and work in physical anthropology. The danger here lies in the fact that centuries, and in places millennia, of contact have radically altered the original situation. Some Bantu-speakers may have become hunters, and the culture of most non-Bantu-speakers became intimately interwoven with that of the newcomers. These problems are serious, but they are also important to a broader understanding of culture change in human history generally.

THE SUDANIC STATE

For more than a century, scholars have noticed that many African states had something in common. In many kingdoms the king was considered to be sacred, to be king by divine law, to be endowed with supernatural power either by the gift of the gods or by doctoring. In his household queen mothers and sisters of queens played a special ceremonial role. Matters of etiquette and symbols associated with the court were often very similar: the king could not see a large sheet of water or cross a specific river. His feet could not touch the ground for fear the crops would burn through his power. He could not see blood or dead people for fear this might affect the fertility of women, animals, and land. He had to be physically without a blemish, for he represented the fertility of the land. If, for instance, the king of Rwanda bent his knees, the country would collapse. If the king became ill he had to be smothered as a sacrifice for the well-being of his land. Among his regalia, drums were very important and one often found blacksmith's tools as well. The king's sisters were married to men who could have no other wives, but these women could keep as many lovers as they wanted, for they represented the fertility of the country. Kings often started their reign by committing incest with their classificatory or even full sisters, which put kings beyond the pale of ordinary humanity and its web of kinship, and therefore made them fit to rule. And many more features can be added to this list.

In fact, the notion of a sacred king, often erroneously called "divine kingship," and the bundle of characteristics it carried with it was described by Sir James Frazer at the beginning of this century and by Arthur M. Hocart before 1930. Most early authors attributed these similarities to a similarity of origin. They postulated that "divine kingship" had first developed in Pharaonic Egypt (3200 B.C.–332 B.C.) and spread from there. With variations, this theory has been repeated to this day. Influential modern anthropologists such as Peter Murdock and Heinz Dittmer or historians such as John Fage and Roland Oliver have supported the notion of a distinct African type of kingship and state: the "Sudanic kingdom." According to the theory, it developed in Egypt and spread from there south to Meroë and from there into the East African lake country, or westward beyond Lake Chad, where it met with another state model of local or North African origin. This process was dated to the first half of the first millennium after Christ.

Although the theory is attractive, it must be discarded. On the one hand some features have been included that are in fact based on functional or structural necessity. Delegation of power from the court to provincial governors or the existence of a capital are features that are functionally determined just as much as the hollowness of a pot. A pot is hollow because it is meant to contain something. Delegation of power in a state is necessary because authority cannot be exercised by any other means over an area larger than a few square miles. Among the functional or structural prerequisites that can have been invented independently over and over again is the notion of the sacredness of kingship, because this constitutes one of the few ultimate justifications for authority that man can devise. That this is so can be shown by the prevalence of sacred kingship in such widely different areas as the ancient Near East, India, East Asia, Southeast Asia, the Inca Empire, and on the Tonga and Hawaiian islands. Even royal incest or marriage with the royal sister was found not only in Pharaonic (and especially Ptolemaic) Egypt, but in Hawaii, Tonga, and pre-Columbian Peru. This explains why social anthropologists in particular have tended to play down the whole concept of a Sudanic state and have argued that wherever a state arises in a preindustrial setting it will show many similar features.

In addition, what is known about innovation either through invention or diffusion makes it unlikely that the blueprint of a state with such details as ideology and court life would have spread as one entity. A culture will only accept features from the outside if it sees a need for them, or at the least if they can be fitted in without requiring a total change in way of life. Pygmies, who are long term neighbors of people with chieftainship and, over the past century or so, of people organized in states, have not copied chieftainly or state institutions. To do so would require them to change completely; their way of life and their value system are effective barriers against diffusion.

Changes are usually made to meet a felt need. If new political features are copied, we can expect to find a local development that needed the support of symbols, roles, or structural elements to bolster its own authority. But the basis for that authority must have been there all along, and it must have had roots in the local society — its economy, its social structure, its religion, its value system. In short, states are born of a long process of innovation within society. Elements from the outside are always reinterpreted to make them fit with what exists already.

Not only are features taken over just when they are needed; a complete political system with all its trappings cannot be taken over all at once. Each feature diffuses in its own way. All features that make up the "Sudanic state" complex, therefore, almost certainly traveled at different times in different directions, and at different rates of speed. The resulting picture conceals a multitude of historical events that happened at different times. Some anthropologists, such as Peter C. Lloyd for the Yoruba, therefore claim that neighboring kingdoms have become more similar because they borrowed features from each other, features that originally had been restricted to one kingdom. In the end, the similarities covered over and hid the diversity of origins. This also happened on a pan-African scale.

While anthropologist Peter G. Murdock overstates his case in claiming that all African kingdoms are as similar as peas in a pod — and is wrong in attributing this "fact" to diffusion from Egypt — many similarities between African states remain. These, however, can be explained by a theory of *saturation*. After the rise of kingdoms in different parts of the continent, they began to exchange ideologies, etiquette, insignia, and roles. After a thousand years or so of diffusion crisscrossing the continent, the kingdoms ended up far more similar than they were at the beginning.

This saturation hypothesis can be supported by such evidence as the diffusion of single and double flange-welded iron bells from West to Central Africa. The bells were only a minor insignium of office, but two diffusions are significant. One was completed by about 800 A.D. and one seems to have ended around 1500 A.D. Together they show that Zambian chiefdoms and states, including even Zimbabwe, had thus been influenced at two widely different times from areas as far away as Nigeria or the Cameroons. The saturation theory underlines once more the fact that African peoples did not live in utter isolation. At least in the last two millennia, intercultural contact has been intensive, and it is one of the major processes explaining culture growth within the continent.

THE RISE OF AFRICAN STATES

Now we can see why Sudanic kingdoms look alike. But we have not yet explained why states originated, or why they originated in so many parts of the African continent. First, the chronology. Archaeological work in Mauritania suggests that between 800 and 600 B.C., an *incipient state* existed in the Tichitt area. It was inhabited by ancestors of the Soninke and perhaps Mande. Later it decayed under the onslaught of nomadic Berbers. But after 300 B.C., the movement towards state formation began again, culminating by 400 A.D., or perhaps even later, with the rise of the kingdom of Ghana. On the Senegal River the state of Takrūr may also be related to this general development and some date its beginning to 100 A.D. By 800 A.D. other states had independently arisen in Gao on the Niger and Kanem, east of Lake Chad.

In the Nile valley and Ethiopia, state formation is of course much older, since the middle Nile was already a state by 1500 B.C. and the earliest Ethiopian states may go back to 600 B.C. In the Bantu-speaking area the notion of territorial chieftainship already existed before the migration began, but evidence for the rise of more complex states comes much later. Chiefdoms existed on the East African coast in the eighth or the ninth century, and a large-scale state (Masudi's) in central Mozambique dates from at least the tenth century A.D. In Shaba or Katanga, the beginnings of dense territorial occupation, and presumably the roots of elaborate political organization, go back to the eighth century A.D., and out of these developed a cluster of states that may have been full-fledged kingdoms by the thirteenth century. The interlacustrine area shows evidence for a large state in the fourteenth and fifteenth centuries. As in the lower Congo, states began earlier than the fourteenth century. Between Kanem and the Nile the Daju had clearly formed a state in Darfur by the middle of the twelfth century and perhaps long before.

The chronological evidence, admittedly still scanty, seems to show that different clusters of states arose independently in different parts of Africa. During the first millennium A.D. states arose all over tropical Africa. How did this happen? In general, two sets of theories have been proposed. The first one, defended by Basil Davidson and Christopher C. Wrigley, deals only with Bantu-speaking Africa but has implications for West Africa as well. These authors maintain that the superiority of iron weaponry, monopolized by a few, made the development of states possible. They follow earlier suggestions, which pointed out that in royal rituals all over the continent links are found between the status of smiths and kingship. The ties are there even in areas where smiths are the most despised caste, as in Wadai. Again it is remarkable that smithing and the tools of metallurgy are so often linked with kingship. But is this to be explained by the superiority in warfare that would stem from the use of iron weapons?

One other possible explanation is that kings and smiths both seemed to control supernatural powers and that the link between them lies in magic and

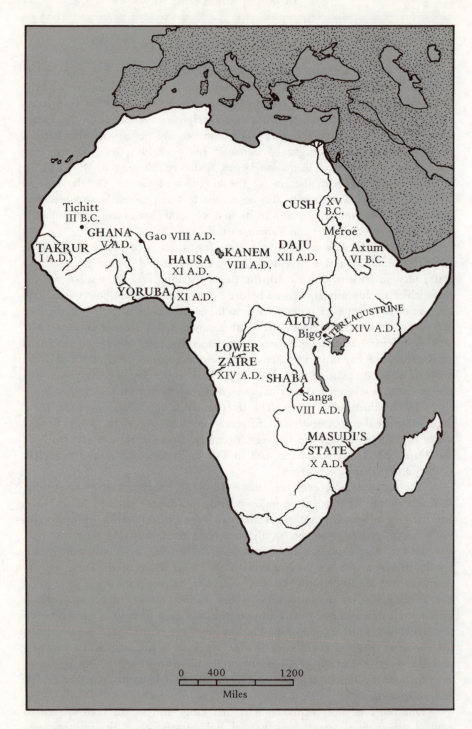

Tichitt
III B.C.

GHANA
V A.D.

Gao VIII A.D.

CUSH

XV
B.C.

Meroë

TAKRUR
I A.D.

HAUSA
XI A.D.

KANEM
VIII A.D.

DAJU
XII A.D.

Axum
VI B.C.

YORUBA   XI A.D.

ALUR

INTERLACUSTRINE
XIV A.D.

Bigo

LOWER
ZAIRE
XIV A.D.

SHABA

Sanga
VIII A.D.

MASUDI'S
STATE
X A.D.

0   400   1200

Miles

The Sudanic States, Eighth Century A.D.

symbolism, rather than in military cooperation. It is not likely that iron weapons were at first a great advantage, because early metallurgy was not efficient and the iron was of uneven quality. In addition, many states elsewhere in the world developed without iron, witnessed in Pharaonic Egypt itself. Some states became quite complex without any knowledge of metals, as on the Tonga Islands. Clearly, then, control of metals is not essential to the development of a state.

Other theories have made much of the link between economic structure and political development. Some hold that states arose where trade flourished and were a consequence of trade. It is clear that trade did flourish in the sahel, on the east coast of Africa, in the gold-bearing lands of Zimbabwe, and in the copper- and salt-producing areas of Katanga. But in the East African lake region evidence of long-distance trade is insufficient to "explain" political development. Trade and the state are, in fact, parallel developments. Traders go to centers and centers are based on more advanced political organization than noncenters. For instance, the Hausa cities were not the earliest points to which trans-Saharan traders went. They evolved as market places only after they were organized as city-states. But a capital city that can function as a market does increase revenue and stimulate further political development.

The other theory, proposed elegantly by the French anthropologist Claude Meillassoux, holds that the key to political development lies in the production of economic surplus, bringing about specialization of labor and a restricted group of "power" goods that could be kept in the hands of a few. Those few could then specialize full time in political affairs and control the rest by redistributing the special goods. These goods were their taxation, labor, and tribute systems, and they took on more and more complex forms as time passed. Gordon Childe had used a similar idea to explain the emergence of cities and states in the Near East and Egypt. Meillassoux's contribution is to show that, by playing on kinship roles, the elders could develop the authority to force their juniors to hand over all economic surplus to them for redistribution, and the first goods to be thus channeled were women and bride-wealth.

This theory has also been challenged. Some point out that the notion of an economic surplus is weak because no one would increase his work load to produce a surplus if he did not already feel compulsion from others or the need for more goods. A call for surplus must come either from people who are already in a position to claim, absorb, and redistribute surplus, or else from a social system in which certain prestige goods are held in esteem by all, so that their possession is the outward sign of status. But once again political specialization, division of labor, and increased production form one constellation in which no priority can be given to a single factor.

Political development grew out of the need for social management of larger and larger groups. Scarcity of some factors of production (such as land or labor) or increasing concentrations of people required more and more sophisticated ways to harmonize their interests, such as better decision-making processes and better-defined channels for the use and devolution of power. The archaeological record shows clearly that state formation was slow. The growth in structures, ideologies, and functions of kinship groups was tied to increasing population, itself inexorably linked with the relation between society and culture, including value systems on the one hand and the environment on the other.

Further evidence of this growth can be found in most African states where kinship still formed an essential part of the political system. The rigid taxonomic approach dividing states from "segmentary" societies has clouded the basic fact that many a so-called segmentary society had specialized political leadership, roles, and procedures, so that kinship "patriarchs" might sometimes govern larger numbers of peoples than some kings did.

The older theory that *all* states originate in conquest must be discarded completely. Once states, or at least chiefdoms, existed, conquest may have played a role, as it did in forming the Zulu nation, for instance (see page 305), but conquest did not often create states in areas where none existed before. Once a state had come into being, it might expand, and expansion sometimes occurred by conquest, sometimes by imitation. Neighbors might transform themselves into a state to hold off the threat of conquest, but they could also accept annexation voluntarily, wishing to participate in the prestige of courts and state rule. The Alur chiefdoms near Lake Albert may have spread in this fashion.

Thus state structures expanded over many parts of sub-Saharan Africa (although in certain cases segmentary or other structures filled the needs of the community as well or better than a state might have done), whereas for pastoral nomads or hunters, the basic residential stability required for a state was still lacking.

CONCLUSION

As soon as food-producing economies had taken root everywhere, Africa had acquired its distinctive character. Its culture areas were already formed. It lacked only the development of states and cities, which were to grow with the increasing complexity of the cultures. Many of the basic canons for sculpture in West Africa go back to the Nok culture that flourished in the first millennium B.C., and, if we can believe Henri Lhote, some masks depicted on rocks in the Sahara are found again 4000 years later among the West African Senufo. Although the continuity in masks may be a little farfetched, there is little doubt about long continuity in the shapes of houses, the layouts of settlements, and the material remains that archaeologists find or artists record on rock.

Stressing this continuity helps us understand Africa's history as well as its present. Each African society represents literally millennia of experimentation and experience, and that experience explains why social systems, values, and cultures did not fade away when European norms were introduced with the colonial period. Yet along with this continuity over centuries, there was constant change. The picture of a "traditional" and unchanging Africa simply reflects our ignorance about much of the detailed patterns of change at early periods.

From the glimpses we do have, however, it seems clear that African societies changed and readjusted at much the same rate as other societies in other parts of the world did between the agricultural and industrial revolutions.

SUGGESTIONS FOR FURTHER READING

Clark, John D. *The Prehistory of Africa.* London: Thames and Hudson, 1970.

Dalby, David. *Language and History in Africa.* London: Frank Cass, 1970.

Fagan, Brian, and Oliver, Roland. *Africa in the Iron Age; c. 500 B.C. to 1400 A.D.* Cambridge: Cambridge University Press, 1975.

Fage, John D. *An Atlas of African History.* London: St. Martin, 1958. This is the only available atlas today. A new atlas by Jacob Ajayi and Michael Crowder is due to be published in 1979, by Longman.

Heine, Bernd. "Neue Beiträge der Sprachforschung für die Afrikanische Geschichte." *Paideuma* 22 (1976): 5–10.

Hiernaux, Jean. *The People of Africa.* London: Weidenfeld and Nicolson, 1974.

McCall, Daniel. *Africa in Time Perspective.* London: Oxford University Press, 1964.

Chapter 2
Northern Africa
in a Wider World

THE HISTORY of northern Africa is so different from the pattern or style of history south of the Sahara that some treatments of African history exclude it altogether, partly because present-day North Africa belongs culturally and linguistically to a larger Muslim and Arabic entity that stretches well beyond the African continent. Historically, North Africa has also belonged for several millennia to the world of urban, literate societies. Egypt, at least, played an important role in the development of early civilization, with relatively intense intercommunication and relatively rapid technological progress. Other parts of Africa no further away than Nubia, Ethiopia, or the western Sudan had some contact with this zone of intense intercommunication, but they and the rest of sub-Saharan Africa were only on the fringes until the nineteenth century A.D. North Africa meanwhile played a role in historical processes common to all the Mediterranean basin, and in the wider world that stretched off to the east.

But the rest of African history was not played out in isolation. The Sahara was not as uncrossable or uncrossed as the pre-Columbian Atlantic; the Red Sea was even less of a barrier. Even if the history of sub-Saharan Africa were the only concern of this book, it would still be essential to fill in something of the history of its neighbors and points of contact with other people. This history therefore carries to the northern limits of the physical continent, with occasional notice of events in Arabia or even further afield. To put the relationship another way, North Africa was long in the core area of intercommunication, and it was customary to write its history with little or no reference to the world south of the Sahara. We would have had a better perspective on the human experience if that older history had not confined itself to the history of "civilization," but the history of sub-Saharan Africa is even less comprehensible without reference to its neighboring regions of more intense intercommunication.

THE GEOGRAPHICAL FRAMEWORK

The physical environment of northern Africa was far more than a back-drop against which history was to be played out. Even more starkly than in many other parts of the world, environment set the limits of what was likely or even possible. The fundamental feature was aridity. The Sahara is the largest and driest desert in the world, and the problem of insufficient rainfall shades off from the desert itself to the *sahel* (Arabic for the "fringe" or "shore" of the desert), and on to the better-watered lands along the North African coast or the Nile valley. It was not simply a crude question of whether or not there was enough rain to grow crops. Oasis conditions made agriculture possible wherever the natural setting supplied surface or underground water, which may have fallen hundreds if not thousands of miles away. Different kinds of society came into existence to deal with different environments, and the interactions of these societies over time form one of the major themes in African history as a whole.

Nor were these interactions peculiar to Africa. Africa is a continent, but it also forms a part of the great Afro-Eurasian land mass. The Sahara is merely the westward expansion of the great Afro-Eurasian dry belt that begins at the Sea of Okhotsk and stretches westward across the Gobi Desert, parts of Soviet Central Asia, Afghanistan, Iran, and Arabia, to cross the Red Sea and what is nearly the widest part of the African continent to the Atlantic coast of Mauritania. This belt cuts off sub-Saharan Africa from the sedentary farmers of northern Africa far more effectively than the Mediterranean Sea separates those sedentary societies from southern Europe. This same desert in Arabia cuts off southern Arabia and Africa from the fertile crescent of the Middle East far more effectively than the Red Sea separates Arabia from the neighboring African coast. For that matter, another arid zone lying to the south of the Ethiopian highlands strikes the Indian Ocean coast along the present frontier of Kenya and Somalia and constitutes a second line of defense, isolating central and southern Africa from the north — and incidentally making the high and relatively well-watered plateaus of Ethiopia and southern Arabia a kind of mountainous island in the desert sea.

In fact, northern Africa is divided into a series of different regions, each separated from the others by zones of comparative aridity. The westernmost is the region now known as the Maghrib, from its Arabic name meaning "the West." As a further token of its separation from the rest of Africa, the Arabs sometimes called it "the western island," thinking of the desert to the south as equivalent to the sea to the north, east, and west. The region includes parts of Morocco, Algeria, and Tunisia, although the present-day boundaries of those countries include much more than the true western island, a strip of cultivable land some 2000 miles long east-to-west but only 70 to 200 miles wide. Even within this cultivated zone, the sharply accented relief of the various ranges of the Atlas Mountains makes for a great variety of smaller subregions. The largest

areas of fairly flat land are found at either end — the Moroccan coastal plains
on the west, northern Tunisia and northeastern Algeria on the east.

The climate of the Maghrib, like that of the far south around Capetown, is
"Mediterranean" in type with winter rains and a long drought in midsummer,
not unlike southern California. As a result, the land is productive in the same
crops that grow on the European side of the sea — wheat, wine, and olives, and
sometimes barley in the drier regions. As in California, differences in altitude
make for great differences in rainfall within a small space, so that many crops
have to be grown on irrigated land that receives little actual rainfall. This kind
of agriculture was especially important historically on the desert side of the
Atlas, where rainfall from the high mountains runs off in streams, some of them
underground, until they finally disappear into the sand. This source of water
makes possible a strip of intense cultivation, a ribbon oasis.

Moving east from Tunisia, the Gulf of Syrte indents North Africa, carrying
the shore south into desert altitudes — too far for continuous cultivation all
along the coast. Only in the vicinity of Tripoli, and again where the coast bends
north to form the bulge of Cyrenaica east of Benghazi, is there enough rainfall
for regular cultivation. Otherwise the region that is now Libya and western
Egypt is steppe and desert broken by occasional islands of cultivation where
oases occur. Some of these oases are important, especially in the region south of

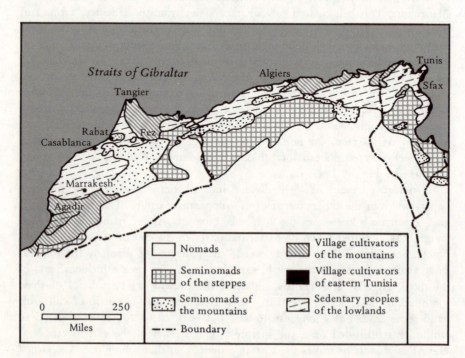

The Setting of North African History

Tripoli called Fezzan and centering on Murzuk, and another oases region south of Cyrenaica. These oases have figured in history out of all proportion to their size or wealth, for they have served as stepping stones for crossing the desert — either in an east-west direction from Egypt to the Maghrib, or north and south from the Mediterranean to the well-watered lands south of the Sahara.

In fact, Egypt itself is an oasis in a region that would be desert if it were not for the water of the Nile, provided by rain that originally fell thousands of miles away in the East African highlands or in Ethiopia. The rest of Egypt has only enough rainfall to support sparse nomadic pastoralism. Historical Egypt is a very long ribbon oasis stretching down from the mountains to the south, but the oasis is not uniform through all its length. In the lower Nile valley of Egypt proper, the river brings water for irrigation of the floodplain on either side. From Aswan to Cairo, usually called Upper Egypt (see page 46), the valley is truly ribbonlike; in Lower Egypt, below Cairo, the river splits into the many branches of the delta, flowing through low-lying and often swampy country until it reaches the sea.

Above Aswan, the character of the river valley is again different. Easy navigation by sailing vessels ends with the first cataract, the lowest of a series of six rock shelves that force the water through rapids or over low falls between that point and Khartoum, where the Blue and White Niles come together. This stretch is the Nubian Nile, where the streambed cuts more deeply into the countryside than in Egypt itself, limiting the area of floodplain irrigation. The natural frontier at the first cataract was the historical frontier between Egyptian and Nubian cultures. It also became a language line; the ancient language above Aswan was ancestral to modern Nubian and belongs to the Eastern Sudanic branch of the Nilo-Saharan language stock (and is thus related to sub-Saharan languages), whereas Coptic or Ancient Egyptian belonged to the Afro-Asiatic language family, related to Berber, Arabic, and Hebrew. In this sense, the southward stretch of Egyptian culture was not to the southern edge of the Sahara but only to the Aswan frontier in mid-desert.

Above Nubia was the savanna country of sub-Saharan Africa, where rainfall agriculture was again possible. This was also the Sudan, in Arabic *bilād al-Sudān,* "the land of the blacks." Along the Nile, the sedentary populations of the Sudan could use irrigation, but that was not common until the twentieth century A.D. The older base here was rainfall agriculture, as it was along the whole east-west belt of savanna country stretching from the Red Sea to the mouth of the Senegal.

Within this belt the northernmost region usable for agriculture has twenty to twenty-four inches of rainfall, and rainfall increases steadily to the south until the forest belt is reached. But this did not mean that populations were denser further south. Desert-side conditions were often just as favorable for agriculture. In the Nilotic Sudan, in particular, the natural environment became more difficult away from the sahel. Further south, the Nile became choked with vegetation and spread out each high-water season across the neighboring grass-

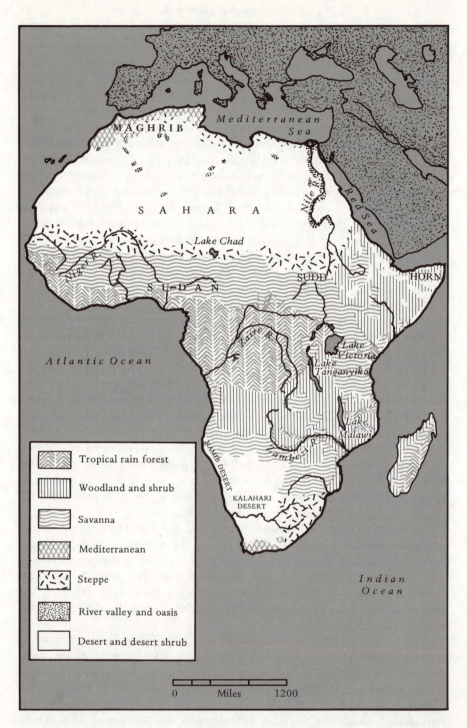

Legend:

- Tropical rain forest
- Woodland and shrub
- Savanna
- Mediterranean
- Steppe
- River valley and oasis
- Desert and desert shrub

Africa: Vegetation

land. Rather than favoring agriculture as similar floods did in Egypt, the result was an environment far more friendly to pastoralism than to tilling the soil. The vegetation-choked reaches of the Nile, called the *sudd,* were also a barrier to further navigation up river, and the annual flooding made travel to the south difficult by land as well. As a result, the dense agricultural populations of the northern Sudan along the Nile were not really a threshold of contact, leading easily to the rest of tropical Africa; they themselves had no intense and continuous contact with other peoples further south. The Nile valley was therefore less than adequate as a transportation route leading from the East African highlands to Egypt.

On the other hand, the lower Nile provided superb transportation at early stages of maritime technology. All during the season of low water from November through the following August, sailing vessels could easily move upstream by using the prevailing northerly winds. The return to Cairo or the delta was equally easy, with the current to help. Above Aswan, the cataracts were not an insuperable barrier, but they made water transportation more difficult.

As a transportation route, the Red Sea is more deceptive. It was not a good route from north to south until the nineteenth-century invention of steamships and the construction of the Suez Canal. The main problem was not the land bridge at Suez so much as navigational difficulties on the sea itself. The same prevailing northerlies that help navigation on the Nile also blow over the northern Red Sea, but they blow all year with no river current for the return trip.

In the southern half of the Red Sea, the wind direction alternated with the Indian Ocean monsoons. In winter, winds on the Red Sea blow from the southeast as far north as Jidda and Mecca, where the northerlies take over. With the southwest monsoon of the summer months, northerlies prevail along the whole length of the sea, making it easy for Indian Ocean ships to return home. This made for easy sea communication in the southern half of the sea, but sailing ships rarely made the whole voyage from one end to the other. It was more efficient to off-load the southern cargoes at some convenient port about midway along either shore. On the western side, it was convenient to transship from a port like Suakin to the Nile below Aswan for the final trip down the river to Cairo or a Mediterranean port. To the east, it was convenient to transship at a port like Jidda for overland caravan by way of Mecca and Medina to Syria or other parts of the fertile crescent. The Red Sea was therefore readily usable in connection with camel caravans, but it never played the same historical role as the Mediterranean in uniting peoples and cultures around its fringes.

The final region of early sedentary population and good rainfall is the combined highlands of Ethiopia and south Arabia. These two regions are on different continents, but the Red Sea has not divided them historically. They are not merely geologically and climatically similar; their cultures also have much in common, with the Amharic and Tigriña languages of Ethiopia closely related to the Arabic of southern Arabia. The very fact that both sides of the straits have long practiced sedentary agriculture separates them from the surrounding nomads. South Arabia is also somewhat cut off from the east by the "empty quarter" of pure desert that occupies the southeast interior of the Arabian peninsula. In much the same way, Ethiopia was cut off from the south by the arid belt of the present-day Kenya-Ethiopian border, and from the west by the sudd of the Nile valley. Yet both southern Arabia and Ethiopia enjoy easy contact with the Red Sea, since the highlands drop off precipitously to the seacoast on either side of the straits. Both have their easiest overland contact to the north — in Arabia, through the caravan route along the eastern shore of the Red Sea, and in Ethiopia by way of routes northwest to the Nilotic Sudan and thence down the Nile through Nubia to Egypt. Although Ethiopia and southern Arabia are clearly south of the great Afro-Eurasian dry belt, these regions tend toward the style of North African history, partly because of their easy contact with the north and partly because of Ethiopia's isolation from the rest of sub-Saharan Africa.

EGYPT: THE FIRST AFRICAN CIVILIZATION

In this book, we often put quotation marks around *civilization* because of its invidious overtones. Westerners have long talked and written about Africa as an uncivilized, barbaric continent — when what they really meant by "civilized" was simply "people like us," and by "barbarians," "people different from us." But the term *civilization* first meant the way of life of people who lived in cities, and the word still can be used in that sense. We prefer to refer to the *intercommunicating zone* in world history as the region where people were in easiest touch with one another, and hence were able to borrow innovations and achieve a rapid rate of technological change. But we might just as easily refer to the origin of this intercommunicating zone as the rise of civilization, in the sense that civilization means life in cities and a greater intensity of intercommunication began with city life.

Afro-Eurasian agriculture appeared for the first time to our knowledge in the Middle East about 10,000 B.C., and the agricultural revolution spread out from there with profound consequences for human society. This new phase is sometimes called the neolithic, or New Stone Age, to separate it from the rougher tools of the hunting and gathering peoples, and from the metal tools that followed.

The next threshold of human technological change was a combination known as the Bronze Age, even though metallurgy was not its greatest achievement. The true secret of Bronze Age achievement was efficient agriculture — efficient enough to leave a surplus over the basic food needs of the farmers themselves. Some food could then be diverted to pay specialized and skilled craftsworkers in other fields. Denser populations were also possible, and concentrations of people began to gather around a point of trade, a royal court, or an important temple. These concentrations were in fact embryo cities. They increased the intensity and variety of communication and provided a stimulus to invention through the exchange of ideas.

The first Bronze Age society was Sumer in Mesopotamia, where the archaeological record shows a rapid development of an urban society between about 3500 and 3000 B.C. The technology that made this possible included irrigation agriculture in the Tigris and Euphrates valleys and improvements in transportation, such as wheeled carts and sailing vessels; refinements in metallurgy and pottery; and finally, in about 3000 B.C., the art of writing. Early Sumerian civilization was confined to irrigable river valleys, apparently because the technology of rainfall agriculture was still not adequate to support a non-food-producing segment of society.

It is also possible, however, that irrigation agriculture made for a more tightly controlled society, where whatever surplus the farmers or fishermen might produce beyond their own needs could be drawn off for the support of priests, rulers, or a nobility. This supposition rests on the reasoning that irrigation works often require a larger scale of work organization than either hunting or rainfall farming. Once ways were discovered for organizing the masses, the rulers could have manipulated the people more easily for their own benefit. Rainfall farmers, on the other hand, normally worked the land in family-sized units. These units were more nearly self-sufficient, hence harder for the rulers to manipulate and less prone to contribute their resources to the cities, temples, or courts.

Other urban societies appeared a little before 3000 B.C., often in distant river valleys where irrigation was also possible, rather than in regions that were nearby but lacked the crucial environment. One of these second-string centers of irrigation agriculture and urban life was the Indus valley in northwest India; another was the Nile in Egypt. The desiccation of the Sahara had not yet begun, and the Nile gave a reliable source of irrigation water, while the neighboring lands were suitable for some rainfall agriculture and for raising sheep, goats, cattle, and donkeys. (Horses and camels were not yet available.)

In the Nile floodplain, early irrigation was comparatively simple. The behavior of the lower river today follows from the fact that the flow from Lake Victoria-Nyanza into the White Nile is fairly constant throughout the year. But the Blue Nile from Lake Tana in Ethiopia, which contributes twice as much water each year, contributes it sporadically — the flow reaching Egypt in August and September is about forty times the flow in March or April, toward the end of the Ethiopian dry season. For Egypt this meant (as it does today) that the Nile flowed over its banks in the summer months. The silt it carried provided renewed fertility for annual cropping, and the earliest form of irrigation was simply to plant the land bared by the receding flood. Residual moisture was enough to carry these crops through to the harvest. The first artificial irrigation simply modified the natural order by building levees and channels to control the flow from the main river, and earth banks to impound it to a depth of one or two meters long enough to guarantee adequate deposits of moisture and silt.

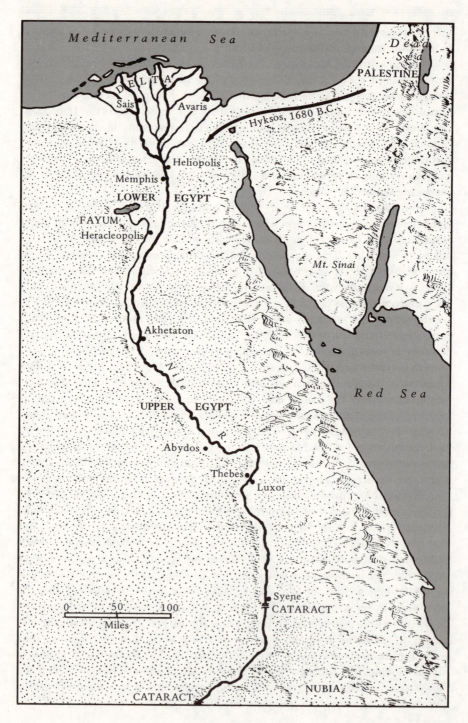

Early Egypt

This system, called *basin irrigation,* could be further improved by various devices raising water from the Nile to the floodplain even in seasons of low water. Some devices depended on the flow of the river itself, others used animal power, and some used human strength alone. The total area in perennial irrigation in early times was very small indeed, but it contributed to the wealth of the valley by allowing a second or even a third crop on the same land. Today the great majority of cultivated land in Egypt is under perennial irrigation, but the dams to store the water, the canals to carry it, and the powered pumps to lift it came only with the nineteenth and twentieth centuries.

Urban society using basin irrigation arose remarkably fast in Egypt, compared to its slow development in Mesopotamia. Shortly after 4000 B.C., copper came into use. After 3600 B.C., technological change became even faster, with borrowing from Mesopotamia in agricultural and craft production, and perhaps in some aspects of social organization. The early cities of sun-dried brick emerged at this time as did long-distance trade at sea and on the Nile, and innovations in the art of writing. In some respects, Egypt began to develop its own style and character. Writing, for example, took the form of hieroglyphs or picture writing, as opposed to the Mesopotamian cuneiform, which worked on an altogether different principle. (A third system, Phoenician writing with symbols that stood for sounds, not ideas, was different again. It was, of course, the ancestor of the alphabet later adopted by the Greeks, Romans, and the Western world generally.) Authorities generally assume that writing spread from Mesopotamia to Egypt by stimulus diffusion, in which the idea of writing came from abroad but the particular technique was invented locally.

In other respects, Egypt moved rapidly past the point reached in Mesopotamia. From about 3600 B.C. to about 3000 B.C., Egypt's basic civilization took shape. The most notable achievement was in political organization. The earliest urban society in the Nile valley was divided into a number of small states. After 3400 B.C., these states grew in size and in social complexity. By 3200 B.C., they had merged into only two; by 3100 B.C., the whole country was united under the first pharaohs. The initial political unity lasted during most of the next thousand years, in spite of periods of disorder and changing dynasties. It was built in part on the natural unity of the Nile valley from the first cataract to the sea, reinforced by excellent water transportation — and by lack of neighbors. The narrow floodplain of the Nubian Nile could not sustain a large population, and potential enemies had to come from across the sea or across the desert from the east or west. Only the nomads of the Red Sea hills or the western desert posed a constant threat, but their land was too poor to give them real power unless the Egyptian state was weak or disunited.

Egyptologists use the label *Pharaonic* for the whole period from the first united kingdom of 3100 B.C. to 332 B.C., when Egypt was conquered by the armies of Alexander the Great of Macedonia. The earlier period is called *Predynastic,* whereas the following period, under Alexander's successors, is called *Ptolemaic,* after the Graeco-Egyptian Ptolemies who ruled until Egypt was absorbed into the Roman Empire just before the birth of Christ. Specialists also subdivide the Pharaonic period, beginning with the Old Kingdom (3100–1640 B.C.), the original united Egyptian state under the pharaohs. A period of disorder followed in about 2180–2080. Then came the Middle Kingdom (2080–1640), then a second intermediate period, and finally a New Kingdom (1570–1090 B.C.). The remaining Pharaonic period is often categorized as the period of the invasions or the era of foreign dynasties, because Libyans, Assyrians, and Persians controlled the country — sometimes with supreme control exercised from their homeland, sometimes merely as dynasties of foreign origin naturalized in Egypt. A further convention divides the Pharaonic period into thirty dynasties labeled in Roman numerals from I to XXX.

It is important to recognize that these separate periods and subperiods are conventions imposed by historians, not a reality that ancient Egyptians themselves would have known. Although they are useful to help make order out of nearly three thousand years of confused history, these conventions can also suggest the misconception that historical change is properly summarized in the political shifts of rulers or ruling dynasties. When art is ascribed to a particular dynasty, for example, all we really know is that it was created when that dynasty ruled — not that the pharaohs were actually responsible for it, directly or indirectly.

Some historical developments seem to mature slowly, but Egyptian culture of the Pharaonic period rose to a remarkable flowering in the Old Kingdom and then retained much of its characteristic style for millennia. It was not changeless, but many Egyptologists believe that established traditions stifled further innovation. Monumental building, for example, reached a kind of peak in about 2600–2500 B.C. (dynasty IV), when some of the most impressive pyramids were constructed, and it continued over the next millennia. Other art styles that first emerged at the beginning of the Old Kingdom can still be traced in art produced two thousand years later.

Egyptian religion, however, is an exception to this impression of monolithic uniformity and stability over time. The earliest pharaohs of the Old Kingdom were regarded as incarnations of the raven god, Horus. Without quite giving up this claim, later pharaohs were also recognized as god-descendants of Re, the sun god, or of Osiris, the god-ruler of the underworld. The accepted explanation is that the original pharaohs came to rule over a country with a great deal of religious diversity, with each of the small original kingdoms having its own gods and local priesthoods. One way to reconcile them all might have been to establish an authoritative account that would show them as members of a common pantheon, where one god was supreme but all found an honored place — and some Egyptian theologians tried this without long-term success. Another solution that worked better for the central authorities was not to worry about primacy among the gods, but to allow each group of priests to go its own way so long as all recognized that the pharaoh himself was a god-king incarnate on earth.

As we have seen, Pharaonic Egypt was one of the many African states with institutions that used to be classified as divine kingship. The god-king was not merely a deity; his personal physical health and well-being were peculiarly and intimately associated with the land, the harvest, and especially with the supply of water by the Nile flood. While anthropologists and historians once postulated that this kind of kingship may have originated in Egypt and passed from there to the rest of Africa, the best present hypothesis suggests that many aspects of sacred kingship were independently invented in several places to justify an accepted structure of authority over society. Other aspects may have been diffused up or down the Nile valley in the distant past, but there is no reason to suppose that they went from Egypt upstream rather than downstream from the Sudan toward Egypt. Indeed, these ideas about kingship were probably accepted at a time before the desiccation of the Sahara, when Egypt had more numerous neighbors where deserts now exist.

Early representations in Egyptian art show pharaohs with symbols of pastoralism like the shepherd's crook, and several authorities believe that their later religious position as god-kings is traceable to an earlier role as magicians and rainmakers among pastoral nomads or seminomads. All of this suggests that the original unification of the Nile valley may have been achieved through conquest by a pastoral nomadic community from the not yet desiccated Sahara. If a nomadic confederation had been formed under religious leadership (as often happened among nomads in more recent history), and if it conquered the sedentary states of the Nile valley (as often happened to other sedentary societies), the resulting administration might well have been similar to that of the early pharaohs — a political structure that was essentially an extension of the god-king's household, imposed from above on localized peasant communities, each with its own local gods and beliefs.

In any event, peasant communities formed the base of Egyptian society. Most peasants were freemen, though a small class of slaves also existed. At least during the Old Kingdom, no important social groups stood between the peasantry and the royal household — no merchants, for example, and only the bare beginnings of a local gentry. The entire organization of the country, including foreign trade and irrigation works, was in the hands of the royal household. The peasantry either had their labor taxed or were conscripted to work on levees, dykes, irrigation channels, and monumental architecture like the pyramids. Tens of thousands of people must have been mobilized each year to create public works on the scale of those that remain, though they may not have worked in such terrible conditions as our mental pictures of "Egyptian bondage" suggest. Before the coming of perennial irrigation, little or no farm work was possible for a few months. Historians now believe that pyramids and irrigation works alike were built by mobilizing labor during this slack season, rather than by keeping thousands of slaves at work on a year-round basis.

After the first millennium of pharaonic rule, the royal household became less efficient. Perhaps it grew too big and unwieldy, or perhaps officials began

to make their offices hereditary. In any case, the centralized kingdom broke
down after about 2180 B.C., creating the first *Intermediate Period* in which
political authority was fragmented. Several local leaders claimed to be the god-
king of all Egypt, though none of them could make the claim stand.

Then, after 2080 B.C., centralized authority returned with the foundation
of the Middle Kingdom, but the consequences of recent localization remained.
Landlords and local priests became an important intermediate group between
the peasantry and the royal household. Egypt also began to lose some of her
previous isolation behind the surrounding deserts. Naval expeditions had already been sent down the Red Sea to southern Arabia, Ethiopia, and the horn of
Africa at the end of the Old Kingdom. With the Middle Kingdom, they became
more systematic and regularized. More intense trade by sea reached out to the
Levant, and overland contact brought systematic and regular relations to the
fertile crescent.

Up the Nile, one or more Nubian kingdoms had already come into existence during the Old Kingdom, and parts of Nubia probably fell under Egyptian domination even before 2000 B.C. These Nubian kingdoms were originally
similar to Egypt itself, with aspects of sacred monarchy associated with rain-
making and fertility of the soil. Later on, during the Egyptian New Kingdom,
the original Nubian institutions were covered over by a systematic cultural
Egyptianization which brought Egyptian gods and hieroglyphic writing. The
web of more intense intercommunication, originating in Egypt, nevertheless
began to reach sub-Saharan Africa at a very early date, and it continued for
many hundreds of years, though sometimes by fits and starts, following political
and military changes.

Egypt's increasing contact with the outer world shot forward decisively in
the Second Intermediate Period (1640–1570 B.C.), bringing new rulers from
Asia called the Hyksos. Historians are divided as to just who these Hyksos may
have been. One possibility is that they were chariot-riding warriors who swept
down and conquered Egypt, as similar charioteers had recently conquered Mesopotamia. But they could have been more simple immigrants from Asia who
infiltrated and then rose more slowly to power. In any event, they founded a
Hyksos principality that ruled most of the delta while a native dynasty continued
to rule over Upper Egypt. Whatever their political role, the Hyksos brought a
new mode of Asian technology, from military chariots to bronze metallurgy, new
textile manufactures, and new musical instruments, even new agriculture (for
example, olive trees and new breeds of cattle).

After 1570 B.C., the New Kingdom began when an Egyptian dynasty
united the entire country. The Hyksos disappeared or were assimilated into the
Egyptian population, but the impact of increased foreign contact remained.
Egyptian foreign policy was felt regularly in Asia, and several Egyptian armies
invaded the fertile crescent. For a time after 1500 B.C., it looked as though
Egypt might unite all the urban societies of the Middle East under her rule,
much as Rome later united the Mediterranean world. At some period in the

New Kingdom, Egypt did succeed in ruling Nubia almost as far as the rain lands of the Sudan. But the Egyptian threat was overtaken by the rise of other states.

Especially after about 1400 B.C., a series of Asian powers came in turn to a position of dominance — first Hittites from Anatolia, then Assyrians, and finally the Persians, just before the Macedonian conquest swept over them all. While Egyptian armies still sometimes marched in Asia, Asian armies also now marched in Egypt. Both Assyrians and Persians ruled Egypt for a time. Other foreigners founded Egyptian dynasties, including Libyans from the west (people ancestral to the present-day Tuaregs of the Sahara), and Egyptianized Nubians from the south. Well before the end of the New Kingdom, foreign elements had a strong impact on Egyptian life and art. Iron metallurgy came in from Anatolia. Even before the Ptolemies and Greek overrule after 332 B.C., such imported ideas had already paved the way for the Hellenistic synthesis that was to pull Egypt more firmly than ever into the intercommunicating world of the Mediterranean and the Middle East.

NOMADS AND SEDENTARIES

Historians generally presume that pastoralism without agriculture was a late specialization that followed the rise of mixed farming in Asia, as it did in Africa. Some early pastoralists were pure nomads without a fixed base where crops could be raised. Others were seminomads who practiced transhumance — sending their stock off seasonally to the high mountains or into the desert during the rainy season. In either case, they were specialist producers. As such, they needed commercial outlets among farmers who would exchange grain, wine, and oil for meat and milk — farmers whose sedentary life made it easier for them to produce the tools and textiles that the nomads also needed. This specialization tended to make early nomads dependent on sedentary society, all the more so before the nomads had horses or camels to give them wide mobility.

This situation gave the sedentary farmers a better bargaining position than the nomads. The less-specialized farmers did not need nomad products as much as the nomads needed their grain, cloth, and tools, and the farmers must have taken advantage of that fact in bargaining about the terms of trade. Nomads, on the other hand, had a chance to redress the balance through force. They were usually organized in bands a good deal larger than a single family, while the single household was often the basic unit of sedentary work-organization. Nomads were mobile; sedentaries were fixed to their plots of ground and their stores of grain for the next planting. The nomads' wandering life of herding and hunting also developed skills that could be turned to military ends. The end product was mutual dependence, tempered by the fact that either side might try to push its advantage over the other.

Nor was the balance of advantage constant through time; it changed with changing technology. Before about 1700 B.C., none of the nomadic groups

living in the shadow of the great urban societies of that time was a serious
military threat. Even though horses were first domesticated about 3000 B.C., the
usual beast of burden was the donkey, and men went into battle on foot. The
nomads' big advantage — mobility to assemble and strike fast with a large force
— came only with the effective military use of horses, and that was slow in
coming.

To use horses for mounted fighting required bits, bridles, saddles, and
stirrups that would enable the rider to control his horse and fight at the same
time. The first military use of horses came with chariotry, not cavalry. A two-
wheeled chariot provided a mobile platform and some protection for an archer
and a driver, but even that was slow to evolve. The first horses were raised for
meat. After a time in Mesopotamia, they were used to pull four-wheeled carts,
but these had fixed axles and the cart had to be dragged around turns. The real
shift to military importance came only a little after 1700 B.C., when horses began
to be attached to a pole leading forward from the chariot. They could then
carry part of the weight and turn the two-wheeled vehicle with ease. About the
same time, reins were invented for steering the horses from the chariot; short
and light compound bows were developed to make the archer more effective;
and chariots themselves were made with spoked wheels, which gave them speed
without sacrificing strength.

By the time chariots were effective, the intercommunicating world of the
Bronze Age "civilizations" had expanded from Egypt and Mesopotamia to include the fertile crescent and the Iranian plateau. Further afield, similar centers
existed in China and the Indus valley. In North Africa and Europe, the agricultural revolution had already come, but with only embryo cities, in spite of the
impressive temple sites of standing stones like Stonehenge in Britain and other
similar sites in Malta and North Africa. More significant was the spread of
bronze metallurgy into the steppelands that stretched across the whole of Asia
from the Black Sea to Manchuria. It was there that chariot warfare was first
perfected.

Between about 1700 and 1400 B.C., charioteers from the steppe attacked
and conquered most of the urban "civilizations" from Mesopotamia to China.
Some of them, speaking Indo-European languages, moved into the north Indian
plain, while others moved into Europe. In both places their languages are still
dominant. The Hyksos who brought an end to the Middle Kingdom in Egypt
were also charioteers, whatever their other role may have been. Further west in
Africa, the Berber-speaking peoples, whom the Egyptians called Libyans, were
using chariots for their raids on the Nile valley as early as 1235 B.C. By that
time, chariots must have been commonly used by all the nomadic peoples on
the fringes of the Maghrib as far as the Atlantic coast.

Chariots must have brought even more drastic changes to the Sahara, which
was then well on its way to desiccation. The most plausible hypothesis holds that
the chariot revolution was seized by the Berber-speaking peoples of northern
Africa. Their monopoly over this military innovation made it possible for them

to drive the desert people off to the south along the whole stretch from Lake Chad to the Atlantic. Whatever languages may have been spoken in northwestern Africa before this time, Berber languages became dominant from the western desert of Egypt to Morocco, south to the Senegal and the Niger bend, and out to the Canary Islands in the Atlantic. In the Sahara itself, a sequence of rock engravings of chariots is found along a route that extends southward from Morocco to the Niger bend, then back to the north by way of the Saharan highlands to end in Tunisia. It is possible that chariots had some role in trans-Saharan communication from a date that could be as early as 1300 B.C. People of the Fezzan in Libya were famous as charioteers in Roman times, so the chariot phase in the western Sahara may have lasted as long as a thousand years. It is unlikely, however, that the chariots were ever transport vehicles. In a region without roads, pack animals are far more efficient than carts, and the chariots must have been limited to military use to protect the slower caravans, but there is no evidence of extensive caravan trade across the Sahara until camels became available.

Meanwhile, the steppe peoples in Asia far to the northeast had been riding horses in an experimental way even before chariots were perfected. Riding techniques improved gradually, but the regular use of cavalry in battle is recorded no earlier than 900 B.C. Then, it came as part of a horse revolution associated with a whole set of social changes on the steppe that made possible a new kind of nomadic mobility. In a military sense, it called for special techniques for guiding a horse in battle and shooting arrows from its back. It also called for new breeds of horses strong enough to carry a man and his supplies over a long distance. Other patterns of nomadism shifted as well, as people could move more stock faster and further with horses to help with the herding.

War chariots gave way to cavalry very rapidly after about 900 B.C., and most rapidly in places where pastoralism encouraged other uses for the mounted horse. It was especially fast, therefore, throughout the Eurasian steppe and again in the Maghrib and the deserts to the south, but slower in Egypt. A little before 700 B.C., for example, Libyans from the west, using mounted horses, conquered the Nubian section of the Nile valley against the opposition of Egyptian forces still using chariots. To the west of the Nile, the cavalry revolution followed the chariot revolution by a delay of about six hundred years; cavalry, in short, spread into that region much faster than chariots had done, an index of the way northwestern Africa was gradually being pulled into the spreading intercommunicating zone.

The last millennium B.C. was also the period when camels finally arrived in Africa, coming first to the area east of the Nile. They were never the principal military animal, but they could carry heavier loads than donkeys, and over longer distances without water. Because the load per animal was greater, a single drover could control a larger carrying capacity, so that the manpower requirements per ton of freight were less. Camels could also graze on more arid land than that usable by cattle, sheep, or even goats.

The camel made its first significant impact in the African region a little before 1000 B.C., when it played an important role in improving communications between northern and southern Arabia. About that time, a series of kingdoms appeared across the straits from Ethiopia, linked by commercial caravan to the "civilized" world of the Middle East. The arid belt became less serious as a barrier than it had been when water routes of the Nile and Red Sea were the principal links from north to south. Camels began to be used on the Egyptian side of the Red Sea as well, toward the end of the Pharaonic period, but they were not used intensively elsewhere in Africa until after the birth of Christ.

The westward movement of camels into the Sahara proper followed a different route from that taken earlier by the introduction of horses. Instead of moving along the North African coast and then out into the desert, the use of camels first diffused along the southern shore of the desert from the Nile valley to Borku and Tibesti, north of Lake Chad, in the first century A.D. By the fourth century, they were very common in the desert region between Chad and Tripoli and had spread even further west. This time, the desert people reversed the advantage that went against them with the introduction of chariotry: camels now favored the desert against the sedentary peoples in the Maghrib, who were then more or less unified under imperial Rome. The Romans were weakening in any case, but they were also forced to fall back from some of their advanced positions in the face of aggressive nomadism, trying merely to hold the nomads outside an elaborate set of fortified lines stretching from Tunisia to Morocco.

Looking back from about the fourth century A.D., the nomads had gained in power steadily through technological increments of chariots, cavalry, and then camels. At that point, the balance of technology against sedentary societies reached a plateau of relative stability, which was to last until the seventeenth-century invention of good field artillery — and even that was not much used in the Sahara until the nineteenth century. But a pattern of nomad-sedentary relations had developed much earlier. Nomads had been raiding sedentary peoples even before the era of the chariot; tensions growing out of complementary production and exchange were equally old; sedentary and nomadic peoples were rivals for the land marginal to either group, even before Cain and Abel came to represent the two ways of life for the Old Testament. At least by the time horse cavalry arrived on the scene, nomadic-sedentary relations had fallen into a pattern that became a major theme in world history between the agricultural and industrial revolutions. It was noticed in the Bible, and again by Ibn Khaldun, the great historian of Tunis in the late fourteenth century. Recently, Owen Lattimore developed it further with his study of *Inner Asian Frontiers of China.*

These authorities noticed first of all the rivalry and complementarity of the nomadic and sedentary ways of life, especially along the natural frontier between the steppe and the sown. Both Lattimore and Ibn Khaldun wrote about recent periods when technological advantage had been relatively constant, yet history seems to have passed from phases of nomadic to phases of sedentary dominance. This alternation took place because either side could capitalize on its natural advantage with good organization. Once organized to act in concert, either could control the marginal lands and thus weaken the other. Lack of organization for common effort was disastrous. The sedentary village was helpless in the face of surprise attack from the steppe so long as each village tried to defend itself with its own resources alone. But sedentary life allowed for a denser population and greater wealth. An organized sedentary state could pool the resources of many villages, defend the frontiers, seize the marginal lands, and, if necessary, police the steppe itself. If the state became weakened or disorganized, however, nomads could raid at will, regain the marginal land, build their own organization, and finally carry their forays into the heart of the sedentary empire.

Nomads under purely nomadic leadership might envy the wealth of their sedentary neighbors without understanding how that wealth could be exploited. In that case, their raids tended to be destructive, but that was all. When nomads fell under another kind of leadership, however, that of men who were marginal to both distinct cultures, another possibility occurred. These men would know enough of the nomadic way of life to command a nomadic following, yet understand how a sedentary society might be made to run for their own advantage. When that happened, raids could turn into conquest; nomadic leaders founded new dynasties ruling over the sedentary society. But once in command of a sedentary empire, the nomad leaders soon found themselves on the other side of the ancient rivalry. Their interests became those of sedentary society, as they, in turn, had to deal with nomads beyond the frontiers — either those who had lost out on the spoils of conquest or others who had come to occupy their former ecological niche. At that point, the struggle was back at square one, with a new victory promised to those who could organize to act in concert.

This style of history is a theme that runs along all the fringes of the great Afro-Eurasian arid belt during the past two thousand years and more, with men like Genghis Khan or Tamurlane as examples of the marginal leader of nomads who built a great empire. Some interpretations would show the Hyksos in Egypt as essentially chariot-riding barbarians who destroyed the Middle Kingdom and rebuilt it under their own control. Ibn Khaldun interpreted the history of North Africa from the ninth to the fourteenth century as a series of nomad-founded dynasties that rose to power and then fell to new nomadic leaders from the steppe. The Saharan fringes of the West African savanna can be used to illustrate a similar process. Changing technology in the last millennium B.C. thus set the scene for a new style of history that was to last nearly to the end of the second millennium A.D.

HELLENISM AND THE RISE OF ROME

One of the myths of African history, only recently dissipated, stressed as a main theme that the isolated and "primitive" continent had been gradually enlightened by the successive spread of "civilization" by increments — each new phase being a greater intensity of contact with the West. The interpretation

is vastly oversimplified. It also carries a false suggestion that African history
was made in Europe, not in Africa, and the overtones of European racism and
cultural arrogance are obvious. Yet there is some validity to a similar interpretation of world history — one that is equally broad, but less value-laden and
centered on Europe. This view stresses the gradual formation and spread of a
series of intercommunicating zones, beginning from small points in the river
valleys and spreading gradually to larger and larger parts of the Afro-Eurasian
land mass.

The lower Nile valley was obviously one of the earliest of these points.
The most significant next steps for northern Africa were the incorporation of
Egypt in the greater Hellenic world, politically articulated by Alexander of
Macedonia's conquests after about 320 B.C. For Egypt the fact of military conquest by Macedonian armies was not crucial; earlier foreign armies had marched
along the Nile, and Egyptians had conquered other Middle Eastern territories
in her turn.

During the next centuries Hellenism spread west in the Mediterranean and
was given new political form by the creation of the Roman Empire, which also
incorporated the island of the Maghrib during the first century B.C. All this
was not so much the spread of "civilization" into Africa as the incorporation of
northern Africa, along with other newcomers, in that part of the world where a
very broad and intense interchange of cultures was taking place.

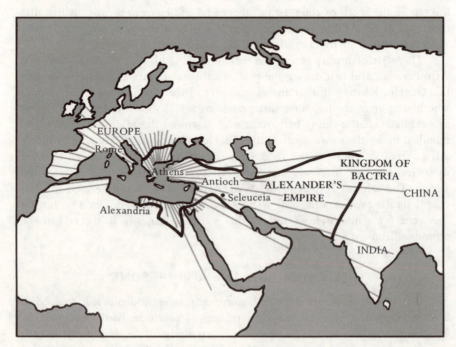

The Diffusion of Hellenism

Greek culture began to expand into neighboring parts of Asia, Africa, and Europe long before the formation of the Macedonian Empire in the 330s B.C. Greek commerce based on the export of wine and olive oil reached into the western Mediterranean, Asia, and Egypt. Another export was the Greek way of fighting in disciplined and armored infantry units — the famous Greek phalanx. Along with this military technique went Greek mercenary soldiers and other Greeks seeking employment in commerce, government, and many other fields. Greeks of this stamp were active in Egypt from the late seventh century B.C. onward, and Egypt gradually merged culturally into the Hellenistic world in the centuries that followed, down to Alexander's conquest. Even though Macedonian political control disappeared after about 280 B.C., the Greek-dominated kingdom of the Ptolemies was one of the most powerful states of the early Hellenistic world, along with a Seleucid kingdom ruling much of western Asia and a Macedonian state that was reduced (though larger than the original Macedonia).

As Greek culture spread into the Middle East, it also changed. Some well-springs of its own originality in the homeland dried up; Greece itself began to absorb cultural elements from abroad, as well as exporting them to others. Exported elements tended to change and adjust to their new environment. In sum, the Greek culture of the fifth century B.C. turned into the Hellenistic culture of the second, a culture that was common to the whole of the Middle East — especially in the cities and in international communication. Older cultures survived in part as a substratum. In Egypt, for example, the city of Alexandria became one of the great centers of Hellenistic culture, perhaps its greatest urban center of all. But the countryside and the older cities up the Nile were less changed. The new government administration was probably more efficient in extracting tax revenue from the peasants than the last pharaohs had been, but that revenue went to pay for life in Alexandria. The cultural mix may not have been very different from that of modern Africa, where Western education and Western institutions dominate the centers of power while aspects of the pre-colonial way of life survive in the countryside with much less change.

Neither the Maghrib nor western Europe were affected by the first phase of Hellenism. Macedonia itself was a frontier territory of the "civilized" world, and its military conquests took it back to the core area of southwestern Asia. The western Mediterranean was a distant fringe, but one that already had commercial contact with the core. This spread of cultural influence from east to west was carried principally by trade diasporas of Greek or Levantine origin. In early phases of cross-cultural trade, some kind of mediation was needed to help open commerce between people of differing cultures. Usually agents were sent out to establish a small trading post or colony in alien society. There they could learn about the local ways of doing business and mediate between the local people and merchants from their own homeland who might follow. The Greeks established many trade outposts of this kind on the shores of the Mediterranean. Many grew into enclaves under Greek control, and these often grew on into Greek city-states populated by colonists from a home city on the Aegean. Some were as far west as Marseille, which tapped the trade of the Rhone Valley. Closer to home, the shores of southern Italy and eastern Sicily were ringed with trade enclaves and cities of Greek origin. Through these activities the Greeks acted as cultural missionaries from the intercommunicating zone.

In North Africa, Phoenicians played a similar role. The original Phoenicians were Caananites from the coastal towns of what is now Syria, Lebanon, and northern Israel. These cities were sometimes dominated by Egypt, Persia, or Assyria during the last millennium B.C., but they kept their separate identity as specialized urban centers oriented toward maritime trade. Their trade diaspora to the west began about 1000 B.C. By about 800 B.C., the main lines of the network were complete — one line of trading posts in coastal Egypt and thence up the Nile as far as Memphis; a major western base at Carthage in Tunisia; and a second major base at Cadiz in Spain, beyond Gibraltar. Smaller bases and trading posts were located at Ibiza in the Balearic Islands, on Sardinia and the western coast of Sicily, and scattered along the North African coast from Tunisia to Morocco.

When the Phoenician homeland in the Levant fell to Macedonian conquest in the 330s B.C., it merged into the broader Hellenic world, leaving Carthage in the west as the main Phoenician base and center of Punic identity for a few centuries more, though Carthage kept a theoretical allegiance to the homeland even after it fell to Macedonia. Carthaginian influence in the Maghrib, however, was much like Hellenistic influence in Egypt of the Ptolemies. It was concentrated in the cities, with otherwise only a triangle of Punic-speaking countryside bounded by the Mediterranean and a line connecting Bône in eastern Algeria with Sfax in central Tunisia. Elsewhere, the hinterland of the Punic settlements was controlled by a number of Berber-speaking states. Their institutions are somewhat shadowy to us, because the only surviving records of their affairs are those left by Romans, but one large state the Romans called Mauritania lay in the far west of Morocco and western Algeria. Present-day eastern Algeria, which the Romans called Numidia, was divided between two other sedentary Berber kingdoms. Carthage seems to have stayed clear of deep involvement with its hinterland as a matter of policy; it was essentially a maritime power and its prime strategic interests lay overseas in its control of trade routes and seaports. The great struggle between Rome and Carthage for dominance of the western Mediterranean in the second century B.C. began when they clashed over which was to dominate Sicily.

Both Rome and Carthage grew to importance as part of a broader process in which the "civilization" of the eastern Mediterranean spread to the west. Just as the Phoenicians carried the culture of the Levant, Greek and Hellenistic culture spread westward along the trade routes, expanding first by Greek settlements in southern Italy and then north through the rest of the peninsula. The process paralleled the timing of the spread of Hellenism into the older urban societies of the Middle East, but in Italy Hellenism met a culture that was only just emerging into the pattern of literate, urban societies. Compared to Greece, Italy had some

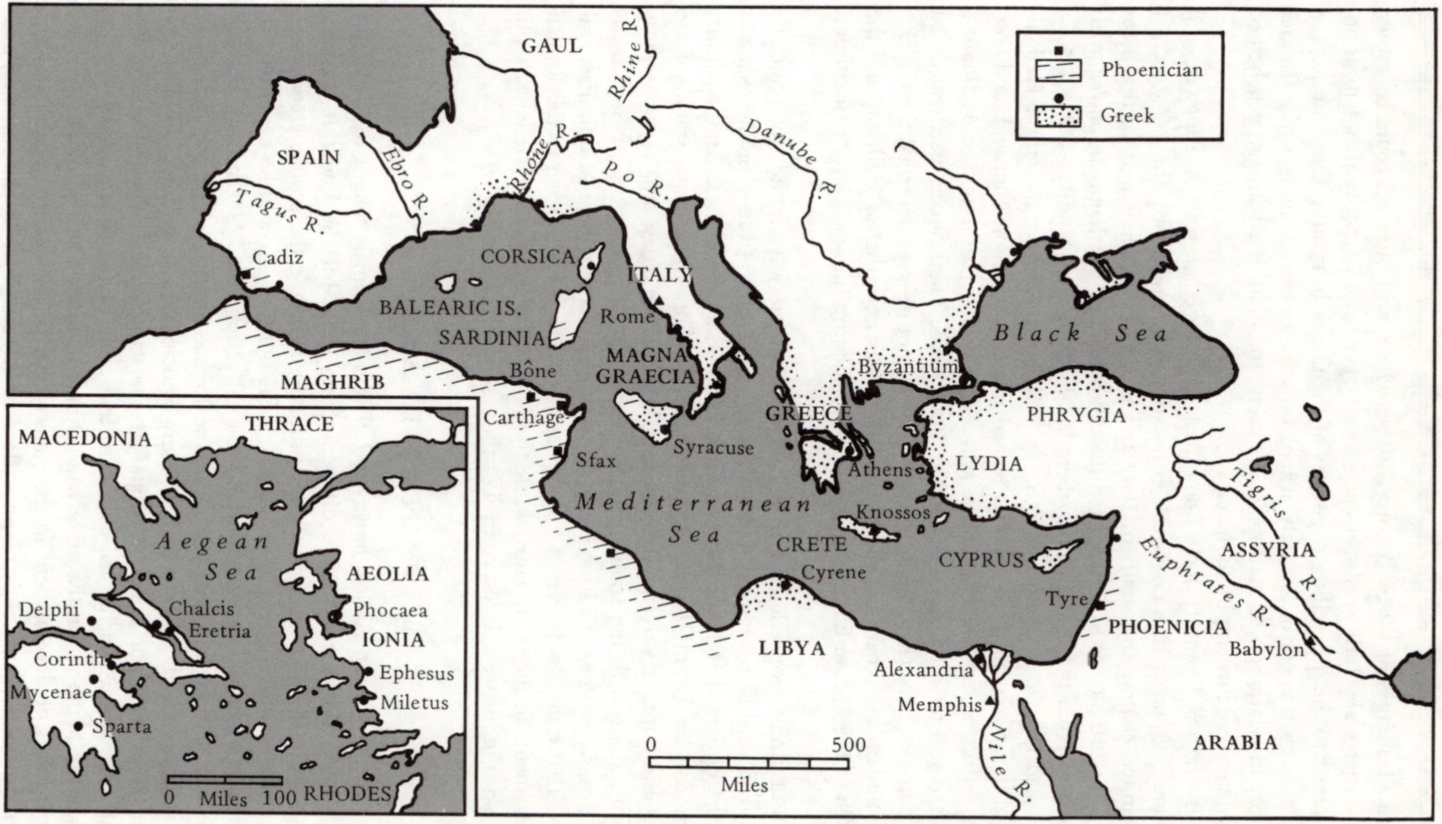
Phoenician
Greek
GAUL
Rhine R.
Danube R.
SPAIN
Ebro R.
Rhone R.
Po R.
Tagus R.
Cadiz
CORSICA
ITALY
BALEARIC IS.
Rome
SARDINIA
MAGNA GRAECIA
Black Sea
Bône
Byzantium
MAGHRIB
Carthage
GREECE
PHRYGIA
Syracuse
Sfax
Athens
LYDIA
Mediterranean Sea
Knossos
CRETE
CYPRUS
Cyrene
Tyre
PHOENICIA
LIBYA
Alexandria
Memphis
Nile R.
Tigris R.
Euphrates R.
ASSYRIA
Babylon
ARABIA
0 500 Miles
MACEDONIA
THRACE
Aegean Sea
AEOLIA
Delphi
Chalcis
Eretria
Phocaea
IONIA
Corinth
Mycenae
Sparta
Ephesus
Miletus
0 Miles 100
RHODES

The Greek and Phoenician Push to the West

of the advantages of a new country. Wine, wheat, and olive oil could be grown on a larger scale. Italy was also open to a larger scale of political organization, in contrast to the quarrelling city-states of the Greek heartland. Once the Roman city-state began to expand in Italy, it took on some of the advantages of a frontier territory in relation to its metropolitan society, the kind of advantage that helped Macedonia build its empire to the east.

In the third century B.C., Rome had advantages of scale, manpower, and economic resources that no Greek city-state could muster. By the 260s B.C., it had united central and southern Italy and moved on to challenge Carthage for Sicily. By 200 B.C., it had completed the destruction of Carthaginian power, with some help from the Numidian Berbers in North Africa. Shortly after 150 B.C., Rome had gone on to conquer Greece as well. From then on, the fringe Hellenization of early commercial contacts turned into a much more thorough and conscious effort to imitate the Greek way. The Roman form of the Hellenistic synthesis still retained characteristic Latin overtones. The Romans were concerned with some matters (law, for instance) that had not deeply concerned the Greeks. The fundamental character of Roman society was nevertheless Hellenic, and the growth of the Roman Empire provided an articulating framework for that cultural synthesis.

But Rome stopped short in one very important way. It did not unite the "civilized world" in the way Macedonia had once done from a similar position on the frontiers of Hellenic culture. Rome captured the Greek heartland, Anatolia, Egypt, and the Levant, but its conquests stopped short at the upper waters of the Tigris and Euphrates rivers. Mesopotamia, home of the oldest urban societies, was left out, along with the Iranian plateau. By the third century A.D., a new Sassanian dynasty in Persia had succeeded in uniting the most ancient Middle East and giving that region a degree of stability and security superior even to the Roman achievements in the west. Thus, while the Roman Empire pushed Hellenism into new lands in the west, it lost control of the east.

ROMAN NORTH AFRICA

All of northern Africa, however, fell into the Roman sphere, although for Egypt with consequences quite different from those for the Punic and Berber territories to the west. Egypt was agriculturally rich, and the economy continued under Rome little changed from its own past. But now it could be exploited for the benefit of the Roman rather than the local ruling class. Alexandria continued to be one of the really great cities of the Roman empire, while the hinterland was integrated with the imperial economy principally as a supplier of wheat for Rome (and later for the new capital at Constantinople). The culture of the countryside was as unchanged as the ancient cycle of the Nile flood.

In the Maghrib, on the other hand, Roman conquest and administration led to new kinds of development in the countryside. In the *tell,* the relatively well-watered coastal plains and inland valleys of Algeria, and in the former Punic

region of northern Tunisia, Roman rule led to the Romanization of at least the
upper classes. Roman towns came into being as administrative centers, surrounded by Roman estates, with large-scale agriculture worked by slave labor.
While this intensification of agricultural development took place in Numidia and
the old Carthaginian territories, a second kind of change came to the high
plateaus that lay behind the coastal plains. This high country was more arid than
the *tell,* and much of it lacked the twenty to twenty-four inches of annual rainfall needed to grow a successful grain crop in that climate. During the first
century or so of Roman occupation, the high plains were still used only for
sparse seasonal grazing. Then, about 100 A.D., Romans introduced olive trees,
and dry-farming techniques made it possible to grow barley on favored sites on
the high plains. Olive trees could survive the hot summer dry season, and they
could grow on ground too steep and rocky to be tilled. Unlike the richer plains
of the *tell,* the land here remained in the hands of Berber smallholders, who
profited greatly from the Roman connection that gave them a distant market for
their oil. The *tell* peoples lived largely on the export of grains to the Roman
world as a whole, but prosperity there passed its peak after the second century
A.D., whereas the high plateaus were still climbing toward their peak of prosperity about the middle of the third.

   Just as the Roman state promoted more extensive commerce in goods, it also
promoted commerce in ideas, and not necessarily from Rome itself. Its role as a
framework for part of the intercommunicating zone made possible the diffusion
of ideas from the fringe to the center and out to all the rest of Roman territory.
In religion, for example, the old paganism with combined Roman and Hellenistic
roots began to decline during the civil wars of the third century. A variety of
new religions appeared as alternatives. Christianity was one of these, coming
from the Levantine Judaic tradition, but with a message more attractive for its
emotional and moral appeal than for the complexity of its theology.

   During the first three centuries of the Christian Era, the new religion was
far more important in the eastern Mediterranean than it was in the west. Rome
was the only western site among the four original episcopal sees, the others being
at Antioch, Constantinople, and Alexandria. Alexandria was, in fact, the most
important early center for the development of Christian doctrine and Christian
education. When the empire was divided for administrative convenience in the
late fourth century A.D. into a western half (based on Rome) and an eastern half
(based on Constantinople), Alexandria lost some of its primacy to the two
capitals, especially to Constantinople. Constantinople's new preeminence led in
the longer run to a rivalry among bishoprics and ultimately to the division of
Christianity into an Orthodox and a Roman Catholic branch, but that issue was
hardly raised before 324 A.D., when Christianity became the favored religion for
the empire as a whole.

   The Maghrib had meanwhile kept to its old ways and retained ancient
Berber and Punic religions until after about 200 A.D., when Christianity began
to penetrate the urban centers and the *tell,* especially the former Carthaginian

territories. Its spread to the Berber-speaking peoples of the high plains and the seminomadic fringes was somewhat slower, though North Africa was to be the home of some of the most important of the church fathers, including Tertullian (d. about 230), the first important Christian theologian to write in Latin, and Augustine (d. 430), whose writings did more than any other to set the theological traditions of the Roman church.

As Christianity moved up from its early position of one among many oriental religions current in Rome, it encountered new problems. Especially after it became the official church of the empire, the question of official tolerance or intolerance became serious. An official and approved Christian view of things began to appear, and those who disagreed with the principal bishops and church councils were branded as heretics — those who had chosen to follow error even where the truth was known and proclaimed. It is hardly surprising that all kinds of social and ethnic differences within the Roman Empire tended to emerge as heresies in opposition to the dominant forces in Rome and Constantinople.

Sometimes it was almost pure chance that particular heresies became the preferred religion of certain minorities. One early view of the relations between God-the-Son and God-the-Father held that the sanctity of Christ was derived from the divinity of God-the-Father, and this view was carried by missionaries to the Germans north of the Danube in the early fourth century. It was called Arianism, and it was later condemned as heretical, but the Germans had already begun to accept it. It therefore continued and grew to be their principal variant of the Christian faith, which they kept even after they entered the imperial territory. It finally came into the Maghrib with the Vandals, after moving more than a thousand miles in space and a century in time from the point where missionaries had first begun preaching it beyond the frontiers.

In much the same way, the Donatist heresy became the doctrinal variant peculiar to the Maghrib. The issue in this case was partly the proper form of church government and partly the question of whether a lapsed sinner could be saved without undergoing martyrdom. The issue itself was not so important as the fact that the Roman government supported the Catholic position, while the dominant Romanized classes in urban Africa, as well as the Berber countrymen, became Donatists. The original schism, indeed, began only shortly after about 300 A.D., just as Christianity was coming to be tolerated in the empire. It did not become really serious in the North African provinces until nearly a century later, when the Donatist church was officially banned. But Donatism lasted in the rural areas until the end of Roman rule and beyond, although the Vandals arrived about 430 A.D. to become the new masters, setting Arianism in competition with Donatism and Catholicism alike. Donatism became the version of Christianity peculiar to Berbers, just as Arianism was peculiar to Germans.

Egypt also acquired its own variant of Christianity. When the Christian division between Rome and Constantinople was separating the Latin-speaking from the Greek-speaking parts of the empire, eastern Christianity itself was being divided between the Greek core with its center in Constantinople and the Syrian and Egyptian fringes, where Hellenism had always been something of an overlay on the non-Hellenic popular culture. This time the local view, ultimately proclaimed heretical, was the Monophysite doctrine that Christ had one nature, wholly divine, that his human appearance was only the appearance of humanity, not reality. The opposing Orthodox and Catholic view held that Christ had two natures, one human and one divine. Even after being declared heretical in 451, Monophysitism continued in Egypt and Syria in spite of occasional persecution by the official government of east Rome. In time, these continued religious tensions were to weaken the empire against foreign enemies.

In spite of internal strains, Christianity became an important cement holding together the various cultural elements that had been merged to some degree by centuries of Roman rule. The spread of Christianity beyond the frontiers was therefore a partial extension of the intercommunicating zone, even though Roman rule might not follow. And Christianity did expand beyond the frontiers, to the Celts in Ireland, to the Germans as Arianism, south of the Sahara into Nubia and Ethiopia in the Monophysite version. In expanding, the faith of Rome was not necessarily accepted intact. In Nubia, for example, the local culture had often assimilated some aspects of the Egyptian way while rejecting others. Even after a superficial Egyptianization under the New Kingdom, Nubia began to drift off in its own directions from about 600 B.C., taking new gods from sub-Saharan Africa and making the Queen Mother into an important constitutional figure. But when Egypt fell to Macedonian and then Roman conquest, it became an early center of Christianity, while Nubia remained as the last holdout for many ancient Egyptian religious ideas. Though Monophysite and Orthodox missionaries visited the upper Nile, they failed to convert the rulers of Nubia until nearly 600 A.D. By that time, three separate Nubian states lay between the first cataract and the savanna country south of the desert. Two of these, Nobatia and Makuria, lay along the Nubian reaches of the Nile as it flows through the desert, but the third, Alwa or Alodia, lay in the south where rainfall agriculture was possible. All three became Christian during the seventh and early eighth centuries.

Ethiopia and southern Arabia were subject to Roman cultural penetration even earlier than Nubia. Commercial contact with Egypt had been at least sporadic since about 2000 B.C., and was reasonably continuous for the last pre-Christian millennium. The commercial attractions of the horn of Africa and southern Arabia were two aromatic gums exuded by trees found in this arid region. Frankincense, the gum of *Boswellia carterii* and *B. frereana*, was especially important for Roman funeral pyres, and myrrh from *Commiphora myrrha* was used mainly for cosmetics and perfumes. The rise of Hellenism and then of the Roman Empire brought prosperity to the ruling class in the Mediterranean basin, and increased the demand for these products. In addition, about 150 B.C., shippers on the Indian Ocean began to make more direct voyages across the Arabian Gulf from Bab el Mandeb directly to India and even on to southeastern Asia, rather than following the coastlines as they had done in the past. They found this comparatively easy by using the alternation of southeast monsoons blowing for half the year, with the prevailing northeast winds blowing during the other half. With that innovation Red Sea navigation, in combination with caravans along the northern shores, was not simply a link across the dry belt — it led to India and the east beyond, or south along the African coast.

These commercial currents carried both Christianity and Judaism into Ethiopia and southern Arabia in the first centuries A.D. The main political force in the region at that time was the kingdom of Axum, based on the Ethiopian side of the strait but having occasional control over Yemen as well. Axum was never under Roman control, but its commercial interests prompted a policy of alliance with Rome. This may be one reason why Axum adopted Christianity as its official religion in about 350 A.D., only one generation after Christianity became the official faith of Rome itself.

Ethiopian Christianity, however, followed the Egyptian or Monophysite

Egypt and Nubia

version, and the Ethiopian church remained attached to the Patriarch of Alexandria after the end of Roman unity, and even after the rise of Islam in Arabia and the Islamization of Egypt itself made the Christian position precarious. Contact was not always easy, but Ethiopia and Nubia alike remained faithful to old beliefs that were losing out in the Mediterranean basin, in much the same way Nubia had earlier held on to the ancient Egyptian religion that was dying in Egypt itself. In the process, Christianity came to be integrated with local culture, which meant that it deviated slightly from the norms of the Mediterranean church, but it also developed the resilience necessary to hold on through long centuries of quasi-isolation from coreligionists to the north.

THE END OF ROMAN UNITY

The "Fall of Rome" was such a complex process that historians still shy away from assigning simple causes or even sets of enumerated causes. In one sense, indeed, "Rome" did not fall. West Rome may have fallen as a political structure, but the other Rome based in Constantinople evolved by stages into the Byzantine Empire and lasted in one form or another until the fifteenth century. By then, Latin Christendom had recovered and given new form and content to the Roman heritage.

But the "fall" of west Rome in the fourth and fifth centuries A.D. was undoubted. Weakened by epidemic disease, economic decline, political instability, and social unrest, it was unable to hold the frontier against the pressure of German "barbarians," who wanted to enter the empire, whether as peaceful migrants, forceful migrants, or mere hit-and-run raiders. These movements have some resemblance to the nomadic-sedentary conflicts in more arid regions, and they can be traced through layers of indirect pressure of one people on another across the Eurasian steppe to the frontiers of China. But the Huns who terrorized Europe from the Hungarian plain in the late fourth and early fifth centuries were the only nomadic peoples to attack Rome from the north or east. The Germans who moved across the frontiers into western Europe were farmers, not nomads, though they sometimes came organized in war bands that resembled the nomads' military formations.

Throughout the fifth century A.D., western Europe divided into a number of German kingdoms with actual power, while Rome still maintained a theoretical claim to rule over the whole. The chief spillover into Africa was the movement of the Vandals into the Maghrib by way of Gibraltar in 429 A.D., after migrating across France and Spain. Once in Africa they settled down, but theirs was hardly a mass movement. Their total numbers (probably exaggerated at that) were no more than eighty thousand, or less than the population of Roman Carthage. Nor were they any more given to "vandalism" than other military of their time. Our word *vandalism* comes from the "bad press" they received in Latin circles, where they were heartily disliked because they were Arians, not Catholics. They nevertheless established their control over the cities and eastern coastal plains that had once been Carthaginian and Numidian. The rest of the Maghrib fell back into the control of Berber leaders who had already been in dissidence, often exercising de facto control ever since the Donatist struggle against the Roman government.

Vandal rule tended to follow the Carthaginian rather than the Roman pattern. Vandal strength lay with their navy, which dominated the west basin of the Mediterranean from about 440 A.D. to 480 A.D. They too neglected the hinterland and concentrated on seaborne control over the Balearic Islands, Sardinia, and Corsica; and they contested Latin control of Sicily just as the Carthaginians had done a half millennium earlier. This pattern of control over North African ports, with a further attempt to dominate the sea lanes, was to recur in the history of the Maghrib, as other conquerors were to seize the ports and small enclaves in their hinterland, paying little attention to the affairs of sedentary rural populations in their rear.

The Vandals themselves were displaced by just such another conqueror in the form of the Byzantine Empire, as the eastern Roman Empire was now called. While the western part of the Roman Empire was overrun by Germans, the Greek-speaking east held its frontiers by borrowing the Persian manner of fighting with heavily armored cavalry. The Byzantines called these troops "cataphracts," and they were similar to the armored knights that were to emerge later on in medieval western Europe. After successful holding action through the fifth century, the emperor Justinian set out in the 530s to build up his naval power, hoping to reconquer the Italian peninsula and Rome itself. This required naval dominance in the west basin of the Mediterranean, which in turn called for a preliminary victory over Vandal naval power. The final assault on Italy failed, but the first step in North Africa succeeded. The Byzantine navy and armies brought the Vandal part of the Maghrib back under Byzantine control for another century and a half — down to the Muslim conquest shortly after 700 A.D. But this return to "Roman" rule was not like the first Roman period. The whole of the far western Maghrib remained independent, as it had been in fact since about 400 A.D.

THE RISE OF ISLAM

The sixth-century Byzantine failure to reunite the Roman world was final. From then on, the Christian world was to be divided, and Islam was to emerge from Arabia in the middle of the seventh century as a third heir to the Hellenic synthesis. Arabia was beyond the formal frontiers of Rome, but it was economically and culturally associated with the Roman world in a number of ways. The caravan route down the east coast of the Red Sea was a key link in Rome's commercial tie to Axum and the Indian Ocean. Communities of Christians and Jews were to be found along the trade route in cities like Mecca and Medina, just as similar communities were to be found still further south in Yemen and Ethiopia.

But these Arabian cities were also in touch with the Sassanian world to the northeast, the other heir to the Hellenic synthesis. Sassanian Persia at that time held the lower part of Mesopotamia and its influence lapped over into eastern Arabia. During a decade or so before 600 A.D., the Persians came further still, drove the Axumites out of Yemen, and set up their own control over the eastern side of Bab el Mandeb. In a long-term struggle between the Red Sea and the Persian Gulf as alternate routes from the Mediterranean to the Indian Ocean, the advantage at that point tilted toward the Persian Gulf.

Arabia in the seventh century A.D. was also a country of nomads, who were especially numerous in the better-watered lands along the Red Sea coast, near the highlands of the south, and along the southern fringes of the fertile crescent stretching from Syria and the Levantine coast to Mesopotamia. Along all of these fringes between the steppe and the sown, the style of history based on competitive reciprocity between nomads and sedentary peoples had been the rule for centuries. Nomads and seminomads from the steppe, the ancient Hebrews among them, had often moved north in the past to found kingdoms in the better-watered lands of the highlands or in the north. In the early seventh century, the northern kingdoms of the sedentary peoples were especially weak. Monophysite Syria and Egypt were disaffected with Greek rule from Constantinople. Similar political problems troubled Sassanian Persia in its domination of Iraq. To make matters worse, Persia and the Byzantine Empire had been locked in a long and expensive war for a quarter century ending in about 630 A.D.

The sedentary empires, in short, were in disarray and ripe for a new nomadic attack, if only the nomads and the marginal people could find effective leadership and organization. A little before 620 A.D., the early basis for this leadership and organization began to be laid through the message of a religious prophet. Muhammad appeared in Mecca with a message from God — and this was not a new god but the God of the Christians and Jews. He made no claim to found a new religion (though a new religion was to be the result), but rather to complete the divine revelation already given humankind in part by earlier prophets in the Jewish tradition — Abraham, Isaac, Jacob, and Jesus as well. He saw himself as the last of the line, "the seal of the prophets." His message also brought in elements of the local Arabian polytheism, such as its reverence for a great black rock, the *kaba,* at the center of Mecca. Both the kaba and the city of Mecca itself, as a holy city, became a central focus of the new faith, and pilgrimage to Mecca became a religious duty for Muslims.

The *Koran,* which contains the corpus of Muhammad's own writings, was not composed as a single volume. It brings together various shorter pieces released in varying circumstances throughout his life, and it is supplemented by oral traditions about his sayings, which were later written down. The whole message was not theologically complex or especially new, and it was congruent with the existing religious traditions of the Middle East. Muhammad held that each individual had a personal relationship with a single God who could guide his way in this life to good fortune or bad and would see to it that he entered paradise after death, if he believed in God and performed a set of fairly simple

prescriptions for conduct and ritual behavior. The message also held a millen-
nial element, in that God would bring the world to an end in the imminent
future. With that final event, all would be judged as ready for paradise or not,
according to their actions in life. Among the principal actions enjoined on those
who accepted Islam were daily prayer at set times, obedience to the Prophet and
the laws He had received from God, giving alms to the poor, pilgrimage to
Mecca at least once in a lifetime, and struggle (*jihad*) against the forces of
error and disbelief.

The first installments of the message were directed at townsmen and sedentary farmers in the oases along the Red Sea coast, not at the nomads of the desert,
and even there, Muhammad met opposition in the early years. In 622 A.D., he
was so opposed by the town authorities of Mecca that he removed himself and
his followers to Medina. This removal, flight, or *hejra* is still taken as the
beginning of the Muslim Era. Once in Medina, Muhammad changed from his
old role as a mere preacher to become the secular as well as the spiritual head
of a community of the faithful. Many followers were Arabs who had left the
nomadic way of life for a sedentary existence in the oases, people who had
found their old religion unsuited to the new way of life. With a larger following,
Muhammad's forces began to win military victories against their local opponents.
Victory itself brought still more adherents. By 630 A.D., Mecca itself accepted
Islam and Muhammad's rule, and the rest of Arabia was united under his
command by the time of his death in 632 A.D. In these early Islamic years, in
short, Muhammad functioned as a marginal man between the steppe and the
sown, a city man by origin, with initial appeal to the sedentary society, but with
an increasing nomadic allegiance that succeeded in uniting the Arabian steppe.

Conquest beyond Arabia was mainly left for Muhammad's successors,
though Muslims had raided north into Byzantine and Sassanian lands even during his lifetime. After his death, his followers first struggled briefly with one
another for succession to his leadership over the community. The first successor,
or *khalifa,* was Abu Bakr, whose main task was to rebuild the Arabian unity
that had faltered on the death of the Prophet. It was Umar, the second *khalifa*
("caliph" in English) who led the successful campaigns of conquest against
the sedentary empires to the north. The Muslims captured Syria in 636; by 651,
they had completed the conquest of the whole Middle East from Egypt through
the fertile crescent to Persia. These operations went far beyond the earlier raids
for booty alone; they turned instead to the other pattern of nomadic conquest
under marginal leadership, founding a new dynasty ruling the sedentary lands.

By the 660s, the new Arab rulers, called the Umayyads (after Umar, the
first conqueror), were firmly established at a new capital at Damascus. The first
rulers were Arabian, but the center of the empire was no longer Arabia, and
the new cultural synthesis that began to be formed took on the Roman heritage
of Egypt and Syria along with the Sassanian heritage of Iraq and Persia. But
this union was not so much the joining together of disparate elements as it was
the reunion of cultures and territory that had once been the center of the Hel-

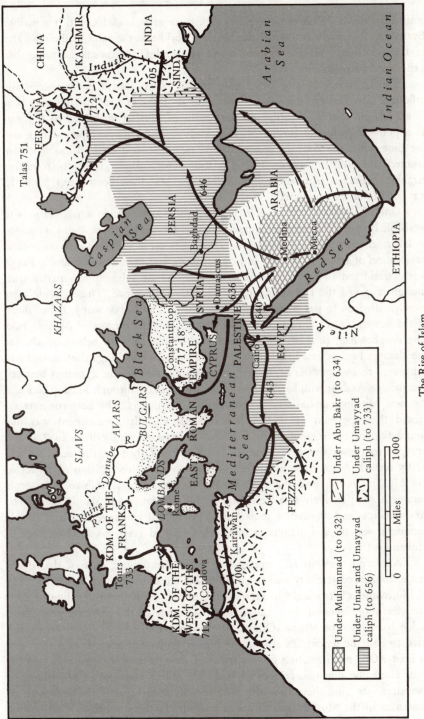

The Rise of Islam

Under Muhammad (to 632)

Under Abu Bakr (to 634)

Under Umar and Umayyad caliph (to 656)

Under Umayyad caliph (to 733)

Miles

0   1000

lenistic synthesis. With the exception of Greece and Anatolia, which remained Byzantine, the new core area of the Muslim world was the same as the core area of the "civilized" Middle Eastern world Alexander had conquered more than a thousand years earlier.

The Umayyad dynasty lasted only until 750 A.D., but it had a special significance, first because it united all Muslims in a single state for the only time in all Islamic history — (although the dream of Muslim unity was to continue as a political goal into the twentieth century). The Umayyad period was also the time when the Arabian conquerors of two sedentary civilizations first confronted the problems of creating a viable new synthesis from their ancient Arabian heritage, their new religious message, and their borrowings from the ways of life of the conquered.

One of the most important new problems was to decide what relations to establish between the Arabian conquerors and the new Muslims who converted to Islam in the conquered lands. The Umayyads avoided forced conversion and persecution of religious dissent. Jews, Christians, and even Zoroastrians in Persia were considered to be "people of the book" whose religion was partly true, though it lacked the full revelation of God to Muhammad. These people were merely called on to pay higher taxes than Muslims paid, but many, if not most, of the new subjects did convert to Islam within the first century of Muslim rule. The Prophet had, furthermore, proclaimed the equality of all believers, whereas the Umayyad rulers based their power on the Arabian tribal organization that had supported them from the beginning. In so doing, they set up a tension between the ancient Arabian emphasis on political organization through kinship ties and the new Muslim emphasis on a community of believers. The new converts resented their position as second-class citizens, and that resentment was one foundation of the revolution that dethroned the Umayyad caliphs in 750 and brought to power the new Abbasid dynasty. From then on the question was partly settled. Arabs were no longer to have an exclusive position of power in the Muslim world, and the descendants of the original Arabian conquerors became a comparatively small element in the population of Islamic states. The Arabic language nevertheless remained as the official language of Islam, largely because it was the holy language in which God had given his final message to Muhammad.

A second division fell among the Arabs themselves: some settled down in the conquered territory and began to assimilate the sedentary values and way of life, while others sought to preserve the nomadic way and the values of their early training. Some of these simply took the booty of the conquest period and faded back into the steppe. Others set their opposition in religious terms and tried to halt the tendencies among the higher leadership toward what they saw as laxity. One manifestation of this trend of thought was an open revolt in the 650s along the nomadic fringes of Iraq. The rebels were called Kharijites, or "seceders," because they chose the direction of heresy against the judgment or consensus of the Muslim community as a whole. In the immediate situation, the revolt failed, but the authorities in Damascus or Baghdad gradually lost control of the Arabian steppe and its nomadic peoples. In the old relationship between nomads and sedentaries, the successors of Muhammad had now crossed to the sedentary side. Kharijism, however, was to continue on the fringes of the sedentary empires with a special importance in Berber North Africa.

A third difference of opinion divided those who thought that the *khalifa* should succeed Muhammad in his religious role and those who wanted a successful politician and military leader. This division was to take many different forms in later Islamic history, but its early form was a dispute over which group was eligible for the caliphate. The religious purists tended to argue that true descent from the Prophet could be traced only to Muhammad's daughter, Fatima, and her husband, 'Ali (who was also Muhammad's cousin). Their claim to office was then joined by a second proposition, that the full word of God was not there for all to see in the Koran. Instead, an esoteric body of knowledge and interpretation was preserved and passed down through the line of 'Ali. This view, with many later variants, came to be known as *shi'a*. Its opposite, the main line of *sunni* Islam, held that the correct interpretation of revelation must be found through the consensus of the community, not through the special powers of particular lineages.

It is possible to see the split between shi'a and sunni as a Muslim variant of the Christian division between Catholic and Protestant, but that parallel has serious limitations. Sunni Islam allowed far more tolerance for differences of belief than any version of Christianity did. The shi'a belief tended to be narrower and less tolerant, although it developed several different versions that tended to change through time and to add to the original points of difference with the sunni majority.

EARLY ISLAM IN AFRICA

The Maghrib was only partly involved in these early divisions. The first phase of Muslim expansion to the west stopped after 641 A.D. with the conquest of Egypt. The Muslims were not strong enough for a frontal assault on the Byzantine Empire, and the Byzantine fleet still dominated the Mediterranean. The Arabs, however, were quick to incorporate the conquered peoples and use their skills. By the 660s, the Umayyad empire had built a fleet that could threaten Byzantium at sea. The real target was Constantinople, but the Muslims began — as Justinian had begun in his sea campaigns against Rome — with a move on Tunisia. By 670 A.D., they had established their hold on the corner of Africa opposite Sicily. (That part of present-day Tunisia had been the "Africa" of the Romans — the name was only later extended more widely. It was now Arabized to "Ifrīqiyah.") The Umayyad empire found itself in the same strategic position as the Romans, Vandals, and Byzantines had before them. The attack on Constantinople failed, but the Muslims moved inland in Tunisia and established a key base at Kairawan, which could serve as a strong point against the non-Muslim Berbers of the hills and a point of safety against the Christians, who necessarily had to come by sea. There the Muslim advance stabilized until after 700 A.D., with Berbers holding most of the Maghrib, Byzantine garrisons in many of the North African port towns, and the Umayyad empire holding central Ifrīqiyah from their base at Kairawan.

By 711 A.D., the Umayyad armies had marched back and forth through most of the Maghrib, but no single controlling authority could surrender in a way that would allow the Arabs to rule through an existing administrative framework, as they had done in Egypt and Syria. The sedentary Berber region, the future Algeria and Morocco, was controlled by a vast number of different Berber authorities. Whatever power might claim to rule the region — whether Roman, Vandal, Byzantine, or Muslim — the Berbers had enjoyed de facto independence over most of the countryside for more than three centuries. Neither the sedentary Berber authorities nor the Berber nomads of the hinterland were willing to give up the reality of power. They might accept a theoretical Umayyad sovereignty, might even convert to Islam. But the full impact of Islam, of Muslim rule and Muslim culture, came only slowly over several centuries, in spite of historical atlases that still sometimes show a solid block of color spreading across North Africa in the late seventh century from Egypt to Morocco.

The Muslim advance in Spain was actually more impressive than in Africa itself. By the early eighth century, Roman rule had long since passed over to Visigoths, who had followed the Vandals across France and the Pyrenees. The Muslim invaders in this case were mainly Berbers from North Africa who had accepted Islam, rather than Arabs from Arabia, although they were reinforced by the Umayyads after their first military successes in 711 A.D. By 720 A.D., they had acquired at least a formal claim to everything south of the Pyrenees and to parts of southern France. (The further advance into western Europe, stopped by the Franks at Poitiers in 732 A.D., was more nearly a raid-in-force than a real invasion attempt.) The hold on Spain was consolidated by the middle of the eighth century — so much so that, when the Abbasid dynasty replaced the Umayyads in Damascus, a member of the Umayyad dynasty managed to retain control over Spain. That act broke the formal unity of the Muslim world, but the aggressive first phase of Muslim conquest was then over in any case. The date 720 is therefore a convenient mark of a new phase in Mediterranean history, when Islam completed its early gains and joined western and eastern Christendom in a three-way partition of the Roman world.

The Muslim drive across North Africa, however weak their actual political dominance over the Maghrib, changed Africa's relation to the intercommunicating world from then onward. Most obviously, it joined all of North Africa to the Muslim world. Since Muslims and Christians were to be chronic enemies for the next thousand years or so, it implied that neither of the Christian heirs of Rome would have much influence on Africa by overland routes. But Christian influence was already established south of the desert in Nubia and Ethiopia, and neither was strongly threatened at first. The very fact that the first Arab outburst went north of the desert meant that nomadic pressure on the southern fringes would be relieved for the time being. Yet the capacity of Ethiopia or the Nubian kingdoms to mediate between the intercommunicating zone and the rest of Africa was seriously weakened. On the other hand, the Muslim world began as the most dynamic and creative of Rome's three heirs. Between 750 and 1500, sub-Saharan Africa was to be far more deeply and permanently influenced by the Islamic world than it had been by Christian Rome over the equivalent period since the beginning of the Christian Era.

SUGGESTIONS FOR FURTHER READING

Abun-Nasr, Jamil M. *A History of the Maghrib*. Cambridge: Cambridge University Press, 1971.

Fairservis, Walter A. *The Ancient Kingdoms of the Nile*. New York: Mentor, 1962.

Gibb, H. A. G. *Mohammedanism. An Historical Survey*. 2nd ed. London: Oxford University Press, 1953.

Holt, P. M., Lambton, Ann K. S., and Lewis, Bernard, eds. *The Central Islamic Lands*. Cambridge History of Islam, vol. 1. Cambridge: Cambridge University Press, 1970.

————. *The Further Islamic Lands*. Cambridge History of Islam, vol. 2. Cambridge: Cambridge University Press, 1970.

Julien, Charles André. *History of North Africa from the Arab Conquest to 1830*. London: Routledge and Kegan Paul, 1970.

Lewis, Bernard. *The Arabs in History*. Rev. ed. London: Arrow Books, 1958.

McNeill, William. *The Rise of the West*. London and Chicago: University of Chicago Press, 1963.

Montet, Pierre. *Eternal Egypt*. London: Weidenfeld and Nicolson, 1964.

Moscati, Sabatino. *The World of the Phoenicians*. London: Cardinal, 1973.

Chapter 3

Africa
North of the Forest
in the Early Islamic Age

HISTORIANS DEAL with North African history from a number of perspectives, and each perspective has its own conventions and terms of reference. At one level, they write about the rise and fall of dynasties named for the founding leader, like the Umayyads, who ruled from Damascus until 750 A.D., followed by the Abbasids with their capital at Baghdad until nearly 1000. But the name of the dynasty refers to more than the actual rulers. It also stands for a period of time, like the dynastic chronology used by Egyptologists. Any periodization of this sort is a form of generalization covering a multitude of events. It is useful, even essential, as a way to cut through masses of detailed political history, but exceptions always exist behind the general facade of a dynastic name and style, and any reference to dynasties always loses a little in accuracy for the sake of generalization.

At a higher level of generalization, historians talk about periods that take a number of dynasties. The Middle Kingdom or the Old Kingdom in ancient Egypt, for instance, were groups of dynasties. In Western history, we have the sequence of ancient, medieval, and modern, with the Middle Ages conceived as falling between ancient and modern and usually given dates of approximately 800 to 1500 A.D. When historians in the West first began writing about Africa, they tended to carry over their Western terminology and to talk about "Africa in the Middle Ages." This is obvious nonsense, because in Africa this period is not a middle between any clearly detectable phases. Yet historians have not yet devised a generally accepted set of terms to deal with the periodization of African history.

The Islamic world is a clearer entity, and a set of terms have been suggested that seem to mark off the main phases after the initial rise of Islam. The first of these is the classical age of Abbasid rule, a period of enormous creativity when Islamic civilization took on its main features. It can be dated to approximately 750 to 1000 A.D. The next period, roughly 1000 to 1500, can be called the

Islamic Middle Ages, roughly coterminous with the European Middle Ages, but "middle" in this case between the Abbasid period and the Age of Three Empires that followed. In political terms, this Islamic Middle Age was a time of political fragmentation after the relative unity imposed by the Abbasids, and it was followed between 1500 and 1750 by a new phase of Muslim unity, but this time unity within three separate segments. The Ottoman Empire dominated in the west, the Saffavid Empire in Persia dominated the center, while the Mogul Empire held the east from the plains of northern India. This chapter deals with the Abbasid period and the Islamic Middle Ages.

We can also consider this a time in terms of another, still broader perspective, that of *world* history as a whole. From that point of view, the period from a few centuries B.C. to the time of Muhammad in the seventh century A.D. was one in which the scattered parts of the intercommunicating zone began to form clusters and within these regions to develop fairly homogeneous cultures. This happened in East Asia, and it happened in the Middle East with the Hellenistic synthesis, continued by the Roman and Sassanian empires. The next period, roughly 750 to 1750 has been called in world history the "Islamic Age." It was a time when Muslim civilization came to the fore as the most successful heir of Rome, and equally as an heir of the Sassanian civilization. In the early part of this thousand years the Muslim world was the most creative of the major "civilizations." It was also so located that it bordered on the rest, and it soon became the intermediary through which the others were able to communicate. Chinese inventions like the compass and gunpowder, Indian inventions like positional notation in mathematics, and the Hellenistic heritage, particularly Aristotle's philosophy, all passed to western Europe by way of Islamic intermediaries. Still other ideas and inventions passed in the other direction or were borrowed from Islamic originals.

In this same perspective of world history, the period that followed was the "European Age," when Europe replaced Islam as the central turntable of world history. Historians differ as to the best date for the transition. In fact, it was gradual. The balance had clearly swung to Europe by 1800, yet the beginnings of the shift can be traced to the maritime breakthrough of the late fifteenth century. As a shift in technology, the maritime revolution was not so important as the scientific revolution of the seventeenth century or the beginnings of industrialization in the eighteenth, but it did give Europeans the capability of reaching every continent by sea. For parts of the world beyond the reach of Islamic culture, the maritime breakthrough itself was the beginning of the European Age in the sense that European mariners were the first direct link to the intercommunicating zone. This was true for the Americas just as it was for the whole west coast of Africa south of the equatorial forest (see the map on page 26). But for Africa north of the forest and all down the east coast to the Mozambique Channel and beyond, the Islamic world remained the vital link with the intercommunicating zone until well into the nineteenth century.

Neither label — Islamic Age or European Age — should be misunderstood.

Both imply for Africa the possibility of cultural borrowing, not complete dominance from abroad. Africans continued to invent new ways of doing things and to modify their old ways for reasons having nothing to do with outside influence. When they borrowed from another culture, they borrowed selectively and fitted the borrowed feature into their own framework.

Some parts of Africa, however, came into the sphere of Islamic culture at a much earlier date, notably Egypt and the core area of Ifrīqiyah around Kairawan even before 750. Between that date and about 1500, the rest of Africa north of the desert had become Muslim; so too had much of the Nilotic Sudan, the nomadic fringe to the Ethiopian highlands, and the *sahel* region across its whole length south of the desert. The role of Islam in the Mediterranean basin was different from its role south of the Sahara, but this chapter will treat all of Africa north of the forest belt, not merely Africa north of the Sahara.

THE GEOGRAPHICAL BASE
OF WEST AFRICAN HISTORY

The geographical background of North Africa, the Nilotic Sudan, and the horn of Africa is already familiar. The great bulk of West Africa south of the Sahara now enters the picture as a major region. Just as the Maghrib has some of the characteristics of an island, with a sea of water to the north, east, and west and a sea of desert to the south, West Africa is like a peninsula, attached to the mass of sub-Saharan Africa at the Cameroon mountains and stretching westward between the Gulf of Guinea and the Sahara. The Arabs called the whole stretch from Mauritania to the Red Sea *bilād al-Sudān,* the Sudan, or "land of the blacks." More recently, "Sudan" has become the generic term for the whole belt of open savanna country just to the south of the desert. It is one of those longitudinal layers of climatic and vegetation zones whose orderly progression from north to south is typical of the west coast of a continental land mass. Beginning with the Mediterranean climate of Morocco, the sequence is desert, savanna, forest — then, moving south of the equator, savanna again, desert again (the Namib and Kalahari of southern Africa), and finally a climate like Morocco's at the Cape of Good Hope.

West Africa embraces only two of these zones, savanna and forest, and geographers discriminate carefully between the vegetation and climatic subdivisions within each of these. Savanna, for example, can be divided into two or three main types having still finer distinctions within each. But the course of history has been modified even more by other features of the environment. One of these is the distribution of tsetse flies, which spread trypanosomiasis to men and animals alike. Trypanosomiasis is serious enough for people, but disastrous for cattle and horses. The flies need the shade of high brush, which is kept down by intensive agriculture. Horses and cattle have been raised in the northern and more arid savanna, but this cannot be done easily in the southern and more humid sections, although the line between these zones has always been subject to change by human activity.

The sequence of zones — desert, savanna, forest — is all too easily conceived in a series of stereotypes. It is easy to imagine tropical rain forest as steaming jungle, and some of it is. But the geographical category is set in terms of "natural vegetation." Man can change that: the forest zone today supports some of the densest agricultural populations in Africa, and it has done so for centuries. The stereotyped savanna is even more of a problem. Technically, savanna grasses predominate over other vegetation, and some call it "grassland," but it is far from being open prairie. Trees and bushes dot the savanna almost everywhere, right to the edge of the desert. Some places have woodland so thick that even in the dry season, when no leaves are on the trees, it is hard to see more than a hundred yards. Curiously enough, the most open and treeless part of the savanna is that nearest the forest, the "derived savanna," or man-made grasslands that were once forest.

The physical explanation for differences in natural vegetation is simply the difference in annual rainfall. In West Africa, it varies from more than 160 inches at a few places along the coast to less than 15 inches at the edge of the desert. Beyond that point, with less than 10 to 15 inches, rainfall agriculture is impossible. With the apparent northward movement of the sun in summer, a tropical air mass moves inland from the Gulf of Guinea, bringing rainfall north until it reaches the southern Sahara in July. Then, as the sun moves south again in fall, the maritime air is replaced by a dry continental air mass. By January, this dry air reaches the Guinea coast, and even the forest region has a brief, comparatively dry season.

As a result of this pattern, the more northerly regions not only receive less rainfall; what rain they do get is concentrated during a brief part of the year. Crops with a long growing season can be grown only in the southern savanna. A forest requires nearly year-round rainfall, whereas grasses can die back, leaving seeds to wait for the return of rain. Savanna trees are species able to survive through a long dry season, if they are not too closely spaced.

Human beings also had to adjust to the short growing season and the long arid period. Much of the savanna belt has annual rainfall roughly equal to that of the American Middle West — thirty to forty inches a year. But when this rainfall comes within a four- or five-month period, rather than being distributed through the year, and when it comes in conditions of heat and in alternation with periods of great aridity, it creates a special problem. Certain types of soil very common in West Africa tend to form a permanent rocky crust if they are cleared of vegetation for tillage. This crust is called laterite, and laterization has gone further in West Africa than anywhere alse in the world. Many sections that once must have been productive are now barren rocky plains, virtually useless to man except for very sparse grazing. Even where laterization is no danger, the pattern of intense rainfall and heat tends to dissolve and carry off the nutrients in the soil. The traditional solution is to practice shifting cultivation, using a field for only a few years followed by long periods of fallow.

Further north, where tsetse flies are less common and cattle more so, the seasonal problem takes another twist. Stock have to be kept alive all year on the grass that only grows during three months or less. In addition, many places have no water for people or animals in the dry season, although they have plenty of pasture and water in the rains. The obvious solution is to have a base with year-round water during the dry season, feeding the cattle elsewhere during the rains. The result is *transhumant pastoralism,* a pattern of seasonal movement with the herds, sometimes combined with cereal cultivation around the base village. This pattern was used in North Africa, where flocks could be taken to the high mountains in summer; it could also be used on the desert fringes. In West Africa, it was often used in places that had enough rainfall for agriculture, but with large tracts of fallow land as well.

Climate influences history in still another way: the difference in rainfall from year to year. In some years the rain zone extends far out into the Sahara, bringing less rain over the savanna. In other years, rain is normal in amount but irregular in distribution, producing too short a growing season. In some years no rain falls over the northern savanna. These variations produce hunger and sometimes famine, as they did all along the sahel in the early 1970s when the rainfall was insufficient for several years running.

Our knowledge of climate history in the distant past is still sketchy, but African chronicles composed in Timbuktu on the Niger bend provide good information for the sixteenth and seventeenth centuries, and the pattern can be traced onward into the eighteenth century from other sources. These records suggest fairly reliable rainfall in the northern savanna during the sixteenth century, followed by a failed harvest every seven to ten years in the seventeenth century, and every five years or so in the eighteenth. In addition, the consecutive failure of the rains for a series of years led to two major disasters. One centered on the years 1639–1643 and the second on the late 1740s and early 1750s. Estimates (inevitably very uncertain for lack of hard evidence) suggest that at least half the population of the northern savanna region died or fled on each occasion. Some desert-edge cities, like Walata, had to be abandoned for a time. A disaster on this scale was averted in the early 1970s only because food could be sent in from the outside, but even then famine could not be avoided.

The one environmental feature that provided a kind of safety valve was the existence of north-flowing rivers like the Senegal, the upper Niger, and the Shari, which flows into Lake Chad. Each is fed by water that falls far to the south, creating a crest of water fifty to a hundred feet higher than average low water, overflowing the banks and carrying both silt and moisture to the surrounding fields. Crops planted on the wet fields as the water level began to recede would grow and ripen during the dry season, as they did where basin irrigation was used in ancient Egypt. But the height of the flood itself varied, according to the amount of rainfall further south. Along the Senegal in recent years, a high-flood year will carry water to more than twice the area reached by a low-flood year. But the water does rise every year whether it rains locally or not; thus, the riverain populations were not in the same danger of being wiped out by drought and famine as were those living away from the rivers. These others simply planted a crop each year and hoped for the best.

At a very early period, certainly well before the beginning of historical records, West Africa had centers of specialized production in addition to the agricultural sector, which included most people. Fishing was an intensive and specialized occupation along the coasts and rivers. Dry-season hunting was a major source of meat in savanna and forest alike. Rock salt was mined in the Sahara, while sea salt was evaporated and packaged along the coast or extracted from salt-concentrating plants like the mangrove. Iron ore is found almost everywhere in West Africa, but some regions with the best ore and the most plentiful charcoal were special centers of iron production and exported to others that were less well endowed. Still other regions concentrated on cotton and cotton textiles, sheep raising, and woolen cloth. As a result, regular patterns of internal trade within West Africa developed by which the surplus of one region could be exchanged for that of another. The vegetation zones — savanna, desert, and forest — practically guaranteed this outcome: the frontiers between them stretched in an east-west direction for thousands of miles, creating nearby regions with differing resource endowments, hence there was a natural advantage in north-south exchange.

PEOPLES AND CULTURES OF THE SUDANIC BELT

The three different environments demanded three distinct systems of human ecology. Because of the importance of man's relation to the land, we might expect to find three different cultures — one for the Sahara, one for the Sudanic zone, and one for the rain forest. In material culture and ecology, this was obviously the outcome, but other aspects of culture are by no means uniform within each vegetation zone; nor do they change sharply on crossing an ecological frontier to the north or south. Instead, each aspect of culture seems to be distributed in its own particular way. If we were to map these distributions we would need a base map of northern Africa with a series of overlays — several hundred of them, one for each important aspect of culture, indeed for each separate aspect of language, political structure, religion, art, family, or kinship. Very few of the overlays would show an identical pattern, and few would correspond closely to the pattern of the physical environment. The total pattern would show a remarkable degree of homogeneity, but with diversity, too, as widely shared cultural features were mixed in different ways.

Even the frontier often drawn between the Sahara and sub-Saharan Africa, one of the sharpest cultural lines anywhere in Africa, is only one step along a continuum. An older view, that the Sahara fringe was a sort of cultural divide, was largely based on racist assumptions: Saharan peoples were generally considered to be "white." It was assumed that they must therefore be culturally different from the "blacks" to the south. This view is mistaken on two counts. First, race has nothing to do with culture; and, second, the racial frontier between "black" and "white" is only roughly coterminous with the ecological frontier. In the west, many "white" and sedentary Moorish farmers live in the Senegal valley today, though they and the desert nomads to the north are very much a mixed race. In the central Sahara, to the north of Lake Chad, the desert nomads are Negroid peoples speaking languages in the same Teda-Daza family as those spoken in the savanna to the south. The people of the Nubian or desert reaches of the Nile are also "black" and so are the sub-Saharan "Arabs" of the Republic of the Sudan. The people of southwestern Arabia, for that matter, look very much like Ethiopians or Somalis on the African side of the Straits.

Language families not only straddle the desert-savanna frontier; they also cross the racial line. Hausa is one of the most widely spoken of all sub-Saharan languages, and its speakers are overwhelmingly both "black" and sedentary. It is nevertheless related linguistically to Arabic, Berber, and Hebrew, not to other languages of black Africa. Again, the Fula language, spoken by the people who are variously called Fulbe, Fulani, or Tukulor, is closely related to Wolof and Serer and other languages of Senegal, though many of the Fulbe are markedly Europeanoid in appearance — just as many Negroid people from Mauritania to the Nilotic Sudan have Arabic as their home language.

In the far west, from Morocco south across the desert and into the western Sudan, pre-Islamic kinship systems appear to have been matrilineal. This block of peoples was contiguous; but it included both sedentary and nomadic Berbers and sedentary peoples south of the desert, and it included both "blacks" and "whites." Then after a thousand years of Islamic influence, these people have all turned to patrilineal reckoning of kinship ties, again regardless of language, race, or ecology.

Elsewhere, other culture traits can be found from the edge of the desert south to the Gulf of Guinea. The Hausa, for example, had a pre-Islamic religion of a distinctive West African type. They worshipped many of the same divinities found far to the south among the Aja and Yoruba of Dahomey and southwestern Nigeria. But other traits of Hausa culture, like the language itself, are far more closely associated with the Tuareg of the Sahara. The same kind of pattern can be found at the eastern end of the Sudanic belt in Ethiopia, where many culture traits are still held in common with south Arabia, whereas others reach out to an African hinterland extending far beyond the highland area itself and taking in people whose physical appearance is not at all Ethiopian.

No simple hypothesis can account for all these cultural patterns, and no true explanation is likely to be simple. The horizon of written and oral history combined hardly goes back more than a thousand years anywhere along the sahel, except in the Nile valley. Add another three thousand years for the Nile valley itself and we still cover only a tiny fraction of human history. Within the time period we know about, however, we have evidence of dramatic changes over a few centuries. Whole regions can and sometimes did change their "mother tongue" without significant influence from mass migration. The Egyptians, for example, went from Coptic to Arabic largely because of the religious prestige of a language closely associated with Islam. Other people moved in mass migrations that took them thousands of miles before they settled down again and began to exchange culture traits with new neighbors. And small-scale, selective borrowing must have taken place continuously along all cultural frontiers. We can only assume that similar things occurred in places beyond the range of our present knowledge.

One of the usual causes assigned to cultural homogeneity is the existence of a large political unit, ruling over a particular territory for a long period of time. In a European example, France created a remarkable degree of cultural unity among people who spoke languages as different as French, Breton, Basque, German, Flemish, Occitan, and Provençal and who were culturally diverse in other respects as well. Similar tendencies can be seen in parts of the Sudanic belt as well. In the valley of the upper Niger, the pattern of Mande languages is indicative. They are a group roughly equivalent to the Romance languages of Europe. Some are fairly closely related; others are more distant, but the language variously known as Mandingo, Malinke, or Bambara occupies a greater territory and has many tens of thousands more speakers than any other. The Malinke-language area is, in fact, very nearly the same as the core region of the ancient empire of Mali. *Malinke* means the language of Mali, and its geographical spread suggests that Malian control encouraged the unification or merger of a number of preexisting regional dialects. Relatively isolated communities that were not brought into the empire also speak Mande languages, and these have tended to grow more distinct with time.

States or empires, however, were not always so crucial to the spread of a language over a wide region. Songrai (or Songhai) another African empire centered further down the Niger near its northern bend, had a home language called Songrai, but that language spread very little beyond its original homeland on the banks of the Niger downstream from Timbuktu. Hausa, on the other hand, was never associated with a large state until the nineteenth century, but it became a home language stretching over an area equivalent to Mali, and its use as a lingua franca reached even further. It would appear, then, that some large empires furthered the process of cultural homogenization, whereas others did so to a much lesser degree, and wide cultural homogeneity could appear without the influence of a large state.

STATES AND STATELESS SOCIETIES

One striking difference between African and Western history is that Western history is uniformly set within the framework of the state. Even during the anarchy and disturbances that followed the fall of Rome, the state remained the norm of aspiration, whatever the reality. Partly for this reason, when Europeans first began to consider African history, they took the state form of political organization as the proper measure of "progress." People with elaborate states were taken to be advanced; those without them were considered backward. Recent authorities, however, suggest that this view is far from accurate. At some levels of technology, state administration may only serve to draw off part of the social product for officials and courtiers who contribute little or nothing to that product. Many Africans apparently reached this conclusion, for states and stateless societies have existed side by side over nearly two millennia, without the stateless people feeling a need to copy the institutions of their more organized neighbors. Whether statelessness was preferable or not, it was clearly preferred.

This fact has left some difficult gaps for historians of Africa. Stateless societies leave few records. Their political operations are far too subtle and complex to be described accurately by early travelers from abroad, whether Arab or European. Oral traditions find no "great men" to celebrate. Genealogies are crucial to the operations of these societies, but their members tend to remember everybody's genealogy for two to five generations back rather than that of the ruling family for thirty. As a result, our only information on the way stateless societies changed is that gathered in the nineteenth and twentieth centuries. And because as many as a quarter of all the people in West Africa alone belonged to stateless societies at the beginning of the colonial period, any work of history necessarily leaves out a large segment of African historical development. The only remedy is to examine statelessness in the recent past for whatever hints it may give of the probable style of life in earlier times.

Political anthropologists, the scholars principally concerned with statelessness, do not always agree as to what characteristics mark a state. And, in reality, political institutions shade off from complex political structures, with full-time rulers exercising authority over every individual within a defined territory — these are clearly states — to societies at the other end of the spectrum in which authority is so dispersed that no permanent group of rulers can be identified. Those who exercise authority do so part-time, over small groups of people, and over only a limited sector of their affairs. Whatever the fine points of distinction along the way, this dispersal of authority is a mark of statelessness. In recent centuries it has been most clearly epitomized by the Tiv and most Ibo of Nigeria, and by many Berber societies in North Africa.

One common misconception is to confuse the kind of political organization with the scale of organization. Some African states were very small, whereas some stateless societies were very large. A few hundred people living together in a village or group of villages could have a full-time ruler drawn from a royal lineage, exercising authority over a territorially defined state and completely independent of other such states. In contrast to a microstate of this kind, some stateless societies settled conflicts between individuals as the Tiv did, by letting each antagonist call on the support of his kin. Thus, one kinship group was balanced against another, and the matter was settled by agreement, arrived at by representatives of the two groups. The size of the kin group called into play varied according to the antagonists' place in the kinship system; each conflict therefore called for a different ad hoc alliance and different representatives for each occasion. But thousands of people could be involved in a conflict between distant kin, and the Tiv system extended to nearly a million people at the beginning of the colonial period.

Stateless societies could work in several other ways, but the key building block in Africa was almost always the lineage, whether matrilineal or patrilineal. Lineages often settled their own internal quarrels, even where the state existed, and the crucial problem was to solve conflicts between lineages. The Tiv system of balancing kinship segments was one way. Another was to assign control over one aspect of life, such as landholdings, to the leadership of one lineage, while other lineages dominated other spheres. Still other societies worked through crosscutting social divisions, such as age grades, which had their own solidarity, separate from that of lineages. In other places, secret societies held both religious and judicial functions. Many forms of organization cutting across lineages were also common in a region of microstates. A secret society, for example, sometimes spread its influence through an area far larger than any state, and used its influence within each state to reduce the dangers of interstate conflict.

In spite of the many advantages of a stateless society, some things were hard to do without a more elaborate political structure. Warfare on a large scale required a command structure. Defense against a numerous enemy called for a concentration of the resources of a large area at a single point. Stateless societies could concentrate for attack or for a short war, as stateless nomadic societies have shown again and again in their raiding operations. But a permanent mobilization for defense — the kind of defense, say, that a sedentary society would need along a steppe frontier — required permanent officials. Second, only a well-organized state could easily regulate and protect trade over a large area. This calls for effective police, a system of law allowing aliens to come and go with security, and perhaps economic regulations to shore up the bargaining position of the society in its international exchange. Finally, only a state with its permanent officials and central direction could easily mobilize the wealth of society for special purposes such as temple building or the support of a priesthood, a nobility, or a royal lineage.

Performing these functions was not completely beyond the capacity of stateless societies, but it was extremely difficult. Sedentary societies living along a frontier with nomads had little choice: either set up permanent states or become tributary to the nomads. Defense in other situations, however, could often work well enough. The British, for example, found the Tiv far harder to conquer than any of the large states that finally made up Nigeria. But the problem in that case was simply that the Tiv had no one in authority capable of surrendering for the entire group. The British had, in effect, to force the surrender of each individual kinship segment. Commerce could also be organized without a state. The Ibo of Nigeria, for example, had a lively commercial system in which periodic local markets were linked by long-distance trade in the hands of specialists traveling under religious protection who were further assisted by a network of fictitious kinship ties. The usefulness of a state's coercive power in concentrating wealth is obvious, but it is equally obvious that wealth can be spent for public purposes in a stateless society as well, even though the contributions are necessarily voluntary. It should be equally obvious that deep social stratification is not likely to be voluntary.

EARLY STATES SOUTH OF THE SAHARA

Africa north of the Sahara had a long tradition of political life in states; these were incorporated in the Roman Empire. But the Berbers of North Africa also had their own tradition of segmentary society. We know almost nothing about the way it operated in the distant past, only that it survived as a living tradition and reappeared alongside states down to the very eve of the European conquests. Other regions with a long history of contact with the Hellenistic and then the Roman worlds also developed their own individual political traditions. This was the case with the Christian Nubian kingdoms of the desert and the Nilotic Sudan, as it was of the Christian states that succeeded Axum in the Ethiopian highlands. It was also true of the states that were to emerge south of the Sahara.

The location of these earliest states in West Africa suggests that they arose, as states have done elsewhere, to meet the needs of trade and the problems of defense. The ecological frontier between nomads and sedentaries, which was a source of friction reflecting different life styles, also held out the possibility of cooperation through trade. The savanna country was very badly supplied with salt of any kind, while several deposits of excellent rock salt lay in the Sahara. The steppe people were in a position to supply cattle and horses, which were especially valuable because they were hard to breed in the humid savanna. The sedentary farmers, in turn, could supply millet. As exchange at the desert edge became linked to more distant trade, the savanna people could draw in gold and (in time) kola nuts from the forest. The nomads in turn could draw in the manufactured products of North Africa.

The earliest states appeared at nearly the same time in a row along the northern fringe of the savanna. By the tenth century, one or more states existed along the middle Senegal, where Takrūr (or Fuuta Tooro) was to be in later centuries. A large Soninke state that came to be known as Ghana occupied the sahel between the northward bends of the Niger and Senegal. Gao, a Songrai state, had already organized its control of the Niger bend. Further east, beyond and to the north of Lake Chad, a certain Sayf bin Dhi Yazan had already united a number of Negroid nomadic kinship groups into a federation. The nucleus of this federation was the Kanuri people, who were later to turn sedentary and to rule over the successive empires of Kanem to the east of the lake and Borno

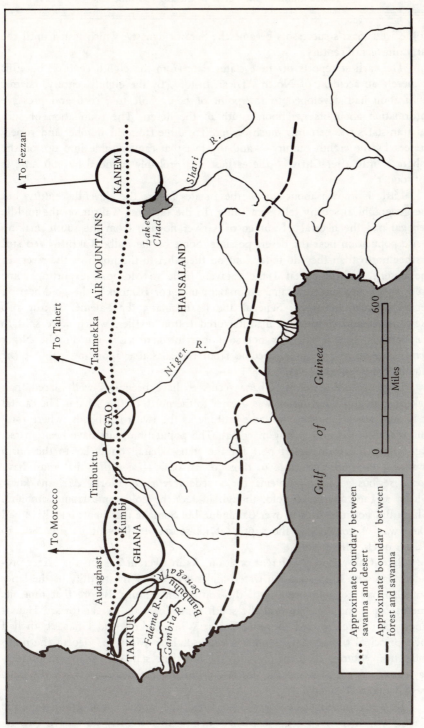

The Earliest Recorded States in West Africa, c. 1000 A.D.

To Fezzan

KANEM

Shari R.

Lake Chad

AÏR MOUNTAINS

HAUSALAND

To Tahert

Tadmeka

Niger R.

GAO

To Morocco

Timbuktu

Audaghast

Kumbi

GHANA

Senegal R.

Falémé R.

Bambuku

Gambia R.

TAKRUR

Gulf of Guinea

.... Approximate boundary between savanna and desert

– – – Approximate boundary between forest and savanna

0   600
Miles

to the west. Sayf's successors became the Sefawa dynasty, which lasted until the early nineteenth century.

The earliest reports of these states date from the eighth century, but this is merely an accident of North African history. By the eighth century, Islamic civilization had developed to the point of being able to record and preserve information about its neighbors south of the desert. The foundation of sub-Saharan states was certainly much earlier. To judge from the number and variety present by the eighth century — and the fact that camels came into use on the Sahara a little after Christ — the earliest was probably founded by 500 A.D., if not sooner.

Little is known about any of these states before the eleventh century, but the geographical setting tells something. In the far west, Takrūr on the middle Senegal had the natural advantage of a river flowing from the south, making dense population near the desert possible. Some of the Fulbe Takrūri lived still further north than they do today, out on the sahel to the north of the river. In the desert, Berbers operated the caravan trade to Morocco, exporting some gold, which undoubtedly came from Bambuhu (or Bambuk), the gold-bearing region between the upper Senegal and its tributary, the Falémé. Takrūr also grew millet and cotton and manufactured cotton textiles, which were sold to the nomads. Desert salt was not so important here as it was on the Niger bend, because salt could also come from the coastal evaporating pans at the mouth of the Senegal River.

In geographical terms, Ghana seems to have been less well placed than Takrūr, though its reputation was greater to the north of the Sahara. The capital at Kumbi was at roughly the same latitude as the two river bends, where rainfall agriculture is now barely marginal. The population must have been sparse. Audaghast, the main desert port for the trans-Saharan trade, lay to the north and west in conditions close to those of an oasis — a setting that must have posed serious security problems for a sedentary state. North Africans knew Ghana as the country of gold, though in fact the gold came from Bambuhu. Ghana did not rule directly over Bambuhu, but Soninke merchants may have had some way of controlling the supply at its source, to prevent its diversion to Takrūr or elsewhere.

Early Gao was in a different position. As in riverain Takrūr, the Niger provided Gao with fish, irrigation water, and silt to renew the fertility of the land. But Gao had no gold trade until the fourteenth century. Before that time, its line of communications toward the south went down the Niger toward Hausaland, not upriver toward the gold fields. While Takrūr and Ghana both had their principal trans-Saharan contacts with southern Morocco, Gao in the ninth and tenth centuries dealt mainly with the Kharijite state of Tahert (in present-day eastern Algeria) using the desert out-port of Tadmekka in much the same way Ghana used Audaghast.

Between the Niger bend and Lake Chad, the largest ethnic group were the Hausa, who then lived a good deal further north than they do today. This region, however, was slower to develop states or to feel the direct influence of the trans-Saharan trade than either Songrai to the west or Kanem to the east. Even Kanem passed through a process of state-building different from that of the western Sudan. The nucleus was a nomadic confederation of peoples speaking separate languages of the Teda-Daza group, probably formed in the ninth century. Nomadic confederations of this kind are common enough in history; the unusual thing is that this one held together. The separate tribes merged culturally to form the Kanuri. Sometime before the early twelfth century, they overran the sedentary lands in Kanem to their south. By the thirteenth century they had become sedentary themselves, with Njimi as their permanent capital. It is likely that they were involved in the trans-Saharan trade well before this, but Kanem had nothing to offer to outsiders so attractive as the gold of the western Sudan. Instead, it had the advantage of lying at the end of one of the most convenient of all the trans-Saharan trade routes. The Fezzan, an oasis region in what is now central Libya, had easy connections to North Africa, which meant that the actual desert crossing was comparatively short. In addition, between the Fezzan and Lake Chad lay a very convenient sequence of well-spaced wells and oases.

Of the region between the Kanuri and the Nubian kingdoms on the Nile, historians know very little beyond the fact that states came into existence at some points before about 1000 A.D. in a pattern similar to the appearance of states further west. That is, in the circumstances of growing trade between the desert and the sown, a focus of political authority was likely to turn up wherever trade was especially intense, as at the southern end of the easy desert crossing from Lake Chad to the Fezzan, or whenever local geographical conditions made possible a denser population or offered a more secure rainfall. These conditions were fulfilled by north-flowing rivers such as the Niger, the Senegal, or the Shari emptying into Lake Chad. They were also fulfilled where altitude both improved the chance of rainfall and made defense against desert raiders easier. The best example is the Marra mountains in the western part of the Republic of the Sudan, almost halfway between the Nile and Lake Chad. There, in the plateau and mountains region of Darfur, with a peak rising to more than 10,000 feet, a series of kingdoms flourished over the centuries. Whatever Darfurian kingdom might exist at a particular time was an important way station in the diffusion of culture across Africa from west to east or from east to west. These kingdoms were in contact with Christian Nubia, for example, as well as with Kanem to the west; they also had direct contact with Egypt by way of an ancient caravan route that ran northwest from the Marra mountains to join the Nile at its westernmost point near the third cataract.

THE COMING OF ISLAM

The influence of Islam manifested itself differently in different societies. Places that were conquered first in the Umayyad period and went on to become Muslim states had one experience, as was the case with Tunisia and Egypt. The rest of the Berber Maghrib had another experience, though it too entered the Muslim world at an early date. Beyond the Sahara, all along the Sudanic belt, in Ethiopia, or down the East African coast, Islam came later, and it came through missionary work and voluntary conversion more often than it did through government pressure. That experience was again different. But even in the core area, the picture of a homogeneous Muslim civilization can be over-drawn. While some parts of Muhammad's message went everywhere and took root with extraordinary uniformity (given the fact that Islam had no specific institutions for enforcing orthodoxy), other aspects of pre-Muslim culture with-stood a millennium of Muslim influence with remarkable tenacity.

One part of the Muslim heritage was the nature of the Muslim state, which owed more to historical experience than it did to the prescriptions of the Koran. Muhammad's followers had founded a universal empire, but it differed from the Roman Empire it replaced. At its head, the caliph was theoretically Muhammad's successor on earth. The Muslim world thus began with a basic trust in the state's capacity to create a good society on earth — not a paradise, but the kind of society in which men could do God's will and earn their salva-tion and in which God's law would be enforced as nearly as possible. Christian Rome and its successor states, on the other hand, looked back to the time when the state had persecuted Christians. A Christian state deserved the allegiance of its subjects, but good Christians still had to be discriminating about what was Caesar's and what was God's. A Muslim caliph was in a different position from a Christian king; it was his responsibility to make sure within his sphere that God's and Caesar's were the same.

Ideals of this sort are rarely realized, of course, but they tend to give direc-tion to the way institutions develop. With Islam, that influence was especially strong in the field of law, which was more closely integrated with religion than it was in the Christian tradition. Since Muhammad had begun as head of a religious community, his message from God was legal as well as theological, although the law set forth in the Koran was not presented systematically or clearly on every point. One of the first tasks of Muhammad's successors there-fore, was to study, elaborate, and systematize the legal framework he had left them, and this task fell to the general group of clerics or learned men, the *'ulamā* (singular *'alīm*), who dealt with faith and law alike. Over the early Muslim centuries from about 730 to 930, the 'ulamā of the Muslim world spent a great deal of their collective effort on legal work. The result was the *shar'ia,* the finished version of Muslim law. In fact, there were three different and equally authoritative versions, but the Malikite view was the one that came to be most respected in Muslim Africa.

In this as in other interpretations of the Koran and the traditions, the 'ulamā had to settle differences of opinion. In theory, differences could only be settled by a consensus of the community of believers; but the consensus had to be represented by someone, and the 'ulamā, as an informal corporation of learned men and judges, took this duty on themselves. They were not a priest-hood, ordained with special powers other men lacked, but their ability to speak in the name of religion and law gave them an important political role in many Muslim societies.

During the Abbasid period, Islam was very much an urban religion. The bedouin, pastoralist element from Arabia became insignificant. The dominant voice spoke from the key cities of Damascus, Baghdad, and Cairo. The 'ulamā reflected and reinforced this urban character, as the caliphate itself became the key institution organizing and supporting religious life. The Muslim message took on a dry and legalistic character, which appealed to the Muslim urban elite but not to the people in the countryside, who conformed when necessary but made their own mixture of new and old religions.

Shī'a, of course, offered a more emotional kind of religion, but *sunni,* or orthodox, Islam had only a few spokesmen along these lines until the time of al-Ghazāli (d. 1111), who found a way to open up a more personal and emo-tional kind of religious experience yet still satisfy the demands of orthodox theology. This new mysticism was called *sufi,* and it emerged at a time when the state was weak and people had reason to doubt that all was well with the world. Many different sufi variants appeared. Some dwelt on specific rituals or actions that would bring the believer into closer contact with God; others went further and incorporated aspects of pre-Islamic belief. Though many of these were far from orthodox, they were tolerated, if not supported, by the 'ulamā.

The organizational form of sufi Islam was the religious brotherhood (Arabic *tarīqa,* pl. *turuq*). The term in Arabic means "path," and each was a different path to a more personal and satisfying religious experience. At first, the *turuq* were simply groups of followers who gathered around a leader whose name and ideas were associated with the order. In time, they tended to form branches in other cities and in the countryside. Suborders sprang up by fission, sometimes lasting only a short while, although several orders have a continuous history from the early centuries to the present. Some came to have branches throughout the Muslim world, like the most famous of all, the Qādirīya, founded in Baghdad by 'Abd al-Qādir al-Jīlāni (d. 1166). Others had a more regional following, such as the Shādhilīya whose founder, al-Shādhili (c. 1258), studied at Fez in Morocco but settled in Alexandria. That movement was espe-cially strong in North Africa, though it also reached southeast into Arabia. The most important Maghribine sufi theologian, however, was Ibn al-'Arabi (d. 1240) of Spain, whose thought influenced many later tendencies of the sufist movement.

After the thirteenth century, when the turuq began to replace the state as the main articulating institution of Islamic life, the office of *shaykh,* or leader of the brotherhoods, rose in importance as the urban 'ulamā declined. It was also the sufis who carried Islam beyond the formal bounds of the Muslim empires. Islam spread into unadministered or lightly administered territory such as Berber North Africa even before the sufi movement came into existence, but sunni Islam was confined to the plains of Ifrīqiyah, while less orthodox versions moved beyond the frontiers, like the Kharijite heresy in the eighth century. Before the end of that century, two Muslim Kharijite kingdoms had already emerged in the oasis country north of the Sahara, one at Tahert in southern Algeria and the other at Sijilmasa in Morocco. Later, about 900 A.D., the shīʻa doctrine also appeared, with special appeal among the Berbers of the Kabylia mountains of northern Algeria. In time it was to spread from that new base eastward into Ifrīqiyah and Egypt.

The Berbers, who earlier had accepted Donatist Christianity, seem to have made a habit of adopting foreign religions heretically; and they continued even after sunni Islam had won out over Kharijism and shīʻa. The Berber country people especially left a wide area in human affairs to supernatural forces other than God. These were mainly survivals of ancient nature spirits, reinterpreted in Islamic terms as *jinn,* or genies. Berber Islam also emphasized the personal power of a saintly man or his descendants, a cult of living saints whose quality of holiness, or *baraka,* gave them power to see the future and perform miracles. Combined with sufi Islam, it was a short step to ascribe magical powers to the shaykh of a tarīqa and to venerate the tomb of a notable saint after his death.

ISLAM SOUTH OF THE DESERT

Islam was carried across the desert to the western Sudan even before the Maghrib itself was fully converted. The Kahrijite center at Sijilmasa was also the main northern terminus of the caravan trade, and townsmen and traders generally were Muslim before most of the rural population had been converted. Some converts were made in "black" Africa even before 800 A.D., and knowledge of Islam spread in the southern sahel region during the next century. The first conversion of a royal court followed in 985, when the Ja (Dya in French) rulers of Gao accepted Islam.

Rulers in the sahel reacted to Islam in different ways. In Gao, for example, they apparently made no effort to force or encourage the conversion of the rest of the population. In Takrūr, the rulers became Muslim in the 1030s and embraced the new religion with more enthusiasm. Further east, the *Mai* (or king) of Kanem became Muslim before the end of the eleventh century, even before the Kanuri became sedentary. Here too the ruler tried to do what he could to spread the new religion, including special encouragement given to the growth of a class of ʻulamā. Conversion to Islam not only helped the flow of trade to the outside world; it also brought the invaluable technique of literacy. In Ghana the rulers rejected Islam for themselves, although they welcomed Muslim merchants. The Soninke merchant class, however, was among the first social group in West Africa to accept Islam, and its members continued to have an important role in trade throughout the western Sudan.

The version of Islam presented to West Africa in these early centuries was obviously different from the sunni doctrine of the Middle Eastern cities, having at first a strong Kharijite influence followed by that of shīʻa Islam, but it appears to have been congenial to the West African religious tradition. This point has to be made with caution, because we lack direct evidence about religion in West Africa nearly a thousand years ago. It is nevertheless possible to pick out some common themes that run through West African religions today, and these should suggest the kind of religion that probably existed in the past. The antiquity of these religious traditions is attested by the fact that they are so widely spread across the continent, and it was these beliefs that had to be adjusted (or abolished) to meet the challenge first of Islam and later of Christianity.

All African religions, as they appeared near the end of the colonial period, were monotheistic in the sense that they believed the world was created by a single God. They differed from Christianity and Islam in holding that the creator God was no longer in active charge — nor was he ever a moral force for good or evil; he simply set the stage and then retired into neutrality. The supernatural forces that counted for something in the world's day-to-day affairs were themselves part of the created world. They too were morally neutral, subject to influences that could make them act for good or for evil. But they also had their own interests, responsibilities, and even personalities.

One group included the spirits of the ancestors, the personal guardians of specific lineages or ethnic groups. They watched over their descendents, but even they were not necessarily beneficent; they required handling through prayer, sacrifice, and ritual. A second group of spirits included the members of a general pantheon, without ties to any particular ethnic group, but with occupational specialties such as the pagan gods of Greece and Rome had. One had special powers over thunder and lightning, another over smallpox; still another was often a trickster with certain evil proclivities suggesting a Christian devil. The number of deities recognized by a particular African society differed widely, from fifteen or twenty to sixty or more. But the individual was not called on to perform rituals for all of them. He might participate actively in the worship of only one or two, working under the supervision of cult leaders who were at least a semiprofessional priesthood, if not full-time specialists.

The principal form of religious activity was ritual observance, the object of which was to put the individual or congregation in close communion with the deity in question. The means chosen was normally a sacrifice, often of an animal that was later cooked and eaten by the congregation. Spirit possession, with music and dance helping the spirit to enter the worshipper's body, was also used. In a trancelike state, the worshipper could then take the spirit's role and communicate to the rest of the congregation in its name. Prayer was a crucial part of ritual and private devotion, as it is with Islam and Christianity. In special circumstances, some African religions called for human sacrifice, but such sacrifice was almost always associated with the particular or family gods, not with the general pantheon.

Alongside the ritual of the cults, most West African societies also practiced some form of divination. Diviners were usually a separate group from the cult leaders and were, like them, at least semiprofessional. Their main task was to give advice, to help the individual deal with the spirit world. A diviner would be consulted, for example, in deciding which cult or deity should be most honored. He could be asked to foretell the future, he could deal with misfortune — both supernatural and man-made. When witchcraft or sorcery was suspected, a diviner could be called in to identify the witch and recommend appropriate countermeasures. The diviner did all this by using a battery of supernatural charms and techniques, although one suspects that common sense and untrained psychiatry were the real secrets of success.

It is obvious that many of these religious ideas — ritual sacrifice, for example — occur also in Middle Eastern religions like Judaism and Christianity. It is generally believed that these resemblances go back to an ancient substratum of religious thought that was common to much of the Old World before cultures diverged. Detailed resemblances between the religious ideas of the Maghrib and West Africa, furthermore, suggest that these two regions were closer to one another in religious culture than either was to the Middle East before the rise of Islam. In both the Maghrib and West Africa, animal sacrifices were the main way of placating the spirits. In both, the blood of the sacrificed animal was the crux of the ritual. Spirits both north and south of the Sahara were thought to live in particular species of tree; wooden objects and living trees often were important in ritual.

These parallels can be extended further to include several forms of divination and much else. They could have been created by close contact before the desiccation of the Sahara, or they could have come from diffusion across the desert in either direction in more recent millennia. Perhaps we shall never know their origin, but the fact remains that Maghribine Islam was the version that came into West Africa, which was already predisposed to receive it. The furthest extension of the Muslim world toward the west was not the Maghrib, but the Sudan.

The movement of Islam into the horn of Africa and the Nilotic Sudan was nearly contemporaneous with its introduction into West Africa, even though these two regions were only a short jump across the Red Sea from Arabia. The original Arab conquest stopped short of Nubia and the Nilotic Sudan after the seizure of Egypt in the 650s, because the caliphate wanted to be free to move in other directions. It therefore arranged a treaty with the Nubian kingdoms, which provided for open trade up and down the Nile and tribute payments in the form of Nubian slaves but otherwise left the frontier where it was. In one form or another, a treatylike arrangement with similar provisions lasted during the next six centuries, until the 1260s and 1270s, when a Muslim Egyptian government once more took up the military advance toward the Sudan. In the intervening period, Islam had advanced without military support. Trade up the Nile made that result nearly inevitable, and bedouin Arabs from Arabia moved increasingly into the desert regions on either side of the Nile. The Nubian Christian kingdoms nevertheless held to their old religion until the fourteenth century, and individual Nubian Christians still made the pilgrimage to Jerusalem until after the end of the fifteenth.

Further down the Red Sea, the process of Islamization was similar: no open conquest but a slow infiltration of Islamic ideas. These penetrated fairly rapidly among the nomadic peoples along the fringes of the Ethiopian highlands, generally by about 1000 A.D. The Muslim infiltration of the highlands was slower. So long as the Abbasid caliphate was strong and had its capital near the Persian Gulf, most trade from the Muslim Mediterranean to the Indian Ocean went through Baghdad, and the Red Sea remained a backwater. Then in the eleventh and especially in the twelfth century, Red Sea trade revived. Muslim merchants began to penetrate the hinterland of Ethiopia, sometimes passing through the Christian kingdom when political conditions permitted, but going around it through the eastern highlands when they did not. By about 1250, the eastern highlands of Ethiopia and all the territory to the east and north of the Christian kingdom were already Muslim or strongly influenced by Islam. From the point of view of the sedentary, mountain Christians, however, Islam was not only an alien religion; it was also the special faith of nomads and merchants, just as it was in West Africa.

TRADE AND ISLAM IN WEST AFRICA

Merchants in long-distance trade were, in fact, the principal carriers of Islam into sub-Saharan Africa, just as Greek and Phoenician merchants in long-distance trade had been the initial carriers of the Hellenistic synthesis into the western basin of the Mediterranean. This role as culture-bearers was common to merchants precisely because they were forced by their occupation to remove themselves, to go and live in culturally alien communities. And yet they also had to keep in touch with the culture of their homeland.

As the importance of trade increased in the western Sudan from the eleventh century onward, the Muslim long-distance traders carried their network of commerce southward from the desert ports on the sahel. They spread as a trade diaspora, sending out emigrants to settle at all the principal points of trade so as to be assured of trustworthy business contacts. The Arabic sources refer to all these traders as "Wangara," and by 1500 at least three separate networks can be distinguished.

One of these was the main line of trade southward from Timbuktu by way of the Niger. This was apparently first operated by Songrai boatmen and Soninke merchants, joining the Niger bend to the Malian metropolitan province. Then, with the attraction of the Akan goldfields in the fifteenth century, and the new entrepôt of Jenné, the network continued overland through Bobo Julaaso (French Bobo-Dioulasso), Kong, Bonduku, and on to Begho just north of the forest. The traders on this route were of Soninke origin, but they soon took on Malinke language and culture. In so doing, they adopted their own ethnic identity as

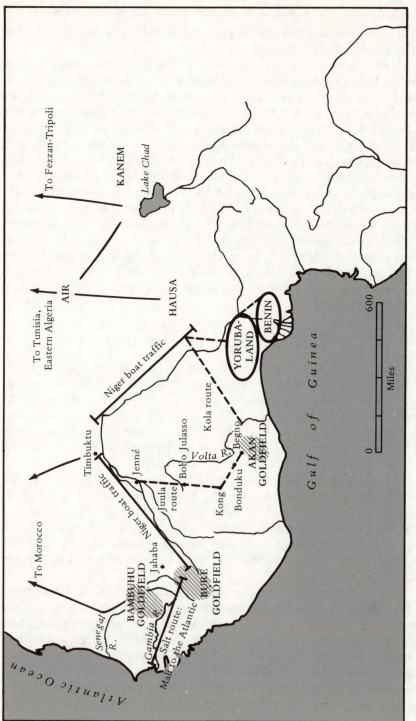

Early Trade Routes in West Africa

Juula (French Dyoula), which is simply the Malinke word for "merchant." Well before 1500, the traders on this route were reaching down to the coast itself.

A second route ran westward from the Niger to the Bambuhu goldfield. Its principal base before 1500 was Jahaba (Diakha-Ba), the functional equivalent of Begho. From there, one branch carried gold back to the Niger bend, but another route ran through to the Atlantic, following the line of the Malian advance to the sea. This route from Jahaba to the ocean could have been opened as early as the fourteenth century; it was certainly working regularly by about 1600. These traders to the west were originally Soninke like the Juula, but they too changed to a cultural pattern that was basically Malinke and began to identify themselves as Jahanke (French Diakhanké). They never had a Jahanke state, but their line of semi-independent villages strung out along the trade route remains as evidence of their trade diaspora.

The third of the early trade networks is also traced to Soninke origins, though it long since became completely Hausa. Well before the fifteenth century, the Soninke known as Wangarawa began to place their settlements in various Hausa towns. A Juula trade route also stretched out as a branch from present-day Bobo-Julaaso eastward through the southern part of Upper Volta. Hausa trade in Hausa hands, however, soon began to spread to the south of the Hausa towns. One line of commerce that was to be extremely important reached to the southwest, toward the forest of present-day Ghana, where kola nuts were a very important export to all of the savanna. Another reached down into the Yoruba states and Benin. Still others reached from the Hausa towns northward to the Aïr massif in the desert, which formed a convenient entrepôt for the Saharan trade, or eastward to tap the trans-Saharan trade entering Kanem.

MIGRATIONS

The most significant migrations in the known history of Africa — the Bantu migrations, the southward movement of savanna peoples into the West African forest, the emptying of the Sahara following its desiccaton — had all taken place long before the eighth century A.D. The main lines of cultural and linguistic geography in northern Africa were set by then. Yet people still moved from place to place in small numbers, as refugees from local drought conditions or political oppression, in search of better land or new opportunities. As they moved, they carried their culture with them. As they settled down among aliens, they created plural societies, with small enclaves of foreign culture that could sometimes last for a century or more before being absorbed in the culture of their neighbors. Meanwhile, their presence created a source of cross-cultural borrowing.

This kind of individual and small-group movement ran parallel to a similar but involuntary movement that occurred in the course of the internal slave trade. Slaves were captured in warfare, but they were rarely kept by their captors because they might easily escape and might be dangerous. They were sold into the trade, taken hundreds of miles from home, and then sold to the people who intended to use their services — if, indeed, they managed to avoid the export trade to North Africa and, later, to the Americas. The early slave trade within Africa has not been studied in detail, and the evidence may be too thin to give a secure picture when it is studied. It is known, nevertheless, that slavery and a slave trade existed in sub-Saharan Africa at a very early time.

The more recent pattern of slavery in sub-Saharan Africa also provides some hints. It was quite different from the economically oriented slavery of the New World. In most places, slavery was an assimilative institution, designed to serve as an artificial kinship tie permitting the addition of members to one's group, village, or society. Newly purchased slaves gradually acquired rights as they slowly became members of the new society. In time they or their descendants settled down as full-fledged members of that society, though often with a subordinate social status. Usually, "slaves" could not be sold after the first generation, so that, in the Western sense of chattel slavery, they were not slaves at all. Although it is clear that the newly purchased slaves usually assimilated the culture of the master's community, what we know about acculturation suggests that the very process of absorbing aliens must also have changed that community's way of life. The influence of this process in building a common West African culture may have been considerable, especially when we remember that in many West African societies half or more of the population was in "slave" status at the beginning of the colonial period.

The major exception to this pattern of individual and small-group interchange was along the sahel, the "shores" of sedentary occupation north and south of the desert itself. Large-group migration still took place on both sides of the line separating the desert from the sown. Nomads tended to be more numerous near the sahel than they were in the central Sahara because rainfall was better and the sahel afforded a valuable opportunity to trade with the sedentary farmers. On the sedentary side of the line, other pastoralists were also present, practicing transhumance with their cattle during the wet season. Because both groups therefore moved each year in any case, they tended to move more often and in larger numbers than their sedentary neighbors did. From the eighth century through the fourteenth, the most important population movements along the sahel were three: Arabs coming west along either side of the North African sahel from Egypt to Morocco and Mauritania; an equivalent but smaller movement of Arabs in the sahel and steppe south of the desert from the Nilotic Sudan toward Lake Chad; and an eastward movement of Fulbe pastoralists along the northern tier of savanna country from the Senegal valley to northern Cameroon.

The Arab movements were the most significant; they, not the original Muslim conquests, brought about the Arabization of the Maghrib, the western Sahara, and the Nilotic Sudan. Several thousand Arabs had settled in Egypt after the first Muslim conquest of the eighth century, but Arabic speech and culture penetrated further west only in the cities and through the religious prestige of Arabic as a holy language. Berber Muslims of the first Islamic centuries spoke Berber, just as most Spanish Muslims at the same period spoke an early form of Spanish. But common use of Arabic and the penetration of Arab culture came only with the movement of nomadic Arab migrants in large numbers, especially in the eleventh century and later. It was not a blanket migration, sweeping the native population before it, but rather a relatively slow infiltration accompanied by a great deal of intermarriage and voluntary culture change.

In origin, these population movements were a continuation of the movement of people out of Arabia into the Middle East, a movement that had begun long before the rise of Islam and continued whenever the sedentary authorities to the north were weak. The Egyptian desert to the east of the Nile was Arabized before the time of Muhammad, and bedouins continued afterward to push into Egypt along the fringes of the Nile valley, sometimes crossing to the western desert, sometimes pushing southward toward the Sudan. The nomadic Beja of the Red Sea coastal region held their own, though they gradually turned to Islam. The Arab immigrants found it easier to move south or west and ultimately to set up a new pattern of life near the Sudanic savanna country or in the far west.

In the first stages, these migrating Arabs had to deal with the governments of sedentary Egypt, sometimes in cooperation or even in alliance against third parties, sometimes in the usual enmity of sedentary and nomadic peoples. In the tenth century, as Abbasid power weakened, the nomadic side became more daring. A little before 1000 A.D., the Banu Hilal and the Banu Sulaym tribes from the central Arabian plateau moved into the eastern desert; then, beginning about 1050, they moved west in force for a major attack on Ifrīqiyah — perhaps at the urging of the Egyptians who wanted to be rid of them, but at least without Egyptian resistance to their crossing the Nile and moving off. In the next centuries, the Banu Hilal and others continued moving until they reached the Atlantic coast of Morocco and Mauritania.

Historians disagree about their long-term impact on the Maghrib. One view, somewhat discredited recently, held the Hilalians responsible for the destruction of classical "civilization" that had survived since Roman times. It pointed to the destruction of irrigation works and the turning of plowed fields into mere pasture for herds, which drove the native Berbers into the mountains. The recent revision holds that the nomads were sometimes destructive but not without redeeming contributions to Maghribine civilization. They sometimes cooperated with sedentary regimes, and they were not alone as a nomadic threat to the sedentary Maghrib; Berber nomads had also been destructive in the past and would be so in the future. Whatever their precise assessment, however, historians today agree that the Arabs were a politically unsettling force in Maghribine politics for centuries to come; and that they accomplished the linguistic Arabization of Tunisia, of most of the plains in Algeria and Morocco, and of a great deal of steppe and desert off to the south as far as the western Sudan.

The second Arab movement into the Nilotic Sudan and along the southern sahel was actually a branch of the first. Although some of the Arabs who moved into the Nilotic Sudan came directly across the Red Sea, most used the route by way of Sinai and Egypt, bypassing the Christian Nubian states as they moved southward parallel to the Nile. In a massive but badly documented migration, they not only occupied the sahel and the steppe just north of it; they also moved into the rainfall lands supporting sedentary agriculture in the Sudanese savanna. In the century from 1250 to 1350, Egypt also applied military pressure to the Nubian kingdoms, which were gradually going Muslim by peaceful conversion in any case. Those stretched along the desert Nile fell to Egypt, leaving only the southern kingdom of Alwa, partly Islamized, to continue a token existence into the sixteenth century.

Some of these Arabs kept to their old role as camel nomads and pushed west along the steppe north of the sahel to occupy the northern plains of Kordofan, Darfur, Wadai, and into present-day Chad. Other Arabs pushed south into regions of sedentary agriculture and mixed with the original inhabitants to create a population that is obviously partly African in physical appearance but

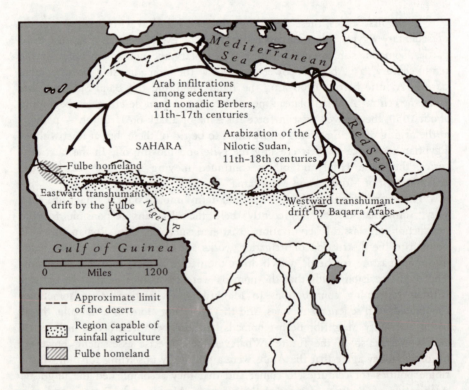

The Arab and Fulbe Migrations

Arabic in language and many other aspects of culture. Later arrivals from Arabia found the land suited to camels and sheep already occupied, so they moved into the sahel country and became cattle nomads called *baqarra,* practicing transhumant pastoralism in a country that could also be used for agriculture. Some of them moved west, living among many other peoples until, in time, they reached the longitude of Lake Chad, where their descendants, the Shuwa Arabs, are still to be found.

While the Arabs were moving along the southern steppe frontier from east to west, the Fulbe (or Fulani) were moving from west to east. They were cattle people like the baqarra, keeping south of the sahel and practicing transhumance rather than true nomadism (that is, they stayed near permanent sources of water in the dry season, moving out with the rains only to return when the pastures and water holes dried up). As a result, they had to be away from home when their farmer neighbors were planting and harvesting. Theirs was therefore a specialized occupation of their particular ethnic group. Fulbe pastoralists are found today scattered through the western Sudan from the Atlantic to Lake Chad, speaking a common language with comparatively small dialectal variation over great distances. Many also have a physical appearance suggesting a European or North African strain somewhere in the background. But all people speaking their language are not pastoral. Sedentary Fulbe are the dominant population along the middle reaches of the Senegal on the Senegal-Mauritania border.

The ethnographers who encountered the Fulbe in Senegal decided that the pastoral Fulbe were a separate "tribe," whom they called Peuhl, while they called the sedentary speakers of the same language Tukolor. This practice, which persists to the present, has caused endless confusion because Europeans who encountered the same people in Nigeria called them all Fulani, no matter what their occupation. To avoid confusion, they will all be called Fulbe here, that being their most common name for themselves.

Many ingenious theories have been concocted to explain Fulbe origins, but the most plausible hypothesis recalls that sedentary Fulbe have long been the dominant population in the state of Takrūr and its successor, Fuuta Tooro, on the middle Senegal. Their appearance is rarely Europeanoid, which means that they look like their Wolof and Serer neighbors, whose languages are also similar. The easiest way to solve the problem of pastoral Fulbe with European-like features is to assume that people who looked European and knew something about raising stock once turned up on the Senegal. Because the Berbers of the desert have been neighbors of the sedentary Fulbe at least since the beginning of our era, the easy assumption is that some of the Berbers moved over and joined Fulbe society as pastoral specialists. The Senegal River made an excellent dry-season base, and the Ferlo wilderness to the south of the river has excellent pasture in the wet season, though lacking both wells and surface water in the dry. If the shepherds who attached themselves to Fulbe society spent the dry season among the sedentary Fulbe and took Fulbe wives, their shift to Fulbe culture would not have taken very long.

The pastoral Fulbe, however, were especially vulnerable to the climatic irregularity of the desert fringes. A series of dry years of the kind that have occurred periodically in the history of the sahel would force pastoralists along the Senegal to shift to a more secure dry-season base to the south. Once shifted, they might not return, though the sedentary people could stay because they depended on basin irrigation when the rains failed. A few pastoralists might remain with them, forming the nucleus of a new growth of cattle and population when adequate rainfall returned. Meanwhile, those who had been driven away kept shifting in response to political pressures, or the lure of still newer pastures. They drifted off, generally to the east and generally staying in the latitudes where transhumant pastoralism was efficient. They appear to have been welcomed, because their type of pastoralism filled an ecological niche not occupied by the savanna farmers.

By the thirteenth century, the most advanced edge of the Fulbe drift appears to have reached Hausa country. Along the way, large numbers settled in Maasina on the upper Niger above Timbuktu, where the desert-river relationships like those on the Senegal were reproduced with variations. Others drifted into close relations with non-Fulbe, which meant that many settled down, became sedentary, and adopted a culture that was partly local and partly from the Senegal. By 1950, the total number of Fulbe in West Africa was estimated at more than five million, several times the population of their homeland in the middle Senegal valley.

Climatic irregularity also caused the dispersion of sedentary farmers. The Soninke or Sarakolé, for example, had an early homeland in the region between the middle Senegal and the Niger bend. It was an area of light rainfall at the best of times, but very well placed for trade northward across the desert. Soninke oral traditions tell of a time when they all lived together in "Wagadu" (identifiable as the ancient kingdom of Ghana), but the displeasure of the gods stopped the rain for seven full years. Wagadu turned to desert, and the people had to flee to the south. The climatic disaster clearly resembled those of the seventeenth and eighteenth centuries or the 1970s in the same region, but this one took place well before 1500. It scattered the Soninke far and wide. Some still live near "Wagadu," but the majority are dispersed through the western Sudan from the Gambia to Upper Volta. Some live in large communities that were able to maintain Soninke-speaking states for centuries. Villages isolated among aliens, however, often took on the culture of their neighbors, though with a Soninke input that is still detectable. The dispersion of the Fulbe is therefore only one of several cases of dispersion caused by climate, but the Fulbe were specialists who moved together in a tight community. They therefore preserved their language and culture over a longer period than was possible for sedentary farmers who settled among new neighbors.

POLITICAL CHANGE IN NORTH AFRICA

For most of the Islamic world, the Middle Ages were marked on the one hand by a breakdown of Abbasid unity and a rise in the importance of the turuq as a key institution guiding religious, and sometimes secular, life. It was, on the other hand, also a period of expansion for Islam, beyond the old frontiers into Southeast Asia, sub-Saharan Africa, and down the East African coast. North Africa fits a little imprecisely into this pattern. The Maghrib never experienced the unity of Abbasid rule, but the main trends from about 1000 to 1500 A.D. were those of the Islamic world at large. That long period can also be divided in the middle. Before about 1270, North African political affairs were dominated by three successive attempts to create a new, universal, Muslim empire: a shī'ite effort based on eastern Algeria and Ifrīqiyah; a nomadic empire-building invasion by the Almoravids of the western Sahara; and a final effort by the mountain Berber Almohad movement of central Morocco. After 1270 and the collapse of the Almohad empire, political life became still more fragmented as each region fell under the control of local forces. In Egypt and the Maghrib alike, secular-minded dynasties rose and fell without claiming the caliphate or universal rule over *dar al-Islam*.

The three earlier efforts at unification also had a good deal in common. Each had a home base and source of major support in a region that was geographically and culturally marginal to the Muslim civilization it sought to conquer. Each called for a purification of Islam and a return to the first principles of religion, though they disagreed about what those principles were. Each wanted to create a good society by breaking the social and political mold to create greater justice based on Islam. Each helped generate a creative phase in the history of art and letters. And each achieved a measure of economic success within its territory, though none was able to create a state with enough unity and administrative continuity to last more than a couple of centuries.

The first of the three empire-building attempts began in the 890s with the following of an itinerant shī'ite preacher among the Berber, Kutuma mountaineers in the eastern Kabylia mountains of Algeria, and it ended with the establishment of the Fatimid sultanate, controlling the eastern Maghrib but centered on Egypt. The founder belonged to a branch of shī'a Islam which believed in an imminent Mahdi or savior who would come to root out injustice and perfect the shar'īa by showing the hidden meanings in Muhammad's message. The result would be a new order on earth, where the state would no longer be required because Muslim law would be followed automatically by virtue of the internal convictions of the faithful.

The rise of the Fatimids began when the movement came out of its mountain base and seized Ifrīqiyah in 909 A.D. It then consolidated its position in the eastern Maghrib, capturing the Kharijite kingdoms of the south in the 950s. By the 960s, it was ready for an advance on the Middle East. It captured Egypt easily enough and campaigned briefly in Syria, but the conquests stopped there. The Fatimids moved the capital to Cairo in the 970s, however, and settled down for two centuries as a mainly Egyptian regime with uncertain control over their former base in the Maghrib.

Their descent on Egypt gave the Fatimids a role in the dissolution of the Abbasid caliphate, but their real importance in Islamic affairs was their reorientation of Mediterranean and Indian Ocean trade. From their base in Egypt, they developed the Red Sea route, providing naval patrols at sea and secure control over the desert caravans from Aswan to the port of 'Aydhab, opposite Jidda and Mecca. This not only diverted trade from the Persian Gulf; it also increased the total east-west trade. Even Christian powers like Genoa and Venice began to profit by coming to Alexandria for goods from as far away as Southeast Asia.

When the Fatimid dynasty fell in the 1170s, Egypt's position in interna-

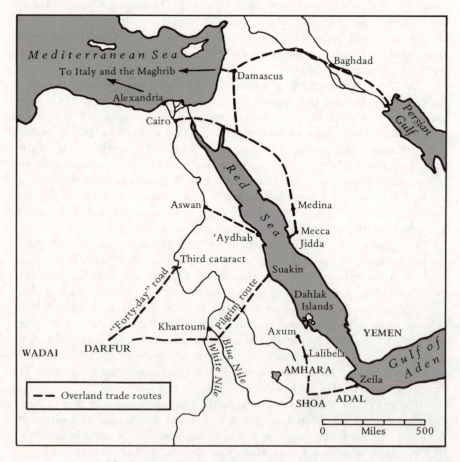

The Strategy of Trade on the Red Sea and Its Vicinity

tional commerce was not affected. Ifrīqiyah was already lost to the Hilalian Arabs in the 1050s. The loss of Egypt was a blow to shī'a Islam, because the next dynasty returned to sunni orthodoxy; but the original Berber ruling class had long since lost real control, as the military forces from the Maghrib were phased out in favor of slave soldiers from Asia or the Sudan. After a brief intervening dynasty, control of Egypt passed to these slave soldiers called Mamluks. They were recruited in childhood by purchase beyond the fringes of Islam and brought up to be professional soldiers. With their monopoly of physical force, it was easy for them to become masters of the state, and new generations of soldiers could be recruited in the same way to carry on. The Mamluks therefore continued as the rulers of Egypt down to its conquest by the Ottoman Empire in the early sixteenth century.

The Almoravid empire, second of the three Maghribine empires, began at the opposite end of North Africa, at much the same time as the Hilalian movement into Ifrīqiyah. Because the Almoravids drew their strength from a nomadic base, the combination of Almoravid Berbers from the southwest and Hilalian Arabs from the southeast brought a nomad crisis to the sedentary Maghrib, beginning in the second half of the eleventh century. The crisis also suggests that the sedentary societies had fallen into a period of weak organization and inadequate defense.

The Almoravid movement first began among the Lamtuna, a nomadic, Muslim, and Berber tribe which controlled one of the caravan routes from southern Morocco to the western Sudan. In the 1040s, they attracted a Muslim preacher from southern Morocco to serve as their spiritual guide. With his leadership, they put together a nomadic confederation that mobilized the military power of the western Sahara in much the same way the original Muslims had mobilized the nomadic power of Arabia. On the intellectual side, the movement called for a return to the primitive purity of Islam, with a strong emphasis on the role of the shar'īa and especially the Malikite version. It was thus at the opposite end of the spectrum of Islamic thought from the sufi movement that was to blossom in the following century. The name, Almoravid, however, comes from the Arabic *murābitun,* meaning men of the *ribāt,* a holy retreat or fortified place for the defense of Islam. That aspect, at least, prefigures the role that holy men and places of religious retreat were to play later on in Maghribine Islam under sufi influence.

Whatever the religious drive of the Almoravids, their early moves reflected their interest in trans-Saharan commerce. In the 1050s, they turned both north and south, first capturing Audaghast, the chief desert port for the empire of Ghana, then turning north to capture Sijilmasa in southern Morocco. This gave them the two main termini of the gold route across the desert. In the late 1050s, however, they failed in another southward move against Takrūr, but their further northward movement took them far into the sedentary parts of southern Morocco. By the mid-1090s, they went on to capture all of Morocco, western Algeria, and Muslim Spain, establishing a new nomadic dynasty in control of the Muslim

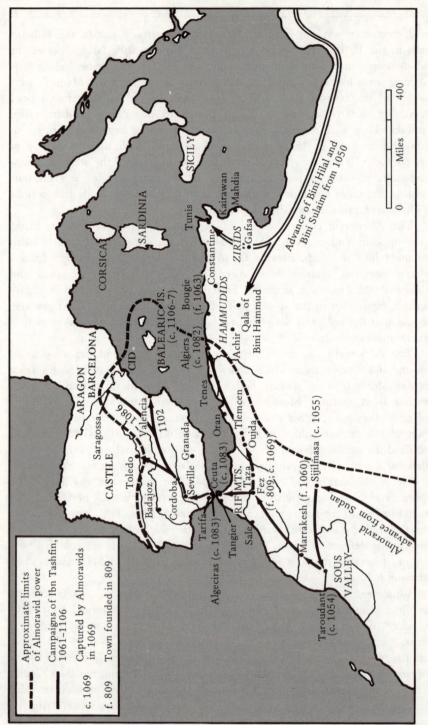

The Empire of the Almoravids (c. 1050–1140 A.D.)

Approximate limits
of Almoravid power

Campaigns of Ibn Tashfin,
1061–1106

Captured by Almoravids
in 1069

Town founded in 809

c. 1069

f. 809

ARAGON
BARCELONA
CASTILE
Saragossa
980?
Toledo
Valencia
1102
Badajoz
Seville
Granada
Cordoba
Tarifa
Algeciras (c. 1083)
Tangier
Ceuta
(c. 1083)
RIF MTS.
Taza
Fez
(f. 809; c. 1069)
Sale
Oujda
Tlemcen
Oran
Tenes
Algiers
(c. 1082)
Bougie
(f. 1063)
Tunis
Constantine
HAMMUDIDS
Achir
Qala of
Bini Hammud
ZIRIDS
Gafsa
Kairawan
Mahdia
CID
BALEARIC IS.
(c. 1106–7)
CORSICA
SARDINIA
SICILY
Advance of Bini Hilal and
Bini Sulaim from 1050
Marrakesh (f. 1060)
Sijilmasa (c. 1055)
Almoravid advance from Sudan
Taroudant
(c. 1054)
SOUS
VALLEY

Miles
0   400

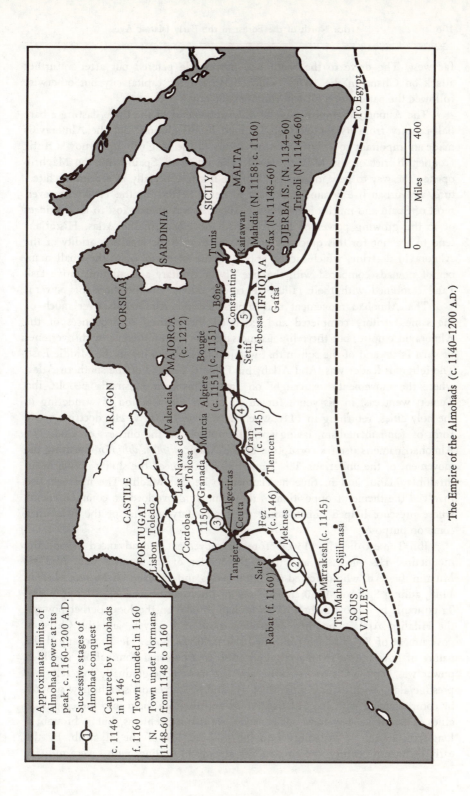

The Empire of the Almohads (c. 1140–1200 A.D.)

Approximate limits of
Almohad power at its
peak, c. 1160–1200 A.D.

Successive stages of
Almohad conquest

c. 1146 Captured by Almohads
in 1146

f. 1160 Town founded in 1160

N. Town under Normans
1148–60 from 1148 to 1160

Miles

0   400

To Egypt

MALTA
SICILY
SARDINIA
CORSICA
Kairawan
Mahdia (N. 1158; c. 1160)
Tunis
Sfax (N. 1148–60)
DJERBA IS. (N. 1134–60)
Tripoli (N. 1146–60)
Bône
Constantine
IFRIQIYA
Tebessa Gafsa
Setif
Bougie (c. 1151)
Algiers (c. 1151)
MAJORCA (c. 1212)
Valencia
Murcia
Oran (c. 1145)
ARAGON
Tlemcen
Granada
Las Navas de Tolosa
Cordoba
1150
Algeciras
Ceuta
CASTILE
Toledo
Lisbon
PORTUGAL
Tangier
Fez (c. 1146)
Meknes
Salé
Rabat (f. 1160)
Marrakesh (c. 1145)
Tin Mahal
Sijilmasa
SOUS VALLEY

far west. The drive to the south had meanwhile petered out after a further attack on Ghana in the 1070s, which destroyed the capital city but otherwise followed the pattern of a hit-and-run nomadic raid.

The Almoravid empire was the most ephemeral of the three, lasting a bare half-century from its conquest of Spain to its dissolution. But the Almoravids made an important contribution to the culture of the Maghrib, up to now a rustic frontier district of the Muslim world. The union of Spain with the Maghrib opened the way to new influences from the north, especially in art and architecture, and urban life became important as never before. By the 1140s, however, most of Spain and much of the western Maghrib was already lost to local princes or to the growing power of the Almohad movement in the Atlas. Historians tend to account for this quick failure by pointing to the legalistic aridity of the Almoravid doctrine, which lacked appeal in the Maghrib, or to the small number of nomads compared with the size of the military and administrative task (and combined with their failure to co-opt others into positions of power).

The Almohad movement that superseded the Almoravids over much of the same territory completed and extended the cultural consequences of the Almoravid empire, but the religious message was quite different, with overtones of shi'a Islam and of the sufism that was just then beginning in the Middle East. The religious leader was 'Abd Allah Ibn Tumert, a native of the southern Atlas, where the movement first caught on among his own Masmuda people. Ibn Tumert went east in his youth for an education and a period of wandering in the holy cities, returning in 1118 when he was nearly forty. His doctrine was a form of fundamentalism, laying special emphasis on the oneness of God. The Almohad name is itself a corruption of the Arabic *al-muwahhidūn,* meaning the movement of the unitarians. Ibn Tumert also introduced the shi'ite notion of an infallible Mahdi and in time he claimed to be that Madhi. The message also involved the theme of opposition to the Almoravid overlords, a common enemy whose presence helped him to unite the segmentary societies of the Atlas in a common purpose.

Ibn Tumert died in 1130, before the movement had advanced beyond the mountains. His successor and the real founder of the empire was 'Abd al-Mu'min ibn 'Alī, who defeated the Almoravids and annexed all Morocco before 1148, adding Spain in 1150 and the rest of the Maghrib as far as Ifrīqiyah and Tripolitania by 1160. In the process he had to take on the local Berber powers, the Hilalian Arabs who then controlled most of Ifrīqiyah, and the Christian government of Sicily which controlled the Ifrīqiyan ports. He also changed the nature of government from a religious effort to a personal domination, in which power was kept in his own family; and the movement gradually lost religious prestige along with its first supporters. He and his successors sought new support by compromising with the Hilalian Arabs and inviting them into the empire as allies. That move may have solved some short-run problems, but it brought a long-term source of instability into the political life of the Maghrib. By the early thirteenth century, the empire was already in decline, with severe military losses to the Christians in Spain and inability to master the government anywhere. By 1250, Almohad rule was effectively finished, and the Banū Marīn, a tribe of Berber nomads, came over the sedentary frontier in 1069 to capture the old capital at Marrakesh and establish themselves as a new dynasty over the Moroccan part of the empire.

The Almohad movement was thus ephemeral; even the complete Almoravid–Almohad sequence was shorter than the two centuries of Fatimid rule in Egypt. Yet the movement had wider significance. It brought about a general revival of commerce, just as the Fatimids had done in the east. At its height it had the best fleet in the western Mediterranean, and it opened the sea to Christian as well as to Muslim traffic. Urban life continued the development begun under the Almoravids, with a new burst of creativity represented by figures such as Ibn Tufayl (d. 1185) in Spain, among the most important of medieval Islamic philosophers and theologians. Ibn Rushd (d. 1198), whom the Christians called Averroes, was even more important for his commentaries on Greek philosophy; his works in translation were to bring new knowledge of Greek philosophy into Europe. The last decades of the twelfth century also witnessed a flowering — some say the finest flowering — of western Muslim architecture in Morocco and Spain alike.

The second half of the Muslim Middle Ages, from the end of the Almohads to about 1500, brought political fragmentation but was not necessarily a general decline. Local political authorities worked with the informal but significant understanding that all belonged to the larger community of Islam. Economic growth in both Egypt and the Maghrib continued until the mid-fourteenth century, and longer in some areas. Art and letters may have lost the outstanding creativity of the recent past, but the courtly arts of polished upper-class life continued in local centers like Granada, the only remaining Muslim state in Spain, and with the Merinids, who ruled much of Morocco from Fez in the fourteenth century.

This was also a classic period for the interplay of nomadic and sedentary pressures, observed and recorded by Ibn Khaldun (d. 1406) of Tunis, an outstanding philosopher and historian who used the past few centuries in the Maghrib to illustrate his theme, which was a form of environmentalism: nomads were tough because nomadic life was hard; sedentary life made for the dissipation and weakness of the ruling class. Nomadic life encouraged collective effort for a common goal; sedentary life allowed the selfish pursuit of personal or family interests. Sedentary kingdoms were therefore liable to become increasingly weak, and so to encourage conquest from the steppes. But a new nomadic dynasty ruling over sedentary society would weaken in its turn. The whole cycle passed through five stages and occupied about 120 years.

Historians today honor Ibn Khaldun for his insight but do not accept his entire set of beliefs. They recognize the nomadic-sedentary conflict as one major theme among several, but they also see a complex web of cooperation as well as rivalry between the two ecological systems. Many would also stress the change from the early to the late Middle Ages, from a phase in which political leaders were trying to create a new empire in conscious imitation of the first caliphs, to a new phase of limited ambitions and limited power in which the rulers represented a particular ethnic group, tribe, fraction, or social class (in the case of Mamluk Egypt). Islamic states, in short, no longer claimed religious as well as secular leadership. The leaders of the sufi turuq had begun to replace them, and secular leaders acquiesced by acting mainly on behalf of their own class and extended family. By the late fifteenth and early sixteenth centuries, these changes contributed to a real weakening of the Maghribine powers and a basic shift of power from Muslims to the Christians north of the Mediterranean.

TRADE AND POLITICS
SOUTH OF THE SAHARA: GHANA

For the political history of sub-Saharan Africa, written sources are hard to come by, so that West Africa emerges slowly through time according to the kinds of source available. Before the tenth century, we have only archaeology, linguistics, and a range of other indirect evidence. From the tenth century to the fourteenth, we have the added element of reporting from North Africa in Arabic, combined with the earliest oral traditions. Then, from the fourteenth century, European written records from the coast are added, followed in about the seventeenth by more and more detailed oral traditions and the survival of written records compiled by Africans on the spot.

The period from about 1000 to 1500 is one of intermittent and partial reporting. Some of the best travelers' accounts of this period, like Ibn Battuta's marvelously detailed report of his trip across the Sahara and south to Mali in 1352–53, tell much more than we know about most later periods up to the eighteenth century. But aliens encountered severe health problems in West Africa, and merchants tended to turn back at the desert's edge. Information reaching North Africa was therefore often at second or third hand, with nothing but silence about some regions for a century or more at a time.

Even if it were desirable to give a consecutive political narrative, it would not be possible. It is possible, however, to see something of the style of international relations — and, behind the recurrent pattern of events, some of the factors that influenced the rise and fall of states. One of the problems facing any sub-Saharan state in this period was implicit in the economic geography of its situation. The point of contact with the trans-Saharan trade was the desert's edge. A sedentary state near the desert would seek to control the desert ports and to control as long a section of the desert-savanna frontier as possible. With an exchange like that of gold for salt, bargaining was open, without a multiplicity of buyers and sellers to establish a market price. Salt could be monopolized because the Saharan desposits were few and easily controlled. Gold could also be monopolized in the same way, at least in theory. But, so far as our meager evidence goes, no sub-Saharan state ever came to control the three principal goldfields in West Africa — Bambuhu between the Senegal and the Falémé, Buré to the southeast near the upper Niger, and the Akan goldfield in the forest and savanna of present-day Ghana. It was rare, indeed, for one of the larger states to control any of these producing areas for long; the same purpose could be accomplished by controlling the desert-savanna frontier, blocking off the Saharan traders from access to the gold. The result would then be a monopoly on each side. If the Sudanese could exercise some control out into the desert itself, they might even break the monopoly on that side and create a decisive shift of the terms of trade in their favor. These considerations are reflected in a recurrent pattern of expansion by strong states on the desert fringe — first east and west from the core area, then out into and across the desert if possible,

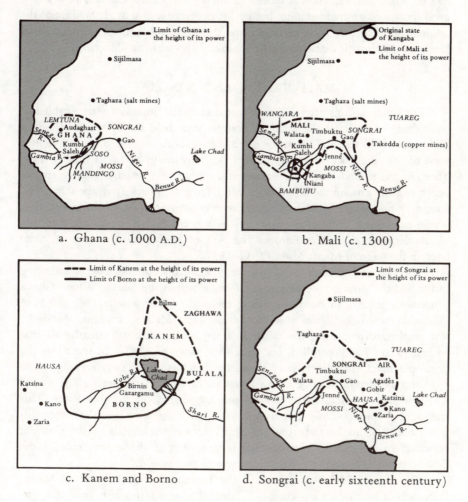

a. Ghana (c. 1000 A.D.)

b. Mali (c. 1300)

c. Kanem and Borno

d. Songrai (c. early sixteenth century)

Ancient Kingdoms of the Western Sudan

with rarely a serious effort to build an empire in their hinterland away from the desert.

If control of the sahel was a way to control trade, the sahel was also dangerous; it was open to nomadic attack and subject to irregular rainfall. Both of these dangers played a role in the fall of Ghana. At the Ghanaian peak of power in the eleventh century, Bambuhu was the only one of the three goldfields already drawn into the Saharan gold trade. Therefore, Ghana's stretch of sahel from the northward bend of the Niger to the upper Senegal may well have been enough to blanket access to the gold; it would have been enough had there been an adequate way to prevent leakage through Takrūr. But then, in the middle of the eleventh century, both Audaghast and Sijilmasa fell to the Almoravids, and the Ghanaian capital was sacked in 1076. That ended Ghana's power as a great incorporative trade empire, but not its existence as a state. It held on to the original Soninke core area until perhaps the thirteenth century, and the final blow was the climatic disaster and the Soninke dispersal from "Wagadu."

MALI, KANEM, AND SONGRAI

For two centuries after Ghana's first decline, no successor state established equivalent control over the sahel. A Songrai state held the Niger bend, and a Fulbe state held the middle valley of the Senegal. A Soso state rose to control some of the sahel between the two rivers, but only briefly and on a smaller scale. Then, in the second half of the thirteenth century a new incorporative empire began to form around the kingdom of Mali, lying well back from the sahel. The legendary first leader of Malian expansion was Sunjaata (*Soundiata* in French), whose position in the oral literature of the western Sudan is equivalent to that of Charlemagne in western Europe. The peak of Malian success, however, came later, in the reign of Mansa Musa (1312–1337 A.D.).

The precise causes of Mali's success remain unclear, but one contributing factor was the growing development of trade within the Sudan. Where Ghana had drawn gold from Bambuhu alone, the trade routes now reached the Buré goldfields, which Mali was able to control. Most Malian expansion, however, was northward to control the sahel. In time, Mali controlled virtually all that ancient Ghana had controlled, but with some new twists. One of these was the development of the Niger River above the bend as a waterway carrying trade right through from the edge of the forest to the edge of the desert. The second was a westward extension to the Atlantic by way of the Gambia River. This westward empire-building left a belt of Malinke-speaking peoples, who still live along the line between the old heartland and the mouth of the Gambia, remnants of an ancient need for salt independent of the desert trade or the Fulbe-controlled route to the Atlantic by way of the Senegal.

The rise of Mali was crucial to the Islamization of the western Sudan. It brought a southward movement of Islam into new territory beyond the normal reach of North African traders, and full acceptance of Islam as the court religion spread the new belief very widely through the empire. Mali apparently accepted Islam just as the state was expanding. Sunjaata is remembered as a Muslim ruler, but nothing in the traditions from that period suggests that Islam was anything but a formality. By the middle of the fourteenth century, however, the Malian court and urban life were described by Ibn Battuta in terms that suggest an ordinary Muslim country of a type the famous traveler had visited many times before. It seems doubtful that Islam had as yet penetrated to the outer provinces or among the rural masses, but that process was beginning.

By the time of Sunjaata, the Kanuri far to the east had moved in from the desert, settled in Kanem, and from that base had begun a military expansion of their own. Their outstanding leader was Mai Dunama Dibbalemi (ruled approximately 1221–1259 A.D.), nearly an exact contemporary of Sunjaata. The two empires, however, were quite different. Whereas Mali began well back in the savanna and expanded to the desert fringe, Kanem began on the desert fringe and expanded still further out into the desert. The Kanuri nation had for some time been assimilating kindred people in the region. The inhabitants of Kawar oasis, nearly halfway across the Sahara, had become Kanuri during the course of the twelfth century. Before the end of the thirteenth, Kanem conquered the Fezzan, an outlier of North Africa, and ruled it directly for a half century, while an offshoot Kanuri dynasty ruled it for another century. A second direction of Kanuri expansion, under Dunama Dibbalemi, was to the northeast, where a trade route first ran eastward along the desert-savanna fringe and then across a corner of desert to reach the Nile and Egypt. Kanuri trade of the thirteenth century reached out this way as far as the Nile and probably to the Red Sea, connecting to the sphere of Mamluk Egypt.

Only partial explanations of Kanuri success emerge from the evidence we now have. One interpretation stresses the role of Islam in the Kanembu state, pointing out that the Mai (kings) had become Muslim, though their authority still depended on many of the pre-Muslim sanctions of Sefawa rule. Dunama Dibbalemi shifted to Muslim sanctions for his rule, destroying the pagan regalian symbols. This move could have been a bid for Muslim support, or simply a sign that he felt strong enough to dispense with pagan support. If so, it may have backfired; the Mai lost power in succeeding reigns, and an anti-Muslim reaction may have been one cause.

Dunama Dibbalemi also innovated with regard to political structure. About this time, the Kanuri developed a system of delegated military command, the successful commander being rewarded by a grant of authority over a section of the empire. Throughout world history this was a very common way of governing newly conquered territory, but it always carried the danger that the military officers would make their positions hereditary and thus transform themselves from a group picked by the king for their achievement and personal loyalty into a hereditary nobility who had turned their public office into private property.

In any event, Kanem did not succeed in governing a vast empire for long. Even some territory and people near the home base remained independent —

the Lake Chad islands, for example, and the peoples immediately to the south of Kanem, even some who were culturally similar to the Kanuri but lived under their own rulers, the Bulala, in contrast to the Sefawa rulers of Kanem. And the Bulala became a serious military problem after Dunama Dibbalemi's death.

Through the maze of political history, some themes emerged after the thirteenth century that were common to both Mali and Kanem — and almost certainly to other states whose political history is less well known. One problem was succession to office: how to find procedures flexible enough to exclude incompetents, but fixed enough to allow the new ruler to take office without fighting a civil war. The problem was not specific to Africa, though polygyny tended to complicate it by increasing the number of possible heirs. In Mali, the problem of succession was solved (to the extent that it *was* solved) by the royal officials. On a number of occasions following the death of a Mansa, they were able to choose between several branches of the royal Keita lineage, depriving incompetents of office but keeping power in the hands of the dynasty. These shifts at appropriate moments appear to be one reason Mali lasted into the nineteenth century as a state, though it was vastly reduced from its former imperial size.

Kanem was far less successful in escaping dynastic quarrels. Over time, many different branches of the Sefawa came into existence. Lacking royal officials who could balance one against another, each branch tried to make its own arrangements for a military following among the nobility. As a result, civil war became endemic over long periods, to the advantage of the Bulala. In the late fourteenth century, just as Mali was reaching its peak of power and well-being, the Bulala drove the Sefawa and their following out of Kanem, first to the southwest of Lake Chad. After a century or so in exile and division, the Sefawa finally reestablished their own capital at Gazargamo, this time in Borno to the northwest of Lake Chad. The local inhabitants assimilated Kanuri language and culture, and, by the first part of the sixteenth century, Borno was able to reestablish a degree of control over the old homeland in Kanem, but the center of control was now in Borno.

This second rise of a Kanuri empire was parallel in time to a new empire in the west, just as the first Kanuri empire rose at the same time as Mali. This new empire had the same Songrai base as the earlier Gao, a contemporary of ancient Ghana. Since then, the Niger bend had fallen under the control of Mali, which not only developed the river trade to its own metropolitan province far up the Niger; an overland route also left the main river at Jenné and passed southward to the Akan goldfields. With these two routes functioning, people at the Niger bend were in a position to tap the trade of both Buré and the Akan goldfield. In addition, offshoots of the Hilalian Arabs were moving into the far western Sahara during the fifteenth century, threatening the position of the Berber nomads and making trade generally unsafe. As a result, Timbuktu became the principal desert port of the western Sudan, even before the decline of Mali. As Malian power shrank in the fifteenth century, Timbuktu's economic advantage remained. Three contestants emerged, seeking to control the strategic Niger bend: the Mossi states within the bend south of Timbuktu; the riverain Songrai; and the Tuareg nomads to the north. Songrai won militarily, and the reign of Sonni 'Alī (1464–1492) marked the passage of Songrai from a small riverain state to a great empire. In the first decade of the sixteenth century, Songrai extended its lateral control westward to the Senegal, thus blanketing Mali's access to the Saharan trade and establishing once more the dominance of the desert-savanna fringe, to last nearly to the end of the sixteenth century.

TRADE AND POLITICS:
THE NILOTIC SUDAN AND ETHIOPIA

In the Nilotic Sudan and the Red Sea region, a different geographical environment produced a different pattern of commercial strategy, but trade and politics were nevertheless linked as clearly as they were in the western Sudan. One strategic link was the desert Nile between the first cataract above Aswan and the junction of the Blue and White Niles near present-day Khartoum. Whoever held this stretch of the Nile could control trade and collect tolls, not only on trade bound for the Nilotic Sudan but also on that which branched off by caravan from the third cataract southwestward toward Darfur. But the Nile was not the only route to the Nilotic Sudan. Caravans could reach the upper Nile from Red Sea ports like Suakin or across a corner of the Ethiopian highlands from mainland points opposite the Dahlak Archipelago.

Because of these routes, the commercial strategy of the Nilotic Sudan was tied to the Red Sea as well as the Nile. The Red Sea trade, in turn, was greatly affected by political factors in Egypt and Iraq. Abbasid control had meant that most trade from the Muslim world to India and beyond passed through the Persian Gulf, and the Red Sea became a backwater, used for local trade only. The rise of Fatimid Egypt brought an Egyptian interest in Red Sea shipping and a rise in the commercial prosperity of all the states that depended on Red Sea trade.

These considerations applied to the Ethiopian highlands as well. During the Abbasid downswing in Red Sea trade from about 750 to 970, the Christian society in the western highlands turned away from the sea. Some people who spoke Semitic languages ancestral to Tigriña and Amharic migrated south along the backbone of the mountain ranges. Christian missionaries also began to work their way south into the regions that were then Cushitic-speaking and neither Christian nor Muslim in religion, including the plateau of Showa where Addis Ababa now stands. A little before 1100 A.D., the political center also moved south from Axum to Lalibela as a new, Zagwé dynasty came to control the northwest highlands.

This was not so much a break with the Axumite past as a reassertion of Christianity further into the interior. The coast was lost to Islam in any event;

Ethiopians no longer had their own ships on the Indian Ocean or the Red Sea. But Christian Ethiopians were able to reach the Middle East. They strengthened their contacts with Coptic Christianity in Egypt. Once the Frankish Christian invaders had been cleared from Palestine in the late twelfth century, Ethiopians were permitted to make the pilgrimage to Jerusalem. The inspiration of these visits can still be seen in the monumental churches carved from solid rock at Lalibela.

About 1270, a new dynasty unseated the Zagwé and moved the political center still further south into Amhara. The more able monarchs of the new series, like Amada Syon (ruled 1314–1354), pursued a self-conscious strategy of trade, first trying to dominate the coast (which failed), then trying to control the main north-south trade routes down the backbone of the western highlands from shore points opposite the Dahlak Archipelago to the regions south and west of Showa. This route, incidentally, ran through the core of the Christian highlands, but the merchants were mainly Muslims from the coast. Their missionary work helped to form a small Muslim minority at a very early date, and the strategy of trade came to be linked to the strategy of religious conversion.

The joining of religious and commercial rivalry was all the more serious because a competing route to Showa began at Zeila on the Gulf of Aden and ran along the axis of the present-day Jibuti to Addis Ababa railroad. This was Muslim territory most of the way, and its western anchor was the small sultanate of Ifat in Showa itself. In the late thirteenth century, when Amada Syon and his successors were trying to consolidate their hold over the north-south route and Christian Ethiopia, the sultans of Ifat were trying to do the same over the east-west route and the Muslim territories generally. The Christians won and established a form of hegemony over the united Muslim confederacy that Ifat had assembled. They went further in the fourteenth century with a series of conquests to the west and south against states that had not yet fallen under either Muslim or Christian influence.

These victories carried the Christian Ethiopian state to a peak of power and centralized control that it would not attain again until the nineteenth century. The Christian kings capitalized on the prestige of their victories. They used the church as a missionary institution to assimilate the conquered provinces, and they drew even more power from the fact that their conquests were fresh. When new territory was annexed, it was sometimes left under a representative of the old ruling family, but most often it was placed under the control of men of known personal loyalty to the king. At the most local level, the king granted these men a form of tenure with the right to collect tribute and personal services due the monarch. In return, they acted as the local government, kept the peace, and appeared with followers for military service when required. At first, these local rulers and the provincial governors above them were appointed for short terms only, but in time many were able to stretch out the appointment and finally to pass it on to their children — as happened in Kanem as well. Thus, the court held tight control during the first generation after the acquisition of a new province; later on, the province gradually drifted into greater and greater autonomy as the royal officials assumed the prerogatives of a local nobility. This tendency toward local autonomy was greatly aided by the terrain, where very deep valleys separated adjoining plateaus into natural fortresses, but it was counteracted by keeping the king and court in periodic migration from province to province so that each in turn would come under direct royal inspection in the presence of the standing army.

Given time, the Christian kingdom might have developed a greater Ethiopian identity on which a genuine merger of the newly conquered provinces could have been based, but it was not given time. The centrifugal tendencies of the local nobility became increasingly strong through the fifteenth century. The Christian religious nationalism sponsored by the court began to meet the opposition of a Muslim religious nationalism from the Muslim minority and the neighboring Muslim states. In the last quarter of the fourteenth century, a member of the ruling house of Ifat (then annexed to the Christian kingdom) went to the eastern highlands near Harar and founded a new kingdom known as Adal, a troublesome neighbor from then onward. Christian-Muslim animosities did not reach crisis proportions until the 1530s, but the Christian kingdom was in decline for at least a half century before that.

A word of warning may be necessary in considering the history of northern Africa through this period: unintended distortion is inevitable from the nature of the evidence. Political change in Egypt and the Maghrib can be traced in detail, and the trends of intellectual and social change are far clearer there than is possible for any region south of the Sahara. Once south of the desert, the great empires of the sahel receive most attention because the men from North Africa who left the records rarely went further. Further south, our knowledge is limited to shadowy outlines. The Hausa-speaking region of northern Nigeria, for example, had already begun to develop extensive towns that served as marketing and craft centers. These towns came into existence as early as 1000 to 1300 A.D., apparently without much direct influence from the patterns of urbanization in North Africa. But Hausa emerged into the light of recorded history only in the fifteenth century, when Muslim influence first began to be important. In this case, Islam did not come directly from North Africa but indirectly by way of Songrai to the northwest or Borno to the northeast. By the fifteenth century, Hausa was divided into a series of walled towns, each ruling over the surrounding countryside; Katsina, Kano, Zazzau (or Zaria), and Gobir were already important.

Other centers of state-building existed still further south. On the Benue, a state had already emerged among the Jukun people, alongside the resolutely stateless Tiv. Still further south, both the Yoruba states and Benin had been founded before the fourteenth century. Their bronze sculpture demonstrates not only great art but also a technical proficiency in metallurgy which suggests that forest people were no less advanced than those of the savanna. Far away in the Ethiopian highlands, we know the names of several states that were neither Christian nor Muslim and that also flourished in this period, but that is all we do know about them. It is important to keep in mind that the record of written history is not what historians think is important, selected from everything that took place. It is merely what they think is important, selected from what they are able to find out about.

SUGGESTIONS FOR FURTHER READING

Ajayi, J. F. A., and Crowder, Michael. *History of West Africa.* Vol. 1. 2nd ed. London: Longman, 1976.

Bovill, E. W. *The Golden Trade of the Moors.* London: Oxford University Press, 1958.

Hasan, Yusaf Fadl. *The Arabs and the Sudan from the Seventh to the Early Sixteenth Century.* Edinburgh: Edinburgh University Press, 1967.

Le Tourneau, Roger. *Fez in the Age of the Merinides.* Oklahoma City: University of Oklahoma Press, 1961.

Levtzion, Nehemia. *Ancient Ghana and Mali.* London: Methuen, 1973.

Mauny, Raymond. *Tableau géographique de l'ouest Africain au moyen âge.* Dakar: IFAN, 1961.

Spaulding, Jay. "The Funj: A Reconstruction." *Journal of African History* 13 (1972): 39–53.

Tamrat, Taddesse. *Church and State in Ethiopia 1270–1527.* London: Oxford University Press, 1972.

(See also the bibliography for Chapter 2.)

Chapter 4

Economy, Society, and Language in Early East Africa

MANY CHARACTERISTIC ELEMENTS of East African life, including the distribution of languages, the ways people earn their livelihoods, and the forms of local social organization, took shape in a time without written documentation. Arabic documents, so important for the early history of the West African savanna and for towns on the East African coast, are almost entirely absent for the eastern interior. Historians have therefore had to turn to archaeology, linguistics, and the study of oral traditions to piece together an account of the formative centuries in East Africa.

LINGUISTICS, ARCHAEOLOGY, AND HISTORY

The startling diversity of languages in East Africa, which may at first appear to be an obstacle to historical understanding, provides useful evidence about early developments. With language, as with oral traditions, complexity and diversity are the raw materials for the historian's reasoning from the known pattern (the distribution of languages and of individual words) to find out about past social change and the interaction of ethnic groups.

East Africa has well over a hundred languages, divided among four major language families. We have seen that languages belong to a single family when they are descended from an ancestral language, or protolanguage, and therefore strongly resemble one another. When speakers of the protolanguage live apart from one another, speech in each locality takes on unique characteristics, and separate local dialects emerge. Later, the dialects become so different that they are no longer mutually intelligible; they have become separate languages. These new languages, in their turn, continue the process of local differentiation. Each early language thus develops into a cluster of related languages or a branch of a language family.

Each of the language families is spread over a large part of the African continent, and, in some cases, beyond the borders of the continent itself. For this reason, when historians refer to linguistic groupings of the peoples of East Africa, they usually refer to subgroups of the larger language families. Dozens of Bantu languages are spoken across East Africa, from southern Uganda and southern Kenya southward. Other chapters show the importance of Bantu-speaking peoples in Equatorial and southern Africa. Yet the Bantu languages are merely one subgroup within a larger grouping (Benue-Congo), which is itself only a part of a language family (Niger-Congo). A second major group of East African peoples speak Nilotic languages, a subgroup of Eastern Sudanic, which ultimately derives from the Nilo-Saharan language family. A very large majority of present-day East Africans are either Nilotes or Bantu-speakers.

The identification of language families, or of subgroups within language families, has a limited, but extremely useful, range of consequences for historical knowledge. First, the limitation. Similarities of language may accompany other similarities between people, but they carry no necessary implications about other aspects of the cultures or about somatic characteristics. This is common sense, but easy to lose sight of. Bantu-speaking peoples in East Africa, for example, are more strongly agricultural than the Nilotes are. The most famous pastoral peoples, like the Maasai, speak Nilotic languages, but the Arusha, who live near Mount Kilimanjaro in northern Tanzania, speak the Maasai language while relying heavily on agriculture like their Bantu-speaking neighbors. The Baraguyu of central Tanzania, who also speak the Maasai language, build rectangular flat-roofed houses, again like those of their Bantu-speaking neighbors, and completely unlike the igloo-shaped Maasai dwellings.

Cooking styles, house designs, even ideas about supernatural spirits can be borrowed from neighbors. Any one culture is therefore an amalgam of bits and pieces from a great many historical sources, and it is often impossible to point to a primary source for a particular culture. A language, on the other hand, does have a single major source. Individual words may be borrowed, but the basic structure of the language — its repertoire of sounds, the regularities in word forms, the syntax in which words are ordered — can have only one ancestral language. All this is clear in American life. Americans have borrowed foods and cooking styles from a great many sources: they eat pizza and Chinese food; they can mix together cooking styles with different origins. But the American language has a single central source; it comes from England. Cooking styles, and most other elements of everyday culture, can be transmitted casually, but languages can only be transmitted through intimate, long-term contact between speakers.

Because speakers of a Nilotic language must have learned the language through intimate contact with other speakers (normally their parents), who in turn learned from still others, and so on back to the protolanguage of a particular branch of Nilotic, and then to proto-Nilotic itself, it is probable that some core elements of proto-Nilotic culture have been transmitted through the generations. But it is equally probable that cultural elements have been reinterpreted, added to, some lost. There can be no easy assumptions about an ancestral culture's characteristics, but it is often possible to sniff them out.

Linguistic analysis provides several kinds of historical information. As we have seen for Proto-Bantu (Chapter 1), a comparison of the variant languages descended from a common source can be used to reconstruct some words in the protolanguage. Knowledge of protovocabulary is of little historical use when expected words like mother and father are reconstructed, but it is of much greater use when household objects or kinds of religious leaders are named. A second use of historical linguistics is to point toward a place of origin for the protolanguage through the spatial distribution of the family's branches. And again, lexico-statistics provides at least a rough indication of the length of time since two languages diverged. Finally, historical linguistics can tell something about early cultural interactions, through the study of the way words are distributed among different languages and the sound shifts that occur when words are borrowed between language families.

Archaeological findings are more reliable than linguistics at locating cultures in time and space, and they give more precise information about material culture. Archaeology and historical linguistics provide partial checks and correctives to one another. When archaeologists find remains of a group whose presence had been already indicated by words borrowed from its language, the high probability of the group's presence is established. When archaeological and linguistic evidence diverge, the mystery deepens.

CUSHITES, NILOTES, AND BANTU-SPEAKERS

Nilotes and Bantu-speakers, the vast majority of East Africa's current residents, completed their occupation of the region no more than two thousand years ago. Their expansion was part of a general trend toward increasing population densities, tied to the evolution of the region's economy as it moved from substantial dependence on hunting and gathering to agriculture and stock keeping. Although hunting and gathering are frequently very efficient at providing subsistence in return for little labor, they support relatively low densities of population. Pastoralism supports higher densities, while agriculture potentially supports the highest of all. As a general rule, land that can support pastoralism is not left to the hunters and gatherers, while land that can support agriculture is not left to the pastoralists. In each case, the ultimate use of the land is the one that allows for the higher density of population, though mixed forms of subsistence do continue at the higher density. Pastoralists and hunter-gatherers can share a single territory, just as farming and stock keeping are very often integrated in a single economy.

The shift from hunting and gathering took place in slow steps, beginning about 6000 B.C. As elsewhere in Africa, the first major changes came in lakeside or riverside settings, where fishing supported more sedentary populations than hunting and gathering could. The spread of cattle keeping was the next impor-

tant development, beginning about 1000 B.C., and cattle bones have been found
at sites in Kenya's Rift Valley and the surrounding highlands, where stone bowls
or stone platters have also been found.

These stone-bowl-using cattle keepers were probably Cushites, speaking
languages forming one branch of the Afro-Asiatic language family. The hypothesis identifying the early stone-bowl cattle keepers with the Cushites is

Major Language Groups of East Africa

based on the survival of isolated Southern Cushites in Tanzania's Rift Valley, as remnants of what must once have been a more widespread community. Cushitic loanwords are also present in a number of Nilotic and Bantu languages. Vocabulary reconstruction indicates that Southern Cushites were very early cattle keepers and probably also cultivators of grain. The evidence for their presence looks very convincing.

The emerging recognition of Cushitic importance is mildly embarrassing to African historians who have spent years trying to slay the dragon of the Hamitic myth. "Hamitic myth" is the term recent writers have used for a racist set of historical ideas, which attributed the great achievements of Africa to light-skinned outsiders who came down from the north. In the words of C. G. Seligman, a major proponent of the idea, "the incoming Hamites were pastoral Caucasians — arriving wave after wave — better armed as well as quicker-witted than the dark agricultural Negroes." [1] This is maddening; it breaks a basic rule of method by mixing race (Caucasian), language ("Hamitic"), and culture (weapons, economy), and further makes the assumption that lighter skinned is quicker witted. Joseph Greenberg has pointed out the one-hundred-percent negative correlation between "Hamitic" languages and pastoralism in West Africa.[2] He succeeded in having the word "Hamitic" dropped from respectable use by discrediting the linguistic analysis on which the grouping was based.

Although the Hamitic myth has been completely abandoned, the importance that recent authorities give to the Cushites is so strongly reminiscent of it that the two hypotheses must be compared directly. The Cushites did indeed enter East Africa from the north (from Ethiopia), and they *do* speak languages of the same large family as Hebrew and Arabic (Afro-Asiatic). The evidence, however, roots the Cushites firmly in African soil. Of the seven branches of the Afro-Asiatic language family, all except Semitic are found only in Africa, from the Berber of the far northwest across to Ancient Egyptian in the northeast. Recent studies show that Semitic languages have been spoken in Ethiopia for at least four thousand years. Some linguists have even suggested that the Semitic languages originated in Ethiopia and spread from there to Southwest Asia, although this is frankly speculative. In any case, the unity of the Afro-Asiatic language family does not support any theory of Asian influence on Africa in historic times.

Within East Africa, the "Hamites" had been described as bringing the civilized arts to a preexisting substratum of cultivators. In reality, the Cushites were among the prior populations who were absorbed and pushed aside, although they contributed institutions, words, ideas, and knowledge of the local

[1] C. G. Seligman, *Races of Africa,* rev. ed. (London: Thornton Butterworth, 1939), p. 156.

[2] Joseph H. Greenberg, *The Languages of Africa,* Indiana University Research Center in Anthropology, Folklore, and Linguistics, Publication No. 25 (Bloomington, Ind., 1963), p. 51.

environment that survived in the languages and cultures of those who supplanted them.

About two thousand years ago, the domain of the Cushites, and of the other early populations of East Africa, began to contract as Nilotes intermingled with and ultimately supplanted the more northerly of these early peoples, while Bantu occupied the south. The Nilotes spread from their homeland, between Lake Rudolf in northern Kenya and the Nile River to the west and northwest. This is an arid belt which supports pastoralism and only the most marginal agriculture. Quite early, the ancestors of three separate language subgroups had divided from one another. The Southern Nilotes[3] occupied the highlands to the west of the Rift Valley of Kenya. The Kalenjin, the most numerous of the Southern Nilotes, say they migrated to escape drought, although it is difficult to know how to interpret such an ancient tradition. In any event, the western highlands of Kenya, where most of the Southern Nilotes settled, enjoyed much higher rainfall than the Nilotic homeland in the north, and grain agriculture became more important in their economy, alongside cattle keeping. Other Southern Nilotes who live in arid areas further south, in Tanzania, rely much more heavily on herding for their subsistence.

The record of the momentous events in western Kenya is much clearer than the explanation of those events. The Southern Nilotes succeeded in supplanting the Cushites and other early inhabitants of the area. But why did they succeed? What was their advantage? Why did the Cushites begin their long decline from being the major inhabitants of much of Tanzania and southern Kenya to their current place as a few isolated remnants? Two kinds of explanations are possible. The first is economic: perhaps the Southern Nilotes found some better way to use the resources of the region and grew at the expense of their neighbors. The second explanation looks to social organization: this may have enabled the Nilotes to conquer or absorb earlier inhabitants. On present evidence, this second explanation is more probable, but both must be weighed.

The economy of the new residents of the western highlands was based on livestock and grain agriculture. The Kipsigis, one of the Southern Nilotic peoples, have a tradition describing a time of famine, when their cattle were fast dying out. Several women found eleusine (a domesticated grass) growing in elephant dung. Their hunger drove them to taste some of the grain. They liked it and used the rest as seed. From the time of that discovery, according to the tradition, the Kipsigis became powerful and superior to other peoples. The early cultivation of eleusine and of sorghum is confirmed by linguistic recon-

[3] The distinction among Southern, Eastern, and Western Nilotes follows J. H. Greenberg's usage in The Languages of Africa, which has also been followed in Christopher Ehret's Southern Nilotic History (Evanston, Ill.: Northwestern University Press, 1971). In Zamani: A Survey of East African History, edited by B. A. Ogot (Nairobi: East African Publishing House, 1974), the Southern Nilotes (Kalenjin, Dadog) are called Highland Nilotes; the Eastern Nilotes (Maasai, Teso, Karamojong) are called Plains Nilotes; the Western Nilotes (Lwo) are called River-Lake Nilotes.

structions. But since the Southern Cushitic economy was also based on livestock and grain agriculture, it is difficult to see where the Nilotic advantage lay.

The second explanation of Nilotic expansion rests on the social institution of the age-set. Christopher Ehret, whose research on Southern Nilotic language history is the basis of our knowledge of the period, has shown that age-set organization was a comparatively early development.[4] The Southern Nilotes and their early neighbors lived in scattered villages without chiefs. Age-set organization made it possible for the Kalenjin (the Kenya branch of the Southern Nilotes) to mobilize armed men on a fairly large scale, extending far beyond the single village. This meant that the Kalenjin could use their extended power to take cattle and, more rarely, land from their neighbors.

A group of adolescent boys who were initiated together would form an age-set, which had its own name, some common rights and obligations, and a sense of unity. A single set was supposed to move through the different grades together. Members of the *Kimnyekeu* age-set, for example, were initiated together, immediately entering the grade of young initiates. When the appropriate time came, the whole of the set moved on to the next grade together, becoming warriors but keeping their set name, while the *Kaplelach,* the next older group, went from the grade of warriors to that of elders. When successive sets had used up each of the seven or eight age-set names (after somewhat more than a hundred years), the cycle would begin again with the first name.

Because similar sets existed among a number of neighboring Kalenjin Southern Nilotes, individuals or small groups who moved from one place to another could easily become part of local village life simply by entering the appropriate age-sets. This meant, furthermore, that aliens could be integrated more easily into Kalenjin society than they could be into a society organized on narrow lineage principles. Because members of an age-set had to treat one another as equals, the sets made attractive points of entry for strangers. Thus, the age-sets caused insecurity, from which they themselves were the means of escape. The ancient inhabitants of the region, who were threatened by the military strength of the age-sets, could, by joining, end the threat.

The historical reconstruction of this process of absorption is based on the existence of age-sets by the time of the early Southern Nilotic spread, perhaps in the first millennium A.D., and on examples from more recent periods. Beginning in the seventeenth or eighteenth century, the Terik, a subgroup of the Kalenjin, offered asylum to neighboring Bantu-speakers on condition that they join the Terik age-sets. In the end, the Bantu were numerically superior to the Terik, but they called themselves Tiriki after their hosts.

Bantu-speakers, spreading from the west, occupied the areas south of the Nilotes in most of Tanzania and parts of Kenya and Uganda. In the Bantu-speaking region, pottery styles associated with the Early Iron Age are very

---

[4] *Southern Nilotic History* (Evanston, Ill.: 1971), p. 45.

similar to one another — dimple-base in the great lakes region, Kwale ware on the East African coast, and other styles in Zimbabwe and Zambia. Their similarity indicates that they derived from a single ancestral style. Many archaeologists assume that this broad distribution of related styles is evidence for the spread of Bantu-speaking peoples who gradually differentiated into local groups, which made variant local pottery styles.

It is not possible, however, to identify these particular potters as the early carriers of Bantu languages, although the coincidence between finds of early pottery and recent language patterns is very impressive. The northernmost dimple-base ware is found between Lakes Kyoga and Albert in Uganda at the northern limit of Bantu speech. Kwale ware on the coast also reaches far to the north, near the limits of Bantu languages, whereas related wares have not been found at all in the Rift Valley and highlands occupied by people who speak Nilotic and Cushitic languages.

The intellectual challenge and excitement of research into the very early history of East Africa comes from the fact that enough evidence already exists to justify the search for a coherent pattern, while new information pours in to test hypotheses. Unlike the field of early Mediterranean history, where historians use similar methods, much of our present-day evidence about early Africa has been found only in the past decade. Just as much new data will probably be found in the next decade, which is a challenge to careful and creative historical thought. Each student of the field can continuously think through the old generalizations, testing each one.

For the Early Iron Age, the testing of past hypotheses and the challenge to create new ones have come from new radiocarbon dates. The spread of the Bantu-speakers in East Africa was usually thought to have taken place beginning about two thousand years ago. This conclusion is based on the broad distribution of Early Iron Age wares during the first millennium A.D. During the past several years, however, many earlier carbon dates have been reported. Dimple-base ware from Buhaya, in northwestern Tanzania, has been given the following dates: 450 B.C., 550 B.C., 1080 B.C., 1250 B.C., 1470 B.C. Kwale ware finds in eastern Tanzania have been dated to 1100 B.C. and 1260 B.C. These dates mean that either the Bantu spread much earlier than historians have thought, or the spread of the pottery styles is not directly related to Bantu expansion. At this point, the challenge is there, but no hypothesis yet explains those data in a satisfactory way.

MIGRATIONS, CULTURAL INTERACTION, AND THE ENVIRONMENT

The cultures of Bantu-speaking peoples in East Africa were closely related to one another in the Early Iron Age, then diverged. Each small area developed its particular local culture. This happened in the early centuries of the second millennium A.D. The change can be seen archaeologically in the emergence of numerous local pottery styles in place of the broadly similar Early Iron Age styles.

For this new period, oral traditions become considerably more relevant, referring as they do to the migrations of peoples and the creation of local cultures. They change the whole style of historical description. It becomes possible to deal with ideas held in each local group about the relationship between past and present, the way in which societies came to be what they are.

Two kinds of migration tradition are important. First, many small lineage and clan groups recount where their ancestors came from, why they moved, and under what circumstances. Second, entire ethnic groups sometimes have traditions of origin, of the movement of a whole people, of the foundation of a way of life. Each kind of tradition has its own historical uses. The traditions of a small lineage tell only about that group, and sometimes only about recent local events or details of land ownership. But tens of traditions, or hundreds, can be fitted together to form general patterns of recent history — as they do when we learn that many groups moved after a particular nineteenth-century famine or war, or when we learn of the more distant formation of local cultures.

The traditions of the highland peoples who live on either side of the eastern Kenya-Tanzania border, for example, tell of the movements of many small groups from one highland region to another, passing across lowlands, even for some distance. Each lineage or clan tells of its own migration, unconscious of that larger pattern which informs us of local economic specialization after the end of the Early Iron Age.

The scattered masses of mountains are wetter than the lowlands, because the moisture-laden air blown in by the Indian Ocean monsoons passes over the lowlands, rises in the mountains, cools, then deposits rainfall. The technological knowledge and agricultural skills of highland peoples came to be adapted specifically to the highlands. Parents taught their children the properties of plants, how to use wild vegetation as indicators of when and where to plant, and how to identify and use different soil types. Learned medicine men of the highland zone today know the names and characteristics of thousands of highland plants. They know the taste of the leaves, roots, and bark of most plants, and which berries and leaves are eaten by birds or animals, which are not. Local plants were often the central symbols of complex rituals, so that a religious event strengthened an individual's sense of belonging in that particular part of the environment. When people were forced to move, therefore, they sought out other places where they could apply their knowledge, avoiding the lowlands.

Although in some rare cases highland peoples moved to the lowlands, this sort of move was more difficult, involving the development of new skills. The Kamba from the southeast of Mount Kenya, for example, expanded from their highland home to the neighboring dry lowlands. As they did so they were forced to become less reliant on agriculture and more so on cattle herding and hunting.

Special adaptation to a particular environment could take physical as well as cultural forms. Epidemiologists now recognize that over the long run of history humans and the diseases that prey on them work out a kind of mutual adaptation. Even in comparatively short periods some special adaptations have been important in African history. Through most of tropical Africa, for example, people tend to have an inherited blood characteristic, called sickle-cell trait from the shape of certain cells under the microscope. Many who have the sickle-cell trait die of anemia before they reach the age of reproduction. Over a long time, the trait therefore tends to disappear from the population. But the sickle-cell trait has another characteristic; it provides protection from falciparum malaria, the characteristic African form especially dangerous to infants and to people who first encounter the disease as adults. Because of this protection, infants with the sickle-cell trait in highly malarial regions tend to escape death in the first five years, while those without it tend to die.

In East Africa, to a greater extent than in any other part of the continent, the local populations have developed optimum incidence of the sickle-cell trait, so that in all places tested the frequency of the trait varies directly with the danger of malaria. In the nonmalarial highlands of Mount Kenya or Kilimanjaro, populations have almost no sickle-cell trait, whereas those who live along the infested southern shores of Lake Victoria have extremely high levels, and intermediate intensities of malaria are matched by intermediate frequencies of the trait. This distribution means that migration from the nonmalarial highlands to the wet lowlands would inevitably increase the death rate. Because it takes about seven hundred years for sickle-cell frequencies to reach optimum levels, it also means that the people of East Africa must have been relatively stable in their choice of environments.

The traditions preserved by large groups, whose members share a sense of identity and a language, contain a very different set of characteristics from those preserved by clans and lineages, although the two kinds of traditions usually exist side by side, clans and lineages being subgroups of the larger unit. Where the lineage or small-group traditions are found in great numbers and great variety telling mainly of local events, the large-group traditions are often found in only one version, which deals with the most central events of the group's history. These latter traditions often explain the sense of a group's cultural unity; they show which institutions are thought to be central, which local groups are closely related to one another and which are strangers or enemies. They are usually rich in literary value and symbolic content. But the power of a myth in shaping perceptions sweeps people along in agreement, so that alternative visions of history become difficult to find. Where small-group traditions are poor in content and rich in numbers, large-group traditions are rich in content but lack variants for critical analysis. Oral historians reconstruct the past by comparing divergent accounts; the more powerful the myth, the more restricted the divergence.

The classic tradition of origin told by the Mijikenda can serve as an example. The Mijikenda are a group of nine related peoples who live in the strip of land paralleling the coast of Kenya and running over into Tanzania. All Mijikenda tell that they once lived in Singwaya, far to the north in the hinterland of the Somali coast. They lived peacefully in Singwaya, all nine groups together with some neighboring peoples of Kenya and Tanzania, until they were driven southward by the Galla, people of the dry areas of southern Ethiopia and Somalia (see page 129).

The story affirms the unity of the Mijikenda, and tells about the origins of the social institutions which are the basis of that unity. When they are asked why the nine peoples are so much alike, Mijikenda often respond, "We came from Singwaya." At the heart of Mijikenda organization was the village built in a special prescribed form for group rituals. The most powerful magic of each village, at its center, was a pot "from Singwaya" full of medicines protecting the group against disaster. The Mijikenda also trace their age-set organization to the first initiations at the time of their conflict with the Galla in Singwaya. The Singwaya story, in short, asserts that some elements of Mijikenda culture are so central they are neither the result of piecemeal development over a long period, nor the actions of an individual, but were brought whole and fully articulated from a cultural source. These are the enduring elements of Mijikenda culture, their "Old Testament."

In addition to its richness as a cultural document, the Singwaya tradition gives evidence about the actual movement of people. Calculations of the number and duration of age-sets places the migration from Singwaya in the sixteenth-century, which corresponds with the date we have for Galla (and closely related Somali) expansion based on documentary evidence.

The difficulty with the Singwaya tradition is not that it is fabricated, for it is not, but that it is a culturally rich crystallization of a historical event. The event was a real one, but the tradition abstracts the relevant details in order to present a coherent picture of the origin of society and its institutions. Details which would confuse the picture, which would indicate that different Mijikenda groups had different origins, or that show more than one source of the central institutions are omitted. In fact, we know from archaeological, linguistic, and documentary evidence that the Kenya coast was occupied by Bantu-speaking people like the Mijikenda long before the sixteenth-century migration. The expansion of the Galla and Somali drove out only the northernmost Bantu-speakers, who migrated southward and merged with the established population. The Singwaya tradition is a stereotyped expression of the importance of the migration for the emergence of Mijikenda society in its present form.

We have one example of the evolution of a unified story because the tradition of the Rabai (one of the Mijikenda peoples) was recorded in 1847. At that time, the Rabai said that they originally came from Mount Kilimanjaro, to the west, that they were on the coast when the rest of the Mijikenda arrived, and that they joined with the Mijikenda to form a single people. By the mid-twentieth century, this story was no longer told; the Rabai now simply claim to have come from Singwaya with the other Mijikenda. In short, the tradition agrees with the reality the Rabai perceive: that they and the rest of the Mijikenda are one people. This social reality is more important than the "truth" of a particular historical detail.

MAASAI TRADITIONS

The pastoral Maasai of the Rift Valley have shaped their oral traditions to accord with the perception of themselves as the only pure pastoralists. They explain how they came to be different from the surrounding peoples who defile themselves by digging the soil or by subsisting on meat from the hunt. For example, a Maasai story about the hunting people called the Dorobo begins when a Maasai elder came upon the first Dorobo. The Maasai, as yet unseen, overhears God telling the Dorobo to come the next day to receive God's gift. The next morning the Maasai goes to see what God will give, but the Dorobo does not appear. According to the tradition, recorded by Alan Jacobs,

> God then let down a bark-rope . . . from the sky and began to let cattle down, until there were so many that they intermingled with those of the Dorobo. Then the Dorobo came, and when he could no longer recognize his cattle among those of the Maasai, he was angry and shot away the bark-rope with an arrow. . . God caused the cattle to stop descending and he moved up into the sky, and was never seen on the ground again. Thus all the cattle which Maasai now own were first given to them by God, and it is because the Dorobo lost his cattle by not listening to God that he must hunt wild animals for his food.[5]

The myth thus makes the point that economic specialization began in the time of origins and is therefore permanent and unchanging.

A related tradition separates the Maasai proper from people they call Iloikop. These are people who speak the Maasai language, are largely pastoral in economy, and live in political groups separate from the Maasai proper. These traditions describe how the Maasai migration began in the north, near Lake Rudolf. According to one version, the Maasai and Iloikop began as a single group, but they separated into two during the migration only to encounter one another many years later. By this time, the Iloikop had changed beyond recognition in their customs, although they still used the Maasai language. Maasai refer to Iloikop as "corpses." According to Jacobs, the Maasai often describe the gluttonous lack of self-control of Iloikop, who, according to the Maasai, kill milk cows to satisfy their taste for meat and are therefore driven to rely on products of the soil. "If only they were prudent like us," the traditions imply, "they too would be able to live as pure pastoralists." According to the Maasai, the later conflicts (in the nineteenth century) between Maasai and Iloikop

[5] Alan Jacobs, "The Traditional Political Organization of the Pastoral Maasai" (D. Phil. thesis, Oxford University, 1965), p. 27.

resulted from the fact that the Iloikop, driven to eating agricultural produce, made war from envy of the pure pastoralist way of life. It goes without saying that the Maasai also despise the Bantu-speaking farmers; the farmers in their turn often hold Maasai customs in contempt. But Maasai reserve their most powerful terms of abuse for those closest to them, the Iloikop, just as European socialist factions once heaped their most extreme abuse on deviant groups of

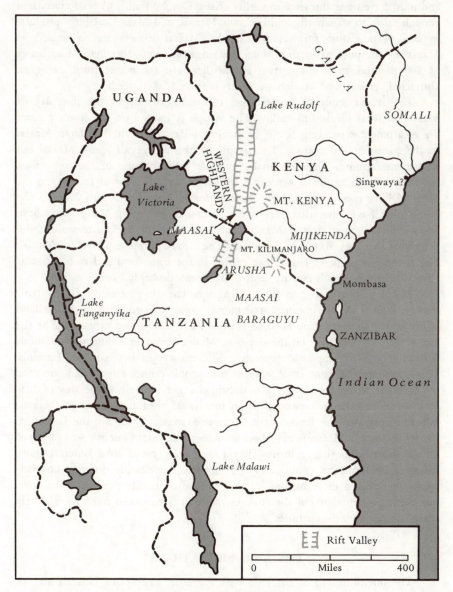

Maasai and Mijikenda Today

fellow socialists who threatened their sense of self-definition, rather than on the capitalists.

Maasai traditions concerning the purity of their pastoral life contrast with a more flexible reality. They could not sustain pure dependence on pastoralism in times of drought, cattle disease, or loss of cattle in war. Some Maasai became hunters after the disastrous outbreak of cattle rinderpest in the 1880s and 1890s, and must have done the same in earlier crises. Dorobo hunters who accumulated enough cattle to start herds could become Maasai, and Maasai eat farm products in bad years. Some farmers who spoke Maasai were even recognized as Maasai by the pure pastoralists. Like the Singwaya myth, the myth of exclusive Maasai pastoralism is not untrue, but neither is it the whole truth, being an abstracted, crystallized version of reality as the Maasai see it.

The recent study of one village, called Pagasi, shows the interplay of Maasai pastoral ideals and reality. The village is located on the lower part of the escarpment separating Sonjo (agricultural Bantu) at the top from Maasai in the plains at the bottom. The people of the village all speak Maasai but subsist on farming. They are unable to raise cattle because of the tsetse flies, but some village members own cattle, which are kept by Maasai relatives in the plains. Of the men in the village, about half were born Sonjo, half Maasai. The Sonjo who live in the village are in the process of becoming Maasai; they have learned the language, joined Maasai clans, and have brothers, sisters, sons, and daughters living as Maasai in the plains. The village is thus a school for Maasai. Nor is the process new. The village existed in the same form and with the same effect in the nineteenth century, and similar ones probably existed earlier.

The Pagasi pattern, in which language change precedes full economic change, reflects the environment and human capacity to adjust to it. Maasailand is not suited to agriculture because rainfall there is low and capricious. At the top of the Rift Valley or on the slopes of Mount Kenya or Kilimanjaro, rainfall is high enough to support a completely different way of life based on farming. This environmental contrast is so great that people cannot move from one zone to the other without making really drastic changes in their whole way of life. In a sense, to become a pastoralist, an individual must first become a Maasai. Where changes in the landscape were more gradual (as among the Baraguyu, the southernmost Maasai), neighbors on either side might borrow some but not all of the neighboring culture. They could grow more alike, interact more intensely, and cultures could change over time. But sharply different environments surrounded most Maasai, so that individual families might move from one culture to another but the cultures themselves remained fixed in relatively sharp contrast over the centuries.

THE LWO MIGRATIONS

The intermingling of the Lwo with the other peoples of Uganda and its vicinity was quite different from the Maasai's maintenance of cultural boundaries. The Lwo, who like the Maasai speak Nilotic languages, began with a mixed economy involving cattle keeping, fishing, and grain agriculture. As they moved down from the north over a long period, they met with many different groups already in place, and both borrowed and donated elements of their culture, social institutions, habits of mind, and economic practices. The migration was enormously complex — not large groups in sweeping movements, but a few individuals moving at a time as part of a larger trend. Whatever the local detail, these migrations were momentous in giving most of Uganda and neighboring parts of Kenya the patterns of population and culture that persisted through the colonial period.

The large groups that speak separate Lwo languages all have oral traditions describing the migrations; smaller subgroups also have their traditions. Each of the many groups, large and small, has its own tales of where it came from, what others it met along the way, who the leaders were. The broad picture of the movement emerges only when the separate traditions are pieced together. And this has not been easy to do, because the people in question live over a vast area, extending more than 900 miles from north to south.

There can be no doubt that these migrations really did occur. For one thing, each local tradition tells only its small bit of the large story. Until recently, no one teller could have been aware of the other pieces or of how they fit together; yet the dozens of separate stories are in fact parts of a remarkably coherent large account. Again, the stories are supported by linguistic evidence. They claim common origins for people who actually do speak similar and historically related languages. Combined, these rich stories with their complex local variations make historical verification possible.

Two geographically separate sets of people took part in these migrations: a northern set who now live in the southern part of the Republic of the Sudan, and a southern set who are now spread over a large part of Uganda, with fringes extending north into the Sudan and into southwestern Kenya. Both sets trace their origin to somewhere in the north; for the southern Lwo, it is an indefinite north, but northern Lwo traditions focus on a great, flat, marshy floodplain near the point where the Bahr al-Ghazal runs into the Nile. Linguistic research by Patrick Bennett supports this location as the general area of the Lwo cradleland, though linguistic evidence cannot be as precise as oral traditions in pinpointing a specific spot.

When we speak of the origin of the Lwo, the word *origin* is used in a very special sense. Any given people who speak a Lwo language have a great many individual origins, just as Americans come from many different places. The Lwo language, however, has a single origin, just as the American language does. Certain clans and lineages also preserve traditions of having been the "original" Lwo, who then intermarried with others to make the present Lwo community. In other words, many of the distinct Lwo peoples speak related languages with a single origin, but within each Lwo community are the individual clans and lineages whose ancestors brought the language from the north. To return to the

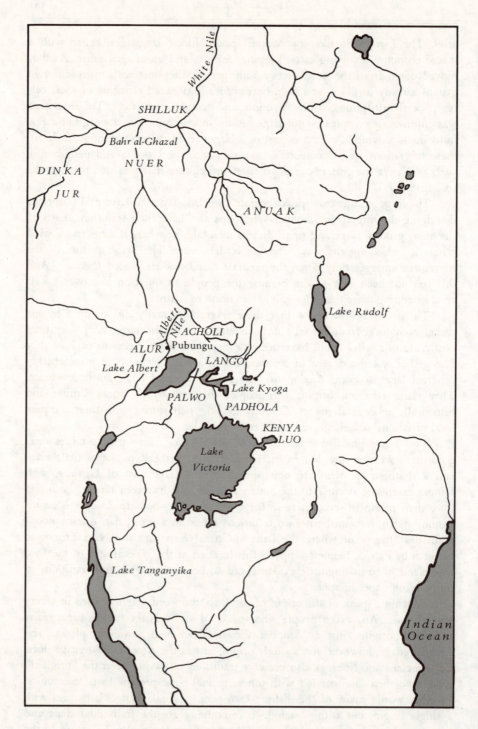

Lwo Peoples and Other Western Nilotes Today

American analogy, each distinct people has its recognized Mayflower descendants.

The traditions of the northern Lwo tell of a time of origin when two or three brothers and their children and grandchildren were living together. After family quarrels broke up the large group, segments went off in different directions. One set of relatives became the Jur; another evolved into the Shilluk; a third, according to some traditions, became the Anuak people. Traditions about the three brothers express these three peoples' sense of cultural relatedness. But the traditions have also compressed a long historical process into one or two generations. It is clear from the linguistic analysis that it was the Shilluk who first moved away from their home area, possibly as a result of the expansion of the non-Lwo peoples who live there today. Then the remaining Lwo split into three: the Anuak, the Jur, and the ancestors of the southern Lwo, who in turn were ultimately to split and give their languages to many of the peoples of Uganda.

While the northern Lwo remained close to their original homeland, and therefore recall their place of common origin, the southern Lwo do not remember the cradleland. It is important to keep in mind that each separate group of Lwo sees the world from where it is now. People understand that they are related to other groups of southern Lwo who speak closely related languages. Their traditions answer this question: how did we come to be separated from our neighbors so that we are no longer one people, but two or three? They often begin by telling of an encampment where they were once a single group, and go on from there. They rarely recall the cradleland, because few southern Lwo know of or need to explain their relationships to the northern Lwo peoples such as Anuak, Jur, or Shilluk. Many trace their origins to a place called Pubungu, just north of Uganda's Lake Albert, on the Albert Nile, where a major split took place.

These southern Lwo separation stories often center on the theme of the spear and the bead. It is a story of two brothers, named in one version Nyipiir and Nyabongo. One day Nyipiir was tending his field near the Nile, to the north of Pubungu, when an elephant broke into the field. Nyipiir grabbed the nearest spear, which happened to belong to his brother, and hurled it at the elephant. The animal ran off wounded, with the spear hanging from its side. Nyipiir offered to pay his brother for the lost spear, but Nyabongo insisted on having it back. Nyipiir therefore set off through the wilderness to hunt for the spear. He finally found it at the legendary home of the elephants together with some beautiful beads that became the royal beads.

After Nyipiir returned, a second episode tells how Nyabongo's baby swallowed one of the royal beads from the land of the elephants. Nyipiir first demanded his bead back, then cut open the baby's stomach to get it. Nyabongo, his baby dead, left with all his dependents, and the other Lwo families also left, driven on by the impact of the tragedy. Some traveled east of the Nile, some west. They sank an axe in the Nile as a symbol of this separation. The axe remains today at a sacrificial shrine, looked after by the headman of Pubungu, whose lineage remained behind to serve as guardians.

The story of the spear and the bead is not, of course, a true account, for it is told over a vast area and in each place it is given as the reason for the separation of different groups. The stock explanation fitted easily into oral tradition, which in any case mixes history with wisdom about man and society. On one hand, the story explores relations between brothers and what happens when extreme, unreasonable demands are made in the name of kinship. But again, because the names of the characters and places can change from one telling to another, the story also preserves historical information. We can therefore accept as fact that Lwo clans did divide to the north of Lake Albert, although the division may have taken place over a long period of time rather than as the result of a single quarrel. But that was not the sole migration; at least one other path followed by many small movements passed near Agoro, far to the northeast, and then to the east of Pubungu.

LWO INTERACTION AND ADAPTATION

The history of the Lwo migrations within Uganda is remarkable for its complexity, with many small groups moving over a long period of time and interacting intensely with other Uganda peoples. These interactions involved people of four distinct and separate language groups: the Lwo themselves as speakers of Western Nilotic, speakers of Eastern Nilotic like the Maasai (though not the Maasai themselves), speakers of Central Sudanic, and Bantu-speakers. Table 1 illustrates the broad pattern of these interactions, but it must be understood as a simplified and partial view of events. One distortion comes from the fact that most large, self-identifying ethnic groups have come into existence only in the past century. At the time when the Lwo interactions were taking place, the Acholi, to take only one example, did not think of themselves as a "tribe" of Acholi but rather as people of a great many different localities, each of which had a local history and a sense of identity. An authentic account of the Lwo migrations would thus give hundreds of histories of small localities.

Another simplification is the recipelike formula for the history of each locality. Take so many people of one origin, so many of another, add them together, and an Acholi group emerges. Ever since Professor B. A. Ogot founded the modern study of the Lwo migrations, historians have understood that each locality took its shape over centuries. In any particular case, Lwo entered at many different times, and other peoples also entered at many times. The account is also partial because the chronology is weak. Dates for events before 1750 are largely guesswork. Some are commonly given in the literature: departure of the Lwo from the cradleland, in the early fifteenth century; departure from Pubungu, about mid-fifteenth; early Padhola settlement, around 1625. But these dates come from a count of the generations reported by oral traditions. That method is an unreliable guide to chronology, because a generation is often remembered only if it contained a known ancestor of a living social group; it is sometimes forgotten if it contained no notable ancestor or recognized founder of a lineage. It is impossible, therefore, to know the exact number of generations from a past event to the present day.

As the Lwo peoples moved across what is now Uganda, in myriad movements by small groups, they covered a wide range of territory with considerable variation in topography and rainfall. Lwo adaptability, their willingness to move from one environmental setting to another, stands in sharp contrast to the pattern of stable environmental specialization found so widely elsewhere in East Africa. One problem is to explain why the Lwo were able to move from one setting to another, whereas the Maasai, for example, abhorred any change in their ecology, and the highland Bantu also clung to a familiar environment. Part of the answer must depend on the probable ecology of the Lwo in their cradleland to the north. Of this, we have no certain knowledge; but the mode of subsistence common to many of the emigrant Lwo offers one clue, while that of Nilotic peoples like the Dinka and Nuer who remained in the cradleland provides another. These Dinka and Nuer were not Lwo, but they speak Western Nilotic languages of the same branch as Lwo. This means that in the moderately distant past the ancestors of the Nuer, Dinka, and Lwo were one people.

The Nuer ecology is very strongly conditioned by their environment, an enormous flat plain crisscrossed by many rivers and having a single very heavy rainy season each year from April to October. In those months, the plain turns into an enormous grass-covered swamp, and people are forced to move with their cattle to any available patch of high land where they can build wet-season villages. Cattle graze and people plant millet on ridges and high points. Then, in the dry season, when the marshes dry out completely, they move to large camps bordering the rivers, where they have access to water. They live partly on animal products, partly on the grain grown in the wet season, and partly on fish caught in the rivers.

We have no conclusive evidence that the early Lwo economy was identical with that of the modern Nuer, although a fundamental similarity may be assumed. Most Lwo peoples claim an environmental basis for their identity by calling themselves *Jonam,* meaning "people of the lakes and rivers," though the Nuer pattern of seasonal transhumance could not be retained fully in the places to which the Lwo moved. The Nuer combination of fishing, cattle keeping, and seed agriculture based on millet was, however, easier to retain in a variety of different settings, and many Lwo retained it, though some lost their cattle. Palwo traditions, for example, describe their loss of cattle through disease. The Anuak also have no cattle because they live in a region infested with tsetse flies, but their vocabulary is still rich in cattle terminology, showing that they must once have been cattle keepers. Southern Uganda, the home of Bantu-speaking people, has two rainy seasons and lives mainly on perennials like bananas rather than on annual seed crops like millet; but most of the Lwo did not get that far, remaining instead where they could keep to their pattern of

TABLE 1. *Ethnic Interactions Resulting from the Lwo Migrations*

Modern Ethnic Group Substantially of Lwo Origin	Language Group	Other Groups Absorbed	Language of Absorbed Group	Character of Interaction
Acholi and Lango	Western Nilotic — Lwo	Groups related to modern Teso and Karamojong	Eastern Nilotic	One integrated society developed in which all people ultimately spoke Lwo, but each clan recalled its own origin. A great many clans were of non-Lwo origin.
		Madi	Central Sudanic	
Alur	Western Nilotic — Lwo	Madi, Okebo, Lendu, Bendi	Central Sudanic	A continuous process of absorption of earlier non-Lwo residents into Lwo-speaking society took place. The non-Lwo languages were still spoken around the partially absorbed fringes. Within Alur society, members of the clans of Lwo origin were chiefs of very small chiefdoms. The non-Lwo were subjects.
Palwo	Western Nilotic — Lwo	Palwo became a peripheral group in preexisting Nyoro society	Lwo at the edge of Bunyoro spoke own language; Nyoro not absorbed	The Nyoro royal dynasty was of Lwo origin, but in the process they became Nyoro (Bantu-speakers). The Palwo survived as a separate group, speaking Lwo, in northern Bunyoro. The Palwo periodically intervened in Nyoro dynastic politics. For the history of Bunyoro, see Chapter 5.

(*Continued on next page*)

millet grown in one rainy season a year. Even the Kenya Luo who moved up into the highlands where bananas thrive continued to rely on grains as their staple.

The Lwo of northern Uganda, who became the Acholi and Lango, found themselves in an environment lacking such dramatic contrasts as the high margins and low bottom of the Rift Valley, where the Maasai lived, and therefore did not create sharp cultural boundaries with their neighbors. Instead, they found a

TABLE 1 (*Continued*)

Modern Ethnic Group Substantially of Lwo Origin	Language Group	Other Groups Absorbed	Language of Absorbed Group	Character of Interaction
Padhola	Western Nilotic — Lwo	Nyole, Gwere, Soga	Bantu	Lwo speakers initially moved into an area of virgin forest, with few prior inhabitants. Later movements into the area included immigration, in small numbers, of all groups listed, except perhaps Sewe. Immigrant women married into Lwo clans, and some men were adopted by Lwo clans. A few Lwo-speaking clans claim Soga, Gwere, or Teso origin.
		Teso	Eastern Nilotic	
		Sewe	Identity uncertain — probably Eastern Nilotes	
Kenya Luo	Western Nilotic — Lwo	Luyia, Gusii, Kagwa, Kanyibule, Waturi	Bantu	Prior inhabitants driven out and some absorbed in Kenya Luo groups. Intense interaction at borders, with members of border groups adopting one another's languages and cultures under some circumstances.
		Terik	Eastern Nilotes	

large and relatively flat plateau, where they interacted with people of other origins, and cultures merged in a way that would not have been possible where special environmental problems required special solutions. Here, all could learn from the rest because they were all trying to cope with the same environment.

But some of the migrating Lwo departed far more drastically from the ecological tradition than the others did. This was especially true of the Alur, the Kenya Luo, and, to a lesser extent, the Padhola, all of whom belonged to the southern Lwo. In all three cases, a portion of the migrants moved away from the water's edge to higher land, where they could no longer fish or keep large numbers of cattle (except among the Alur) and where bananas and root crops did well. This movement presents a puzzle, because it appears that these people gave up the expertise they had accumulated over generations in order to adapt to a new environment.

We are fortunate in having a good suggestion as to the probable reasons for these alterations; the Kenya Luo made a similar move in the nineteenth century within the range of recent and detailed memory. At the beginning of this move, the Luo occupied the narrow belt of grassland on the shores of Lake Victoria, a region suitable for cattle rearing, seed agriculture, and fishing. The economy of that period included a wide range of activities, among which an individual could choose in time of crisis. The crisis period began about the middle of the nineteenth century with crowding and overpopulation. The first response was for younger sons who did not expect to inherit much cattle to make for the nearby highlands. The highlands were thought to be less healthy for cattle than the lake shore, but rainfall there was more abundant and better distributed through the year. A poor man could go to the highlands, plant two crops a year, and build up his capital for the purchase of cattle, the most prestigious form of wealth.

Then, in about 1890, rinderpest arrived as a new disease and wiped out the cattle herds on the lake shore. Formerly rich elder brothers and fathers moved up to join those who had pioneered highland agriculture in an attempt to recoup their cattle losses. That indeed was their only alternative other than fishing or growing millet on limited land. Thus some of the Kenya Luo were forced into the highlands by bad times, not attracted there by an obvious opportunity.

This case of the Kenya Luo suggests that in earlier moves, Lwo peoples like the Alur were both drawn by the rich possibilities of the highlands and driven by diseases affecting cattle or people. Rinderpest, which reached East Africa only in the late nineteenth century, is ruled out; east coast fever is one possibility, but trypanosomiasis is even more likely. This is the disease carried by the tsetse fly, called nagana when it affects cattle and sleeping sickness among humans. It would have been a new disease for the Lwo, because their cradleland is unique in its complete freedom from the tsetse. Tsetse flies live in almost any kind of vegetation, except the total absence of wooded cover. Even very sparse wood is adequate for tsetse. But the Nuer plain was almost totally treeless.

The species of fly that breeds along Uganda's riverbanks is usually harmless to cattle, although it causes occasional epidemics among humans. The flies that were deadly to cattle, and bred in the grassland, were isolated enough in their distribution so as not to cause continuous outbreaks. The cattle herders came to know which sections of the countryside were dangerous and avoided them. But sharp fluctuations in rainfall or in the distribution of wild animals on which tsetse feed could cause the flies to move into new areas and come into contact with people and cattle. Many twentieth-century examples show ecological change leading to outbreaks of trypanosomiasis. It is highly probable that similar outbreaks occurred in the past. Palwo traditions describe the loss of cattle to trypanosomiasis and other diseases. The Alur movement up from the Nile valley to the highlands quite probably followed the pattern of the Kenya Luo. Poor individuals moved up first, then, at a time of cattle disease, their relatives followed. This is speculative history, but it is supported by evidence on the precolonial distribution of tsetse flies and by a careful appraisal of the riverside economy.

The Lwo intermingling with other peoples thus took place in two quite different settings. In some places, the terrain was relatively flat and uniform and the economy of the Lwo and their neighbors was relatively similar. In others, sharp differences in altitude separated the cattle-keeping Lwo from their high-land neighbors, and the Lwo had to learn a new technology as they moved uphill. In either case, the result was that Lwo and non-Lwo came to live side by side and to learn from one another. This interchange took place at all levels from religious ideas to ordinary crafts. The Padhola of southeastern Uganda, for example, share designs for a wide range of everyday objects with their Bantu-speaking neighbors to the east. The Alur of northwestern Uganda share similar elements of material culture with their Central Sudanic–speaking neighbors, while sharing other elements with related Lwo peoples. In this way, the objects still produced by Lwo craftsworkers are continuing evidence both of the migrations and of Lwo ability to adapt and learn in their new homelands.

THE COAST

The movement of people and of ideas differed radically between the East African coast and the interior. In the interior, small groups of people moved from place to place as conditions affecting subsistence changed. New ideas moved freely between neighboring areas and could ultimately be communicated from one neighbor to another and on to a third neighbor across vast stretches of East Africa. But individuals did not regularly travel long distances except in time of crisis, such as drastic famine. Very few coastal trade goods have been found in the interior for the period before 1500. The few seashells and other goods found at sites of the Late Stone Age onward were probably passed from hand to hand into the interior, with no one individual serving as a long-distance trader. On the coast, by contrast, once maritime skills were developed, traders moved regularly and rapidly among the East African towns as well as to distant ports of the Indian Ocean. The coastal towns assumed a dual identity: their overland ties developed through the slow movement of populations and the arduous transfer of trade goods over short distances; their maritime links spanned thousands of miles and tied together diverse cultures.

The great contrast between sea and land travel lasted into the era of caravan trade between the coast and the interior in the nineteenth century. The accounts of European explorers document the difference. In 1848 and 1850, Johann Krapf, the missionary explorer, traveled first on land, then in a small Swahili coasting boat, then in an Arab ship sailing overseas. He made about 6 miles a day on land, 25 miles a day along the coast, stopping at small ports along the way, and over 100 miles a day on the long-distance voyage. Krapf found it easier to travel 1,600 miles to Arabia than to visit his neighbors in the not very distant coastal hinterland.

Maritime trade on the Indian Ocean developed much earlier than it did on the Atlantic, going back at least to the second century B.C. for the beginnings of a regular traffic linking Africa, India, and Southeast Asia through the alternation of prevailing northeasterlies and the southwest monsoon. Northeasterlies blow from November to March, carrying ships from India, Arabia, and the Persian Gulf. In April, the wind starts blowing from the southwest for the return journey. Persian Gulf and Arabian ships in East Africa prefer to leave in April because of the stormy conditions that develop at the horn of Africa in May.

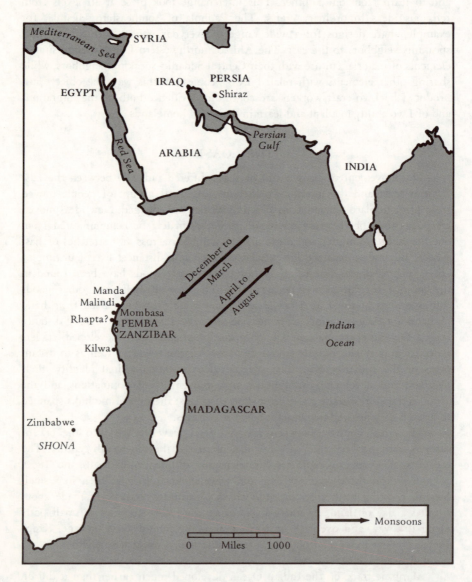

The Indian Ocean to 1500

Those ships not leaving in April must wait idly until the late part of the monsoon in August.

The pattern of winds and sailings favored the northern coast of East Africa as a destination for overseas traders. The crucial question was how far south sailors could get before the northeast winds lost their force, always remembering that ships needed to leave by April for the return voyage. Toward the end of their season, the northeasterlies blow with constancy only on the northern sections of the coast — further north with each successive month. They blow with constancy as far as Mombasa in February but only to the Somali coast in March. Given the normal time required for a trip from Arabia or Persia, Zanzibar was usually the southern limit of navigation. Mariners who wanted to reach Kilwa on the southern Tanzanian coast had to sail past Zanzibar by January before the northeasterlies had lost their force and regularity. Anyone sailing south of Kilwa had to wait from April to August in East Africa, because the currents made an immediate return trip impossible.

These geographical factors shaped the history of the East African coast. The sailing patterns show why Kilwa became an important coastal town at a time when the most important products traded there came from further south, beyond the limits of a return trip in the same season. They show why Mombasa and Malindi, with poor and barren hinterlands but easy return sailings, occupied central positions as trading towns, and why Zanzibar, the preferred southern sailing limit, has historically been a major entrepôt.

All over the Indian Ocean, coastal and overseas shipping existed side by side. East African coastal sailing, which could continue through most months of the year, was essential for trade within East Africa and for assembling goods destined for overseas markets. Long-distance traders from the north stopped at major ports only in the brief period before the changing of the monsoon. They therefore required goods already bulked through the agency of either the coastal trade or local land-based trade. East Africans were, for the most part, involved in the coasting trade, whereas Arabian and Persian Gulf mariners dominated the long-distance trade by virtue of having home bases convenient to overland and sea routes that connected India, East Africa, the Red Sea, the Mediterranean, Central Asia, Syria, Iraq, Persia, and Egypt.

Between the time of Alexander the Great (356–323 B.C.) and the rise of Islam (seventh century A.D.), Indian Ocean trade was directly linked with the trade of a unified Mediterranean in a way that would not be repeated until modern times. Alexander's vast conquests in Asia tied the two worlds together. Spices, rare woods, and ivory were taken from India and East Africa to the Red Sea and on to Egypt and the Mediterranean trade. Ivory prices in the Mediterranean dropped significantly between the fourth and third centuries B.C., no doubt as an indirect result of the linking of the Mediterranean and Indian Ocean worlds.

The earliest account of East Africa's involvement in the trade is given in a Greek merchant's guide, called the *Periplus of the Erythraean Sea* — that is, the Red Sea and Indian Ocean. The guide, written about the end of the first century A.D., describes the journey down the East African coast to a market town named Rhapta. The remains of Rhapta have not been found, although it is clear that the town was located somewhere along what is now the Tanzanian coast, very probably on its northern half. Small ships from south Arabia stopped at Rhapta. Arab captains and crews stayed long enough to intermarry and to learn the local language. While Rhapta was loosely dependent on a south Arabian state, the other trading towns of the coast farther north were completely independent, each under its own chief.

Through all the vast political and economic changes over almost two millennia, between 100 A.D. and the nineteenth-century colonial conquest, some basic patterns in the organization of coastal life were continuous, reflecting long-term continuities in political organization and in geographical and economic conditions. With the long-distance sea trade in the hands of Arabs, but with East Africans dominating access to the products of their own country, it was natural for the Arabs to settle in East Africa in order to establish regular and continuous trade relations. The autonomy of most of the individual market towns, each ruled by its own chief, came from a pattern of sea trade in which ships could easily bypass any one market town and find the same products at another.

We have documentation for East Africa's relations with the Graeco-Roman world, but other overseas connections, on which the documents are completely silent, existed at the same time. Indisputable evidence of a link with Southeast Asia is found in the Malagasy language, spoken on the large island of Madagascar off the southern coast of East Africa. Malagasy is a Malayo-Polynesian language, closely related to one of the languages of Borneo, 8,000 miles away.

Bananas and other Southeast Asian food crops, which were essential to the early Bantu adaptation to the forest environment, are further evidence of the connection. Bananas have been cultivated in the great lakes region of East Africa for a very long time. The coconut palm, which came from Southeast Asia, was planted on the East African coast by the first century A.D. Such evidence points to an Indonesian migration around two thousand years ago. The Indonesians probably sailed in short steps along the Indian Ocean coastline, although the archaeology of the East African coast shows no signs of Indonesian settlements.

The great age of the East African coast — the age of royal courts and stone palaces, of mosques with coral carvings, of imported luxury goods — began gradually in the ninth century, with increases in trade and urban growth going on until about the fifteenth century. Individual African towns rose and fell, but the general pattern was continued growth with few interruptions.

The ninth-century increase in trade was related to the increasing importance of the Persian Gulf, which came with the movement of the Abbasid capital from Syria to Iraq. The goods exported from the East African coast tell something of its history, helping to explain the rise and fall of particular towns and to assess the impact of long-distance trade on ordinary people.

Ivory was important in the Islamic period, as it had been in the Graeco-Roman period and continued to be into the twentieth century. As the Roman demand for ivory declined, the slack was taken up by Indian buyers, who preferred East African to Indian ivory because it was soft and easy to work and because the tusks were large enough to be used for making the bangles worn by Indian brides. When either the woman or her husband died, the bangles were destroyed, thus ensuring continuous demand. The Islamic lands also took some ivory, and, by the tenth century, substantial quantities were being shipped around India to China.

Slaves were another export of the coast, partly because the enslavement of Muslims was prohibited in the Islamic world, which thus created a demand for slaves from beyond its fringes. Many slaves were also taken to India, and some to China, but most went to the lands around the Persian Gulf. Large numbers were already exported by the ninth century. In the Middle East, they were called *Zenj,* the word for East Africa, although some of those called Zenj undoubtedly came from other places. Many were put to work draining land for the planting of sugarcane in southern Iraq; they revolted in 869 A.D. and held out for fourteen years before they were suppressed. Afterward, the slaves were used in the army but not usually for agricultural labor.

Gold was an increasingly important export from East Africa between the tenth and fifteenth centuries. It was brought from the region of Zimbabwe to the southern portion of the coast, then taken north by sea. The quantities were very small before the tenth century, but they grew over time. A Portuguese factor at the port of Sofala in the early sixteenth century estimated that 130 pounds of gold were passing through the port each year. Gold winnings in the interior may have been as high as a thousand pounds a year, though not all of this would have passed through Sofala.

Other, more ordinary products were also shipped from East Africa. The treeless Persian Gulf coast bought the straight mangrove poles of the East African coast for house building. Food grains were undoubtedly also exported from East Africa.

The archaeological evidence for imports shows pottery from the Persian Gulf, Chinese porcelain, and glass beads. Trade to the Far East must have been extremely important, for porcelain from China was more common than Islamic ware in fifteenth-century Kilwa. But the durability of ceramics and glass distorts the archaeological picture; large quantities of cotton cloth were imported from northwest India and from China without leaving any equivalent remains.

Northern coastal towns were dominant in the East African trade up to about the eleventh century; but they slowly gave way to southern ports like Kilwa. The changes came from the growing importance of gold. As long as ivory was the most important export, trading towns could develop at any one of a number of points up and down the coast, because elephants were found almost everywhere. Given a choice, long-distance merchants from overseas always chose the northern towns because of the difficulty of return in a single season from further south.

This preference for northern ports accounts for the importance of Manda on the northern Kenya coast between the ninth and thirteenth centuries. Manda was wealthy from the start, with stone buildings and rich imports. Fifteen percent of the ninth-century pottery found at Manda was imported from outside Africa, showing how well it could afford expensive goods from overseas.

When gold began to be a more important export, the ports of the northern coast tried to control the trade in order to retain their predominance. By the end of the twelfth century, however, the trade was in the hands of Kilwa, in southern Tanzania. Kilwa, rather than Sofala, still further south, served as the great port of the gold trade, because Sofala was beyond the point of return in a single season; Kilwa was the sailors' southernmost limit.

The localized sources of gold, in contrast to the wide distribution of ivory, made political centralization possible but not inevitable in the gold-digging regions. A leader who could control a substantial piece of gold-working territory could concentrate in his hands the goods with which to reward supporters. Monopolistic control over gold also gave such leaders leverage in dealing with powerful outsiders from neighboring societies.

The contrast between the large empires of the Shona gold region and the small states and sometimes stateless towns of the coast shows that state-building is not simply a function of trade. In the goldbearing regions of southern Africa the localization of an extremely valuable resource made state-building possible, just as control over the desert trade routes and scarce resources such as gold and salt made empire-building possible in West Africa. But it was not possible to control the East African sea routes as it was the desert routes of the Sahara. A ship could sail past one port to the next, and therefore monopoly was not possible without maritime dominance.

The cultural and social synthesis on the coast was related to patterns of trade. The Arabic language and Islamic culture tied the towns to distant Indian Ocean ports. Bantu language (or languages) and culture integrated the towns with their local settings, on which they were dependent for provisions, for some trade goods, and possibly for political security. A mixed culture developed as alien settlers arrived on the coast, were absorbed into East African life, and intermarried locally. Their children were the local hosts to later generations of immigrants. Today's Swahili language is heir to the centuries of interaction. It has a Bantu structure and a remarkable number of Arabic loanwords. In the same way, Swahili culture is strongly East African, yet also Islamic.

This process of interaction between local and exotic cultures went on from the ninth century to the fifteenth and later, but we know almost nothing about the local language of this period. The first definite documentary evidence of Swahili comes hundreds of years later, in the early eighteenth century. Bantu languages, however, were already spoken on the coast by the ninth century, and they must have resembled modern Swahili.

Oral traditions describe two sets of immigrants during the formative years of the coastal towns. The earliest were the Debuli, probably from Debal, a port near the mouth of the Indus River in modern Pakistan. Then came the Shirazi from the Persian Gulf. Today, many coastal Africans who look like mainlanders, speak Swahili, and share the culture of East Africa still call themselves Shirazi. Their genealogies begin with mythical ancestors from the Islamic heartlands. Their traditions on the origins of particular lineages are not historically accurate; they are, rather, ideological statements of the importance of an overseas Islamic heritage in the culture of the coast.

The connections between the people of the East African coast and Arabia or the Persian Gulf thus exist at several levels. Some individuals really have come in recent times from Southwestern Asia; others are the descendants of individuals who made the migration a hundred years ago; still others trace mythical links based on a sense of spiritual kinship. A similar range of variation must have developed gradually during the early Islamic period. No evidence of Islam is found before the twelfth century. Beginning at about this time, Persian settlers arrived on the Somali coast. Other "Shirazi" later established themselves further south, but as they moved from town to town, married local women, and learned local customs, they developed an Afro-Islamic culture.

Just as East Africa shaped the migrants and their descendants, Islam and the alien culture helped to shape East African coastal culture. It was more than the Africanization of Muslims and the Islamization of the coast. After local cultural compromises had been worked out, the process began all over again with the arrival of a new set of migrants — sometimes to a new section of coast. While the descendants of the first migration were moving southward, other people brought new techniques directly from the Islamic heartland. The great palace at Kilwa, for example, was built in the latest Islamic architectural styles of its time.

Outside the towns, in rural villages on the coast and in the hinterland, lived Bantu-speaking peoples who did not accept Islam at all. In spite of this cultural difference, ties of economic interdependence developed. There was probably no long-distance overland trade, except in the south near the Zambezi, and the towns relied on their hinterland neighbors for the products of the mainland. Each of the major towns appears to have had its own sources of ivory. The towns of the Tanzania and Kenya coasts relied on their hinterland neighbors for agricultural products. According to Idrisi, a twelfth-century geographer, Malindi carried on an extensive trade in dried fish, which must have been sold on the mainland. Remains found at both Manda and early Kilwa contain grooved blocks used for the manufacture of shell beads, one of the products most commonly traded to the hinterland. This trade could have been carried on, as similar trade has been in more recent times, through the initiative of hinterland peoples who came to town with their products, or at periodic markets just behind the coast.

In the absence of long-distance trade, it is possible that some goods nevertheless came a long way indirectly, passing from one trader to another.

The place of the coastal trade in the historical evolution of hinterland peoples is impossible to know. The ivory trade, for example, could have been dominated by chiefs who used commercial wealth to reinforce their power, but it could have been carried on just as easily by small bands of hunters who had no significant role in the political organization of the surrounding cultivators. Ibn Battuta, the great Muslim traveler, describes Kilwa's raids on the coast for slaves, but in other places the trade may have been limited to criminals and to prisoners taken in wars having local causes. All that we know is that the coast exported slaves, surplus food, and the products of surplus labor, and, for the most part, the people of the coast and hinterland received what they saw as luxury goods in return.

SUGGESTIONS FOR FURTHER READING

Azania: Journal of the British Institute of History and Archaeology in Nairobi. London: Oxford University Press, 1966–. The articles in this journal provide a continuing account of archaeological research in East Africa, covering both the coast and the interior.

Ehret, Christopher. *Southern Nilotic History.* Evanston, Ill.: Northwestern University Press, 1971.

Freeman-Grenville, G. S. P. *The East African Coast: Select Documents from the First to the Earlier Nineteenth Century.* Oxford: Oxford University Press, Clarendon Press, 1962.

Ogot, Bethwell A. *History of the Southern Luo.* Nairobi: East African Publishing House, 1967.

Ogot, Bethwell A., ed. *Zamani: A Survey of East African History.* Rev. ed. Nairobi: East African Publishing House, 1974.

Oliver, Roland, and Mathew, Gervase. *History of East Africa.* Vol. 1. Oxford: Oxford University Press, Clarendon Press, 1963.

Sutton, J. E. O. *The East African Coast: An Historical and Archaeological Review.* Historical Association of Tanzania Paper No. 1. Nairobi: East African Publishing House, 1966.

Chapter 5

Political Culture
and Political Economy
in Early East Africa

EAST AFRICAN ORAL TRADITIONS tell of hero kings, of great hunters or herds-men with miraculous powers, who came, often as strangers, to found kingdoms. Their successors emerged from the time of fabled magical deeds to conquer local clans, to fight wars against neighboring kings, and to bring famine or plenty. These great tales tell more than the history of royal rule; they also indicate the changes that took place in the lives of ordinary people — changing rituals and cultivation, alterations in lineage life, tribute payment, and trade. The history of politics is thus a key for unlocking the history of more elusive and more profoundly important developments.

ORIGINS OF POLITICAL CULTURE

The culture of royal rule encompasses the myths told about early kings, the way in which royal courts were built, the rituals of fertility and of a king's accession and burial, the praise names, royal titles, and regalia. Striking simi-larities in all these matters are found within certain sections of East Africa and, in some cases, across the whole region. The similarities are clearest at the end of the nineteenth century — a period for which documentation is strong, but before the major changes of the colonial period had occurred. The broad distri-bution of cultural elements, however, undoubtedly had its origins in much earlier periods. The crucial historical problem is to explain how these similarities came about.

As with the Lwo, local culture often took shape through a continuous series of movements by small groups of people. As they moved from place to place, they retained and adapted inherited ideas and learned others from new neighbors; some emerged as rulers, others became commoners. The people of western Tanzania, for example, are grouped together in three large but vaguely defined ethnic groups — Nyamwezi, Sukuma, and Kimbu — and they are divided into a great many small chiefdoms. Their deep cultural similarities developed from countless movements over the generations. The environment over much of the area could not support permanent villages; as the land in one spot was exhausted people moved on to begin farming again elsewhere. In any one section, immigrants appear to have come from every point of the compass. The chiefly lines of the Nyamwezi recall having come from the west (Rwanda, Buha, Burundi), from the south (Kimbu, Ugalla), and from the distant east near the coast (Sagara, Zaramo). A similar widely scattered pattern emerges for the history of Kimbu chiefs.

This multiplicity of small movements led to the overlapping of titles and of chiefly symbols over broad areas, as can be seen from the titles given Kimbu chiefs. Their primary title, *mwami,* is the same as the king's title in Rwanda, far to the northwest; they also shared another title with the Nyamwezi just to the north — *mtemi,* ultimately derived from the verb *-tema,* meaning to "cut," possibly because the chief (as the only person who could order the death of a subject) cut people down. A third Kimbu title was *mwene,* the same as was used by peoples further south between Lakes Malawi and Tanganyika, though it was also used near the Tanzania coast much further east, and again to the west in some of the kingdoms of southern Zaïre. Political culture had been communicated in all directions over an enormous area.

Often the basic ideas of kingship originated locally, even when early rulers came from somewhere else, for the simple reason that early kings were forced to justify themselves and their actions convincingly to their subjects. As a result, similarities in royal culture among neighboring kingdoms often reflected deeper similarities in the nonroyal elements. *Mwami,* we have seen, was a title shared by the Kimbu and the kingdom of Rwanda. It extended still further among Rwanda's neighbors west of Lakes Tanganyika and Kivu, and in the kingdom of Burundi. The history of the word leads back to a time before any known kingdoms; it existed (according to linguistic evidence) from the very early years of the Bantu expansion, thousands of years ago. Its original meaning was probably not "king," merely "notable person." Even today, when the word is examined in its full distribution across the societies of East Africa, it carries no *necessary* implication of kingship or of large-scale political organization. Among the Lega of eastern Zaïre, for example, a mwami was any person who had been initiated into a ritual secret society, while for the Nyanga west of Lake Kivu the title was used by every minor headman even if his political following included only a few households.

The kingdom of Rwanda is an excellent test case for hypotheses about the local formation of political culture. The social distance between rulers and subjects was fairly great; in recent centuries the king and his relatives remained separate from and did not intermarry with the subject population. Even so, traditions show that royal rituals grew out of rites practiced before the establishment of the ruling dynasty. These rites were essential to the fertility of the land, had been developed by those who lived on the land in the earliest period, and

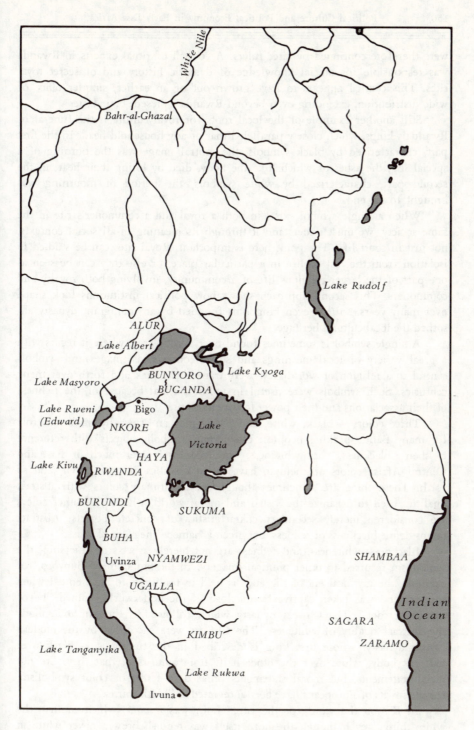

White Nile

Bahr-al-Ghazal

Lake Rudolf

ALUR

Lake Albert

BUNYORO

Lake Masyoro

BUGANDA

Lake Kyoga

Lake Rweni
(Edward)

Bigo

NKORE

Lake
Victoria

HAYA

Lake Kivu

RWANDA

BURUNDI

SUKUMA

BUHA

Uvinza

NYAMWEZI

SHAMBAA

UGALLA

Indian
Ocean

SAGARA

KIMBU

ZARAMO

Lake Tanganyika

Lake Rukwa

Ivuna

Some Peoples of East Africa

were therefore continued by later rulers. A council of ritual experts in Rwanda was responsible for official knowledge of dynastic history and of secret royal rites. This council appears to have grown out of an earlier, simpler office of wide distribution, extending even beyond Rwanda's present boundaries.

Still another example of the local roots for royal culture is the funeral of Rwanda's kings, which closely paralleled that of any household head. In the first part, characterized by black symbols, the central image was the burning of a special log, the ashes of which, like the body, died by losing their heat; in the second part, characterized by white symbols, the period of mourning was brought to an end.

When a single symbol exists in both a royal and a commoner's rite in the same society, we must understand it through its meaning in all social contexts, not just in court life. The point here is important. Royal rites can be studied in isolation from the rest of life in a particular place, or else they can be seen as one part of the larger religious life of a community, involving both royalty and commoners. This second approach shows how political institutions took shape over many years, so that even kingdoms founded by an immigrant dynasty absorbed the local cultural heritage.

A single symbol is sometimes found over a wide area, where it recurs with a great variety of local meanings and social contexts, as images and symbols central to a religion or world-view were transmitted back and forth over many centuries. Such symbols were useful in political ritual because of the richness of their associations and their power to stir emotions.

Three colors — black, white, and red — play an especially important role for many Bantu-speaking peoples: they group symbolic objects with reference to their "blackness," or "whiteness," or "redness." Over much of East and Central Africa colors are held to have moral qualities of purity, evil, and so forth. These three are sometimes thought of as primary colors with abstract qualities used to organize the visual and moral world, whereas all other colors are considered merely secondary characteristics of concrete objects. Abstract nouns define blackness or redness, but green is named "the color of grass."

Blackness, whiteness, and redness are not merely aspects of chiefship; the symbolism recurred in other political imagery. In the kingdom of Bunyoro, for example, the mythical era of the gods is held in traditions to have ended when the last god was taken captive by the lord of the underworld, named "he of the black soot." The Chwezi dynasty which followed is thought to embody the abstract quality of whiteness. The Chwezi were succeeded by the modern Nyoro dynasty, whose first king is described in the traditions as black over half his body, white over the other half. It is quite clear that these are not racial statements, but moral statements phrased in terms of color symbolism, for the spirits of Europeans have been integrated as "black spirits."

In Kimbu the word for the ritual horn was *imbutu,* which means "the white thing," even though the horn itself was reddish brown, never white in color. Each chief had at least one of these long wooden "ghost-horns," inherited from his ancestors and blown only on the most solemn ritual occasions associated with "the honor of the earth." Its name came from its moral qualities, and the supreme being in Kimbu is called "the white one." In Sukuma, just south of Lake Victoria, on the other hand, when councillors assembled after the death of a chief to elect his successor, they would examine a certain part of a chicken's stomach for each candidate to decide whether he would bring fertility to the land. If it was blackish, symbolizing rain clouds, the omen was a good one. If it was whitish for dry earth, or reddish for hot sun, then the candidate was rejected, for he would bring drought and famine. Almost everywhere, white systematically opposed black, and red was often somewhere between; but the moral qualities of the opposed colors changed from place to place and from one situation to another, according to the world-view of the particular society. Color symbolism illustrates once more how similarities in the culture of royal rule across East and Central Africa were merely secondary elaborations of a deeply rooted common cultural heritage.

The theme of the hunter-king was as common and drew on symbols as widely recognized as the royal black-white-red symbolism. The traditions of many kingdoms throughout tropical Africa tell of dynasties founded by a heroic wandering hunter. In East Africa, they include many Kimbu, Nyamwezi, and Sukuma chiefly lines. Shambaa traditions of northeastern Tanzania tell of a founding hunter-king who distributed meat to the people and killed the wild pigs that had destroyed the crops. Still other hunter-founders are remembered in the small states west of Lake Victoria, as well as in Buganda, the largest kingdom north of the lake.

These traditions do not mean that an army of hunters marched across the region founding states. But hunter myths seemed particularly appropriate in describing kingship and political power. Their meaning may have differed slightly from one place to another, but the same broad themes are found in most. Hunting is first of all a powerful masculine activity, and the myth was often used to explain male dominance within a village. In farming societies, men were responsible for protecting their land from wild animals, in much the same way that the king protects his territory from invaders. This is one reason the Shambaa king is described as a hunter of wild pigs that destroy crops, and why the term for the guard of Kimbu chiefs recalls the word for guards against marauding baboons. Just as an ordinary man hunted for his family, the king or chief collected cattle and distributed meat at his court — whether the cattle came from tribute or as booty from raids. Some Nyamwezi chiefs were addressed as *wanyama,* "of the meat."

The king's power to take cattle from his subjects, to eat meat, to act as the supreme hunter was like that of a lion which could enter a village at night, kill a cow, and leave. In states with the hunter myth, lion imagery is also very important for kingship — with lions' claws in headdresses, the king ritually smeared with lion fat, or called "the lion." Success in the hunt was also a sign of magical power, since hunters without magic could spend days looking for game without killing anything. The king (or chief) was the only person who could order the death of a subject, and rites of kingship are often explicit in describing the hunter-king as a killer. Public ritual in East and Central Africa is strikingly different in this respect from the public ritual of societies with a European political heritage. Centralized power obviously rests on the power to kill criminals or traitors, and external enemies through warfare. Yet public rituals in the United States such as inaugurations, campaign speeches, or national holidays usually allude to the protection of citizens and the maintenance of peace. Precolonial African public rituals tell of these things, too, but they are more honest in laying bare the deadly basis of power.

The hunter symbols themselves are older than the states where the myths were told. They appear in many contexts, even in stateless areas. In eastern Tanzania, where the hunter-chief myths were very common, the Ngulu give the hunter a key symbolic role in girls' initiation rites, which have nothing to do with political leadership but are associated with the defense of territory. In the same region, the hunter Sheuta ("father of the bow") is invoked as the first ancestor from whom all lineages are descended, with strong evidence that early Shambaa kings simply borrowed the Sheuta myth in order to apply it to their founding hero.

A similar process of taking on an ancient myth probably occurred in Bunyoro, where Ruhanga is the Creator God but the name *Hangi* is also remembered in some clan traditions as a hunter and the first man to settle in Bunyoro. The hunter-founders of the most recent dynasty are therefore heirs to a long legendary tradition.

THE CHWEZI

The traditions about hunter-kings are called myths because they express basic truths about society, yet they sometimes (not always) have a basis in historical fact. The Kimbu myths of founding chiefs, for example, have expressive value, but many are also historically correct in describing early chiefs who were hunters. Myths and the history of myths, as we saw in Chapter 4, can yield historical knowledge. The history of the Chwezi dynasty can serve as an example, for it is a classic case. Bunyoro and Nkore (Ankole) in western Uganda are the most prominent kingdoms with Chwezi traditions, and among the oldest in East Africa. Historians seeking to date their origins have often begun with the Chwezi traditions.

The myth, as told in Bunyoro, places the Chwezi in the middle of three historical epochs — the first dominated by the gods, the second by the Chwezi, the third by the Lwo from the north. The center of power in Chwezi times lay to the south of central Bunyoro, in the kingdom remembered by the name *Kitara*. According to the myth, the Chwezi takeover began during the reign of Isaza, the last of the earlier dynasty, part gods, part kings descended directly from the Creator God. The lord of the underworld sent out his choicest cattle to tempt Isaza, who kept and treasured them. One day the cattle wandered off, but the king followed them into a deep pit. When he tried to get them out, the earth swallowed him up, and forever after Isaza was a captive of the underworld.

Meanwhile, the kingdom was run by Isaza's humble gatekeeper, who became the founder of the Chwezi dynasty, though he is not remembered as a Chwezi. Instead, the myth gives his descendants legitimate royal origins by having Isaza's son return briefly from the underworld as a hunter. He encountered the gatekeeper's daughter, impregnated her, and thus fathered the first Chwezi king. In fact, only two Chwezi kings are remembered. The myth has it that they ruled in succession until local strife and evil omens convinced the last to leave. When the Chwezi disappeared, their place was taken by Lwo from the north, founders of the dynasty that held power until the twentieth century.

Of the three phases of Nyoro traditional history, only the Chwezi period is subject to profound historical controversy. No responsible historian thinks the story of the gods before Isaza has any accessible historical meaning; nor do scholars question the real existence of the modern line of kings descended from the Lwo. But the Chwezi exist in the half-light tantalizingly near to historic events, yet disturbingly mythical in their actions and origins. Many mythical episodes cannot be accepted as factual — such as the indentations in the rocks remembered as footprints made by the Chwezi, the "people of the moon," on their way out of the country, where the last ruler is said to have disappeared down the crater lakes of western Uganda.

One does not need to accept the reality of the footprints, however, to find historical clues in the myths. Two kinds of evidence suggest that a kingdom really did exist. First, a great many clan traditions within the Nyoro successor kingdom supply circumstantial details about the activities of local social groups during the Chwezi period. Some clans remember being allied with the gatekeeper, others with the gatekeeper's Chwezi successors. Clan traditions suggest, moreover, that the Chwezi period was no brief interlude of two reigns, but a longer time of continuing change. The two named Chwezi kings were possibly symbols of longer periods.

The second piece of evidence for the historicity of the Chwezi is the capital site at Bigo. Large earthworks that have been excavated here reveal a structure resembling more modern royal enclosures, with a large area for keeping cattle. The structure suggests political centralization, because it would have taken several thousand men a period of years to move the volume of earth used in Bigo's construction. Bigo's radiocarbon dates point to about the sixteenth century.

The tradition's combination of historical probability and historical impossibility, of living people and supernatural spirits, is a product of the long history of the myth itself. It probably began before the royal period with tales about nature spirits. At the time of the Chwezi kings the tales were already being told. With the death of the kings, the history of their reigns took the form of earlier legends. This is why major Chwezi heroes usually have a dual character. One of the first rulers, for example, is remembered not only in royal traditions, but also as the spirit of smallpox which must be propitiated. The nature spirit and the historical figure are joined in a story about an epidemic of smallpox (or possibly some other disease characterized by pustules) which struck that king's army. His Mubende Hill shrine is important in Nyoro royal rituals, and it is also remembered as the residence of a pre-Chwezi priestess to the god of smallpox.

The assimilation of spirit cults to historical events can be seen from recent examples. The Nyoro divide spirits into two types, white and black. The Chwezi are called white, but the black spirits are more numerous, though less benevolent. A number of black spirits have been added in the twentieth century, including the spirits of "Europeanness," of the army tank (called "rhinocerosness"), of the airplane, and of Mpolandi (the spirit of Polishness, discovered during World War II when a large camp of Polish expatriates was established nearby). Black spirits existed long before the airplanes or the Poles, but the actual historical experience was incorporated into a continually developing spirit world.

The remarkable work of Peter Schmidt in the Haya states further south more fully documents the way in which ancient myths become joined to traditions about later historic figures.[1] The traditions about King Rugamora Mahe are strikingly similar to the Chwezi legends, and here too the royal line appears to have associated itself with earlier shrines to strengthen its legitimacy. Rugamora Mahe, whose capital site was near a tree named "the ironworker's hut tree," was said to have ordered the construction of an iron tower. When Schmidt excavated the capital site, he found the remains of an iron smelting furnace (the tower?) and of an ironworker's hut, with the ironworkings carbon-dated to the sixth century B.C., older than any other Early Iron Age site of the great lakes region. The tradition was therefore passed on continuously for over two millennia; along the way, it absorbed elements of the Chwezi myth as well as details of Rugamora Mahe's royal line.

Much of the scholarly literature on early East African history has to do with the earliest kingdoms and the spread of kingship. Historians have returned again and again to these questions: Where did the Chwezi come from? Where did they acquire the institution of kingship? And where did they carry it after they were driven from Kitara? But these are unproductive questions. Even if we were able to learn the "origin" of the Chwezi, which seems extremely unlikely, the origins of the institution of kingship probably lie in the period before detailed traditions began. The story of Rugamora Mahe shows that some early events are remembered for millennia, but the descriptions are so compressed and elliptical that evidence outside the traditions must be found for historical reconstruction. Possibly some pre-Chwezi gods were actually kings. We shall never know.

[1] Peter R. Schmidt, *Oral Tradition and Archaeology* (New York: Africana Publishing Company, forthcoming).

The Chwezi case also illustrates two important points. First, ideas, symbols, and myths that have great meaning and emotional power enter into life at all social levels, from the royal court down to the most ordinary household. Nyoro mediums communicated with Chwezi spirits both at the court and in isolated villages. The spirit medium at the court attempted to insure the well-being of the state, while the mediums among ordinary people were concerned with the prosperity of the household and appealed to an individual Chwezi called the "household spirit" or the "trusted thing of the household."

Second, cultural elements that could be used to build kingdoms were often carried from one society to another by ordinary people. Humble practitioners, often women, who traveled from place to place healing and initiating new mediums carried the cult of Chwezi mediumship and respect for the spirits over hundreds of miles. In some new areas, it had no association with kings and chiefs. Given the adaptability of the ideas about spirits, Chwezi mediumship could possibly have moved from one place to another as a healing cult of ordinary people, only to be used later by intrusive kings whose origins were not associated in any way with these spirits.

AUTHORITY ON THE COAST

The Muslims of the coast are a special case in African political culture, because coastal rulers claimed overseas origins and their political forms and rituals were clearly Middle Eastern. While hosts and strangers in the interior grew more alike each year in ritual and symbolic usage, alien cultural elements on the coast were periodically renewed and returned to their original forms. This periodic renewal was possible, first of all, because the speed and ease of sea travel brought new groups of visitors in successive generations. Islamic culture was not left to develop local forms, but was reintroduced over and over again. In addition, the Koran and other Islamic writings made it possible for religious leaders to identify departures from orthodox practice and to prove the legitimacy of their demands for a return to the earlier way.

The rites and myths of the interior or those of the non-Islamic cultures on the coast, by contrast, were transmitted orally. Non-Islamic ideas and customs changed over the centuries, but the alteration in any one year was imperceptible. Lacking adequate records of past practice, no one individual fully perceived the magnitude of change. With Islam, writings were an independent standard of religious thought and practice that preserved the unique features of the religion, prevented it from merging with local practice, and created a religious duality between Islam and the local religions, as happened in West Africa as well.

This religious duality was also preserved through the growth of appropriate political and economic institutions. The small Islamic coastal towns had close ties of mutual dependence with the non-Islamic peoples of the coastal region, but each group had its own specialized functions that separated the two populations and the two ways of life. Until the eighteenth century, for example, the Muslims of the towns (except in the extreme south) specialized in sea trade and made no attempt to enter the interior, while the mainlanders monopolized overland trade without attempting to compete with the Muslims on the sea. Coastal towns and mainland peoples had separate chiefs who made formal agreements to divide their spheres of authority. In rare cases, the chief of the coastal town agreed never to go into the interior, while the mainland chief agreed not to see the water's edge.

Yet even with institutionalized separation and with the book to correct deviation, the two groups borrowed religious practices from one another. Spirits entered the bodies of Muslims and non-Muslims alike, demanding propitiation or responding to exorcism. Some Muslims went to mainland medicine men when they became ill, swore blood brotherhood like the mainlanders, and adopted local initiation rites for their young people. Aspirants to prestige and power in the coastal towns acquired histories of descent from overseas Muslims. The Persian or Arabian pedigrees, like the hunter stories of the interior, were sometimes rooted in fact; however, even when a dynasty had originated abroad, its living heritage came from generations of intermarriage and cultural exchange in East Africa.

Just as Muslims never became part of the allied mainland societies, few non-Muslims lived as freemen in the towns. Local religions within the towns were supposedly confined to slaves. If a mainlander converted to Islam, his family could move into the urban upper classes only if its pedigree was accepted; preferably, this would show its descent from the Prophet Muhammad. But it was possible to be a Muslim yet not a *mwungwana,* or true noble, or yet a "Shirazi," with origins in Shiraz on the Persian Gulf.

The combination of Islamic practice and alien pedigree in the Swahili city-states along the coast bred a society based on rigid class lines, similar to the pastoral society of central Rwanda. It grouped together the ruler and the more prestigious and powerful members of society and gave this entire elite separate symbols of identity. Class, in either place, was determined by birth rather than by achievement. In Rwanda, both classes spoke the same language. On the coast, the Swahili language (and its ancestors) was East African in origin and was spoken by all members of society. The crucial difference was that the oral transmission of culture in Rwanda led to a homogeneous culture, whereas the partially literate transmission of culture on the coast preserved sharp religious differences.

LINEAGE POLITICS AND INEQUALITY

As in Central and West Africa, East African political units over the past thousand years varied enormously in size, ranging from large kingdoms down to autonomous self-governing lineages in societies commonly called stateless, which resembled those of the Tiv and most Ibo in West Africa. Most of the East

African kingdoms were located north and west of Lake Victoria, while small chiefdoms and self-governing lineages predominated over much of present-day Kenya, Tanzania, and northern Uganda. But great diversity in size masked fundamental similarities, for lineages were as important in large states as they were in areas of decentralized political authority. Almost everywhere in Africa the lineage rather than the individual paid tribute or answered to the court of law. In East Africa as in West, the right to supply the ruler or to exercise some other political function was often assigned to a lineage. It is therefore important to look at African lineages in some detail — in the immediate context of East African history, though with broader implications for the continent as a whole, for the institution is found from the Berbers of the far northwest to the Zulu of the far southeast.

Kinship is, indeed, much alike in all human societies, but kin groupings were more important politically in Africa than they were in most European, American, or Asian societies. In most societies, a person who thinks of close kinfolk thinks of a mother, father, sisters, and brothers, though the group of close relatives is larger where polygyny is practiced. The crucial political distinction, however, is the line between kinsmen and nonkinsmen, and that line is drawn very differently in Africa from the usual practice in Europe, America, or many parts of Asia. African lineages, unlike Euro-American kin groupings, have precise boundaries between members and nonmembers and make a clear distinction between those who assume joint responsibilities and those who do not.

When most Europeans or Americans consider the limits of kinship, they think in terms of widening circles, of an ever larger group of cousins, aunts, and uncles until, in the end, those who are "too distant" are left outside. "Distance" in this sense is reckoned according to how far back one must go before finding a shared ancestor. The closer the shared ancestor, the closer the relative. Sisters and brothers — children of the same parents — are the closest. People who share grandparents are still very close. But the limit is vague. Do all the descendants of your great-grandparents count as kinfolk? Of your great-great-grandparents? Politically significant kin groupings are weak because of the shading off with distant relations. Without clear borders, the kin group as a whole cannot assume joint obligations or act as a corporation.

An arbitrary border might be laid down were it not for a second characteristic of Western and much of Asian kinship. Male and female links count equally in the chain of reckoning, back to grandparents or great-grandparents and then down again to cousins. Seen from the point of view of an individual, one's mother's relatives and one's father's relatives are in every sense equivalent. But, seen from the point of view of the relatives themselves, each group regards the other as mere relatives by marriage, not true kinsmen. This happens because husband and wife are related to one another "by blood" in only a single way — through the birth of their children. Only full siblings, therefore, can agree on a full set of common relations. To all others, at least half are excluded, as related by marriage.

FIGURE 1.

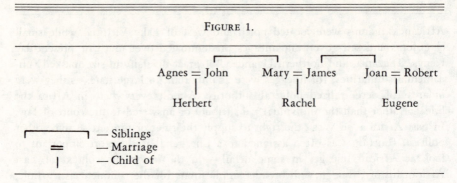

Agnes = John   Mary = James   Joan = Robert
      | | |
   Herbert   Rachel   Eugene

┌─────────┐   — Siblings
    =   — Marriage
    | — Child of

This is shown in Figure 1. Rachel's cousins include Herbert and Eugene, although Herbert would say that Rachel is a cousin but that Eugene is not, while Eugene, for his part, would not recognize Herbert as a kinsman. It is impossible therefore for kinsmen to assume legal obligations because each individual defines the group differently. If a law were passed, for example, that kinsmen must make equal contributions toward the payment of university tuition fees, then all three would pay for Rachel's but only two of the three would pay for either of the others.

In a lineage, the reckoning of kin starts from a single dead ancestor and includes all his or her descendants either through male links (in which case the system is patrilineal) or through female links (matrilineal), rather than starting from a living individual and working back to multiple ancestors. All the people in Figure 2, for example, as descendants of Hamza, are members of a single patrilineage. Notice that Rehema is a member, even though she is a woman, because she is descended from Hamza through a male. But Rehema's children will not be members of the lineage, because they will be related to it through a female; instead, they will belong to the lineage of Rehema's husband.

A lineage as a whole can assume a legal obligation because it is a bounded group with a clear membership. Thus, a rule could require that should any one of the descendants of Hamza commit a crime, then all the descendants of Hamza

FIGURE 2.

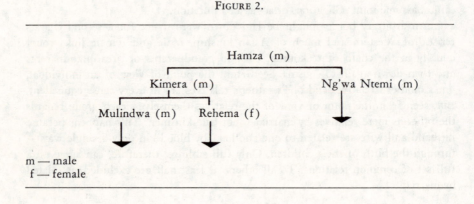

Hamza (m)

Kimera (m)   Ng'wa Ntemi (m)
      | ↓
Mulindwa (m)   Rehema (f)
      ↓   ↓

m — male
f — female

would be held responsible for paying a fine. If the lineage were too large and unwieldy for some governmental purposes, then a segment might assume the responsibility. While all the descendants of Hamza would pay a fine, the descendants of Ng'wa Ntemi might be required to send one man to the king's army, the descendants of Kimera another. Once the lineage grew beyond a certain size, each segment would become a separate lineage — the descendants of Ng'wa Ntemi and the descendants of Kimera, with Hamza quite possibly forgotten.

Lineages often provided essential insurance to individual householders. In case of partial, local famine, for example, an individual's survival was threatened. Cheap transportation was not available to bring in food, and individuals had little accumulated wealth with which to buy their way out of a crisis. The lineage, as a larger group, could share its resources. Kin who were more fortunate would lend food or use lineage wealth to buy food, expecting similar aid for themselves in case of need. This often meant the margin of survival to an individual householder.

Members also relied on one another for help in times of political uncertainty or individual crisis. Where no state apparatus existed, an individual attacked by an outsider could usually depend on his or her lineage for defense, or for help in arguing a case before the local joint council of lineage elders. In times of general insecurity, the lineage was often the key to the individual's survival. It could provide armed men for protection. When a member was taken captive in a raid, a fund of common lineage wealth was sometimes used to pay the ransom.

As prisons were virtually unknown in the East African interior, the lineages in association with the state (where it existed) controlled criminals. Among self-governing lineages, if one person injured another, the lineage whose member had suffered would demand the punishment of the offender or compensation. Even where kings and chiefs held courts of law, lawbreakers were normally called to justice by the lineages of the persons harmed, and the most common judgment required criminals or their lineages to pay compensation to the victims. If compensation could not be paid, lawbreakers were taken by the chief as slaves, so that a lineage's willingness to pay determined whether a person would lose his or her freedom for a criminal act. Here again the lineage provided insurance; those who paid a relative's fine were paying the equivalent of a premium, so that they themselves would be insured in their own time of trouble.

The range of variation in African social organization, as in so much else, should not be underestimated. Not all societies were strictly matrilineal or patrilineal. Some had elements of both: land, for example, might be transmitted through male links, and ritual leadership through female links. Others resembled European kinship systems. Pure lineage forms of organization, although vital for understanding many African societies, are one end of a continuum of social forms.

In most African societies, fines, famine food, or ransoms were paid in special goods that served as stores of value but that did not normally enter everyday exchange. In much of East Africa, special lineage payments were made in livestock, either cows or goats — but this varied from one society to another, the only clear rule being that high-value lineage goods needed to be rare or they would lose their value. In some places, where iron was very scarce, iron hoes were used to pay lineage debts; in other places, cowrie shells from the Indian Ocean were used. Ownership of great quantities of these special goods conferred prestige, which was somewhat separate from the day-to-day business of food production or survival.

Lineages, because they used the wealth of all members to insure individuals against some predictable risks, were usually seen as egalitarian. In fact, important kinds of inequality could exist within ordinary lineages of farmers and herders. In many cases, as we shall see, the stratification of kingdoms was merely lineage inequality writ large.

Unequal power within the lineage usually derived from unequal control of prestige goods. These goods were used not only in crises but also as bridewealth, the payment made by a man or his lineage segment to some members of his wife's lineage. Because most African societies were (and still are) polygynous, bridewealth served to control the distribution of wives, for some mechanism must exist to determine who will have many wives and who will have none. A man who wished to marry not only had to possess enough prestige goods to pay the bridewealth; he also had to have enough left over for lineage obligations and household crises.

A young man who wished to marry could begin to save bridewealth by selling his surplus crops for hens, then his hens for a goat, and later his goats for cattle. But bridewealth might be set so high that a young man could almost never pay on his own. He would need the help of someone with inherited wealth, usually his father. Sometimes the bride's father would also demand that the young man's father help negotiate the bridewealth, to ensure that his daughter entered a harmonious family.

All this meant that older men were in positions of control, because they decided when young men could marry and achieve full status as adults. In many polygynous societies, older men used this power to take a disproportionate share of the women, leaving men in their twenties wifeless. Where women did a very large share of the farming, as in most of East Africa, a man with more wives had access to a greater share of productive labor. The system tended to preserve equality of wealth among lineages (at least in patrilineal societies), since the richest lineage would take the most wives and its wealth in the next generation would then have to be divided among a greater number of children.

Inequality between old and young men was general in African lineage systems. While a young man might often work harder than his father or other elders, access to wives was determined not by current earnings but by access to prestige goods. The young man knew, however, that some day he would inherit his father's wealth, take more wives, and assume authority over his sons in turn.

The inequality between men and women was more fundamental, because women did not usually own prestige goods in sufficient quantities to make decisions about marriage age or about which men would be polygynous, although in most cases a woman could refuse to marry any particular man. In the majority of East Africa's agricultural societies, men decided where and how to farm, while women did most of the regular day-to-day work once men had cleared the farmland. Men hunted, went to war, argued court cases, arranged lineage affairs. Men's authority was especially clear in polygynous households, where the man as lone decision-maker could settle disputes and decide a course of action for two or more wives, while the women had to reach a unanimous decision to exert equal influence.

THE PROCESS OF DOMINATION

Another kind of early inequality occurred among lineages. With the emergence of early states, the king's lineage and closely associated lineages became comparatively rich and powerful. And the process could be reversed; just as states sometimes came into being when a lineage could dominate previously independent lineages in its neighborhood, large states sometimes broke down into small chiefdoms, and, in some rare cases, returned to self-government at the lineage level.

Of these processes, state formation has received the most attention from anthropologists and historians. Conquest once seemed the obvious explanation for lineage dominance, but that solution was too simple. Conquest presupposes that a few could dominate many through force of arms, but before firearms came to Africa, rulers and subjects usually had similar technologies. Because autonomous lineages were capable of banding together to resist an external threat, a small group of fighting men would have experienced great difficulty conquering unified resistance.

The evidence points to much more subtle processes. Although we will never know the exact events surrounding the emergence of the earliest East African states, we do have fuller evidence for developments in somewhat later periods — in post-Chwezi Uganda, for example. We have already seen that the Lwo migrations were decisive in the settlement of large areas of Uganda and neighboring lands. One by-product of these migrations was the emergence of a great many petty chiefdoms, even though the Lwo had a clearly articulated system of patrilineages, and in some places remained chiefless.

Our knowledge of the spread of Lwo chiefdoms is fullest for the Alur of northwestern Uganda and the nearby parts of Zaïre, because Alur expansion was still going on in the late precolonial period. It is therefore a useful illustration, even though the process was not the same everywhere. Alur chiefs and commoners today speak a Lwo language, but when the Lwo-speaking ancestors of chiefs first arrived in the area, they found people speaking languages very distant from Lwo — Madi, Lendu, Okebo — and these are still spoken at the edges of Alur society and beyond.

Expansion meant the proliferation of small-scale units. Multiplication of chiefdoms was a multiplication of lineage segments, and it took place in much the same way as the expansion of an ordinary lineage in most African societies. In an ordinary patrilineal household surrounded by unoccupied land, the farms cleared by the father belonged to him. Depending on the rule of inheritance, they would ultimately belong to one, or several, or all his sons. No matter what the rule, the one plot would not be large enough for a number of sons. One or two sons would count on inheriting the old man's farm, perhaps expanding it a bit. The others would move out, farming an adjacent or a distant plot depending on their personal relations with their father and the availability of good land. Ultimately, the father became the ancestor of a lineage; his sons became the ancestors of segments.

In an Alur chiefdom, the chief was the father of a household of minor chiefs. He would give some of his sons outlying portions of his territory to govern under his authority. Because chiefs usually took many wives and had many sons, some sons would be left without a piece of the old man's territory. Some would go without office, ultimately merging with the commoners. Chiefs often sent troublesome, unruly sons to govern territories at the very edges of the chiefdom, where they would either prove themselves or fail. At times, neighboring Lendu or Okebo would invite the chief to send a son. This happened, for example, when one of a pair of feuding Lendu lineages allied itself with an Alur chief in order to dominate the second. At this point, the second would ally itself with a second Alur chief, provoking a third competing lineage to seek its own ally. Under these circumstances, an invited chief could make only the smallest demands on his subjects, but informal chiefship became stronger with the passage of years. After a time, one of two things happened to a minor son at the border: if he prospered, he could make his territory the center of a new expanding chiefdom; or, with his father's death and the succession of his brother at the old center, he might be replaced by his brother's son, in which case he would seek a new territory beyond the fringes of the old chiefdom. The cumulative effect of sons seeking territories was the constant expansion of the area under Alur domination, even though no one chiefdom ever grew to be very large.

It is impossible, of course, to know how the very first Alur chiefdom began, but three overlapping possibilities are evident. First, it is possible that some Alur attracted followings because of their reputations as rain magicians. Certainly Alur chiefs of more recent periods have enjoyed the support of subjects who expected to benefit from chiefly control of the rains. The second possibility is that the Alur came as predatory lineages, lineages that were larger than those of the Lendu, Okebo, or Madi, and were therefore able to dominate the original population, ultimately absorbing more and more territory and client populations.

The predatory lineage is one potential answer to the general question of domination in lineage-based society, because lineages everywhere vary widely in size and internal differentiation. The third possibility was for a clever leader to make alliances tying together several lineages. Perhaps the Lwo immigrants allied themselves with one side in the lineage feuds among earlier inhabitants. Factions form and break up continuously in lineage-based society, but a faction in permanent control was the core of a chiefdom.

This process can be seen with the greatest clarity in the case of the Shambaa kingdom in northeastern Tanzania. The kingdom was founded in the eighteenth century, which is very late for centralization in East Africa, but it took place in an area where there were no large kingdoms. It is more certain here than in the great lake kingdoms that the political unit was not an offshoot of an earlier state, but grew out of lineage-based society.

The territories that ultimately became chiefdoms (that is, subordinate governmental units within the kingdom) had been tightly knit social units *before* political centralization took place. These protochiefdoms were clusters of permanent large villages, with each cluster in the middle of a piece of land about ten miles across, fairly empty of population at the edges. This clustering came from the Shambaa pattern of mountain farming. Villages were placed near the crest of the escarpment so that some members of each lineage could farm in the plains below, while others farmed in the highlands. These village clusters were more permanent than many others in East Africa because they were at the midpoint among scattered farms. Because most productive land was far from home, soil exhaustion did not create pressures to move the village.

Within each village cluster, political integration built on the social integration that already existed because of the marriage pattern. Representatives of two lineages in a particular generation would make blood pacts swearing loyalty to one another, then make a great number of marriages between their members. Their rules for marriage then forced children of the next generation to seek alliances in some other, as yet unrelated, lineages within the cluster. This led to a pattern in which most people were related to most others. The early chiefs thus took control of tightly knit social units.

The founding king entered this society at a time of conflict between the Shambaa and new immigrants who did not accept Shambaa ways of marriage and of settling local conflicts. He created a larger political unit by choosing two or three significant village clusters and then making alliances with the most influential lineage in each by marriage and the blood pact. Continuity was assured when he placed his capital in one important territory, making a member of its most influential lineage a court official, but then named his son by a wife from a second territory the royal heir.

This outline of political consolidation by predatory lineages (with the Alur) or multiple interlineage alliances (with the Shambaa) is, of course, a form of oversimplification. It says nothing about the actual exercise of power, the subtle day-by-day play of political strategy, or the personality or emotional sources of support available to early leaders. Nor does it describe the particular historical circumstances in which people felt the need to expand the political scale. These circumstances necessarily vary from case to case. With both Alur and Shambaa, however, the state arose when people of drastically different cultural and linguistic backgrounds came to live side by side and needed either to merge cultures and form a single social organization or else to let one group dominate the rest. The Alur spoke Western Nilotic languages and came to live alongside the earlier Central Sudanic speakers, while the Shambaa were Bantu-speakers among whom Cushitic migrants had recently settled.

Once the kingdoms had been founded, lineage dynamics continued to have profound influence. All lineages go through periodic crises as generations succeed one another. When the structure of the royal lineage was the framework of the state — as it was among the Alur and the Shambaa — these crises were amplified and became recurrent crises in the life of the state. Each Shambaa king, for example, attempted to make his sons rulers of the subordinate chiefdoms. Once the sons were in office, the king's word was obeyed through the land, because his authority as a father over his sons reinforced that of a king over his chiefs. The chiefs paid tribute to the royal court, joined in the united army of the kingdom, and allowed their subjects to appeal judicial verdicts to the king and his council. But when such a king had ruled successfully for a period and finally died, the senior son who became the next king found himself in a difficult position. He tried but invariably failed to become a centralizing father-king. The existing chiefs were his half-brothers, who saw no reason to obey someone of their own generation. They knew that if they united in resistance to his authority, they would all survive in power. Their close kinship made combined action easy. They paid no tribute, kept completely independent armies, and maintained their own courts of final appeal. In effect, the kingdom broke up into a number of temporarily self-sufficient minikingdoms.

This fluctuation between centralization and decentralization could take place only when every function of government was duplicated at the lower level, when a local capital was a full replica of the central capital. The local chiefdom duplicated the king's apparatus for collecting tribute, his judicial organization, and his army. This pattern contrasts sharply with the government of any twentieth-century nation, in Africa or elsewhere, in which particular functions are specifically reserved for central or for local government.

The strengthening of the central state apparatus, where it occurred, took two forms. First, kings sometimes separated the affairs of the royal lineage from those of the state. In some cases, a senior son became king while another took charge of ritual lineage affairs. In others, all state officials were members of commoner lineages, a system denying a power base to royals. In virtually all cases, the king underwent rites of passage that separated him and made him seem different from his close relatives. Second, kings might try to monopolize some governmental functions that were not duplicated at the local level. It then became more difficult for subordinate units to withdraw and proclaim their independence.

The clearest separation of the king's lineage from governmental affairs was found in the kingdom of Buganda, north of Lake Victoria. Clans (descent groups larger than lineages) were politically important in Buganda, but no royal clan was allowed to exist. Ganda clans and Ganda kingship were patrilineal, but the king took his mother's clan name and clan symbols, so that each king had a different clan from his predecessor; in this way, no continuity of royal clan interests developed. Buganda therefore emerged by the eighteenth century as one of the most powerful kingdoms of the region, capable of expanding at the expense of its neighbors and achieving a very stable centralized authority. Not only were close kinsmen of the king prohibited from becoming territorial chiefs; by later precolonial times, princes were even forbidden to live at the court of any chief, and, in some cases, the king's brothers were killed to eliminate the threat of rebellion.

The other possibility, that of keeping some important functions in the hands of the central government alone, was most effective when the king could build a standing army directly under his control, one that was not called up at the first instance by the individual subchiefs. Buganda tried to move in this direction in the mid-nineteenth century, after firearms were introduced, but the most famous example was to be the Zulu kingdom of South Africa in the early nineteenth century.

TRIBUTE IN THE ECONOMY OF EARLY KINGDOMS

Almost everyone in early precolonial East Africa worked at producing food for household consumption, but famine struck often as a result of drought, locusts, or cattle disease. In this setting it was a burden to support specialists of any kind, whether a political elite, blacksmiths, medicine men, or kings. Medicine men and blacksmiths were not a serious problem; they often farmed part-time, and they were thinly dispersed over the countryside. But a royal court was a nonfood-producing concentration in a single spot, even though a surprising number of the elite found time in their daily rounds to tend gardens.

Some East African kingdoms solved this problem by placing the court in the richest, most fertile region with the greatest possibility of a surplus. In others, the entire capital was moved periodically, so as not to exhaust the resources of any one locality. In still others, a centralized fighting force enabled a king to raid his neighbors for the court's upkeep. Some kingdoms and chiefdoms, especially in the nineteenth century, lived off profits and commissions from trade. Still others, however, collected tribute, like water from a rock, in poor and unproductive regions.

Where tribute (rather than plunder or profit from trade) was the main source of support, a limited variety of payments was found all across East

Africa. One kind was paid in the prestige goods also used as bridewealth — usually livestock, but sometimes iron hoes or other products. These goods helped the king to reward his friends and helpers, sometimes to gain new supporters; for example, he might help a poor but loyal young man to marry or, more rarely, buy the services of young bachelors by promising to pay bridewealth in the indefinite future. A second kind of tribute was nonprestige food items such as flour, plantains, or the like to be used for the court's day-to-day subsistence. Third, subjects provided service by working on the chief's farms or maintaining paths, building houses at the court, or serving in the military. Fourth, in some cases tribute was paid in regional specialties. In Buganda, for example, where chiefdoms within the larger kingdom extended inland from Lake Victoria, the fishermen at the lake's edge were responsible for supplying fish. Specialized hunters in many places were required to give the chief one tusk of every elephant killed. Finally, some special goods of no great subsistence value were respected as chiefly symbols to be paid as tribute whenever found. Subjects of the Chewa kingdoms of Malawi, for example, were required to give their rulers the red feathers of certain birds.

In states that collected tribute, two quite different economic relationships tied subjects to the king, though both could coexist in a single kingdom at the same time. One was a territorial relationship, found almost everywhere, in which each lineage or segment within the state's boundaries had to pay tribute. In return, the king assumed a set of general obligations to all his subjects. A second, patron-client relationship might also exist, in which the king or chief had a special relationship with some lineages but not with others. It usually began with a gift from the king or chief to the head of a lineage segment. That segment in turn owed special obligations to its benefactor.

In Bunyoro and in the Shambaa kingdom, the economic relationship was territorially based. A number of chiefs appointed by the king collected tribute in their separate localities. In the Shambaa kingdom, the chief's representatives would travel from village to village collecting livestock to be delivered to the court after they had taken a portion for themselves. Some tribute collectors would go out on their own initiative, so that the chief first learned of their efforts when they brought the livestock to his court. Wise subjects paid up, but some also insisted on accompanying their payments to court so as to be credited by the chief and spared additional exactions. The chief also sent word when food was needed at court, and some subjects would voluntarily bring food after a good harvest. Chiefs in turn passed tribute on to the king, though he also received direct tribute from the small region immediately around his capital.

These payments were important, not only as support for the political establishment but also as symbolic statements of loyalty. A lineage head's refusal to pay tribute to his chief, or the chief's refusal to pay the king, were acts of rebellion. In the Shambaa case, a chief's refusal meant war, while for the commoner it could lead to his execution and the enslavement of his family. Nineteenth-century travelers' reports describe the king's soldiers hunting through the forests to find rebels who withheld tribute. Verbal assurances of loyalty were easy to make, but tribute was the real test. This situation is familiar in America, where "money talks." The resources used must be scarce to have meaning. It is for this reason that wealthy Americans receive high salaries for important jobs, even though their need is minimal and the needs of others desperate. If they were not given money that other people need, how would we know they were important? Thus, even in industrial society, payments have a crucial symbolic meaning.

Once tribute reached the chief's or king's court, it was used first to support political specialists, who in turn provided essential services for the benefit of all: defense, justice, sometimes religious rituals or magical ceremonies to keep the land prosperous and healthy. A second use, hard to disentangle from the first, was political: to pay off specific privileged groups whose support was essential for the exercise of power. In some cases, these were commoners living near the royal capital who were the king's first line of defense; in others, they were leaders of influential clans or lineages whose word carried great weight or who commanded armed men. Because the crucial political figures were those closest to the capital, payoffs of this kind went to those at the center, forcing the people of the fringes to subsidize the core region.

Ordinary subjects everywhere expected to pay the state more than they received directly in return. According to a proverb in Bunyoro, "What is given to the king does not return." The Shambaa expressed the same idea differently by calling the king the "owner of the land." They said he could not be bribed, for everything belonged to him. When you paid him, you were only giving him something that was already his.

PATRONS AND CLIENTS: RWANDA AND BUGANDA

The patron-client relationship, where it existed, functioned alongside territorial tribute collection. It emerged with the greatest clarity in a number of kingdoms west of Lake Victoria, and it has been most extensively described for Rwanda, where the occupational specialization of pastoralists and farmers heightened the interdependency of social groups and the complexity of the system. Rwanda's rulers were drawn from a stratum of society called Tutsi; the great majority of subjects were called Hutu. The Tutsi of central Rwanda thought of themselves as pastoralists who governed Hutu agriculturists. As so often when identity is based on economic activity, reality was much more complex than the accepted image; some Hutu were quite wealthy in cattle. But the image of Tutsi pastoralist rulers had ideological power and was true in many cases. As in many stratified societies, the social separation of Hutu and Tutsi was heightened by barriers to intermarriage.

The patron-client relationship in Rwanda was called *buhake,* derived from the verb meaning "to pay one's respects to a superior in his court." A person created the tie by approaching a richer, more powerful man to beg for "milk" and protection. "Be my father," he would say, "and I will be your son." The superior, if he wished to accept his client, would give the man a cow as a mark of the relationship. *Buhake* is best known from documents and traditions about the nineteenth century, and historians have been debating whether it existed in earlier centuries during the growth of the Rwanda kingdom. In these later times, when land became scarce, it is also clear that a form of clientship through the award of land existed alongside clientship through the award of a cow.

The king, a Tutsi, ruled through a complex administrative structure, with several different kinds of chiefs, virtually all of whom were Tutsi at the higher levels. In some cases, the network of patron-client relations ran parallel to the system of administration, so that the man who governed also served as patron to many of those he administered. In other cases, patron-client ties were used to create a network of political relationships cutting across the governmental hierarchy.

When a Hutu was client and a Tutsi chief his patron, he was expected to give service and loyal support. In return, he gained protection from other predatory Tutsi and exemption from some of the dues he would have owed the chief who was now his patron. The cow he received was a personal pledge of protection, very different from the impersonal provision of defense by a chief in a territorial tribute relationship. Until recently, anthropologists thought that the peasant gave loyalty, service, and tribute in return for the cow and the dairy products it provided. But recent studies of Rwanda diet show that milk and beef have had minimal importance in the farmers' subsistence. Nor could the cow be seen as an exchange for tribute, because the subjects who paid the most tribute were the ones who received nothing from their chief. The farmers without patrons were worst off because they had to do without protection and also without exemption from arbitrary demands for service. A Rwanda proverb says, "A dog is feared not for his fangs but for his master." Just as bridewealth was a mechanism for rationing wives, the payment of cows was a way of rationing clients among patrons in Rwanda. Each client normally had only one patron, but a wealthy and powerful patron had as many clients as he had cows for distribution. The number of a man's clients and supporters, limited only by his wealth in cows, was the clearest indication of his power.

The fact that cattle keepers ruled over farmers in Rwanda and Nkore led to speculation among earlier historians of Africa that the Tutsi may originally have been a separate people with their own language and culture, who long ago swept down from the north and conquered the tillers of the soil. In this view, all the pastoralist dynasties of the region — not only Rwanda and Nkore but also the mythical Chwezi — were originally invaders who brought the idea of the state with them and imposed their institutions by conquest. In fact, this view is simply another misconception about African history that was very heavily influenced by the Hamite myth. It is now thoroughly rejected.

Critics have shown that the "Hamitic" languages were incorrectly classified, and in any case, the pastoralists of the lake kingdoms speak the same Bantu languages as the farmers with whom they live. Linguistically, the Tutsi are no more "Hamitic" than the Hutu. Nor does the picture of pastoral conquest fit the Chwezi traditions, in which the mother of the first king was named *Nyinam-wiru,* which means "mother of the agriculturalist." Her father had been the royal gatekeeper, of humble origins, and her son the first king was brought up by a potter, and potters were members of the farming class.

Some critics went even further to argue that farmers and herders had a single origin back in the mists of time. Richer men became herders, while the poor farmed, so that the political institutions of Rwanda or Nkore could be considered simply government by the rich over the poor. This approach has important evidence in its favor. Agriculturalist war leaders in Nkore sometimes acquired livestock in battle, after which their descendants could become pastoralists. And each of the many Rwanda clans is mixed, including both farmers and herders who claim common descent. The difference in stature between the tall Tutsi and the shorter Hutu would then have to be explained by great differences in the animal protein content of their diets. But this explanation is weak from the point of view of biology. The two communities have a different distribution of blood types suggesting a long-term separation, if not a separate origin. Even this evidence is not conclusive, however. The distributions of A, B, and O blood types, for example, could have been inherited from separate distant ancestors; but they could have been caused just as easily by variations in the survival value of different blood types in diverse disease environments.

Another kind of biological evidence is the fact that lactase (the enzyme for digestion of milk sugar) is more frequently deficient among farmers in the kingdom of Buganda than it is among either Hutu or Tutsi. This difference might indicate separate origins for farmers and herdsmen, but it might also show long-term adaptation to the environment. If, at some distant time, both Ganda and Tutsi had had low frequencies of the lactase gene, lactase-deficient Tutsi who tried to live on a largely pastoral diet would have had a smaller chance of survival than those with lactase, having less nutritional benefit from imperfectly digested milk. Over the long term, those with the lactase gene would tend to survive and to pass it on to their children, while lactase deficiency would not have been so important for Ganda, whose main staple was the starchy plantain, related to the banana.

The meaning is clear. The pastoralist and agriculturalist communities of Rwanda and neighboring states have been separate from one another — have not intermarried in significant numbers — over a long historical period. Their separation fits the pattern of other groups in the region that developed specialized economies with cultural and even biological adaptations to particular microenvironments. In the extremely varied environment of Rwanda and Nkore, some of the landscape was appropriate for agriculture, other parts for herding. Specialized farming and herding groups lived side by side, each in its own environmental niche. These bits of pastoral and agricultural land, however, were interspersed, so that the interaction was more frequent than was possible on many other pastoral-sedentary frontiers, such as the fringes of Maasailand or of the Sahara. It is impossible to know, on the basis of current evidence, whether the pastoralists and agriculturalists all began as a single Bantu-speaking community whose economies became increasingly specialized with the passage of time, or whether they had diverse linguistic and cultural origins.

The large kingdoms ruled by pastoralists, like Rwanda, grew out of earlier symbiotic relationships (which survive today in some localities) between neighboring herdsmen and farmers. Pastoral rule over agriculturalists was not the invariable outcome. In Buganda, for example, the kings identified with the agricultural majority of their subjects, but gave their cattle into the care of herdsmen who occupied a weak and insignificant position in Ganda society. In Bunyoro, the herders enjoyed high prestige but were completely separate from the kings and princes. Perhaps the emergence of pastoral domination resulted from intense interaction in areas with fairly dense populations of herders.

While clientage in some lake-area kingdoms was established by paying a cow, patron-client relations based on land were relatively rare — in sharp contrast to medieval Europe's land-based feudal system. Cattle were more important than land in East Africa because of the combination of low population densities and poor, light soils. Unused land was easy to come by, and its preparation for planting did not usually involve a large labor investment. Each chief had an abundance of unoccupied land on which new subjects could quickly begin supporting themselves with their own crops. Land was not, therefore, a useful measure to determine which competing chiefs would win the most clients. The general point here is that control of a resource could be used to win control of people (whether through bridewealth or clientage) only if it was a *scarce* resource. When land was a *free* resource it could not play this role.

The few East African cases in which land was scarce and therefore served as the basis of royal domination are revealing illustrations. The most famous example is Buganda, where the king "owned" almost all the land and controlled people through control of the land. When he assigned an administrative territory to one of his chiefs, the appointment implied control over land used by ordinary cultivators. The king also created a separate and special class of chiefs (called *batongole*) who received independent estates within the domains of administrative chiefs. A great estate was a power base, for a chief could grant land to minor chiefs, and they to ordinary cultivators, all in return for political allegiance and tribute ultimately collected from the peasantry.

Buganda's banana and plantain gardens were the key to the economic, and therefore political, value of land. The climate of Buganda is unusually well suited for the cultivation of these plants, which not only are eaten as fruit but form the starchy staple of the diet and are even the main ingredient in brewing beer. Banana gardens require a considerable initial labor investment: the soil must be cleared and usually another, preparatory crop planted before the young banana plants can be put in and grown. In Buganda, once the plants are producing, however, they go on for decades with relatively little attention. Ordinary cultivators in Buganda therefore had a substantial investment in their land; moving to new land meant losing that investment. The fact that banana groves required a comparatively large investment and gave large yields meant in turn that the population was comparatively dense and stable. It then became worthwhile to make a further investment in infrastructure such as communications. Thus, each important chief used the labor owed by his subjects to construct footpaths four feet wide between his own seat and the capital.

As with cattle in Rwanda, land in Buganda took on a symbolic value as well. A person who lived on a chief's land was dependent on him and owed him loyal service as well as tribute. The most ancient and honored clans of Buganda had some land of their own, which did not come from the king, and were to that extent independent of the king's authority. It was clearly more important for those clan members to retain their own lands rather than to receive twice as much as the gift of the king — and sacrifice independence. One of the greatest rewards a king could bestow on an important chief was an estate exempt from royal taxes, which was therefore an independent power base. In the nineteenth century, if not earlier, ordinary peasants sometimes left their land to move to another place, where a kinsman was chief and political conditions more favorable. Transactions in land, in short, were not only economic but political, and the political relationship was sometimes valued more highly than the land payment that was its justification.

REGIONAL AND EXPORT TRADE
IN THE POLITICS OF THE INTERIOR BEFORE 1750

Regional trade networks across the East African interior existed through most of the Iron Age, with iron, salt, pottery, and grain exchanged for one another and carried from market to market. In the archaeological record and the record of traditions for the period before 1750, the nodes of the network, the most important centers of commercial production and trade, were not located on a political basis — at the courts of kings — but rather on the basis of production and transportation. Trade centers sometimes formed at lake ports for canoe traffic, or at the juncture between two climatic zones where growers of different food crops met, or where farmers in a hungry season could buy food from their neighbors whose crops had already been harvested.

Unlike the western Sudan, where large empires were closely related to trade, many of the richest trading networks in early East Africa thrived amid very small chiefdoms and in the border areas between kingdoms, where no one authority held supreme control. Evidence for early trade networks has been found, for example, at points where exploitable concentrations of salt or iron ore were located, often far from the major states. The archaeological excavation of Ivuna and Uvinza, two salt-producing sites in western Tanzania, shows evidence of extensive local trade from the thirteenth century, with no hint of state growth. Uvinza's political organization is known only for the nineteenth century, hundreds of years after the trade began. The salt springs were located where the borders of three chiefdoms converged, beyond the exclusive control of any one leader. In Uganda, evidence for the richest early trade based on salt and iron comes not from the great kingdoms but from a no-man's-land around Lakes Masyoro (George) and Rweni (Edward) — to the west of the kingdoms of Nkore and far to the north of the kingdom of Rwanda. Examples of trade within a kingdom, as in the fish for farm-produce trade of Buganda, have been taken incorrectly to show that political centralization makes commerce easier. Trade like this was, in fact, carried on all across East Africa wherever local specialties were found, whether within political boundaries or across them.

Control of trade goods contributed to the development of political authority only in the extreme southern part of East Africa, near the Zambezi, where long-distance trade between the coast and the Shona goldfields developed very early. By the fourteenth century, extensive trade passed between Ingombe Ilede, just north of the Zambezi, and the Indian Ocean coast over four hundred miles away. Archaeological excavations reveal that Ingombe Ilede (meaning "the place where cows sleep") was part of a local network of trade in salt, copper ornaments, and subsistence goods, as well as a long-distance network in goods of much higher value. The burials there show great differences in wealth between notables and ordinary people, with the richest dressed in cotton cloth, wearing copper and iron bangles on their arms and legs, and strings of gold, shell, and glass beads around their necks and waists. While some cloth was made locally, the gold was imported from the south, the shell and glass beads from the coast, and copper (which came in standardized ingots) from the mines of Zaïre and Zambia in the north. Local exports appear to have been mainly ivory and salt.

In the sixteenth century, the Portuguese, having rounded the Cape of Good Hope to make contact with the Indian Ocean world, sent representatives up the Zambezi in an attempt to wrest control of the gold trade from the coastal Muslims and the kings of the interior. While they directed their attention to the goldbearing regions south of the river, their presence provided a market for ivory collected in the developing Malawi kingdoms in the north, between the Zambezi and Lake Malawi.

The Malawi kingdoms represent the first clear case of trade-based political power in the East African interior. While the earliest leaders of the Malawi kingdoms relied on tribute, the monopoly that each king was supposed to hold over external trade in ivory became increasingly important. With the shift in political economy came a shift in the relative power of the competing kingdoms, in favor of those best placed for trade. By the seventeenth century, much of the ivory exported through the Portuguese Zambezian trading settlements originated in the Malawi kingdoms.

Here is the first glimmer of what was to become so important a development in later centuries: the ruler's reliance on external trade instead of internal tribute as a means of generating the political wealth used in rewarding his followers. The shift from tribute to trade, which had its faintest beginnings

near Lake Malawi, was momentous because, once completed, the stability of a
king's rule would depend not on his relations with tribute-paying subjects but on
his relations with outside traders. In any conflict of interest a king would be
forced to choose between outsiders who controlled the trade and citizens whose
lives and livelihoods might be at stake.

The difficulty of maintaining control in a trade-based state became clear in
the Malawi case. By the late seventeenth century, increasing numbers of Portuguese were meddling in Malawi affairs, so that even minor subchiefs had alien
trading partners and therefore independent sources of authority. The successful
Malawi trading kingdoms therefore began to break up because it was impossible

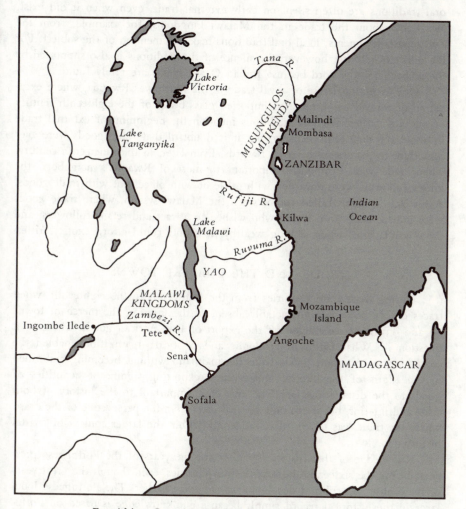

East African Coastal Politics and Export Trade, 1500–1750

to maintain a royal monopoly when alien traders were free to enter the land.

As the Malawi kingdoms weakened, their role in the trade also declined. In the late seventeenth and eighteenth centuries, the Yao, to the east of Lake Malawi, traded directly to the coastal ports of northern Mozambique, replacing the Malawian links with the inland Portuguese settlements on the Zambezi. Yao political organization was more decentralized and therefore better able to absorb the shocks of changing trade conditions. Minor leaders rose and fell along with their success in trade.

The increasing importance of trade goods for political leadership in the Zambezi-Lake Malawi area appears to have no close parallel in the regions to the north. The negative evidence, however, is very difficult to interpret, since oral traditions are often silent on early external trade, even when it did exist. We know about the trade in the Malawi kingdoms, for example, from the Portuguese documents; local oral traditions make no mention of the subject. For the northern interior, however, the silence of the traditions is also supported by the archaeological record because Indian Ocean goods are rarely found.

One exceptional case of royal trade in the north was Rwanda, where excavation of a royal grave revealed imported glass beads of the eighteenth century or perhaps earlier. Rwanda traditions mention the beginning of external trade in about the eighteenth century, but it is doubtful that trade goods were ever important to the system of royal rewards. Even later, in the nineteenth century, when trade was enormously important to most of Rwanda's neighbors, the king's followers were rewarded with cattle or with office, not with trade goods. A distinction seems called for between the Malawi system, where trade goods were indispensable to a leader who wished to attract and retain followers, and the Rwanda case, where a king wealthy in tribute could afford exotic rarities.

TRADE AND THE COASTAL TOWNS

During these same centuries from the fourteenth to the eighteenth, when traces of overseas trade are notably absent in the interior, the merchant towns up and down the coast lived off the export of East African goods. The crucial question is: What forms of economic and political organization enabled the coastal towns to export goods from the mainland without becoming embroiled in the affairs of the interior and without exporting significant quantities of goods to the distant interior? The answer is important to the history of both coast and interior, but it can only be answered from the perspective of the coast, where the trade was taking place, and only within the larger context of coastal history.

Knowledge of that history is fullest for the years of the Portuguese presence during the sixteenth and seventeenth centuries, even though the great years of mercantile and cultural development had come earlier. The Portuguese loom large in the historical record simply because our knowledge is based on Portuguese sources, beginning with the record of Vasco da Gama's exploration of the east coast in 1498. Not many Portuguese lived in East Africa at any one time, and few of those settled north of what is now the Tanzania-Mozambique border. In 1586, nearly ninety years after Vasco da Gama, the total number on this enormous coast was about fifty. Clearly, they were unable to administer affairs on a day-to-day basis or even to make a minor impact on the culture of the coastal towns. But scattered Portuguese could still intervene powerfully in East African political and commercial affairs because of the superiority of their seaborne cannon to any arms produced or used in East Africa. Their ships, of much heavier construction than the Indian Ocean vessels, were floating platforms for heavy cannon. In other respects, Indian Ocean and Portuguese seamanship were roughly comparable. The local pilot who joined Vasco da Gama on the Kenya coast to guide his ships to India knew how to use the navigational instruments on board. Throughout the sixteenth and seventeenth centuries, the principal naval base and capital of all Portugal's Eastern operations was Goa on the west coast of India. The Portuguese actually in East Africa at any given time were too weak to maintain their position by force, but coastal leaders who fought the Portuguese could expect punishment by a fleet from Goa.

All this meant that the Portuguese were much more capable of destroying than of building power on the coast, especially in the sixteenth century. Kilwa, for example, had been the most important trading town between the late twelfth century and the end of the fifteenth century. It resisted the Portuguese intrusion and went down to defeat in 1505. But the Portuguese victory was not the beginning of extended rule. They could do little more than tax the place. Within three or four years, the inhabitants had moved out to competing coastal towns. By 1512, when the Portuguese withdrew from Kilwa, the town had been reduced to insignificance.

Conquest of a town was not equivalent to control of its trade. After Kilwa declined, the Portuguese traded at Sofala, further south. As soon as this happened, a major part of the trade moved to a competing town, Angoche, just beyond the reach of the Europeans. Only by establishing posts up the Zambezi to control the interior sources were the Portuguese able to take over a significant portion of the trade.

In most places, they were forced by their poverty in manpower to accept the continuation of trade patterns as they were. Gujarat in northwest India, for example, had supplied much of East Africa's cloth, and Gujarati merchants had been important in the overseas trade. They remained influential. Portuguese attempts to sell European goods failed, so that even Portuguese merchants dealt in Indian cloth and beads, while Gujaratis continued to participate in the trade on into the twentieth century.

The coastal towns of present-day Tanzania and Kenya no doubt continued the ivory trade with the interior much as they had done before the Portuguese arrival, although very few details are known. The coastal merchants did not make trading expeditions into the interior, as they were to do in the nineteenth century.

Two possible forms of commercial organization are hinted at, either in the records of the period or by the institutions of later periods, which may well have existed at the time. First, we know from political history that each town had its allies among the non-Muslims of the coastal strip and its immediate hinterland. Mombasa, for example, regularly made large payments to people called Musungulos, undoubtedly predecessors of the modern Mijikenda, who live just behind the coast. In return, the Musungulos provided military assistance, and they may have carried ivory to the coast. The second possibility is that small bands of specialized hunters, relatively separate from the major populations of the interior, hunted in an area extending to about 200 miles inland and then brought their ivory to the coast. Traveling bands of Kamba hunters from central Kenya carried on this kind of hunting and trade on the mainland opposite Zanzibar in the eighteenth century. It may have been done in much the same way earlier.

In any case, most people of the interior were insulated not only from contact with the Portuguese but even from contact with the coastal Muslims. They were probably ignorant of the coastal value of their ivory. They were certainly ignorant of its exchange value in India. Within any given historical context, only an economic actor who has the fullest possible information is able to strike the best bargain. Because Indian Ocean market information was unavailable in mainland East Africa, the African producers were paid with goods that would have looked paltry in any other segment of the trade. The middlemen, whether African coastal Muslims, Portuguese, or Gujaratis, made a healthy profit, but the trade appears not to have generated a wide range of productive economic activity inland.

The Portuguese profited from their position as the only major armed sailing power with full knowledge of the trade. They tried to prevent the spread of information to other European powers, including technical knowledge about sailing the Indian Ocean. For this reason, they spread stories of the terrible cannibals in the East African interior; the more horrible the dangers, the less likely competitors were to make contact. They even convinced the people of Zanzibar in the late sixteenth century that the English were cannibals.

In politics as in trade, the Portuguese were forced to accept, and adapt to, preexisting patterns. The coastal towns had always competed with one another. Except for the brief interludes when visiting Portuguese warships ruled supreme, this pattern continued, although the Portuguese completely eliminated some players from the competition. In the long-term pattern of coastal politics, the small island towns, which were incapable of mustering substantial armies themselves, sought allies among hinterland peoples for fighting men, trade goods, and provisions, and among overseas traders for ships and some supplies. Patterns of shifting alliances and factions continued throughout the Portuguese period and beyond it. Each town entered a special relationship of alliance with and dependence on the mainland peoples. According to the Portuguese records from the time of their first arrival, whenever the European intruders threatened a town, mainland archers, usually with poisoned arrows, appeared to help. The leaders of the merchant towns made substantial annual gifts to their mainland allies, like Mombasa's payment of several bales of cloth each year to the mainland Musungulos.

The forms of the mainlanders' political involvement in the life of the towns become clear from the better-recorded alliances of a later period, after the departure of the Portuguese. Each of the Mijikenda peoples was allied with a particular Swahili subgroup of Mombasa. When the Swahili representative took office, he made a substantial payment to his hinterland allies. Each Mijikenda *kaya,* or ritual center, had an ambassador to the allied Swahili group. During the Portuguese period, as later, the mainlanders were probably capable of overthrowing town leaders; and, in one instance, they betrayed Mombasa's king for 2,000 cloths.

At some places outside Mombasa the consent of mainland allies was required before a new town could assume office. In others, authority on the mainland and the seacoast were strictly separated. On the central Tanzanian coast, authority was divided between the coastal Muslim chief "who does not see the [setting] sun" and the hinterland chief "who does not see the water." It was probably this form of alliance that was offered to the uncomprehending Portuguese when they attacked Mombasa in 1589. At that time, the people described in the documents as "Zimba" appeared and asked for free passage across the ford to the island, offering to divide the conquest between the Portuguese as rulers of the sea and themselves as rulers of the land.

After the decline of Kilwa the two most important towns on the northern half of the coast were Mombasa and Malindi, her neighbor further north. These two were engaged in a bitter competition that drew in mainland allies and smaller towns up and down the coast. Since Mombasa and Malindi were accustomed to throwing their nets wide in the search for allies, they naturally saw the Portuguese, from the time of their first arrival, as seaward counterparts to their mainland friends. Malindi greeted the early Portuguese explorers with assistance and warm assurances of friendship. By 1500, the king of Malindi complained to the head of a visiting fleet that his friendship with the Portuguese had earned him the enmity of Mombasa. Malindi's strategy was successful. The Portuguese joined against Mombasa and destroyed that city several times during the sixteenth century, with the final great battle near its end, provoked by Mombasa's enthusiastic welcome of a small Turkish fleet which had come down from the Red Sea. If Malindi had drawn Christians into the coastal competition, why should Mombasa not draw in Portugal's great Muslim enemy?

The final war between Mombasa and Malindi reveals the full complexity of the coastal alliance system. Several major towns joined Mombasa in welcoming the Turks. In the counterattack by the Portuguese fleet, Malindi and her mainland allies, the Segeju, entered the battle. Mombasa fell, and the Portuguese decided in 1593 to fortify and garrison the town, while the king of Malindi moved south to become the new king of Mombasa.

After the Portuguese had destroyed Mombasa's power and built their own fort there, their position north of Cape Delgado became much stronger than it had been earlier in the sixteenth century. On the other hand, their presence made little real difference to the pattern of coastal politics, in which they simply became another player in the game of alliances. They, like other East African coastal powers before them, collected tribute from towns up and down the coast, but they also assumed Mombasa's old obligation of paying tribute in turn to its mainland allies, the Musungulos. With Mombasa's old power broken, the king of Malindi (and Mombasa) became a rival of the Portuguese. In 1614, a Portuguese commander arranged to have a king of Mombasa murdered, and in 1631 the ruler of Mombasa massacred the Portuguese garrison in his turn.

As the seventeenth century wore on, Portugal lost its early leadership among Europeans in the Indian Ocean trade — first to the Dutch, then to the English as well. As a consequence, the Portuguese also lost out to shippers from the Persian Gulf who began to appear more and more frequently in East African ports. As they did, they stepped into the position Portugal had once held. When one faction among the competing towns found allies among the Portuguese, the other faction turned to Portugal's maritime rivals, most often the Turks or Omani Arabs. Even within a single town like Pate on the northern Kenya coast, one political faction supported the Portuguese and its rivals turned automatically to the Arabs. From the coastal perspective, the old game went on; when Arabs drove the Portuguese from Mombasa in 1697, it was simply the replacement of one sea power by another.

SUGGESTIONS FOR FURTHER READING

Beattie, John. *The Nyoro State*. Oxford: Oxford University Press, Clarendon Press, 1971.

Feierman, Steven. *The Shambaa Kingdom*. Madison: University of Wisconsin Press, 1974.

Karugire, Samwiri Rubaraza. *A History of the Kingdom of Nkore in Western Uganda to 1896*. Oxford: Oxford University Press, Clarendon Press, 1971.

Kimambo, Isaria N. *A Political History of the Pare of Tanzania: c. 1500–1900*. Nairobi: East African Publishing House, 1969.

Kimambo, Isaria N., and Temu, Arnold J. *A History of Tanzania*. Nairobi: East African Publishing House, 1969.

Ogot, Bethwell A., ed. *Zamani: A Survey of East African History*. rev. ed. Nairobi: East African Publishing House, 1974.

Oliver, Roland, and Mathew, Gervase. *History of East Africa*. Vol. 1. Oxford: Oxford University Press, Clarendon Press, 1963.

Roscoe, John. *The Baganda*. 2d ed. London: Frank Cass, 1965.

Southall, Aidan. *Alur Society*. Cambridge: W. Heffer, 1956.

Strandes, Justus. *The Portuguese Period in East Africa.* Translated by Jean F. Wall-work. Edited with topographical notes by J. S. Kirkman. Nairobi: East African Literature Bureau, 1961.

Twaddle, Michael. "Towards an Early History of the East African Interior." *History in Africa* 2 (1975): 147–184.

Plate 1. Prehistoric rock painting of herdsman and cattle at Tin Tazarift, Sahara, from a time when the Sahara was lush pasture-land. (From *Tassili N'Ajjer,* éditions du Chène, Paris. Photo by Jean-Dominique Lajoux)

Plate 2. Terra cotta head from the Nok culture in Nigeria, 500 B.C.–200 A.D. (Federal Department of Antiquities, Lagos, Nigeria)

Plate 3. Terra cotta statue of a king or nobleman from Ife (Nigeria), probably dating from early in this millennium. (Collection Musée de l'Homme)

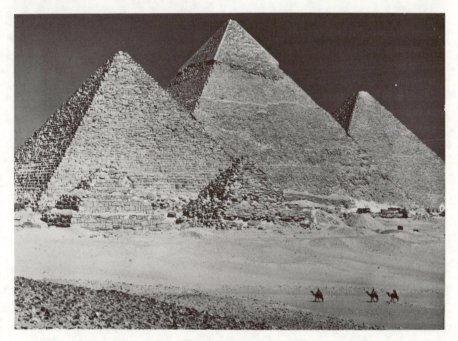

Plate 4. The pyramids of Gizeh. (Photo Researchers: George Holton)

Plate 5. Giant steles of Axum, as much as 110 feet high. These were probably built between the second century B.C. and the fourth century A.D. (Werner Forman)

Plate 6. Villa at Utica, Tunisia, the only Roman villa still standing in Africa. (Werner Forman Archive)

Plate 7. A church carved from rock at Lalibela, Ethiopia, thirteenth century A.D. (P. D. Curtin)

Plate 8. Bab Mansur, gate in the city wall of Meknès, Morocco, constructed early in the eighteenth century. (P. D. Curtin)

Plate 9. At left, a Fulbe man and woman of the Senegal valley, early nineteenth century; at right, a Wolof prince of the early nineteenth century. (From Boilat, *Esquisses Sénégalaises*)

Plate 10. Kneeling woman holding a bowl, from Luba, Zaïre, Buli workshop. Such statues were used by Luba kings. White porcelain clay with supernatural powers was kept in the bowl. This is a utensil of sacred kingship. (Musée Royal de l'Afrique Centrale)

Plate 11. Statue of a noble hunter, from Chokwe, Angola, representing Prince Ilunga, the hero who came from Luba country, married the Lunda princess, and thus founded the Lunda empire. The statue represents the ideal hunter for the Chokwe of the middle nineteenth century. (Museum für Volkerkunde. Staatliche Museen PreuSSischer Kulturbesitz, Berlin [West])

Plate 12 (below). Ruins of Great Zimbabwe. (Courtesy, Rhodesian National Tourist Board)

Chapter 6
Africa
North of the Forest
(1500-1800)

THE FIFTEENTH AND SIXTEENTH CENTURIES witnessed a new phase in the history of northern Africa, marked principally by the rise of powerful and pushy neighbors. The year 1500 has no particular significance. It is simply a convenient date that will serve as a marker for trends that began far earlier but took on weight and importance about this time. The most spectacular change was the emergence of the Ottoman Turkish Empire as one of the three Muslim empires that were to divide the Islamic world in the sixteenth and seventeenth centuries. Turkish nomads from central Asia had captured Baghdad in the eleventh century. A Turkish state under the Ottoman dynasty appeared in Anatolia in the fourteenth century, crossed over into Europe, and began the conquests that ultimately gave it control of the territory that had once been Byzantine. Even that phase was finished when the Ottomans captured Istanbul, the former Constantinople, in 1453. New Turkish naval power in the Mediterranean, the Turkish seizure of the Levant and then of Mamluk Egypt gave them importance in Africa. By 1550, they had become dominant in all North Africa except Morocco.

But the Turks were not the only source of pressure. Western Europe also moved to a new position of importance in the world, based on remarkable technological advances going back to the eleventh century. In these centuries, technology had been matched by scholarly work in the sciences, as Europe appropriated all the mathematical and scientific knowledge available from anywhere in the intercommunicating zone. The fact that much of this knowledge came through Islamic transmitters is a small irony in the major transition from an Islamic Age to a European Age in world history. That transition was not complete until the mid-eighteenth century, but it began for the Maghrib in the fifteenth century with Spanish and Portuguese military pressure on the coasts.

Meanwhile, the main political trends in the Maghrib led toward fragmentation of power and lack of unity in the face of either the Turkish or the Iberian threat. The successor states of the Almohad Empire were in full decline by the fifteenth century. Central government almost everywhere had become only a legal fiction, as real political power devolved into the hands of Muslim holy men, Arab lineage authorities, Berber segmentary societies, or small Muslim states.

Seen from the southern shore of the Sahara, these political changes in North Africa foreshadowed an important shift in Africa's relation to the world. A great Muslim empire, whose heartland was far away in southeastern Europe and Anatolia, now commanded the northern coast of the continent from Suez to the Atlas. In sixteenth-century Morocco, a new dynasty consolidated its power in reaction both to the Turks and to the Christian infiltration from the north. Furthermore, both the Ottomans and the Moroccans were armed with firearms, which were all but unknown south of the Sahara. Both had diplomatic relations and chronic military conflict with the states of western Europe. During the sixteenth century, Ottoman and Moroccan diplomacy and force reached across the desert. At least indirectly, states to the south of the Sahara — from Ethiopia in the east to Jollof and Fuuta Tooro in the west — were pulled into the fringes of a web of international relations that linked them, however distantly, to Europe.

In the longer term of history, these changes in the sixteenth century spelled the beginning of the end of Africa's isolation. But the longer term of history needed several more centuries to be played out. Firearms in the service of alien conquerors *would* bring an end to African independence — but only after 1880. The Ottomans and the Moroccans were armed in the same manner as the Europeans, but the effectiveness of sixteenth-century firearms is often overestimated. Sixteenth-century battles in Europe were won by highly trained and disciplined infantry whose key weapon was the pike, not the musket; and the Turks' most effective unit was unarmored cavalry. Artillery was decisive only as a siege weapon until at least the 1630s when light, rapid-fire field artillery became available.

CHRISTIANS, TURKS, AND NAVAL POWER IN THE MEDITERRANEAN

The Christian threat from the north and the Turkish threat from the northeast reached the Maghrib mainly in the form of naval power. In this respect, they followed a pattern of Mediterranean history that was already old. Nonnomads who had successfully conquered the Maghrib or some part of it always did so from the sea. That had been the route taken by the Phoenicians, the Vandals, the Byzantines, and the first Muslim caliphate. In essence, this was simply the result of the Maghrib's islandlike situation. The sea then became even more of a frontier when the Christians held the northern shores and the Muslims the southern, and the defensibility of this frontier was related to the level of government organization, much as it was on the desert frontier against nomads. When Maghribine society was well organized, the ports were linked to a productive economy in their hinterland; they could be strong at sea with the combined resources of the whole society. But when political authority was fragmented, the ports were on their own, prey to the superior mobility of a seaborne enemy — in the same position, in short, as a sedentary outpost on the *sahel*. This jeopardy, however, was equally true for the Christian coasts to the north, which were also subject to raids from the sea when the Muslim powers were strong.

Partly as a result of this pattern, the coastal Maghrib passed back and forth between a condition of relative safety and prosperity and one of instability and danger. The theater of this action, however, was not the Mediterranean basin as a whole but individual regions within it. The Almoravids successfully built their empire and captured Muslim Spain at the same time the Christian Crusaders were capturing Jerusalem at the other end of the sea. To some degree, the Mediterranean basin west of Italy was a single unit, but the strategic places there were the narrow seas — the straits between Sicily and Ifrīqiyah and the straits of Gibraltar. From the twelfth century onward, control alternated between Christians and Muslims.

On the Sicilian channel, for example, the Fatimids once controlled Sicily, but they weakened. After the eleventh-century incursions of the Hilalian Arabs, the port towns of Ifrīqiyah were left to fend for themselves, and the Sicilians captured most of the coastline by the 1120s. With the push of Almohad power into Ifrīqiyah, Muslims recaptured the ports from the land side, and the Christians were expelled by 1160. This time, however, the Almohads left Sicily alone, though Sicilian aggression resumed a century later with French support (it was then that a French king who was also a Christian saint, Saint Louis, was killed trying to capture Tunis). After that, Ifrīqiyah held its own until nearly 1490, but Christians and Muslims raided one another's seaborne commerce and still raided the opposing coasts, even though peaceful trade across the Mediterranean also increased.

At the very end of the fifteenth century, the dynasty ruling Ifrīqiyah was weakening, just at the time when Ferdinand and Isabella, monarchs of Aragon and Castile respectively, married and united Spain. They captured the one remaining Spanish Muslim kingdom, Granada. Sicily too fell to Spain, so that Spain could now threaten the Maghrib from Gibraltar to Tripoli. From the late 1490s to about 1610, the Spanish descended on the Barbary Coast in a series of raids and captures that gave them Melilla and Oran in the west, Mers-el-Kébir near Oran at the center, Bougie in Ifrīqiyah, and Tripoli still further east. For a time, it looked as though the Spanish monarchs were about to repeat the Vandal success of a thousand years earlier and conquer the Maghrib from the sea.

In fact, Spain's ambitions lay in Italy. She was also checked in North Africa by the emergence of Ottoman seapower, which became important about 1503 with the Turks' victory over Venice in a prolonged war. After that, they moved into the Levant and conquered Mamluk Egypt in 1517. By that time, private Ottoman commerce raiders had already appeared in the western basin of the Mediterranean. The most famous were Aruj and Kair-ed-Din, two brothers whom the Christians called the Barbarossas for their red beards. They began harassing the Spanish from about 1510, privately at first but with increasing support from Istanbul. As time passed, they and the Turkish navy that came to their aid captured the North African ports one after another. At first, they simply replaced the Spanish — a process mainly completed by the 1570s, when they turned to the hinterland as well. Thus, it was the Ottomans, not the Spanish, who actually stepped into a position of suzerainty over the Maghrib from Tripoli to western Algeria; and the coastline once held by the Byzantine Empire from Constantinople once again fell into the hands of an empire ruling from Istanbul.

While the substitution of Ottomans for Spanish was played out in the northeastern Maghrib, another struggle took place west of Gibraltar. There, as along the Mediterranean coast, ships of the opposing religion had been fair game, and opposing coasts had been subject to raids in peacetime as in wartime. Christians and Muslims might allow alien ships in their ports, but the open sea was the scene of international anarchy in the absence of any moderating conventions of international law. In 1399, a Castilian force had crossed over and sacked Tetuán, killing half the population and enslaving the rest. A Portuguese force seized Ceuta opposite Gibraltar in 1415, but neither of these moves was the beginning of Christian predominance. Granada in Spain itself was still a Muslim country. Rather than ushering in the European Age, the coastal seizures represented one more temporary shift in the balance of power across the straits.

Muslim Morocco moved still further toward full collapse in the second half of the fifteenth century, with no capacity to organize a united defense of its ports. Portugal therefore acted on the Atlantic coast, as Spain did on the Mediterranean, picking up Tangier, Arzile, and Larache, mainly in the 1470s, and adding Safi, Agadir, and Azemour in the early sixteenth century. In time, Morocco would retrieve most of these, but simultaneous with this short-term rise of Portuguese power was a far more significant period of experimentation off the African coasts that led to the major breakthrough of the maritime revolution.

PORTUGAL AND THE MARITIME REVOLUTION

The maritime revolution of the fifteenth century affected all of Africa. Over the short period between 1433 and 1488, Portuguese mariners opened direct access to the western coast of the continent from Tangier to the Cape of Good Hope. A dozen years later, their rounding of the Cape gave them access to the eastern shore as well. The change was revolutionary in the sense that maritime technology could suddenly accomplish voyages at sea that had once been impossible. But it was not so revolutionary for political relations, because the Europeans could not yet dominate the states and peoples among whom they traded.

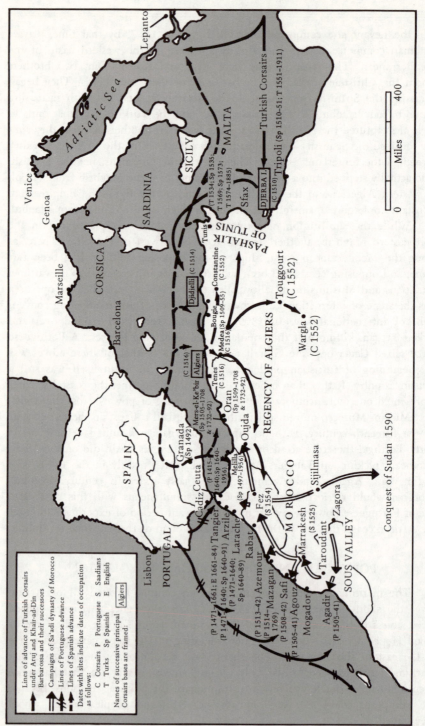

Turks and Hispanic Powers in the Maghrib

Legend (map key):

Lines of advance of Turkish Corsairs under Aruj and Khair-ad-Din

Barbarossa and their successors

Campaigns of Sa'adi dynasty of Morocco

Lines of Portuguese advance

Lines of Spanish advance

Dates with sites indicate dates of occupation as follows:

C Corsairs P Portuguese S Saadians
T Turks Sp Spanish E English

Names of successive principal
Corsairs bases are framed: Algiers

Place labels:

Lepanto

Adriatic Sea

Venice

Genoa

Marseille

Barcelona

CORSICA

SARDINIA

SICILY

MALTA

Turkish Corsairs

Tripoli (Sp 1510-51; T 1551-1911)

DJERBA (C 1510)

Sfax

(T 1534; Sp 1535; T 1569; Sp 1573; T 1574-1885)

Tunis

PASHALIK OF TUNIS

Constantine (C 1552)

Bougie (Sp 1509-55)

Djidjelli (C 1514)

Tenes (C 1516)

Medea (C 1516)

Algiers (C 1516)

Mers-el-Kebir (Sp 1505-1708 & 1732-92)

Oran (Sp 1509-1708 & 1732-92)

Oujda (S 1554)

REGENCY OF ALGIERS

Wargla (C 1552)

Touggourt (C 1552)

SPAIN

PORTUGAL

Lisbon

Cadiz

Granada (Sp 1492)

Ceuta (P 1415)

Tangier (P 1471; 1661; E 1661-84)

Arzile (P 1471-1640; Sp 1640-1956)

Larache (P 1471-1640; Sp 1640-89)

Azemour (P 1513-42)

Mazagan (P 1514-1769)

Safi (P 1508-42)

Agouz

Mogador

Agadir (P 1505-41)

Melilla (Sp 1497-1956)

Fez (S 1554)

Rabat

MOROCCO

Marrakesh (S 1525)

Taroudant

SOUS VALLEY

Sijilmasa

Zagora

Conquest of Sudan 1590

0 ————— 400

Miles

In 1444, the first European reached as far south as the Senegal River and sailed back to Europe. The important feat was the return, because the Mauritanian coast has an unfavorable northeast wind and current during the whole year. It was accomplished in the first instance by noticing that the winds blew slightly onshore during the day and offshore at night. By sailing in a series of long tacks to take advantage of these changes, it was possible to return against wind and current.

But this was not the significant discovery. Sometime between 1444 and the 1470s, Portuguese mariners now unrecorded found that by sailing on a single long tack to the northwest, keeping as close as possible to the trade winds, one would soon arrive at the latitude of the Azores, where the winds were variable but generally westerly and fair for the Portuguese coast. This discovery did far more than merely make it possible to sail easily to Cape Verde and back. It was the first recognition that the ocean wind pattern tended to be circular, with easterlies prevalent within about thirty degrees of the equator, and westerlies in the forties and fifties of north or south latitude. Once this pattern was known, it was possible to sail nearly anywhere in the world with a favorable wind.

In the first phase of exploiting this breakthrough, the Portuguese in the 1470s and 1480s explored their first corner of the broader Atlantic pattern. Before 1470, no European ship had sailed beyond Sierra Leone. By 1490, the Portuguese had regular trade relations with the Gold Coast, enough to justify their expensive castle at Elmina (built in 1481 more for protection against European interlopers than against the Africans), and they had reached beyond the forest to the southern savanna. This brought them into the world of the southeast trade winds, where the north Atlantic pattern was repeated south of the equator.

Other sailors explored further applications of the wind patterns that carried them across the Atlantic and into the Pacific and Indian Oceans. This phase began with Columbus on the Atlantic in 1492 and ended in 1522, when Sebastian del Cano brought Magellan's fleet back to Spain, having discovered that trade winds are uniform and tend to blow in the same direction all over the world. Once that was known, Europeans could go nearly anywhere.

THE PORTUGUESE IN WEST AFRICA

Because the Portuguese were the first to achieve this maritime breakthrough, theirs was the first move, the first chance to experiment, to innovate in search of national or personal advantage. During the first period, the Portuguese learned what was and was not possible in the African trade. They learned, for example, that it was not practical to try to enter the inland trade. African merchants with developed commercial networks were already on hand; easier and more profitable exchanges were possible if the Europeans dealt with them only at coastal points. In West Africa, Europeans also learned that slaves could usually be bought and that direct raids on African villages would only bring reprisals on the next European ship to appear. They also learned that trade forts were useful in some places, but only if they had the cooperation of the African authorities. It was therefore customary to pay these authorities an annual fee, which Africans and Europeans variously interpreted as tribute, rent, or license fee.

The Portuguese also learned in these first decades that they suffered enormously high death rates in West Africa; 25 to 50 percent died within a few months. They nevertheless tried several different experiments with the African trade, which served as precedents for other Europeans who were to follow.

One important effort involved the gold trade. The knowledge that North Africans drew gold from across the Sahara was a key motive luring the Portuguese down the African coast in the first place. Well before 1500, they had learned the main lines of West African geography. They knew precisely where the gold came from, and explorers whose accounts have since been lost visited all three of the important goldfields as well as the court of Mali.

The Portuguese began by trying to sell European products in return for gold and other African exports, but they soon learned that they could also sell their shipping services, being paid in gold for taking goods from one part of Africa to another. West Africans were ready to buy woolen cloth and cavalry remounts from Morocco as well as copper and brass from Europe. The Portuguese were able to supply both by sea, in competition with the caravan trade. Once on the Guinea coast, they could sell the metals at a place like Benin in return for beads, pepper, and slaves. The pepper went to Europe, but the beads and slaves were exchanged for gold on the Gold Coast. This trade in slaves from one part of Africa to another ended after the slave trade across the Atlantic became important, but a European carrying trade from one part of Africa to another remained. Later Europeans took cotton cloth, for example, from one part of the coast to another, and the Africans demanded non-European as well as European products for centuries to come — cowrie shells from the Maldive Islands in the Indian Ocean, which served as a major West African currency, or Indian cotton textiles, which were more important than European cottons far into the nineteenth century.

The map on page 187 illustrates a further major change in the strategy of trade. Even though the Portuguese turned most of their attention after 1505 to the brighter promise of Indian Ocean trade, the West African coast was open to navigators, and it was only a matter of time before someone would seize the opportunity. Some of the peoples who had been furthest from possible contact with the intercommunicating zone now became among the closest.

Further inland, a balance had to be struck between the old routes across the Sahara and the new routes by sea. Long-distance through trade from North Africa to the Gulf of Guinea existed before 1500 at two points, perhaps more. One was the Gold Coast, where the Juula trade route from the Niger at Jenné reached through the Akan goldfield to the sea. Another, somewhat less direct route led south from Hausa to the Yoruba cities, which in turn had commercial relations with the coast at Dahomey and Benin. From coastal points like these, the mari-

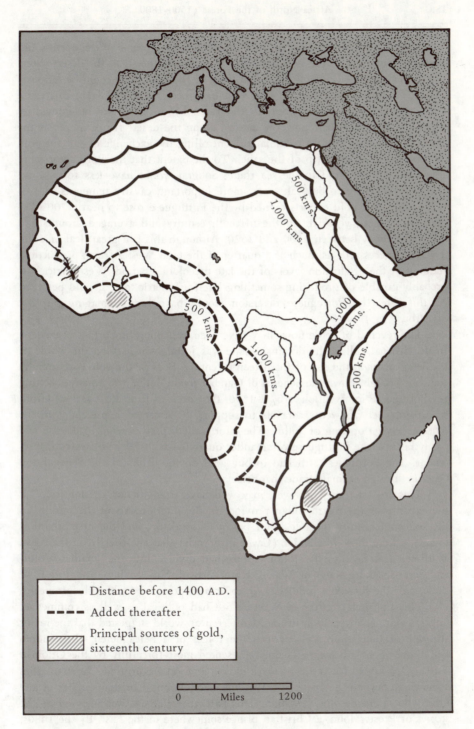

Distance from an Ocean Port

time revolution could reverse the direction of flow along some of the north-south overland routes, attracting gold toward the seashore rather than the desert shore. When this happened, inland states that lived by the gold trade could be seriously affected. Songrai, for example, may well have been weakened from this cause during the sixteenth century. Sonni 'Alī (ruled 1464–1492) and his immediate successors extended their power westward along the desert fringe as far as the Senegal, following the old formula for controlling the exchange of salt for gold by controlling a long strip of the sahel. To the extent that the Portuguese were able to divert the gold to the sea route, Songrai would have less foreign exchange with which to buy salt — or, more important, cavalry remounts.

Gold Coast gold exports carried by the Portuguese rose to nearly 700 kilograms in a peak year late in the fifteenth century and averaged around 410 kilograms yearly between 1500 and 1520. Although this is a great deal of gold, it was not necessarily as much as a quarter of the total West African production. Judging by the production levels of the late precolonial period, West Africa was probably capable of producing something like four metric tons of gold per year. At this rate, the Portuguese diversion would have been damaging but not disastrous.

The reversal of trade flows may have been even more important elsewhere. In the Senegal valley, the dominant state was Jollof, which ruled the whole of the Senegambia at the end of the fifteenth century. Because the gold of Bambuhu could be brought down the Senegal or Gambia rivers, Jollof was a natural setting for Portuguese intervention. About 1590, they decided to make a serious effort, sending a fleet of twenty caravels to support the cause of a pretender to the office of *Burba* or king of Jollof. The effort failed, partly owing to disease and partly because the Portuguese commander quarreled with Jelen, the African pretender. The Portuguese still had to buy gold on the banks of the Senegal and Gambia through ordinary trade channels.

This coastal trade, however, may well have strengthened coastal Jollof at the expense of the metropolitan province in the interior. About the middle of the sixteenth century, greater Jollof began to break up, and the first provinces to secede were those like Kajor (Cayor in French) that lay directly on the coast. Within a few decades the Jollof empire had divided into the smaller Wolof- and Serer-speaking states of Waalo, Kajor, Bawol, Siin, Saalum, and Jollof; of these, only the shrunken Jollof lacked sea or river ports for trade with Europeans.

This Portuguese effort in West Africa had political as well as commercial implications. Their position in the Mediterranean world suggested that the major struggle of their time was between the forces of a beleaguered Christendom and those of an advancing Islam, represented most forcefully by the Ottoman Turks. One hoped-for result of maritime exploration was to find Christian allies somewhere beyond the encircling Muslims — or, failing Christians, allies of any kind who might become Christian. This particular chimera was inspired by the stories of Prester John, a Christian prince somewhere in the East. By the 1480s,

Portuguese agents had already visited the Ethiopian court and discovered that a Christian prince did in fact rule to the east, beyond Islamic lands, and the effort to find African allies was especially strong in the 1490s. Portuguese military support for Jelen's effort to seize power in Jollof was just such an attempt to put a Christian king on an African throne. In the kingdom of Kongo south of the lower Zaïre river, a more peaceful approach had greater success. Christian missionaries arrived there in 1491 and soon converted a candidate for the throne. In 1506, he actually took office as Affonso I, the first of a line of Christian monarchs who were to lead an interesting effort at modernization. The early promise of the effort prompted a favorable Portuguese response to another diplomatic initiative from the African side. In 1514, the Oba of Benin sent a mission to Lisbon, hoping to arrange to buy firearms. The Portuguese answered by sending missionaries, who made a few converts but failed to convert the Oba. He, in turn, got no firearms, the missionaries died, and the effort was apparently abandoned on both sides. Meanwhile, the Portuguese continued their missionary work in Kongo, but West Africa was not to receive serious missionary attention until the nineteenth century.

TURKISH RULE IN
SIXTEENTH-CENTURY NORTH AFRICA

When the Turks first began to challenge the Spanish hold on Maghribine ports, the people of the hinterland were hardly affected. They were far too divided among themselves to resist the Turks, even if they had wanted to do so. The only strong resistance came from the Spanish masters of the ports, the only people who were actually threatened at first. For the rest, Turks were no worse masters than the Spanish, and they had the advantage of being Muslim. They also took pains to cultivate the *'ulamā* in the urban centers, sometimes asking their collective advice about matters of state. In the interior, Turkish authorities tended to work through rural religious leaders like the heads of the *sufi* brotherhoods, and a broad current of collaboration between the Turks and the brotherhoods lasted through the sixteenth century.

Such collaboration was easy enough to maintain, since the Turkish strategy was directed toward maritime affairs, with no serious effort made to control the hinterland until the last quarter of the sixteenth century. It was only then that three provinces or regencies came into effective existence, ruled from capitals at Algiers, Tunis, and Tripoli respectively. Each was placed under a *pasha* directly responsible to Istanbul, a division that led ultimately to the present territories of Algeria, Tunisia, and Libya.

The first pashas were Turks sent out for relatively brief terms of office so that they would represent Istanbul's interests in these distant outposts of empire; but as the Maghrib was too far away for close control, each regency soon began to go its own way. The pashas were still dependent on Turkish military support, especially against the Europeans across the sea, but they began to extend their terms of office. After about 1610, they began to act like independent monarchs, though recognizing the theoretical authority of Istanbul.

As the pashas became more independent of the distant sultan, they were obliged to compromise with local sources of power. Each regency had a local council called a *dīwān,* designed at first to represent the officers of the garrison and other important Turkish residents. With time, however, others had to be taken into the circle of power, either informally or formally as members of the council. In Algiers and Tripoli, and to some extent in other port towns as well, the most powerful voice came to be that of the commerce raiders, who were organized in regular guilds. The Turkish presence in the Maghrib had begun with the Christian-Muslim rivalry at sea. As time passed, the Europeans became dominant in peaceful commerce, which left commerce raiding against the Christians as the most viable alternative for the Maghribine ports. This was the beginning of the "Barbary pirates," as the Europeans called them, though Christian pirates from Malta and elsewhere also lived by raiding Muslims. The Barbary raiders' guilds became the dominant voice in the regency governments of Algeria and Tripoli in all matters having to do with commerce, captured Christian slaves, or diplomatic relations with Europe. They were less important in Tunis, however, because that capital had a more fertile hinterland within easy reach of the port and hence a greater concern for the hinterland.

Elsewhere, the pashas tried to govern by a form of indirect rule. They appointed a *caïd,* or governor, for each important town, leaving the rural areas under a very diverse local leadership, roughly supervised by Turkish clerks. The caïds themselves bought the office, collecting what taxes they could and passing a stipulated amount to the pasha at the port, who was usually more concerned with milking inland sources of revenue than with inland government. His control was therefore real enough in the towns but minimal in the country-side, which felt his authority only when the caïd borrowed troops from the port for a systematic tax-gathering expedition. These expeditions were partly a show of Turkish strength intended to overawe the populace, partly institutionalized robbery that kept the countryside in chronic revolt through the middle decades of the seventeenth century. After a time and especially in Algeria, these raids became so important that their military leaders, bearing the title of *bey,* became more important than the caïds themselves. The whole Algerian hinterland came to be divided into administrative territories called beyliks, each marking off the raiding territory assigned a particular bey.

After the 1660s, the link between the pashas and Istanbul weakened still more. In Algiers, the Turkish garrison revolted against the pasha, and the commerce raiders in their turn revolted against the garrison. They still claimed a form of allegiance to the Ottoman state, but they insisted on electing their own ruler with the title of *dey.* By the eighteenth century, Istanbul recognized this situation, confirmed the elected deys, and granted them the powers of a pasha; but effective control had passed to the dey — and to the three beys, who had meanwhile managed to make their offices hereditary, reducing the tie to Algiers even as Algiers cut the tie to Istanbul. In Tunisia and Tripolitania, the course of events was similar. Commerce raiding was less important, but deys and beys of local origin replaced pashas appointed by Istanbul. But here the dominant oligarchy included more local landlords and heads of Arab lineages.

Egypt was immensely more important to the Ottoman Empire than the Maghrib was, but Ottoman rule became localized there as well. The first administrative expedient was to keep Egypt under tight control through a viceroy enjoying more prestige than an ordinary pasha, though he was assisted by a dīwān representing other officials and military officers. Each important source of wealth was also assigned to an official whose job it was to supervise that aspect of the economy as well as to keep the revenue flowing in.

In the first instance Turkish rule seems to have improved Egyptian administration and strengthened the economy. In any event, Egypt became a more efficient source of government revenue than it had been in the last years of Mamluk rule. On the other hand, most of the early officials and tax farmers were Turkish Janissaries. That is, they were slave-soldiers or slave-administrators equivalent to the Mamluks themselves. Over time, they tended to seize the reality of local power as the Mamluks before them had done. By the end of the sixteenth century, the new Mamluks were in effective control of local government and dominated the viceroy's dīwān. Those who had been tax farmers gradually turned themselves into landlords with control over the land equivalent to ownership, so that less of the revenue passed on to the central government and more of it went to support a local gentry.

By the early seventeenth century, Istanbul recognized the new Mamluk order, at least informally, though it kept better control over the viceroys than it did over the Maghribine pashas. These officials were still appointed from Istanbul. They might face a council with an independent source of power, but they still kept some room for political maneuver. Egypt also remained an important source of Ottoman revenue, and it carried out important functions for the Ottoman Empire as a whole. It was charged, for example, with controlling the Red Sea, garrisoning the Red Sea ports, governing the holy cities of Mecca and Medina, and suppressing any piracy that might affect the pilgrim traffic. It was not until the nineteenth century that Egypt moved as clearly out of the orbit of de facto Ottoman control as the Maghrib had done by the early eighteenth.

MOROCCAN RECOVERY

At the beginning of the sixteenth century, political disintegration had gone further in Morocco than it had in any other region of the former Almohad Empire. Yet the Moroccans managed to keep their independence from the Turks on their eastern frontier and from the Spanish and Portuguese to the north. Part of the explanation lies in the structure of Maghribine government. Large states like that of the Almohads were not a monolithic whole whose collapse meant

the collapse of all government. They were a form of overrule that left the constituent parts intact. A governing dynasty might be too weak to defend the ports
against the Iberians, but the hinterland had its own resources for defense,
whether or not there was a strong central government. More organization was
needed to defend themselves against the Turks in Algeria, but a new dynasty
arose in the course of the sixteenth century to provide that organization.

This new dynasty, the Saadians, came to power through a special configuration of nomadic pressure and religious politics. It would have been natural
to raise the cry of danger from infidels in order to oppose the Spanish and
Portuguese attacks from the sea. But the Moroccan 'ulamā of the late fifteenth
century were too closely tied to the failing power of the old regime to rally a
mass movement of any kind. The other source of religious authority, the Muslim brotherhoods, or *turuq,* were divided among themselves. Some proposed a
holy war against Spain, but the largest of them opposed any such scheme. This
left the rallying point in defense of Islam to a new force in Moroccan politics,
the *shurafā* (sing. *sherīf,* plural often written shorfa in English), or the direct
descendants of Muhammad.

By this time in Islamic history, whole tribes of Arabs traced their ancestry
back to 'Ali and Fatima through the male line, and these people were held in a
kind of esteem that tended to turn them into specialists in religious knowledge
and law. The most prominent lineage of this kind in sixteenth-century Morocco
was the Sa'adi, who had migrated westward across North Africa to settle during
the twelfth century in the Dra Valley on the Saharan side of the Atlas. All
shorfa were not religious leaders; the Sa'adi had a military force of their own as
well as the ability to rally others to the defense of Islam. About the middle of
the fifteenth century, they had begun active military pressure against the Portuguese on the south coast. About 1515, they began to move north in Morocco,
conquering the country by force and persuasion. By 1534, they had captured
Marrakesh and unified the south. This put them in a position to expel the Portuguese from the southern ports and enter maritime contact with the outside
world, especially with England. By mid-century, the Saadians had conquered all
Morocco. This is not to say that they had day-to-day administrative control everywhere, because no Moroccan regime had that kind of power before the twentieth century; but they were recognized everywhere as nominal rulers and as
de facto rulers in the more accessible parts of the country.

Nor did their victory over the infidels give them a monopoly of religious
authority within Morocco. The sufi brotherhoods were still strong, especially the
Qādirīya with its headquarters for the Maghrib in Algiers and very close links
with the Turkish authorities there. The most important rival order was the
Jazūli, which supported the Saadians. Once in power, the Saadians needed money
and it was only natural for them to tax their opponents, especially if these opponents claimed religious authority of a different kind from their own. They
therefore set out systematically to expropriate the great wealth of the rival

brotherhoods and to reduce the authority of reputed holy men. They succeeded to a degree, but they also won a reputation for antisufi tendencies that was to come back to haunt them reign after reign. In the longer run, they had to compromise with one after another of the strong turuq in order to gain their support against the Turks and the Iberians. The result was a Sherifian dynasty, but one that had to tolerate a great variety of religious authority and practice.

The need to compromise grew in part from Saadian military weakness. The Sa'adi were a small lineage in a kinship-dominated political system. Their following of relatives and secure allies was chronically arrayed against other and larger family interests. When they could point to an infidel threat, however, it was possible for them to rally an important response from the whole country. That happened in 1578, when Portugal invaded northern Morocco, only to be defeated decisively at the battle of al-Ksar al-Kebir (Alcazarquivir in English, sometimes called the battle of the three kings). Sebastian of Portugal and the Saadian sultan were both killed. The Portuguese crown passed to the Spanish monarch from 1580 until 1640, and Ahmad al-Mansūr (1578–1603) came to the Moroccan throne.

Even after his victory, the new sultan had to face the fact that the central government could not count on a regular and faithful military force. He therefore tried a number of expedients. One was to hire Turkish and European mercenaries as a standing army. Another was to use slave-soldiers imported from sub-Saharan Africa, on the model of the Janissaries of Turkey or the Mamluks of Egypt. In the short run, this policy strengthened the regime at home and abroad, though it courted the long-range danger that a standing army might take power into its own hands.

Al-Mansūr's greatest military and political achievement was to preserve Moroccan independence. That may seem to be more than other sultans had done, but this was the period when the Spain of Philip II nearly dominated the whole of western Europe. It was also the period when the Ottoman Turks were still strong in the Mediterranean, when the reality of their power in Algeria was nearly at its peak. In fact, Morocco would probably not have been defensible if either one of these potential enemies had decided on an all-out attack. What saved the country, as it was to do many times in the future, was the rivalry of its opponents. Most of the time, al-Mansūr could count on some English support against Spain, on Spanish support against the Turkish threat, and on Turkish support against a potential Spanish invasion.

Al-Mansūr was also involved in the western Sudan with his one great adventure in foreign policy, the cross-desert attack on Songrai in 1591. It was not really a major invasion, though it brought about the downfall of the Songrai empire. The Moroccans were able to dominate the Niger bend for a time, but their forces there soon slipped out of control. The Moroccan government made some short-term gains in improved gold trade, but the main importance of the trans-Saharan strike was that it marked the beginning of nearly two centuries

in which sub-Saharan Africa was to be a serious concern in Moroccan international relations — not least because it was the most convenient source of the
slave-soldiers that were an important element of the standing army.

Al-Mansūr's immediate successors, however, were to lose the degree of
control he had created. For a time, the country was divided between rival
Saadian princes, and the religious brotherhoods returned as informal rulers
over much of the countryside. It was, indeed, the beginning of the end of power
for the Saadian dynasty, though not for the shorfa as a broader group. The next
dynasty, the Alawī, were also Arabs from the Hilalian invasions, shorfa who
had settled in the oasis region of Tafilelt beyond the Atlas to the south of Fez.
After a slow buildup of power there on the fringes during the mid-seventeenth
century, the Alawī emerged under Mulai ar-Rachid to capture Fez and found
a new dynasty.

Like the Saadians before them, the Alawite dynasty rose rapidly to a pinnacle of power represented by the reign of Mulai (or Prince) Isma'īl (ruled
1672–1727), followed by several decades of political fragmentation and dynastic
rivalry. Like al-Mansūr before him, he built a slave army, mainly recruited in the
western Sudan. This meant that he too became involved in sub-Saharan affairs.
He led one expedition across the desert in person in 1689, married into the
Sudanese aristocracy, and established at least a nominal Moroccan control over
the whole of the western Sahara. After his death in 1727, however, real power
passed to the sub-Saharan soldiers of the royal guard, just as it passed to the
equivalent body of Mamluks in Egypt. The guard made and unmade sultans at
will for the next three decades, and it was only gradually that central power was
partially restored by the rise of new Alawī power under able sultans in the
second half of the eighteenth century.

THE CENTRAL SUDAN

Other African states, this time south of the desert, were like Morocco in
experiencing and reacting to the rise of the Ottomans without actually falling
to Ottoman conquest. In the central Sudan on either side of Lake Chad was a
region beyond the influence of the Atlantic trade, at least until the last decades
of the eighteenth century. The Hausa states and Borno therefore continued their
orientation toward the north. As political power in Hausaland was consolidated
around its set of fortified cities, the Tuareg region of the steppe was also consolidated into the Sultanate of Aïr, more nearly a nomadic tribal federation than a
true sedentary state but nevertheless having a capital in the oasis city of Agadès.
The main function of Aïr was to provide an institution for organizing Tuareg
relations with their sedentary neighbors, and some kind of organized relations
were necessary for the good of all who profited from the caravan trade.

The new and important sedentary power throughout the sixteenth century was Kebbi, on the frontier between Songrai and Hausa culture, and ruled
by Songrai until the early part of the century. Once independent, however,

Kebbi came to rival the "big four" among the Hausa states — Gobir, Katsina, Kano, and Zazzau — and reached out briefly to establish its control over Aïr and the steppe. To the south of Hausa, the Jukun state of Kwawarafa also grew more powerful in the sixteenth century in the Benue valley, remaining staunchly anti-Muslim. Jukun raids against the Hausa states and Borno alike were an increasing problem through the late sixteenth century, though they only reached their greatest extent in the seventeenth.

Borno, meanwhile, responded to the Turkish challenge with a new intensity of commerce across the desert. The Kanuri position had begun to stabilize even before the Turkish seizure of Tripoli. Mai 'Ali Gaji had reestablished a fixed capital at the very beginning of the sixteenth century, and Borno slowly extended its authority over Kanem to the east. It was already in diplomatic contact with Tripoli, and, when the Ottomans seized Tripoli in the 1550s and began pushing out into the desert, the contact was maintained. Through this channel, Borno became the first state to bring firearms south of the Sahara, and it even secured the services of a few Turkish mercenaries. It is possible that the Turks and Borno later clashed over control of the cross-desert route. If so, the conflict was postponed until the 1570s, when Borno was already familiar with firearms and Ottoman power was reaching its limits everywhere.

By that time, Borno was moving toward a second peak of power and success in the world, equivalent to an earlier peak in the reign of Dunama Dibbalemi in the thirteenth century. The early reign of Mai Idris Aloma (ruled 1580–1617) is chronicled in a contemporary account in greater detail than that of any other Sudanese ruler. This account, by Ibn Fartua, pictures a pious Muslim monarch much concerned to improve the mosques and extend the judicial system. It also pictures a countless round of military activity against recalcitrant minorities within the kingdom and against foreign enemies in all directions. The kindest interpretation is to see this constant raiding as the necessary path toward political consolidation and the creation of a Kanuri nation. Another view suggests that this was Borno's response to the Turkish challenge. Guns and powder had to come from the north; but here in the Chadic region, where there was no gold to earn foreign exchange, slaves had to serve instead. It is also possible that it was easy to acquire slaves in this period, when Borno had guns and her neighbors did not.

The region east of Kanem barely began to emerge into the light of historical knowledge in the sixteenth century. One or more states had already existed in the Marra mountains of Darfur, but between there and the Kanuri center near Lake Chad we can only guess that some small states may have existed side by side with stateless societies and the various kinship-based political organizations of pastoral peoples. This region apparently absorbed some Islamic ideas and institutions by way of the Kanuri, along with Kanuri political refugees and other offshoot population movements. A new state of Bagirmi was founded about 1500 immediately to the southeast of Kanem; it was absorbed into Borno during the reign of Idris Aloma and then resurrected as an independent state.

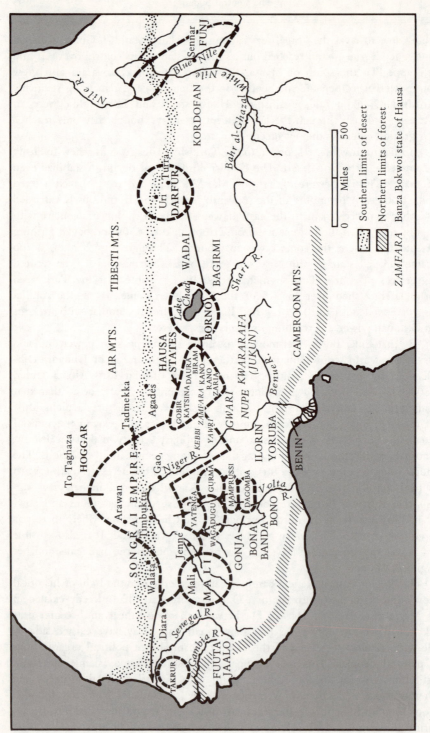

The Sudan in the Sixteenth Century

ZAMFARA Banza Bokwoi state of Hausa

Southern limits of desert
Northern limits of forest

0   Miles   500

A decade or so into the seventeenth century, Wadai appears as a newly Islamicized state further east, under a dynasty that maintained itself in power until 1911. A new Islamic state also emerged or reemerged in Darfur about the 1630s. All three of these states had some contact across the Sahara with North Africa, but they tended to operate even more on a commercial and diplomatic axis that ran east toward the Nile valley and west toward Borno. When Borno was strong, they were pulled that way, only to be attracted in the opposite direction when there was a strong power in the Nilotic Sudan.

THE FALL OF SONGRAI

It is hard to avoid being struck by the contrast between Songrai and Borno in the late sixteenth century. Each increased its contact with a new power to the north of the desert. For Borno, the result was to reinforce her political and military influence. For Songrai, it was military defeat of disastrous consequence for much of the western Sudan.

Part of the difference has to be explained simply as a matter of timing. Borno met the Turks at the end of more than a century of continuous Ottoman expansion, when Turkish resources were wearing thin. Songrai met the Moroccans only shortly after their great victory over Portugal at al-Ksar al-Kebir in 1578 — not perhaps at the peak of Moroccan military and political achievement but at least at a time when they had checked the Europeans and were looking for a cheap conquest that might help pay for the chronic struggle against their Hispanic and Turkish enemies. While Borno appears to have assimilated the new weapons before it had to meet actual Turkish pressure, Songrai had struggled for nearly a century with unresolved internal conflict.

After the spectacular reign of Sonni 'Alī (ruled 1464–1492), the secular-minded Sonni dynasty was driven from power by a Muslim party that stressed the clear Islamic obligation to convert all people to the word of God. The first important ruler of the new dynasty was Askia Muhammad (ruled c. 1493–1528). He not only stood firm against the pagan practices of the countryside; his pattern of conquest also suggests a possible ambition to make himself ruler of a united and Islamic western Sudan. If so, he failed; he was finally deposed by his own sons, and his legacy was a long period of religious strife.

Economic pressures also appeared. The Portuguese effort to reverse the trade routes and export gold by sea may have made some difference, but Songrai gained control of the salt-mining areas in the Sahara early in the sixteenth century. This move should have made her trade position as secure as possible under the circumstances. It was impossible to prevent the drain of gold southward to the sea, but the terms of trade could have been protected and it might have been possible to increase gold production. But the Moroccans began in the 1580s a series of maneuvers directed first at the salt supplies in the desert, then, in 1591, at Songrai itself.

The Moroccan army sent across the desert was small by Sudanese standards, only about 4,000 men, but it was enough to defeat a Songrai army many times its size — a victory followed by the occupation of the Niger bend. The Moroccan victory is sometimes credited to the use of firearms, which were loud and spectacular; and the Moroccan forces came to be called *Arma,* from the Arabic *ruma,* meaning "musketeer." But the key to success was more likely the use of disciplined mercenaries and slave-soldiers against the uncoordinated mass of the Songrai army. The recent economic pinch in Songrai could also have caused a serious remount problem — since horses were imported from the north. In any event the Moroccan success was limited. The Arma were strong enough to seize and keep the desert ports like Timbuktu and Gao, but they were not strong enough to recreate the Songrai empire. The Songrai homeland on the Niger below Timbuktu was only sporadically under Arma control, and Arma showed a greater interest in moving upstream toward the goldfields, where they were sometimes able to control the Niger valley as far as Jenné. But their power to expand within the Sudan was limited, while the Moroccan power to keep them under metropolitan control was even more limited. The local commander soon became an independent sovereign in all but name. By the 1610s, the Arma had taken local wives and made themselves into an independent ruling class, receiving no support from and accepting no orders from Morocco. They and their descendants stayed on as rulers of Timbuktu and its vicinity until 1737, sometimes controlling a little of the surrounding country. The whole episode is reminiscent of Kanem's trans-Saharan conquest of Fezzan in the thirteenth century; Kanem also lost control after a few decades but left a Kenembu dynasty ruling Fezzan for about a century and a half.

Some authorities have seen the fall of Songrai as a calamity for West Africa, the beginning of disorder and decline that lasted well into the nineteenth century. It is true that no great empire rose in the place of Ghana, Mali, or Songrai, and this made a real difference to the people of the sahel west of the Niger bend. Without a strong state to mobilize the strength of the region, it was prey to chronic warfare and nomadic attack. The whole sahel also experienced severe drought and famine from 1639 to 1643 and again from 1738 to 1756.

But the sahel was not all of West Africa, not even all of the western Sudan. We have no evidence of a similar time of troubles among the second-tier states well to the south of the desert-savanna frontier. The Hausa states appear to have prospered in the seventeenth and eighteenth centuries, perhaps gaining some of the trans-Saharan trade diverted from the Niger bend. Upstream from Timbuktu, in the first half of the eighteenth century, a new state rose to power in the Niger valley, based on the city of Segu. It was ethnically Bambara and non-Muslim by religion. It took on imperial proportions by encroaching on the declining power of Mali to the south, establishing its dominance over the Fulbe herdsmen in the internal delta of the Niger to the north, and finally by expanding toward the desert edge. Thus Segu finally mastered the whole length of the Niger from Timbuktu to Jenné, and so was able to control the flow of trade from the forest toward the desert. In the last decades of the century, Kaarta, a second Bambara offshoot of Segu, rose to power in the sahel itself between the Niger and the Senegal and began a career of expansion westward toward the Senegal valley, following the ancient strategy of seeking to control as long a section of the desert edge as possible.

The key military institution in both Segu and Kaarta was the *tõ jõ* (corporate slaves), a standing army of slave-soldiers that began as an association of slave raiders who gradually built their power into permanent rule over the region. In this respect, they were not very different from the Arma. Their rise to a position of military dominance paralleled the decline of the Arma, and Kaarta, alone of the desert-edge states, was successful in putting up a united defense against the Moroccans operating to the north of the Senegal.

Elsewhere, we often know only the outlines of political history — too little for confident generalizations about the health and well-being of society. At times, a military offensive may indicate strength, though military power can hardly be taken as an index of social health. The territory within the Niger bend, in present-day Upper Volta and northern Ghana, for example, was the home-land of the seven states that made up the Mossi complex — Tenkodogo, Waga-dugu, Yatenga, Fada Ngurma, Mamprussi, Dagomba, and Nanumba. Led by Yatenga, they emerged briefly into the international forum of the northern tier in the fifteenth century with a bid to seize control of the sahel and the Niger bend. As it turned out, Songrai won. The Mossi lost and dropped back to their old homeland.

TURKS AND CHRISTIANS IN EASTERN AFRICA

The Ottomans conquered Egypt in 1517, but they made little effort to reach up the Nile into the Sudan. Their furthest stretch in that direction was to Nubia, where they briefly controlled the Nile valley south of Aswan, only to see their own officials turn themselves into independent rulers. Further south, the Funj kingdom of Sennar came into existence at the beginning of the six-teenth century, quite independent of Turkish moves in Egypt or the Red Sea. Very little is known of this state or its history other than that the Funj seem to have originated along the White Nile just below the *sudd* region. They first made themselves a ruling aristocracy in the *gezira* (the long peninsula sepa-rating the White and Blue Niles just above their confluence) over subjects who were partly Arabian and partly of local Sudanese origin. At some time, prob-ably quite early in their rule, they converted to Islam, and at their seventeenth-century peak of power they controlled the whole region from the Red Sea west-ward to Kordofan.

The Turks were far more interested in the Red Sea and the valuable trade of the Indian Ocean than they were in the upper Nile, but the Indian Ocean was already contested by the Europeans. In 1505, the Portuguese arrived in strength and established bases on the East African coast. In the decade that followed, they made good their naval supremacy and tested it against the best fleets the Egyptians and other Muslim naval powers could muster. They also found the limitations of their sea power: they were unable to secure a base capable of blocking the straits of Bab el Mandeb and closing off the Red Sea. Once in control of Egypt, the Turks built ships on the Red Sea and soon established their naval supremacy there, but they were unable to extend that power into the Indian Ocean.

This standoff between Portuguese and Turkish sea power had immediate consequences for the Ethiopian highlands as well as for the port towns on the Red Sea and the Gulf of Aden. In the early decades of the sixteenth century, the Christian monarchy of the western highlands was still the strongest state in the region. Adal remained as an Islamic state, but it was only a minor power confined to the eastern highlands. By the 1520s, the Portuguese-Ottoman conflict at sea cut heavily into the trade and prosperity of the whole region. The Turkish presence may also have acted as a new encouragement to Muslim aggression. The Sultan of Adal, Ahmad ibn Ibrahīm al-Ghāzi, called Grañ (ruled 1506–1542), began to rebuild his power mainly from a sedentary base in the highlands. He also began to gather a following among the nomads of the lowlands — Somali to the east, 'Afar and others in the Danakil depression to the west. In 1527, he declared a *jihad*, or holy war, against the Christians, using some firearms acquired from the Turks but relying mainly on the nomads' response to the call of Islam and the lure of booty. The Portuguese countered by sending musketeers of their own, but the Muslim cause was generally successful. By 1541, Amad Grañ had virtually completed the conquest of the Christian highlands, though he died in battle the following year. With that, the coalition fell apart, the nomads turned to raiding in their own interest, and gradually, through the 1540s, the Christians reconquered their country.

The disintegration of Ahmad Grañ's nomadic following left his own country open to attack by other nomads — not the Muslim Somali who had followed the jihad but the Galla, who had not yet become either Christian or Muslim and had been moving slowly outward from the southern highlands for some time. During the 1540s, they poured into the eastern highlands that had once been Adal, not so much raiders as nomadic pastoralists come to settle on any land they could take. The western highlands were also subject to Galla infiltration, weakened as that region was by the long war of the jihad. By 1563, a third of the Christian kingdom was in Galla hands, and they continued to threaten all the Ethiopian sedentary states off and on for the next three centuries. Over time, however, many Galla turned sedentary, often adopting either Islam or Christianity and other aspects of the highland sedentary culture.

Meanwhile, the Portuguese military intervention in aid of Christian Ethiopia had opened the country to more extensive contacts with the West. The Jesuit order sent a mission in the hope of converting the Coptic Ethiopians to Catholicism. In time, the missionaries succeeded in converting the Emperor Susenyos (ruled 1607–1632), and he in turn embarked on a program of modernization coupled with the doctrinal reformation of the church. The program made some gains, but it ran into bitter opposition from the Ethiopian clergy and the people at large. The result was civil war leading to the abdication of Susenyos and finally the expulsion of the missionaries. Ethiopia was then more isolated than ever, faced with the problem of continued Galla migration and infiltration through the seventeenth and eighteenth centuries, and with the growth of provincial power at the expense of the monarch. By 1770, Christian Ethiopia was a single kingdom in name only.

THE TWILIGHT OF TURKISH RULE IN NORTH AFRICA

The reality of Ottoman rule over North Africa was dissipated gradually, but the decade centered on 1710 saw crucial changes that made Turkish over-rule little more than a fiction. The Bey of Tunis made his regime hereditary, founding a new dynasty that was to last two and a half centuries, though the Turkish claim to ultimate sovereignty was not denied on either side. The Dey of Tripoli did much the same with the consent of his dīwān, founding the Karamanli dynasty that lasted until the Turks reconquered Tripoli in 1835. The oligarchy of Algiers expelled the Turkish pasha at about the same time but failed to achieve the kind of stability a hereditary monarchy might have brought in its place. The office of dey passed from hand to hand with the play of local political forces. Of the thirty-odd deys who ruled between 1671 and 1818, fourteen gained office by killing the predecessor.

The international relations of eighteenth-century Barbary were still characterized by rivalry with the Christians and the ancient pattern of mutual commerce raiding across the Mediterranean, but the regencies were now independent enough to fight one another. Tunisia's greatest threat came from Algiers, which tried several times to force Tunis into a tributary position. Tunis meanwhile threatened Tripoli in much the same way.

All three regencies nevertheless kept a shadow of Turkish rule. The Karamanli of Tripoli were themselves of Turkish origin, though they had intermarried for several generations with the local Arab ruling families. The Turkish garrison in Algiers continued as an important force, with soldiers recruited from Anatolia as late as the early nineteenth century. Tunisia alone took on the appearance of a fairly homogeneous state with a centralized monarchy having a semblance of control over the countryside, though this came about partly because the Tunisian plains were situated geographically in the hinterland of the port. Tripoli, by contrast, was little more than a port city with a narrow hinterland backed up against the steppe and desert. Algiers had a mosaiclike hinterland of Arabs and Berbers in the *tell,* Berbers in the mountains, still more Arab and Berber nomads in the far hinterland, and the Turkish oligarchy in the capital.

By coincidence, Egypt also passed into a new political phase with a civil war in 1711. The Mamluks were once more victorious over the Turkish forces, with a resultant cutback in the viceroy's powers. But here the degree of change was different from Barbary; Ottomans could still exercise power on occasion. Major policy changes had to have the acquiescence of Istanbul, if not its prior consent. The Mamluk oligarchy was also reduced through time to a total of twenty-four officers with the title of bey. Each of these officeholders competed with the others for imperial preferment, and the viceroy kept a measure of real power according to his ability to play off one against the rest. From time to time, one or another combination of Mamluk political forces would try for true independence on the order of the Maghribine regencies, but the Ottomans still had enough power to send an expeditionary force from Turkey and restore the old equilibrium.

As the end of the eighteenth century approached, the broader international situation began to change in ways that prefigured the nineteenth-century dominance by Europe. The balance of military power had been shifting slowly. In the sixteenth century, Turks had been a serious threat to eastern and southern Europe. In the seventeenth, Turkish armies could still march on occasion to the walls of Vienna, but no eighteenth-century Muslim empire had power equivalent to that of a large European state. By the 1760s, the British East India Company had already replaced the Mogul Empire as the strongest power on the Indian subcontinent, and the Dutch East India Company was stronger than any one of the Muslim sultanates of Southeast Asia. In 1798, Napoleon successfully invaded Egypt, an important sign of changing times even though other Europeans soon forced him to relinquish his dreams of North African empire. The colonial period was still some decades off, but the threat was already implicit in the new differentials of military power.

RELIGION AND REFORM IN NORTH AFRICA

This rapid growth of European power in the eighteenth century calls for a retrospective explanation from historians, and the answer usually turns on the European development of industrial technology. It also called for an explanation from thinking Muslim leaders of that period. One response was technological, to consider borrowing what the Europeans had invented. Another, and probably the dominant answer in the eighteenth century, was religious. Religion was, after all, the factor that defined being Christian and being Muslim. If Muslims won, it was attributed to Islam; if Christians won, it must be on account of their Christianity. More to the point, if Muslims lost, or seemed to be slipping behind, it must be that something had gone wrong with the *kind* of Islam they practiced. The most orthodox religious authorities in the eighteenth-century world of Islam thought they could detect the fault: failure to follow exactly the way set out by the Prophet. And the most common source of that failure was the tolerance of semipagan practices, especially ones that had grown and spread with expansion of the sufi brotherhoods.

By the eighteenth century, the sufi turuq existed in great numbers and great variety. They were especially strong in the Berber west, in the northern parts of the Ottoman Empire, and in India — in precisely those parts of the Muslim world that were newest to the faith, beyond the range of everyday Arabic speech, beyond the core area of Islam represented by the Abbasid Empire. It was only to be expected that relatively newly converted people could hold on to some of their older beliefs, fitting them into the Islamic framework much as the Christians of northern Europe adapted the pagan Christmas tree.

But sufi thought and organization also moved in common directions by mutual borrowings throughout the Muslim world. Almost all the sufi brotherhoods were affected in one way or another by the theological teachings of Ibn al-'Arabi in thirteenth-century Spain. Orthodox Muslims had accounted for the existence of evil in the world by accepting the idea that an omnipotent and merciful God allowed evil to exist for his own reasons, though evil acts would be punished in the life hereafter. Al-'Arabi and his followers sought a very intense and emotional love of God, and they were unable to reconcile their emotional state with the notion that a perfect God would allow any evil at all. Their solution was to deny that the apparent evil people experience *is* evil. Because of God's essential goodness, they argued, what appears to be evil must be good in some ultimate way that mere mortals cannot understand.

Doctrines that shared this tendency could lead some to reject the earthly world and spend their time in study, prayer, and contemplation of God's greatness. Some sufi doctrines took that direction. But it was also possible to begin with al-'Arabi's teachings and move to a kind of fatalism under the conviction that whatever happens must ultimately be for the best. Still another possibility was to adopt an amoral attitude, arguing that because people act as God wills, God could hardly punish someone in the next life for doing what He himself has ordained, however much that action might seem contrary to common morality. The more extreme versions went beyond any reasonable definition of Muslim orthodoxy, but these sufi teachings were nevertheless tolerated in the Ottoman empire alongside those of the urban 'ulamā.

The sufi brotherhoods also became more elaborate institutions as time passed. From their beginnings as informal groups which happened to follow and propagate the teachings of a particular mystic, they became societies with formal membership and rules of behavior as well as ritual. Sometimes the members lived together in a special retreat house or monastery called *ribāt* or *zāwiya* in Arabic. Those who did not reside together were often expected to pay calls at these religious centers from time to time, if only to maintain their personal contact with the head of the order or his regional representatives.

The turuq officials were far more than recognized men of learning, as the 'ulamā were. They had a kind of institutional authority over their followers, and they were thought to possess special powers others lacked. These powers were usually conceived as emanating from the original founder of the order and passed on through a mystical chain of benediction. A laying on of hands or a ritual testament transmitted the special holiness, or *baraka,* of the founder along a chain of authority called a *silsila*. An important sufi religious figure could recite his silsila as a chain of transmitters of learning and holiness back to the head of his order and beyond to someone who had known and learned from Muhammad himself — usually 'Ali, as the person closest to the Prophet. The chain of almost esoteric transmission, the possession of a permanent organization, and a permanent headquarters or set of regional headquarters all helped to give the sufi clerics, or marabouts, of North Africa a secular as well as religious authority. It was a different kind of power from that usually exercised by a state, but the extent of power could be as great, and some orders could stand within a particular region as the functional equivalent of a state.

Some historians have argued that sufism met a genuine and felt need for religious experience; others claim that it also encouraged religious charlatanism, saint worship, and fatalism, all of which corrupted the morals and body politic of the Ottoman Empire and Morocco alike during the eighteenth century. Whether this charge is justified or not, several religious reformers of that century saw the broad currents of sufism as a cancerous growth that had to be removed from the original body of Islamic belief.

The most important reform movements of this kind began in central Arabia about 1744 with the teachings of Muhammad ibn 'Abd al-Wahab, at once primitivist, puritan, antisufi, and supported militarily by the Arabian house of Sa'ud. The Wahabis conquered most of Arabia including the holy cities and then moved north against the Ottoman Empire. As they moved forward on the battlefield, their doctrine also changed by passing beyond its original attack on sufi excesses to attack the orthodox 'ulamā as well for their tolerance of those excesses.

Though Wahabi power was broken militarily in 1818 and never recovered, the doctrine spread far more widely; and the tendency toward a purification of Islam spread more widely still. These broader ripples were felt most in the core area of the Ottoman world, including Egypt, and they were to merge in the nineteenth century with other varieties of Islamic reformism. In the Maghrib, however, sufism was and remained far stronger than it was in the Middle East, and a new sufi order, the *Tijānīya,* was founded by Ahmad al-Tijāni in southern Algeria as late as 1781. But even there the reform movement gained some adherents, including at least one Alawi sultan of Morocco, though the Moroccan situation was complicated by the fact that the sultans claimed one kind of baraka through descent from Muhammad, while the sufi leaders claimed another through the silsila of their orders.

RELIGION AND SOCIETY SOUTH OF THE DESERT

Muslim religious reform took on another meaning south of the Sahara, especially in West Africa. There, Islam had been introduced directly, rather than through the agency of the state, into a society that was not so urbanized as either North Africa or the Middle East. Islam was therefore sufi almost from the beginning and dominantly so ever since. It was also more than a religious message promising salvation to those who would do God's will. Islam meant literacy for serious Muslims, and this opened a small window onto the literatures of the intercommunicating zone. It also carried ethical standards, injunctions, and a body of law that was (or should have been) enforced by the state on believers and unbelievers alike. Acceptance of the new religion therefore meant an acceptance of social change. But society could change a religion even as religion could change a society, and Islamic practice changed in its West African setting. This is not to say that Islam in the western Sudan became less "pure" than the Islam of North Africa or the Middle East; its purity is beside the point for historical analysis. The point is that people adjusted to the new religion, not by splitting the difference between the new orthodoxy and the old paganism, but by changing their beliefs and actions in different directions and in several areas of thought and life. The new religion was made secure in the new society by shaping it to some degree and by adjusting to it as well.

Islam came to West Africa as a merchants' religion and was identified with commerce from the start. It was only natural that West African merchants would be among the first to convert. It was they who had the closest contact with Muslim merchants who came down from the north, and their own travels through West Africa carried them beyond the effective range of local deities who were associated with particular places or particular lineages. A more universal message suited their widening range of experience. Rulers also had close contact with the alien merchants, and they too were among the early converts — they and the people of the towns and the court.

But a ruler could not change his religion as a private act, either as a whim or from deep personal conviction. Where the masses were still non-Muslim, his conversion was a political act simply because of the long association between religion and kingship. Just as the head of a lineage was often the oldest male member and was seen as the natural intermediary between the ancestral spirits and the living members of that lineage, so too it was common in African states to conceive of the ruler as having a special ritual position in relation to the gods, particularly to the gods below the universal pantheon who were especially concerned with a particular people. A king who became a Muslim could compromise, of course, and carry out his ritual functions in regard to the old gods alongside his obligations to the One God. He could even encourage Islam, support scholarship and learning, but still fall short of the full enforcement of Muslim law. Many Muslim rulers were forced into this position, where their private beliefs might be most orthodox yet their public acts were not. A ruler might equally well be unorthodox in belief, but in any event he was caught in a position where actions measuring up to the highest standards of Islam were very difficult.

Not so for the merchants as a class. They were under no such pressure to compromise. They might even see an advantage in the status of religious specialist. The best kind of Muslim education carried literacy, of undoubted use in commerce. Religious prestige, and especially the reputation of power to manipulate the spirit world, had obvious uses in pagan as well as Muslim territory. Like some of the commercial specialists in nineteenth-century Iboland who were able to pass back and forth through a stateless society partly on account of their religious position, Muslim merchants sometimes encouraged a belief that Islamic learning brought them secret powers over the spirit world. As Richard Jobson, an English merchant, reported of his Jahanke fellow-merchants whose route ran inland from the upper Gambia in 1625: ". . . they have free recourse through all places, so that howsoever the Kings and Countries are at warres and up in arms, the one against the other, yet still the Marybucke [Marabout, or Muslim cleric] is a privileged person, and may follow his trade or course of travelling, without any let or interruption of either side."

It was also in the merchants' interests to insulate themselves from the society through which they traveled. People connected with trade diasporas had tended to do this from ancient times by setting up autonomous enclaves whenever possible. Within these enclaves, they enjoyed the right to live under their own laws and to have a representative to deal with the host government on their behalf. The western Sudan had a similar practice from a very early date. The capitals of Ghana and Gao were double cities as early as the eleventh century — one city for the king and court, the other for the merchants. Since the merchants were often Muslim, the separation was sometimes drawn on religious lines, as it was in Ghana before the court converted to Islam. Later towns with a strong reputation for Muslim piety and learning were sometimes granted autonomy by the state. Jaxaba (in French, Diakha-Ba) on the Bafing near the Bambuhu goldfields was a Jahanke town that had such a grant from the government of Mali.

Long before the eighteenth century, this division between the political and religious elites, each with its own sphere of activity, became very widespread in the western Sudan. On the religious side, it was often accompanied by the ideal of pacifism and a suspicion that political rule was unworthy of a truly religious person. Although the distinction between the two elites may have originated in the need of the clerical and commercial group to protect itself in its position as a minority, the ideal may also be associated with certain aspects of North African sufism, and it also has Kharijite overtones. Whatever its origin, it made for a deep division between secular and religious leadership in the western Sudan.

As time passed, this division became a source of conflict. In the first instance, it was felt by Muslim rulers who were pushed by their Muslim subjects, if not by conscience, to enforce Islam. This placed a Muslim ruler on the horns of a dilemma. If he took the prescriptions of his religion seriously, he was obliged to try to impose Islam on the people and fully enforce Muslim law; but this course was likely to alienate many of his subjects, and it might well destroy the pre-Islamic religious ideology that so often supported and justified West African rulers in the first place. If, on the other hand, he ignored pagan practices or tolerated religious syncretism, he was likely to stir the wrath of the clerical community. Even though that community was likely to be small, it was powerful; it contained the literate, the merchants, and those with the closest ties to the greater world beyond the borders of a single state.

Signs of this tension appear early in history. Dunama Dibbalemi, the great thirteenth-century ruler of Kanem, chose one horn of the dilemma and opened the *mune,* a container of sacred regalia that was supposed to protect the dynasty only so long as it remained closed and hidden. Symbolically, he thus denied his sacred role as a ruler — and the justification of that rule in the eyes of his pagan subjects. There is some evidence that this denial seriously weakened the Sefawa dynasty and ended the rise of Kanem. Later, at the end of the fifteenth century, Sonni 'Alī of Songrai took the opposite course. Though he was formally a Muslim, he capitalized on his prestige as a sacred figure in the traditional religion, at the price of serious opposition from the clerical community in Timbuktu. This Muslim opposition was one reason for the fall of the Sonni dynasty and its replacement by the Askias.

These two instances suggest that the outright seizure of either horn of the dilemma was likely to be disastrous. Yet the Muslim ruler had little choice: the most delicate compromise between Islam and paganism was, to a pious Muslim, a decision against the full teachings of the Prophet. The orthodox view of sunni Islam held that the ruler had an obligation to see that Muslim law was fully enforced. Yet most Muslim rulers were decidedly tolerant of pagan practices, and the cry for religious reform demanded state action, not just personal action. It was an easy step from the cry for reform to the cry for revolution, from the demand that rulers should do as the 'ulamā said, to the demand that the 'ulamā themselves should rule.

The revolutionary force of Islamic reform grew with the passage of time. It was implicit in the change of dynasties in sixteenth-century Songrai. It became explicit in the seventeenth century with the idea that tolerance of paganism was tantamount to paganism itself. Jihad could then be declared against rulers who were actually Muslim, and a sequence of jihads on that basis began and continued far into the nineteenth century. Before the movement had run its course, scores of governments were overthrown, their secular rulers being replaced by Muslim clerics. The clerics often emphasized the religious nature of their new office by taking the title of *Imam* or its derivatives in African languages, like the Fulbe *Almaami.* In normal usage, Imam is simply the title of the leader of prayer at the Friday mosque, hence its suggestion of religious guidance. In Africa it was often coupled with *amīr al-Mu'minīn,* commander of the faithful, the title used by the Umayyad caliphate when all Muslims were united in a single state, hence the suggestion of a militant and united Islam.

Just as Islam itself came to the western Sudan by way of the Sahara, the reform movement also came across the desert — and was transformed in the process by the imprint of Saharan social and religious patterns. In the distant past, the Sahara had been occupied by the camel-using Berbers. Beginning in the fifteenth century, the western Sahara was changed once more by the arrival of Arabs of the *banū Maʿqīl,* a tribe that had drifted across the northern fringe of the Sahara at the time of the Hilalian invasion of the Maghrib and now began drifting south into the desert. During the fifteenth and sixteenth centuries, they gradually replaced the Berbers as the dominant nomadic people in the Sahara west of the Niger bend, defeating them and reducing most Berbers to a status of respectable subordination. Though not quite tributaries, the Berbers were nevertheless forced to pay a form of protection money to the victors.

During the obscure centuries of this shift in nomadic populations, a crucial change took place in the social and political relations of the desert tribes. The Berber nomads had a strong religious tradition going back to the Almoravid movement, and they began to lay special emphasis on their function as Islamic teachers and religious specialists, at the same time rejecting political and military roles as inappropriate to their clerical status. The Arab immigrants meanwhile claimed political dominance and the military role for themselves. By the early part of the seventeenth century, nomads of the western Sahara were divided into two groups. One, called *zwāya,* was clerical, normally of Berber extraction but even then beginning to shift to Arabic speech and some aspects of Arabic culture. The other was the military group descended from the banu Maʿqīl. A similar division in the Sahara may have existed even earlier, because it clearly reflects the ancient West African tendency to separate the clerical, mercantile, and religious roles from the political and military. Tuareg society, for example, was divided into a warrior group called *Imazegen* and a clerical group called *Ineslemen* (literally, "Muslim"), but no suggestion of two separate waves of immigrants.

The earliest of the jihads against states deemed incompletely Muslim occurred in the setting of this division between zwāya and Maʿqīl in the southwest Sahara, just to the north of Fuuta Tooro and the Wolof states. The reform movement began in the 1660s under the leadership of a zwāya cleric who took the name Nasīr al-Dīn. He began preaching personal reform and purification, asking his followers for a more complete personal submission to God and His law, and he built a substantial following on both sides of the ecological frontier. Then, in 1673, he began to demand that secular rulers surrender their powers to him as Imam and amīr al-Mu'minīn — in effect as founder of a new theocratic Muslim state. Rulers who refused to surrender were the targets of his call for jihad. At first, the movement was a spectacular success. It swept the zwāya of southern Mauritania and overturned the rulers of Fuuta Tooro, Kajor, and Waalo among the sedentary states to the south. The secular rulers soon rallied, however, under the leadership of one of the Maʿqīl. Nasīr al-Dīn himself was killed in battle in 1674, and the movement was defeated everywhere, but not without leaving a legacy for the future.

A generation later, in the 1690s, a Futaanke cleric named Malik Si took the title of Imam and established his rule over Bundu, a region just beyond the southeastern frontier of Fuuta Tooro. He recruited followers where he could

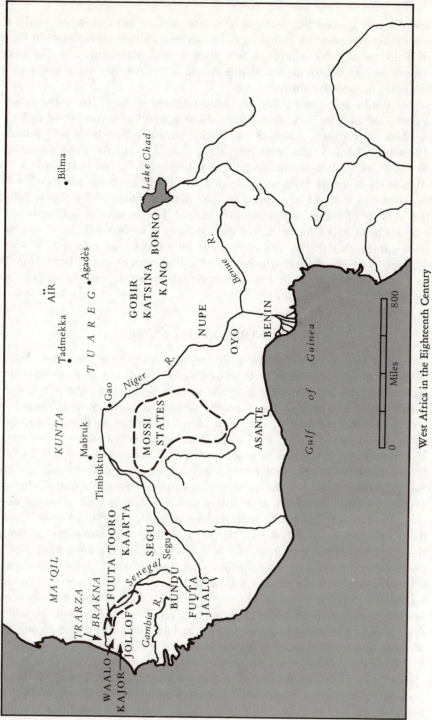

West Africa in the Eighteenth Century

and declared a jihad that was partly a state-building movement and partly an attempt to dispossess the Malinke (and partly non-Muslim) inhabitants in favor of Fulbe immigrants. Within a few years he was successful, and the Sisibe dynasty he founded continued to rule Bundu under the title of Almaami until late in the nineteenth century.

A third revolt under Fulbe leadership followed in the 1720s, in the pattern set by Malik Si. The Fuuta Jaalo highlands were occupied at that period by large numbers of emigrant Fulbe living among an older population of Yalunka (French Djallonké), who were generally pagan. The call for jihad was issued by two Fulbe leaders, Karamoko Alfa and Ibrahima Sori, and it resulted in the Almaamate of Fuuta Jaalo, ruled from then on by an alternation in office of two dynasties founded by the two leaders. Both in Bundu and in Fuuta Jaalo, the ideology of Islamic reform was maintained, but genuine dedication to religion seems to have dropped below the standard set by Nasīr al-Dīn. Some historians think that the cry for reform was little more than a facade for state-building by emigrant Fulbe who happened to find themselves as a large minority in a non-Fulbe society, and a secular aspect was to accompany the religious in many of the later jihads.

THE NOMADIC FRONTIER

After Songrai fell to the Arma, the sedentary societies of the western Sudan seemed unable to respond in an organized way to the danger of nomadic attack. Nomads became more active during the seventeenth century, and in the eighteenth they began raiding deep into the savanna country, moving forward to occupy the marginal land of the sahel. Morocco also reentered the scene from across the desert. Starting with Mulai Isma'īl, whose mother was Sudanese, Moroccan rulers again took a serious interest in Sudanese affairs, but Isma'īl turned from the Niger bend to the sahel further west and especially to the Senegal valley. This time the Moroccans contented themselves with "informal empire," without attempting to establish Moroccan control over sedentary societies. By the early eighteenth century, leaders of the Ma'qīl, descended from those who had defeated Nasīr al-Dīn, recognized a vague Moroccan suzerainty down to the Senegal River itself, and Morocco kept a military force permanently stationed on the southern fringe of the desert, raiding at will along the savanna-desert frontier from the Atlantic coast to Kaarta, a distance of some 500 miles. Called *orma* (plural *ormankoobe*) on the Senegal, these Moroccan troops were as hard to control from home as their predecessors, the Arma, had been. The caïd in command nevertheless intervened in local politics; for many years the Moroccans virtually controlled the office of Saatigi of Fuuta Tooro.

Over the decades of insecurity, the frontiers of sedentary control gradually contracted to the south. By the late eighteenth century, Fuuta Tooro, which had once extended fifty to a hundred miles north of the Senegal, was confined to the south bank of the river. In its place on the north bank stood new emirates

founded by Ma'qīl: the Trarza opposite the lower Senegal, and Brakna opposite the northern bend. Both recognized Moroccan overrule at first, but as
the Alawites weakened in the late eighteenth century they became independent.

A similar southward move by the nomads took place at the Niger bend.
The Arma had once been successful in keeping some measure of control over
the neighboring Tuareg, as Songrai had done even more forcefully in the more
distant past. In the Adrar uplands, out in the desert, removal of sedentary control made room for a prolonged struggle over the grazing land between two
Tuareg tribes, the Kel Aulimadan and the Kel Tadmakka. In the 1650s, the
Tadmakka lost and retired southward, where they took up new lands to the
south of the Niger within the bend. Tuareg nomads also seized control of Aïr
early in the seventeenth century. Their Sultanate of Aïr reached a peak of independent power late in that century, when the Tuareg drove the northernmost of
the Hausa southward into Gobir. Before the end of the century, the Kel Aulimadan also moved south, taking up land north of the Niger and downstream
from Gao. There they pastured their flocks and practiced extortion on the
riverain Songrai, much as the ormankobe were doing on the Senegal to the
west. Finally, in 1737, the Kel Aulimadan defeated the Arma for one last time
and took control of Timbuktu themselves, introducing almost a century of
nomadic control over the Niger bend.

This southward movement of the nomads is clearly associated with climatic
change. We know, for example, that the sahel had generally favorable rainfall in
the sixteenth century; this was followed by recurrent drought and famine in the
seventeenth and eighteenth. These changes are associated with a cool phase in
European climate history between 1600 and 1750, just as the great sahelian
drought of the 1970s was associated with a cool phase in the northern hemi-
sphere. Although we know little in detail, it seems clear that the southward push
of the nomads in the eighteenth century was not so much a return to the ancient
pattern of nomad response to sedentary weakness as it was a southward movement of the natural frontier between sedentary and nomadic occupation.

THE BACKGROUND OF RELIGIOUS REVOLUTION

The jihad of Nasīr al-Dīn in the 1670s began with no apparent stimulus
from the Muslim world at large. No general demand for religious reform existed
in North Africa or the Middle East. The reformers simply drew on local traditions of piety, some of which may well have gone back to the period of the
Almoravids. By the 1770s, all this had changed. Reform movements were alive
in many parts of the Muslim world, sometimes antisufi, sometimes carried by the
more conservative sufi religious brotherhoods. The Qādirīya in particular was
active in North Africa and began a new phase of growth and importance in the
second half of the eighteenth century. Its spread across the Sahara was closely
associated with the Kunta, an Arab zwāya tribe, whose principal base was then
at Mabruk, about a hundred miles north of Timbuktu. The Kunta's reformist

preaching began in the 1750s, and by the 1770s the tarīqa had a very broad
following in both the desert and the savanna. Much of its appeal was the personal magnetism of Sidi Mukhtar al-Kunti, who reorganized and reformed the
order and developed a very broad, if informal, political influence through his
role as religious adviser to many of the nomadic tribes. His teaching would
provide the background for a new generation of Fulbe jihads in nineteenth-
century Maasina and Hausaland.

Meanwhile, in the 1770s, another revolt took place on the Senegal, where
the new influence of the Qādirīya merged with the century-old legacy of Nasīr
al-Dīn. A clerical party, led first by Suleiman Bal and then by Abdul Kader,
replaced the secular-minded Denianke dynasty with a new Almaamate of Fuuta
Tooro. This was not quite a repetition of the earlier jihad, since Fuuta was
only one of the countries that had rallied to Nasīr al-Dīn, but the goal was not
simply religious revolution in one country. The Futanke reformers tried to expand their movement by military means, though they failed against Kajor, and
the first Almaami was killed fighting Bundu. The reform movement still lacked
the broad appeal that was to enable it to spread so rapidly and so widely in the
nineteenth century. After its first burst of expansion, Fuuta Tooro settled down
as a third Almaamate, controlled by an electoral council of five or six important
figures who had more real power than the Almaami they appointed and so
frequently removed.

This and the earlier Fulbe jihads of the seventeenth and eighteenth centuries clearly foreshadow the great religious revolutions to come, but they represent a much smaller scale of political change. The most significant success of
Islam in the Sudan of the sixteenth, seventeenth, and eighteenth centuries was
quiet conversion combined with the spread of new organizations like Qādirīya,
and this quieter kind of expansion was an important precondition of the empire-
building movements of the nineteenth century.

SUGGESTIONS FOR FURTHER READING

Cissoko, Sekéné-Mody. "Traits fondamentaux des sociétés du soudan occidental du
    xixe siècle." Bulletin de l'IFAN, Ser. B, 31 (1969): 1–30.
Gray, Richard, ed. From c. 1600 to c. 1790. Cambridge History of Africa, edited by
    J. D. Fage and R. Oliver, vol. 4. Cambridge: Cambridge University Press, 1975.
Hopkins, Anthony G. An Economic History of West Africa. London: Longman,
    1973.
Raymond, André. Artisans et commerçants au Caire au xviiie siècle. 2 vols. Damas-
    cus: Institut français de Damas, 1973–74.
Shaw, Stanford J. The Financial and Administrative Organization and Development
    of Ottoman Egypt, 1517–1798. Princeton: Princeton University Press, 1962.

(See also the bibliographies for Chapters 2 and 3).

Chapter 7
The West African Coast
in the Era
of the Slave Trade

HISTORIANS in Europe and America have had a long-standing tendency to over-
emphasize the importance of the slave trade as a factor in African history. That
may have been natural enough because the slave trade was undoubtedly the most
important form of African commerce for Europeans between 1650 and 1850,
and the humanitarian campaign to abolish the slave trade in the nineteenth
century made it an important public question in most western European and
American countries. But in fact, the present Republic of South Africa was hardly
affected by the trade at any period; and East Africa from Tanzania to Ethiopia
was not seriously affected until the nineteenth century, not, at least, as seriously
as West Africa was. In almost any part of the continent, the slave trade was only
one among a number of currents of long-distance commerce. Even at the height
of the trade, it was far from being the only African export by sea. Gum and
hides from Senegambia and Sierra Leone and gold from the Gold Coast or
Zimbabwe were important at any period. Many other minor currents of trade
also played a role.

In this book, however, we are going to continue the overemphasis on the
slave trade, and by intent. Although we are trying in general to look at African
history from the African perspective, we are writing mainly for American
readers, and the slave trade was the greatest historical tie between the Americas
and Africa, not merely in populating these continents but also for its contribution to American culture of all races.

From the broadest perspective, the slave trade was part of a more general
exchange of plants, diseases, and people following the worldwide maritime
revolution of the fifteenth and early sixteenth centuries, though the process was
slow to unfold. In spite of the fact that the great discoveries began with Portuguese experimentation off the Saharan coast, the full impact was delayed. Up to
1600 or so, European influence in Japan or the Moluccas was greater than it was
in West Africa, and some of the most important consequences for Africa were

indirect, growing out of the general redistribution of people, crops, and diseases within the Atlantic basin. New crops from the Americas made it possible for tropical Africa, and especially the forest regions, to sustain populations several times larger than those of the past. Maize, peanuts, and manioc — to name only three — permanently altered the relation of Africans to their environment. But they only came to be known gradually, even on the coast, and the diffusion of knowledge into the interior was hardly complete by the late nineteenth century.

The movement of people and diseases brought about equally basic, time-consuming changes. The first movement of Europeans and Africans to the New World took with it diseases that were unknown in the Americas. Within a century, they had wiped out most of the Indian communities of the tropical lowlands and reduced highland populations to less than half their pre-Columbian levels. This was to be important for Africa; in the longer run, Africa was to be the source of their replacements.

The same mechanism of differential immunity to disease was also important in Africa itself. The underlying process depends on the fact that diseases tend to alter very rapidly, developing new strains and new types of infection. Human communities that have been isolated for long periods therefore tend to be subject to different sets of diseases. Furthermore, in each community individuals tend to develop countervailing immunities against the prevalent diseases of the region, with some inherited immunities against those known to their ancestors and even more against those they may have had as children. This means that people will be relatively immune to the diseases prevalent in their childhood disease environment, but more susceptible to strange diseases — and far more likely to die once they are infected.

Most of Africa had close enough contact with the rest of the Afro-Eurasian world to have acquired the same diseases, and hence enjoyed a degree of safety in its contacts with strangers. An unfamiliar disease might occasionally be imported, followed by an epidemic that would seriously injure the population in that generation, without impairing its ability to recover in the next. The cholera epidemics of the nineteenth century did this kind of damage, and similar epidemics may well have followed the early European voyages to western Africa. Some African peoples, however, were so isolated from the rest of humankind that they were susceptible to the same kind of devastation that occurred in the Americas. The isolation of the Khoikhoi peoples of South Africa, for example, left them open to the series of eighteenth-century smallpox epidemics that destroyed their ability to survive as a separate community.

In West Africa, the epidemiological weakness lay on the other side; Europeans shared most of the African disease environment, but not the diseases peculiar to a tropical climate. Yellow fever and falciparum malaria were especially serious. Yellow fever is rarely fatal when contracted as a child, and one attack brings lifelong immunity; but it is often fatal when contracted as an adult. Falciparum malaria is one of the most frequently fatal varieties of malaria, and it is hyperendemic in most of tropical Africa, so much so that the new arrival can hardly hope to stay as long as a year without receiving an infective mosquito bite.

In the past, these conditions made for extremely high death rates among new arrivals from Europe — death rates that could often run to more than 50 percent a year before efficient tropical medicine was known. Similar death rates had been reported from the beginning of European trade on the West African coast, and the North African merchants also sustained high death rates if they went far into the savanna country. This suggests that the fifteenth-century pattern was similar to that of the recent past, when the most active vectors for malaria and yellow fever were mosquitos that flourished in the open savanna and were not confined to forest or swampy country. These disease conditions help to explain why the maritime revolution had so little impact on the West African coast for such a long time. Any European activity there exacted an enormous price in European mortality, but the indirect impact of Europe was nevertheless very important.

THE RISE OF THE SOUTH ATLANTIC SYSTEM

A little before 1500, the Portuguese seized the island of São Thomé in the Gulf of Guinea, almost on the equator some 200 miles west of Gabon. There, they set up plantations to produce sugar for the European market, under European direction but using the labor of slaves imported from the adjacent coasts of Africa. This form of production was not entirely new; it was modeled after similar plantations on Madeira and in southern Portugal itself, and it served in turn as a model for still other plantations run in the same way — first in Brazil in the late sixteenth century and then in the Caribbean during the seventeenth and eighteenth centuries. These plantations created the economic demand for slaves from Africa, a demand that was to make the African slave trade of later centuries the largest intercontinental migration up to that point in history.

The whole system of plantation agriculture is sometimes called the South Atlantic System. Its productive centers were mainly in the Americas, supplied by slave labor from Africa, managerial staff from Europe, and producing tropical staples for the European market. Its origins go back to the Mediterranean during the period of the Crusades, when the Europeans first discovered cane sugar, which had long been produced in the Levant and North Africa. After the Europeans were expelled from the Levantine mainland, they continued to produce sugar under European control on Cyprus, then in plantations based on eastern models in Sicily, southern Spain, and Portugal. The overseas production of exotic crops was an important economic innovation, based largely on improving maritime technology and the nascent capitalism of the Italian cities, especially Genoa, which supplied much of the capital and managerial skill.

Sugar production was a business that posed unusual problems. It was partly agriculture in the form of cane cultivation and partly manufacturing, to reduce the cane juice to semirefined sugar. The whole process was very labor-intensive, which meant that comparatively large numbers of people had to be concentrated to work a small piece of land. No ordinary agricultural population was dense enough to provide such a concentration of manpower, which meant that massive labor migration was always called for wherever the sugar industry was introduced. In the Mediterranean, the institution for forced labor migration in the Middle Ages was slavery. Unlike in northern Europe, where slavery had given way to various forms of serfdom, in the Mediterranean basin it survived among Christians and Muslims alike. A small-scale slave trade carried war prisoners and other unfortunates for sale as domestic servants, as rowers in the galleys that still dominated maritime warfare, or as laborers in mines and plantations. Most agricultural labor was controlled in other ways, but it was only natural to continue the slavery of workers secured through the slave trade.

Slavery also gave the early plantation owners a degree of control over their workers that was rare for medieval agriculture. The ordinary village in Mediterranean Europe required very little detailed management. Custom controlled the sequence of operations and the distribution of the product. New plantations, on the other hand, called for careful supervision simply because they were new and because the operations were unfamiliar to the workers. Sugar plantations also needed precise timing in the delivery of cane to the mill. As a result, organization on Mediterranean sugar plantations took the form of gang labor, which worked under constant supervision day after day, hour by hour. The unskilled workers were easily thought of as interchangeable labor units, and this dehumanizing element of supervised gang work distinguished plantation slavery from other forms of social subordination and forced labor.

At first, the slaves on Mediterranean plantations were mainly war prisoners taken within the region, principally in wars between Christians and Muslims. In time, however, the demand for mobile labor exceeded the local supply, and slaves were drawn from a distance, especially from the seaports of the northern and eastern coasts of the Black Sea. By the fourteenth and fifteenth centuries, "black" Africans from the trans-Saharan trade were also sold in larger numbers to southern Europe.

As Europeans moved out into the Atlantic, the plantation complex moved with them. The Spanish set up sugar plantations in the Canary Islands. In 1455, the Portuguese began to plant sugar on Madeira — with Genoese capital and Sicilian technicians — and the next step carried them on to São Thomé. Sixteenth-century moves led from the Canaries to Hispaniola in the Caribbean, and from Madeira to Brazil.

Each onward movement raised new problems of labor supply. Canary Islanders and American Indians died in large numbers from European disease. The Europeans were accustomed to enslaving non-Christian prisoners of war, but that could hardly solve the labor problem. The Portuguese voyages down the African coast, however, showed the way to an alternate supply. Just as it was possible to short-circuit the trans-Saharan gold trade, it was also possible to short-circuit the trans-Saharan slave trade and purchase slaves on the Guinea coast. During the second half of the fifteenth century, even before an American demand for slaves appeared, Africa appears to have exported about 500 to 1,000 slaves a year to Portugal and the Atlantic islands.

Each forward move of the sugar industry brought a larger scale to plantations, designed according to the most modern technology known. Advantages of scale and technology soon made it possible for the more distant centers of production to compete effectively with the old centers closer to the European market. During the second half of the sixteenth century, the trans-Atlantic shift was completed: old centers on Madeira and São Thomé gave way to new production from Brazil. As Brazilian production grew, Brazil itself was forced to shift more and more from the labor of American Indians to that of African slaves. By 1600, the fully formed South Atlantic System was in place, not yet with the scale or geographical extension it would assume over the next two centuries, but with all the main elements present.

The system's further transfer to the Caribbean was largely the work of the Dutch in the mid-seventeenth century. As they became supreme in the maritime

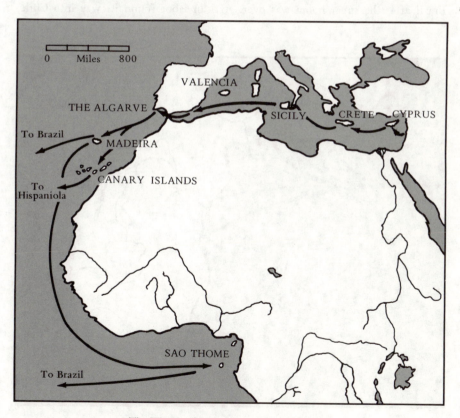

The Westward Migration of Sugar Planting

carrying trade, they tried to seize the Portuguese sphere of operations in the East and West Indies alike. During a fifteen-year occupation of northeast Brazil, they mastered the technology of the South Atlantic System. They captured some of the Portuguese posts on the African coast, including Elmina. Even after being driven from Brazil in the 1640s, they could still offer their knowledge and a supply of slaves to the English and French, who were then trying to colonize some of the Lesser Antilles. The Dutch themselves were content with the profits of the carrying trade, leaving the actual planting to others. The result was a "sugar revolution" in the Lesser Antilles in the 1640s and 1650s, and the revolution spread westward by the early eighteenth century to Jamaica and Saint Domingue, the later Haiti. With the new phase, Dutch supremacy passed, as Portuguese supremacy had done before; the English and French began to carry their own trade, including the trade in slaves from Africa.

With the forward movement of the South Atlantic System and its increasing weight in the economic patterns of tropical America, the very fact that the plantations used slaves tended to produce a spin-off of slaves into other kinds of enterprise. African labor mined the gold and diamonds of eighteenth-century Brazil after the sugar boom was over. African labor found its way into Chile,

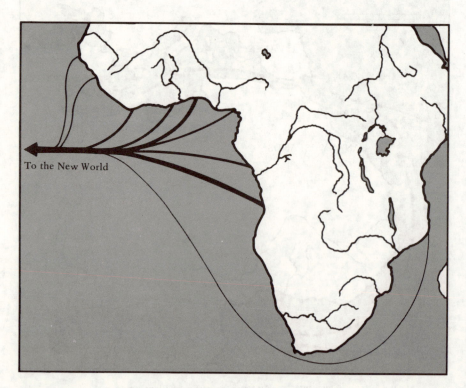

Origins of the Eighteenth-Century Slave Trade

Mexico, and Peru, as well as the circum-Caribbean region of Spanish America. In North America, a sector of the South Atlantic System came into existence in the British mainland colonies, alongside a quite different sector of European settler agriculture in which farmers of European origin did their own work. All of these fringe areas absorbed some of the export of people from Africa, but over the whole history of the slave trade at least 80 percent of the total went to the tropical plantations.

THE HISTORICAL DEMOGRAPHY
OF PLANTATION SLAVERY

The forward movement of the slave plantations was not so much a leapfrog as a process of continuous growth behind moving frontiers. The older, outmoded plantation areas were sometimes left behind with diminished production, but the system as a whole continued to expand. The growth in the slave trade tells part of the story. From an estimated annual average import of about 2,000 slaves to the Americas in the sixteenth century, the figure rose to an annual average of more than 80,000 in the 1780s, the first peak decade of the trade. It then declined, but rose once more to a new peak in the 1840s, in spite of American and European legislation progressively outlawing the trade after 1808. Its effective end came only in the period of 1850–1870, and occasional shipments took place later still.

In some respects, this curve of intercontinental migration was not very different from the later sweep of European migration overseas, which reached an even higher peak in the first decade of the twentieth century. Demographically, however, the two groups of migrants were very different. The Europeans, once overseas, tended to increase in numbers faster than the populations they left behind. The African slaves, however, failed to increase naturally; deaths exceeded births in most slave populations of tropical America. This was not so in the British North American colonies, nor was it so in parts of southern South America; but it was dramatically so in Brazil and the Caribbean, where slave imports were concentrated.

Even though we still lack a full explanation of this demographic peculiarity, some of the contributing causes are clear enough. Planters tended to buy slaves as labor units, without either expecting or encouraging them to reproduce. They regularly bought more men than women, usually in a two-to-one ratio but occasionally much higher. Even if the resulting population had had a reasonably high birth rate per female, its total birth rate per capita would have been low; but the birth rates per female were low, and infant mortality was high. Women slaves apparently knew some methods of abortion and birth control and some tried not to have children. Planters kept them working during pregnancy, which must have increased the rate of miscarriage, and sent them back to work shortly after they gave birth. It seems likely that the pattern of net natural decreases among slave populations owed at least as much to low birth rates as it did to high death rates.

But death rates also played a role, and this role was crucial among slaves born in Africa. Movement from one disease environment to another normally exacted some price in higher morbidity and mortality. Planters of the eighteenth century and earlier recognized a period of "seasoning" for newly arrived Europeans and Africans alike. Data are scarce, but a few samples show that young Africans newly arrived in the American tropics died at about twice the rate expected for their age group in Africa itself. For Europeans, however, movement to the West Indies brought increases in mortality by a factor of ten to twenty. These European death rates of 125 to 250 per thousand per annum among the newly arrived were far milder than they would have suffered in West Africa, but they were still high compared with the equivalent rate of about 30 per thousand among newly arrived Africans. These comparisons help to explain why a labor force from Africa appeared desirable to American planters, and they also explain why a slave population with a high proportion of African-born tended to have high rates of net natural decrease. The native-born (or "creole" in West-Indian English) were comparatively safe. Creole populations, whether Afro-American or Euro-American, could grow from net natural increase, but the usual pattern for slave populations was net natural decline, sustained only by a continuous stream of forced immigrants from Africa. In this way, the South Atlantic System consumed people, just as other industries consume raw materials. It used up slaves from Africa, and it used up managers from Europe at an even higher rate.

These demographic patterns are related in curious ways to economic development or the lack of it. When an immigrant population from Europe or Africa was set down in the New World, its first response to the new environment was a sharp decline in numbers as a result of "seasoning." After a few generations, however, it would level off and then begin to rise slowly. But one-shot immigration of this kind was a sign of comparative economic stagnation. Wherever the plantation economy showed signs of vigorous growth, further immigrant population was added so rapidly that the stage of net natural growth was constantly put off, in most cases until after the effective end of the slave trade. Barbados, however, was a small island where the plantations soon occupied all available land. The slave population, which began to grow about 1640, ended its first phase of rapid growth in the 1680s and stabilized after about 1750. Thereafter, slaves were imported only to supply the difference between births and deaths. By about 1805, the slave population had become self-sustaining and largely creole — and few new slaves were brought from Africa.

The demographic pattern in Barbados was repeated with variations in other colonies. Everywhere in the plantation zone, the volume of the slave trade was tied to the rate of economic growth, not by a direct ratio but by a variable function that increased with the increasing pace of economic growth. While sugar production, to take an example, was directly related to the labor supply, sugar production could have increased at the same rate as natural population growth without *any* additional slave trade, once a creole slave population had been established. But to increase sugar production faster than this rate required *new* labor, and it was precisely the imported workers who died at exceptional rates and drove the slave population as a whole into negative rates of natural increase. Thus each economic boom in the Americas multiplied the cost to Africa in human suffering, while economic backwaters in the New World had little or no demand for immigration.

THE ECONOMICS OF THE ATLANTIC SLAVE TRADE

In retrospect, the Atlantic slave trade seems irrational as well as immoral. It is hard to imagine why Europeans of the seventeenth and eighteenth centuries were willing to send young men to the African coast, where their life expectancy was hardly more than a year. About a quarter of the crew of each slave ship died on the voyage. The life expectancy of a young immigrant from Europe to the West Indies was only five to ten years. The explanation, of course, lies in the fact that the decision to build and run the South Atlantic System was not made by a whole society; it was made by individuals filling a limited number of roles, and these individuals responded, decade after decade, to an array of conditions that made the system appear profitable — at least to themselves.

One of the apparent irrationalities of the system was to locate the plantations in America, given the fact that the labor to work them was in Africa. The more natural solution was to plant in Africa where labor was available. But Europeans died in Africa even more rapidly than they did in the West Indies; little African land was suitable for sugar; and good sugar land lay unpopulated in the New World. The decision therefore favored the Americas as soon as the comparative values of Brazil and São Thomé were known. Though Europeans tried several times in later centuries to set up plantations on the African coast, most failed until the twentieth century.

But the American tropics had to draw population from somewhere. The Indians were dying; Europeans died too; but Africans had some degree of immunity to the general range of Afro-Eurasian diseases as well as to those peculiar to the tropics. Africa was obviously the most desirable source of people for the New World, but there was a question of costs. If voluntary emigrants had been anxious to leave Europe in large numbers, cheap but inferior European labor might well have been preferable to high-cost slave labor from Africa. But voluntary emigrants were no more available in Europe than they were in Africa. Most Europeans sent overseas to work the plantations were political prisoners, convicts, and other unfortunates. They were expensive and supplies were limited. Most of the labor force came from Africa, and at low prices.

The low real cost of a slave purchased on the African coast was a crucial factor in the economics of the slave trade. West Indian planters of the early eighteenth century believed that the price of slaves was so low in Africa that it actually cost less to buy a newly imported field hand than it did to pay the cost of subsistence for a child from birth to working age at about fourteen. It now appears that they were generally correct in early decades in spite of the expected high death rate of the newcomers. But about the middle of the eighteenth century, the rising price of slaves began to suggest other alternatives. Especially from the 1770s, planters began to advocate having equal numbers of each sex in a slave gang. Some began to give time off for pregnancy and prizes for motherhood. They shifted, in short, to a policy of seeking to increase the number of slaves by natural growth rather than by importation.

This policy may have been sufficiently common toward the end of the eighteenth century to affect the demand for slaves from Africa. Its timing would make it appear so, as the long-term trend to slave imports first turned downward in the 1790s. On the other hand, a self-sustaining slave population would have come about in any case with the passage of time and increasing proportions of creole slaves. A planter's decision to shift from importing to encouraging natural growth among the slaves would merely accelerate this tendency.

The long-term increase in the real prices paid for slaves during the eighteenth century was important to the African side of the slave trade as well. It seems clear that the real price of slaves rose steadily from about 1680 to the 1840s, with a fivefold increase over the century and a half. These rising prices were an important influence on the economics of enslavement. It has to be kept in mind that most slaves exported to the Americas had been free people or belonged to nonsalable categories of social subordination before their capture and sale into the trade. Most were war captives; the remainder were condemned criminals, political prisoners, kidnap victims, relatives sold for debt or for food in time of famine; only a few had been slaves from birth who were sold by their masters. Just as the economic operations of the South Atlantic System involved a planter's decision whether to import slaves or breed them, it also involved African decisions about the way people might be enslaved.

Some of the economic reality can be clarified by setting up abstract models to illustrate the economic forces at play. The total purchase price finally paid for a slave delivered to an American plantation had to be divided among those who performed the various functions in the trade along the way. Part went to the African merchants who brought the slaves to the coast from their place of capture. Part went to the European merchants who brought them across the ocean. Part went to the men who performed the act of enslavement. The probable economic behavior of the original captor presents the most serious problem. Two abstract, hypothetical, and extreme circumstances can be laid out to illustrate the possibilities. If we assume the captor was a ruler or commander who made war for political reasons having nothing to do with the slave trade, his supply of captives would simply be a by-product of the war; they would have no assignable costs. His only "cost" would be the possible value of whatever use he might have for the slaves if he chose not to sell them into the trade — what economists call the opportunity costs. If this hypothetical circumstance were normal, the supply of slaves to the trade from any particular part of Africa would have a very low price elasticity; that is, it would not respond to increases in the price offered, but only to political conditions in the region. This possibility can be called the "political model" of enslavement.

The opposite pole of possibilities would be another model, an "economic model." This time, the hypothetical commander or ruler is assumed to be in the business of enslaving people as an economic enterprise. If we assume that he made war only to capture prisoners for sale, then the costs of warfare were actual costs that had to be set against the final selling price of the captives. If this circumstance were normal, the supply of slaves to the trade from any part of Africa would have had a high price elasticity; that is, rising prices would encourage a higher rate of capture so long as the price was higher than the marginal cost of enslavement.

Whichever model is assumed, it would describe supply conditions and their probable response to price changes at the point of enslavement. That is, to the degree that reality resembled the "political model," the supply of slaves would be unresponsive to price changes; to the degree that it resembled the "economic model," it would be much more responsive.

But this leaves the merchants out of the picture. They, both African and European, also received a share of the selling price of a landed slave in the New World. They could be expected to behave along the lines of the economic model. Because their costs of transportation were related to distance, rising prices would make it possible for them to travel further into the interior or to reach toward the more distant coasts of Africa in search of slaves for sale. In economic language, the price elasticity of the supply of slaves would be moderately high with respect to the service and transportation components of the selling price, even if the political model prevailed at the point of enslavement.

But rising prices would cause another kind of change. As the price of slaves rose, a commander mainly following the political model of enslavement would nevertheless begin trying to maximize the number of prisoners so as to pay some of the costs of the war. At *some* price, enterprising men would be tempted to take up the function of enslavement following the economic model. The function of enslavement would be subject, in short, to another kind of elasticity — the price elasticity of movement along the continuum from the political to the economic model of enslavement. In theory, then, rising prices would extend the geographical area supplying the slave trade, and they would also increase the incidence of slave raiding as opposed to by-product enslavement.

Life and decision-making in the era of the slave trade was far more complex than these simple abstractions suggest, but the abstractions nevertheless help to explain some changes in the historical course of the slave trade. One of the clearest of these was the inland penetration of the slave traders, from the second half of the eighteenth century, in response to increasing real prices. Where the slave trade of the sixteenth century had drawn its victims almost entirely from a band within a few miles of the coast, the trade of the late eighteenth and early nineteenth centuries drew many slaves from the western Sudan and many from the southern savanna in the heart of Central Africa.

In addition, the early history of the slave trade was marked by a tendency to jump erratically from one source of supply to another in response to periods of warfare or political upheaval. This pattern, combined with the very low real price paid for slaves, suggests that the political model of enslavement was probably dominant at the beginning of the slave trade and for some time afterward. At the present state of our knowledge, it is impossible to say when or to what degree the rising price of slaves made the economic model a possibility. It may *never* have been a possibility in the full sense that the sale of slaves could pay the full cost of warfare, but occasional African societies after the first third of the eighteenth century began to behave in ways that suggest enslavement had become at least partly an economic enterprise. The kingdom of Dahomey may have been one such example. The organized extraction of slaves from Iboland may have been another. The Bambara states of Segu and Kaarta may have been a third, and still other possibilities are found in Central Africa. Our information on any of these, however, remains uncertain.

It is hard to disentangle the function of enslavement from the business of slave trading, which certainly was an economic enterprise. The second half of the eighteenth century nevertheless seems to be marked by a rising price, an increasing flow of slaves from Africa, a further reach into the interior, and a greater incidence of enslavement approaching the economic model. By curious coincidence, the rising real price of slaves, which introduced this final and most damaging phase in Africa, simultaneously made planters in the Americas try to encourage naturally growing slave populations, and natural growth dampened the demand for slaves.

THE INSTITUTIONAL PATTERN
OF THE SLAVE TRADE

Until the end of the sixteenth century, the Portuguese dominated West African maritime trade in spite of sporadic rivalry from other European powers. During this period, a body of Afro-European commercial custom came into existence, with patterns of exchange and cross-cultural behavior that were to be remarkably stable until the second half of the nineteenth century. By 1600, the Portuguese had stopped pursuing some of the initiatives they had taken early in their acquaintance with West Africa — a precedent their competitors and successors from other parts of Europe accepted.

By common consent, Europeans gave up the kind of massive intervention in African military and political affairs that was represented by the Portuguese Jollof expedition of 1490, though the Portuguese continued to play a more modest military role to the south of the Congo and in the Zambezi valley. The

Portuguese gave up their early effort to support Christian missions and provide technical assistance, as they had done at first in the Congo, and the other Europeans followed suit. Except for isolated efforts in scattered places, the Christian missionary effort in West Africa stopped after the first half of the sixteenth century. São Thomé became a failed plantation society; neither the Portuguese nor any other Europeans were to enter agricultural management on a similar scale until the nineteenth century. Where the Portuguese had begun with an emphasis on the gold trade, after about 1700 they and their successors thought first of the slave trade.

Certain patterns of trade laid down before 1600 became fixed. One was the convention in West Africa (though not for Central Africa or Mozambique) that European traders should stop at the waterside and not move into the interior. The Africans insisted on this as a way of protecting their position as middlemen in the trade to the interior; Europeans had to accept it because they already had enough trouble manning the waterside posts in the face of fantastic death rates among the newly arrived. Their only long-term inland penetration in West Africa was to the head of navigation on the Senegal and Gambia rivers.

Governments, both African and European, tried to exercise as much control over trade as possible — often with monopoly as a goal, though this they rarely achieved in the face of opposition from private traders, both African and European. European governments thought first of a monopoly over the national sector of the trade as a means of shoring up their national power and wealth against competing European nations. Not that the African trade was ever an important part of the total, but the sugar colonies were dependent on a steady supply of slaves, and these colonies were believed — probably mistakenly — to be the most valuable part of any European empire overseas. Even beyond the usual mercantilist arguments against buying from foreigners, each European state considered it important to supply its own colonies with slaves, for fear a foreign supplier might cut off the trade at some later date, with disastrous results. Spain alone was content to leave the slave trade to others most of the time, though she controlled the importation of slaves into Spanish America through a system of permits, or *asientos*. The other powers also surrounded the slave trade with their own cloud of laws and regulations. Many granted a monopoly over the national sector of the trade to a single, chartered, joint-stock company, endowed with certain governmental powers. The companies were expected to use their monopoly profits as a subsidy to repay the cost of maintaining fortified trading posts in Africa. In this way, the burden of defending the slave trade in wartime was passed over to a private firm — at least in theory.

In fact, it was impossible to enforce the monopoly rights. Planters were always willing to buy slaves from foreigners rather than pay a monopoly price. Private shippers were always willing to enter the African trade as "interlopers" infringing on the legal monopoly. With six thousand miles of coastline open to trade, all the interlopers had to do was to stay clear of the fortified trading posts. Against such competition, the chartered companies found their profits insufficient to pay for the upkeep of the forts. This was the probable outcome even if the company's employees in Africa had been honest, which they rarely were. The employees, after all, went to Africa with less than a fifty-fifty chance of returning home; few were willing to take such risks for the sake of a small salary. In the end, all of the principal monopolistic companies failed financially. Some were kept going by state subsidies, but the great bulk of the slave trade after the seventeenth century was carried by independent shippers in fierce competition with one another. This competition, in turn, caused the Europeans to bid up the real price of slaves, in spite of occasional half-hearted attempts to keep it low by joint action.

The mode of trade between the seaborne Europeans and the African merchants was remarkably uniform over long stretches of coastline, perhaps because the Europeans picked up the customs of one trade area and then spread them more broadly. All along the coast, bargains were struck in a currency of account that was neither a European currency nor the usual African currency of the region, though some trade currencies came into general use over time. One such currency was the "bar," originally a bar of iron weighing about twelve to thirteen kilograms. These bars were about three meters long, but they were usually notched for subdivision into smaller units of twenty-five to thirty centimeters each, a size corresponding to an ancient form of iron currency used on certain parts of the upper Guinea coast before the period of maritime contact. Bars became the currency of account from the Senegal River south and east to the present-day Ivory Coast. The next currency area centered on the Gold Coast, and here the local currency and the trade currency alike was gold dust for large transactions. In the course of the seventeenth century, a new fictitious currency came into use — the "trade ounce" with half the value of a measured ounce of gold dust. In the course of the eighteenth century, the "trade ounce" spread further east until it reached into present-day Nigeria, displacing earlier currencies of brass and copper and a currency of account that represented the value of a slave. The Bight of Biafra used a great variety of different currencies, changing through time and including a horseshoe-shaped object in brass called a "manila," cowrie shells from the Indian Ocean, and a form of cloth currency based on the value of a standard piece of handwoven African cotton. Two or more currencies were sometimes used in the same place, and cowrie shells were often used for minor purchases where the currency of account had an inconveniently large value.

Whatever the trade currency, it rarely filled the same role as a modern all-purpose currency. One of the main problems was the inflexibility of certain prices. The prices of African exports varied according to market conditions, but those of African imports tended to be set by custom at an early date and then remained fixed for long periods — up to a century or more. A "bar" or an "ounce" worth of slaves or ivory depended on a bargain struck between buyer and seller, but a "bar" or an "ounce" worth of guns or iron or textiles was a fixed quantity. At some time, perhaps in the early seventeenth century, the bar values of these products must have corresponded to their actual cost in Europe, but this was no longer the case in the late seventeenth or eighteenth centuries. One bar worth of blue bafts, an Indian textile, might represent a prime cost several times that of a bar worth of brandy. In effect, no single exchange rate expressed the relationship between "bars" and any European currency. Instead, a separate exchange rate prevailed for each of the commodities imported into Africa.

This system of multiple exchange rates greatly complicated the process of striking a bargain. Buyers and sellers had to agree first on the price to be paid for the export products — gold, wax, slaves, and so on. Then they bargained once more about the "sorting" or actual makeup of the bundle of goods to be taken in payment. The African merchant would insist that as much as possible be paid in "heavy bars" like blue bafts, while the European would try to pay as much as possible in "light bars" like rum.

In addition, European visitors to the coast paid a variety of fees, duties, and other charges. The African state where trade took place normally charged for the privilege and imposed additional fees for anchorage, wood and water, and the like. Ceremonial gifts were required at the opening and closing of a bargaining session, and a variety of brokers, interpreters, and other service personnel had to be paid. These charges varied greatly from place to place, depending on the local commercial culture and the kind of control the African authorities exercised over trade. This, in turn, depended on the political circumstances in each region along the coast.

SENEGAMBIA

The first region to the south of the Sahara was Senegambia, traditionally the shores of the Senegal and Gambia rivers and the country lying between them. It was the first sub-Saharan region to enter into maritime contact with Europe, and it was especially important in the first centuries of the slave trade — furnishing perhaps a third of all the slaves exported from Africa before 1600. This temporary boom in the Senegambian slave trade followed the mid-sixteenth-century breakup of the Jollof empire into a reduced Jollof and a number of successor states. Once the new political situation stabilized toward the end of the sixteenth century, Senegambia took on new importance as the closest maritime approach to the Bambuhu goldfields. The Gambia River was navigable by oceangoing ships for some two hundred miles and river shipping on the Senegal could reach four hundred miles into the interior. These rivers contributed to Senegambia's prominence in a mixed trade, where gold and slaves were often second in importance to cotton textiles, hides, beeswax, ivory, and gum. After the seventeenth century, most of the slave exports from this region originated in the far interior, beyond the head of navigation on the two rivers.

The organization of trade changed through time. In the sixteenth century, the Portuguese neglected the Senegal in favor of trade along the coast from

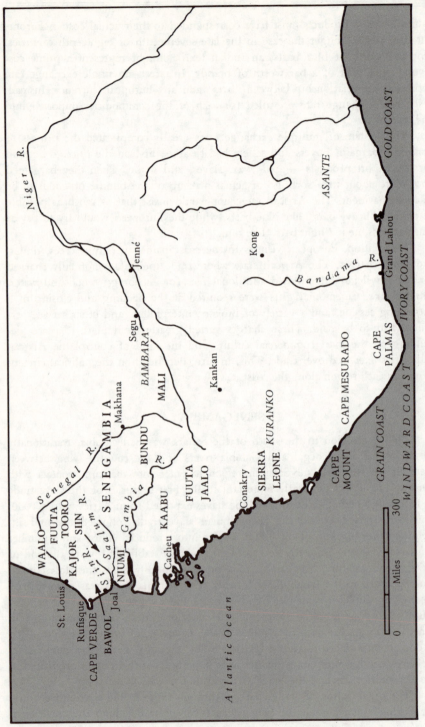

Senegambia and the Windward Coast

Cape Verde to the Gambia and up the Gambia River. On the open coast, they dealt at a series of small ports — Rufisque in Kajor, Portudal in Bawol, Joal in Siin, Kawon and other points on the Saalum River for Saalum. On the Gambia, the political setting was also one containing several successor states to a great empire of the past — Mali in this case rather than Jollof. A series of small Malinke-speaking states lined the banks of the river, and at least one of these, Kaabu, was still a functioning province of Mali at the earliest period of Portuguese trade.

Rather than having a fortified factory on the coast itself, the Portuguese tried to organize their trade with Senegambia from their base on the Cape Verde Islands, but many individual Portuguese, contrary to official policy, went to live on the mainland. By the end of the sixteenth century, all the principal port towns had an Afro-Portuguese community descended from these early traders and identifying themselves as Portuguese and Catholic, though their appearance was African and their way of life was a Luso-African mixture. By the early seventeenth century, the Afro-Portuguese constituted the main trade community on the coast and up the Gambia; willing to trade with any ship, regardless of nationality, they had a trade network that reached to the head of navigation on the Gambia and all its tributary creeks.

Long-distance trade from the further interior, however, lay outside their sphere. The overland caravans represented another kind of specialization, and the caravan leaders sometimes came right through from the upper Niger to the coast at Rufisque or Joal. More often, they stopped at a convenient point on the middle or upper Gambia, where their goods were transferred to the waterborne transport of the Afro-Portuguese. In addition to the slaves and ivory for overseas export, these caravans brought down iron, cotton textiles, and kola nuts for the Senegambia in return for Senegambian mats, textiles, and salt for distribution to the interior. This long-distance trade therefore represented regional exchanges within Africa as well as overseas trade, and the overseas aspect was almost certainly a fifteenth-century addition to an already existing commerce.

However obscure its origins, the trade route eastward from Gambia to the upper Niger was dominated in the seventeenth and eighteenth centuries by the Jahanke (French Diakhanké). These people were never part of a single state: they were, instead, a people whose sense of nationality was born of a trade diaspora that had originated, according to tradition, in Ja near the Niger bend. By the seventeenth century, they lived in separate villages that were semiautonomous from the local political authorities and linked by ties of nationality and kinship to other Jahanke villages, no matter how distant. In many respects, they resembled the Juula of northern Ghana, the Ivory Coast, and Upper Volta, who were also traders living in scattered towns who traced their origins to Ja, claimed Soninke ancestry, and spoke a dialect of Malinke. The Jahanke cultivated the role of the clerical, pacifist, politically neutral, and commercially oriented mercantile community. The remains of their former trade network can be seen today in a string of Jahanke towns running in a line eastward from the

Gambia to Segu on the Niger, and north and south through Bundu connecting the desert edge with the kola forests of Fuuta Jaalo.

The middle decades of the seventeenth century were a period of commercial uncertainty for Senegambia, with the Afro-Portuguese serving all comers, while the Dutch, French, English, and even such unlikely contenders as the Duke of Kurland (in later Latvia) tried to tighten their grip on part of the trade. It was only at the end of the century that a relatively stable situation emerged. The British came to be normally dominant on the Gambia, attempting to control the trade of the river from James Island, a few miles from the river's mouth; the French held a similar position on the Senegal, which they controlled from the island of Saint Louis. In fact, neither post was very strong; both fell at various times to European enemies or even to mere pirates, though they were always reoccupied by their usual owners.

The Gambia was tidal to the normal head of navigation. The British sometimes bought from the Afro-Portuguese, who sailed the river in large "canoes" capable of carrying ten to twenty tons, and they usually maintained a series of unfortified factories upriver, served by sloops that carried the goods back and forth from their main post at James Island. The island lay within the territory of the north-bank state of Ñumi or Barra, and it had no independent supply of fresh water. Most of the time, Ñumi was content to milk the trade by taxing passing ships, exacting payments from the British and from the French who often kept an unfortified post at Albreda, also in Ñumi, a little below James Island. The result was constant bickering between the Europeans and the African authorities, largely because the Europeans were never strong enough to overawe the Africans, while no single African state was strong enough to control the passing trade.

The Senegal, on the other hand, was not tidal and it was consequently less useful as a transportation route. Seagoing ships could hardly go beyond Saint Louis; even river craft could reach the upper river only during the few months of high water — though they could then go some four hundred miles toward the heart of the western Sudan. In the 1690s, the French placed a fortified post at Makhana, not far from the present city of Kayes in the Republic of Mali. With a permanent store of trade goods on the upper river and annual expeditions to maintain contact with the coast, the French had a viable alternative to the British commerce on the Gambia. African merchants coming down from the interior had a choice of trading partners. Competition between the two river routes affected African states as well, because no single state could cut off both routes. Thus, while all states charged tolls on passing caravans or boats, the amount they could exact was limited by the fear of driving traffic to the other route.

The Senegal route also lacked an Afro-Portuguese community to serve as middlemen. Partly as a result, an Afro-French community grew up at Saint Louis. Even when the Compagnie des Indes tried to exercise its monopoly over the river trade, it used African boatmen and commercial agents. By the second half of the eighteenth century, the "French" trade on the Senegal had fallen completely into the hands of the Saint-Louisians — men who were generally Wolof in language and culture, at least formally Muslim by religion, and African in appearance. Only a few were racially Afro-European, but the whole community gradually blended more European traits into its culture with the passage of time. The Afro-Portuguese of the Gambia, by contrast, were originally of European descent, but gradually became more African in culture as well as descent.

The Senegambia was never a major source of slaves after the sixteenth century, and the Senegambian slave trade reached a peak in absolute numbers about the beginning of the eighteenth century. As it declined thereafter, it became an even smaller fraction of the whole. The Wolof states, the main source of slaves in the mid-sixteenth century, now sent as few as fifty or a hundred a year from each state, normally sold by the king as a royal monopoly. Fuuta Tooro generally tried to prevent the sale of its own people into the slave trade; and the policy was successful as far as the Atlantic trade was concerned, though the anarchy of Moroccan military operations must have meant a fairly large drain of captives across the Sahara to the north. The only eighteenth-century slave trade of real consequence was *through* Senegambia, not *from* it. The victims came from the far interior and were largely Mande in culture, captives taken during the rise and expansion of the new Bambara states.

UPPER GUINEA AND SIERRA LEONE

To the south of the Gambia, the open savanna gives way first to thicker woodland and then to high forest. The coast is deeply indented by a series of drowned river mouths and numerous offshore islands. Political organization was also different; the legacy of former empires such as Jollof or Mali or of persistent state structures like Fuuta Tooro was missing. Instead, the region was one of microstates intermixed with small stateless societies. Nor was Islam the major religious force it was in Senegambia, though Muslim-controlled trade routes reached down into the forest in search of local specialties like kola nuts.

During the period of Portuguese dominance, this coastal region was one of the most important for the slave trade. Perhaps a third of the slaves exported by sea during the sixteenth century came from here, even though the Portuguese had no fortified posts on the coast itself until nearly the end of the century, when they built a fort at Cacheu. Their trade was organized from the entrepôt of the Cape Verde Islands, and much of it was carried by individual Portuguese who went to live on the mainland under African jurisdiction and there collected slaves and bulked local produce for sale to passing ships. In time, they too became a separate Afro-Portuguese community, similar to those on the Gambia further north.

Although the southern part of this region, the present Republic of Sierra Leone, was only on the fringe of the Portuguese trade zone, it was briefly a large contributor to the slave trade in the mid-sixteenth century. In the early part of that century, this was a region of microstates inhabited by culturally similar people whom the Europeans called Sape. They were, in fact, the ancestors of the present-day Bullom, Temne, Limba, Baga, Nalu, and Landuma. About the middle of the century, the region was swept by a series of invasions by people called Mane, now recognized to have been an offshoot of the Mande people of the savanna. It was not so much a military conquest as a migration by the Mane and their allies, some of whom were related to the Kru of present-day Liberia. The resulting warfare was a major producer of slaves for sale until the situation finally settled down early in the seventeenth century, leaving a new configuration of small states, many of them ruled by descendents of the invaders. A new pattern of culture also appeared, as Mane and Sape merged to form ethnic groups ancestral to the present-day Loko and Mende.

Once the Mane invasions had stopped, the region dropped from the mainstream of the slave trade. During the seventeenth century and into the eighteenth, it depended partly on the sale of local products such as beeswax, camwood, and ivory and partly on transshipping inland products like the gold of Buré and Bambuhu. Some slave trade continued, but at less than half the value of the total exports. It recovered briefly at two points in the eighteenth century — in the 1720s through the 1740s, reflecting the fighting associated with the Fulbe jihad in Fuuta Jaalo, and again in the 1780s and 1790s — but the region's contribution to the total slave trade of the century was even less than that of the Senegambia and less than 5 percent of the total.

Perhaps because the slave trade was comparatively unimportant, Upper Guinea and Sierra Leone attracted little attention from the major slave trading companies. Instead, private traders of several nationalities came to settle on the coast, as the Afro-Portuguese had done in the past. Some of them married into important local families, which made it possible for their children to inherit chiefdoms. In the vicinity of Sierra Leone, the dominant politico-mercantile figure of the early eighteenth century was the Afro-Portuguese leader Jose Lopez de Maura, but in the second half of the century he was joined by a number of powerful Afro-English families — the Rogers, Caulkers, Clevelands, and Tuckers. Trading forts began to appear in the Sierra Leone estuary only late in the century, with the French on Gambia Island and the English on Bruce Island.

THE WINDWARD COAST

Further east, beyond Cape Mount, was the region the English called the Windward Coast — to the windward, that is, of the permanent fortified posts on the Gold Coast, though it was sometimes called the Grain Coast in its western section and the Ivory Coast in the east. Its principal distinguishing characteristic is the absence of natural harbors or even of good landing spots in the lee of rocky promontories, so common along the Gold Coast. Instead, the beach is characteristically very steep, with heavy surf close to shore and poor anchorages further out. Maritime trade was mainly what the Europeans called a "ship trade," without resident Europeans on shore. Instead, a ship would call here and there along the coast, or simply sail along watching for a signal that Africans on shore had something to trade.

One result of this kind of contact was that Europeans rarely stayed long enough to find out much about the country or people, and historical sources are more meager here than they are for any other part of the African coast. If there had been large African states in the area, oral traditions might fill the gap; but traditions carrying back 200 years or more are rarely preserved unless they serve some political function, usually connected with a state or a royal lineage. Nothing recorded so far among the maze of stateless societies and microstates backing the Windward Coast goes back as far as 1700, though oral traditions preserved to the north of the forest belt make it possible to fill in the outlines of historical change in the western Sudan, and more may someday be possible in the forest as well.

Partly because of the lack of natural harbors, trade along this coast was fragmented, divided among many small ports or shipping points. One French survey of 1783 listed thirty-five ports of call in this region, none of them evaluated as normally supplying more than a few hundred slaves a year. It can be assumed that most of these ports drew on their immediate hinterland within the forest. Yet some of these points also drew slaves from the savanna country, especially during two particular periods in the eighteenth century.

A heavy export from the region of Cape Mount and Cape Mesurado (the neighborhood of modern Monrovia) occurred from the 1720s through the 1740s. This spurt may be associated with the warfare that accompanied the Fulbe jihad in Fuuta Jaalo in the 1720s and afterward, but the natural outlet for Fuuta Jaalo would have been further west to Sierra Leone. Instead, this one seems to be associated in part with the eastward expansion of the Kuranko into the upper part of Guinea-Conakry. It may also be associated with very important commercial changes occurring still further in the interior. Kola nuts had long been exported from the forest regions northward to the savanna country, especially along the north-south trade routes from the Akan goldfields to Jenné. In the seventeenth and eighteenth centuries, similar trade routes carried south into the forests of Sierra Leone, Guinea-Conakry, and northwest Liberia. By the eighteenth century, they penetrated through the forest to the coast, so that European goods entered the flow of trade to and along the Niger.

One political reflection of these commercial changes was a set of movements sometimes called the "juula revolution" — that is, a political revolution run by men whose principal activity was commerce. Just as the traders already controlled many of the towns along the routes southward from Jenné, traders now began to establish their own control over political units south of the upper Niger. One of the most important crossroads was the town of Kankan in upper Guinea-Conakry. In the late seventeenth century, the juula, or merchants, who worked that region were dominantly Muslims of Soninke origin but now Malinkized in speech and other aspects of their culture. That is, they were very similar to the Juula of the Jenné-to-Akan route, or to the Jahanke who worked the trade of the Gambia. Sometime in the late seventeenth century, they seized control of Kankan and its region and set up the independent city-state of Bate — an important stepping-stone for the trade headed toward the kola region or the coast, and an example to other juula who had trouble dealing with the non-Muslim and nonmercantile microstates through which they had to pass.

A second spurt of trade from the Windward Coast took place in the 1770s and centered on the export of slaves from the port of Grand Lahou at the mouth of the Bandama River in the present-day Ivory Coast. This increase was again associated with a new trade route through the forest along the line of the Bandama River. It was, in effect, a new branch of the main north-south route from the Akan region to Jenné. Increased slave exports of the late eighteenth century seem to be associated with the westward expansion of Asante, but the hinterland of the Bandama route had already experienced its own "juula revolution" earlier in the century. About 1700, juula forces under a certain Seku Watara began to create a new state based on the trading city of Kong. By the 1730s, it had become the largest empire created so far in Africa south of the Niger River, with control stretching to the fringes of Asante, north nearly to Jenné, and westward to the Bambara kingdoms. Some of Kong's military operations carried as far as Bamako on the Niger. But the polity was fundamentally weak, a domination by juula over people of great ethnic diversity spread over a large area. It was also divided between juula Muslims and the mass of the population who were not Muslim. Asante and the Bambara kingdom of Segu finally defeated it in battle, and it fell back into its constituent units after about 1740.

It is not clear what role the fall of Kong may have played in the flow of trade through the forest to the coast, but that trade declined abruptly after the end of the eighteenth century. The Windward Coast as a whole simply dropped out of the slave trade, even though the illegal slave trade continued to flourish elsewhere. It is likely, however, that trade that had once passed through to Cape Mesurado went to Sierra Leone instead, while that of the Bandama route was diverted to Asante and then down to the Gold Coast.

THE GOLD COAST

The Gold Coast had the greatest density of European military architecture and trading posts anywhere on the coast of Africa. It was the gold trade, however, and not the slave trade that made for all these forts. At least in West Africa, European trading posts were rarely fortified unless they traded in gold, and they were designed for defense against Europeans, not Africans. (The African authorities had the easy option of simply cutting off trade if their guests became too demanding.) And the danger was not merely an enemy naval force in wartime; pirates might also appear at any time. Slaves were an inconvenient mark for raiders, and other African products were hardly better, but gold was easy to carry off and easy to dispose of. This is one reason why the first Portuguese fortification, begun in 1481, was called simply Elmina, "the castle of the mine." Rival trade forts began to rise in the neighborhood only in the seventeenth century, but, by the eighteenth, the coast was dotted with twenty-five major stone forts, separated from one another by an average of only ten miles — and even less if the numerous lightly fortified or unfortified factories and outstations are taken into account. There was, of course, no real need for that many forts, but each European power felt that it had to have its own set, as the Dutch, English, Danes, Swedes, and Brandenburgers all tried to follow in the footsteps of the Portuguese.

The goldfields also influenced the pace and character of political change in African society. Gold was a magnet that attracted traders from the south, and Juula had reached as far as the coast by the fifteenth century. In addition, kola from the Gold Coast forest was especially choice, and the value of the kola exports to the north may have been even greater than that of the gold trade. The new commerce made a larger scale of political organization desirable. The forest had been mainly organized in tiny states, while stateless societies were more common in the savanna immediately to the north. One of the first, if not the very first, Akan state to reach toward a larger order of magnitude was Bono, which grew up in the early fifteenth century in the gold-producing area. It lay near the frontier between forest and savanna, and it was closely associated with the Juula town of Begho, then the principal commercial center serving the Akan goldfield.

Formation of other states just north of the forest was even more closely associated with the pull of the goldfields. Gonja was founded in the early sixteenth century by the commanding officer of a cavalry force sent into the region from Mali. He broke away with some of the troops and set himself up as an independent ruler. Later, in the mid-seventeenth century, Gonja spread still further by conquering nearby microstates and stateless peoples, until it became a major force in the region between the Akan states of the south and the Mossi complex to the north.

On the coast itself, the attraction of the gold made this one of the earliest regions to have intense contact with Europeans. It was therefore one of the first African territories to acquire crops from America; maize and manioc quickly became important food crops in the Akan forest. They were clearly of the greatest importance in increasing people's ability to use the tropical forest. The immediate influence must have been a major change in population densities throughout the forest zone over the course of the sixteenth and seventeenth centuries.

The developing trade to the coast during the seventeenth century also influenced the scale of political organization near the coast. The first spectacular change was the rise of Akwamu, a new state founded by the Abrade people, an Akan group who moved, about 1600, to the immediate hinterland of Accra. At first, they were clients of the Ga-speaking rulers of Accra; but their new territory lay across the trade route from the interior, and they were able to combine military and commercial pressures to force trade through their own capital at Nyannaoase. By the late 1670s, Akwamu had accumulated enough wealth from the flow of trade to become powerful as well. It then turned to military aggression against its neighbors, forcing the defeated into a tribute-paying relationship.

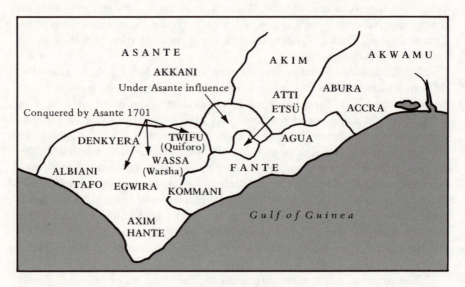

The Gold Coast in 1729

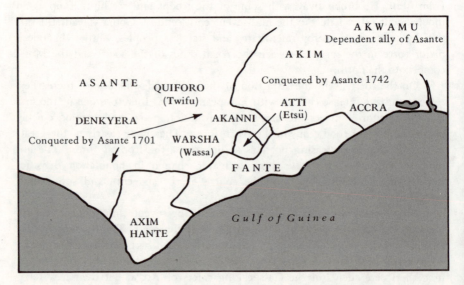

The Gold Coast in 1750

By the 1690s, its dominance extended over most of the coastal region to Cape Coast in the west, north into the beginning of the savanna country, and eastward across the open savanna of the Benin gap as far as the frontiers of Dahomey. Only the core area of Accra, however, was closely integrated with the state. The outlying conquests were autonomous regions that could break away again at the first sign of military weakness. Akwamu's institutions for controlling these peripheral territories proved to be too weak to prevent ambitious local magnates from taking slaves within the empire itself, just at a time when the gold trade was giving way to a much larger trade in slaves. About 1730, the whole structure came apart; Akwamu was conquered by Akim, its neighbor to the west, though some of the Abrade royal lineage moved off to the northwest, where they founded a new and much smaller Akwamu.

The rise of Akwamu was not so much an isolated phenomenon as an example of a general pattern. Denkyera, lying behind the western Gold Coast, rose to power at very nearly the same time as Akwamu, and its success rested on a similar basis of first engrossing trade and then moving on to military conquest. The pattern was repeated with similar timing in the rise of trading states to the east (such as Allada) and with slightly later timing in the rise of Asante.

The Asante state was founded about 1680 with the election of a certain Osei Tutu to the leadership of a number of matrilineages around the present city of Kumasi and the region immediately to the south. By 1700, after Osei Tutu defeated Denkyera, Asante became a major power. More important still, he (or his advisers) carried through a series of creative innovations to produce a larger scale of political integration among the kinship-oriented microstates that had been the usual Akan institution up to that time. One of these changes was the institution of a new all-Asante council, the Kotoko council, as the ruling body. New judicial institutions, with a wider sphere of jurisdiction than had existed in the past, were also introduced. The development of a new national ideology was more important still. Each of the formerly independent divisions of the kingdom, including Kumasi itself, had a ceremonial stool of office, which was far more than a throne; each stool represented the ties of kinship that gave ultimate sanction to the authority of the ruler. Osei Tutu introduced a new stool, "the golden stool," which stood for the national unity of the whole state. In effect, it was a fictitious extension of kinship so that a temporary alliance could become a permanent kingdom, and that kingdom could incorporate some of the territory it conquered.

This is not to say that a larger and more unified state immediately sprang into existence. One of the continuing themes of Asante history in the eighteenth and nineteenth centuries was the struggle to consolidate the larger unit, and Asante territorial expansion compounded the problem. In practice, the Asante rulers tried to incorporate only those conquered states that were Akan in culture, and even these were sometimes reluctant to join. Several serious wars of attempted secession took place even within the Akan culture area. Non-Akan states, like Gonja and Dagomba in the north, were left with their separate identities and merely required to pay tribute. Others, like the Ga states and a few outlying Akan states, were under Asante domination and were watched more closely, though they were not invited to join the Asante union.

The period just before 1700 was also one of crucial change in the economic history of the Gold Coast. Ever since the opening of maritime trade in 1481, this region had been a source of gold, only rarely of slaves. In the second half of the fifteenth century and far into the sixteenth, the Gold Coast had imported slaves brought by the Portuguese from Benin or Kongo. Even later, the Portuguese and then the Dutch had discouraged and even prohibited the export of slaves for fear of interfering with the gold trade. By the 1660s, however, the slave trade began to grow in importance, first from Accra and associated with the rise of Akwamu. By the 1680s, slave exports had risen to 75 percent of total export value. By the 1720s, the Gold Coast sometimes actually *imported* gold in exchange for slaves, though the main pattern of the eighteenth century was to export both, and the volume of the slave trade rose and fell with the rhythm of the Asante military activity in the hinterland.

Meanwhile, the long contact between European and African merchants near the coastal trade castles produced a network of contact and interchange between cultures. Western education, at least to the level of literacy and commercial arithmetic, was important for traders, and many Africans were able to use their business connections to secure hospitality for a few years' residence in Europe. One African, Philip Quaque of Cape Coast, received an education in England, was ordained as an Anglican priest, and returned with an English wife to take up a post as official chaplain of Cape Coast Castle. From the European side, Richard Brew of Anomabu spent thirty years on the Gold Coast and founded an Anglo-African family that became an important part of the local elite down to the present. The process as a whole was not so much "Westernization" as the creation of a culturally mixed community that would later be able to mediate between the two parent societies.

THE BIGHT OF BENIN

The Bight of Benin refers to the southward bend of the coast east of the Volta River and to the body of water within the open bay. By extension, Europeans of the slave-trade era used the term to refer to the whole coastal region between the Volta and Benin rivers — roughly the present-day Togo, Dahomey, and western Nigeria. It was a region with ancient cultural homogeneity, part of a cultural continuum that reached from the Gold Coast to eastern Nigeria. Thus, the Ewe and associated peoples of Togo and eastern Ghana have some similarities to their Akan neighbors and others to the peoples of southern Dahomey, who can be grouped together as the Aja. These Aja, in turn, had even more in common with the Yoruba of southwestern Nigeria, including centuries of historical interaction. The most important recent Aja state, the kingdom of Dahomey, was an outlying part of the Yoruba Oyo empire during much of its history. On the other side of the Yoruba states, the Edo kingdom of Benin has been ruled for most of the past four centuries by a dynasty claiming Yoruba origin. Benin also fits into the pattern of urbanization that was common to the Yoruba and Aja alike, though in other respects Edo culture seems closer to that of the Ibo to the east or the Igala to the northeast. Authorities will differ as to where the most important discontinuities in this sequence may be located, but contact over thousands of years has produced a marked cultural continuity.

This continuity also stretches into the interior. The sharp environmental change from forest to savanna has no counterpart in most aspects of culture. All of the language families now found in this part of the forest zone are also found in the savanna north of the forest. It is usually assumed that they were originally spoken by savanna people, some of whom moved into the forest after the coming of agriculture. Other aspects of culture also suggest ancient ties to the north. Yoruba sculpture, for example, has strong stylistic similarities to the Nok figurines made to the north of the Benue River before the birth of Christ. Some deities of the Aja religion are strikingly similar to those worshipped among the non-Muslim Hausa. These and other traits found both north and south of the forest-savanna frontier may recall the ancient southward movement of settlers, or they may simply be a reflection of cultural diffusion along the trade routes. A developed flow of trade connecting the coastal region with the Hausa states and the Songrai portion of the Niger valley was already present when the Portuguese arrived.

This pattern of commerce may have been much older still, and it may be connected with the fact that this coastal region had larger and more elaborate states, and at an earlier date, than any other coastal region short of Senegambia in one direction and the kingdom of Kongo in the other. For the Yoruba and Edo, states may go back to the eleventh century or even earlier, and the elaborate technology necessary for the Ife and Benin bronze statuary suggests an even earlier date for the introduction of advanced metallurgy into the forest zone. The older view that the savanna peoples were somehow "more advanced" than those of the forest cannot be sustained, even though the existence of states was not necessarily a sign of "advancement," and this is one part of Africa where large states, small states, microstates, and stateless societies have existed side by side for centuries.

Our best historical information nevertheless concerns the larger states, and three of them — Benin, Dahomey, and Oyo — illustrate part of the range of options available to an African state responding to European trade. The lack of correspondence between the former and present names for these countries is a serious problem. The African kingdom of Dahomey gave its name first to the French colony and then to the independent republic of Dahomey, but in 1975 the republic changed its name to Benin. The new name has to do with the Bight of Benin which washes its shores, and nothing at all to do with the ancient kingdom of Benin, which was further east. To avoid confusion, we will use the terms Benin and Dahomey to refer to the long-standing units of that name, using "République du Bénin" only for Dahomey after 1975.

Benin was the first to attract serious attention in Europe, partly because it was expanding to a peak of military power in the sixteenth century. It was the scene of early Portuguese missionary efforts and continued to be one of the African states best known in Europe. But Edo relations with the Europeans were not especially close. It was not really a coastal state at all, though its port of Ughoton on the Benin River could be reached by sailing inland through the territory of the Itsekiri and western Ijo. Although Benin at one time made itself overlord of the coast as far west as Lagos, the Edo were normally far more concerned with the north — with Nupe, Igala, and the Yoruba states.

Benin also stayed out of the large-scale slave trade. In 1516, the *Oba* (or king) began to restrict the export of male slaves, and the restriction soon became a complete embargo on exporting males that lasted until nearly the end of the seventeenth century. Because the Europeans wanted mainly male workers for the American plantations, the embargo cut back the maritime trade of Benin to the export of pepper, African-made cotton textiles, beads, and ivory. Even this trade was conducted as a royal monopoly, which may have made Benin less attractive to Europeans than other ports were, though the monopoly became harder to enforce as the internal power of the Oba declined during the seventeenth century. By that period, the royal officials appointed to trade with the Europeans had come to be more like brokers, who helped them (for a fee) in the conduct of their business.

In the eighteenth century, the embargo on male slaves was lifted, but the slave trade nevertheless remained a minor current. Prices were high, and the Europeans had cheaper sources elsewhere. From time to time, the Oba forced the Europeans to buy a batch of war prisoners or political prisoners as a condition for being allowed to trade in other goods, but the total numbers traded over the years were very low. In the late eighteenth century, when the slave trade as a whole reached its first peak, exports from the whole region of the Benin River reached only about a thousand slaves a year, and most of these were supplied by the Itsekiri. In the early nineteenth century, Benin dropped out of the slave trade altogether. It survived nevertheless as a major state until almost the end of the century. If this experience over four centuries can be taken as a lesson, it seems that one option open to a major African state was simply not to participate in the slave trade at all. Insofar as firearms were a necessity for survival in competition with other states, they could be acquired by selling other goods.

Dahomey, on the other hand, apparently tried to make the slave trade pay, even to make it the principal support of the state. Regular trade with Europeans came comparatively late with the Aja. The first trading state, Allada, was founded before 1530, though the Dutch began to trade there toward the

end of the century, and Allada soon became the chief center for European trade
to the Bight of Benin. In the second half of the seventeenth century, however,
Ouidah began to compete for trade while Dahomey rose in the hinterland with
a position equivalent to that of Akwamu in regard to Accra. In this location
it was only natural for Dahomey to consider the possibility of controlling trade
for the profit of the state.

The original Dahomean constitution was similar to those of the Yoruba
states. That is, the *oba,* or ruler, was the supreme official, but he was not free
to act on his own. Instead, his powers were strictly circumscribed by a set of
councils, some representing lineages, others professional groups. One council
normally chose the oba from among the eligible members of the royal lineage.
Another usually had the power to order the oba to commit suicide. Once in office,
an oba could appoint some officials and councilors, but these royal appointees
were always balanced by others who represented particular interests or particular lineages. The personal ties that counted most in this society were first of all
the ties of kinship, secondly the ties to fellow members of a professional or oc-

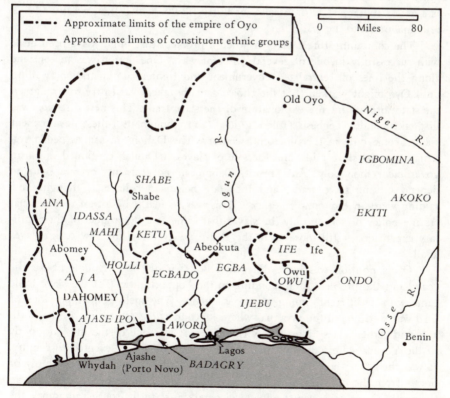

Yorubaland about 1800

cupational group. Only after that was the individual bound to give loyalty and obedience to the oba.

The Dahomean constitution began to depart from this pattern early in the eighteenth century, intentionally subverted by a succession of rulers who used their control over firearms to convert the state into a despotism. By the 1730s or so, they had created a new political order in which each individual was directly and personally subordinate to an all-powerful ruler. This new regime was not originally designed to serve the slave trade. But, in the 1720s, Agaja, the king, led Dahomey in its most successful drive toward the coast, capturing Allada and Ouidah and giving Dahomey its first direct contact with the European slave dealers.

But just when Agaja had succeeded in dominating the coast, Oyo began to threaten the independence of Dahomey itself. Oyo had a strong cavalry force, which turned out to be superior to the Dahomean musketeers. In 1730, Oyo forced Dahomey into a tributary relationship, though Dahomey kept its political integrity and Agaja remained in power. Dahomey was even allowed to keep some of its coastal conquests, although Oyo organized other coastal territories as a new tributary state of Ajashe, or Porto Novo, which then became Oyo's principal outlet to the sea.

The continuing threat of Oyo posed a problem that might have been dealt with successfully in one of several different ways. One option was to continue along the lines of centralized government and tighter administration, waiting until Oyo might weaken. But the choice actually taken was to try to strengthen the state through intense exploitation of the slave trade. This new direction was first taken under Tegbesu (ruled 1740–1774), though its fullest development was to come only in the nineteenth century. The Dahomean armies began systematic annual slave raids, and the sale of slaves at Ouidah continued as a firm government monopoly. As a result, Dahomean government revenue came to depend on the slave trade, and the state began to behave as though slave raiding were an economic enterprise. This was in marked contrast to the usual Asante policy of selling only the slaves that came as a by-product of their military expansion — still more so to the Benin policy of selling few or no slaves at all.

Oyo's position was quite different from that of the kingdoms nearer the coast, and the problem of responding to the "opportunities" of the slave trade came with a different timing and consequence. The metropolitan province of Oyo was well out in the savanna, where its connections lay mainly to the north and with other states along the Niger River. It was one of the most northerly of the Yoruba states, and not the most important until the seventeenth century. It was then that the Oyo cavalry was perfected; this arm required a supply of horses from the northern parts of the savanna, which strengthened Oyo's ties to the north. Oyo then began to expand, generally toward the south and among the other Yoruba kingdoms. In time, Oyo annexed thirteen other kingdoms, which then became provinces of the Oyo empire, stretching into the Egba forest to the south and west of the present city of Ibadan. But coastal Yoruba states, like Ijebu, remained independent, and Oyo had only indirect commercial contact with the coast until her descent on Dahomey. Even then, coastal trade was comparatively unimportant, and Oyo's major trade lay either with the Hausa states or northwest along the Niger toward the bend. These were the strategic sources of remounts, and Oyo still depended on cavalry well into the nineteenth century.

From this time, one can only speculate about the motives and directions of Oyo aggression. As the southernmost cavalry-using power, her advantage lay in moving still further south against states whose archers could often be overwhelmed. Movement into the forest, however, would have been very dangerous on account of the tsetse fly, but the "Benin gap," a corridor of savanna breaking through the forest belt in Togo and Dahomey, opened the way to the use of cavalry against Dahomey. Oyo military activities in the Benin gap began in 1698 with an attack on Allada, and the next half century saw not only Oyo's triumph over Dahomey, but a similar hegemony extending as far west as the frontiers of Asante.

During this period, the first slaves captured by Oyo began to find their way into the Atlantic slave trade, and Oyo began to face the problem of responding to the possibilities and dangers of getting caught up in the trade. Oral traditions still reflect some of the tensions between the military and the merchant's council — one arguing for still more military expansion, the other wanting to pursue peace for the sake of trade. In fact, neither of these possibilities seems to have been pursued consistently. For several decades before 1774, the *bashorun,* or supreme military commander, became more important than the *alafin,* whose powers were usually so circumscribed by councils as to make him a mere figurehead. Then the Alafin Abiodun won a brief civil war and built new power for his office. Abiodun had once been a merchant and he apparently sought to develop his power on the basis of the slave trade, which increased enormously in the 1780s, while Oyo's military power declined. By the late 1780s and early 1790s, some frontier provinces became strong enough to break away. In 1796, military failures led a council to require Alafin Awole to commit suicide, as provided by the constitution. But this time a new alafin able to command a broad sweep of general support could not be found, and a long interregnum, accompanied by further decline in the administrative structure of the empire, lasted into the nineteenth century.

With Oyo, imperial expansion began and continued for many decades before military aggression came to be linked to the slave trade, but once the link was made, the decade of the 1780s was both the peak decade for Oyo's export of slaves and the beginning of its internal crisis. The slave trade was at least one element contributing to decline, but it was not alone.

Comparisons with the political development of Dahomey and Asante suggest that other causes were more fundamental. During the eighteenth century, it is clear that both Asante and Dahomey were struggling in their own ways to adapt old political institutions to the new challenge posed by European trade. The way chosen in Asante was to create a new and larger national unit and to articulate that nationality through a newly developed political structure. In Dahomey, the first change of direction was a constitutional revolution abolishing the old way of balancing lineages through councils. This, in turn, cleared the way for a second set of moves integrating Dahomean economic and military policy with the service of the slave trade. Our evidence is less firm for eighteenth-century Oyo than it is for Dahomey or Asante. Oyo appears to have first built an empire and then begun the large-scale export of slaves without first changing its forms of government. As a result, the checks and balances of the traditional Oyo constitution failed to work, and Oyo was not able to respond adequately to the new commerce, to the rebellious provinces, or (in the longer run) to the threat of militant Islam beyond the northern frontiers. Whereas Asante and Dahomey were to continue as viable states until the European conquest in the last decade of the nineteenth century, Oyo collapsed so completely in the 1820s that the nineteenth-century slave trade drew more heavily on Yoruba than on any other nationality, though Yoruba slaves had been practically unheard of in the Americas before 1750.

THE NIGER DELTA AND THE CAMEROONS

East of the Benin River lies the delta of the Niger, a land of myriad channels, creeks, and mangrove swamps. At the seaward fringe, the delta forms a sand ridge, high enough for villages of fishermen and salt gatherers. In the upper delta, inland beyond the salt water and mangrove swamps, is a region of freshwater swamp with some higher land suitable for agriculture. Long before the beginning of European trade, conditions in the delta itself encouraged trade between the seaward settlements and the agricultural areas of the upper delta and its hinterland. By 1500, one of the villages at the lower fringe of the delta was reported to have a population of 2,000 people and an active commerce through the system of creeks and lagoons. (Two thousand people would hardly make a large city today, but it should be kept in mind that Oporto, the second largest city in Portugal, had only 8,000 people at that time.) Similar conditions existed further east, where the estuary of the Cross River again provided an opportunity to exploit maritime resources and trade these products with the hinterland. In spite of ethnic differences between the Ijo of the Niger Delta proper and the Ibibio, Efik, and others to the east, political and historical circumstances were similar as far east as Mount Cameroon.

People along this coast had been trading with the interior in their large "canoes" before the Europeans appeared on the coast, and they traded occasionally with the Europeans in the sixteenth century, though the Europeans set up no regular shore establishments. Until the second half of the seventeenth century, however, the slave trade here was very small indeed. But then the coastal

societies changed radically, adapted their organization to the demands of the
slave trade, and made contact with others in the hinterland who were making
similar adjustments. The result was a commercial organization that supplied
far more slaves per mile of coast or square mile of economic hinterland than
any other part of eighteenth-century Africa.

Some of these adaptations were political. At the beginning of maritime
contact, the eastern Ijo of the delta were divided into a series of lineages, each
bearing the name of an eponymous ancestor and settled in a series of interrelated villages. Each village, however, was independent of the rest and was
governed by a council and one or more headmen exercising minimal executive
powers. Extensive trade required a more powerful organization, capable of defending the routes to the interior. By the late seventeenth century, these formerly

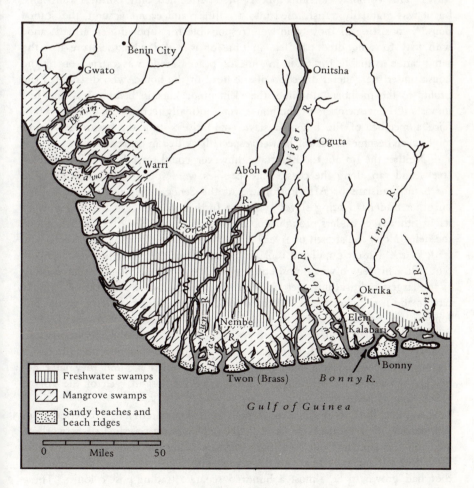

The Niger Delta

independent villages had regrouped to form a series of small monarchies, each under a royal lineage and centered on a principal trading town — Bonny, Nembe or Brass, Kalabari or New Calabar, among others.

The Efik of the lower Cross River also developed a more consolidated form of government, but in a different way. There, the separate villages continued to be independent, each ruled by a chief and council and constituting so many microstates. But they also had a common government in the form of a secret society, the *ekpe,* or leopard society, which extended to all the villages and was able to enforce common action in most circumstances requiring such action.

New economic institutions came along with these constitutional changes. One of the subunits in the older political order was the *wari,* or "house," actually an extended family made up of a man, his wives, some relatives, and their slaves. This corporate kinship unit at first performed only political functions, but it was gradually transformed into a military and economic unit, the "canoe house," consisting of those who were responsible for supplying an armed canoe with fifty to a hundred paddlers in time of war and who therefore had the same canoe available for trade in time of peace. Trade was carried on by the house under the general direction of the head of the house, who distributed the profits to the members. In time, the element of kinship became less and less important. New members of the house were normally recruited by purchase, but, once a member of the house, a slave could rise within the organization and might even become its head if he were especially skilled in trade and war.

Neither the Ijo nor the Efik trade, however, could reach beyond the maze of creeks and ran along the coast. Both peoples were specialized navigators, like the Saint-Louisians or Afro-Portuguese of the Senegambia, and they depended on other traders to bring slaves from the further interior. On the Niger River itself, other river traders brought goods down the river to markets a little above the delta, along the stretch of river between present-day Onitsha and Aboh. The trade of the densely populated Iboland to the east of the Niger was more important still. This region was almost entirely stateless, with the village group serving as the largest political unit, yet lacking the centralization of authority that might have made it a microstate. Local trade took place within the village group, but long-distance trade was left to outside specialists. One such group of long-distance traders were the people of Awka, who began traveling as priests and diviners connected with their Agbala deity. Their religious role made it easier for them to pass safely through a variety of jurisdictions, and they later developed a network of fictitious kinship ties with a host in each of the village groups they visited.

Another Ibo group, the Aro, worked with similar religious protection from Ebinokpabi, their great oracle. And theirs was a closely coordinated network of Aro colonies stretched out as a trade diaspora along the trade routes. Some of these Aro settlements go back to the seventeenth century, and by the nineteenth they had grown to be almost a hundred separate trading-post colonies. These were linked together by Aro who moved along the trade routes, and they were further linked by four-day trade fairs, alternately held at two central points every twenty-four days.

Both the Aro and the Awka trade networks were beyond the range of European observation during the period of the slave trade, and Ibo oral traditions have too shallow a depth in time to be satisfactory. It may therefore be impossible to explore the detailed history of Ibo trade. The Ijo and Efik dealers on the coast (and presumably their suppliers) were nevertheless exceptional in their ability to maintain a supply of slaves to the Atlantic trade that was both numerous and steady one decade after another, while the supply from other regions fluctuated widely in response to political or military changes in the hinterland. This fact, plus a scattering of other evidence, suggests that the dominant form of slave catching in this region may not have been warfare but kidnapping combined with the manipulation of oracles, so that human sacrifices could be called for and the victims then quietly shipped off to the Americas.

THE SLAVE TRADE IN AFRICAN HISTORY

One of the striking ironies of African history is the fact that maritime contact, which ended Africa's long isolation and brought all coasts of the continent into contact with the intercommunicating part of the world, should also have led so rapidly to a situation in which Africa's main export was her people. And the full impact of the slave trade on African history remains hard to assess. It is obvious that enslavement and exile to the New World were terrible experiences, that the dehumanizing institutions of plantation slavery were worse still. The violence of capture and the dangers along the way surely meant that at least as many were killed as were delivered to the plantations, and the waste in human life continued as the plantations failed to achieve an excess of births over deaths. But terrible as these consequences were for the people who were enslaved, they tell little about the impact of the slave trade on African societies themselves.

This assessment is even harder to make because the incidence of the trade was so uneven. Some small ethnic groups were completely wiped out. Others suffered heavily for a time — a few decades of political instability — but were otherwise untouched by the trade: most Yoruba and most Wolof had this kind of experience. Other societies, like Benin, were very lightly involved for centuries on end, but too lightly for the trade to have made a really serious impact. Still others, like Dahomey, may have profited from the slave trade, though at the expense of their African neighbors. Elsewhere on the continent, large regions, like most of the present-day Republic of South Africa, were simply not involved in the trade at all. With these differences, it is virtually impossible to strike a balance. But some things appear to be clear. The sheer physical destructiveness of the trade was not significant enough to produce a general and striking difference in social health and progress between areas where the slave trade was prevalent and those where people suffered only from the usual run of war, plague, and famine. Its most serious damage to African society was probably not physical destruction and loss of life, nor the drain of population but rather a warping of social purposes to serve destructive ends. The total impact of the trade therefore has to be measured not by what actually happened, but against the might-have-been if Africa's creative energy had been turned instead to some other end than that of building a commercial system capable of capturing and exporting some eighty thousand people a year.

SUGGESTIONS FOR FURTHER READING

Akinjogbin, I. A. *Dahomey and its Neighbours, 1708–1818.* Cambridge: Cambridge University Press, 1967.

Curtin, Philip D. *The Atlantic Slave Trade: A Census.* Madison: University of Wisconsin Press, 1969.

———. *Economic Change in Pre-Colonial Africa: Senegambia in the Era of the Slave Trade.* Madison: University of Wisconsin Press, 1975.

Curtin, Philip D., ed. *Africa Remembered. Narratives by West Africans from the Era of the Slave Trade.* Madison: University of Wisconsin Press, 1968.

Daaku, Kwame Yeboa. *Trade and Politics on the Gold Coast, 1600 to 1720.* Oxford: Oxford University Press, Clarendon Press, 1970.

Davies, K. G. *The Royal African Company.* London: Longman, 1957.

Latham, A. J. H. *Old Calabar, 1600–1891.* London: Oxford University Press, 1973.

Ryder, Alan F. C. *Benin and the Europeans, 1485–1897.* London: Longman, 1969.

Chapter 8
Equatorial Africa before the Nineteenth Century

EQUATORIAL AFRICA stretches over huge spaces from the *sahel* of Chad to the Victoria Falls on the Zambezi. Only two basic landscapes predominate in this vast area. The tropical forest straddles the equator and extends roughly four degrees north and south. Here, in the second biggest forest of the world, the canopy of the giant trees towers over two levels of vegetation and the sunlight reaches the ground only in small golden specks, for everywhere hungry leaves above drink it up. Some flora and fauna are adapted to the ever-humid shadows, others to the forest edges, especially near the patches of open savanna (*esobe*) found frequently in the western two-thirds of the forest. People also live in the woods, but many prefer to dwell near the placid, meandering rivers that cut a majestic swath through the forest, ultimately to rejoin the father of them all, the mighty Zaïre (Congo). They also dwell on the edge of the esobe, along the huge marshes near the equator, or along the smaller swift rivers that hurry to the Atlantic.

The second basic landscape takes in the rolling domains of the grasses north and south of the forest. There, as far as the eye can see, an ocean of grasses bends with the wind, but most of the year the eye does not see far, for the clumps of grass reach well above human height. Only in the dry seasons, when fires level it all, do the distant horizons appear. Where the forest is still near, its outlines can be followed along the river valleys and even in the copses crowning the ridges. Farther north or south, the fingers of the gallery forests thin out and disappear while the grasses grow to a lesser height. In this environment, new species of trees are found, at first scattered, then more dense as the savanna turns into woodland. To the south, this landscape reaches the Zambezi. In the north, the grassy woodlands are broken by low-lying marshes, infested with mosquitoes. These are the lower Shari and Salamat basins in the west and the *sudd* in the east. Only south of Darfur and in Adamawa to the west do the woodlands go over into parkland, and ultimately into sahel and then desert.

The whole of Equatorial Africa is somewhat separate from the rest of Africa, and the savanna south of the forest was especially isolated before the Portuguese arrived along the seacoast. Yet within the southern savanna, movement was not hampered at all, not even by the small mountain chain that follows the Atlantic coast. Its earlier contacts with the outside, however, were directed toward the Zambezi and the east coast and through the forest toward the north. Although the forest constituted a barrier, it was not an absolute wall; within the forest, communication by water was easy wherever the rivers were broad and slow-moving, and cultural similarities in this environment can be traced back to the hydrography. North-south travel was fairly easy along the coast and along the Ubangi, Sanga, and Congo (Zaïre) rivers, as it was also along the Lomami and Lualaba rivers. The patches of esobe also made travel easier than might at first appear.

North of the forest, the savanna once again forms a cultural unit up to the tenth parallel, the northern limit of the tsetse fly and the area where extensive bogs and marshes cut the area off from the Chadian sahel. Only along the Shari in the west and toward the Nile in the east was there an easy opening to other

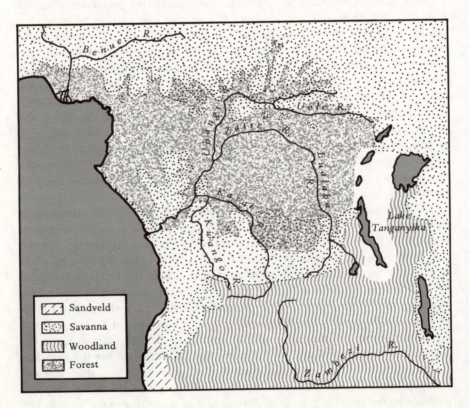

Equatorial Africa: Vegetation

parts of Africa. Elsewhere, the mighty mountain barriers of East Africa, with the rift valleys and the great lakes, tended to isolate Central Africa, though leaving bridges of comparatively easy communication along the Zambezi River or between Lakes Tanganyika and Malawi. To the northwest, a similar bridge stretched across the Adamawa plateau and the grasslands to the south. As a result, Equatorial Africa falls naturally into three self-contained regions — the forest itself, and the savannas to the north and south, with each of these regions having only limited access to the outer world.

THE LATER IRON AGE
IN THE SOUTHERN SAVANNA

For the period up to 1500 A.D., the history of the forest and southern savanna depends mainly on archaeological evidence. So far, little or no archaeological work has been done in the equatorial forest or the northern savanna, so that these regions only enter firmly into the historical picture when written records are available. Many archaeological sites are already known, however, and it is now clear that the so-called Uelian neolithic remains from the northeast of the Zaïre Republic represent a full-fledged Iron Age. It also seems likely, though still on slender evidence, that the Early Iron Age in the north may have changed quite rapidly into a more advanced Late Iron Age.

In the southern savanna, excavations make it appear that the Early Iron Age styles lasted for as long as a thousand years and only gave way to the Late Iron Age after 1000 A.D. Some remarkable evidence, however, has been found in the great necropolis uncovered at Sanga in Zambia and at the related archaeological sites in Shaba (formerly Katanga). These sites reveal the beginnings of art styles and ways of doing things that appear to be directly related to the later Luba and Lunda empires, which emerged as political entities before 1500 A.D. In this area, the Sanga and Katanga sites have been occupied continuously from the eighth century to the nineteenth, and the preexisting Late Stone Age levels appear to be followed directly by Late Iron Age levels.

Sanga was a huge agglomeration inhabited by fishermen and hunters. Physically, these people could well have been the ancestors of the present-day Luba. They spoke a Bantu language. The virtuosity of the metalworkers, whether they dealt in iron or copper, is astonishing. Their potters were also skilled at making vessels especially as funerary goods. We can assume that these workers were specialized artisans, evidence that a surplus in food production made specialization possible. Under such circumstances, one would expect to find royal tombs, but none have appeared thus far, even though the cemetery is immense. Inequalities of wealth are evident in the tombs, however, among both adults and children. Other evidence, suggestive of chiefly institutions, takes the form of a different pottery from Katoto, where the evidence for chieftainship is stronger; and some graves at Sanga contain richer than ordinary grave goods, including emblems typical of the regalia of later Luba chiefs. A number of graves apparently belong to traders in copper crosses, as appears from the fact that crosses are only found in a small number of graves which also contain special pottery not found elsewhere. Sanga appears to have been trading with the south, at least 150 miles away, and indirect connections with the Indian Ocean are revealed by a few cowrie shells and a number of glass beads.

Archaeologists conclude that the Sanga culture flourished without diffusing very far and that foreign influence here was insignificant. After the Stone Age, the sites indicate a succession of three different cultures: Kisalian, Kabambian, and the historic Luba culture. Continuities between the earlier two and the later Luba culture are amazing, including such similarities as types of bells and headrests, regalia, mutilation of the teeth, and general physical characteristics. Unfortunately, archaeologists have not yet assigned dates to each of these cultures. To the west of this area, undated chance finds in northern Angola, taken along with present-day pottery types along the upper Kasai and Lungwebungu rivers, point to a similar continuity of early and later populations, stretching from about 1000 A.D. down to recent populations like the Lunda.

LUBA AND LUNDA EXPANSION TO 1800

The Luba and Lunda empires that arose in Central Africa a little before 1500 can probably be traced back to intensive cross-fertilization among the many different traditions that met and mingled in the Lualaba valley between the eighth century and the fourteenth or fifteenth, when these kingdoms began to spread their influence and sometimes their political control over large parts of the southern savanna. Unfortunately, this development remains largely inaccessible to the archaeologist. We also miss the kind of reporting by people literate in Arabic that helps to illuminate the history of the western Sudan at this same period. Oral traditions are available, but oral traditions of the distant past often have a mythic quality: they sometimes express people's ideas about the past and their justification of the present social order in words that are to be understood as symbolic rather than as literal accounts of the events that actually took place.

This is especially true within the larger Lunda culture area, where people's ideas about the past and their expression of those ideas are profoundly influenced by the institutions of perpetual succession and positional kinship. Perpetual succession is the practice whereby each successor to a particular office takes the title or name of the original holder of that office. If an official who bore the name and title of Kinguri died, his successor was also called Kinguri. This was something more than a tricky way of naming people; it implied that the new Kinguri *was* Kinguri, too, and took on the personal identity of the original holder of that office. This identity is underlined by the companion institution of positional kinship: the kinship ties of the original officeholder are fictitiously adopted by all his successors. Thus, the original Kinguri was brother of a certain Chinyama, then all succeeding Kinguri are considered to be brothers of all succeeding Chinyamas. In this case, "brother" expresses a historic kinship tie, but it also expresses a current relationship that could be translated "chief of equal rank." Within this framework of thought and expression, to talk about the death of Kinguri refers not to the death of a person but to the abolition of the office, position, and title of Kinguri.

These institutions may have existed from ancient times among the whole range of peoples from the Bemba of eastern Zambia westward to the upper Kwango, and they have led historically to a certain uniformity among this group of societies and to a contrast with the Luba who lived to the north. The contrast is heightened by the fact that the southern groups were matrilineal, while the Luba have been patrilineal as far back as memory goes. The Luba and Lunda peoples are nevertheless linked in their myths of origin.

These myths begin with the reign of a certain Nkongolo over the central Luba kingdom. He was of the Songye ethnic group and an uncouth person who was driven from office by a handsome hunter from the east, Ilunga Kalala. Ilunga Kalala enlarged the state, invented its organization, perfected its ideology and etiquette. The myths of origin of the Kaonde peoples to the south tell of other Luba chiefs who departed and came to settle among them and provided

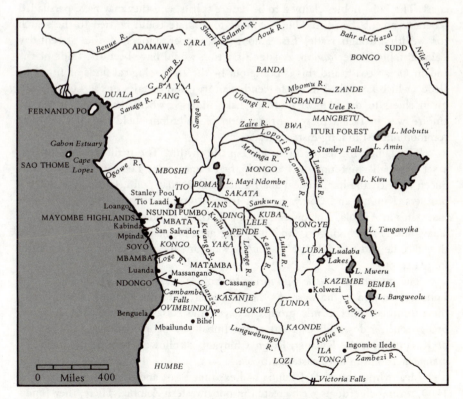

Peoples of Equatorial Africa in the Eighteenth Century

their first framework of organization as a state. Bemba legends tell a similar story of Luba nobles migrating to the east and founding the Bemba state. The central Luba tradition says little or nothing about these emigrants, but it does tell how another handsome hunter, a nephew of Ilunga Kalala, went among the Lunda and founded a kingdom of the Luba type. Present-day cultures show some Luba influence among the Kaonde, Bemba, and Lunda, but the detail in these myths of empire may not be factual, except perhaps for the personal names. Nkongolo may represent one man, but he may equally well represent a whole dynasty of Songye rulers that was replaced by a new dynasty founded by Ilunga Kalala; or Nkongolo may represent a world-view rather than a genuine historical person or dynasty.

In any event, the Lunda empire must be older than 1490 (on other evidence traceable to the coast, where it was recorded by Europeans), and the central Luba kingdom may be even older. The most likely hypothesis at present is that the sites of Sanga and Katoto represent the core towns of very early states, ancestral to the Luba kingdom, which probably grew out of a set of small chiefdoms in the Lualaba valley. The success of the Luba leaders in making themselves kings over non-Luba peoples may be explained in part by the prestige of the Luba court. The Luba nobles claimed to be nature spirits, and they may have persuaded others to accept the idea. The incentives to migrate could be tied to the search for wealth through trade, first among the copper miners of the present-day Zaïre-Zambia border region. A later attraction would have been the trade of the Indian Ocean coast, and this is borne out by the archaeological finds of Ingombe Ilede (which flourished in the fifteenth century) and by tales of the Luba having given chiefs to the Malawi south of Lake Malawi, where the so-called Maravi empire was in fact a loose confederation of chiefdoms held together by their common interest in long-distance trade.

The Lunda myths of origin are equally mythic. The main story holds that a set of small chiefdoms first united, then came under Luba influence when a queen married the handsome Luba hunter. But at that point, two of the queen's brothers, Kinguri and Chinyama, left for the west where they founded Lunda-like states in Angola. The queen's son by the Luba hunter was known as Mwaant Yaav, and he, like Kinguri and Chinyama, gave his name to a perpetual title for the office he had first filled. Mwaant Yaav became the royal name for the central Lunda empire.

The movement of the Kinguri into Angola makes it possible to trace this Lunda expansion to the west. As those who left with the Kinguri moved about, they absorbed other ethnic groups between the Kasai River and the Atlantic, finally settling down about 1620 as the Imbangala people ruling over the state of Kasanje near the Kwango River. Chinyama's followers became the nuclei of many chiefdoms in northeastern Angola.

Meanwhile, the central Lunda had expanded east and south as well. Around 1700, several chiefdoms were created in northwestern Zambia. There, they found the Lozi kingdom, which could resist them. This kingdom had been created by a single or a few Lunda who had left one or more generations earlier and had incorporated existing chiefdoms. These chiefdoms left an obvious imprint on the new state, which itself may have been subject to social and cultural influences from the polities in Zimbabwe south of the Zambezi. Throughout the eighteenth and early nineteenth centuries, the Lozi themselves expanded gradually, first along the Zambezi River valley, where they assimilated a rival Lozi state, and then on both sides of the Zambezi over the adjacent plateau. Thus they subjected the peoples living between the Zambezi and the hook of the Kafue River.

Early Lunda expansion eastward aimed at control of the important salt-producing area of the Lualaba near Kolwezi. From there on, a general, or *kazembe,* was sent to occupy valuable salt pans and copper mines in Shaba and also perhaps to establish control over trade with the lower Zambezi. By 1750, this led to the creation of the kingdom of Kazembe centered on the Luapula valley, which was to become almost as powerful as Lunda itself. Guns from Europe had facilitated this conquest in its later stages, and trade linking Kazembe to the Portuguese posts on the lower Zambezi after 1780 helped the new country to prosper.

From the Yaka people on the Kwango, this loose Lunda empire stretched to Kazembe to the Luapula. Most of the local peoples had accepted Lunda rule and participated in further expansion because their leaders had readily been granted Lundahood, symbolized by a cowbelt. The nucleus kingdom with the Mwaant Yaav was recognized as the senior partner; presents called tribute were sent on occasion by even the farthest-removed kings, but the area was too far-flung to be closely controlled from nuclear Lunda. In practice, Kazembe and the Yaka were especially autonomous, but only the Lozi and the Luba remained outside the Lunda commonwealth.

THE LUBA AND LUNDA CULTURES ABOUT 1800

The earliest picture of Luba or Lunda culture as a working entity dates from the period of the first detailed European reports, which can be read back into the past for only a short distance in time. We therefore have to be content with the knowledge that earlier Luba and Lunda have lived in a similar way — though not in exactly the same way, because these cultures were constantly changing.

About 1800, the basic social and political unit of the Luba was the local patrilineage with its clients — that is, people who calculated their descent from the father's side, hence lived together with a number of unrelated hangers-on, servants, and the like. These groups had their own villages with their own lands, though this was not the case with the other Luba who were still matrilineal, as the central Luba must also have been in the more distant past. With the central Luba, a number of patrilineal villages were joined together into a chiefdom ruled by the head of a particular patrilineage. The kingdom, with its own royal patrilineage at the head, was the sum of several chiefdoms. The particular *kilolo,* or chief, was dependent on the king for his office, even though he had to belong to the chiefly patrilineage. Some provinces were governed directly by the king, while others were grouped under a close relative named either for life or for only a short period of time.

The king's power was concentrated on his capital, the *kitenta*. There he ruled with a host of titleholders and followers, who also formed the core of his army. Each new king appointed titleholders, and most offices were held by his relatives on his mother's side. Kingship was based on the concept of *bulopwe*, a mystical call to rule. Bulopwe resided in the blood and was transmitted patrilineally from the time of Ilunga Kalala. It made the king a *vidye*, or spirit-hero, and all the great rituals, the protocol, and the emblems stressed this sacred quality.

The court was the center of a vigorous artistic life. Different provinces had separate styles in sculpture, ranging from the soft naturalism found among the Hemba in the east to the almost strict cubism popular with the independent Songye in the north. Among the masterworks of sculpture were the *mboko*, female statuettes holding bowls, royal stools, and other emblems. But much sculpture was associated with the secret or closed associations of a religious nature, which were the real counterbalance to the chief. Most of the Luba masks belong to this sphere. But sculpture did not originate with the founding of the kingdom, nor indeed was the best sculpture always found at the highest court. From the stylistic diversity, it is evident that the traditions of this great art go back to remote times.

Luba verbal art was based on a tradition of beautiful and elaborate praise poetry, *kasala*, while the epic of Ilunga Kalala had become a major work of art. Luba polyphonic music was also an important cultural achievement. Religion centered around the ancestors, who could reach mortals through divination and messages spoken through cult media. This, like the closed associations and the initiations for boys and girls, was based on a complex and luxuriating symbolism. It differed from other religions and value systems mainly in its dramatic flair and suggestion of violence.

The Lunda state, by contrast, had been built up from preexisting tiny chiefdoms based on matrilineal succession. Several of these were grouped in a district headed by a *cilool*. At the capital, government was in the joint hands of the emperor and his council, or *citentam*. This council was composed of ritual titleholders, some of whom represented the aboriginal chiefs and some of whom were Luba imports. Others were administrative officers and representatives of the tributary kingdoms.

The originality of the Lunda system lay in its use of the two legal fictions, positional succession and perpetual kinship. Because the descent system was less relevant than the pattern of preferential marriages, which kept the influential families linked to one another in stable relationships, it could be expressed in an idiom of kinship that defied the passage of time. It allowed for incorporation of new foreign elements; and it was completely separated from the underlying social system, so that it could thrive in either matrilineal, patrilineal, or bilateral societies. This adaptability explains ultimately the success of the Lunda expansion. Whereas the Luba could not integrate newly conquered groups into the ruling bureaucracy, the Lunda could do so, and, by achieving Lundahood, the subject chiefs came to have a stake in the system.

But material culture and economic structure were far less developed among the Lunda than among the Luba. Most Luba were industrious farmers, whereas more of the Lunda remained hunters. Their villages were smaller; their techniques, including weaving and ironworking, were poorer; even their clothes and appearance were much humbler. Their religion, also based on ancestor cult, was much simpler and the social and religious associations were not so important. They had no significant sculpture or literature. Their culture, in short, revolved almost exclusively around political values, whereas the Luba world was much more varied, valuing religion and art as much as politics. No wonder, then, that so many elements of Luba culture spread among the Lunda.

Among the peoples in the Luba-Lunda orbit, two cultures deserve separate mention. The Songye were Luba in origin but already separate by the mid-sixteenth century or before. Most of them lived in agricultural cities of many thousands, sometimes grouping a whole ethnic unit in one settlement. These towns were governed by a religious association, the *bukishi*, which held power alongside the hereditary kings. The bukishi held a huge store of esoteric knowledge and ritual, and it represented an explicit theory of political rule, rather like the bulopwe belief of a mystical calling to rule. But it also incorporated a complex cosmogony presented in a myth of creation. Songye society was remarkable for the high rank it accorded its skilled smiths. Smithing reached a peak of skill here, and the status of smiths was correspondingly high: they formed an endogamous group, equal to the chiefs.

West of the Lunda, the Chokwe people, then a small group, were famous for their ironwork and for their hunting. They also possessed a distinct tradition of sculpture which flourished at the courts of their Lunda chiefs and was inherited from pre-Lunda times. Chokwe art influenced the whole Kwango valley, not only by its style but also by motifs in which scenes of daily life and animals of the bush are common. This art was also characterized by great versatility in representation and by selective borrowing from Angola, probably by way of Kasanje, of Renaissance and rococo motifs, adapted to fit Chokwe esthetics.

By 1800, a process of cultural expansion and cross-fertilization was under way all over the Luba-Lunda area. Institutions, symbols, values, objects were spreading from one end of the area to the other. The title *kilolo*, for instance, may have been of eastern Luba origin, but by 1880 it had come into use among the Yans near the mouth of the Kwilu. The Luba initiation ceremonies for boys, the *mukanda*, spread to the Lunda and then north to the Pende, Luba Kasai, and Kuba peoples before 1650! The *cisungu* for girls covered eastern Angola, Luba-land, and most of northeastern Zambia. The use of a small talking drum, the *mondo,* was found from the Kwango to the Luapula rivers, but only among the Lunda, the Luba having a different one.

Many more examples of this continuous exchange of cultural items are known, ranging over the whole spectrum of culture. Yet many cultural features did not spread, either because (as in the case of the talking drum) the other culture already had a satisfactory element or because too much change would be involved in accepting the new institution, although that was rare. Perhaps this explains why Chokwe sculpture did not spread among the Lunda, although similar styles existed along the upper Kasai River down to the Kuba people in the north.

THE ATLANTIC REGIONS SOUTH OF THE FOREST: THE KINGDOM OF KONGO TO 1575

From the Early Iron Age onward, the Atlantic regions south of the forest and west of the middle and upper Kasai seem to have developed very much on their own. Archaeological work here is still in its infancy, but enough is known to deny close connection with regions further east. The first solid historical information comes from oral traditions set down mainly in the seventeenth century.

According to available data, a principal center of political development lay on the southern fringes of the forest north of the River Zaïre. To begin with, this whole region between the ocean and the middle Zaïre was organized in tiny chiefdoms, each the size of an English parish, where a local Lord of the Land saw to it that relations with the nature spirits were not disturbed as he performed the proper rituals and enjoyed a prestige derived from these functions. His office was hereditary and, in effect, his possession of a link to the spirit of the territory was the key to the office. Gradually some of these lords built up their real power and subjugated others in the name of their spirits, who, they claimed, were superior to other territorial spirits; or they set themselves up as political chiefs and left the ritual business of the local parish to the vanquished lord. This, of course, implied a special status for the spirit who had helped the overlord to his victory.

In time, chiefdoms became larger and more complex in political organization. Eventually three main states emerged: Loango on the coast north of the mouth of the Zaïre; the Tio kingdom — it can hardly be called a state — north of the Stanley Pool (Malebo); and the kingdom of Kongo. The whole evolution may have begun very early, perhaps even in the first millennium. Its last stages, when Kongo's conquest of its six main provinces was secure, probably dates from the fourteenth century.

Meanwhile, south of the River Zaïre, in the valley of the middle and upper Kwango, similar developments led to the emergence of chiefdoms where both ancestral spirits and charms played an important ideological role. First came the

Pende chiefdoms, then Matamba, and finally (around 1500) Ndongo with its titled king, the *ngola*. It is possible that this pattern was merely a variant of the one north of the river; but the southern group developed more slowly, so that Ndongo rose to power only after Kongo had become the superpower of the whole region. The rapid development in the north owed something to the favored position on the fringe of the forest and savanna, just as some savanna states derived a commercial advantage from their location on the border between savanna and desert. The northern group would also have gained from the fact that canoes had to transship at the Stanley Pool because of the Zaïre rapids below that point, while the only economic advantage for the south was a group of salt ponds on the Kwango.

At the time the Portuguese landed in 1483, the ruler of Kongo was Nzinga Nkuwu. Relations between the two powers started well. Soon the king was baptized and a Portuguese expedition helped him fight the Tio or a related

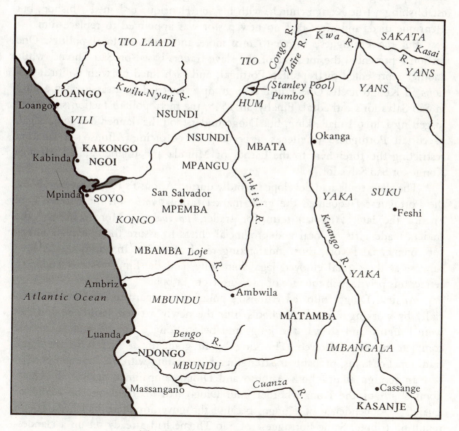

The Kingdoms of Kongo and Angola
in the Sixteenth and Seventeenth Centuries

people near the Stanley Pool. Later on, possibly as a result of persistent slave raids by other Portuguese based on the island of São Thomé or because the king realized that adherence to Christianity implied a total change in Kongo's political traditions, Nzinga Nkuwu returned to his former faith. A faction led by his younger son Affonso remained Catholic and, after the king's death in 1506, Affonso defeated his brother and the pagan faction. A period of collaboration between Portugal and Kongo followed, with Affonso asking for technicians of all sorts and King Manuel of Portugal obliging, but requesting payment in copper, ivory, and slaves. Gradually the Kongolese became disenchanted, mostly because of Portuguese behavior in Kongo and their realization by the early 1520s that the slave trade was undermining the king's authority, that it led to the kidnapping and enslavement of free people, even of members of the royal family. Affonso could also see the special Portuguese interest in exploiting gold and copper mines. Yet he remained a staunch Christian, continued to ask for missionaries, made Catholicism the state religion and fount of the royal authority, thus replacing some of the sacredness of kingship. He almost succeeded in establishing a true Kongo church, with his son Henrique ordained a bishop, but Henrique died, and after that no new pastor was appointed to replace him.

But the Portuguese began to mix more and more in local politics. One faction represented the interests of the slave traders based on São Thomé, while another represented metropolitan Portugal; and each lined up with political factions in Kongo itself. One Portuguese group even tried to assassinate the king in São Salvador's cathedral. Finally, in 1545, the metropolitan faction succeeded in getting Diogo I made king, but Diogo understood the danger. He soon began to curtail Portuguese privileges, especially by enforcing Affonso's regulation restricting the foreigners to the harbor of Mpinda and to the capital, *Mbanza Kongo*, or São Salvador.

The slave trade had developed rapidly during Affonso's reign. By the 1530s, the Portuguese frequented the great market called *pumbo* on the Stanley Pool (hence the later Angolan term for trader, *pombeiro*). More seriously, the traders made gifts to local and provincial chiefs to assure their help in return for commercial favors, thus endangering royal authority. In addition, the Portuguese at the capital enjoyed legal immunity, and the king was never able to retract this privilege in the face of pressure from Lisbon.

At first, Diogo followed Affonso's policy with regard to the Church, especially by working for better schools. But the newly arrived Jesuit missionaries were haughty and so was the king, and before long a quarrel and an almost complete rupture followed. The king began gradually to return to the more traditional customs, probably to strengthen his standing with the common people.

In foreign affairs, both Affonso and Diogo campaigned against the chiefdoms south of the Kongo border, and Diogo had marched on the island of Luanda, a dependency of Kongo, because the governor there had been lax in remitting tribute. Some Portuguese of São Thomé had already set up a clandestine slave trade in that area, principally in collaboration with the chief or king of Ndongo, the ngola. In 1556, the ngola, with Portuguese help, rebelled and defeated Diogo in the field. Immediately afterward, the king of Ndongo sent an embassy to Portugal by way of São Thomé asking for trade and missionaries. Kongo had indeed lost control over the south. Kongo was isolated. After Diogo's death, the local Portuguese imposed his successor, but the populace rose up and killed the Portuguese. It took years for the Kongo to recover from its resulting reputation for xenophobia and the consequent boycott by Portuguese shipping.

A little later, two monarchs in succession were killed in battle near Stanley Pool (Malebo) by Tio or related people, no doubt in a war to achieve control over the growing markets of this area. Following these deaths, a large number of Kongo peasants, perhaps a majority, rebelled against the aristocracy. This rebellion is remembered as the Jaga invasion of 1568. The regime tumbled like a house of cards. The king and his government had to flee to an island in the mouth of the river, where they could be protected by Portuguese ships. The rebellion was motivated by steadily increasing levees and taxes, of which signs appear as early as 1526. It was not so much that Kongolese were sold into slavery, for not so many were. It was the appetite for foreign luxury goods at the court and the provincial capitals and even at the local aristocratic level that led to such a burden being imposed on the peasants.

The Portuguese called in by the new king fought for years to reestablish royal authority. At the same time, they assured themselves of control over the country, where they remained in force until 1576, the year after the foundation of Angola. As the insurgents were subdued or chased away, some settled north of the river, while others rallied in the Kwango valley and organized themselves in new chiefdoms. Here they were to be conquered later by the Lunda and to become Imbangala.

The name *Jaga* came to be applied by the Portuguese to all mobile hostile forces, though at a later time it was applied primarily to the Imbangala when this people was formed between the Cuanza and Kwango rivers. This led to considerable confusion in the historiography of Central Africa. The small Humbe state in southern Angola, for example, is said to be of Jaga origin, although it was probably much closer to the Ovimbundu people of the Angolan highlands. For the Portuguese, however — and, by 1620, for the kings of Kongo as well — Jaga had come to mean "savage, cannibal, inhuman barbarian." These views helped to crystallize Portuguese racial views and to justify their expansion in Angola.

PORTUGUESE EXPANSION IN ANGOLA

In 1575 Paul Dias de Novaes landed with a small fleet and the Portuguese king's permission to conquer Angola for himself and his country. He knew Ndongo, having lived at the ngola's court as a prisoner for several years. He first settled on Luanda island, where many traders had their homes. Then he founded Luanda on the mainland. His intention was to proceed up the Cuanza River to the fabled silver mines of Cambambe, but, when he did so, he started a hundred-year war with the ngola.

In a first period, the Portuguese succeeded in holding Luanda and in founding Massangano, but in 1591 they were defeated in the field by an African coalition. The *conquista* had floundered. But the Africans were unable to capture the two towns of Luanda and Massangano. As a consequence, Portugal revoked the concession, declared Angola a colony, sent troops in, and muddled on. The Portuguese reached Cambambe but discovered that the silver did not exist. Nevertheless, it was too late to withdraw, and already the slave trade and raiding were yielding high profits to the army captains and the traders. As a result, a cease-fire signed in 1604 was soon broken. The war went on and turned in favor of the Portuguese, thanks to a Jaga alliance. By the end of 1622, the Portuguese had taken Ndongo, driven the ngola into hiding, helped cause a famine, killed hundreds of petty chiefs, and defeated an army sent by the king of Kongo. But the Vatican upheld Kongo's protestation that Portugal had fought a brother Christian country with the help of "Jaga cannibals." In addition, Kongo mobilized and forced Portugual to sign a truce.

Kongo had been able to retrieve some of its former might. After 1576, it had first forced the retreat of the Portuguese, then resisted their demand to build a fort at the mouth of the River Zaïre. Kongo then entered into trade relations with the Dutch and established independent relations with the Vatican, the only supranational arbiter of the day. It also obtained its own bishopric. Trade relations with the Pool and the great market of Ocanga on the Kwango enriched Portuguese merchants in Kongo, who therefore tended to side with Kongo against the settlers of Angola.

But in 1623 the king of Ndongo died. His sister Anna Nzinga succeeded. Because the conditions of the truce were not carried out, she allied herself with the Jaga, incited soldiers to desert, slaves to flee, and chiefs who were now vassals of Portugal to rebel in her name. Luanda was undergoing a Dutch scare and could not react immediately, but the situation grew so serious that finally a force was sent against Nzinga. Defeated and retreating, Nzinga captured the kingdom of Matamba, reorganized from that base, withstood another campaign, and returned to her former territory. Finally, she allied herself with the king of Kasanje, a new power on the Kwango, and Luanda sued for peace. Kasanje accepted it, though Nzinga rejected the overtures. At this point, in 1641, the Dutch captured Luanda.

Portugal now found itself at war with all the African powers, Kasanje and Kongo included. In this predicament, the Portuguese held out at Massangano until 1648. Just as a combined offensive was about to crush them, Brazilian reinforcements under Salvador de Sa recaptured Luanda. The reconquest then began. Kasanje sided with the Portuguese, and by 1650, its marketplace, Cassange, had become the major emporium for trade with the interior, a position it was to maintain for two centuries. Nzinga and Kongo sued for peace; both finally obtained an honorable settlement that safeguarded their independence.

Meanwhile, Kongo entered another period of greatness. Dynastic strife had weakened the country until 1641, when Garcia II, helped by his Dutch alliance, managed to restore the royal authority. Soon afterward, he accepted the first Italian Capuchin missionaries, who began an intensive effort to convert the Kongo countryside. They, in turn, helped him to obtain favorable peace terms from Portugal after 1648, even though Garcia in his later years turned away from alien innovations to trusted values and customs.

But the Angolan Portuguese still believed that there were gold mines in Kongo and were determined to have them. They launched a successful invasion in 1665, but they were not strong enough to occupy the country. That invasion marked the beginning of civil wars that would last until 1710 and destroy the old political structure. Kongo then disappeared as an active force. The Portuguese had already moved on to liquidate the remnants of Ndongo and of Matamba, the state of Nzinga. Ndongo was easily subjugated, but Matamba held out, and a lasting peace ended the century-old war only in 1683. Angola was now bordered on the east by two powerful states, middlemen in the slave trade, Matamba and Kasanje. To the north, the political collapse of Kongo had led to anarchic slave raiding, which in turn gave way to trade organized by the Vili people of Loango, whose caravans reached as far south as Matamba. Portuguese Angola thus had lost most of the northern slave trade to the ports north of the Congo or Zaïre River, and to its Dutch, French, and English rivals.

In Kongo, anarchy formed the background for the decline of European and Christian influence unmixed with older traditions. One phenomenon was the growth of an important millenarian movement — a turn away from this-worldly solutions to the country's pressing problems toward a new hope for supernatural intervention. The movement began when a Kongolese girl claimed to be St. Anthony. She announced that she had come to teach the true religion: priests were impostors, God and his angels were black, and the kingdom of heaven was especially close to Kongo, for Christ had really lived and died in Kongo country. She believed that her mission was to restore the kingdom and anoint the true king.

The movement was not unique; there had been forerunners as much as a century earlier. But it was the first Zionist African Church; earlier movements had been more limited, seeking mainly to Africanize the clergy. Its very existence shows the depth of the ideological and emotional impact of European thought and religion. It dramatically illustrated the clash of cultures, as well as the collapse of the Kongo order founded on its unitary kingdom.

When the founder of the movement was executed, Antonianism slowly collapsed; nevertheless, Christianity did not regain the position it had held formerly. When kingship was restored it was mainly symbolic, and a new kind of society came into being in which Kongo was fragmented into many independent chiefdoms; and Christian elements came to be mere bits of religious belief embedded in the older Kongo religion.

KONGO CULTURE IN THE SIXTEENTH AND
SEVENTEENTH CENTURIES

The splendor of Kongo in these centuries was linked intimately with its court, which capped a social structure based on matrilineal corporate groups organized in villages. Each village was the residence of a few older male and female members of the lineage surrounded by their children, client lineages, and slaves. By 1650, as a result of the slave trade, slaves belonged to two strata: domestic servants and trade slaves for export. Each district was governed by a headman named by the king or provincial governor. These headmen were judges and administrators who called for taxes or labor when it was needed, transmitted orders from the capital, sent back reports, and led their men in war. They could be deposed at will by their superiors, but some districts were directly under the court, whereas others belonged to the six provinces, whose governors fulfilled the same duties on a larger scale and acted as advisers of the king. In two provinces, the governorships were hereditary, and one of these, Soyo, broke away from the state after 1636. In the other provinces, the governors were always close relatives of the king, and from 1614 to 1641, the governors of Mbamba and Nsundi in particular were responsible for most of the wars of succession.

At court, a galaxy of titled officers administered and judged. The *mani lumbu* was head of the royal residence, the *mani vangu* was supreme justice, and so on. After 1512, one of the most important of the titleholders was a Portuguese councilor, in later years usually the royal confessor, and after 1575, many Portuguese titles and trappings came to augment the local finery. After 1600, the canons of the episcopal see of São Salvador constituted yet another level of councilors.

Kingship was the summit of the whole system. Any male descendant of a former king was eligible, although after Affonso only his descendants had this right. Even so, the number kept increasing with each generation, so that by 1665 the *infantes,* or princes, had become so numerous that they formed a social class by themselves. Theoretically, the king was elected by a special body of nine to twelve nobles, including the *mani kabunga,* the former pagan religious authority who retained a right of veto. But in practice the electors did not act until the strongest contender was obvious to all. Each generation, the struggle for succession became more complicated and finally led to the civil war of 1665–66 and the general political collapse.

At the start, royal authority was based on divine right and a conception that royalty was sacred. Later on, a single papal bull and proper ointment by a cleric affirmed this sacred character. Possession of the bull was essential for recognition. But even if he was supreme in theory, the king was limited in practice by the opinions of his electors, governors, and major dignitaries, all of whom held some power. Royal power rested ultimately on the guard, which was formed during the seventeenth century, recruited among the Hum of the Pool area and Tio, and armed with muskets. The governors also had their guards, but only in Mbata on the Kwango border did they have firearms. For war or work, the general population could be called up. Because they fed themselves, campaigns were short and collapsed easily through hunger and desertion. Military tactics were more sophisticated than the supply system, at least by 1600. The army formations had wings and tried pincer movements. Attack could be organized in waves and some troops held as a strategic reserve.

State income derived from tribute in goods, fines in court, and tolls levied on roads or river crossings. The king controlled the currency, which consisted of *nzimbu,* a particular type of seashell (*olivancillaria nana*) that was found only near Luanda island. But the government followed no clear fiscal policy and inflation was constant and rampant. This was so in part because nzimbu were not acceptable for the European trade, which was based on slaves. Even though all government officials and missionaries were paid officially in nzimbu, slaves often had to be substituted. Tribute was collected once a year at a grand ceremony held in the capital on the feast day of St. James Major. At that time, the king would also confirm his officials in authority for one more year or else replace them.

Centralization was greater in Kongo than in neighboring kingdoms because all its officials could be deposed; but the good functioning of the state was too dependent on the personality of the king, and the ambiguous rules for succession constituted a fatal flaw. In neighboring Loango, provincial governors could not be removed. The governors were royal heirs, with the first heir apparent ruling the first provinces, the second heir the second province, and so on for all four provinces. Whenever a king died, every governor moved up a step. The succession was clearer than in Kongo, but centralization was less effective.

The Tio state was believed to be larger than either Kongo or Loango, but its component chiefdoms were practically autonomous. The king had neither army nor bodyguard, no central court of justice nor uniform administration. In fact, tribute was the only link that tied all the Tio chiefs to the king. The kingdom was never seriously attacked, mainly because its core area consisted of almost waterless plateaus. Other people could not live there easily because they lacked the techniques adapted to this very special environment.

Kongo religion and values came to be strongly influenced by Christianity, but only by certain Christian values that were in keeping with preexisting Kongo values. An ancestor cult existed and probably grew stronger with the collapse of the realm. Belief in sorcery and witchcraft was so strong that even some missionaries succumbed to it. The Kongolese used charms and practiced collective fertility rituals such as *kimpasi* or *kitomi,* in which the priest of the land gave powers to the governor. Later, in the eighteenth century, the cross itself would become the strongest of charms, while the statues, mainly of St. Anthony, became fertility charms. Yet the Catholic faith never completely died out in Soyo or around the capital, even though it became an adjunct to traditional ritual.

Foreign technology also had an influence. Between 1548 and 1583, maize came into use, and shortly after 1600 cassava spread slowly. Before 1695, the "canned preparation" known as *kwange* was invented. It consisted in compressing cooked cassava flour into loaves. These then remained edible for up to six months. With this preparation, fishing and long-distance trade on the Zaïre River became easier. Tobacco also came into use toward the end of the seventeenth century, and pottery came to be molded on a wheel rather than by hand. But in iron technology the Kongo had nothing to learn from the Portuguese; rather the reverse was true. Other metallurgical techniques were advanced enough for copper bracelets to be made with the lost wax process.

Kongo art of the seventeenth century is directly known through *mintadi* (funerary stone statues of chiefs), through metal objects, through decorative motifs on pots and cloth, and especially through crosses and statues in exquisite taste. The sculptural styles and techniques then existing remained almost unchanged until the end of the nineteenth century. The freedom of posture given to the human body is a remarkable feature of Kongo art. Music and dance were highly valued and no ceremony took place without a performance. Only descriptions of musical instruments, without transcriptions of the music played, have come down to us. These included a hand piano and an instrument not unlike a guitar, which indicates that melody played an important part in Kongo music. The music played on these Kongo guitars was adapted to the European guitar in Brazil, where it developed and absorbed further elements and was finally exported to Zaïre in the twentieth century.

THE COAST IN THE EIGHTEENTH CENTURY

The eighteenth century saw a massive extension of the slave trade, although very little political change was taking place on the coast. Angola lived by the trade, and its territorial organization — on many points a copy of the former Ndongo system — required tribute in people to feed that trade. But most of the slaves came from inland, imported through the middlemen markets in Kasanje, Matamba, and, after 1750, northern Ovimbundu (see the map on page 253). The high profits enjoyed by colonial settlers and government officials alike explain their refusal to develop any of the other natural resources of the territory. The trade also explains the chronic rebellion of Africans who did not participate but were plagued with epidemics, raids, and constant levies in people. Still, Angola's richest period was over; all the trade north of the Bengo River went to the British and the French by way of the Vili of Loango or the coastal Kongo. Angola tried several times to occupy part of this area, just as it fought other wars in the hope of breaking Matamba's middleman position, but no lasting success came from either endeavor. In 1783, its most ambitious move was the occupation of Kabinda, north of the Zaïre, but it met stubborn resistance and ended after a year, when a French fleet captured the place.

From 1764 onward, Angola tried periodically to diversify the economy, restructure the administration, and attract immigrants, but all failed. The one success was unintentional. As early as the 1680s, and with official disapproval, *sertanejos,* or "bushtraders," moved across Ovimbundu plateau and away from Portuguese control. By 1800, they had reached the upper Zambezi in Loziland and made Benguela, their coastal base, as important an exporter of slaves as Luanda was.

In the next century, the *sertanejos,* with the Ovimbundu, would finally break Kasanje's monopoly of the slave trade. But before 1800 the middlemen stood firm, especially Kasanje. The Matamba and the Ovimbundu states of Bihé and Mbailundu protected their position by their ability to go raiding farther into the interior and thus bring more slaves to the market. These raids strengthened their authority and furthered centralization, because the kings controlled the trade, the new wealth, and the new weapons. The weapons themselves came by way of the Vili state of Loango, because the Portuguese sold very few and were unwilling to buy ivory, which had great value to the north European traders but not to the Portuguese settlers, since it was a royal monopoly.

Both the Vili and coastal Kongo profited from the trade in slaves with the Yaka, Stanley Pool, and the Tio. But here the effects of wealth and guns were very different, because chiefs or kings could not maintain an effective monopoly over the trade. Self-made men began to oust the hereditary chiefs, simply because they could buy more followers and acquire more guns. Gradually the situation deteriorated into open political competition, with the political units becoming smaller and smaller as a sort of anarchy took over. By 1800, the process had weakened Loango, though the king there still wielded some real power. For Kakongo, Ngoi, Soyo, and the Kongo, however, the process of disintegration had already run its course.

The last of the middlemen states was the Tio kingdom of Makoko, north of the Pool. It was one of the rare places in Africa where ordinary persons, not criminals, were sold into slavery. This was the consequence of the Tio social structure and its notion of adoption; social groups were strong when they had a large membership, and membership could be extended by buying slaves to be adopted. A variety of reasons might later force people to sell. Wealth was required to achieve political success, and heavy fines were payable in the case of feuds or accusations of witchcraft, which were inevitably made whenever someone died. The Tio might then sell their own people to the traders.

But they also controlled the trade upriver toward the Kasai, and, in the eighteenth century, ivory and slaves came down from as far as Lake Mayi Ndome (formerly Lake Leopold II) and the lower Ubangi. The middleman position did not, however, reward the king as much as one might imagine. The kingdom had always been very decentralized, and the king could only control the market on the Pool — not the trade in the west from Loango to the plateau of the upper Alima, where commerce was in the hands of the independent Tio Laadi.

This growing independence of the western chiefs found political expression around 1800 and shortly thereafter when they introduced a new political institution, the *nkobi.* This consisted of a basket with charms that could be bought. Its owner then held political power, not because it was delegated from the king, but directly from his charm, just as the king himself held power because he was the keeper of the age-old charm associated with the great Spirit of the Tio country as a whole. At the same time, Tio material culture was impoverished because imported items began to replace local products such as canoes, nets, salt, cloth, guns, and fine pottery. On the other hand, tobacco was grown after 1700 and became a major export. This counterbalanced to some extent the seventeenth-century loss of the copper and lead mines at Mindouli, which had fallen into Kongolese hands.

By 1800, the lands south of the forest presented a surprisingly unified picture for such a vast area. Much of Zambia and the lands between Lake Tanganyika and the Kwango participated in a single great cultural tradition — that of the Luba and the Lunda. Along the coast from Loango to Benguela and inland to the Kwango, the Kongo cultural tradition, mixed with Portuguese features especially in Angola, held sway. Between the Kwango and Kasai rivers, people mixed some features from both traditions, while the Ovimbundu of central Angola developed a different tradition of their own.

To the north, however, along the forest from the Bateke plateaus to the Sankuru River, a fringe area escaped absorption by these great cultural traditions. Here, each group had a stronger individuality, although they were influenced by forest cultures. The Ila-Tonga along the middle Zambezi, in the far south, represented another fringe, while the Lozi had retained considerable originality despite Lunda influence. Further east in Malawi and beyond the Zambezi, the dominant cultural patterns were southeast African, linked to and in part derived from the former empire of Mwene Mutapa.

PEOPLES OF THE FOREST

No Iron Age archaeological site has yet been found in the forest. Stone Age remains, however, suggest that this environment has been inhabited by humans for a very long time, though written evidence goes back only to the fifteenth or sixteenth century and is so sparse that little can be said in detail for any period before 1900. Historical reconstructions are therefore uncertain and rest principally on ethnographic accounts written at the end of the nineteenth century or at the beginning of this one.

Geographically, the forest environment is highly uniform from the East African lakes to the Atlantic, but it falls into three subdivisions: mountains and hills between the lakes and the Lualaba River; a central depression between the Lualaba and the Ubangi and middle Zaïre rivers; and higher land again west to the Atlantic.

Culturally, the forest people share a remarkably uniform way of life. Pygmies are found over the whole area mainly as hunters alongside non-Pygmy farmers and fishermen. All speak Bantu languages, with the exception of one Central Sudanic–speaking area in the Ituri forest. The agricultural economy rests principally on bananas as the staple crop, which probably replaced dependence on yams. Kinship ties are unusually strong and uniformly patrilineal. Residence is normally in hamlets grouping a single lineage, with several hamlets making up a village. In religion, most peoples are alike in believing in nature spirits, ancestor worship, the efficacy of medicines, witchcraft, and sorcery. Some quite specific beliefs and practices can be traced from the Atlantic to the Ituri forest, indicating that the broad cultural homogeneity was not a result simply of similar environment but of long-standing east-west contacts across the forest zone. The long east-west reaches of the Zaïre River no doubt contributed to this result, but more remains to be explained.

In the eastern forest, the best-known people are the Lega, who spread eastward from the Lualaba River to the shores of Lake Kivu at least several centuries ago. In the process they absorbed preexisting Pygmy populations and themselves differentiated over time into a number of variant cultures. The most striking feature of the central Lega culture is the *bwame* association that provided government, ethical guidance, religion, and sanctions for prestige differences. It was also responsible for the ivory and wood carvings that are considered one of the highlights of African art. In Lega society, a man aspired to be granted a rank in the bwame association and then to climb up the ladder of rank to the very top. To do this required the support of his whole lineage, and any lineage with several high-ranking bwame members acquired reflected prestige. Women could also attain rank, but political and judicial authority belonged to male members in the higher ranks. The main function of the bwame association, however, was to preserve and act out rituals concerning the esoteric lore of the group in such diverse realms as morals, medicine, and religion.

To the northeast, in the Ituri forest, complicated wandering fusions and dispersals of population give the impression that seminomadic instability has been the rule for many centuries, with Bantu-speakers sometimes dominant over Central Sudanic–speakers, and sometimes the reverse. Most people were non-Pygmy who lived symbiotically with the Pygmies but did not mix with them. Each non-Pygmy village claimed "its pygmies" in the depths of the forest. From time to time, the little men came to exchange meat for bananas and iron arrow-tips. To them, this was not a link to a *master* village; in fact, they thought of non-Pygmies as rather bulky and slow-witted folk who had to be humored when one needed their products. Otherwise they were to be avoided. In fact, the bands of Pygmy hunters were protected by their own mobility, which could take them to another part of the forest and put them in contact with another village.

On the northern fringes of the forest, west of the Ituri, lived the Bwa and related peoples. Their normal political structure was a segmentary system of clans subdivided into lineages and sublineages. The structure was so elaborated that senior lineage members ruled over hundreds if not thousands of people. But at least one centralized chiefdom, the Mangbele of Aruwimi River, also arose among the Bwa to flourish in the eighteenth century, moving eastward to rule over Central Sudanic–speakers as well. This state was to be a model for the more celebrated Mangbetu state that was created after 1800.

The central forest belt was the home of a large cluster of ethnically related peoples known collectively as the Mongo, who seem to have occupied this section for more than a thousand years. In spite of our general lack of information, a historical pattern of some importance is faintly visible here and should become clearer with more research. In this instance, shortly after 1000 A.D., one group of Mongo from the lower Lomami River valley migrated westward and became ruling lineages over the existing, or "old," Mongo and their Pygmy neighbors. In time, this movement reached the neighborhood of Lake Mayi Ndombe, where they founded a chiefdom about 1450. Other chiefdoms followed in this same region, and one movement across the forest fringes became the Kuba kingdom with a civilization very different from the others.

Some elements of Mongo history suggest a tentative outline of the ways in which the forest cultures changed over time. Unilineal descent was and is weak among the Mongo, though political succession may once have been matrilineal well before 1500 A.D. But wives also went to live in their husbands' village, which meant that the village could not be ruled by the head of the matrilineage. Another principle of authority was therefore called for, and that principle of authority supported a king or chiefs who were hereditary Lords of the Land rather than heads of the lineage. This may explain why many other peoples between Mongo country and the Atlantic also had Lords of the Land and why the Tio title for king is Mongo in origin. But sometime before the sixteenth century, the Mongo began to change to the patrilineal mode of reckoning descent, which opened the possibility of a very broad and complex shift from political organization centered on Lords of the Land to political organization centered on the patrilineage. In recent times, many and diverse mixtures of the two systems are still to be found, showing that one gave way incompletely to the other.

In this case, complex cultural features spread without any significant migration of peoples. Similar change could come about when peculiarly mobile specialists moved back and forth over considerable distances. The Elinga, or fishermen of Mongoland, maintained a communications grid along the many tributaries of the Zaïre River, and this may explain why the language remained so uniform over such a vast area. The Bobangi, an ethnic group of specialized fishermen and river traders, dominated the Zaïre upstream from the Stanley Pool. In the 1780s, they were only beginning to establish their trade network, but it spread over a wide part of the Zaïre basin in the coming century, under a form of government that was really a plutocracy in which power lay with the big traders.

West of the Zaïre in what was to be the Middle Congo, some peoples related to the Mongo were to be found, of which the most important were the Mboshi. But further west, in the Cameroon and Gabon forests, history is little explored. One reason for our ignorance is the movement of the Fang peoples from the northern fringes of the forest, near the source of the Sanaga and Sanga rivers, downstream toward the coast. This movement began as early as the sixteenth century but with increasing pressure from the late eighteenth; the Fang simply absorbed previous populations as they moved slowly south and west.

The coastal populations of the forest zone are better known because of European records. Except for the Duala of Cameroon, who came from only a short distance inland about 1770, these peoples have lived where they now live ever since European ships first began sailing these coasts. Here, the political pattern was one of small kingdoms, and the principal occupation was to act as middlemen between the interior and the Atlantic trade. This commercial connection probably began with trade in sea salt to the interior, long before European ships arrived. It also included an early seaborne coastal trade that seems to have linked the region of Loango just north of the Zaïre mouth to West Africa at least as far as the Bight of Benin. This coastal navigation seems to account for the spread of cultural features such as the polychrome sculpture shared by the Yoruba and Loango, or the single artistic tradition in masks and statuary that involved the whole of western Gabon. With the opening of European contact, these same peoples began selling local products like pepper, ivory, camwood, even firewood and beeswax, as well as slaves in increasing numbers from the late eighteenth century onward. But they were not big contributors to the slave trade at its height.

THE KUBA AND LELE
OF THE SOUTHERN FOREST FRINGE

The peoples on the fringe between the forest and savanna were not a clear unit in the way the forest peoples tended to be. From west to east, they included such peoples as the Tio, the Boma, the Sakata, the Yans-Ding group of cultures, the Lele, the Kuba, and the Songye. Some aspects of this whole zone indicate links with Tio culture at a very distant time. Others show varying degrees of contact with the forest, especially with the Mongo, if they were not actual migrants to the forest fringes. The Kuba, for example, are one group that moved by slow stages to the south of the Sankuru River, settling among a population of Pygmy hunters and farmers who spoke a form of Luba. Several of the immigrant chiefdoms united and subjugated the local people, who were then absorbed (along with some of their way of life) into the new Kuba synthesis.

This Kuba kingdom was neither very big nor very important until the period 1625–1640, when a certain Shyaam aMbul aNgoong became king. He may originally have been a trader on the routes that reached downstream toward Kongo. In any event, he became the true founder of Kuba civilization by mixing or encouraging cultural features from the western region, some from as far away as Kongo. This cultural revolution continued under his successors to about 1680. The result was unique in the region: a sacralized strong kingship, founded on complex ritual symbolism, with the most complex administration in Central Africa; a court system with institutions resembling a jury; and special representation to the court from all interested parties. Southern influences were also borrowed, including boys' initiation ceremonies with strong Lunda influences. The unique quality was the way these diverse elements were fitted into a new synthesis, which incidentally gave the arts, of which sculpture is the best known, a crucial role in ceremonial and daily life.

The Kuba state reached its peak about the middle of the eighteenth century and remained strong for some time. Its power rested first of all on the absolute military superiority of the ruling segment of the population, the *Bushong*. After 1700, agriculture developed to the point that output per family doubled. This surplus made trade with all its neighbors possible, and contact with the Atlantic coast had already begun through intermediaries in the seventeenth century.

The neighboring Lele had almost the same Mongo origins as the proto-Kuba, but they evolved in quite a different direction — illustrating in one well-known case how important the process of historical change must have been in other parts of Africa where our ignorance makes us imagine a static "traditional" society. Where the Kuba had developed a centralized administration, the Lele moved toward greater and greater decentralization. In the system ancestral to both, the principle of authority had been age, but the Kuba developed their new administration by creating removable officials who were called *kolm,* or elders, whatever their actual age. Lele, however, kept to authority based *only* on age, where the oldest of a set of age-grades ruled in a virtual gerontocracy, but only at the village level and through the bonds of matrilineages, so that each village was virtually an independent state. The economic consequence was a less organized agriculture, with less collaboration and division of labor, and an agricultural underproduction as spectacular as was the Kuba surplus for sale abroad.

THE NORTHERN GRASSLANDS

The historical study of the northern grasslands is still in its infancy, but the culture of this region showed many similarities as of 1800, in spite of intrusive movements of aliens within the past millennium or so. In more remote times, for example, the grasslands people spoke Central Sudanic languages, like Bongo, the Sara spoken in the Shari basin, or the Mangbetu and related languages spoken on the fringes of the Ituri forest. But then people speaking Adamawa-Eastern languages came in from the west — that is, people who were not Bantu-speakers, but whose languages belonged to the same broad Niger-Congo language family that includes the Bantu languages. The descendants of these intrusive peoples would be the present-day Gbaya, Ngbandi, Zande, and Banda, stretching east to the border between the republics of Zaïre and the Sudan.

The most spectacular historical movement was that of the Zande. Their ruling clans trace their descent from a migration that began somewhere in the north, in Darfur or Kordofan, in perhaps the fifteenth century. Once in the region of the Ubangi and Uele rivers, they began a slow expansion to the east that ended in the creation of a dozen different kingdoms. But these were not mass migrations, pushing the local people ahead of them. They were, rather, the imposition of Zande clans as rulers over the local people, who still retained their culture and transmitted much of it to their new rulers. In the process, the Zande and their subjects evolved complex institutions that permitted the rapid mutual assimilation of "foreigners" to the body politic.

By 1800, the cultural similarities across these northern grasslands outweighed the more obvious division between stateless peoples like the Gbaya and others like the Zande states. Most people lived in dispersed settlements, cultivating sorghum in the north and bananas in the south. Villages were small, usually no more than an extended family; political organization was loose even in regions with states, so that society was often disturbed by feuds and quarrels, mitigated by the distance between settlements. Religion was mainly an ancestor cult centering on certain sacred objects kept in shrines and guarded by lineage elders; these objects were the ultimate sanction for correct relations between individuals and groups. Even though the ultimate origins and historical changes in these cultures are not known, they are very similar to the kinds of society found in central Cameroon. This similarity again shows that intercommunication must have existed over the past millennia, even in such sparsely settled and comparatively isolated regions of Africa as this one, because the people obviously have borrowed from others.

CULTURE CHANGE AND HISTORY

It is evident that throughout Equatorial Africa and, indeed, throughout all of Africa, profound change was taking place among human societies, even though we are ignorant of most of it. Some of the impetus to culture change was external, but much of it was internal, as one part of a people's way of life adjusted to changes in another sphere. The Kuba, for example, once believed that there were nature spirits in the sun, but the belief gradually died out. At present, our best hypothesis for explaining this change is that these spirits were attached to the cultural identity of ethnic subgroups within the kingdoms. Once the kingdom became strong, these local spirits were invoked less and less often. Finally they were no longer included in public worship. The change was gradual and probably unconscious. In time, adults no longer thought it worthwhile even to pass on the names of the nature spirits to their children.

But internal innovation could also be conscious. A man or woman might have a new idea or suggest a new custom. If the idea or custom caught on, it became a part of the culture. Some innovators were no doubt persons of high rank, but others might have been quite humble. Many innovations were not so much new inventions as the discovery of ways to make use of new patterns without completely revolutionizing the way of life that people already followed. The spread of cassava among the Tio is one example. Before cassava was adopted, maize had been the main crop. Maize was planted in the forest by the men, while women grew yams. Because cassava seemed more like yams than like maize, women began to grow cassava as well. But as the share of cassava increased, and maize fell, women found themselves doing more work. It altered the division of labor between the sexes and the fundamental relationships within every household. At the same time, cassava came to be essential to commerce because it was a food that was easily preserved for long trips and freed men from agriculture for commercial pursuits. The change to cassava thus set in motion economic changes that were absolutely crucial in forming a new way of life.

The acceptance of a new plant might encourage other kinds of innovation as well. Cassava contains a violent poison that must be removed before the plant can be eaten. When the plant came from Brazil to the Kongo, the technique for removing the poison did not come with it. Instead, the Kongolese turned to another technique they already knew for removing poison from certain local wild yams and adapted that to cassava. Partly as a result, they obtained a kind of cassava flour that could be used for familiar dishes in substitution for cereal flour or banana flour. In this case, invention was required to preserve the traditional cuisine.

External stimulus could also cause change, and the easiest way for human culture to move from one place to another is for the people to move — in short, migration. But the movement of cultures in this way could be greatly varied, depending on the mixture of populations at the end of the road. Immigrants might assimilate little or much of the culture of their new home. A lot of immigration occurred on the fringes of particular cultures, as when women married across ethnic borders or from one village to another. Most Central Africans seem to have accepted this kind of interethnic marriage, and the movement of wives between villages had a continuous tendency to prevent cultural divergence, even when villages were at some distance from one another. In this context, it is important to remember that women were the normal agriculturalists who could take new techniques or new crops with them. Because women also practiced medicine and served as priestesses in many of these societies, their knowledge touched really significant aspects of life.

Of course, diffusion could also take place by stimulus alone, as when a people saw their neighbors with something they wanted or observed a better way of doing things. Antiwitch cults apparently spread in this way. Other features, in art for example, could spread across ethnic lines without first having been adopted by all the people of the ethnic group in which they were invented. Thus, a style of mask invented in a particular Pende village spread to the villages of two nearby ethnic groups without spreading to all the Pende. Certain institutions could also spread very widely. The *elombe,* for example, was an official medicine man who made war magic. Variants of the name and office occur in the northern savanna, right through the forest, and in the southern savanna among people whose cultures are otherwise quite distinct. They all apparently wanted more effective war magic and so borrowed their neighbors' way of getting it.

Trade was especially important in the dissemination of ideas, customs, or artifacts. Long-distance trade, of which the slave trade was the most important branch, was responsible for the introduction of guns from the Atlantic as far east as Kazembe. It also furthered the spread of maize, cassava, and other American crops. Maize was first assimilated in Kongo in the sixteenth century. After 1600 it began to move beyond Kongo, and by 1800 it was in use throughout virtually all of the Zaïre basin. Cassava started later but by 1700 its processed form was commonly used by fishermen and traders along the rivers of the entire basin, and its cultivation spread rapidly among forest peoples.

Trade could also carry alien diseases, of which smallpox is a striking example. If it was known to Equatorial Africa before the arrival of European ships, it was not endemic enough to provide a widespread immunity. The disease thus struck in epidemic form with special virulence in the sixteenth century. By 1620, the Tio country and the whole of Portuguese Angola were affected, and similar attacks, with corresponding population decline, must also have occurred among the peoples of the interior.

Trade also affected culture by altering political structure. Where the slave trade was intense, middleman states were strengthened while the states that furnished many slaves were weakened — if, indeed, their weakness was not the reason they furnished slaves in the first place. The slave trade in some coastal areas also brought the decline of hereditary authority and the rise of new classes of wealthy traders who ended by making themselves rulers.

Finally, political structures themselves could influence the way of life of their subject peoples. In broad terms, larger political units tended to produce a more homogeneous culture among their subjects, however diverse their original cultures may have been. This happened among the Zande, the Lozi, the Kuba, and especially in Portuguese Angola. It also happened through conquest with the spread of Lunda and Luba culture influence over a wide area. More elaborate political structures also called for change in the courts, titles, and bureaucratic devices — followed by art and spoken literature to celebrate the new class of kings or nobles.

Of all these factors, trade and political elaboration were clearly crucial. In the southern savanna, political change seems to have been the primary agent of cultural change; in the forest, trade appears to have been more important. Further north, in the northern savannas before the Zande conquests, more humble border interchanges together with the travels of a few slaves or medicine men were probably more important than either political change or the kind of long-distance trade that existed in the forest or southern savannas.

States and trade networks, in short, acted as infrastructures that opened local societies to the flow of foreign influences while they created the need for new institutions to meet the new challenges. Historians for a long time have recognized that these were a very important part of the cultural history of Africa in the nineteenth and twentieth centuries, when the external influences were mainly European. They are now beginning to learn that similar conditions on a different scale were already at work, changing the cultural outlines of the African continent long before any Europeans appeared along its shores.

SUGGESTIONS FOR FURTHER READING

Patterson, K. D. *The Northern Gabon Coast to 1875.* Oxford: Oxford University Press, 1975.

Roberts, Andrew. *A History of the Bemba: Political Growth and Change in Northeastern Zambia Before 1900.* London: Longman, 1973.

———. *A History of Zambia.* London: Heinemann, 1977.

Vansina, Jan. *The Tio Kingdom of the Middle Congo: 1880–1892.* London: Oxford University Press, 1973.

Chapter 9
Southern Africa
to 1795

THE SOUTHERNMOST PART of Africa — the region bordered on the northwest by the tropical grasslands and on the northeast by the Zambezi River — has had a different historical experience from that of the tropical middle belt across the continent to the north. The western half of the region is similar to the northernmost parts of Africa; the climate of the area around Cape Town is classified as "Mediterranean" and is not unlike the climate in northern Morocco. Further north, it becomes more arid, just as the climate of North Africa becomes more arid as one moves into the Sahara. Along the Atlantic coast, there are true desert conditions, with less than five inches of rain a year. As one travels eastward the rainfall gradually increases; but it is less than twenty inches a year, and the natural vegetation is merely sparse scrub, until one is beyond the modern towns of Mafeking, Bloemfontein, and Queenstown. There, on the high plateau, are temperate grasslands in the Orange Free State and the Transvaal. The Limpopo valley is arid, but there are more temperate grasslands in the highlands of Zimbabwe. Between the eastern escarpment and the Indian Ocean, most of the coastal lowlands have good summer rains. Almost everywhere throughout the region, however, there are great climatic variations from year to year, with periods of severe drought, so that people can never be sure whether there will be enough rain for a good harvest. No wonder the traditional Sotho greeting is "Pula!" (Let there be rain!)

Southern Africa's location at the southern extremity of the Afro-Eurasian land mass made for a history different from that of North Africa as well. Whereas the Nile valley, partly because of its proximity to the fertile crescent of western Asia, became the scene of a major ancient civilization and the Mediterranean shores were vitally affected by the civilizations of the Muslim Middle East and western Europe, southern Africa was far removed from contact with the outside world before the maritime revolution of the fifteenth century. It was at the end of the line for the exchange of information and culture with other people, in much the same way that Patagonia in South America and Tasmania in Australasia were at the end of the line at the southern extremities of their continents.

Nevertheless, southern Africa was not as isolated as those other extremities. It received Bantu-speaking immigrants with knowledge of ironworking and mixed farming, while the inhabitants of the southern ends of America and Australasia still depended on hunting and food gathering and on implements of stone and wood. Its Bantu-speaking peoples also became familiar with many of the diseases from the heartland of Afro-Eurasia. As a result, when closer seaborne contact with the outer world was established in the fifteenth century and later, the Bantu-speaking peoples of southern Africa had some immunities to help protect them from the European diseases that decimated the people of Patagonia and exterminated those of Tasmania.

Moreover, the environments of southern Africa and North Africa were similar in the sense that Europeans could survive in both these regions more easily than they could in the tropic lands between. Consequently, the southern and northern extremities became the two regions of Africa to receive the densest immigrations by European settlers. They acquired the largest colonies of overseas Europeans, both in absolute numbers and in proportion to the number of people sharing cultures that had been domiciled on the African continent for millennia. That development, however, came to its full flowering only in the nineteenth and twentieth centuries.

THE CULTURAL MAP
OF SOUTHERN AFRICA TAKES SHAPE

As we have seen in Chapter 1, southern Africa was sparsely populated and all its inhabitants were still hunters and collectors of wild foods until about 2,000 years ago. Then, during the first millennium A.D., new farming practices spread from the north and the population increased. The effects were most pronounced in the eastern half of the region — in the temperate grasslands of Zimbabwe, Transvaal, and the Orange Free State and in the coastal lowlands east of present-day Port Elizabeth. In much of that sector ironworking was possible, and so was mixed farming — crop production as well as sheep- and cattle-raising. Even so, in the valleys of the Zambezi and the Limpopo and their tributaries, and in Mozambique north of Inhambane, the human population was kept down by the anopheles mosquito, and the cattle population by the tsetse fly.

Crop production did not spread into the western half of the region for lack of water, and, with few exceptions, ironworking did not spread there for lack of timber to make charcoal. Both crop production and ironworking had reached their limits by about 1500 A.D., except that they had not crossed the arid coastal sector around Port Elizabeth into the Mediterranean climatic zone in the south-west corner of the continent.

Cattle and sheep had spread further west than had crop production and

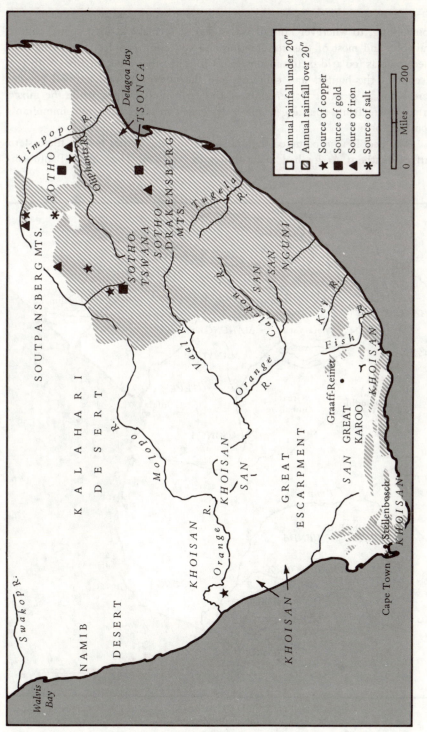

South of the Limpopo

Key (legend):
- □ Annual rainfall under 20"
- ▨ Annual rainfall over 20"
- ★ Source of copper
- ■ Source of gold
- ▲ Source of iron
- ✳ Source of salt

0 — 200 Miles

Map labels:
Walvis Bay, Swakop R., NAMIB DESERT, KALAHARI DESERT, SOUTPANSBERG MTS., Limpopo R., SOTHO, Olifants R., Delagoa Bay, TSONGA, SOTHO, SOTHO-TSWANA, DRAKENSBERG MTS., Tugela R., NGUNI, SAN, Caledon R., Vaal R., Molopo R., Orange R., Orange R., KHOISAN, SAN, GREAT ESCARPMENT, Keī R., Fish R., Graaff-Reinet, SAN, GREAT KAROO, KHOISAN, Stellenbosch, Cape Town, KHOISAN, KHOISAN

ironworking, to wherever rainfall was sufficient to make at least sparse pasture available; and most of the true hunting and collecting peoples were being confined to areas too arid or too mountainous for any other mode of life. With few exceptions, the hunters and collectors and the nonagricultural pastoral peoples were Khoisan-speaking descendants of the earlier inhabitants, while the mixed farmers were Bantu-speaking peoples, descended in large part from immigrants from the north.

The people who occupied the grasslands and the coastal belt of the eastern part of southern Africa had many things in common. They spoke Bantu lan-

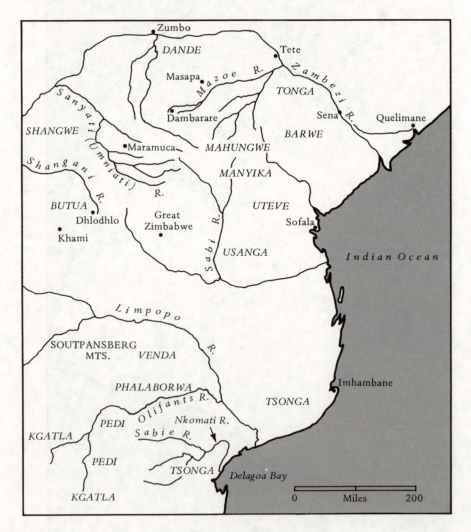

South of the Zambezi

guages. They grew sorghum, owned cattle and sheep, and used iron-headed spears. They were polygynous and traced descent in the male line. And, with one important exception, they were organized in small, autonomous chiefdoms.

There were also significant differences among them. We can distinguish three major cultural groupings (as well as several smaller ones). For convenience, we shall give them the modern names Shona, Sotho, and Nguni, although these names were not in fact used in this sense until the nineteenth century. The crucial distinction among the Shona, Sotho, and Nguni peoples was linguistic. The Shona people could all understand each other's speech, although they spoke different dialects; likewise with the Sotho and Nguni peoples. But a person who spoke Shona could not communicate effectively with a person who spoke only Sotho or Nguni. Other differences tended to follow the linguistic divisions; and though the coincidence was not exact, it was close enough to enable us to talk here of the Shona, Sotho, and Nguni subcultures as being variants of a culture that was common to all the mixed farmers of southern Africa.

Shona occupied the greater part of the present territory of Zimbabwe and, in addition, the area between the Sabie and Pungwe rivers down to the Indian Ocean in modern Mozambique. Sotho occupied most of the present Transvaal, Orange Free State, and Swaziland, and also the eastern part of Botswana and the Lesotho lowlands. Nguni occupied the area between the Drakensberg mountains and the Indian Ocean, from the vicinity of Delagoa Bay southward to near the Fish River.

When we compare the cultures of these three major communities, we find provocative similarities and differences. The Shona and the Sotho had several traits in common that were not shared by the Nguni. For example, the Shona and the Sotho lived in large villages with populations reaching several thousand in some cases, whereas the Nguni lived in scattered homesteads, each containing a single patrilineal family of two or three generations. Also, Shona and Sotho descent groups (clans) bore names, often of animals that were taboo to members of the clan. Thus, members of the Kwena clan among the Sotho were not permitted to harm crocodiles, and if they did so had to perform elaborate purification rituals. The Nguni had no such totems. Again, the Shona and the Sotho were generally better craftsworkers than the Nguni. They made more and finer metalware; they were superior workers in wood and ivory; and they took more pains in making karosses (rugs) from the hides of cattle and wild animals. The Shona and the Sotho also conducted a larger volume of trade from village to village and from chiefdom to chiefdom than did the Nguni. Some of them even had moderately systematic trade relations with the Arab settlements on the east coast, whereas Nguni external trade was at most sporadic.

In several other respects, however, Sotho customs were closer to those of the Nguni than to those of the Shona. Neither Sotho nor Nguni ate fish, while the Shona had no such taboo. Both Sotho and Nguni had ceremonies for the initiation of young men into adult status, and the men who had been initiated together formed a cohesive group for the rest of their lives, while the Shona had no system of age-grades. Among both Sotho and Nguni, a chief was succeeded by his senior son (though the rules for determining seniority differed); among the Shona, by contrast, the succession often went from brother to brother before it passed to the next generation. Sotho and Nguni chiefs played the central roles in the rituals of their people, who believed that the ancestors of the chiefs were able to influence the welfare of the living community. Among the Shona, on the other hand, many religious centers were separate from the political centers, and the chiefs did not necessarily dominate the priests.

Some customs were even shared by the Shona and the Nguni but not practiced by the Sotho. For example, no Shona or Nguni was permitted to choose a wife from his own descent group, whereas Sotho were allowed to marry within their own clan and even gave preference to marriages between cousins.

We do not know much about the ways in which these three subcultures developed. The fact that the three languages are distinct shows that the main bodies of the three peoples must have lived for a considerable period as separate communities in relative isolation from one another. And the fact that each of the three languages has maintained its essential unity shows that within each community the members must have kept in fairly close contact with one another. The oral traditions of these peoples confirm these deductions. The genealogies of Sotho and Nguni chiefs go back many generations (for example, nineteen generations from the middle of the nineteenth century in the case of the Thembu, a Nguni chiefdom); and yet scarcely any Sotho and Nguni traditions associate the founder chiefs with long-distance migrations. Consequently, these peoples must have occupied parts of their present terrain for many centuries.

One has to be cautious about drawing historical inferences from cultural phenomena. It seems probable, however, that the Shona subculture in its various forms developed between the Zambezi and the Limpopo rivers as a result of interactions among the Late Stone Age cultures of the region and Bantu-speaking immigrants from the north and northwest. It is also probable that Sotho culture and Shona culture were both derived mainly from a common source north of the Zambezi; but Sotho culture developed distinctive characteristics in the South African high veld environment when it came in contact with local Stone Age cultures and Nguni culture.

It is more difficult to account for the emergence of the culture of the Nguni people. The Nguni language, though Bantu, does not seem to be strongly related to any particular Bantu language spoken north of the Limpopo before the nineteenth century, when Nguni-speaking warriors fled northward from Zululand to escape from Shaka (Chapter 10). This reinforces the evidence for a long Nguni occupation of the territory below the Drakensberg mountains. Monica Wilson, a social anthropologist, has also pointed out that the strength of the cattle complex among the Nguni may reflect a strong association between the Nguni and the cattle-keeping peoples of the East African highlands.

In most periods, the political systems of the Shona, the Sotho, and the Nguni were very much alike. The basic political unit was the independent chief-

dom, headed by a hereditary chief who exercised executive and judicial authority in consultation with some of his relatives, with commoner councilors, and
with territorial subchiefs. His authority was limited because if he tried to act
arbitrarily his disaffected followers could transfer their allegiance to another
chief.

For many centuries, the Bantu-speaking farmers who settled in areas previously occupied only by indigenous Khoisan people were so thinly spread out
that each village or cluster of homesteads or villages formed an autonomous
political community. As the density of population increased, however, a particular lineage tended to gain control over a territory and to incorporate the previous inhabitants. By the end of the eighteenth century, the Xhosa chiefdom had
incorporated most of the Bantu-speaking settlers as well as the Khoikhoi inhabitants of the coastal territory between the Buffalo and Fish rivers; and chiefs
of the Kwena, Khatla, and Taung lineages had incorporated most of the Bantu-
speaking settlers and many of the Khoisan inhabitants of the high veld between
the Vaal and the Caledon rivers.

These ruling lineages did not create centralized states, however. When a
chief died, an ambitious brother or son, who had already established a territorial
base with the support of his initiation age-mates, often disregarded the authority
of the heir. Contrary to previous opinion, it now appears likely that the senior
Xhosa chief continued to claim to be — and was to some extent recognized as —
the paramount chief over all the Xhosa territory, though he lacked the means to
enforce his will over the outlying parts. Among the southern Sotho, on the
other hand, each dominant lineage split up into several wholly independent
chiefdoms; people knew which chief was genealogically the most senior of his
lineage, but the chiefs who were related to him did not allow their followers to
appeal to his court against their decisions, nor did they perform any of the services due a superior.

By the end of the eighteenth century, the expansive movements of both the
Sotho and the Nguni peoples were being arrested. The Sotho had reached the Maloti mountains (outliers of the Drakensberg escarpment) in the south and the
Kalahari desert in the west; the Nguni had encountered gun-carrying *trekboere,*
nomadic stock farmers of European descent. Chiefdoms were competing for land
more intensively than hitherto, and in some cases they were amalgamating. This
process culminated among the northern Nguni in the early nineteenth century.
First, Dingiswayo, the Mthethwa chief, tried to organize a confederation of the
chiefdoms in his area; then, between 1816 and 1828, Shaka created a military,
centralized Zulu kingdom out of all the northern Nguni chiefdoms. Similar
amalgamations then took place among the northern Sotho (the Pedi) and the
southern Sotho. Among the Shona, on the other hand, population led to an
amalgamation of chiefdoms at a much earlier time, because the Shona had no
thinly peopled farming country to expand into outside the Zimbabwe highlands.

Of the other Bantu-speaking communities in southern Africa, two are particularly interesting as examples of adaptation to the limitations imposed by

the natural environment. The Tsonga occupied the northeastern coastal belt between the Sabie River and St. Lucia Bay. Though some of their lineages claim to have had genealogical relationships with Nguni, Sotho, or Shona lineages, all the Tsonga spoke a single and distinct language. Unlike the Nguni, Sotho, and Shona, they were watermen and fishermen. They traveled, traded, and fished on the Limpopo and the other rivers in their area. Tsetse made it impossible for them to breed cattle in most parts of their territory, but they had fowls and goats and they grew sorghum.

While the Tsonga were Bantu-speaking food producers who adapted to an environment where cattle could not thrive, the Herero — the only Bantu-speaking people who lived south of the tropical grasslands on the arid western side of the subcontinent — adapted to an environment where crop cultivation was not possible. Their antecedents are obscure. Some of their lineages had traditions pointing to an early association with western Sotho peoples in the Okavango area, at the southern end of the tropical grasslands, before it was settled by its present inhabitants, the Ovambo. These traditions tell of a migration westward to the Kaokoveld under pressure from the Tswana (western Sotho) in about the sixteenth century, and of a final move southward to the vicinity of the Swakop River in about the eighteenth century. When European visitors encountered them in the nineteenth century, the Herero were herders with no knowledge of ironworking and no tradition of crop cultivation.

THE GOLD TRADE AND
STATE FORMATION IN ZIMBABWE

In September 1871, Carl Mauch, a German explorer-prospector based in the Transvaal, came upon the awe-inspiring ruins of Great Zimbabwe, seventeen miles southeast of the modern Rhodesian town of Fort Victoria. Great Zimbabwe is the most impressive monument in the African interior south of the Nile valley and the Ethiopian highlands. Covering more than sixty acres of ground, it consists of two complexes of dry-stone buildings, which Europeans have misleadingly called the Acropolis and the Temple. The former is a series of enclosures atop a hill; the latter includes a large number of buildings half a mile away in a valley, many of them encompassed by a massive circular wall (32 feet high and 17 feet thick at its maximum), which incorporates 900,000 large granite blocks. During the 1890s, after Mashonaland had been occupied by settlers under the auspices of Cecil Rhodes's British South Africa Company, prospectors systematically despoiled the ruins of everything that could conceivably yield a profit, including several thousand dollars worth of worked gold. Looting continued into the twentieth century until the Rhodesian government put a stop to it.

In the early published accounts of Great Zimbabwe, Europeans often insisted that it must have had an exotic, non-African origin. Europeans said the same thing about the bronzes of Ife and Benin and about other impressive human achievements in Africa. To this day, some local Europeans cannot bring themselves to credit Africans, let alone the ancestors of the modern Shona inhabitants of the area, with the capacity to construct such elaborate buildings. They assume that some forgotten "whites," inspired by Jewish or Arabian models, must have built them. In fact, it has been demonstrated by a series of professional archaeologists who have worked at the site, notably David Randall MacIver in the 1900s and Gertrude Caton-Thompson in the 1920s, that Great Zimbabwe was the headquarters of an indigenous African state that flourished for several hundred years. Now, thanks to more recent work by members of the Rhodesian Historical Monuments Commission, supported by carbon-14 dates, which correlate with documents written by Portuguese who visited the Zambezi valley (but not Great Zimbabwe itself) in the sixteenth and seventeenth centuries, and by oral tradition freshly obtained from the Shona peoples, some of the history that lies behind the physical monument at Great Zimbabwe has been unraveled, though many aspects of it are still uncertain.

There was a persistent buildup of the population in the Zambezi-Limpopo region during the first millennium and a half A.D. This was the result of successive economic advances, as shown in the archaeological record: the introduction and spread of crop cultivation, cattle-keeping, and metallurgy, along with changes in the quality and design of pottery and in the materials and styles of buildings. At all stages, cultural variations within the area were related to differences in the local environments; but these were variations between peoples who were in contact with one another and who ultimately came to speak one of the mutually intelligible dialects of the Shona language. Archaeology has also revealed rather abrupt shifts in the material culture at specific sites, and occasional layers of ash indicate destructive episodes. We cannot interpret these shifts and breaks precisely. Informed opinion now lays greater stress than formerly on the dynamics of change within the established population of the area, and there is less insistence on the advent of new types of peoples as a necessary explanation for every fresh cultural trait.

Originally, a great deal of gold ore lay near the surface in a broad belt running from the Mazoe River in the northeast to beyond the Limpopo River in the southwest. There was also alluvial gold in the Zambezi tributaries. The inhabitants were washing alluvial gold by the tenth century A.D. and by 1000 A.D. they were also recovering and working gold ore. They mined in open stopes sloping downwards, eventually reaching as far as a hundred feet below the surface. They split the rock cover by alternately heating and cooling it; they then cut out the ore with iron picks and took it to the nearest stream, where they crushed and panned it in running water. The Shona continued this method of goldmining until the nineteenth century. By then, the ores that could be worked by these methods were virtually exhausted, but small quantities of alluvial ore were still being recovered in the twentieth century.

Great Zimbabwe lies some distance south and east of the auriferous belt. Iron Age people occupied the hill for a period during the first millennium and, after an interval, it was reoccupied during the eleventh century. For the next four hundred years, it was the political and religious center of a considerable empire. The inhabitants enclosed the hilltop, which probably contained a sacred shrine, with dry-course stone walls, using the local granite which splits easily into regular sheets about six inches thick. Because their building methods included features not to be found anywhere north of the Zambezi, theirs was probably an independent invention, free from external aid or influence. From the thirteenth century onwards, they improved their building techniques and completed the Great Enclosure, which was probably the royal palace, in the valley below the hill. The Great Zimbabwe site has yielded local pottery of good quality and design; ornaments made of copper, bronze, and gold; remarkable figures of birds carved from soapstone; and also ceramics of Asian origin, including a piece of glazed Persian faience that has been dated to the thirteenth century, and several Chinese celadon dishes of about the fourteenth century.

Great Zimbabwe was clearly the capital of a considerable empire. Its wealth must have been derived from its location on the long-distance trade route between the gold-producing reefs to the north and the west, and Sofala, a Muslim trading port subordinate to the city-state of Kilwa, on the Indian Ocean to the east.

During the fifteenth century, Great Zimbabwe somewhat abruptly went into decline. Most of the inhabitants left the area, perhaps because it had been overexploited and was no longer able to produce enough food for a large population. Some of the people migrated northward and settled in the valley of the Mazoe, a tributary of the Zambezi, where alluvial as well as reef gold was available. From that nucleus, they created an empire in the tradition of Great Zimbabwe. Its rulers bore the title Mwene Mutapa, which passed into European documents in the form Monomotapa. Like their predecessors at Great Zimbabwe, the Mwene Mutapa dynasty profited from the gold trade, which now became diverted from the route via Great Zimbabwe to Sofala to a route down the Zambezi valley to new ports on the Indian Ocean. The Mwene Mutapas controlled the alluvial gold supplies and the northern section of the gold-bearing reef; and they claimed dominion over the valley and escarpment south of the Zambezi from Zumbo eastwards to the sea, including the Muslim trading posts on the Zambezi.

The population of the empire of the Mwene Mutapas was sharply stratified. The majority of the people were peasants whose style of life was already very similar to that of the Shona of the nineteenth century; but at that time they were also responsible for mining the gold and fighting the military campaigns for the Mwene Mutapa and his aristocracy. The system seems to have worked fairly well under the founder king and his immediate successor, but they were not able to create lasting institutions that would hold the empire together after they had died. Instead, they adopted the practice of appointing their male relatives as provincial governors; and by the end of the fifteenth century, some of these men were acting as independent rulers. When the Portuguese made contact with the northern Shona, they found the Mwene Mutapa living in isolation from his subjects and served by young men of the aristocracy who, on reaching mature age, became invested with various titles that the Portuguese rendered into terms intelligible to themselves, such as captain-general and majordomo. But these Portuguese accounts described the Mwene Mutapa monarchy when it was past its prime. It was not necessarily like that in the fifteenth century. In the seventeenth century, several Mwene Mutapas acknowledged Portuguese overrule, but the Portuguese were never able to control them absolutely.

Meanwhile, further south, in the vicinity of modern Bulawayo, the Changamire dynasty gained power over a large territory and remained completely free from Portuguese penetration. The Changamire dynasty exerted a tighter control over gold production and the gold trade in their area than any other rulers in the Zambezi-Limpopo region managed to do. Their capitals at Dhlodhlo and Khami had impressive stone buildings and accumulated vast quantities of finely wrought gold ornaments. They systematically collected tribute from their subjects and they had the final say in the succession to their vassal chieftaincies. Their state flourished until it was overthrown by invaders from Zululand in the 1830s.

THE PORTUGUESE IN SOUTHEASTERN AFRICA

Vasco da Gama opened up the sea route from Europe to Asia via the Cape of Good Hope and the East African coast in 1498–99. During the next decade, the Portuguese harassed the Arab traders in their East African bases and at sea and gained partial control over the commerce of the Indian Ocean. They established their overseas capital at Goa on the west coast of India, built fortresses at Sofala (1505) and on Mozambique Island (1507), and instructed their commanders to locate and exploit the gold of the interior. Reports by travelers to Shona country, such as Antonio Fernandez (1514), whom the Portuguese government sent to report on the origin of the gold exported from Sofala, showed that "Monomotapa" was no Eldorado. The country of the Shona was difficult to reach and its gold output was modest by Mexican standards. Nevertheless, throughout the sixteenth and seventeenth centuries, the major Portuguese objective in southeast Africa was to exploit the gold resources of the Shona.

The Portuguese impact on the Shona peoples is a classic example of what could be called "creeping imperialism." The initial Portuguese intentions were exclusively commercial. Trade routes to the gold-producing areas were to be opened up from the coastal establishments at Sofala and Mozambique. The Swahili traders were to be ousted, but the rights of the indigenous Africans were to be respected. By the end of the sixteenth century, these commercial objectives had been partially fulfilled. Using the Zambezi River as their principal route to the interior, the Portuguese founded, fortified, and garrisoned townships on the banks of the river at Sena, about 160 miles from the mouth, and at Tete, another 160 miles upstream. They also took over the old Swahili trading posts and founded new ones in the goldbearing area southwest of Tete — at Masapa,

Luanze, Dambarare, and Ongoe, and even at Maramuca nearly 300 miles from Tete. These steps enabled them to acquire the lion's share of the gold trade from the Shona country. But they were disappointed in the volume of gold they obtained and Swahili traders siphoned off some of it along trade routes to coastal settlements north of Mozambique, where they usually contrived to evade the Portuguese patrols and ship the gold to Arabia or India.

By the time the Portuguese arrived in East Africa, the empire of Mwene Mutapa had begun to disintegrate. His hold over the eastern Shona was becoming tenuous, as local and collateral lineages claimed their autonomy. Impressed by Portuguese firearms, the sixteenth-century Mwene Mutapas used the Portuguese as allies against their dynastic rivals and insubordinate regional chiefs; but the alliance was not stable. In 1561, overzealous Jesuits obtained a footing at the royal court and even contrived to baptize the Mwene Mutapa and many of his relatives and councilors. When reaction followed, Father Silveira with fifty of his Shona converts were killed. The Portuguese believed Swahili traders had poisoned the minds of influential persons at the Mwene Mutapa's court. That may have been a factor; more likely, conservative forces in Shona society, notably the Mwari priesthood, were outraged by the activities of the Jesuits and needed little prodding by foreigners.

In 1569, a new Portuguese king, Sebastião, sent a thousand men under Francisco Barreto with orders to gain control of the gold mines, to see that they were properly exploited, to expel the Swahili traders, and to secure safe access for Portuguese missionaries. The expedition went up the Zambezi to Sena, where most of its members succumbed to malaria. This episode showed that with their sixteenth-century firearms, the Portuguese could occasionally make impressive military demonstrations, at great cost in men, but they were unable to exert permanent control over the Shona.

Another major crisis occurred in 1628, when Kapararidze, a new Mwene Mutapa, tried to reunite his kingdom and to expel the Portuguese. The Portuguese responded by helping Mavura, a rival claimant to the succession, to oust Kapararidze. In return, Mavura acknowledged himself a vassal of the king of Portugal. A further anti-European outburst followed, but a Portuguese military expedition reestablished Mavura as Mwene Mutapa. From then onward, he and his successors depended on Portuguese support. If they tried to act independently, they were overawed. The price of their alliance with the foreigners was a drastic reduction in the size of their territory and in the number of their followers. Finally, in the 1690s, the Changamire invaded and conquered most of the northern part of Shona country, ousting the Portuguese from the entire area of the goldfield. They never returned in strength.

One reason the Portuguese had not made better use of their opportunities in southeast Africa was their failure to create an efficient system of local administration. Most local officials, from the captain of the fort at Mozambique downward, like their counterparts elsewhere in Africa and Asia, used their offices for private profit rather than to promote the interests of the Portuguese

government. In the interior, except for occasional military expeditions, the
Portuguese presence consisted of private individuals pursuing their own interests first and foremost and acting as Portuguese officials only secondarily, if at
all. In the middle of the sixteenth century, a Portuguese adventurer settled at
the court of the Mwene Mutapa and gained some influence over him. The
viceroy in Goa capitalized on this relationship by giving him the title Captain
of the Gates and making him the representative of the Portuguese monarch at
the Shona court. This precedent became the norm.

From time to time, Portuguese kings and their advisers conceived the idea
of planting a colony of Portuguese settlers in the country of the Shona, to
bolster Portuguese power there. In 1677 an expedition of settlers was actually
dispatched from Portugal, but little is known of its fate, except that it had no
significant results. European settlement in the Zambezi valley was always cur-
tailed by a heavy mortality rate. The number of settlers reached a peak of
perhaps two hundred early in the seventeenth century, but dropped to not more
than fifty in 1700. Most of these were absconded soldiers and sailors, along
with a scattering of Dominican and Jesuit monks, orphan girls, and prostitutes.
Indeed, Indian immigrants from Portuguese Goa became more numerous than
Europeans in the Zambezi valley. Nevertheless, some of the Portuguese and
Indian settlers founded families whose achievements were the most enduring
and significant by-products of Portuguese power in all of East Africa before the
twentieth century.

During the sixteenth century, the Mwene Mutapa granted the Portuguese
officials who commanded the forts at Sena and Tete jurisdiction over the lands
and the inhabitants of the vicinity. By the end of that century, private Portuguese
individuals were acquiring similar titles to land and jurisdiction from the Mwene
Mutapa and other African chiefs in return for favors rendered, usually military
assistance against African enemies. This process continued during the seventeenth
century, especially after the Mwene Mutapa became dependent on Portuguese
protection, for that protection was provided by settlers rather than officials. The
forces that intervened in the crisis of 1628 were the private armies of Portuguese
settlers, who exacted wholesale concessions from the Mwene Mutapas thereafter.

Early in the seventeenth century, the crown began to acknowledge the
rights acquired by these estate-holders. After 1629, when the crown obtained
pseudolegal sovereignty over the Mwene Mutapa's realm, it tried to regularize
relations along lines that had initially been devised to promote settlement in
Brazil. The estates (*prazos*) granted Portuguese individuals (*prazeros*) by
African authorities could remain in the hands of families subject to the payment
of an annual quitrent for three generations. After that, they were to revert to
the crown. Later in the seventeenth century, the crown decreed that new estates
should be created and allotted to Portuguese orphan girls and inherited in the
female line for three generations. In the eighteenth century, further decrees
limited the size of estates, prohibited absenteeism and pluralism, and obliged
heiresses to marry men from Portugal.

These regulations were generally ignored. Some prazos grew in size until they covered a thousand square miles or more. Successive generations of prazeros married spouses who might be Africans, Indians, or members of other estate-owning families. By the nineteenth century, four or five family groups of mixed descent — we might almost call them clans — owned vast stretches of land on either side of the Zambezi River, from Chicoa to the Indian Ocean. These families wielded virtually unlimited power throughout that area. Neither the neighboring African rulers nor the Portuguese government were able to control them.

Their power derived from their African military followers and their ability to import firearms and ammunition. Two classes of subject peoples lived on a prazo: the descendants of the Africans who had occupied the land at the time it became a prazo, and the slaves whom the prazero had bought, or received as presents from chiefs, or captured in raids. The local people were administered through the heirs of their traditional chiefs and headmen, who were responsible for organizing the payment of tribute in local produce and labor. The slaves provided the prazero with domestic and specialized labor, and the male slaves also served in the prazero's private army.

By the nineteenth century, the distinctions between the two types of dependents were becoming blurred. Indeed, separate historical studies by Allen F. Isaacman and M. D. D. Newitt have shown that the prazos became more like African chiefdoms as the years went by. The prazeros and their families continued to use Portuguese names and titles and to profess Christianity; but they were barely literate, they spoke local African languages more than Portuguese, they were polygynous, they believed in witchcraft, and they performed the functions of African chiefs, including in some cases the ritual functions. In this way the Portuguese elements were gradually assimilated into the local African culture. They were, however, exceptionally turbulent chiefs. With their armed followers, they were a constant menace to the surrounding African chiefdoms and to one another. Thus the most enduring consequence of Portuguese activity in East Africa during the three centuries following Vasco da Gama's dramatic first voyage was the emergence of a new and independent power structure in the Zambezi valley.

HUNTERS AND HERDERS
IN SOUTHWESTERN AFRICA

In the fifteenth century, the western half of southern Africa did not experience the full effects of the food-producing revolution and the associated migrations. Some people there were still hunters and collectors; others were also pastoralists, with sheep, cattle, or goats. Europeans have called these peoples Bushmen and Hottentots. Sometimes they have used these names indiscriminately; at others, they have tried to distinguish between the hunters, whom they called Bushmen, and the herders, whom they called Hottentots, regarding them as distinctly different peoples. These names have stuck in popular usage to this day; but they have acquired derogatory connotations, and the indigenous names San and Khoikhoi are preferred. Moreover, we should be clear in our minds what we mean when we talk of the San and the Khoikhoi, because there was no precise correlation between the linguistic, physical, and economic variations among these peoples as a whole. Here, we shall treat the economic distinction as the crucial one, calling the hunters San and the herders Khoikhoi — a usage now customary among scholars, as is the habit of calling them jointly the Khoisan peoples.

The hunters were descendants of the ancient human populations of southern Africa who continued to practice a Late Stone Age mode of living. By the sixteenth century, they had retreated before the farmers and herders to mountainous and arid areas and to some sections of the seaboard that were not coveted by others, mainly in the western half of southern Africa. There they lived off roots, plants, insects, game, and fish. They were organized in small hunting bands of kinsmen, rarely more than a hundred strong. Each band stuck to a defined territory, wandering around in a continuous search for food, perhaps using a cave shelter as headquarters in bad weather.

Bands of hunters who have survived to the present day are remarkably well adapted to their natural environment and psychologically well adjusted. Generally short in stature, they are physically tough, with exceptional powers of endurance. They are deeply versed in the habits of their prey and skilled in extracting lethal vegetable and insect poisons, which they smear on the bone heads of their arrows. They no longer practice the arts of painting and engraving, but their predecessors did both until the nineteenth century and have left their record for posterity on innumerable caves and rock shelters from Zimbabwe to the Cape of Good Hope — paintings and engravings that show great imaginative power, a wide variety of styles, convincing portrayal of animal and human forms, a lively sense of humor, and also a sense of awe. The hunting bands that have been studied by modern research teams represent only one variety of the vast range of Stone Age peoples who formerly inhabited southern Africa. Theirs is the conservative tradition of the bands that avoided confrontation with the forces of change by retreating to areas in Botswana and Southwest Africa that are too arid for even the most extensive pastoral farming.

We know very little about the relationships between farming and hunting peoples north of the Limpopo; by the time European travelers entered that area they found Bantu-speaking farmers occupying nearly all of it. Until the nineteenth century, however, hunting bands continued to hold out in several areas in the eastern half of South Africa and we can reconstruct their relationships with the farming peoples.

The first groups of farmers to occupy an area were usually outnumbered by the local bands of hunters. In these circumstances, the two cultures were able to coexist without much interaction or tension. In the course of time, however, the farming populations became more numerous. Two types of interaction then took place. Farmers took San wives and brought up the children of such unions like any other member of their village community, and they acquired the farming culture. In this way, the Nguni and the Sotho peoples acquired the genes of the ancient populations of South Africa. Farmers also became patrons of individual hunters. A patron would protect his client and supply him with grain or milk and with pots and ornaments; in return, the hunter would trap or shoot game for his patron as well as for himself.

In some cases, relationships like this became general. This is what happened in Botswana, where the temperate grasslands merge into the Kalahari thornveld. There, to this day, Sarwa hunting bands remain bound to Tswana chiefdoms in systematic symbiotic relationships. Further east, where water is more plentiful, however, the farmers had less need to establish permanent relationships of this sort. In that case, as the farming populations became numerous, the hunters found that they were losing control over the water supplies and that the wild animals were being exterminated. They treated the farmers' sheep and cattle as game. Farmers retaliated, and relations between the two peoples turned to hostility. In the long run, the farmers triumphed because of their greater numbers. Some hunting bands might retreat for a time, but in the eastern half of South Africa, the farmers caught up with them sooner or later and annihilated them.

We have good information about this process in Lesotho. In about the sixteenth century, when the first lineages of farmers moved into the Caledon River valley, they were few in number; they lived amicably with the local hunting bands with a great deal of intermarriage until the middle of the nineteenth century. Moshweshwe (1786–1870), the southern Sotho king, and several of his senior kinsmen took San as well as Sotho wives as a matter of policy to strengthen their claims to authority throughout the area. By the beginning of the nineteenth century, however, pressure on the land increased, and the hunters began to retreat into the Maloti mountains. Later, when the Sotho themselves had lost much of their land to European settlers, they were obliged to establish cattle posts in the mountains. There, they came to blows with the San and eventually exterminated them.

The Khoikhoi were the product of another type of contact between different cultures in southern Africa. Contrary to earlier beliefs, it is now recognized that their ancestors were predominantly indigenous southern African hunters who at some stage had acquired sheep and cattle from neighbors and modified their social and political institutions as a result of this change in their material culture. Where and when the crucial transfers of sheep and cattle took place we do not know for sure. It must have happened comparatively recently, perhaps early in the second millennium A.D., because all the Khoikhoi seem to have understood each other's language. The historian Richard Elphick has shown that the hunting communities which first acquired sheep and cattle in southern Africa probably did so in central Botswana. The donors would have been Bantu-speaking mixed farmers. Once this change started, it developed a momentum. Pastoralists formed larger-scale communities with more complex institutions than hunting bands had, and they expanded into the better pasturelands throughout the western half of southern Africa, including the zone of Mediterranean climate at the Cape. In so doing, they generated a series of new political units through a process similar to that experienced by the Nguni and the Sotho, and they also incorporated numerous members of the hunting communities. But the change from hunting to pastoralism was not unqualified. In good seasons, hunters acquired cattle and sheep and became pastoralists; but in time of drought or warfare, people lost their livestock and again became wholly dependent on hunting and collecting.

When the Portuguese and the Dutch began to explore the country in the sixteenth and seventeenth centuries, they found Khoikhoi herders occupying the better pasturelands from the lower Orange River southward to the Cape of Good Hope, and from there eastward to the area between the Gamtoos and Buffalo rivers, where they were in contact with the southern Nguni chiefdoms. Their political units included several thousand people under hereditary heads who adjudicated disputes and enforced decisions, therefore justifying the title of chief.

A broad belt of country between the Gamtoos and Buffalo rivers formed a frontier zone where Nguni and Khoikhoi made contact. Their relationships seem to have been more intimate and more egalitarian than were those between hunting and farming peoples. This was probably because the herders' material culture and social organization had more points of similarity with those of the farmers. A network of reciprocal relationships was established. During the sixteenth century, when Khoikhoi were perhaps more numerous than Nguni in the contact area, a Xhosa chiefdom split, the new chiefdom entered into symbiotic relations with a Khoikhoi chiefdom, the two chiefs became linked by marriage alliances, and the Xhosa adopted the culture of the Khoikhoi. During the seventeenth century, however, Nguni numbers increased in the contact zone as a result of population movements from further east. Khoikhoi chiefdoms then became dependent on Xhosa chiefdoms, and their members were eventually incorporated into Xhosa society, to form the Gqunukwebe subchiefdom.

In short, the interactions among farming, herding, and hunting peoples in southern Africa produced a rich variety of responses, including a number of eccentric but revealing cases. The Dama of Southwest Africa, for example, are a people of Negroid appearance who are hunters and collectors; they have a subordinate symbiotic relationship with the Nama, a Khoikhoi-speaking herding people; and they themselves speak Khoikhoi and no other language. This shows how various the relationships among physical type, language, and material culture can be.

When we stand back from the details, however, we see that a single trend was manifestly paramount in southern Africa during the millennium and a half that preceded the Dutch settlement at the Cape of Good Hope. Bantu-speaking farmers were expanding slowly but inexorably at the expense of the other inhabitants, none of whom was as powerful. The hunting peoples, the herding peoples, and even the Portuguese settlers in the Zambezi valley were being

eliminated as autonomous communities, some by assimilation, some by reduction
to dependent status, some by outright extermination. Had the Dutch not occupied
the Cape and spawned the self-reliant and expansive Afrikaner people, more of
the Bantu-speaking farmers might have adapted to living in areas where it was
not possible to grow crops, as the Herero had done, and eventually Bantu-
speaking chiefdoms might have dominated all the western as well as the eastern
parts of southern Africa.

THE DUTCH IN THE CAPE COLONY:
THE ORIGINS OF A PLURAL SOCIETY

A very different type of society emerged as a result of Dutch initiative in
the southwestern corner of Africa. French, English, and Dutch ships began to
round the Cape of Good Hope toward the end of the sixteenth century. In 1602,
the Dutch merchants, who had hitherto been competing with one another, pooled
their resources and founded the Dutch East India Company, with a charter from
the States-General of the Netherlands that gave the company a trade monopoly
and administrative powers from the Cape of Good Hope eastward. Whereas the
Portuguese had established their Asian headquarters at Goa in India, the Dutch
concentrated on the Indonesian spice trade and placed their governor-general in
Batavia (Jakarta), Java. During the first half of the seventeenth century, ships
of many European nations often put in at the Cape of Good Hope to refresh
their crews and to barter sheep and cattle from the local Khoikhoi peoples. In
1648, a Dutch ship, the *Haerlem,* was stranded at the Cape, and some of its
crew spent a year ashore before they were picked up by the next season's return
fleet. On reaching Holland, a member of the party recommended that the company establish a permanent base at the Cape so as to reduce the extremely heavy
mortality in ships. In 1652, the directors dispatched an expedition of about
ninety men under the command of Jan van Riebeeck, who was instructed to build
a fort and a hospital, to grow vegetables and wheat, to breed sheep and cattle,
and to set up navigation marks for ships — and to thus provide a safe anchorage
and refreshment station approximately halfway between the Netherlands and
Batavia. During his ten-year term of office, van Riebeeck accomplished these
tasks and founded what became the city of Cape Town.

The directors of the company had no intention of creating a New Holland
in South Africa. They never regarded the Cape as performing any useful function beyond that of a refreshment station, and they always treated it as an
outlying and subordinate part of their eastern empire. Expeditions from Cape
Town showed that no gold, no silver, and no copper were to be had in the
vicinity. Consequently, the Cape establishment might have acquired no more
significance in African history than the Portuguese forts along the East African
coast had. In fact, however, a community of overseas Europeans developed there
as a by-product of the Dutch presence. These were the embryonic Afrikaners,
whose descendants now control the Republic of South Africa.

Two factors led to the creation of a settler community at the Cape. One was the calculation of van Riebeeck and the directors that the company would save money if it persuaded some of its employees at the Cape to go off the payroll and instead cultivate land on their own account. The company could then buy their surplus produce and fix the prices, for there would be no other markets available to them. Accordingly, in 1657 nine men were freed from their service contracts and allotted land at Rondebosch, five miles from the fort; others soon followed them. The second factor was ecological. Unlike the Zambezi valley, the Cape, located at 34° south latitude, was free from anopheles mosquitoes, tsetse flies, and other carriers of tropical diseases. Moreover, the indigenous inhabitants of the area — the thinly spread, politically disunited, seminomadic Khoikhoi herders and San hunters — were not able to prevent the occupation of the land by men who had firearms and could call on the resources of the company's garrison in an emergency. Consequently, a community of European men, women, and children took root and developed strength and self-reliance in the vicinity of Cape Town in the second half of the seventeenth century.

The so-called free burgher community was recruited mainly from among the company's servants, who were predominantly Dutch and German. Some brought their wives from Europe; a few married orphan girls transported by the company; many of them failed to acquire European wives. A French element was added in 1688–89, when the company provided passage for about 150 of the Huguenots who had fled to the Netherlands following the revocation of the Edict of Nantes in France. The company dispersed the Huguenots among the Dutch-speaking farmers and made Dutch the only official language and the Dutch Reformed Church the only church in the colony. Consequently, the children of settlers of French or other foreign origin spoke Dutch and were assimilated by the Dutch colonial majority. As early as 1679, the free burghers were more numerous than the company servants at the Cape. In 1699, they numbered 402 men, 224 women, and 521 children. A century later, they were about 17,000, and because at all stages the majority of the new immigrants were male, men outnumbered women in the free burgher population of the colony. Today, their descendants number more than two million and form over 60 percent of the European population of the Republic of South Africa.

During the seventeenth century, company officials tried to confine the settlement to the Cape peninsula and the area around Stellenbosch (thirty-five miles from Cape Town), which was founded in 1679. The colonists were expected to concentrate on agriculture, with stock raising no more than a sideline. By the end of the seventeenth century, however, they were producing more wheat and wine than the company needed for the garrison and passing ships. The problem was accentuated by the conduct of senior officials. The governor and others had acquired large farms and were working them for personal profit, using company labor and ensuring that the company bought their produce before it began to buy the produce of the colonists' farms. The result was that some

of the colonists began to move farther afield, and, by specializing in sheep-
and cattle-raising, they became more self-sufficient and less dependent on the
company. When they needed firearms, ammunition, clothes, or groceries, they
could sell or barter sheep or cattle to Cape Town traders or their agents, but
they no longer had the problem of selling their harvests in a market controlled
by the government. The company facilitated this dispersion by relaxing its land
policies and recognizing the right of each stock farmer to occupy three thousand or more acres of land, provided he paid a small annual license.

During the first three-quarters of the eighteenth century, *trekboere* (nomadic stock farmers) continued to spread outward from the agricultural belt
in the Cape peninsula and its vicinity, avoiding the dry karoo, or tableland,
and occupying land wherever there was enough pasture and water for their
stock. Further expansion was then impeded by natural and human obstacles. In
the northwest, beyond the Oliphants River, the land was too arid. In the northeast, bands of San hunters carried out raids on their stock from fastnesses in
the Sneeuwberg mountains and made white settlement insecure. In the east, the
Bantu-speaking southern Nguni farmers formed an impregnable barrier.

The Afrikaner people were never completely self-sufficient. From the start,
they were the dominant element of a plural society. When Jan van Riebeeck
planned the settlement of the first free burghers on the land, he intended that
they should have the services of slaves. Because slaves were used for manual
and domestic labor at virtually every outpost of the Dutch East Indian Empire,
it was natural for a company official with Eastern experience to extend the institution to South Africa. So slaves began to be imported by sea to Cape Town in
1657, and importations continued through the seventeenth and most of the
eighteenth centuries. Some came from Indonesia, India, Malaya, and Ceylon;
many of these were Muslims. Other were Africans from Madagascar or tropical
East Africa. At the Cape, the company used some slaves and sold others to
colonists. The economy of Cape Town and the neighboring agricultural belt was
consequently based on slave labor. Slaves virtually monopolized the roles of
domestic servants, artisans, and manual laborers. Most Cape Town tradesmen
owned a slave or two; a few prosperous farmers owned as many as a hundred.
Consequently, the trekboere who moved away from the agricultural belt in the
eighteenth century came from a community that was already accustomed to
using unfree workers of another race.

Long before 1652, the Khoikhoi chiefdoms in the vicinity of the Cape
peninsula had adjusted their mode of life to the opportunities created by the
intermittent visits of Europeans. When a ship arrived, Khoikhoi brought sheep
and cattle and bartered them for tobacco, alcohol, beads, or metal goods, though
misunderstandings were common and sometimes led to bloodshed. After 1652,
contacts became permanent and more intense, and the pattern of relationships
gradually changed. The Khoikhoi, resenting the entrenchment of a white community on their land, pilfered sheep and cattle from the company. Van Riebeeck

tried to prevent this by building a series of strongpoints around the settlement and linking them at one time with ditches and at another with a thick almond hedge. The southernmost Khoikhoi chiefdoms then found they were denied the use of some of their pastures. They also lost their monopoly on the role of middlemen when the company sent expeditions to explore the interior and trade directly with other chiefdoms. When fighting occurred in 1659–60 and again from 1672 to 1677, however, the Europeans took advantage of the divisions among the Khoikhoi, and, with Khoikhoi allies, defeated those who resisted. By the end of the century, many Khoikhoi had become detached from their chiefdoms and incorporated in the colonial society. Van Riebeeck employed a Khoikhoi girl whom he called Eva, and she married the company surgeon. Other Khoikhoi became the clients of farmers in the Stellenbosch area. Nevertheless, several chiefdoms survived as autonomous polities until after the end of the seventeenth century.

During the eighteenth century, however, the remaining Khoikhoi chiefdoms in the Cape Colony disintegrated. Trekboere occupied the best pastures and gained control of the best water supplies. By barter and pilfer they also obtained Khoikhoi sheep and cattle. Disintegration was accentuated by smallpox epidemics that swept through the Cape Colony in 1713, 1755, and 1767. Smallpox took a heavy toll of the Europeans and the slaves, but it had a catastrophic effect on the Khoikhoi who, in their comparative isolation, lacked the degree of immunity that previous contact provided for Europeans, Indonesians, and people from tropical Africa. As they lost their land and their stock, the Khoikhoi chiefdoms broke up into small family groups, most of which became clients of the Europeans. This suited the trekboere very well; Khoikhoi made satisfactory shepherds and herdsmen and cost very little. Trekboere simply allowed Khoikhoi families to live as their dependents, provided they worked when ordered. These events went largely unrecorded because they took place beyond the purview of company officials; but when Governor van Plettenberg toured the colony in 1778, he did not find a single independent Khoikhoi community.

Not all the surviving Khoikhoi became incorporated in the colonial society. Mixed bands were formed containing Khoikhoi, absconded slaves, freedmen, offspring of European fathers and Khoikhoi mothers, and also an occasional European. Such bands operated on the northern fringes of the area occupied by trekboere, obtaining guns, ammunition, and horses from trekboere or traveling traders. They lived in much the same way as some of the trekboere did — by hunting, stock-farming, and raiding weaker communities for sheep and cattle. As the trekboere advanced, they pushed these bands further northward, until by the end of the eighteenth century two main groups, who became known as Griqua and Kora (names derived from names of former Khoikhoi chiefdoms), had established themselves on either side of the middle section of the Orange River, in contact with the colonial society to their south and the Tswana chiefdoms to their north.

COLONIAL SOCIETY
IN THE EIGHTEENTH CENTURY

By 1795, the Cape Colony had a population, in addition to the garrison, of about 17,000 free burghers, 26,000 slaves, 1,000 African freedmen, and 14,000 Khoikhoi. The colony had four distinct socioeconomic zones. Cape Town itself was the only urban community in the colony — the sole port of entry and the principal commercial and administrative center. Besides the civil and military employees of the company, its population included traders and small business-men, a few freedmen, and nearly 10,000 slaves. The neighboring agricultural belt, extending to Paarl, Stellenbosch, and Roodezand (Malmesbury), was dominated by European landowners who employed slaves and a few Khoikhoi clients. Beyond that was a vast thinly populated zone dominated by trekboere, who owned a few slaves and controlled most of the Khoikhoi who lived inside the colony. The trekboer zone in turn merged with the lands dominated by the mixed bands of hunters and herders.

The company's authority diminished with the distance from Cape Town. Nearly all of its salaried officials resided in the town. Their major concerns were to enforce the company's monopoly over the external trade of the colony and to regulate and tax the colonists who conducted the internal trade. The Council of Policy, composed of the governor and other senior officials, was responsible for administration, subject to occasional instructions from the company's directors in the Netherlands, the governor-general and his council in Batavia, and senior officers who stopped at the Cape on their way to or from the East. Besides officials, a few colonists known as burgher councilors sat on the Court of Justice, and they were consulted by the Council of Policy on matters affecting the colonists. When a burgher councilor's term of office expired the Council of Policy appointed as his successor one of two men proposed by the remaining burgher councilors.

Beyond the Cape peninsula, the company had no interest in spending money to create an efficient administrative system. It appointed *landdroste,* as general-purpose district officers, to Stellenbosch in 1679, to Swellendam in 1746, and to Graaff-Reinet in 1786. A landdrost was allowed a clerk or two and perhaps a handful of soldiers, but he could do very little without the cooperation of the colonists in his district. The men who sat with the landdrost on the district court, which had minor jurisdiction in civil cases only, and who represented the government in each subdistrict were colonists and were not paid for their ser-vices. This system placed very few curbs on the European community. Undoubt-edly many crimes went unpunished because of the difficulty of collecting evidence and bringing suspects and witnesses to Cape Town for trial, and many colonists neglected to pay their land taxes.

A similar mixture of monopoly and parsimony was evident in ecclesiastical and educational matters. The company stationed ministers of the Dutch Re-formed Church at several places in the colony and paid their salaries. It supervised the work of the church councils and barred other denominations from operating in the colony until 1780, when a Lutheran church was founded in Cape Town. Each minister was meant to conduct a primary school for his congregation, and some did so. But children who were not European were normally excluded from these schools. Moreover, many European children lived too far from the church centers to attend the schools, and any instruction they received in reading and writing was provided by their parents or by traveling teachers. The only secondary school in the colony during the company regime was founded at Cape Town in 1714. It failed within a few years for lack of support. Later in the century a few of the more prosperous colonists sent their children to Europe for their secondary education, but the vast majority had no such opportunity.

The colonial society was a plural society. In the Cape peninsula, and there alone, it was dominated by the Dutch officials, who became increasingly estranged from the colonists during the eighteenth century. Elsewhere, the embryonic Afrikaner people were dominant. Their power was derived from their control of the basic sources of wealth — land, livestock, and capital; labor, their formal and informal influence over the officials in Cape Town and their virtual control of local administration; their near-monopoly of firearms and ammunition; and their practice of forming commandos, or organized bands of mounted musketeers, to destroy the indigenous hunters who raided their livestock.

The status of the subordinate groups in the colonial society varied. Slaves were regulated in great detail by law. As in other societies based on slavery, the laws were designed primarily to prevent insubordination and insurrection. Besides recognizing the right of slave owners to punish their slaves, the government exercised its authority to maintain their subjection. Slaves were prohibited from owning firearms; they were not allowed to assemble in groups of more than two; they were obliged to carry passes signed by their owners when they were absent from their owners' estates. These laws are of lasting historical interest because they formed the precedent for legislation that was subsequently applied to Bantu-speaking Africans in the nineteenth-century Transvaal and Orange Free State republics and in the twentieth-century Republic of South Africa. On the other hand, the company issued very little legislation that applied to the Khoikhoi clients of Afrikaner patrons. Their status was essentially customary, for it was generally beyond the purview of the officials.

There were tensions and contradictions within the embryonic Afrikaner community on racial questions. Like other slave-owning societies, Afrikaners despised menial functions; and like most communities in which slaves had different physical characteristics from slave owners, they tended to equate differences of status with innate racial differences. Neither the civil authorities nor the Dutch Reformed ministers often opposed these attitudes. To a considerable degree, therefore, the embryonic Afrikaners viewed society in terms of racial categories.

On the other hand, the social and psychological distance between the races in the Cape Colony was not as absolute as has sometimes been assumed. For one thing, subtle and complex processes of acculturation were at work. The slaves had been forcibly detached and deported from their original cultural milieus; the Khoikhoi had witnessed the collapse of their indigenous social system. As dependents of Europeans, they adopted the manners and, insofar as possible, the style of living of the dominant class. But the acculturative trends were by no means exclusively in one direction. Colonists were influenced by their slave and Khoikhoi nurses and domestic servants. The strongest evidence for these interactions is the fact that slaves and Khoikhoi, as well as colonists, had a part in creating a new vernacular language, Afrikaans, which was mainly derived from Dutch but which had a greatly simplified syntax and morphology owing to its use by nonnative speakers.

Nor did the three communities remain biologically distinct. Though marriages between colonists and slaves were prohibited, there was a great deal of concubinage. Many colonists had sexual relations with slave women, and so did visiting soldiers and sailors. At times, indeed, the company officials allowed the main slave depot in Cape Town to be used as a sort of brothel. The children of slave women generally inherited the status of their mothers; consequently, the slave population in the Cape Colony became an ethnically mixed population.

In the trekboer region, European men often cohabitated with Khoikhoi as well as slave women. Some of the offspring were absorbed by the trekboer community; but the majority were rejected by their fathers' kin. Such people either became clients of trekboere or joined the mixed bands that were to become known as Griqua and Kora. Mixing continued to occur in later generations. In recent years, the government of South Africa has tried to draw a hard-and-fast line between the dominant community, which it regards as "pure white," and a subordinate community of slave, Khoi, and Caucasian ancestry that is comprehensively labeled "Coloured."

However common or even legal these terms may be within the Republic of South Africa, they are unsatisfactory for the objective description of South African society as it evolved through history. The historical literature for southern Africa is filled with misnomers. The European "settlers" in South Africa or the "colons" in North Africa were not necessarily people who either settled or colonized. With the passage of time, most of them were born in Africa, yet the term lived on, to be applied to the second and later generations as well. Nor is "white" a satisfactory term for the European immigrants and their descendants. "White" and "black" as terms for social groups are also misnomers, suggesting a false polarity based on the social antagonisms that exist in the United States, where pinkish and brownish people are fitted into a two-caste racial division. South African society came to be still more sharply divided, and its social distinctions are more complex. Where all Americans speak the same language and share the same basic culture regardless of race, South Africa came to have crosscutting distinctions based on racial appearance, language, and other broader cultural divisions. Perhaps the most accurate term for the so-called "whites" would be "overseas Europeans," to set them within a much broader group of emigrants from Europe who carried European culture to the Americas and Oceania as well as Africa.

In South Africa, these overseas Europeans came to be divided between the Afrikaans-speaking descendants of those who arrived before 1795 and the English-speaking descendants of most of those who came later. But the Afrikaans-*speaking* community was not limited to "whites"; it came to include almost all the Coloured as well. The racial group, in short, became divided linguistically, while the linguistic group became divided racially. The Coloured, as well as the Afrikaans- and English-speaking overseas Europeans, became basically Western in their way of life, as distinguished from other cultural communities of indigenous Bantu-speaking Africans and the East Indians who arrived in the late nineteenth century. In this complex situation, nomenclature is sensitive. For our purposes in this volume, we will use the terms European (including those whose ancestors came from Europe generations ago), Coloured, Indian, and Bantu-speaking African, recognizing that they are all to some extent misnomers but nevertheless that they are the least ambiguous terms in the South African context.

CRISES IN CAPE COLONY

Toward the end of the eighteenth century, the tensions that had always existed in Cape colonial society were exacerbated by new developments, both local and extraneous. The European Enlightenment, the American Revolution, and the French Revolution made some impact on the minds of the more sophisticated colonists in Cape Town and the agricultural belt, who always resented the narrow, mercantilist system to which they had been subjected. At the time, however, the company was facing bankruptcy and its directors were more concerned to raise additional revenues from the colony than to relax the existing controls. Finally, the trekboere, who had hitherto coped with their own problems without government assistance, came up against the Nguni chiefdoms in the Fish River area and found that the Nguni were numerous and powerful enough to check the expansionist movement on which they had thrived. The result was a series of crises that produced a sharpened awareness of identity and common interest among the Afrikaners and confirmed their psychological alienation from their European roots.

In 1779, 404 European colonists who lived in Cape Town and the adjacent agricultural belt signed a petition deploring the company's mercantilist policy, exposing the selfish and autocratic conduct of its officials, and demanding reforms that included the removal of the restrictions on private trading and the grant of an effective share of political power. In response, the directors made tardy and inadequate concessions. Economic conditions improved during the early 1780s, when a French garrison occupied the Cape peninsula to assist the Dutch against British attacks. The economic boom collapsed after the construction of defense works ceased in 1785, and it was followed by a profound depression. By 1795, when a British force attacked and occupied the Cape peninsula, the Afrikaners of Cape Town and the agricultural belt were irrevocably estranged from both the Dutch East India Company and the Netherlands.

The crisis in the eastern part of the colony was different. Although trekboere had made frequent hunting and trading expeditions deep into Nguni country during the earlier part of the eighteenth century, it was not until the 1770s that the buildup of the Afrikaner population in the neighborhood of the Fish River was sufficient to produce a general confrontation between the two societies: trekboer and Xhosa. They began to overlap. Some Nguni occupied land west of the Fish River, some trekboere east of it. Trekboere detached themselves from their own people and settled at the Great Places of chiefs and headmen; Nguni became clients of trekboere and worked for them. Previously, the colonial government had tried to prevent this intermingling by ordering its subjects to stay west of a series of frontier lines. In 1778, Governor van Plettenberg toured the frontier area and tried, equally vainly, to persuade trekboere and Nguni to recognize the Fish River as a dividing line between the two societies. Quarrels over cattle led to fighting in 1779, when a group of trekboere applied to the Nguni the military techniques they had devised to deal with San hunters. They soon found that they were not strong enough to impose their will on the more densely settled Nguni, who by this time had acquired guns and horses and could fight in the same manner. Some of the trekboere then appealed to the government for help.

The government placed a landdrost at Graaff-Reinet in 1786, with orders to try to keep the peace; but it did not provide him with any military force, and he could neither control the irresponsible element among the trekboere nor stabilize the frontier. The first landdrost, M. H. O. Woeke, soon fell foul of the trekboere in his district and was recalled. The second, H. C. D. Maynier, was the first company official to become seriously concerned with the harsh way in which some trekboere treated their Khoikhoi clients. He allowed Khoikhoi to come to his office and register complaints. He also tried to curb the trekboere from making further attacks on the Nguni, at least until the San bands who were still harassing the trekboere in the northern part of the district had been overcome. A trekboer faction in the south, however, ignored his instructions and launched an attack on the Nguni, whereupon many Khoikhoi abandoned their white patrons, taking with them a number of horses and firearms, joined forces with the Nguni, and with them devastated the homesteads and raided the stock of the trekboere in the southern part of the district. This collapse was followed by a trekboer rebellion against the colonial government. Armed bands ousted Maynier, refused to admit the president of the Court of Justice who had been sent up from Cape Town to investigate, and proclaimed the district of Graaff-Reinet an independent republic. Much the same thing then happened in Swellendam.

Thus the regime of the Dutch East India Company in the Cape Colony ended in disaster: with economic collapse in the west, outright rebellion in the east, and the general alienation of most sections of the Afrikaner people from a government they regarded as distant, oppressive, and negrophilic. The company's legacy in South Africa was a European community of some 17,000 men, women, and children that was deeply entrenched at the southern end of the continent, adapted to the local environment, and accustomed to using servile labor.

SUGGESTIONS FOR FURTHER READING

General Histories

De Kiewiet, C. W. *A History of South Africa: Social and Economic.* Oxford: Oxford University Press, 1941.

Muller, C. F. J., ed. *Five Hundred Years: A History of South Africa.* Pretoria and Cape Town: Academica, 1969.

Walker, Eric A. *A History of Southern Africa.* 3rd ed. London and New York: Longmans, Green, 1957.

Wilson, Monica, and Thompson, Leonard, eds. *The Oxford History of South Africa.* 2 vols. London: Oxford University Press, 1969 and 1971.

Special Studies

Elphick, Richard. *Kraal and Castle: Khoikhoi and the Founding of White South Africa.* New Haven and London: Yale University Press, 1977.

Elphick, Richard, and Giliomee, Hermann, eds. *The Shaping of South African Society, 1652–1820.* London: Longman, 1978.

Garlake, Peter S. *Great Zimbabwe.* London: Thames and Hudson, 1973.

Isaacman, Allen F. *Mozambique: The Africanization of a European Institution: The Zambezi Prazos, 1750–1902.* Madison: University of Wisconsin Press, 1972.

MacCrone, Ian D. *Race Attitudes in South Africa: Historical, Experimental and Psychological Studies.* Johannesburg: Witwatersrand University Press, 1957.

Marais, Johannes S. *The Cape Coloured People, 1652–1937.* Reprinted from the 1939 ed. Johannesburg: Witwatersrand University Press, 1957.

Thompson, Leonard, ed. *African Societies in Southern Africa: Historical Studies.* London: Heinemann, 1969.

Chapter 10
Southern Africa
(1795-1870)

IN THE EIGHTEENTH CENTURY, Bantu-speaking people held virtually all the land in the better-watered eastern half of southern Africa. In the Zambezi valley, the inhabitants of the *prazos* still possessed vestiges of Portuguese culture; at Mozambique Island and Delagoa Bay, the Portuguese still maintained small bases; and the Cape colonists were in contact with southern Nguni chiefdoms in the vicinity of the Fish River. Elsewhere, the Bantu-speaking peoples were relatively immune from alien influences. Many Sotho, for example, had never seen a gun or a European.

Between 1795 and 1870, radical changes took place throughout southern Africa. There were two major developments. One was the *mfecane* — a series of profound disturbances among the African communities centered in what was to be Natal, with repercussions extending as far north as modern Tanzania. The other was a continuation of European expansion eastward from the Cape of Good Hope, at the expense not only of the Khoisan peoples, as before, but now also of Bantu-speaking Africans.

THE MFECANE

By 1795, the Africans were running short of land. It was no longer easy for groups of people to hive off from a chiefdom to occupy unclaimed land beyond the established settlements. The Sotho had reached the borders of the Kalahari desert in the west and the foothills of the Maloti mountains in the south. The Nguni were wedged in the narrow strip between the Drakensberg escarpment, the Indian Ocean, and the Cape Colony. The customary cattle raids among neighboring villages and chiefdoms were developing into lethal contests for control of water, pasture, arable land, and hunting grounds, and innovative leaders were beginning to amalgamate previously separate chiefdoms. The social and political order that had been a natural concomitant of centuries of expansion was incapable of meeting the challenge now presented by population growth.

The old order broke down initially in the country of the northern Nguni, between the Tugela and the Pongola rivers — according to some scholars because, in addition to pasture on the land, the people in that area were competing for control of trade with the Portuguese base on Delagoa Bay. Changes began to take place around the turn of the century, when the chiefs Dingiswayo and Zwide created two rival confederacies, loosely incorporating chiefdoms they had subjected by force or by threat of force. Dingiswayo's most enterprising warrior was a man called Shaka, an illegitimate son of the head of the small Zulu chiefdom. In 1816, Dingiswayo assisted his protégé to seize control of the Zulu chiefdom from his senior legitimate half-brother. Two years later, Zwide killed Dingiswayo. Shaka succeeded to the leadership of Dingiswayo's confederacy, defeated Zwide, and rapidly conquered all the Nguni between the Tugela and Pongola rivers.

Shaka then created a completely new phenomenon in southern Africa's history: a powerful, centralized, militaristic kingdom. The men were conscripted for service in a standing army that numbered about 40,000 warriors organized in age-regiments. Each regiment lived in a stockaded village, segregated from the rest of society. The shattering victories of the Zulu warriors were due to their exceptionally rigorous training and discipline as well as to the fact that Shaka armed them with short stabbing spears in addition to the customary long spears, or assagais. They used these short spears to close in on an enemy for hand-to-hand combat by disciplined units similar to a Roman legion. Such tactics were previously unknown in local warfare. Shaka had the chiefs killed, the enemy people driven away or subjugated. The women, the children, and the old men of the kingdom did the routine work of stock-raising and crop production in the villages, while the army was sent on annual expeditions, farther and farther from the Zulu heartland, primarily to capture cattle. By 1828, Shaka's regiments had devastated hundreds of square miles south of the Tugela together with parts of the high veld across the Drakensberg mountains, killing thousands of men, women, and children, destroying crops, seizing cattle, and forcing the survivors to flee or to take shelter in inaccessible mountains and forests.

Shaka's regime provided many benefits to his subjects. The men were elated by their victories; the kingdom was enriched by the booty in cattle; and national festivals, such as the annual first fruits ceremony, promoted national cohesion. But Shaka was an autocrat. Whereas Nguni chiefs had previously ruled in consultation with their councilors and headmen, Shaka made his own decisions. By 1824, he was killing his subjects on the flimsiest of pretexts and had become isolated from his people. They were obsequious in his presence and he seemed to have no respect for them. After his mother died in 1827, many thousands of innocent people were butchered in a wave of mass hysteria. In the following year, he sent his army on an arduous campaign to the south and then, with scarcely any respite, he ordered it far to the north, while he remained at home. There, on September 24, 1828, he was assassinated by two of his half-brothers. One of those assassins, Dingane, managed to hold the kingdom together until he was confronted by Europeans with firearms.

Modern estimates of Shaka vary greatly. While all informed historians acknowledge that he possessed exceptional military and organizational talents, some regard him as having played an essentially destructive role. They cite evidence that he suffered from serious psychological disorders derived from insecurity in his childhood, and they consider that his kingdom was inherently unstable because, contrary to custom, he ruled it autocratically and because his system of permanent mobilization depended on annual campaigns against other Africans, which could only produce diminishing returns. One might add that by causing the devastation of the country south of the Tugela and north of the mountain escarpment, Shaka paved the way for European seizure of what would become Natal and the Orange Free State. To others, he is a heroic figure, a symbol of "Black power" in a region that has become dominated by "whites"; and this interpretation has been given wide publicity through an imaginative, fictional biography by the Sotho author Thomas Mofolo. There can be no doubt that Shaka was a military innovator, and one's reaction to his brutal methods should be tempered by an understanding of the context in which he lived and an appreciation of the fact that he, more than anyone, was responsible for the creation of a new political system in southeastern Africa after the old system of small, fissiparous units had broken down.

By the time Shaka died, many northern Nguni had fled. Some traveled as more or less disorganized fragments, such as those who moved in among the southern Nguni, where they became known as *Mfengu* (beggars). Others migrated as military bands, equipped with the stabbing spear, to carry devastation far and wide throughout much of southeastern Africa. The most successful leaders of these bands incorporated local people and set up conquest states modeled to a greater or lesser degree on the Zulu prototype: Sobhuza in Swaziland, Soshangane in southern Mozambique, Zwangendaba and his successors in Malawi and Tanzania, and Mzilikazi first in the Transvaal and then in Zimbabwe.

Already before the rise of Shaka, Sobhuza, one of the northernmost Nguni chiefs, had been driven with his followers into the mountains north of the upper Pongola River. There he and his successor adopted the short stabbing spear and a variant of the Zulu regimental system. They managed to preserve their independence and to incorporate numerous Sotho as well as Nguni groups. In so doing they created a multiethnic kingdom whose people were knit together by crosscutting loyalties to their clans, their patrons, their territorial chiefs, their age-regiments, and the King and Queen Mother. This was the origin of the state still known as Swaziland, named for Mswati, who ruled from 1840 to 1875.

As a result of Shaka's victories over Zwide, several of Zwide's officers fled northward with their regiments. One was Soshangane, who, incorporating later waves of refugees from the Zulu kingdom and maintaining a tight regimental system, succeeded in dominating Mozambique as far north as the Zambezi River

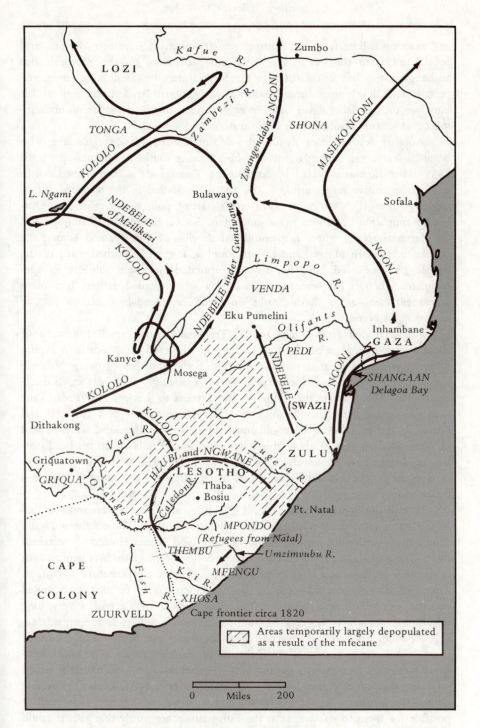

Main Movements of the Mfecane

and exacting tribute from the Portuguese settlements at Lourenço Marques and Sofala and from the Portuguese forts and the prazos on the Zambezi. But Soshangane was less successful than the Swazi rulers in assimilating conquered peoples and developing durable political institutions. Beyond the core of his kingdom on the Sabie River, his power depended on the presence of his regiments, which could not be everywhere at once.

Another dependent of Zwide who fled northward was Zwangendaba, who began to carve out a similar military kingdom in southern Mozambique until 1831, when he was defeated by Soshangane. Zwangendaba then moved northward in successive stages until, in the 1840s, he settled in the western part of modern Tanzania, 1,200 miles north of his starting point as the crow flies. During his migration he caused havoc among the Shona, between the Limpopo and the Zambezi rivers, where he annihilated the Rozwi dynasty, and among the peoples of modern Malawi and eastern Zambia. He, too, absorbed many of the people he conquered; and he, too, incorporated his male subjects in age-regiments, though his were mobilized only when needed rather than on a permanent basis, as in Shaka's Zulu kingdom. Zwangendaba's subjects became known as the Ngoni.

Mzilikazi fled from Shaka to the Transvaal with a small following of about two hundred people in 1822. There he absorbed fresh northern Nguni refugees and incorporated many conquered Sotho into his growing Ndebele kingdom. His regiments made frequent forays against his neighbors in all directions — the Shona across the Limpopo, the Tswana to the west, the Pedi to the east, and the southern Sotho beyond the Vaal — capturing women, children, and cattle. By the mid-1830s, he could muster four to five thousand warriors and he dominated an area of about thirty thousand square miles from his headquarters at Mosega near present-day Zeerust. The Nguni elements formed the upper class in the Ndebele kingdom, but many Nguni men married Sotho women and their children were regarded as Nguni.

Not all the Bantu-speaking people of southeastern Africa were incorporated in the states created by northern Nguni warrior leaders. The southern Nguni chiefdoms — including the Mpondo, Thembu, and Xhosa clusters — remained intact. Some of these people had already borne the brunt of the Afrikaner attack from the west, but their frontier position gave them a compensating advantage. They had already adopted some of the Afrikaner way of fighting as mounted infantry using European muskets. The guns then available had a very long reloading time, which was compensated in eighteenth-century European warfare by close-order drill and volley firing by ranks, sometimes followed by a bayonet charge similar in character to the Zulu use of stabbing spears. The usual Afrikaner tactic was to substitute the mobility of rapid advance, and retreat if necessary, for that of disciplined firing. By taking over the Afrikaners' guns and horses, the southern Nguni gradually came to a way of fighting that made it possible for them to stand against the Europeans more firmly than others could do using the Zulu tactic.

Several Sotho chiefdoms, such as the Pedi, survived intact in their mountain fastnesses in the eastern Transvaal, and so too did the westernmost Tswana
on the fringes of the Kalahari desert and some of the Shona in eastern Rhodesia-
Zimbabwe. But several Sotho leaders also founded larger political units than had
previously existed among them. Some became migrant warriors themselves, such
as Sebetwane, who fought his way northward and created a conquest state in
western Zambia. Others occupied defensive positions that became rallying points
for survivors of the wars. This process was most effective among the southern
Sotho in the valley of the Caledon River. During the early 1820s, militant bands
of Nguni refugees from Shaka and Sotho groups whom they had driven from
their homes devastated the Caledon basin. Families, village communities, and
chiefdoms were completely broken up; many people were slaughtered, and most
of the survivors lost all their sheep and cattle as well as their grain; some even
resorted to cannibalism. By the time of Shaka's death, the Nguni invaders had
lost control of the Caledon region, and the surviving inhabitants, Nguni as well
as Sotho, were attaching themselves to one or another of two Sotho leaders:
Sekonyela, heir to a relatively large chiefdom, and Moshweshwe, who had
started life as the senior son of the head of a small autonomous village community. Both these leaders managed to preserve some cattle and to increase their
herds by raiding the southern Nguni across the mountains to the south, and both
of them occupied mesalike mountains that formed natural strongholds: Sekonyela
on the north bank of the Caledon near modern Ficksburg, and Moshweshwe
forty miles further south at Thaba Bosiu. Both gradually built up their military
capability by procuring guns and horses from the Europeans. Sekonyela and
Moshweshwe repulsed several attacks by Nguni invaders and became rivals for
control of the Caledon basin. Moshweshwe was the abler of the two and eventually he prevailed, although it was not until 1853 that he finally captured
Sekonyela's stronghold.

As a result of these tumultuous events, society throughout southeastern
Africa was transformed by the 1830s. Innumerable people had been killed;
others had been uprooted from their homes; large areas had been partially depopulated; and new and larger political communities had been created. The
rulers of the new states had imposed their authority over the surviving members of numerous small chiefdoms; people speaking different Bantu languages
and dialects were intermingled to a much greater extent than previously. There
was also an accentuation of social inequality. Men who had lost their cattle
became clients of men of property, and in most cases conquering warriors
formed a dominant class. The authority of the rulers was most effective in
relatively small core regions; beyond that, territories occupied by subordinate
chiefs shaded off into territories whose chiefs were semi-independent allies. The
structure and style of the states differed immensely. The traditional order was
most radically changed in the Zulu kingdom, where the men of fighting age
were conscripted into age-regiments and segregated from the rest of society until they reached the age of about forty, and where the traditional liberties of

the people were sacrificed to the interests of the state as determined by the king and his military officers. In Lesotho, at the other extreme, traditional family and village life was revived, the men were mustered for warfare only when necessary and fought under their territorial chiefs rather than in nationwide regiments, and the state was a fragile association of chiefs and their followers, held together by the personality and skill of Moshweshwe.

EUROPEAN POWER IN THE CAPE COLONY

While these dramatic events were taking place in the east, European power was increasing in the western part of southern Africa. The Cape Colony changed rulers several times during the French Revolutionary and Napoleonic wars. It was conquered by the British in 1795, returned to the Dutch (the Batavian Republic) in 1803, and reconquered by the British in 1806; and British rule was confirmed by the European peace settlement of 1815.

Down to 1870, British interest in southern Africa was primarily strategic. Like the Dutch before them, the British used the harbors of the Cape peninsula as bases for controlling the sea route between Europe and Asia. British investment in southern Africa, British imports of southern Africa produce, and British exports to southern Africa amounted to a very small fraction of British investments in and trade with Europe, or North or South America, or Asia. Nevertheless, the colonial economy grew modestly until the 1860s, when there was a severe depression. Cape wine producers prospered until they lost their preferential tariff in Britain in 1831; then wool became the main export. Wholesale houses, chambers of commerce, banks, and insurance companies also laid some of the foundations of a modern business economy, but by 1870 there were still less than seventy miles of railroad track and most of the banks had collapsed during the depression.

The increase in European population was not spectacular. The descendants of those who had arrived during the Dutch period continued to be a large majority of that community. Speaking their distinctive Afrikaans language, they were conscious of forming a separate group under alien rule, like the French in Canada. Only a small proportion of the many thousands of people emigrating from Britain chose the Cape Colony as their new home. The largest such group consisted of about five thousand men, women, and children who settled in the eastern part of the colony in 1820 with assistance from the British government, which intended them to practice intensive agriculture and to form a compact barrier against the southern Nguni chiefdoms. The planned agricultural settlement was not a success, but, after early setbacks, some of the British immigrants became prosperous wool farmers. Others became traders and professional men in Cape Town and other towns and villages of the colony.

The European population, numbering about 180,000 in 1865, comprised two distinct communities: a majority of Afrikaners, descendants of the settlers who had left Europe in the Dutch period, had established deep roots in the colony, and were still predominantly rural and preindustrial in outlook; and a minority of British settlers, a cross section of post-Enlightenment, early industrial British society, who regarded themselves as forming an overseas extension of that society. The dichotomy between Afrikaners and British South Africans, sustained by linguistic and cultural differences, persists to the present day as the major cleavage within the European population of South Africa.

The colonial government tried to diminish this cleavage by introducing British institutions. It appointed magistrates to replace the Dutch district courts, which had included colonists. Members of the high court, traveling regularly on circuit to the district headquarters, administered the law more effectively than it had been in the past; English trial procedures, including the jury system, were introduced; government schools, using English as the medium of instruction and syllabuses that emphasized British history and culture, were founded in the towns and villages; and Scottish ministers were imported to serve the Dutch Reformed congregations. In the short run, these innovations did succeed in producing at least a fringe of Afrikaners who became more or less thoroughly anglicized; but their net effect in the long run was to stimulate an anti-British cultural and political reaction.

The British colonial regime also came gradually to grips with the problem of the status of the subject races. Initially, its policy was conservative. In 1809 the legal status of Khoikhoi and other dark-skinned people who were not slaves was defined in such a way that most of them were obliged to work for Europeans, though they enjoyed some protection in having written contracts of service and access to the courts; and, in 1812, European landowners became entitled to apprentice children whom they had raised on their farms for another ten years from the age of eight, a ruling that immobilized their parents also. By that time, however, the London Missionary Society was active in the colony. During the 1820s its local superintendent, John Philip, shocked by what he found there, collected evidence on the abuse of power by white farmers and the collusion of local officials. The humanitarian lobby in England supported his demand for reform, and, in 1828, "Hottentots and other free persons of colour" were freed from their restrictions and placed on the same legal footing as Europeans.

Soon afterward, the British Parliament put an end to slavery throughout the British Empire. After first making the slave trade unlawful for British subjects in 1807, the British government had then tried to ameliorate the condition of slaves, but in the Cape, as well as the Caribbean colonies, the slave owners had succeeded in making these reforms ineffective. The antislavery movement then shifted its objective from amelioration to outright emancipation, and in 1833 Parliament passed an Emancipation Act, which included a transitional period of apprenticeship and partial compensation for slave owners. When apprenticeship ended in 1838, the Cape slaves stepped into the legal status already acquired by "Hottentots and other free persons of colour."

The elimination of the legal bases of racial discrimination was a step forward. But, as American experience after 1865 would also show, legal equality does not necessarily lead to economic or social equality. In the Cape Colony, Europeans retained effective control over the economic resources, including the land, and the Cape Coloured People, descended from Khoikhoi, slaves, and Europeans, became a rural and urban proletariat dependent on working for wages in cash or in kind, which, by and large, they remain to this day.

Initially, the British governor exercised autocratic powers in the Cape Colony, subject only to his superiors in Britain. After significant numbers of British settlers had arrived, however, some of them took the lead in demanding reforms. Following a struggle with the governor, freedom of the press was conceded in 1827, followed by freedom of assembly, so that political issues could then be debated in the newspapers and at public meetings. By 1853, Lord Durham and Lord Elgin, in coping with the Canadian situation, had broken the ideological impasse that had led to the American Revolution, and the Canadian example became a precedent for constitutional development in other British settlement colonies, in two stages: first, "representative government," in which power would be divided between an executive branch subordinate to the British government and a legislative branch elected locally; and second, "responsible government," with an executive cabinet drawn from, and responsible to, the local legislature (but with Britain keeping control over the colonies' external relations until well into the twentieth century). Was the Cape Colony to be treated as a colony of settlement and subject to this evolutionary development? Or was it, rather, a dependency like India, with a preponderance of alien inhabitants to be ruled autocratically for the foreseeable future?

After some hesitation, the British government opted for the settler prescription, its doubts having been allayed by the grant of equal status before the law to the Coloured people. In 1853, the colony was granted representative government — a legislature with two houses, both consisting entirely of elected members; and, in 1872, it acquired responsible government, with a cabinet responsible to the legislature. The franchise for both houses of the Cape parliament was open, regardless of race, to any man who occupied property worth £25 or who earned £50 a year. In politics as in social and economic affairs, however, the forms might be color-blind, but the substance was very different. The net effect of the constitutional changes was to transfer political power from the British officials to the European section of the colonial population. No Coloured man ever became a member of the Cape cabinet or parliament; colonial juries were entirely or predominantly European. Only a small fraction of the Coloured men registered as voters, and those who did never formed an effective pressure group; their economic dependence made them deferential to their white employers.

THE NGUNI DEFENSE OF
THE SOUTHERN FRONTIER

Until 1811, the Bantu-speaking Africans and the Cape colonists were evenly matched in the frontier zone on either side of the Fish River, where the two societies began to overlap during the eighteenth century. The subjects of the

Xhosa cluster of chiefdoms in the vicinity of the frontier zone were far more numerous than the colonists in the eastern districts of the Cape Colony, and they drove the colonists out of the area for the second time in 1802. But the colonists had more horses and guns than the Xhosa did, and they regained lost ground with the assistance of Dutch troops during the short-lived regime of the Batavian Republic.

Power tilted decisively toward the Europeans in 1811–12, when British troops took part in another round of fighting and then built forts along the Fish River boundary and garrisoned them. In 1820, the strength of the resident Europeans increased once more with the arrival of the 5,000 British settlers. This was the beginning of the conquest of the southern Nguni — a long drawn-out process marked by successive wars and successive advances of the colonial boundary. Most of the wars started with a Nguni invasion of the colony aimed at regaining lost territory; most ended with a counterattack staged by British troops, European and Coloured colonial levies, and their African allies, destroying crops and villages and capturing vast herds of cattle. The Europeans won each of these wars, after the initial setback, because they were drawing on the resources of a powerful industrial state, whereas the Nguni had no such metropolitan backing and were always seriously impeded by their own disunity. No leader succeeded in imposing his authority, as Shaka had done over the northern Nguni or as Moshweshwe did over the southern Sotho. The endemic rivalries between chiefdoms and opposed segments of chiefdoms were compounded in 1835, when the colonial government made allies of 17,000 Mfengu. They had recently arrived in the area as refugees from Shaka, and the Cape government settled them on land conquered from the Xhosa. Nevertheless, the southern Nguni put up a prolonged and often heroic resistance, waging wars in 1819, 1834–35, 1846, 1850–53, and 1877–78, by which time they were a conquered people.

As the conquest proceeded, the boundary of British territory shifted farther and father eastward and incorporated more and more Nguni territory. At the beginning of the century, it was fixed at the Fish River; in 1819, it advanced to the Keiskamma; in 1847, to the Kei; in 1858, to the Mbasha; and in 1878, to the Mthatha. When the Mpondo country was annexed in 1894, the Cape boundary met the boundary of Natal along the Mtamvuna River, which thus brought all the southern Nguni under European administration.

West of the Kei, most of the annexed territory was divided up into farms for European settlers, interspersed with reservations that would form the Ciskei "homeland" in the second half of the twentieth century. Even in the Ciskei region between the Fish and Kei rivers, however, Bantu-speaking Africans still made up the vast majority of the population, not only on their reserves but also in the towns and as workers on the European farms. The Xhosa on the frontier were not so much rolled back as overwhelmed and subjugated by the political power of the Cape government and the economic power of the European settlers who had come to own much of their former land. North and east of the Kei River, how-

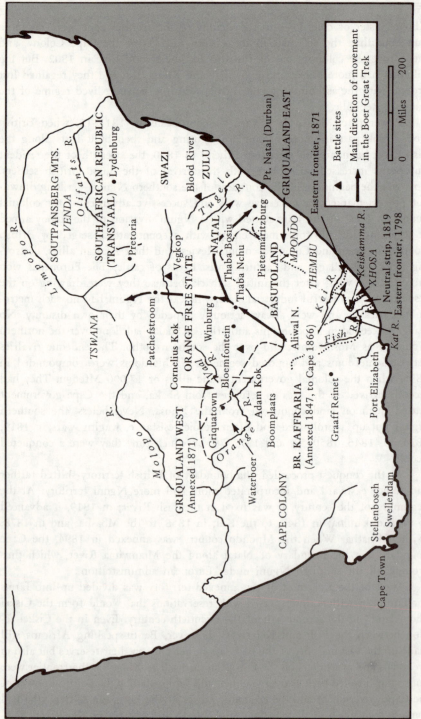

Colonial South Africa and Its Frontiers

ever, the Africans held on to the land. Europeans came into positions of power but not as settlers in the rural areas, except in a small region around Kokstad, which had passed first into the hands of Griqua — under Adam Kok — who migrated there from the interior in 1860–63 and then into the hands of European settlers who displaced the Griqua.

In the Ciskei reserves and the Transkei alike, the southern Nguni were exposed to three categories of alien intruders: officials, traders, and missionaries. Magistrates appointed to district headquarters in the conquered territories gradually undermined the authority of the chiefs, transforming them into subordinate officials with limited powers. Traders, selling commodities such as sugar, tea, blankets, and iron posts that Africans rapidly came to regard as necessities, created a chain of shops throughout the territories. Missionaries of several Protestant denominations — Congregational, Methodist, and Presbyterian — created another chain of stations in which they taught Christian theology in combination with nineteenth-century British cultural values and denounced local customs such as initiation, polygyny, and the transfer of cattle on marriage (*lobola*) that were fundamental to African social solidarity. They also founded schools in which Africans acquired a western education in conjunction with religious instruction.

Each magistracy, each trading station, and each mission became the nucleus of a new social grouping of Africans who detached themselves from traditional society and adapted to the presence of their conquerors. Economic imperatives accentuated the process. People who could not provide for their needs on the lands that remained to them went out from the reservations to work for European farmers, and although some returned to their homes after a year or two, others remained away.

The results for African societies were uneven. Many of the Mfengu, whose social system had been disrupted by Shaka and who had fled southward and received a privileged status from the colonial authorities, adapted most eagerly to the new order. So did individuals and segments from the Xhosa and Thembu chiefdoms. But other individuals and groups continued to resist the new order psychologically, even when they had been physically overcome. In the war of 1819 and again in the 1840s, Xhosa prophets invoked traditional magic to oppose conquest. Then in 1856 — three years after the end of the longest and most devastating war — a young Xhosa girl named Nongqause reported that she had had a vision: the people should destroy all their cattle and their grain; when this was done, the ancestral heroes would be reborn, choice cattle and grain and also guns and ammunition would appear, and a great wind would drive all the Europeans into the sea. This report was taken seriously by many of the Xhosa and by early 1857 they had destroyed over 150,000 cattle. But instead of the millennium, there was mass starvation. Nearly two-thirds of the inhabitants of the affected chiefdoms between the Fish and the Kei rivers are estimated to have died or to have fled into the Colony seeking food and employment.

As people reacted in different ways to their changing circumstances, new cleavages opened up in Nguni society. Rivalries between chiefdoms and ethnic groups were accentuated by the differential treatment they received from their conquerors, notably the division between the Mfengu and the rest. There was also a division between those who persisted in trying to reject alien goods and customs and those who attempted to make use of their new opportunities, such as they were, by mastering the conqueror's knowledge and adopting his customs; these people accumulated imported goods, wore Western clothes, attended mission schools and hospitals, abandoned traditional rituals, and were baptized. Europeans called these modernizers "School" Africans and the traditionalists "Red" Africans, because the latter continued to use red ocher for facial decoration. Chiefdoms and families split along these lines, and the division has persisted. But it was never absolute: every individual was subjected to similar forces and experienced the contrary tugs of tradition and modernization.

The modernization process would have been more successful in pointing the way toward a harmonious colonial society if those Africans who conformed most closely to their missionaries' prescriptions had received the benefits that were implicit in the Cape colonial legal system. When the colonial reforms were enacted in the 1820s and 1830s, and even when the terms of the franchise were set for the Cape parliament in 1853, few Africans lived inside the colonial boundary; the land between the Keiskamma and the Kei was then administered as a separate colony. Later, after the Keiskamma-Kei territory was incorporated in the Cape Colony in 1865, followed by other large blocks of territory with African inhabitants, additional parliamentary constituencies were created there, but steps were taken to ensure that few Africans became registered as voters. Consequently, while some of the early Christian converts were quite enthusiastic in adopting alien ways, by 1870 it was becoming apparent that Cape European society would not accept them as equal, even if their way of life was as "civilized" as that of most Europeans.

THE GREAT TREK

Between 1835 and 1841, about six thousand Afrikaner men, women, and children trekked northeastward from their homes in the eastern districts of the Cape Colony, crossing the colonial boundary in the vicinity of the village that was later founded at Aliwal North. Later, this emigration became known as the Great Trek, and the emigrants as *voortrekkers*. They traveled in organized groups of kinfolk and neighbors, with their Coloured servants and their ox wagons, cattle, sheep, and other movable property, determined to establish new homes for themselves beyond the limits of British control, either in Natal or on the high veld on either side of the Vaal River.

They emigrated for a variety of economic, political, and psychological reasons. Many felt that they were treated unsympathetically by the British administrators who had deprived them of their roles in local government and were introducing English legal procedures and founding schools with a British bias. There had been a minor explosion as early as 1815. A frontier farmer had ignored a summons to appear before the circuit court on a charge of ill-treating his Coloured servant. After he had fired on a mixed force that was sent to arrest him, a Coloured sergeant had shot him dead. Some of his friends and relatives had then raised a rebellion, but they had been rounded up quickly and the ringleaders hanged in public. Although not many frontiersmen took part in this episode, the use of Coloured men to arrest an Afrikaner rankled. Later, the emancipation of the Khoikhoi and the slaves from their legal restrictions shocked the Afrikaner farmers' sense of propriety and temporarily dislocated their labor supply. Moreover, those who had owned slaves felt cheated by the fact that their compensation could only be claimed in London, which placed them in the hands of British agents, who charged high commissions.

Most of the voortrekkers came from the eastern districts of the colony where the Nguni blocked their expansion eastward, making it impossible for the new generation to acquire what they considered to be their birthright of several thousand acres per family. Some of them suffered severe losses during the Xhosa attack of 1834, and during 1835 they were appalled to hear that the British Colonial Secretary was giving credence to the views of John Philip, the missionary who had already accused them of ill-treating their Coloured servants. Now the Secretary was blaming them rather than the Xhosa for starting that war and was instituting a policy of treaties with the southern Nguni chiefs that, in their opinion, could only lead to further troubles. In short, they emigrated because they wished to continue the way of life of their parents and grandparents, independent of an alien government that seemed bent on meddling in their relations with their dark-skinned servants and neighbors.

Nevertheless, only about one-eighth of the total Afrikaner population left the Cape Colony before 1841. Many others felt much the same way about British rule; but they remained inside the Colony where they accommodated more or less successfully to the British reforms, and after 1853 they gradually learned to take advantage of the parliamentary institutions.

During 1834 and 1835, small parties of Afrikaners made reconnaissance expeditions to Natal and the high veld. They returned to report that both regions had spacious territories that were apparently unpopulated — the lush subtropical lands below the mountain escarpment and the fertile grasslands on either side of the Vaal River. These reports were fairly accurate as far as they went (though they overestimated the extent of depopulation); but their authors did not realize that both regions had recently contained quite dense populations of mixed farmers and that the leaders Dingane and Mzilikazi were keeping them depopulated by military raids. The voortrekkers' plans to settle there inevitably brought them into conflict with the Zulu and the Ndebele.

Ever since Mzilikazi had settled north of the Vaal River, he had been attacked several times from the south — not only by Zulu armies sent by Dingane, who still regarded him as a rebellious subject, but also by Coloured horsemen armed with muskets operating from bases north of the Orange. Consequently, when his spies reported that considerable numbers of Europeans with vast herds of cattle and flocks of sheep were occupying land on either side of the Vaal, he sent his regiments to attack them. By 1837, however, there were enough voortrekkers in the high veld to mount an offensive. With Coloured and African allies, they drove Mzilikazi northward from Mosega early in 1837 and later that year sent him fleeing with his followers into the country of the Shona across the Limpopo, where they carved out a new Ndebele kingdom. Having conquered the conquerors of the African inhabitants of the high veld, some of the voortrekkers proceeded to found settlements on either side of the Vaal River.

By 1838, however, the majority of the voortrekkers had decided to settle in Natal, because its coastline provided an opportunity for trade with continental Europe and the United States, in preference to the landlocked high veld, where they could only replenish their supplies of arms, ammunition, and groceries through the Cape colonial network. One of their leaders, Piet Retief, entered into negotiations with Dingane for a grant of land south of the Tugela. But Dingane had already been made suspicious of Europeans by the erratic behavior of a small group of British traders at Port Natal (Durban), who were haboring refugees from his kingdom, and he was well-informed about the fate of Mzilikazi. He regarded a voortrekker settlement in Natal as a threat to his kingdom and he determined to prevent it.

In February 1838, after he had put his mark to a document purporting to cede the territory of Natal, Dingane's warriors massacred Retief and his party and attacked the voortrekker encampments below the Drakensberg. In all, they killed over three hundred and fifty Afrikaners and over two hundred and thirty of their Coloured servants, and they temporarily extinguished European power in Natal. In December, however, a voortrekker force, revitalized by fresh leadership, repulsed a massive Zulu attack with heavy losses by forming a laager with their wagons. About three thousand Zulu perished in that engagement, which became known as the Battle of Blood River. The Zulu nation then began to disintegrate. Mpande seceded from his half-brother Dingane with a large following and allied himself with the voortrekkers, and in 1840 Mpande's regiments crushed Dingane's army and sent the king fleeing northward to his death. Mpande then assumed control over a weakened Zulu kingdom, while the main body of voortrekkers carved farms out of the lands south of the Tugela and applied to the British authorities to be recognized as an independent state.

They nearly succeeded. During the middle years of the nineteenth century the British government did not favor the annexation of an overseas territory unless there were strong commercial or strategic reasons. The Cape Colony itself, with its incessant and costly frontier wars, was regarded as a burden necessarily borne for the sake of the harbors on the Cape peninsula. Natal had much less to offer. The trade conducted there by a few British subjects since 1824 was negligible, and a sand bar made the entrance to the harbor of Port Natal (Durban) inaccessible to all but the smallest ships. Before the voortrekkers arrived, the government had had no hesitation in rejecting requests by the traders and their Cape colonial backers for the annexation of Natal.

In 1842, however, the government changed its mind. A voortrekker commando had raided southward against a chief whose neighbor, the chief of the Mpondo, had appealed through his missionary for British protection, and the *voortrekker volksraad* (legislature) had passed a resolution for the forced removal to the south of numerous Africans who had returned to their original homelands in Natal after the defeat of Dingane, and who were deemed to be "surplus" to the labor requirements of the Afrikaners. The British government concluded that these pressures would have disturbing effects throughout southern Nguni country right down to the Cape colonial frontier; it was also influenced by the humanitarian lobby, which was denouncing the voortrekkers' dealings with Africans. Accordingly, a British military detachment was sent to Natal where, after some sharp fighting, the republican authorities submitted to British rule in 1842. But, during the next few years, the majority of the voortrekkers who had settled in Natal harnessed their oxen again, recrossed the Drakensberg, and made their homes on the high veld.

By the late 1840s, numerous European settlements were scattered across the high veld, from near the Orange River in the southwest to the foothills of the Soutpansberg mountains near the Limpopo in the north. Each settlement comprised a small village surrounded by large pastoral landholdings and formed a distinct community, usually with a nuclear group of families who had left the Cape Colony together. The relations between the settlements were often far from cordial. Differences of opinion on matters such as whether a British missionary or an unordained Afrikaner should conduct religious services and how they should organize themselves politically, compounded by personality conflicts, gave rise to serious quarrels. Near the Cape colonial border in the southwest there were further complications; that area included independent Griqua communities, of mixed Khoikhoi and European descent, and also a considerable number of Afrikaners who still regarded themselves as colonial subjects and were not imbued with the independent spirit of the voortrekkers.

For a while, the British were sucked into the territory between the Orange and the Vaal. In 1843, consistent with the policy they were then pursuing on the eastern frontier of the Cape Colony, they made treaties with the East Griqua chief, Adam Kok, and the southern Sotho chief, Moshweshwe; and, in 1848, an impetuous governor, Sir Harry Smith, annexed the entire territory between the Orange and the Vaal, including East Griqualand and Lesotho. But he had overreached himself. Smith's annexation went against the grain of contemporary British policy and the government in London grudgingly accepted it as a *fait accompli,* but refrained from providing sufficient funds for effective administration of the territory. Moreover, the man Smith appointed as local administrator ineptly became involved in local communal conflicts, eventually forming a military alliance with the Europeans and the smaller African communities against Moshweshwe, who defeated him. The British government then sent out commissioners to examine the situation on the spot. In 1852, they signed a convention with representatives of the Transvaal voortrekkers, recognizing their independence. Two years later, another British commissioner made a similar agreement, known as the Bloemfontein Convention, with representatives of the European population of the area that was to become the Orange Free State.

The Great Trek was a remarkable feat. Previously, white settlers had been confined to the more arid western half of southern Africa, where they had flourished at the expense of the relatively weak and thinly spread Khoisan hunters and herders. The voortrekkers broke through into the better-watered eastern half of the continent, where, taking advantage of the fact that the African inhabitants had recently been scattered and disrupted by the mfecane wars, they were able to occupy vast areas. They defeated the aggressive Zulu and Ndebele kingdoms that had dominated the region and, although Britain annexed Natal, voortrekker independence was recognized in the interior. More than that: in the conventions, the British also recognized that Europeans should be permitted to purchase arms and ammunition in the British colonies, but prohibited such trade with "native tribes," and revoked the British treaty with Moshweshwe.

To modern Afrikaners, the voortrekkers were heroic figures who had brought "white" Christian civilization to darkest southeastern Africa. The Day of the Covenant is a public holiday commemorating the Battle of Blood River. In the 1930s, the celebration of the centenary of the Great Trek was exploited by politicians to intensify Afrikaner nationalism, and a massive Voortrekker Monument was erected outside the capital city of Pretoria. To modern Africans, on the other hand, the voortrekkers were ruthless conquerors who set the stage for their systematic exploitation. There are ironies in both views. Shaka, the symbol of African power, was the agent for the disruption of the African peoples that paved the way for voortrekker settlement. And, while the trek was taking place, the main body of Afrikaners remained in the Cape Colony and were skeptical of the voortrekkers' achievements.

THE AFRIKANER REPUBLICS

The European population of the territories the voortrekkers occupied in the interior grew slowly by natural increase and immigration from the Cape Colony and Natal to number about 45,000 in 1870 (at a time when the Cape Colony had nearly 200,000 white inhabitants). Most of these were still essentially trekboere, or seminomadic pastoral farmers. They claimed vast expanses of land without cultivating it, lived off their herds and flocks, and produced little else for exchange. People of British, continental European, and Jewish descent sold them colonial and imported goods obtained from merchants in the Cape Colony. A few other foreigners were employed by the voortrekker governments as clergy, teachers, and officials.

The voortrekker communities remained fragmented. The extended family evoked more loyalty than the regional group, the regional group more than any larger community. African chiefs as well as British officials often manipulated these divisions, while the Europeans in turn exploited the cleavages among Africans.

Two states gradually took shape in the interior: the Orange Free State (OFS) between the Orange and the Vaal, and the South African Republic (SAR) north of the Vaal. External influences were somewhat stronger in the OFS, which formed a cultural as well as geographical bridge between the British colonies and the SAR. Both republics adopted constitutions that confined citizenship to European men; the Transvaal document bluntly declared that "The people are not prepared to allow any equality of the non-white with the white inhabitants, either in Church or State." The constitutions also provided for the election of presidents and unicameral legislatures. Although there were a few salaried officials in each little capital town, Bloemfontein and Pretoria, and one or more in each district headquarters, neither state had the means to create an efficient bureaucracy, and local administration was mainly in the hands of unpaid, part-time, military officers, elected by the local citizens from among themselves. After a shaky start (the first president was removed from office by force), the OFS eventually achieved stability under President J. H. Brand (1864–1888). The SAR remained chronically unstable. Indeed, the various Transvaal factions were not formally united until 1860, and even then they fought among themselves intermittently for another four years.

The voortrekkers never contemplated living without the use of dark-skinned people as domestic servants and herdsmen. Needing many more dependents than the Coloured people they had brought with them from the Cape Colony, they turned to the local African populations. Commandos often made a point of capturing African children as well as cattle for distribution when a campaign was over, as colonial commandos had formerly captured San children. Voortrekkers also obtained African children by barter from adults who had no food. Captured and bartered African children were called apprentices and, as with Coloured children in the early years of British rule in the Cape Colony, they were meant to become free at the age of twenty-five (twenty-one in the case of girls), but often did not do so. In addition, many African adults as well as children simply stayed where they were as labor tenants when Europeans occupied their land. By methods such as these, the voortrekkers secured an ample supply of African labor.

In most of the areas where they settled, the voortrekkers soon found themselves confronted with a security problem. Numerous northern Nguni who had lived south of the Tugela before the time of Shaka drifted back to their home areas after the fall of Dingane; similarly, numerous Sotho moved back to their home areas on the high veld after Mzilikazi was driven northward across the Limpopo. The voortrekkers tried to deal with this influx by passing laws limiting the number of Africans to four or five families on each farm; prohibiting Africans (and also Coloured people) from owning firearms or horses, or being at large in white areas without a pass signed by a white employer; and placing all "surplus" Africans in reservations under headmen who were made responsible for their good behavior and for providing additional labor on demand.

The Republic of Natal began to formulate such a policy, but in attempting to cope with the "surplus," it set in motion the chain of events that led to British intervention. In the SAR, too, the government lacked the means to enforce its laws systematically. The reservations were not delimited and relations between Europeans and Africans varied considerably from region to region and over time. Generally, the Africans who lived on the reservations had security of life and limb and the opportunity to produce their own food in return for the obligation to provide intermittent compulsory labor for white farmers; but where the Europeans were particularly capricious, there was anarchy. This was always the case in the northern Transvaal, where the European community lacked internal discipline and its officials were themselves guilty of the most flagrant abuses.

The areas where Africans were effectively subjected to white control shaded off into areas where they remained autonomous. Initially, voortrekker leaders tried to acquire titles to land by negotiation with chiefs, and they continued to make treaties when it seemed expedient; but after they defeated Mzilikazi, they saw themselves as having won by conquest his entire Transvaal empire, which they construed in the largest terms as embracing everything between the Vaal and the Limpopo and between the Kalahari desert and the mountain escarpment. They claimed to have liberated all the African inhabitants from Ndebele oppression and to be justified in treating them as vassals.

The Africans saw things differently. Some had never been ruled effectively by Mzilikazi, others had been only partially subjugated, and in either case they strove to achieve and maintain their independence after the Ndebele had been driven out. Several British traders and missionaries, including David Livingstone, encouraged them to adopt this attitude, and increased their capacity to resist republican demands by selling them arms and ammunition. But, located as they were around the periphery of the trekker settlements and divided as they were by traditional feuds and personal rivalries, the African chiefdoms had to depend very largely on their own resources, and the republican authorities were generally able to deal with them piecemeal. The SAR also exploited the fissiparous nature of African chiefdoms by giving sanctuary to the rivals of incumbent chiefs, thus splitting several chiefdoms into two parts — one autonomous, the other under republican control.

Three clusters of chiefdoms managed to preserve their independence from the SAR until 1870 and later. On the borders of the Kalahari in the west, the SAR failed to conquer several of the Tswana (western Sotho) chiefdoms, which became combined into a British protectorate in 1885 and formed the independent state of Botswana in 1966. In mountainous country in the east, the Pedi chiefs rallied the survivors of many northern Sotho chiefdoms that had been disrupted by Mzilikazi and Soshangane, and they repulsed European attacks until 1879, when they were defeated and incorporated in the Transvaal. In the Sout-

pansberg mountains in the north, the Venda actually reversed the tide of encroachment in 1867, when they defeated a commando led by Paul Kruger and
caused the Afrikaners to abandon almost the entire Soutpansberg district. It was
not until 1898, when Kruger was president of a much more powerful SAR,
enriched by gold discoveries, that a republican force of nearly four thousand,
with Swazi and Tsonga allies, finally conquered the Venda.

THE BRITISH COLONY OF NATAL

After Natal was annexed by Britain in 1843, an extreme variant of colonialism developed there. It is estimated that in 1872 the population of the colony
numbered about 320,000, of whom nearly 93 percent were African, less than
6 percent European, and about 2 percent Asian (a balance of cultures that would
be repeated in Rhodesia in the twentieth century). The African population of
Natal continued to rise steeply after the collapse of the voortrekker republic.
Some of these Africans were returning to the neighborhoods they had abandoned during the time of Shaka; others were fleeing from the Zulu kingdom as
a result of internal tensions that reached a peak in 1856, when rival factions led
by two sons of Mpande fought a tremendous battle near the Tugela. The European population consisted of a few voortrekkers who remained in Natal when
the others left for the high veld and a majority of British immigrants who began
to arrive in substantial numbers in 1849. The Asians were imported from India
by the Natal government in the 1860s to work for European planters on the
sugar estates along the coastal belt.

The British annexation proclamation of 1843 included a high-sounding
commitment to prohibit racial discrimination: "That there shall not be in the
eye of the law any distinction of colour, origin, race, or creed; but that the
protection of the law, in letter and in substance, shall be extended impartially
to all alike." The early history of the colony is largely an account of how the
tiny European community subverted that commitment and obtained substantial
control over the entire territory.

The division of the land was a crucial issue. One of the first acts of the
British administration was to appoint a commission to deal with this problem,
with the result that about two million acres out of a total of nearly twelve and
a half million in the colony were eventually defined as African reservations
("locations"). The rest became the private property of individual Europeans
or European companies, or remained in the public domain ("crown lands").
Most of the African inhabitants were placed in the reservations; some squatted
in the public domain; others became tenants of European landowners, including
absentee landlords who merely collected rent, a practice known as "Kaffir
farming."

The African inhabitants were administered by Theophilus Shepstone from
1845 to 1875. He controlled them through chiefs and headmen, of whom some
had prescriptive claims to their offices while others were new men. The chiefs

and headmen were made responsible for keeping law and order in their reservations, subject in theory to the governor of Natal, who was proclaimed Supreme Chief, and in practice to the Secretary for Native Affairs, Theophilus Shepstone. He allowed them to apply customary Nguni law in civil disputes among Africans, but criminal cases and disputes with Europeans were tried by the magistrates in accordance with Roman-Dutch law adopted from the Cape Colony. The Africans paid an annual hut tax as well as customs duties on imported commodities they bought from traders — payments that amounted to more than the government spent on their administration. This method of administering Africans contained many of the features of Indirect Rule, which was to become the orthodox practice of British administrators in tropical African colonies in the twentieth century; it also contained the germs of the apartheid system that prevails in the modern Republic of South Africa.

Economic growth was slow in Natal, and with little material development for the African population. Missionaries founded a few schools and hospitals, but their resources were too meager to have a significant impact. Europeans who lived inland were mixed farmers, who employed African labor in return for low wages or tenant rights. Along the coastal belt, experiments were made with tropical crops, and, by 1870, sugar was being produced on a commercial scale for export. Because Shepstone was not willing to force Africans to become plantation laborers — a very different type of activity from the cattle-herding and grain production to which they were accustomed — the planters used their political influence to persuade the government to make arrangements for the importation of laborers from India and to allot public funds for this purpose. Recruiters employed by the Natal government persuaded Indians to sign contracts ("indentures"), by which they undertook to serve Natal employers for five years, after which they had the option of entering into new contracts or making their own way as private persons. Ten years after arrival, they became entitled to free passages back to India, but they were not obliged to return. The first batch of Indians, who completed their ten years in 1870, set an example that was to be followed by their successors until the indentured system was abolished in 1911: only a small minority returned to India; the rest remained in Natal, where they became market gardeners, shopkeepers, and service workers in and near the two main towns, Durban and Pietermaritzburg.

The economic advantages of the European settlers were promoted and buttressed by political power. By the 1850s, the influence of the humanitarian lobby in England was waning, and British public opinion was becoming reconciled to granting representative institutions to settler communities. For South Africa, the precedent was created in the case of the Cape Colony in 1853. Accordingly, in 1856 a Natal legislature was created with a majority of its members elected by the white settlers. Although there was a reserved civil list, meaning that the salaries of the senior officials could not be reduced by the legislature, and although those officials remained responsible to London until 1893, this was a decisive step toward full settler control of the colony. The use the colonists would make of their political power had been foreshadowed by a commission of settlers who reported on "native policy" in 1854. The commissioners categorized Africans as "savages" — "superstitious," "crafty," "indolent," "bloodthirsty and cruel," "debased and sensual." They described the Africans as "foreigners" with no right to occupy land in Natal; and they declared that since "Natal is a white settlement," the prohibition of racial discrimination in the annexation proclamation had become "utterly inapplicable." [1]

MOSHWESHWE'S LESOTHO

We can illustrate African responses to white expansion in this period by turning to the career of a remarkable man, Moshweshwe, who was born about 1786 and died in 1870. Lesotho occupied a central position in southern Africa and we probably know more about Moshweshwe than we do about any of his African contemporaries in this area, because missionaries got to know him unusually well and wrote quite perceptively about him, and he himself dictated numerous letters. These sources have to be interpreted judiciously, however; the writings of the missionaries were affected by their cultural assumptions and evangelical goals, and we cannot be sure how accurately the letters attributed to Moshweshwe reflect his meaning, for he spoke in southern Sotho, whereas his scribes, who were missionaries or mission-educated Africans, wrote out his dictations in English or French. We can remedy these deficiencies somewhat by drawing on the traditions still current in Lesotho and by using several studies that modern anthropologists have made of aspects of Sotho society.

The senior son of a semiautonomous village headman, Moshweshwe had repulsed several African attacks on his mountain stronghold, Thaba Bosiu, and was incorporating numerous Nguni as well as Sotho survivors of the mfecane wars into a loosely structured kingdom by 1833, when the first Europeans settled in Lesotho. He attracted followers not only because he was a master of defensive warfare, but also because he restored the morale of peoples whose lives had been disastrously disrupted. He put an end to cannibalism and encouraged people to settle down again in villages and resume their customary mode of life as mixed farmers. But, whereas before the wars they had been divided among numerous separate chiefdoms, they now looked up to him as their great chief. He and his councilors heard appeals from the decisions of their local courts and from time to time he summoned all the initiated men to Thaba Bosiu, where he discussed public affairs with them and announced his decisions.

The first Europeans to settle in Lesotho were French Protestant missionaries. Moshweshwe himself had sent messages inviting them. Coloured bands based in the Griqua chiefdoms west of Lesotho, equipped with horses and firearms obtained from the Cape Colony, were raiding his outlying villages and he had heard that missionaries were men of peace who possessed magical powers. As

[1] Colonial Office, 879/1, Public Record Office, London.

Moshweshwe was their patron, his missionaries had an interest in helping him to stabilize and extend his kingdom. His favorite, Eugène Casalis, founded a station immediately below Thaba Bosiu. Moshweshwe consulted him frequently and used him as his secretary and interpreter. He placed other missionaries alongside his subordinate chiefs at strategic points, where their presence deterred potential enemies from attacking them. He also encouraged his people to attend the mission services and schools. By the end of 1847, the Paris Evangelical Missionary Society had nine stations in and near the Caledon valley, and the missionaries had baptized several of Moshweshwe's councilors and close relatives — sons, half-brothers, and wives.

Moshweshwe also made several far-reaching concessions to his missionaries: he adopted Christian burial customs, he ceased to hold initiation schools, and he granted divorces to some of his wives who had been converted. However, he refused to yield to his missionaries' denunciations of the traditional systems of polygyny and clientage, for he himself had many wives and many clients — people who had lost their property during the wars — and he regarded them as essential attributes of his kingship. In the absence of a money economy, they were necessary to cultivate his fields, to look after his cattle, and to prepare food for himself and his numerous guests. Moreover, although he frequently attended services in the mission churches and became very well-informed about the Bible and sympathetic to the moral code of the New Testament, he declined to be baptized, realizing that if he did so he would alienate his more conservative subordinate chiefs, councilors, and relatives (including his aged and respected parents), as well as the Sotho doctors and prophets who had vested interest in the traditional beliefs and rituals.

Traders from the Cape Colony, bringing wagon loads of merchandise to Lesotho, followed the missionaries during the 1830s and 1840s. In the 1850s, they began to build shops at the principal mission stations, buying grain and cattle and selling manufactured clothing and metalware. The Sotho responded by producing a considerable surplus of grain for the market. Moshweshwe himself set an example by using imported ploughs in his own fields and by planting wheat as well as sorghum and corn. He and his people were also quick to appreciate the significance of horses and firearms. By the 1850s, many young men owned horses and muskets, and Moshweshwe had a large ammunition store on Thaba Bosiu. Although the trade in guns and ammunition was frowned upon by European opinion and prohibited by the Bloemfontein Convention (1854), there were always farmers and professional traders who were prepared to take advantage of the Sotho demand. Horses flourished in Lesotho; but the firearms were mostly inferior muskets manufactured in Birmingham specially for the African market. While Moshweshwe encouraged trade, he also took steps to control the traders. He himself, like his father, never drank even the mildest Sotho beer, declaring that a chief should keep a clear head. He agreed with his missionaries in deploring the demoralizing effects of the colonial brandy that traders were selling his people, and in 1854 he issued a law prohibiting the sale of trade alcohol. Five years later, he issued another law asserting his unqualified jurisdiction over traders and prohibiting them from owning any land in Lesotho.

Moshweshwe was able to control the French missionaries and colonial traders because their interests very largely coincided with his own; but the interests of the voortrekkers with their insatiable appetite for land, were almost entirely antithetical. By the early 1840s, Afrikaners and Africans were becoming intermingled in the triangle between the lower Caledon and the Orange as well as further north, and the situation was further complicated by the presence on the north side of the Caledon of several Coloured and African communities, including Sekonyela and his people, who did not recognize Moshweshwe as their king. After the voortrekkers defeated Mzilikazi and Dingane, and as they came to occupy more and more land on the high veld to his north and west, Moshweshwe realized that they constituted a serious threat to his state, whereas the British seemed to have no intention of depriving him of his territory. Accordingly, he sought a British alliance through the medium of his missionaries. In a treaty concluded in 1843, Sir George Napier, Governor of the Cape Colony, recognized Moshweshwe as the ruler of all the land between the Orange and the Caledon and also of a strip twenty miles wide on the right bank of the Caledon (except for Sekonyela's territory at the northeastern end).

But Moshweshwe's relations with the British authorities soon deteriorated. Napier's successor persuaded him to allow settlers in the triangle between the lower Caledon and the Orange. Then, when Sir Harry Smith annexed the territory between the Orange and the Vaal, including Lesotho, he personally assured Moshweshwe that the British regime would not interfere in his internal affairs or with his territorial rights, but the officer whom Smith appointed to administer the territory succumbed to pressures from the Europeans — including the Wesleyan missionaries who served the Coloured and African chiefs on the northern side of the Caledon, who claimed to be independent of Moshweshwe. First, he proclaimed a series of boundary lines that separated the territories of those chiefs from Lesotho. Then, when skirmishes broke out among the affected groups, he organized a coalition of the European, Coloured, and African communities against Moshweshwe and his allies. Moshweshwe, however, defeated this mixed force, repulsed an attack by British regular troops, and defeated Sekonyela and incorporated his people. This prompted the British to disannex the entire Orange-Vaal territory, leaving Moshweshwe face to face with the infant Orange Free State, without an agreed boundary between them.

The inevitable result was friction. Europeans and Africans raided each others' cattle and vied for control over disputed territory. In a war that broke out in 1858, the OFS commandos invaded Lesotho but broke and fled rather than attempt an assault on Thaba Bosiu. By the time fighting was resumed in 1865, however, Moshweshwe was aging and losing control over his subordinates; the OFS, by contrast had a young and vigorous president in J. H. Brand and a European population that had grown considerably. The OFS forces gradually got the upper hand by systematically destroying Sotho villages and crops, storming Sotho strongpoints, and persuading the chiefs to agree to treaties that deprived them of nearly all their arable land. But the commandos never managed to capture Thaba Bosiu, nor were they able to follow up their victories by effective occupation of the land they claimed to have conquered. Bands of Sotho maintained a spirited guerrilla resistance even after their chiefs had come to terms with the invaders. Moshweshwe, meanwhile, had repeatedly applied to the British authorities for protection, and this was granted in 1868 when Sir Philip Wodehouse, the High Commissioner, annexed "Basutoland." Moshweshwe died two years later. By that time British and OFS representatives had agreed on a boundary line that gave the OFS everything north of the Caledon and a considerable area between the lower Caledon and the Orange, leaving a truncated Basutoland consisting mainly of mountains, with only a narrow strip of arable land on the southern side of the Caledon.

The case of Moshweshwe and the southern Sotho illustrates the importance of three variables in the early contact situation: the style of African political leadership, the condition of the African society at the moment of the first substantial contact, and the class of Europeans who provided that contact. Because Moshweshwe was an exceptionally humane and intelligent man, and the southern Sotho were just recovering from the mfecane wars, and the first Europeans who settled in Lesotho were fairly sympathetic missionaries, Moshweshwe eagerly grasped their evangelical teachings as well as their material culture. But Sotho conservatives challenged the honeymoon relationship from the first because they resented missionary interference in their customs, and a reaction swept through the society when it became apparent that Afrikaner settlers were infiltrating their territory with the connivance of British officials, and that the missionaries were not capable of stopping them. By the end of the 1840s, nearly all Moshweshwe's councilors and kinsfolk who had been baptized had left the church and resumed the customs the missionaries had banned. During his later years, Moshweshwe himself revived the initiation schools and seems to have placed greater reliance on traditional remedies than on Christian precepts; and, though both Catholic and Protestant missionaries implored him to accept baptism as he lay on his deathbed at Thaba Bosiu, Moshweshwe died unbaptized.

CONCLUSION

By 1870, European power had increased considerably in southern Africa. The settler population of about 260,000 was slightly larger than that of Algeria at the same date. About 70 percent lived in the Cape Colony, most of the others in Natal and the two Afrikaner republics. Nevertheless, the scale of European migration to southern Africa was minute by comparison with that to North America. In the Cape Colony, from the west coast eastward to the Fish River, the Europeans were distinctly outnumbered by the Cape Coloured people. East of the Fish River — and in Natal and the Afrikaner republics — Bantu-speaking Africans formed a majority of the inhabitants in every district and on virtually every "farm." In the region as a whole (including the independent African territories south of the Zambezi as well as the colonies and republics), Bantu-speaking Africans outnumbered the Europeans by at least twelve to one.

In 1870, moreover, the entire region was still only peripheral to the capitalist economy of Europe and North America. The Cape Colony, as Hobart Houghton has said, was still "a sparsely populated country largely engaged in pastoral farming and self-subsistence agriculture, too poor to advance rapidly by domestic capital formation, and lacking any exploitable resources to attract foreign capital." [2] Cape Town, with about 30,000 people, was the only town with more than 10,000 inhabitants; internal communications were over rough roads, impassable after heavy rains; manufacturing industries were few and small; exports consisted exclusively of unprocessed primary produce, notably wool, and their value amounted to only about £2.5 million a year; and over 80 percent of the external trade was carried by British ships to British ports. Conditions were similar in Natal. In the republics, most Afrikaners were even more tenuously connected with the European or American economy; but they, too, were dependent on British trade channels for manufactured goods, for they had not been able to develop a trade route through the tsetse-infested country to Delagoa Bay.

The South African Europeans, like those at home or overseas in the United States, already assumed that they were biologically and socially superior to darker skinned peoples, even though pseudoscientific racism was to grow in virulence during the final third of the nineteenth century. But they themselves were divided. The British settlers saw themselves as offshoots of metropolitan British society and continued to look to Britain, in the last resort, for economic and military support. The Afrikaners had long since severed their connections with Europe, and, except for a fringe that was becoming anglicized in the colonies, they were suspicious of Great Britain and the colonial bureaucracies.

All the independent African chiefdoms were experiencing European influences by 1870. They were frequently visited by hunters and traders, and most of them had resident missionaries. Although the chiefs employed messengers to keep themselves informed about what was going on elsewhere, they never managed to combine to resist the intruders. In every phase of expansion, Europeans benefited from the divisions within and among chiefdoms. In 1835, voortrekkers were assisted by a Tswana chief when they drove Mzilikazi north of the Limpopo; in 1840, Mpande's followers fought the decisive battle that overthrew Dingane; Mfengu played major roles in the conquest of the southern Nguni; and the OFS used African allies in their wars against the southern Sotho.

By 1870, many African farmers were taking advantage of their new economic opportunities. As Colin Bundy has shown, many southern Nguni in particular were becoming peasants, in the sense that, while they continued to

[2] Monica Wilson and Leonard Thompson, eds., *The Oxford History of South Africa,* vol. 2 (New York: Oxford University Press, 1971), p. 4.

produce most of the food they consumed, they were also producing a surplus of grain, which they traded for imported goods. This development often began on mission stations where, freed from control by conservative traditional authorities, they experimented with new implements such as ploughs, new crops such as wheat, and new agricultural methods such as irrigation. The Mfengu were particularly eager innovators because their social system had been thoroughly disrupted by the mfecane wars. The southern Sotho also had a large grain surplus by the 1850s. Many Europeans in the eastern Cape and the republics acquired most of their grain from African cultivators.

But the capacity of African communities to become self-sufficient peasants, producing grain for exchange with white pastoralists, was offset by their land losses and by European demands for African labor. Wherever they settled in southern Africa, British immigrants as well as Afrikaners used dark-skinned laborers. In the eastern districts of the Cape Colony, Africans, not Coloured people, formed their main labor supply as they did in the republics and Natal (except for the coastal planters who employed Indians). In the Cape Colony, labor relations were regulated by Masters and Servants legislation, which did not overtly discriminate against people on racial grounds but which nevertheless assisted employers by making breach of contract a criminal offense. There, African farm laborers received rations and about $2 a month in cash or the equivalent in kind, such as a cow for a year's service. In the SAR, at the other extreme, farm officials were entitled to compel Africans to work for Afrikaners, and wages, if paid at all, were almost invariably in kind.

The Africans' response to Christianity varied with the efficacy of their traditional norms and institutions. So long as they were self-confident, they found no greater use for missionaries than as informants about the wider world, as scribes for communicating with European authorities, and (if possible) as suppliers of firearms and ammunition. This was still the case with the Zulu under Mpande. Mzilikazi, too, admitted a few missionaries to his kingdom north of the Limpopo, but he kept them isolated and did not allow his subjects to be baptized. But when an African community's confidence in its traditional norms and institutions had been seriously shaken, its members became interested in the missionaries for additional reasons — as sources of new magical powers and new social and political ideas that might help them to accommodate to their new circumstances.

Moshweshwe responded positively to the missionaries in 1833 because the confidence of his people had been shattered by the mfecane; but when it became apparent that his missionaries were not preventing other whites from encroaching on his territory, he confined them to subordinate roles and relied primarily on traditional sources of power. It was only later in the nineteenth century, after the southern Sotho had been brought under alien administration, that they became converted to Christianity in substantial numbers.

Few southern Nguni were converted so long as they felt capable of resisting conquest by military action. In the 1850s, after military resistance had failed repeatedly, some resorted to the drastic remedy of cattle killing — in obedience to the orders of their ancestors as revealed in a prophetic vision. The failure of that remedy made it clear that their traditional physical and spiritual resources no longer sufficed, and during the 1860s, for the first time, large numbers of southern Nguni adopted Christianity as a means of accommodating to the wider world.

SUGGESTIONS FOR FURTHER READING

Macmillan, W. M. *Bantu, Boer and Briton: The Making of the South African Native Problem.* Rev. ed. Oxford: Oxford University Press, Clarendon Press, 1963.

————. *The Cape Colour Question: A Historical Survey.* London: Faber and Gwyer, 1927.

Marais, Johannes S. *The Cape Coloured People, 1652–1937.* Reprinted from the 1939 ed. Johannesburg: Witwatersrand University Press, 1957.

Omer-Cooper, J. D. *The Zulu Aftermath: A Nineteenth Century Revolution in Bantu Africa.* London: Longman, 1966.

Ross, Robert. *Adam Kok's Griquas: A Study in the Development of Stratification in South Africa.* Cambridge: Cambridge University Press, 1976.

Thompson, Leonard. *Survival in Two Worlds: Moshoeshoe of Lesotho, 1786–1870.* Oxford: Oxford University Press, Clarendon Press, 1975.

Thompson, Leonard, ed. *African Societies in Southern Africa: Historical Studies.* London: Heinemann, 1969.

Van Jaarsveld, F. A. *The Afrikaner's Interpretation of South African History.* Capetown: Oxford University Press, 1964.

Walker, Eric A. *The Great Trek.* 5th ed. London: Black, 1965.

(See also the bibliography for Chapter 9.)

Chapter 11

North Africa
in the Shadow of Europe

(c. 1780-1880)

NORTH AFRICA, like southern Africa, met the European threat several decades before it became apparent to the people of the tropical belt between the Sahara and the Limpopo — but the threat was met early for different reasons in the north and south. The southern tip of Africa had been comparatively isolated from the intercommunicating zone until the maritime revolution of the fifteenth century, whereas North Africa had made contact with a wider world at an early date. Where the seventeenth-century establishment of a European community at the Cape was a new thing in African history, the Napoleonic invasion of Egypt in 1789 simply brought one more Frankish army to the Levant, where Frankish armies had marched from time to time since the eleventh century — just as North African armies had marched in Spain and Sicily and North African navies had often dominated the Mediterranean sea lanes. But the reappearance of European power at the end of the eighteenth century was something more than another swing of the pendulum. Europe was then beginning to enter the industrial age, which was to give the leading European states a new advantage in military power compared to the rest of the world. By the 1780s or so, Europe's technological advantage was great enough to be apparent to all but the most backward-looking, but Europe's potential power was not yet effective power. For North Africa, it became effective during the century that followed, first and most intensively for Egypt, last and most weakly for Morocco.

OTTOMAN REFORM

These developments must be seen in a broader perspective than that of Africa alone, even of North Africa. In theory, at least, the whole of North Africa other than Morocco was simply a set of Ottoman provinces ruled from Istanbul. In spite of its weakening control during the eighteenth century, the Ottoman Empire remained the pivotal political and military defense against the

Christian menace — not only for North Africa but for the Muslim world as a whole. The Ottoman state was a religious state, in a way that no Western state was. The sultan was not only a temporal ruler; he was also the recognized *khalifa,* the successor on earth of Muhammad himself. He ruled in his two different capacities — as administrative head and as a religious leader — through two separate sets of officials. One was the ordinary bureaucratic structure of government administration over provinces and their subdivisions, which was theoretically exercised through slave-administrators but in practice was exercised by local men whose de facto authority had to be recognized by Istanbul. The other was the religious and judicial hierarchy, drawn from the class of *'ulamā,* or Muslim clerics. These men supplied the *qadi,* or judges in Muslim law, both temporal and spiritual. Their hierarchy reached its own peak with the office of chief mufti, or seyh-ül-Islam, who could depose the sultan himself for a breach of Muslim law. The significant point is that the 'ulamā were a social and political body with power independent of the sultan.

After the mid-eighteenth century, central control tended to weaken throughout the empire, even as it did in the Maghrib and Egypt. Provincial magnates known as *âyan* increased the powers they had acquired through their wealth, land, or government positions as tax farmers. Some were provincial officials who, like the Karamanli family in Tripoli, made themselves virtually independent. But as the power of the royal slave-administrators declined, that of the slave-soldiers, or Janissaries, increased. Recruited as children from beyond the frontiers in much the same way as the Egyptian Mamluks or the sub-Saharan *'abid* forces in Morocco had been, the Janissaries constituted the core of the standing army. It was all too easy for any of these military groups to translate its physical power into political power that eventually came to be recognized and imbedded in the informal constitution of the state.

The external threat to the empire came first of all on the land frontiers with Austria and Russia. The first important territorial losses in Europe went back to 1699, and further cessions were made to Austria in 1718. In 1774, the Ottoman Empire experienced its first significant loss of Muslim-populated territory when the Crimea fell to Russia. In 1787–1792, the Ottomans recovered militarily in the war against Russia and Austria, but it was already clear that the Ottoman state would have to be thoroughly reformed if it was to survive over the long run.

For nineteenth-century commentators, "reform" meant much the same thing as "modernization" means today; it implied some adaptation of Western technology, at least military technology, in that the end purpose was to make the Ottoman Empire defensible against a major Western attack. The first really serious reform effort was made in 1792–93, when Sultan Selim III issued a comprehensive set of administrative and military regulations known collectively as the *Nizam-i Cedid,* the New Order. The immediate objective was to create a corps of regular infantry, trained and equipped along the same lines as European infantry of the period. This force needed officers trained in a new way, which

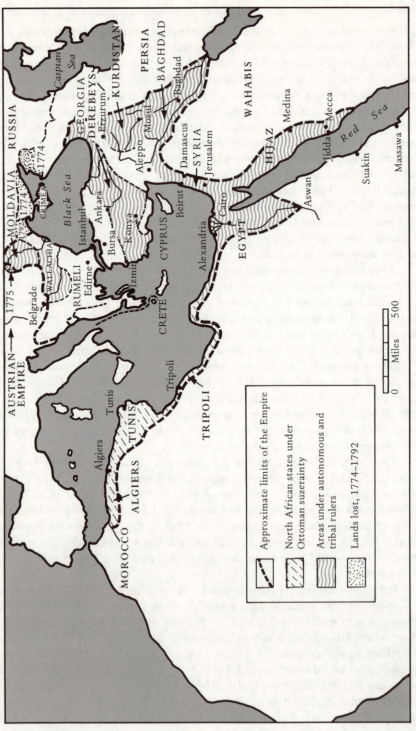

The Ottoman Empire, c. 1790

called for new military and naval schools, staffed initially by French officers. It also cost money, because it was intended to supplement rather than replace the Janissaries, and that in turn called for administrative and fiscal reform.

This effort produced two consequences that were to crop up again and again whenever the Ottoman government — or a North African government — tried to put through military reforms. First, it created a new class of people with power: the military officers with specialized Western training, many of them trained in western Europe. Second, it produced a desire for modernization; along with their technical training, these officers inevitably came into broader contact with Western culture, and they often came to admire some aspects of it. They might not end as avid Westernizers, but they were impressed by Ottoman military weakness in the face of Western power; and they were especially impressed, as the nineteenth century wore on, by the material wealth of industrial societies. In present-day terms, they would be called *modernizers* in the special sense of that term which regards the goal of modernization as the creation of one of the several kinds of societies capable of high levels of production and consumption — levels equivalent to those found in the most developed, technological societies of the time. Modernization in this sense could be many things to many people, not necessarily slavish imitation of the West.

The New Order thus introduced a modernizing military elite into Ottoman society, and it threatened the old order in several ways. By increasing the central government's need for money, it tightened the relaxed fiscal relations between the âyan (provincial magnates), and the central government. Fiscal reform alienated important people. Military reform threatened the Janissaries even more directly. Others saw the new technology as a possible source of contamination for Islam itself, because the new knowledge was infidel knowledge, and this fear was most prevalent among the 'ulamā. Military modernization, in short, might be essential to save the Ottoman state, but it also threatened to redistribute political and economic rewards within the state. The sultan and the New Order (as the new units were soon called) would gain, while the âyan, the Janissaries, and the 'ulamā would lose a little. In 1807, the conservatives rallied against the reforms, drove Selim from the throne, and returned to the old order. Thus, with modernization silenced for a generation in the Ottoman homeland, Egypt and the Maghrib were left to deal with Muslim weakness and Western strength in their own ways.

EGYPTIAN MODERNIZATION: THE FIRST STEPS

It was the province of Egypt, not the Turkish homeland, that took the first lasting steps toward modernization. Egypt was also the first major African state to be subdued militarily and occupied by a European power, and the two "firsts" were connected in ways that made the Egyptian experience a precedent for some and a warning for others, though it had special features that were uniquely Egyptian. The new kind of European threat began with the French occupation of 1798 to 1801, an event more directly tied to the strategy of the Napoleonic wars than it was to French intentions in Egypt itself. The Anglo-French wars of the eighteenth century were part of a worldwide competition for empire stretching from India to North America. The French move on Egypt was connected to the Indian strategy, and it was ended by British naval pressure on the French supply lines — not by an Ottoman counterattack.

The French occupation took place at a time when Egypt was peculiarly open to outside influence. Mamluk rule had reached a nadir in the 1790s. The Egyptian social structure found itself divided between the Mamluk aristocracy at the top and the ordinary peasants, or *fellahin,* at the bottom, with few in between to act as mediators. Some merchants had wealth, but their political power was insignificant. The 'ulamā had more power, but mainly through their religious prestige and command of the educational structure, at the apex of which was the mosque and school of al-Azhar. In these circumstances, the French presence was at once an example of Western power, visible to all, and of Western technological progress, visible only to some. It also disrupted whatever might have been left of the Mamluk political order.

After the French withdrawal, Istanbul once more sent in an effective military force. This balanced the remaining power of the Mamluks and opened the way for an enterprising individual to become the autonomous ruler of the Egyptian province. Muhammad 'Ali began as commander of the Albanian battalion of the Ottoman expeditionary force, a part of the New Order. Through astute maneuvering, he worked with the local 'ulamā to mobilize the middle ground of Egyptian opinion, taking advantage of factional divisions among the Mamluk aristocrats and representing himself as the champion of Egyptian interests against the alien authority of Ottomans and Mamluks alike. Istanbul acquiesced, as it had done so often in the past when confronted by local magnates, and appointed him *wali* of Egypt in 1805. His real power, however, began in 1807 after he had weathered a British naval landing at Alexandria. Selim III's deposition the same year left him free to run Egypt in his own way until his death in 1848.

Muhammad 'Ali's program in Egypt was a direct outgrowth of Selim III's New Order. The changes Muhammad 'Ali made were clearly designed to modernize and strengthen the military force, but military power was not necessarily an end in itself. It is less clear what Muhammad 'Ali had as his ultimate goal. It was certainly not Egyptian greatness or national independence, nor even an early form of Arab nationalism against the Turks. Muhammad 'Ali and his group ruled whatever Arab provinces they could control, but they recognized ultimate Ottoman suzerainty, and the language of administration continued to be Turkish, not the Arabic speech of the country. It could of course be argued that strengthening Egypt was a step toward strengthening Islam against the infidel Europeans, but Muhammad 'Ali was willing to work with Europeans when it suited his purposes, and to work against Ottoman power most of the time. His actions suggest that he was mainly interested in establishing his own power and that of his friends over as large a section of the Ottoman Empire as they could comfortably control.

The intermediate goal of military modernization itself called for sweeping changes in Egyptian society. Some of the most crucial were in education. The existing educational system was based on the village Koranic schools. Higher levels of study led on to the training given the 'ulamā to fit them for leadership in religious and judicial affairs. None of this met the need for military officers and bureaucrats conversant with Western technology. Muhammad 'Ali simply bypassed the existing system without seeking to reform it, creating instead a system of secular state schools modeled on those of Italy and France. Initially, they were staffed by Western teachers, then by Egyptians trained in Europe, and finally, after the mid-century, by Egyptians trained in the system itself.

The government created ancillary services to supplement the new educational establishment. A state printing press brought out books in Arabic — with the help of a translation bureau to make Western knowledge more readily available — military technology at first, then the sciences, and finally even literature. The program also included specialized higher education, with a medical school to begin with, followed by an engineering school modeled on the French Polytechnique. By 1849, its director was a Western-trained Egyptian engineer.

A secular, modernizing program of this kind might have appeared as a threat to the 'ulamā, especially to those attached to al-Azhar mosque. Similar programs *were* seen as a threat in other Muslim countries and would be, later in the century, in Egypt, but, in the first instance, important Azharites looked on Western learning as a way of reforming al-Azhar itself. Egyptian literature and scholarship had a deeply pessimistic tone in the last decades of the eighteenth century. People were alarmed for the safety of Islamic society; but they were not alarmed enough to loose their belief in the ultimate value of the Arabic language and Islamic culture; and Western knowledge, it was thought, could help rejuvenate older traditions. The translation program, for example, called for new attention to Arabic language studies. It began at the technical level with a search for the Arabic equivalent of Western scientific concepts, but it moved on into a much broader renewal of Arabic literary studies, with attention to classical Arabic as well as the language of ordinary speech, which began to take on literary form through the rise of a newspaper press.

Economic development was an obvious necessity for military modernization. Muhammad 'Ali began with a program aimed at wide industrialization, with government-operated factories turning out products as diverse as textiles, sugar, paper, glass, arms, and chemicals. Later, emphasis shifted to the more lopsided development of long-staple cotton for export in return for European manufactures. This required capital investment of another kind to make possible summer cultivation during the season of the low Nile. Animal power and some water-powered devices had been used for centuries to raise water to the fields when the Nile was low, but extensive cultivation called for mechanical pumps, or else canals to carry the water from dams far upstream. All this required enormous capital investment, and Egyptian conversion to year-round cultivation was only begun in Muhammad 'Ali's time. The most important spurts were to come later, during the British occupation toward the end of the nineteenth century, and again, after independence was regained, with the building of the Aswan high dam in the 1960s. The decision to concentrate Egypt's resources on production for export rather than on diversified industry may well have been correct in terms of short-run gain for the Egyptian state. In the long run, however, it slanted the economy toward a dangerous and fragile dependence on one crop with minimal protection against shifts in the world market.

The government also needed to redistribute the national income so that more would go to the state to pay for all these programs, and less to private citizens. The first and easiest step was to expropriate the wealth of the Mamluks and other tax farmers left from the old regime. In addition, Muhammad 'Ali revolutionized Egyptian land tenure. Where tax farmers had once been virtual landlords drawing unearned income from the work of the fellahin, now a new land survey made it possible to tax the peasants directly. This increased state revenue, though it may have decreased the real living standards of ordinary farmers. Some of the land was also given to Muhammad 'Ali's family and other supporters, who held it tax-free. State monopolies provided another source of government revenue. The government monopolized all exports, buying agricultural products at a fixed and low price and selling them on the world market at a much higher price.

Though Muhammad 'Ali is usually called a modernizer, he was one only in a restricted sense of the term. The end product was a modern army in the European fashion, but, at mid-century, the Egyptian economy and society were less, not more, able to move on toward the autonomous development of a balanced economy capable of high productivity and high consumption. Raising agricultural production through state action set the stage for a later weakening of the class of small tradesmen, of the merchant class, and of the 'ulamā, while simultaneously it strengthened the power of the bureaucracy, the army, and foreign commercial interests. That result, however, was hardly apparent until the final third of the century.

Meanwhile, Muhammad 'Ali's payoff was a military establishment strong enough to enable him to assert his independence within the Ottoman Empire and then to expand his control beyond Egypt. In the 1810s, he sent military expeditions into Arabia against the Wahabi movement; this gave Egypt control of the holy cities of Mecca and Medina. Later, in the 1830s, Egypt occupied Syria and Palestine and threatened a successful attack on Istanbul itself. The prospect of Muhammad 'Ali as a new Ottoman sultan, however, brought in the balancing mechanisms of the European state system. Britain had traditionally supported Istanbul against other powers, especially against Austria or Russia. France, for its part, had patronized Muhammad 'Ali. Now France and Britain stopped his drive to the north by a private agreement that he should not be allowed to take

Istanbul; but they did allow his claim to the hereditary pashalik of Egypt — later under the superior title of khedive — while recognizing the ultimate, if theoretical, sovereignty of the sultan.

SECONDARY EMPIRE IN THE NILOTIC SUDAN

Meanwhile, from the 1820s, Muhammad 'Ali's forces had been active south of the Sahara, and this push up the Nile into the Sudan had a different character from the struggles over Ottoman provinces. The new conquests lay beyond any previous Ottoman territory, and they fit into a pattern that was to be extremely common to tropical Africa in the nineteenth century — new conquests that have sometimes been categorized as "secondary empires." This type of empire-building was secondary in the sense that African states expanded against their neighbors by using the new technology whose ultimate source was Europe, yet the empire builders, whether Africans or overseas Europeans, were free from direct European control.

Viewed schematically, the process was simple, though capable of infinite variation. Again and again through history, people who suddenly gained command of a military innovation could lord it over those who remained ignorant. It had happened with the first use of chariots, again with the first cavalry, still later with armored heavy cavalry. It happened repeatedly during the nineteenth century as rapid-fire weapons were carried beyond their source in Europe. It was not, perhaps, inevitable that those who first gained control of the new weapons should use them to create large territorial units — that they should become empire builders — but the temptation was always present.

The position of these empire builders on the periphery was also different from those at the center — in this case, from the Europeans whose technology created the new differentials in military power. Because the Europeans had the knowledge and the industrial plant to create new devices and thus to preserve their lead, they had an advantage that was to be available for decades and even centuries. On the periphery, by contrast, whoever first came into control of European weapons had a comparatively ephemeral advantage, good only until his neighbors had done the same. In the Ottoman Empire, for example, the first to master the use of New Order troops gained an advantage, as Muhammad 'Ali did for Egypt, but others could and did follow the same path within a few decades. (Muhammad 'Ali's power in Ottoman affairs was also always limited to what states at the center of industrialization, like Britain and France, were willing to put up with.) On the periphery, in the Nilotic Sudan, guns and European tactics were still unfamiliar. The Egyptian advantage was that much greater there, even though it was still temporary. This transitional quality may help to explain why people with a windfall advantage were tempted to use it before it disappeared, and why new military techniques spread so rapidly beyond the original center of diffusion.

This phenomenon was not confined to the offshoots of industrialization.

The Zulu technique of fighting in disciplined infantry, or *impi,* formations owed nothing to Europe, yet it spread through southern Africa from the first decade of the nineteenth century in the great mfecane, laying a train of secondary empire–building stretching from Natal northwest to western Zambia and north more than a thousand miles into what was to be central Tanzania. In southern Africa, nearly simultaneously, European settlers developed an effective tactic of fighting partly on foot, partly on horseback for mobility. They could beat the Zulu impi, as it turned out, but their technique had less revolutionary effect when employed against the Xhosa beyond the Fish River frontier, because the Xhosa themselves had adopted the same tactics. In this case, the periphery of diffusion had passed beyond the periphery of settler expansion before the Afrikaners were able to capitalize on their advantage. With the Great Trek, however, the Afrikaners could catch up and outdistance the periphery of diffusion by moving onto the high veld and down into central Natal. There, they could enjoy the same kind of advantage the Zulu had enjoyed against undisciplined infantry a generation earlier. One possible interpretation, therefore, is to see both the offshoots of the mfecane and the offshoots of the Great Trek as secondary empires, one with its roots in Zululand, the other based partly on the distant technological center in Europe and partly on innovations carried out by European settlers in the Cape Colony and its fringes.

The Egyptian conquest of the Nilotic Sudan was more distinctly based on European models, and it foreshadowed more clearly the kinds of secondary empire–building that were to follow in tropical Africa during the nineteenth century. The military innovation again involved firearms, as it did with the Boer mounted infantry, but the problem of slow reloading time for muzzle-loaded muskets was met in a different way. This time, musketeers were given intensive training in disciplined loading and firing by ranks, and this was combined with the use of mobile field artillery.

These tactics, already used in Europe during the eighteenth century, were to change in the nineteenth with the invention of newer, more accurate, and faster-firing guns. In effect, Europe was on the eve of a permanent revolution in military technology that would give secondary empires a longer lease on life. Those with access to the latest European weapons after 1850 or so could count on meeting enemies with the last generation's weapons in their hands. In the immediate situation of the 1820s, however, Muhammad 'Ali's modernized armies fought with the weapons and tactics used in Europe during the Napoleonic wars, though at this point nothing quite so elaborate and overpowering was actually required against the peoples of the Nilotic Sudan.

The rain-watered land south of the desert and the desert fringes then comprised a patchwork of different political organizations — some sedentary along the Nile valley, including the desert Nile through Nubia, others nomadic in different ways. Arab infiltration had produced a change in language and culture over recent centuries. Although the net Arabian contribution to the gene pool of the present-day northern Sudan is estimated at only about 5 to 10 percent, most of the nomadic peoples and some of the sedentaries had become Arabic-speaking by the nineteenth century. The result was similar, in fact, to the Arabic impact on the Maghrib, where about the same addition to the population had also brought a widespread change in language. As in the Maghrib, where Berber persisted in the mountains and some of the desert fringes, islands of Nubian speech persisted at a few points on the Nile and in some highland regions. The Beja nomads of the Red Sea hills also kept their original language and much of their older culture, though they too had long since become Muslim. Other nomadic cultures were more strongly Arabian, especially that of the camel nomads who occupied the desert fringes from the latitude of Sennar to the great southward bend of the desert Nile. The *baqarra*, or cattle-keeping nomads, occupied another ecological niche in better-watered lands further south, equivalent to that of the Fulbe of West Africa; they too took on a good deal of Arabic culture along with the Arabic language.

The Nilotic Sudan in the Nineteenth Century

The Arabian cultural penetration was much weaker among sedentary people, and it stopped somewhat short of the point where the *sudd* blocked the Nile as a viable transportation route. The people here and further south were mainly Nilotes, related to the Lwo who had moved off into East Africa (see Chapter 4). The Shilluk lived along the White Nile, principally on its west bank, and were densely settled in a society estimated at about a million people in the early nineteenth century. Although the effective political unit was the village, the Shilluk also had an elaborately stratified society with a complex political ideology and institutions of a central state in which the god-king was intimately related to the fertility of the earth. If he became ill or old, he was killed and a more fitting man set in his place.

To the south of the sudd and on to the west of the main Nile lived other Nilotes in stateless societies like those of the Dinka and Nuer, with a complex adaptation to their difficult environment with its seasonal alternations between drought and flood. These and similar ill-organized peoples had long been subject to sporadic slave raids from the northern Sudan, which fed the trickle of slaves exported north to Egypt or across the Red Sea to Arabia. The main agents of the slave trade — and the main agents of Muslim cultural penetration to the south — were merchants, usually called *jallaba,* the Sudanese Arabic word for petty trader. Many were Ja'ali, Arabized Nubians from the desert reaches of the Nile. They claimed aristocratic ancestry in Arabia, but their physical appearance and most of their culture were more Nubian than Arabian. A few still spoke Nubian, but most had shifted to Arabic as the home language. Political troubles in their Nubian homeland in the eighteenth century had driven many of the Ja'ali to the south and west, some as far as Darfur and others up the White Nile, where they were to play an increasingly active political and economic role in the nineteenth century.

In 1820–21, when Muhammad 'Ali began his attack up the Nile, the region's political structures were even weaker than they had usually been in the past. The Funj state of Sennar was limited to the *gezira* itself, the area between the Blue and White Niles. Kordofan to the west was under the vague hegemony of the Sultanate of Darfur. The Nubian Nile was politically divided, with some sections under nomadic Arab domination, while the region around Dongola had fallen to refugee Mamluks from Egypt. Muhammad 'Ali's first objective was this remaining center of Mamluk power, because a buildup of Mamluk power in the south could constitute a political threat at a later moment of crisis. Once he controlled the Nubian Nile, he could tap the source of slaves among the Nilotes, and slaves were important as military manpower to an Egyptian state that preferred not to draft the native fellahin.

Muhammad 'Ali's initial expeditionary force was only 4,000 men, roughly the size of the army Morocco had sent against Songrai in the sixteenth century. It had to fight the Mamluks for control of Nubia, but at the mere threat of force the Funj sultanate surrendered. The Egyptians then detached Kordofan from Darfur and added it to the core of a new empire. By the mid-1820s, they had recruited another army by purchase in the far south and trained it to serve as the occupying force. Khartoum, where the Blue and White Niles join, became the capital of the Egyptian Sudan, but the new government was not very active otherwise. It confiscated many slaves belonging to the former Sudanese aristocracy, reopened trade up and down the Nile valley, but made no serious effort to change either the society or the economy. Even the frontiers first established were left virtually unchanged until the 1860s.

GOVERNMENT AND SOCIETY IN THE MAGHRIB: THE OTTOMAN REGENCIES

The external threat to the Maghrib was much the same as it was to Egypt and the Ottoman Empire, and it posed much the same problems. At the heart of these problems was military weakness, but military reforms cost money. New revenue would require administrative and political change, raising once more the basic question: Who should control the power of the state? This last question was even more complex in the Maghrib than it was in Egypt, because here the distribution of political power was more diverse.

In Tripoli, the Karamanli family continued as hereditary pashas acting under their own authority, but they succeeded only by balancing off the quasi-independent power of important groups such as the commerce-raiders' guilds and other merchants in the port against the influence of the nomads and seminomadic leaders from the hinterland. During the long reign of Yusuf Karamanli (1795–1835), European naval powers began to take a stronger stand against commerce raiding. Even the distant United States mounted counterraids against Tripoli during the Napoleonic wars. After Waterloo, the British and French consuls became more active in Tripolitanian affairs. In this situation, the Karamanli did nothing to modernize the military establishment, thus becoming potential prey to any power that did. The Anglo-French rivalry kept both from acting on their own, but the revived Ottoman power, the Bey of Tunis to the north, or even Muhammad 'Ali of Egypt were potential and increasing threats to the Karamanli after the 1820s.

The crisis came in the early thirties, with the nomads of the steppe, the Tunisians, and the threat of British or French intervention all playing a role. The victory, however, went to an expeditionary force from Istanbul, which deposed the Karamanli dynasty and reimposed direct Ottoman rule. That situation was to last until the Italian invasion of 1911–12, but Turkish control was hardly more extensive than that of the Karamanli themselves, and the hinterland of Cyrenaica soon fell under the effective control of a religious brotherhood based on desert oases.

In the second half of the eighteenth century, Tunisia too had settled down under its own dynasty, though here the beys, unlike the Karamanli, still recognized Ottoman authority in theory. By 1800, the Tunisian beylic had moved further away from Turkish influence than either of the other two regencies had.

Turkish presence in military and court circles was weaker. The ports were better articulated with the life of the hinterland and less dependent on commerce raiding. Yet the European threat was felt earlier and more strongly here than it was elsewhere. In spite of Anglo-French rivalries, the consuls forced the Tunisian beys to change some of their policies and to concede important trade and economic advantages, including the abolition of slavery in 1819. Partly to counter this pressure, Tunis moved faster than either of the other regencies to modernize its army and to abolish the remaining Janissaries, though these reforms still came later than they did in either Istanbul or Cairo.

The prosperity of the Deylic of Algiers, built on commerce raiding, had declined sharply after 1750 or so, as the Christian powers were better able to protect their commerce and less willing to pay protection money. Spain still controlled a series of port towns, or *presidios,* scattered along the Moroccan-Algerian coast from Ceuta east to Oran, but Spain relinquished Oran in 1791, and Algiers was less disturbed by consular pressure on government affairs than Tunis and Tripoli were.

But Algiers had special problems in its hinterland. By 1800, the dey himself had become the political tool of the Turkish garrison and certain factions of the local port oligarchy, and his direct authority was recognized only in the province of Algiers. Further afield, the country had fallen under the control of three beys, each exercising within his own beylic the same kind of authority the dey exercised over his own province. But the dey and the beys together controlled only about a sixth of the present republic. Arab and Berber nomads controlled the desert fringes to the south. The Kabylia, a densely populated mountain area, was an independent Berber-speaking enclave stretching east from the vicinity of Algiers nearly to Constantine. Similar Berber mountaineers in the Aurès mountains were independent in fact most of the time, often in theory as well. Still other regions were autonomous under the leadership of important Muslim brotherhoods, and many important family heads could assert an independent power against the authority of a bey or the dey himself. It was not merely that the power of Algiers gradually dwindled with distance from the port; the whole territory was pockmarked with different kinds of local government, each differently related to the authorities in Algiers or even completely independent.

THE SHERIFIAN EMPIRE OF MOROCCO

Morocco was similar in having a variety of authorities variously related to the central government, the crucial difference being that here a local dynasty stood at the head of the government, whereas the authority of the deys and beys derived from the Ottomans. The sultans of the Sherifian Empire of Morocco found still another source of support in their descent from the Prophet, the prestige of religious authority giving them a shadowy national leadership. The idea of nationality is so suggestive of nineteenth-century Europe that it can be misleading to use the term "nation" of any African state. Yet nineteenth-century Morocco had some of the attributes of nationhood; people over a vast stretch of territory recognized their ultimate allegiance to the sultan and identified themselves with the Sherifian Empire — not only in present-day Morocco but in what was later to be the Spanish Sahara, Mauritania, and large parts of southern Algeria and northern Mali. But the territory of allegiance and the territory of effective government were quite distinct, and they were so recognized at the time. In either Asante or Buganda, the king's authority reached more uniformly to the frontiers than it did in Morocco, where the zone of close control was known as the *bled el makhzen* (literally "government country"), and the wider regions of more tenuous allegiance as the *bled es siba*. The latter term is usually translated as "country in dissidence," but that translation obscures the main point; people in these regions might not always obey the sultan or pay taxes, but they did recognize his authority.

Makhzen, as a collective term, was not simply the government of the·day. It was a social and political group centered on the sultan but including in the first circle of power his ministers, a council of notables, the *caïd* (provincial governors), and the *qadi* (judges in Islamic law). It was also overwhelmingly Arabic or Arabized Berber in speech and culture. Because the *makhzen* was such a broad group, the sultan's personal will could not be fully enforced, even within the bled el makhzen. Some members of the inner circle had their own independent sources of authority. They were therefore hard to control and even harder to remove from office. It was taken for granted that they and most other officeholders would try to enrich themselves, but they were also representatives of broader circles of interest in which the sultan's immediate lineage constituted only one element. This broader circle included the 'ulamā, who formed a pool of trained manpower and who supplied men to the post of qadi. It included the urban commercial people, who also occupied some government posts, especially in finance. And it included four specific extended lineages of nomadic Arabs, descended from those who had come to the Maghrib with the Hilalians in the eleventh century and later. These "tribes" were known collectively as the *gish* (literally "army"). They had a special obligation to support the sultan in case of need. Earlier, in the eighteenth century, the officers of the corps of slave-soldiers recruited in sub-Saharan Africa would also have counted as an important element in the makhzen, but they were not important in the nineteenth.

The makhzen, then, governed the bled el makhzen in much the same way the Dey of Algiers and his following governed the province of Algiers. This bled el makhzen changed size and shape from time to time, but/it normally included two great areas of comparatively flat and fertile land: the triangle Fez-Meknès-Rabat and north along the coast to Tangier, and a second triangle from Rabat southward to Marrakesh and west to the Atlantic at Mogador. Fez was the nineteenth-century capital, but Meknès, Rabat, and Marrakesh were also imperial cities that had once served that role. The four together formed the urban core of the bled el makhzen, along with Tangier, where the European consuls kept their residences and where most foreign relations were conducted.

The bled es siba lay beyond, governed by other authorities in other ways. Some of the siba territory was just as tightly controlled as the bled el makhzen, but it was governed differently. A large part of it was the land of the sedentary Berbers of the Atlas and Rif mountains, just as similar people in the Algerian Kabylia and Aurès went their own ways. Much of the rest was nomadic or semi-nomadic. In either case, the underlying political system was based on patri-lineages of varying depth. Among the nomadic and seminomadic peoples, the ultimate patrilineage could be very large, including thousands if not tens of thousands of people, usually calling themselves by the name of their earliest common ancestor, such as the Banu Hillal in Arabic or the Aït Atta in Berber, meaning in either case "the children of Hillal" or the "children of Atta."

The very largest lineages, however, were usually too big to be effective po-litical units. People still recognized an allegiance to the larger kinship units — sometimes called "tribes" or "confederations" (the terminology is not standard-ized) — but more effective governance came through more manageable subsec-tions. Nomads generally had larger effective kinship units than sedentary peoples did. Among sedentary Berbers, the most effective large unit was usually a patri-local village, ruled by a council made up of the heads of lineage subsections, although more intimate aspects of social and economic life were governed by the extended family that could actually live and work together. Villages, in turn, could be grouped together in units of three or four, managed collectively by a similar council. Even so, the unit rarely exceeded eight hundred or so extended families, and larger units tended to break down if they grew much beyond that size.

At the local level, the sedentary Berber political system operated very much like the segmentary political systems south of the Sahara, say, among the Tiv or the Ibo of Nigeria. The point of departure was the fact that only one line of descent, the male line, was taken into account. Each person therefore belonged unambiguously to a single lineage, but that single lineage could be defined by breaking off at one of several possible points up the line toward more and more remote ancestors. It could include merely the children of the same father, or the same grandfather; but, the further back the ancestor, the larger the politically effective lineage.

Lineage units of this kind could play many different roles in many different kinds of societies, and they could also take the place of regular government. Peo-ple naturally join together when threatened by outsiders. When insiders and outsiders were defined by kinship, a threat to one individual became a threat to that person's kinfolk as well, and in a segmentary system, people tended to respond according to their place on the ladder of kinship. If, for example, one of a set of brothers was attacked by his cousin in the male line (father's brother's son), the brothers, along with any junior kinsmen, would be expected to come

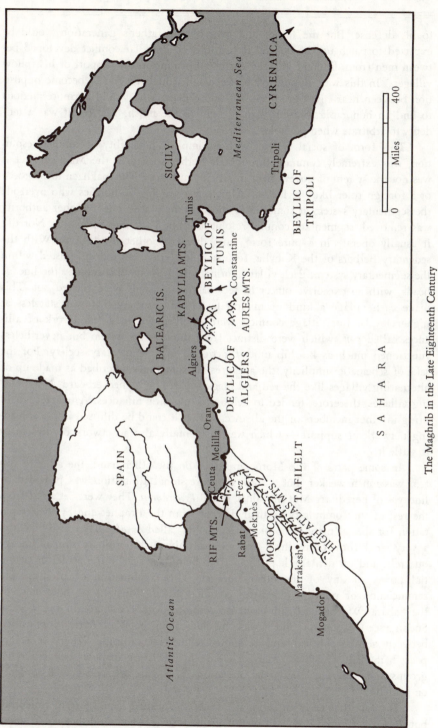

The Maghrib in the Late Eighteenth Century

to his defense. But the father and men of the father's generation would be expected to patch up the quarrel if possible. If a similar conflict developed between men from different villages, each could count on the support of his fellow villagers. In this way, opposition between individuals tended to become opposition between near-equal groups — including many who would be more anxious to find an honorable solution than to fight to the finish. The result was a tendency to arbitrate when possible.

This form of social system, with its implicit possibility of conflict resolution, was extremely common throughout Berber society in the Maghrib, but it was not the system of government in all circumstances. The makhzen in Morocco or a foreign ruler like the Dey of Algiers were higher authorities who overrode the segmentary system at some times and in some places, but if higher authority was removed, segmentary conflict resolution came back into operation. Nor did it usually operate in a pure form, unmodified by other institutions. With the sedentary Berbers of the Kabylia, for example, permanent officers existed within the segmentary system. Each village normally had a council chosen by the lineage heads, with an executive officer to see that its decisions were carried out. This made each village a kind of microstate within a society that was stateless at higher levels. Intervillage conflicts were resolved within a framework of alliances called ςoff, which were distinct from the kinship system but nevertheless functioned much as kinship units functioned in a segmentary society. For the sake of schematic simplicity, the alliances are sometimes described as made up of alternating villages like the red and black squares on a checkerboard. Neighboring villages, therefore, tended to belong to opposing alliances. A quarrel would bring in other members of the alliance, so that it could be diffused into a spreading network of support — which was incidentally also a network of diplomacy to settle it.

In some parts of the Moroccan Atlas, on the other hand, the alliance system was much weaker, but a form of professional arbitration was provided by lineages of hereditary Muslim saints, called *Igurramen*. They were set apart from the rest of the community by their descent from the Prophet and by their reputation for special piety or holiness, the quality called *baraka*. They also practiced a very strict form of pacifism that set them above the ordinary run of lineage quarrels, and incidentally kept them from being a threat to the actual or potential power of any of the other lineages. This combination of pacifism and renunciation of political office was common among Muslims on both sides of the Sahara. We have already seen it combined with commerce in the western Sudan (see Chapter 6), and it was one element in the West African opposition between secular-political and religious-commercial callings. Wherever it appeared, it made possible a role for clerics in mediating disputes between other groups and generally easing the operations of a stateless society that bordered on anarchy.

The fact that their sanctions were merely spiritual kept Igurramen neutral, but they nevertheless exercised real, if disinterested, power, and they could sometimes make a bid for direct secular power — as, indeed, had happened with the Alawite dynasty still ruling in the nineteenth century.

The kind of power exercised by these communities of saints shaded off into another kind of religious power exercised by the heads of the sufi brotherhoods. The headship of a brotherhood was not necessarily passed by inheritance from father to son as sainthood was, and spiritual and political leadership was held by only one man, not by the whole community; but whenever central governments weakened these orders tended to make themselves into governments or quasi-governments. Even within the bled el makhzen, the important marabouts, as the French were to call them, were men to be consulted by a wise ruler.

Alongside regions of segmentary society and those with strong clerical influence, a more secular and autocratic kind of chiefdom was also found in the Moroccan bled es siba. Off to the south, a number of large nomadic Arab lineages dominated the region toward the Atlantic and on down to the Senegal valley, where the Ma'qil leaders of the Trarza, Brakna, or the Mbarek occupied the steppe and barely recognized the distant sultan. In the equivalent steppe position to the north of the desert, the Aït Atta, a very powerful Berber confederacy, dominated both the steppe and the important oases based on the flow of mountain rainfall toward the Sahara. In the Berber-speaking Atlas itself, powerful chiefdoms existed alongside stateless areas. These came into existence when a particular lineage played the politics of segmentary opposition so successfully that it became dominant within its region. In the late nineteenth century, a leader of this kind dominated the eastern Rif mountains from Tetuán to Tangier, while the western Rif was stateless. In the high Atlas, four great Berber rulers of similar origins shared control over the mountains with pockets of segmentary society.

Relations between the makhzen and any of these principalities or stateless areas were highly variable. The great lords of the Atlas were sometimes at war with the sultan or in open rebellion. At other times, the sultan would give one of them an official appointment as caïd over the territory he controlled in any case on his own authority. The sultan's main authority over the siba country was religious, inherited by descent from the Prophet, accepted and respected by the urban 'ulamā. As a result, his actual influence was largely diplomatic rather than political, but indirect influence could be supplemented by an occasional show of force. Periodically, he would call out part of the army for a *harka*, or military procession through some part of the bled es siba. The operation was partly a way of collecting taxes, partly a show of the sultan's power and prestige, but mainly a way of putting him in touch with important people who were normally beyond his control.

Some sultans were more successful than others, and the size of the makhzen, as well as the sultan's influence within it, rose and fell. Among recent centuries, however, the nineteenth was generally a period of strong makhzen. Mulai Hassan (1873–1894) was among the most successful of all. At a time when so much of the rest of Africa was falling under foreign control, he brought in military and administrative reforms to strengthen the regime within its own territory, and he carried out an active military and diplomatic program on the periphery. By that time, however, France was not simply a distant power overseas; it had become an established neighbor on the Moroccan-Algerian frontier.

THE FRENCH IN ALGERIA

The French attack on Algiers in 1830 seems out of its proper time. The main conquest of Africa took place only after 1880. Even in the far south, the Great Trek had not yet begun. European concern with North African affairs in the early nineteenth century centered further east on Cairo, Istanbul, or even Tunis. The Ottoman Empire was a part of the European state system, and it lay at the core of the "Eastern question." In European eyes, Algiers, Tangier, or Tripoli were merely weak nests of commerce raiders, and the French attack on Algiers began in the same style as the American raid on Tripoli — as an application of European muscle to force weak states to toe the line, without territorial acquisition as a conscious goal. On this occasion, it started with an unsettled debt. The Dey of Algiers then insulted the French consul. France demanded redress with a naval blockade that was allowed to escalate into a military attack on Algiers and two other ports, at which point the dey surrendered, ceding all his powers to the French government. Having acquired something that looked valuable, French officials were then tempted to keep it; and the circumstances of French politics made it possible for them to do so.

In fact, France acquired only what the dey had had, which was a great deal less than control over Algeria. For that matter, a good deal of the dey's diplomatic influence in the hinterland disappeared when he vanished to a well-heeled exile in Italy. The French conquest of Algeria therefore began only *after* the seizure of Algiers itself, and it lasted at least until 1872 and the final military operations against the Kabylia. During these four decades, the French military leaders not only carried out extensive military operations; they also began to create piecemeal a series of policies that were to form an important precedent for French colonial rule in other parts of Africa.

The Algerians, for their part, sometimes collaborated with the new regime, even as they had collaborated in part with the Turks in Algiers. Sometimes they resisted French aggression, and again their resistance was of the same order as the Moroccan siba country's resistance to the makhzen. It.was, of course, heightened by the fact that the French were infidels, but the religious difference was not always crucial. Few Algerians were imbued with the idea that a united and powerful Algerian state was desirable. For most, the political unity of a large territory was a deplorable emergency measure, to be ended as soon as possible once the emergency was over.

Resistance to the French was endemic from the beginning; sometimes it involved armed resistance by the existing political authorities, sometimes wider movements organized under religious leadership. These were important in the early 1830s, but they were superseded in the late 1830s and on to 1847 by a new and larger movement centered in western Algeria. It was both anti-French and pro-Muslim, and it was also revolutionary in its attempt to create a new state with a modern administration and army.

The leader of this movement was ʿAbd al-Qādir, son of the local head of the Qādirīya, the most important of Muslim brotherhoods. He began with a center of power south of Oran, a little beyond the immediate reach of the French armies. His first effort was not so much to drive the French into the sea as to contain them in the ports they already controlled. But ʿAbd al-Qādir realized that this would require a new kind of state with a more effective administration than the contemporaneous Moroccan makhzen. It would mean in the longer run an end to the complex lineage institutions of the old political order, and it called for a new-style military organization to enforce unification as well as to resist the French. It called, in short, for the kind of military modernization that Muhammad ʿAli had undertaken in Egypt.

Meanwhile, ʿAbd al-Qādir had to use the symbols of power that already existed. At first, he did not even claim political independence but put himself under the temporal and spiritual protection of his neighbor, the Sherifian Sultan of Morocco. He also took the title of *amīr al-muʾminīn,* commander of the faithful, the same title used by contemporaneous leaders of religious revolution south of the Sahara. And he set out to create a regular government administration that would combine some aspects of a bureaucratic hierarchy with recognition of the power that was. For each district he appointed a deputy of *khalifa.* They in turn recognized and worked through the existing authority of lineage chiefs and others who would join the cause. These men were appointed to the title of *agha,* so that they could act in the name of the central government; but they were also controlled to a degree by agents ʿAbd al-Qādir assigned each of them to supervise fiscal and military affairs.

Up to 1841, the French did not engage him in all-out war, and he used the respite to organize and establish his authority. In the process he had to force some tribal groupings into submission, and he had to fight the *shaykh* of the important and rival sufi order, the Tijānīya. The core of his military power was a small standing army of about 10,000 men, trained by European advisers and fighting with recent-model weapons. But his chief tactic against the French was to avoid open combat insofar as possible and instead to depend on hit-and-run raids against French strongpoints. This gave a certain fluidity to the battle lines, but, at the height of his power, ʿAbd al-Qādir was recognized as ruler of about two-thirds of Algeria north of the desert.

After 1841, the official French policy of limited occupation turned to one of outright conquest, including a direct confrontation with ʿAbd al-Qādir's new order. It turned out to be a harder task than anyone in France expected. By 1844, the French were forced to attack Morocco as well in order to cut off outside support. By 1846, they had put some 110,000 troops into the field, or a third of the entire French army. In 1847, they finally defeated 'Abd al-Qādir, who was betrayed to the French and carried off as a prisoner.

But the end of 'Abd al-Qādir was not yet the beginning of full French rule. Even where the French did rule, they often did so by recognizing a local authority as *bashaga,* just as 'Abd al-Qādir had done in his own zone. This meant that their ability to enforce their orders varied a good deal according to the time and place. Religious leaders continued to organize sporadic revolts. The French garrison had to face a "rebellion" somewhere almost every year from the late 1840s through the 1850s. The most serious of these came in 1871, in circumstances that were more nearly those of initial conquest over a region forced to submit to French rule for the first time. It began with a comparatively minor incident, with one of the local bashagas launching a limited campaign that was partly anti-French and partly an attack on a rival *çoff,* or alliance grouping. That outbreak, however, triggered a rising of the whole Kabylia under the shaykh of the Rahmanīyya, who managed to rally a number of other religious fraternities to his cause. Within a short time, the rebels had captured the whole mountain region from the outskirts of Algiers some 200 miles east along the coast, and south to the edge of the desert. But these people lacked the arms and training 'Abd al-Qādir had tried to organize thirty years earlier. The French army moved in with a swift and punitive repression, though it cost them nearly 3,000 men to crush the rebels.

The two decades on either side of 1870 were the period when French Algeria crystallized into the political and social order that was to persist through the colonial period. One question early asserted itself: Who was to run the government, and in whose interest? In the early phase of conquest, military officers were the effective government, and they continued as such in the outlying districts. They were also the main rulers of the Muslim population. Special agencies called *bureaux arabes,* or Arabic Offices, were staffed by men with special language training. Although military rule could be oppressive, many officers in the bureaux arabes learned through their contacts with the local population and tended in time to regard them as their special wards. They were far from suggesting that Algerians should be treated as equals, but they did form the idea that France had an obligation to rule Algeria well, and fundamentally in the interests of the Algerians themselves. For a time in the 1860s, they succeeded in bringing the French government in Paris around to their point of view.

Their principal opponents and principal rivals for ultimate control over French Algeria were the European settlers who had begun to immigrate from the 1830s onward in the wake of the French armies. At first, the movement was separate from official policy. It began simply because the French administration could make land available to individual Europeans. Other Europeans came because they found economic opportunities in the towns, often in connection with the administration or the army. About half these foreigners were from France, the rest from Malta, the Balearic Islands, or the Spanish mainland. Over time, they adopted the French language and culture and came to think of themselves as French, but as French whose permanent home was Algeria. Unlike the soldiers or administrators, who came out for a period of work as part of a career leading to retirement in France, they expected to live and die in Algeria. By the end of the nineteenth century, more than half were Algerian-born.

Unlike the colonial situation in sub-Saharan Africa, where colonized and colonizers were instantly distinguishable by physical type and skin color, the European settlers in Algeria were set apart by their culture, especially their religion. The French response was to recognize Christians of all origins as a separate legal group of French citizens, with greater rights than the French subjects who made up the vast majority of the population. French citizens came under French law and enjoyed many of the legal and constitutional rights they would have had in France. French subjects, by contrast, came under Muslim law, which meant that their personal and property rights depended on a different set of rules; but they were also subject to special and discriminatory laws and regulations created especially for them by the colonial government. For a time, Algerian Jews were in a third religious category, but in 1870 they were made French citizens, rather than subjects. Inequality before the law came to include inequality in education, in civil rights, and in economic opportunity. The French citizens resident in Algeria jealously guarded their privileged position. They became cultural chauvinists of the most extreme kind, tending to see the differences between their culture and that of the Muslim Algerians as an innate "racial" inheritance.

Up to the 1860s, the army kept the upper hand, with the settlers increasingly resentful. The coming of the Third Republic in France in 1870, however, brought a settler victory. In the name of democracy and republicanism, the French citizens of Algeria were thereafter allowed to elect deputies to the National Assembly in Paris. Algeria was formally annexed to France. The officers of the bureaux arabes were subordinated to the civilian government in each district, and the voice of the settlers became more and more important in deciding French policy. But, as in South Africa, "victory for democracy" in this case meant victory for a democracy confined to a small minority, and the turning point can be located in the 1870s and 1880s.

The importance of the settler community became visible somewhat earlier, with 130,000 Europeans resident by the 1850s. The community grew slowly through the sixties and seventies, with another burst of new arrivals in the eighties that carried the European population beyond the half-million mark before the end of the century — making them about 13 percent of the population as of 1900, about the same proportion they were to remain until the end of the colonial period.

Although most of the settlers lived in towns, their main impact on the Algerian economy was through their acquisition and control of the land — even though Algerians still did most of the agricultural work. The colonial government made a regular policy of securing land from Algerians and then making it available to European settlers. Up to 1851, it had redistributed some 1,400 square miles, an area half again the size of Rhode Island. Nearly half of this land had belonged to the Regency government, but nearly a fifth had been grazing land held by nomadic or seminomadic lineages, who were now forced to settle down as sedentary farmers. Nearly 15 percent was confiscated from government opponents like 'Abd al-Qādir's followers. In this first phase, many of the settlers were given small plots and worked the land themselves, while some 36,000 Algerian families lost their land and had either to move away or to take work as landless farm workers.

After mid-century, still more land changed hands. The French confiscated another section about the size of Rhode Island in the wake of the great rebellion of 1871, and made it available to Europeans. Europeans also began to buy land, and this was the period when they started to move strongly into large-scale agriculture, using dry-farming techniques for grain production in the more arid, yet tillable regions, or cultivating large vineyards where rainfall was adequate. By the end of the century, a pattern of efficient, highly capitalized agriculture under European control was beginning to emerge, alongside the less efficient, undercapitalized agriculture still carried out on the fragmented landholdings of Algerian farmers.

EGYPT'S LOSS OF INDEPENDENCE

In the second half of the nineteenth century, while France completed its formal empire over Algeria, Egypt gradually fell into the informal empire of the Europeans. "Informal empire" is a useful term for that shadowy area in international relations where two states of vastly unequal power were theoretically equal sovereign states, but where the stronger of the two nevertheless exercised more power over the weaker than was common within the European state system. Especially in the nineteenth century, European states often tried to exercise informal control overseas while avoiding the full responsibilities of formal annexation. That exercise of power might be no more than pressure exerted to induce the weaker state to pass a particular piece of legislation or to set tariffs at a favorable rate. In more extreme cases, Europeans sometimes gained control of part of the judicial system — say, the control of cases involving their own nationals. Or they might manage whole government departments, such as the treasury or foreign affairs, leaving the rest of the internal government in local hands.

One problem with the term "informal empire" is that so many different degrees and different forms were possible. Egypt in the nineteenth century passed through several of these. During the first half of the century, it managed to enjoy some of the fruits of modernization, like a strong army, without paying a very high price in the form of European influence. Egypt enjoyed French patronage at that period, but the French consul had nothing like the kind of influence French and British consuls exercised in Tripoli. The slide toward informal empire came only after the 1860s, though some of it can be traced back to Muhammad 'Ali's failure to create a strong and balanced economy. The new khedives, Saïd (1854–1863) and then Ismaïl (1863–1879), were more active modernizers than Muhammad 'Ali had been. Saïd's government built the railroads from Alexandria to Cairo and from Cairo to Port Saïd on the Red Sea. It began a new and more active drive for irrigation works that would make perennial agriculture possible. It commissioned a French engineering firm to begin work on the Suez Canal, which was completed in 1869. Ismaïl was even warmer and less critical in his admiration of Europe, where he had traveled and lived for a time in his youth. He pushed ahead on these same fronts, only more rapidly.

This activity raised several serious problems. The Suez Canal changed the strategic situation in the eastern Mediterranean, opening up a water passage to the Indian Ocean just when steamships made the Red Sea more useful to navigation than ever before. Britain began to be more concerned about Egypt as a strategic route to its Indian empire. To make matters worse, these improvements were made with borrowed money — not only borrowed, but sometimes borrowed at excessive rates of interest and invested in ways that brought no return, such as in monumental architecture intended to beautify Cairo on the model of Napoleonic Paris. Total Egyptian indebtedness rose from about £7 million sterling in 1860 to more than £100 million in 1876. By that time, the annual interest payments flowing out of the country came to £5 million a year, or more than a third of the value of the annual exports. It was manifestly impossible either to pay off the debt or to pay interest on it without demanding a great sacrifice from the Egyptian people, and the need to export in order to pay the interest gave Egyptian economic planning still another bias toward production for export.

The speed of economic growth in the export sector also opened opportunities for foreigners. It was not simply that Muhammad 'Ali's modern educational system could not meet the demand for skilled people, though that was true, too. The legal position of foreigners actually gave them an advantage over Egyptians in all kinds of commerce and in some other fields as well. The foreigners' judicial position dated back to the so-called Capitulations agreed to by the Ottoman Empire. These gave European consuls jurisdiction over disputes between Westerners, and they provided special privileges for Westerners tried on criminal charges before Ottoman courts. In the first instance these privileges were voluntary concessions based on the Ottoman practice of letting each religious or ethnic community look after its own internal affairs. In the course of the nineteenth century, however, new extensions crept in. Marginal cases tended to be brought to the consular courts rather than to Egyptian courts. After 1873, Europeans won the right to have even criminal cases tried by the appropriate consul, and mixed Egyptian-consular courts were set up to hear civil cases in which one litigant was Egyptian and the other foreign. By the 1870s, the number of foreign residents had increased to about 2 percent of the total population, though most were not from western Europe. Alongside the technicians, economic opportunities attracted many Greek and Levantine people of working-class background.

By the 1870s, a second kind of pressure for informal empire was apparent: European creditors, mostly bankers, appealed to their respective governments for help in recovering their loans to an Egyptian government now badly overextended. In 1876, the khedive was forced to appoint four prominent Europeans to posts in his own government as "Commissioners of the Debt." With that, Egypt was clearly within the informal empire of France and Britain, with France the senior partner.

The Egyptian debt then entered the broader network of European international relations that centered on the problem of Ottoman weakness. By the 1870s, the powers anticipated an Ottoman collapse more strongly than ever. They were concerned with the division of the spoils, not the fortune of the sultan. Russia and Austria in particular were rivals for the Ottoman provinces in the Balkans. Russia also hoped for an open and uncontested right of passage through the straits from the Black Sea into the Mediterranean. Germany, France, and Britain were all worried that Russia might upset the balance of power by swallowing the whole Ottoman Empire, though France and Britain were also rivals for influence in Egypt and in the eastern Mediterranean generally. In 1876, a successful Russian war on Turkey touched off a new crisis. Britain threatened naval intervention to stave off a complete Turkish collapse. That led, in turn, to a general European diplomatic meeting, the Congress of Berlin in 1878.

At that meeting, the powers managed to avoid a general European war by dividing the spoils so that each of them got something. Russia made territorial gains. Romania and Serbia were detached from the Ottoman Empire as independent states. Britain promised to defend Turkey from further Russian aggression and received Cyprus as compensation for Russian gains. France received permission to occupy Tunisia, though the actual occupation was put off until 1881.

Egypt came into the picture as an Ottoman province, however autonomous. If the powers felt free to dictate to Istanbul, they felt equally free to do the same to Cairo. In 1878, they forced Ismaïl to appoint one French and one British member to his cabinet, and the web of informal control closed a little tighter. But even this disguised rule from overseas was unpopular with many Egyptians. Heavy schedules of interest and capital repayments proved even more so, and Ismaïl reacted by dismissing the foreign cabinet ministers. The powers in turn reacted by ordering the Ottoman sultan to dismiss Ismaïl himself, and the crisis deepened. Late in 1881, Egyptian troops led by 'Urabi Pasha seized power in Cairo as part of an antiforeign movement. That left the Anglo-

French coalition with a choice between armed intervention or loss of their informal control — with all that implied for their strategic position at the Suez Canal.

On the initiative of the French government, they chose intervention, but then the French National Assembly withdrew its support. That left the British to act alone. In 1882, Britain sent a military expedition, fought and won the decisive battle, and thus found itself in control of Egypt. But this control was far from happy. To withdraw would endanger the Suez route to India, but to stay left Britain rather than the khedive face to face with Egypt's creditors in Europe. The result was an informal British protectorate that lasted until 1914 under a variety of legal fictions, a protectorate that amounted in time to British control of Egypt, but with international pressures from other European powers that severely limited Britain's freedom of action.

THE APOGEE AND COLLAPSE
OF SECONDARY EMPIRE IN THE NILOTIC SUDAN

From the 1850s through the 1870s, Egypt greatly expanded the range and degree of control it exercised in the Sudan. This was another part of Saïd's and Ismaïl's modernization program. Like the rest of the program, it stretched the country's resources beyond the breaking point, but it scored what looked like successes along the way. In fact, two kinds of expansion took place simultaneously, one official and the other private. The official moves followed the line of the Red Sea and the strategic logic dictated by the Suez Canal already under construction. Egyptian moves along the Red Sea coast, the Gulf of Aden, and into the Ethiopian highlands began in 1865 with the acquisition of the previously Ottoman-owned posts at Suakin and Massawa (now in Ethiopia). In the 1870s, the drive continued with an Egyptian occupation of Zeila (now in Somalia) and Harar (now in the eastern highlands of Ethiopia) and two frontal assaults on Ethiopia itself — with a disastrous defeat for Egyptian forces each time.

The second kind of advance was made up the line of the White Nile and west of the upper Nile, but it was carried out by private armies generally under the control of the jallaba, or petty traders, acting as a secondary empire within a secondary empire. The jallaba had been moving toward the south with their trading posts for some decades, but they received a strong assist from 1839 to 1842 when it was discovered that steamboats could sail up the Nile past the sudd and past the relatively well-organized Shilluk. During the next three decades, jallaba, principally from Nubia, became more active than ever as slave traders and slave raiders among the stateless peoples like the Dinka and Nuer. They set up fortified camps, or *zariba,* in the south, manned by slave-soldiers armed with modern weapons. They were not interested in administering the societies that surrounded them, only in trading and securing the passage of goods along the trade routes. It was, in short, an armed trade diaspora like that of the French in seventeenth-century Canada or the Russians in seventeenth-century Siberia, or the contemporaneous Zanzibari in the East African interior. In time, their furthest posts reached as far south as the present frontier between Uganda and Zaïre, and west into the Bahr al-Ghazal region to the south of Darfur. Most of the jallaba were originally Egyptian subjects, and Egypt sometimes recognized their authority in the south, but their real power derived from the fact that modern arms conferred power indiscriminately on whoever first had an opportunity to use them against those who had none.

From the 1860s onward, Cairo tried to deal with the problem of frontier anarchy. It opened a new district capital at Fashoda among the Shilluk, tried to establish an official connection with the prominent jallaba leaders by appointing them as government officials, and sent in prominent English mercenaries to take command of the southern armies. Egypt's final push for control was simultaneous with the financial crisis in Cairo. In 1877, Ismaïl appointed Charles Gordon Pasha as governor-general of the Sudan and simultaneously signed an antislave-trade convention with Great Britain. Gordon was supposed to suppress the slave trade, but instead he lost control of the jallaba altogether, as the southwest and other fringe provinces lapsed into chronic revolt.

But the final collapse came at the core of the Egyptian Sudan, in the gezira between the Blue and White Niles. In 1881, a certain Muhammad Ahmad organized a revolt, declaring that he was the expected Islamic savior, or Mahdi. His forces captured Khartoum and killed Gordon Pasha in 1885. He and his successor then founded a new state that was to rule over the Nilotic Sudan until the British conquest in 1898.

By the 1880s, the movement for Islamic purification and reform had been flourishing for more than a century, and the expectation of a savior was common in the Islamic world. The Mahdi's revolt was one of a series of revolts in Africa and elsewhere that sought to overturn governments judged to be incompletely Muslim. Examples go back in time to Nasīr al-Dīn's effort to build a new Muslim state in southern Mauritania and northern Senegal in the seventeenth century, or to the Wahabi movement in eighteenth-century Arabia. The Mahdi's regime in the Sudan also had overtones suggesting 'Abd al-Qādir's effort to build a new state in western Algeria as a makeweight against European pressure.

Muhammad Ahmad came originally from the desert Nile in Nubia, but he had long since moved south to the gezira as a Muslim cleric of the Samanīya order, one of the reforming brotherhoods founded in Arabia during the eighteenth century. By 1880, he had become the local head of the order with a broad following throughout the gezira and westward into Kordofan. In 1881, he had a series of visions telling him he was to be the Mahdi, not merely for the Sudan but for the entire Islamic world, and he called for a holy war to accomplish this end. The first enemy was the Egyptian regime, locally identified as "Turks," though in fact by this time most officials were Egyptian Muslims, with a sprinkling of Coptic Christians and Europeans like Gordon Pasha. The regime was, in any event, alien enough to raise the fears of those who felt that Islam was in danger, and the Mahdi's original, prerevolt following had been people of unusual religious zeal marked by a streak of puritanism.

The first successes in Kordofan brought new followers with other reasons for opposition to the Egyptian regime. Some of the old Sudanese ruling class who had once accepted the "Turks" began to have second thoughts. Khedive Ismaïl's financial problems and his gradual slide into informal empire were known of in Khartoum, as they were in Cairo. The khedive's effort to establish genuine control over the Sudanese periphery also threatened local interests, especially those of the southern jallaba, and they had friends and relatives in the core area as well. The appointment of an infidel governor-general made it easier still to associate the cause of Islam with specific interests, and the British seizure of Cairo in 1882 meant that the later stages of the war, from 1883 to victory in 1885, were fought against troops under European command. By that time, the movement stood out more clearly than ever as one of Muslim resistance to Western encroachment.

The Mahdi himself died in 1885. His successor, the khalifa Abdullah, carried on, though he gradually changed the nature of the regime. The main support within the country still came from the religious enthusiasts, from the commercial classes, and from many of the baqarra, or cattle nomads, of Kordofan and the west. But success whittled down their influence. The ideal of building a universal Islamic state was quietly allowed to drop. Disciplined slave-soldiers replaced the irregular and largely nomadic forces that had won the first battles, and the khalifa retained many of the administrators who had run the Egyptian government. He also became more tolerant of religious differences within Islam, cooperating when it seemed politic with other brotherhoods less puritanical and orthodox than his own. Toward the end, it was clear that he intended his own son to take over after he died. What began as a religious reform movement, in short, increasingly became just another Muslim state, no more religious than the rest, based on the sedentary societies of the sub-Saharan Nile valley and Kordofan.

But the tendency in that direction was cut short once more in 1898 by foreign intervention. Though the British officials in Cairo had been willing at first to let the Sudan go its own way, competitive annexation elsewhere in Africa raised the danger of another European power occupying the Nile valley and threatening the British position at Suez and on the Red Sea. French plans to send an expedition across Africa from the west coast helped to bring on a new Anglo-Egyptian conquest of the Sudan so that the British drive from the north met the French move from the west at Fashoda. Armed conflict between England and France was avoided, but England concluded that the Nilotic Sudan would have to be annexed to protect her strategic interests. The result for the Sudan was a second period of government from Cairo, this time by an Anglo-Egyptian condominium that was to last until 1955, though ultimate power always lay with the British side of the partnership.

THE FALL OF TUNISIA AND MOROCCO

With a renewed Turkish regime in Tripoli and the French in Algeria, Tunisia's position became increasingly difficult after the 1830s. Either neighbor could threaten the bey's continued quasi-independence. He sought to modernize the army, but at the usual risk of falling into the trap of informal empire in the process. The Tunisian government not only borrowed more in Europe than it could easily repay, it also borrowed at such exorbitant rates of interest that any effort to repay — or even to keep up the interest charges — forced it to raise taxes at home. The heavy borrowing therefore added European bondholders and Tunisian taxpayers to the existing pressures. To complicate matters, substantial numbers of French, Italian, and Maltese settlers moved into Tunisia during the second half of the nineteenth century, in much the same way that foreigners moved into Egypt at the same period. As in Egypt, their presence brought still more pressure from the French, Italian, and British consuls (since the Maltese were British subjects).

By the 1850s, Tunisia could be counted as part of the French informal empire, and the French in fact planned a limited occupation in the late 1860s in order to assure their control. British and Italian protests, however, forced France to agree to turn Tunisian finances over to an international commission. Partly as a result, the Tunisian economy recovered somewhat during the 1870s and the formal French protectorate was put off until a suitable configuration of international relations at the Congress of Berlin removed the opposition and allowed the French to march in, in 1881. Tunisia's line in confrontation with Europe, in short, was very much like Egypt's and the result was much the same.

Morocco, on the other hand, seized the other horn of the dilemma of modernization. Given a choice between military modernization at the price of a large foreign debt, or military weakness with an old-fashioned army, Morocco stood by the old ways. And the policy worked reasonably well, in spite of military defeat at the hands of France in the 1840s and again at the hands of Spain in the 1860s. International rivalries among the Europeans limited the demands that any one of them could make on the sultan. Morocco was open to European economic penetration in the second half of the century, but that penetration was comparatively slow. About 1870, when Egypt already had 100,000 resident foreigners and Tunisia had nearly 10,000, Morocco had only 1,500. Sultan Mulai Hassan (1873–1894) was especially skillful in preserving the balance of the old political system. He had a small force of European-trained soldiers, but the mainstay of his army remained the old combination of slave-soldiers and military levies from privileged tribes. With a more powerful force, he might have been tempted to extend the makhzen's power over siba country; but lack of power reduced the temptation, and Mulai Hassan's revenue matched his expenses to the end of his reign.

This comparatively happy situation may have come from luck as well as from wisdom, because Great Britain had the largest stake in Moroccan trade and acted as an informal protector of Moroccan interests against the Spanish and French on the frontiers. After 1900, however, the old balance began to break down. A new sultan moved toward modernization, which brought on a conservative revolt in the region east of Fez. That, in turn, brought firmer action from France, which sidestepped British objections by promising Britain a free hand in Egypt. Spain was bought off with the promise of a zone of Spanish influence in northern Morocco. By 1904, France had lent Morocco large sums of money and had already taken over the customs and postal services. The slide into informal empire had already begun, but Germany had to be bought off as well before France could formalize the protectorate. Even earlier, the puppet sultan began to lose power internally and France had to bail him out with military support or see him deposed by his enemies. Finally, in 1912, France and Spain divided Morocco into two zones of formal control, though the sultan continued as theoretical ruler under European protection.

This final failure stands in contrast to Morocco's comparative success in keeping out the Europeans, but the Moroccan makhzen nevertheless held out longer than any other government in North Africa. Parts of the bled es siba remained independent of real French control until 1934, nearly the last sections of Africa to be conquered by the Europeans, and the Sherifian sultans continued as heads of state into the late 1970s. In spite of European pressures in the nineteenth and twentieth centuries, the old institutions and loyalties were remarkably resilient.

SUGGESTIONS FOR FURTHER READING

Abir, Mordechai. *Ethiopia: The Era of the Princes.* London: Longman, 1968.

Evans-Pritchard, Edward E. *The Sanusi of Cyrenaica.* Oxford: Oxford University Press, 1949.

Gellner, Ernest. *Saints of the Atlas.* London: Weidenfeld and Nicolson, 1969.

Holt, P. M. *The Madhist State in the Sudan.* Oxford: Oxford University Press, Clarendon Press, 1958.

———. *A Modern History of the Sudan.* London: Weidenfeld and Nicolson, 1961.

Ling, Dwight L. *Tunisia from Protectorate to Republic.* Bloomington: Indiana University Press, 1967.

Miège, Jean Louis. *Le Maroc et l'Europe, 1830–1894.* Paris: Presses Universitaires, 1961.

Montagne, Robert. *The Berbers: Their Social and Political Organization.* London: Cass, 1973.

Vatikiotis, Panayiotis J. *The Modern History of Egypt.* London: Weidenfeld and Nicolson, 1969.

Chapter 12

The Commercial and
Religious Revolutions
in West Africa

THROUGHOUT AFRICA, the precolonial century was a period of revolutionary change in external trade. For tropical Africa, the impact of new trade was so pervasive as to give the false impression that trade and its consequences would explain everything else that took place. But other trends were also running strongly, and these were separate even though some of their nineteenth-century momentum came from long-distance trade.

One such tendency was a growth in the scale of economic systems. Regional economies in many parts of Africa were the most important influence organizing space until well into the nineteenth century. Throughout tropical Africa, increases in trade led to tension between the well-sheltered local and regional communities and the broader institutions that joined them to their neighbors.

A second general tendency was the accelerated pace of culture change. All sorts of cultural features from hairdos to new crops and new cults diffused at a faster pace than ever before, and this rapid diffusion tended to make for common and wide-ranging cultural entities that were also expanding in scale. Both these trends had been present in African history in earlier centuries, but they were now reinforced by world events — specifically, by the industrial revolution in Europe and by African responses to it. And the African side is important, for if Africans had not wanted European goods, the story would have been different.

West Africa's experience in the precolonial century was similar to that of other African regions in the shadow of industrialized Europe, but here the common trends were mixed together in ways that created a number of special patterns. Coastal West and Central Africa had a longer and more intense experience of maritime trade than any other part of sub-Saharan Africa. Their leaders were familiar with European ways and European arms. They had imported tens of thousands of muskets and incorporated them into their military systems. More Europeans came to live on shore after the 1780s, but strategic surprise could not play the same role it played on the upper Nile or in the East

African lake region. Having been innoculated with the virus of European weapons, West Africa had already built up a partial immunity to the dangers of secondary empire–building. European military encroachment was also less serious in these decades than it was in either northern or southern Africa. And though Western cultural penetration took place, its agents were more often Western-educated Africans than European settlers.

But other trends common to Africa as a whole were especially strong in their West African versions. One such was the movement for Islamic reform and rejuvenation. Reformers and revolutionaries who set their programs in a religious framework had been important since the seventeenth century from the middle Senegal to the highlands of Fuuta Jaalo. These movements actually antedated the Middle Eastern reform movements that became increasingly important during the eighteenth century. The new directions from the Middle East combined with local factors to influence a series of political movements couched in a religious ideology. From the 1770s onward, they changed the entire political map of the western Sudan, and the locus of political power in those societies shifted beyond recognition.

Revolutionary change in commerce also swept West Africa. All of Africa experienced enormous increases in overseas trade, but for West and Equatorial Africa the change in scale was simultaneous with a change in the principal exports. With the winding down of the trade in slaves, the new "legitimate" trade (as the Europeans at the time liked to call it) was not merely a substitution for the old; it shifted the centers of wealth and power, as those in a position to profit from the slave trade lost out and new wealth flowed to those who could supply gum-Senegal, palm oil, or peanuts.

RELIGIOUS REVOLUTIONS: THE QADIRI PHASE

Whereas the center of religious revolution in the seventeenth and early eighteenth centuries had been Senegambia and its Fulbe offshoots south and east to Fuuta Jaalo, a new center of reformist preaching and influence appeared in the mid-eighteenth century on the desert fringe just north of Timbuktu. The organizing force behind this movement was the same reforming Qādirīya order that had supplied the organizational base for 'Abd al-Qādir in Algeria. The Qādirīya was a *sufi* order, but it differed from many in being far more orthodox. In the nineteenth century, it was to be near the mainstream and participated in the Muslim call for a return to the purity of primitive Islam. The West African head of the order was Sidi Makhtar al-Kunti, whose reform preaching was effective from the late 1750s to his death in 1811. He made no bid for territorial authority, though his influence was enormously important throughout the southern Sahara and the western Sudan; and the reform message spread along the trade routes from Timbuktu up the Niger through Maasina to the heartland of Manding culture, and downstream toward Hausaland in present-day Nigeria and on beyond, into the Oyo empire in northern Yorubaland. Along the desert fringe, it stretched into what is now southern Mauritania in the west, down into Senegambia, and eastward to the Tuareg of Aïr.

Islam had been gaining gradually throughout the western Sudan in recent centuries, but its gains had taken the form of increasingly important pockets of adherents, not a broad expansion across the countryside. The peasants — the vast majority — clung to their old religion, to the gods attached to lineages, places, or protective functions under a powerful but aloof High God, who had once created the world but had since withdrawn from its day-to-day affairs. Islam, on the other hand, attracted those whose lives were directed outward from the home village, along the trade routes, and into the courts of the rulers. Many rulers were formal adherents of Islam, but they had a largely non-Muslim populace to deal with, and few of them made a serious effort to convert the general public or even to enforce Muslim law throughout the territory.

New tendencies within Islam meant far more to clerical and commercial circles. Islam was, after all, the religion of commerce, and it appealed to ethnic groups with a commercial calling, like the Soninke and their offshoots (the Juula, Marka, and Jahanke among others), who were scattered from the Niger bend south to the forest and west nearly to the Atlantic. The Muslim Fulbe (sing. Pulo), who served as cattle keepers from the Atlantic to Lake Chad, were also sprinkled throughout the region as itinerant clerics in courts, towns, and cattle camps. Elsewhere in the Sudan, however, non-Muslim religions were virtually untouched, especially in the southern, or pre-forest, savannas, but also in such large blocs of "pagan" population as the two Bambara kingdoms or the Voltaic states within the great bend of the Niger.

Nor had the first almaamates, spawned by the *jihads* of the seventeenth and early eighteenth centuries, turned into centers of Muslim power. The rulers of Bundu, founded in the 1690s as a clerical state, kept the title of Almaami, but were no longer trained as Muslim clerics. Bundunke clerical offices and judgeships were reserved for Jahanke clerical lineages who had their own autonomous villages. In Fuuta Tooro, where the first jihad had failed in the 1680s, a second began in the 1770s. In the 1780s, Abdul Kader ('Abd al-Qādir in Arabic) emerged as Almaami, but his armies failed to spread the movement to neighboring states. In 1806, he and the original aims of the revolution died together, defeated in war by the combined forces of Bundu, the pagan state of Kaarta, and a powerful faction within Fuuta itself. The victors preserved the office of Almaami and the fiction of Islamic reform, but the Futaanke clique that betrayed the revolution set itself up as a kind of electoral council that appointed and removed the Almaami at will.

The almaamate in Fuuta Jaalo had a similar history. After the first victories in the second quarter of the eighteenth century, the clerical party became a secular-minded oligarchy whose principal interest was to command the flow of trade from the upper Niger to the coast (in what are now Guinea-Conakry and Sierra Leone). The rulers were Muslim, but they did little more than convert their slaves, and they turned more and more to chronic civil war between

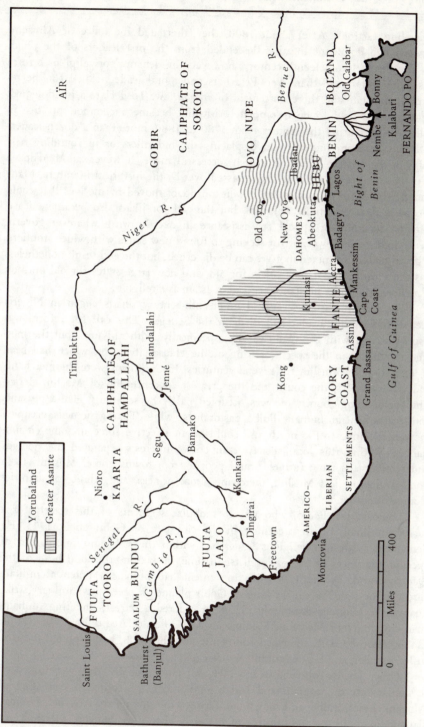

West Africa in the Early Nineteenth Century

quarreling factions. After about 1800, they alternated the office of Almaami between two dominant lineages descended from the first leaders of the jihad.

By the early nineteenth century, however, the demand for religious reform was more widespread than ever. Preachers and moral leaders called for the reform of the state and the enforcement of *shar'īa* law. To declare a jihad against a government held to be incompletely Muslim became a common practice in political life. During the century from 1780 to 1880, more than a dozen leaders with this program succeeded in displacing the old rulers or in founding new states in the western Sudan. For each successful move, however, another dozen or more failed in palace coups now passed over by the historical literature. Many leaders, successful or unsuccessful, were no doubt moved by motives that could be qualified as essentially religious, but the call for jihad also became a least-common-denominator appeal for assistance in overthrowing whatever government might be in power, or for seeking to found new states with wider frontiers. A broad pattern of mixed motives can be discerned, but the end result nonetheless was the substitution of new rulers for old, and new large states for old ones on a smaller scale, and a substantial spread of Islam as a religion.

The new phase of successful nineteenth-century jihads began in Nigeria even before Abdul Kader had died on the Senegal. This call for reform was also associated with the Qādirīya and, specifically, with al-Kunti, but the message was heard in the specific setting of the Hausa city-states, which had been at least formally Muslim for several centuries. In the towns were the merchants and craftsworkers, the court, and the greatest concentration of Muslim clerics. The surrounding countryside was occupied partly by sedentary Hausa peasants and partly by transhumant Fulbe pastoralists, while Tuareg nomads occupied the desert fringe to the north and could be an effective force in some circumstances. Within this local society, competitive interests separated the nomads and seminomads from farmers, rural people from townspeople, Muslims from non-Muslims or less Muslim, merchants from princes, and ethnic communities from one another.

Usuman dan Fodio, who was to mobilize segments of this society for a successful jihad, began preaching in the city-state of Gobir about 1775. He demanded a stronger religious leadership within the state and complained of specific grievances of the pastoralists. In time, he became the local head of the Qādirīya, and, by the 1790s, his movement had become a potential military threat to the state. When the king of Gobir planned a preemptive military strike against the religious community, Usuman ordered a retreat, imitating Muhammad's flight from Mecca to Medina. In 1804, he declared a holy war against Gobir, returned with an armed following, and, by 1808, had captured the city, killed its ruler, and begun building a new capital at Sokoto.

Other revolts followed in other Hausa states. Usually, they were based on a similar reform program and had a similar core of followers consisting of Muslim clerics, Fulbe, and sometimes Tuareg from the north. At times, Usuman dan Fodio could use the prestige of his early victory to influence the choice of leaders elsewhere; he often favored a scholarly Muslim cleric as flag-bearer, usually a Pulo like himself. But other leaders emerged on their own and applied to Usuman for recognition. The movement was never identified as a purely Fulbe drive to dominate the Hausa majority, though the rebels attracted more support from serious Muslims, merchants, and herdsmen than from other groups. The enemy was defined as the old Hausa-speaking ruling class, now condemned as pagan. The mass of the peasantry apparently remained neutral; the bulk of the actual military operations involved two minorities — the rebels and the old aristocrats they expelled from power. Nor was the rebellion in any sense the growth of a secondary empire. Most of the fighting involved sieges of fortified towns, and the dominant force was cavalry supported by archers. Guns, long used nearer the coastal sources of supply, were not important at first. They came into use only gradually as the fighting developed into a state of near-anarchy through much of what was to be northern Nigeria — only to settle down gradually as Usuman dan Fodio was recognized as *shaykh,* or *shehu,* and a general government took form.

The new political order that emerged in the late 1810s and early 1820s was mainly the creation of Usuman's brother Abdullahi, and his son Bello. The head of state was recognized as the *khalifa* of Muhammad on earth, with a principal capital in Sokoto under Bello and a subordinate and semiautonomous western region based on Gwandu under Abdullahi. Each individual flag-bearer was recognized as emir over the territory he had conquered. In practice, this meant that the central government could not easily remove the emirs from office, much less control in detail the internal workings of their subordinate governments. Thus, although Usuman dan Fodio had begun with a detailed blueprint of the kind of society he wanted to create and had some ideas about the means he planned to use, his successors lacked the power to follow through. Whatever its intentions, the central government could use advice, diplomacy, but only occasionally force to correct an especially difficult situation. Even within the area under closer control from Sokoto, old social structures revived under new names. The aggrieved herdsmen drifted back into seasonal transhumance, while a Fulbe and Muslim aristocracy replaced the old Hausa governments in the towns, and the tight social stratification of the old regime reappeared with new men at the top.

Similar politico-religious movements appeared nearly simultaneously, but were independent of and even hostile to Sokoto. The ancient kingdom of Borno, near Lake Chad, was almost captured by an unofficial offshoot of Usuman's movement, though Borno ended by going its own way. At the beginning of the nineteenth century, the ancient Sefawa dynasty was still in power, though much reduced in strength since its apogee at the end of the sixteenth century. Its core area was the region just west of the lake, with a variety of tribute-paying subordinate states north into the steppe and eastward to the Sultanate of Wadai, the next truly independent neighbor. With an impetus from the Fulbe jihads in Hausa country, the Fulbe also rose in Borno. By 1808, they had captured the capital at Birnin Gazargamu, and it appeared for a time that they might over-throw the Sefawa. But a local cleric, Laminu al-Kanemi, came along with a counterreform movement. Independently of the Sefawa dynasty, his forces first regained control of the capital and the western lands lost to the Fulbe. With a following of Shuwa Arabs, Kanembu from the east of Lake Chad, and other seminomadic peoples, Laminu al-Kanemi became a kind of clerical warlord and political arbiter able to appoint and dismiss the *mai*, or king, representing the official dynasty. From the early 1820s, he was solidly entrenched with his own private army under slave-commanders who would follow his orders alone. He and his successors ruled through puppet mai until 1846, when one of them made a bid for real power by calling in the Sultan of Wadai. Laminu's son then had the last mai killed and established his own family as the new dynasty in theory as well as in fact.

To the west of Sokoto, an independent offshoot took still another direction. The setting was Maasina in the Niger valley above Timbuktu, where the river breaks into a thousand branches that form an internal delta over a distance of nearly three hundred miles, from Jenné downstream nearly to Timbuktu. Each wet season, the river rises and spills over its banks to create a shallow lake up to fifty miles wide, though it leaves many bits of high ground that become islands, to which people can bring their cattle until the flood recedes. Then the moisture and silt left by the river create rich pastures across the plain, as well as the possibility of planting a dry-season grain crop. Like the similar environment of the Dinka and Nuer on the Nile thousands of miles to the east, it was well suited to pastoral occupation, mainly by Fulbe in Maasina proper or by Tuareg just inside the Niger bend — but not to pastoralists alone. Somono rivermen fished the Niger waters and carried the important trade that flowed south from the desert edge to Jenné and other transshipment points for the overland trip toward the forest. Riverside commercial towns like Sansanding, Jenné, or Mopti attracted a variety of people from all over the western Sudan, while the agricultural region just above the delta was dominantly Bambara in culture, non-Muslim in religion, and attached to the empire of Segu.

At the beginning of the nineteenth century, Islam was strong among the townspeople and river boatmen, while many Fulbe clerics in the towns had connections among the pastoral Fulbe as well. Political control in the delta, however, belonged to the Fulbe Dikko lineage, which was theoretically Muslim but acted more like a predatory war band with a weak allegiance to the rulers of Segu. The court at Segu, like other western Sudanese courts, was also touched by Muslim influence, though the Bambara countryside was not. In spite of this checkerboard of conversion to Islam, Muslims here had been greatly influenced by the reformist teaching of the Qādirīya center of the Kunta shaykhs near Timbuktu.

News of Usuman dan Fodio's successes in northern Nigeria inspired a more active reformist movement under the leadership of a Fulbe cleric, Ahmadu

Lobbo. Though he followed Shehu Usuman's teachings in some respects, he was more intransigent toward deviation from a strict and puritanical standard of Islamic virtue, and identified more strongly with the Fulbe as an ethnic group. About 1816, Ahmadu began to prepare a jihad that was to be partly a civil war against the Dikko rulers of the Fulbe, partly a war of liberation for all Fulbe from the Bambara of Segu, and partly an effort to create a rightly guided Muslim state. He succeeded against the Dikko in 1818, then against Segu, and in 1821 set up a new state with a new capital at Hamdallahi.

The Caliphate of Hamdallahi differed from its neighbor in Sokoto. It was much smaller, without subordinate emirates, and with far more of its administrative apparatus in the hands of Muslim clerics. It was also limited to a single geographical region with an ethnically homogeneous population. Though Ahmadu Lobbo and his successors sometimes fought their neighbors — they captured Timbuktu itself in 1826 — their policy was generally nonexpansive. As a result, the caliphate lasted fairly peacefully into the early 1860s as the jihad state most faithful to the original Islamic reform program, though its puritanical fundamentalism was also somewhat suspect to the bulk of the West African 'ulamā.

THE COMMERCIAL REVOLUTION

The term *revolution* has been applied to the end of the slave trade and to the growth of other exports from Africa. It has also been used for the rapid growth of West African trade in the first decades of the colonial period, and it could have other meanings for East Africa or the upper Nile, where the nineteenth century brought an increase, not a diminution, of the trade in slaves. A wide perspective on the economic changes in Africa during this period should begin with the overwhelming fact of industrialization in Europe; from that perspective, we can then distinguish a variety of reflexes with different timings and somewhat different consequences for parts of Africa.

Such a perspective can be misleading, however, if it suggests that economic change in Africa took place entirely or mainly because of external stimulus. For most parts of sub-Saharan Africa, overseas trade was only a small fraction of the total trade. The evidence for West and Equatorial Africa from the late eighteenth century onward to the colonial period suggests that total long-distance trade within Africa was increasing more rapidly than overseas trade. That, in turn, suggests that the internal economy was changing rapidly for reasons independent of the European stimulus.

But external stimulus was undoubtedly present as well. From the last third of the seventeenth century to the middle of the nineteenth, the prices offered by Europe for African exports increased steeply — including the price for slaves, which began to rise first. Rising slave prices were simply a reflex of the increasing profitability of slave-grown tropical agriculture in the New World, which in turn reflected the willingness of Europeans to buy more coffee and sugar at higher prices. The greater European wealth, caused ultimately by the industrial revolution, therefore led to a continually increasing demand for slaves, especially for slaves to staff new plantations in Cuba and Brazil.

In time, the search for alternate sources of labor was to bring tens of thousands of East Indians to the Caribbean along with increased European immigration to Cuba and Brazil, but the slave trade ran into opposition earlier. Humanitarian sentiment was increasingly important in Europe in the late eighteenth century. The democratic revolutions in France and the United States and the broadening franchise in Great Britain brought political power to middle-class voters who were moved by the inhumanity of the trade. The northern states of North America abolished slavery in the wake of the American Revolution. France abolished both slavery and the slave trade for a time during the 1790s, though later governments restored both. The Dutch slave trade in effect came to an end about 1795, while the Danes abolished theirs, with small exceptions, in 1803, followed by Britain and the United States in 1808. The rest of Europe followed after 1815. The last legal slave trade in the Atlantic basin was abolished by Brazil in 1830.

But the legality of the trade was not always the crucial question. Shippers from many countries found it profitable to trade in slaves, whatever the law might say, and several countries like Brazil and Cuba were slow to enforce laws they had been forced to pass by international pressure. After 1815, however, Great Britain began using its navy in a large-scale attempt to suppress the trade at sea. In time, France and the United States joined in with small squadrons of their own. These efforts were not enough to stop the slave trade, but they did succeed in capturing some 160,000 slaves at sea, amounting to about 8 percent of those shipped from Africa between 1810 and 1870. That alone raised the cost of slaves in the New World and reduced the size the trade might otherwise have reached. The effective end of the Atlantic slave trade came only when American countries began to enforce their own antislave-trade laws, as Brazil did after 1850, and as Cuba did after the late 1860s. The American Civil War ended the trickle of illegal imports that had continued to add slaves to some southern states through the early nineteenth century.

Meanwhile, "legitimate trade" had already begun to replace the trade in slaves. For that matter, slaves had never been the sole source of West Africa's trade; in the seventeenth century, gold from the Gold Coast and hides from Senegambia had been more important exports. Even during the eighteenth-century boom in slave exports, West Africa sold abroad substantial quantities of timber, gum, palm oil, beeswax, gold, hides, and even a few manufactured products like beads or cotton textiles. Production and commercial facilities therefore existed to be stimulated by rising prices, even before the slave trade declined. Gum from the desert fringe was used in Europe for confectionery and in the textile industry. The price per ton doubled between the 1730s and 1780s, then doubled again by the 1830s. Prices offered for hides and ivory increased tenfold between the 1780s and 1830s, and the price of beeswax increased threefold. Palm oil prices fluctuated widely in short-run swings, but the general level began to rise after 1815, approximately doubling between the 1820s and 1850s. These changes prompted even sharper changes in the volume of exports. Palm oil from West Africa to England alone rose from about 1,000 tons a year in 1820 to 30,000 tons a year in the 1850s. Peanut production from Senegambia rose from negligible quantities before 1840 to around 40,000 tons a year by the late 1880s.

While the prices and quantities of particular African exports were rising very rapidly, the prices of European goods sold in Africa rose only slowly or, in the case of cotton textiles, even declined somewhat as machine production drove down costs. This meant that the terms of trade generally shifted in favor of West Africa from the late eighteenth century to about 1860; West Africans received more goods than they had in the past for a given quantity of exports. But the rise of legitimate trade had some specific and peculiar economic consequences. The total value of West African exports in the 1790s has been estimated at about £4 million sterling; exports other than slaves reached about the same value by the 1850s. On the surface, then, it would appear that an equivalent in legitimate trade had been found to replace the slave trade. But most of the new exports flowed in comparatively small quantities and came from closely defined regions: gum from northern Senegal and southern Mauritania, timber from the riverbanks of Sierra Leone, palm oil from the tropical forests of southern Nigeria. Regions that had profited from the slave trade were also limited and concentrated but they were different regions. Even the illicit slave trade moved to new places as old suppliers like the Gold Coast or Senegambia dropped out altogether. After the 1820s, new sources like Yorubaland became major suppliers to the trade for the first time in their history.

In any case, the economic and social consequences of slave and legitimate trade were different. The society whose people became enslaved was, of course, a net loser, but even the captors received a comparatively small percentage of the total price paid on export. Most of it went to the merchants who moved the slaves to the coast and held them until a European ship appeared. These merchants could sometimes shift to new commodities, but only if they happened to live near one of the zones of new production for export. Otherwise they had to leave commercial activity or shift to the nonexport trade.

With the new exports, the payoff went in part to merchants, but also to new social groups who controlled production. They might be members of an old ruling class, like the Mauritanian lineage heads who controlled semidesert woodlands where their slaves collected gum. Or new production might divert income to new people. The Senegambian peasants who grew peanuts profited directly, and so did large numbers of free migrant workers who began to come annually to work at peanut growing near the Senegal coast or the Gambia River. In the palm oil regions it was again slaves who did much of the work while their owners, the merchants, and the political authorities took most of the new income. But again, it is important to remember that most economic activity was not for export, nor were all new currents of trade bound for Europe. It is probable, for example, that the nineteenth-century kola nut trade from Asante to the savanna country increased even more in value than did the palm oil exports from the Gold Coast.

THE "EUROPEAN" PRESENCE

The influence of European culture along the West African coast grew even more rapidly than the growth of overseas trade might indicate. Legitimate trade required more European residents than the slave trade had done. More accurately, the degree of culture contact on the African coast in the era of the slave trade was unusually low, partly because the slave-trade posts were very lightly manned and partly because the European death rates were so high. Most European posts of the eighteenth century, moreover, were more Eur-African than European. Where the typical European strength might vary from a dozen to a few hundred, the African population associated with the post was always much larger, including many descended from European fathers and African mothers. These Afro-Europeans and others of purely African descent occasionally went to Europe for an education, like Philip Quaque, the Anglican chaplain to the main English fort on the Gold Coast. He and others like him helped to found schools teaching a smattering of European languages and a little commercial arithmetic. These schools were often ephemeral, but, by the turn of the eighteenth century, a scattered, partly European population of permanent residents could be found along the coast from Saint Louis du Sénégal to Benguela in southern Angola. Saint Louis in 1810 was representative, with only about 10 Europeans but 500 Afro-Europeans, another 500 free Africans associated with the post and partly Europeanized in culture, and around 2,200 slaves as a culturally African working class.

By the nineteenth century, these Afro-Europeans had become some of the most important members of local "European" society, partly because the Afro-Europeans stayed on, while Europeans typically came for a few years only. Thomas Joiner of the Gambia had been a slave in Virginia, but he returned to Banjul after the Napoleonic wars and became the largest shipowner and one of the most prosperous merchants in the Gambia. On the Gold Coast, the Brew family, descended from an Irish trader of the mid-eighteenth century, provided a dynasty of Anglo-African merchants and officials for more than a century. Indeed, the last three decades of the precolonial century were the pinnacle of economic success and power for Afro-Europeans all along the coast. Only in the 1880s and later they were pushed aside by Europeans fresh from Europe. By that time, colonial regimes with exclusive, racialist policies had replaced the more informal life of the trading enclaves.

But a new and greater intensity of European activity along the coasts was already evident a century earlier. In the 1780s, a dozen or so new settlements were planned for the African coasts, often with an agricultural component alongside the more common pattern of a fortified trading post. Most of these plans came to nothing, or, if tried, they failed and disappeared. But the British settlement at Sierra Leone had a disproportionate influence all along the West African coast. First established in 1787, it began as a philanthropic project to provide a home for the "black poor" of London, but the plan soon broadened into a projected agricultural colony and a base for "legitimate trade." Through several changes in emphasis and management, it was used successively as a place of settlement for black American loyalists and Jamaican rebels — both groups of returnees from the New World being Western in culture. Then, from the first decade of the nineteenth century, it became a place for the reception and settlement of slaves recaptured at sea by the British navy. It was then the focus of a broad, humanitarian effort to promote Christianity and Western culture in Africa through the agency of Westernized recaptives. Missionary societies sent a higher ratio of personnel to potential converts than they had ever done before. A government-sponsored educational system was soon training a higher proportion of school-age children than were trained in England itself at that time. In 1827, Fourah Bay College opened its doors for the education of an African clergy. The result was a new Anglo-African society, small at first, but increasingly capable of assimilating thousands of new arrivals when the stream of recaptives reached a peak in the 1840s.

A second settlement of returnees had meanwhile been established nearby. In 1822, the American Colonization Society founded a small colony of Afro-Americans at Cape Mesurado. The settlement grew into the city of Monrovia and the colonization effort eventually became the Republic of Liberia. It was unofficially supported by the United States government, but the major effort came from private citizens. Some acted from genuinely philanthropic motives, but others simply wanted to rid the United States of its free Afro-American population, which they regarded as racially undesirable. Other private colonization societies sponsored settlements along the coast south and east of Monrovia, until some 5,000 settlers had arrived before 1850. They were later joined by recaptive slaves landed by the United States Navy, and these settlements became a flourishing set of Afro-American communities. In 1847, the Monrovia settlement sought to clarify its relationship with the United States by declaring its independence. By 1856, the other settlements joined to form an independent Liberia, and most of the European powers recognized the former colony's new status in international law, though informal American influence usually made the new country less independent in fact than it was in theory.

The old trading posts also began to change after 1815. The British returned to the mouth of the Gambia in 1817 after several decades of absence and founded a settlement at Banjul (known as Bathurst during the colonial period), while the French made elaborate plans for the Senegal valley, including a new fortified post at Bakel in 1819, 400 miles inland, and the first use of steamboats on African rivers. They tried in the 1820s to encourage plantation agriculture in the neighboring state of Waalo, but the scheme was undercapitalized, the European managers died, and the Africans were unwilling to work for the wage rate Europeans wanted to pay.

In the 1840s, the British tried an even more elaborate scheme on the Niger, but with similar components. They brought out steamboats for the river trade and planned a plantation colony at the junction of the Benue and Niger rivers in open savanna country, about 250 miles from the sea. They hoped to encourage large-scale cotton production under the direction of an Afro-American specialist hired for that purpose as one aspect of a scheme for economic development, partly in European-controlled territory, but including an effort to persuade African authorities to set up their own plantations along European lines. The economic aspect was coupled with a missionary effort aimed at "Christianity and civilization" on the model of Sierra Leone.

This project failed in short order because of high mortality among the European personnel. It nevertheless illustrates the kind of political, economic, and cultural influence Europeans wanted to exert in Africa at that time. They were emphatically not interested in the form of direct annexation that was to take place after the 1880s. Instead, the goal was informal empire of a limited kind. After the failure of the Niger expedition, for example, the British retained hope that they might find a strong African power — perhaps the Caliphate of Sokoto — that would accept subsidies and advice in return for providing a protective shield over British commerce as it spread into the interior.

France, the only other European country active in West Africa at mid-century, followed a similar set of goals, and placed similar limitations on conquest or annexation. In the 1840s, France too began to set up new trading posts to foster legitimate commerce, such as Grand Bassam and Assini on the Ivory Coast and Libreville in Gabon. Some of the French hoped to establish plantations, especially in Gabon, where they landed the recaptives their navy had taken from slavers at sea, but they had no more agricultural success than the British had had in Sierra Leone or on the Niger. Especially in the 1850s and 1860s, they too used armed steamboats on the Senegal as a road to the interior and as a means of putting force behind their goal of informal empire over the riverain states. And they too hoped for a special relationship with some large interior state as an umbrella to cover the advance of French influence. At first they had in mind the Bambara states of Segu and Kaarta, later the new states established on the same ground by the continuing religious revolutions.

Meanwhile, Liberia and especially Sierra Leone became centers for the less formal penetration of Western culture. Though neither developed the hoped-for agriculture, the settlers in both turned very successfully to trade over networks that reached well beyond the present republics into Guinea-Conakry. Both also developed an important seaborne trade along the coast, sometimes buying condemned slave ships for the purpose. This trade opened a route for many of the recaptives to return to their homelands, especially to Yorubaland in western Nigeria. Because this movement began only in the 1840s, many of the returnees had already spent several years in Sierra Leone. They therefore carried home their knowledge of Western ways. By the 1850s, the stream reached more than a thousand a year in peak years.

Many returnees found it impossible or impractical to resettle in their home village, even if it had survived the wars. Most were associated, in any event, with trade or missionary work and settled first at coastal points like Badagry or Lagos, which became a British government post in 1861. Others made their way inland, many going to Abeokuta, which was already a rallying point for the Egba, a Yoruba subgroup whose cities and towns had been largely destroyed by the wars. Concentrated groups of returnees like those in Abeokuta were soon able to play an important role in local affairs, while those who originally settled on the coast often circulated widely through Yorubaland as commercial travelers, catechists, or Christian missionaries.

By the mid-nineteenth century, other returnees also began to drift back from the New World to Yorubaland, especially from Brazil and Cuba. These "Brazilians," called *amaro* as distinct from the *saro,* or "Sierra Leoneans," also turned to commerce and settled for the most part in coastal towns from Lagos west through Dahomey to the later Republic of Togo. There, they merged with an existing community of Afro-Portuguese who had preserved the Portuguese language and Catholic religion. They developed their commercial position so successfully that French colonial officials of the 1890s estimated that more than half the merchants in Dahomey were "Brazilians."

Some of the returnees were illiterate or barely literate, relatively untouched by the West. The ordinary home language in Sierra Leone was not English but Krio, a new language with an African grammatical base and words derived from many sources, though heavily English. Most ordinary returnees had picked up a new African culture abroad, with a few associated aspects of Western culture. But others were fully educated in the Western manner, including education in Europe. Dr. J. Africanus B. Horton, the son of an Ibo recaptive, became a British-trained medical man who served from the 1850s to his retirement in 1880 as a regular member of the British Army Medical Service. He contributed research reports on tropical medicine to British medical journals, and he published even more widely on African affairs. Samuel Crowther began life as a Yoruba, was captured as a boy, enslaved, then recaptured by a British cruiser and landed in Sierra Leone. He went on to become one of the first students at Fourah Bay College and later the first African bishop of the Anglican Church, founder of an all-African missionary effort along the Niger River, author of a number of books about Africa, including geographical explorations and a study of the Yoruba language.

None of the returnees from Brazil achieved such intellectual distinction, but several of the Afro-French community on the Senegalese coast published books in French. Abbé Boilat, who went to France for his education, published a book-length study of Senegalese society in the 1850s. Other Afro-French rose in the government service, including General Dodds, the French military commander at the conquest of Dahomey in the 1890s.

Africans who reached this level identified with Europe and accepted European culture on its own terms. They admired the technological superiority of the West and often ended by accepting Western cultural chauvinism as well. They saw the appropriate future for Africa in the direction labeled "Christianity and civilization," and they were generally proud to have a part in leading Africa to that salvation. Few suspected at mid-century that a colonial period lay ahead. They assumed that more and more authority would pass into the hands of Western-educated Africans like themselves. By the 1870s, however, a certain disillusionment began to set in. Men like J. A. B. Horton began to worry about the political future, and the educated group were made even more anxious by European expressions of pseudoscientific racism. Their disillusionment was muted at first, but it deepened in the 1890s. By that time, it was abundantly clear that "Christianity and civilization" meant European rule, and European rule by Europeans from Europe — with diminished roles for people like themselves.

POLITICAL MODERNIZATION AND INFORMAL EMPIRE: THE GOLD COAST AND ABEOKUTA

Men like Horton and Bishop Crowther were far more clearly "modernizers" than Muhammad 'Ali had been in Egypt; they understood the West far better than he had done, but they were not in command of independent African governments. Those Africans who did hold power were rarely able to plan ahead over a period of decades. Most of them lacked a clear understanding of the European threat. European warships were present along the coasts; consuls conducted diplomacy with naval power in the background; but European pressure was intermittent. Even the push for informal empire on the Niger or Senegal was sporadic. Elsewhere, the Europeans encroached only gradually with a new trading post here and there.

Some African governments, however, learned how to meet the West more nearly on its own terms, and they learned mainly from the pressure for informal empire and the local response this inspired. Local European commanders in the early nineteenth century tended to mix more actively in African politics than their predecessors had done. On the Gold Coast, for example, the British governor sent diplomatic missions to Asante in the interior. From 1824 to 1826, he abandoned a time-honored neutrality and entered a war against Asante on the side of the Ga and Fante coastal states; this was the beginning of an informal alliance which ultimately made the coastal rulers dependent on British support. In the 1830s, however, the London government decided to reduce its commitment to African trade. It turned the Gold Coast forts over to a committee of merchants, but the committee's main official on the coast, George Maclean, soon began to arbitrate quarrels among the rulers of the microstates in the hinterland. This arbitration gradually grew into a kind of legal jurisdiction, in which a British official, with African consent, acted as judge between African litigants, enforcing African law with a few changes to bring it into line with "civilized" practice. When the British government resumed control of the forts in 1843, it therefore found an informal judicial protectorate functioning as a constitutional device to increase the scale of political life. It was, in short, a step toward political "modernization," though designed to meet a potential threat from Asante rather than Europe. In 1844, the British formalized this informal arrangement by asking each participating state to sign a "bond" authorizing the British governor to act for it in certain judicial matters. The Asante danger forced their compliance, but it was a clear step toward informal empire, even toward colonial rule, because later British officials acted as though they had turned the alliance into a protectorate.

Afro-Europeans and Western-educated Africans also worked with African governments behind the Gold Coast forts. Several times in the 1850s, they advised the traditional authorities in ways that helped them to resist informal empire, and they worked to create modernizing institutions independent of British control, such as a commercial court projected for Cape Coast.

A new phase began in the late 1860s, when King Aggrey of Cape Coast resisted British jurisdiction on the advice of the Western-educated community. The British deposed and exiled him in 1866, but this act showed many people the need for a larger and more powerful political organization, partly to resist British encroachment but also for protection against Asante if, as was widely expected, the British were to withdraw from the Gold Coast altogether. J. A. B. Horton was one of the leaders of this movement; others were African clergymen and schoolteachers associated with the Methodist Church. Between 1868 and 1873, they mobilized local opinion to support the project of creating a new state that would join all the Fante and other coastal peoples in the central and western Gold Coast. The projected constitution assigned a formal role to the traditional rulers of the existing microstates, but it balanced their power against that of the new, Western-educated elite. The new state, sometimes called the Mankessim Confederation from its principal meeting place, recruited a military force and set up a rudimentary administration, but the British, neutral at first, decided to annex the coastal states, creating the Gold Coast colony in 1874.

The Fante Confederation achieved little, but it was an important straw in the wind showing where African opinion was tending. Nor was it alone. A similar Ga-speaking Republic of Accra was also suppressed in 1873 by the British occupation. Nearly simultaneously, the Egba United Board of Management, founded by J. W. Johnson, a Sierra Leonean returnee to Abeokuta, made a similar effort at political modernization, balancing a continuing role for the old elite with a secure place for the Western-educated. It held real power in Abeokuta from 1865 to 1872, almost the same period as the Mankessim Confederation, but it failed in the longer run because it was unable to muster the unified support of the Egba; it also lacked the military power to withstand British pressure from Lagos.

None of these constitutional innovations had the importance of the routine day-to-day participation of educated Africans in the affairs of the European posts.

The distant roots of the movement for African independence, indeed, can be traced back to the political efforts of Western-educated Africans within the European sphere, often working for the colonial governments — even before the colonial period had begun for most of Africa.

COMMERCE AND POLITICAL CHANGE: OYO

Countries undisturbed by the religious revolutions or by the direct influence of Europeans along the coast nevertheless felt the impact of the commercial revolution. Three West African societies from Asante eastward to the Niger can exemplify the possible social and political responses to the new flow of commerce. Broadly speaking, people with commercial interests rose in wealth and power by comparison with the old political and military elites, but generalization at this level can mask a great variety of actual change.

In Yorubaland, the overriding political event of the precolonial century was the collapse of the old empire of Oyo and the growth of a new Yoruba state system to replace it. Commerce was especially important in the later stages of this process, but the fragility of Oyo's political constitution was more crucial to its initial collapse. Eighteenth-century military expansion had left a structure that was neither homogeneous nor united. At the core was the original kingdom of Oyo, from which the expansion had begun. It was culturally Yoruba, fairly homogeneous and united. Beyond were other Yoruba states under Oyo's control, but not under its day-to-day administration. Each had its own *oba,* or king, and went its own way. Each was ruled through a system of councils representing important lineages in much the same way that lineage power was checked and balanced in the core kingdom. Still further afield were a number of diverse non-Yoruba tributary states — Borgu and parts of Nupe in the north, Dahomey and other Aja-speaking states in the west as far as the borders of Asante. These were still harder to supervise, and they tended to break away in times of crisis at the center.

In the central government, an oba bearing the title of *alafin* was balanced against a principal council called the *Oyo Mesi.* The president of the council was the *bashorun,* or military commander, and its members represented the principal nonroyal lineages of the capital. The alafin had been in chronic conflict with the Oyo Mesi throughout the eighteenth century. Much of his power came from his constitutional role as ruler over the provinces and subject kingdoms. The council meanwhile drew its power mainly from Oyo itself, and it was usually dominant. It sometimes ruled without any alafin, allowing the bashorun to become the chief executive officer.

The final crisis came in the 1820s, precipitated by a military revolt under a certain Afonja, who had built up a private military force of local Muslims, aided from time to time by offshoots of the Fulbe jihad based on Sokoto. Afonja not only made himself independent of the central government but detached a substantial part of northern Oyo to create the emirate of Ilorin, dependent on Sokoto. Afonja's success then prompted other provincial leaders on other fringes to revolt and to go their own ways.

The running conflict between the Oyo Mesi and the alafin kept the center from taking effective action until it was too late to pull the pieces together again. The outer provinces all fell away into independence during a period of confused anarchy and fighting that lasted well into the 1830s. Many of the savanna-dwelling people of the metropolitan province around the city of Old Oyo moved south into the forest belt for greater security from roaming cavalry. In savanna and forest alike, walled towns became centers of refuge and power and they began to fight one another for domination over particular regions. Victory meant the destruction of the enemy towns and the enslavement of their inhabitants, which in turn fed the illicit slave trade to Brazil and Cuba.

In the 1840s and 1850s, the worst of the anarchy was contained and a new constitution began to take shape for Yorubaland. Monarchy was meanwhile restored in Oyo, but the new alafin soon found the old location of the capital untenable. He therefore retreated to the south and established New Oyo at the edge of the forest. New Oyo was recognized as suzerain over most of northern Yorubaland, though real power still belonged to a series of towns controlling their own regions. These new towns were larger than Yoruba towns had been in the past, having populations of twenty to sixty thousand people for greater security and often consolidating several older towns into one. Abeokuta, for example, brought together the remnants and refugees from more than a hundred Egba towns and worked out a new combined constitution. Influenced in the 1850s by Christian missionaries and returning saro, this led to the Egba United Board of Management. Other towns were newly founded, like Ibadan, which began as a war camp but stabilized into a city, and Ibadan's constitution reflected its military origin. From the 1850s to the 1870s, Ibadan seemed close to gaining hegemony over all Yorubaland, but the threat inspired other towns with the fear of being gobbled up. The result was a new period of chonic warfare lasting from 1877 to 1892 and centering on Ibadan's drive for power.

Meanwhile, the slave trade ended in the 1850s, and legitimate commerce began to be important. The new flow of trade shifted income from those who captured slaves to those who had palm oil for sale. It also shifted income to communities in a position to profit as middlemen — first to ports directly on the sea like Badagry and Lagos, then to Yoruba states further inland, like Ijebu on the land side of the coastal lagoon or Abeokuta still further inland. While new trade brought new wealth, it also brought new dependence on the ports and a web of informal Lagos influence, which attenuated as it stretched inland. When the British finally decided in 1892 to turn this influence into formal empire, it required only a quick demonstration of power against Ijebu. After that, treaties were imposed on most of the remaining Yoruba states. Though these were not yet treaties of outright annexation, they nevertheless gave the Lagos government so much informal control that annexation could follow whenever Lagos decided the time was ripe.

ASANTE

The Asante experience was somewhat different. The impact of the new commerce was stronger and came earlier in the century. Asante was also smaller than Oyo, more homogeneous in culture, with a more efficient bureaucracy and a less cumbersome constitutional balance between king and council. In most circumstances, the ruler or *Asantehene* had more power to exercise his individual leadership than the alafin had. Asante was nevertheless a lineage-based state, just as Oyo had been. People's fundamental connection to society was through membership in their matrilineage. Matrilineages were internally self-governing within a village, and villages were nearly self-governing within the broader state. The state was regarded as having only limited functions, namely, to maintain law and order internally and to protect the populace from foreign attack. In fact, the state in the eighteenth century had done a good deal more than that. Its expansion northward out of the forest had brought gains from tribute and from slaves for sale to the coast, in a setting where both trade and warfare were monopolized by the central government.

Within government circles of the early nineteenth century, the research of Ivor Wilks has shown two discernable parties: an imperialist party that wanted the state to enrich its citizens through military aggression, and a peace party that wanted the same goal through state trade. A different group of citizens was likely to profit from either alternative. Military leadership stood to be rewarded by imperial advance, whereas state traders would profit from a peace policy, though the Asantehene had a theoretical monopoly of all foreign trade. In fact, trade was controlled by a Company of State Traders under the head of the treasury, with trade chiefs directing the actual movement of goods; but individual merchants carried out their own operations on their own account. The Asantehene supplied each important trader with a regular advance of capital in the form of gold dust, which the recipient could invest himself or pass on to subordinate agents. He was expected, of course, to make an accounting, and most of the profit went back to the treasury; but everyone who was engaged in trade, down to the lowliest caravan porters, expected to make a private profit as well, and the Asantehene sometimes left a segment of the trade open to private enterprise.

The end of the export trade in slaves after 1810 therefore shifted income from the war party to the peace party, and the growth of legitimate trade favored it even more. From the 1840s, the Asantehene began allowing wealthy traders to invest their own capital alongside the state investment, thus shifting somewhat from state capitalism to a mixed system with a degree of regulated private capitalism. Even before these changes, a few men had been able to amass great fortunes from their connections to the state trade apparatus. They were much respected and honored by the state, and they came to own many slaves, because slaves and gold dust were the main forms of transferable property. But they were less secure than they would have liked to be, because the Asantehene had the right to inherit any property held in gold dust.

After mid-century, the commercial group became richer and stronger and began to demand the end of the inheritance tax, and of government regulation it thought was crippling trade. The merchants also picked up chance allies among the underprivileged, both slaves and free, who were strongly opposed to the existing system of military conscription, hence to the military group as a whole. The commercial group and its allies were especially strong in the 1870s, and they began to look south to the newly created Gold Coast colony as a model of a better society. In 1883, they staged a coup that brought down the government of Asantehene Mensa Bonsu, but the alliance of rich and poor turned out to be fragile. Their coup was followed by a series of countercoups, while no unifying leadership emerged among the rebels.

This situation left an opening for the Gold Coast government to intervene actively in Asante politics. Refugees from whomever ruled in Kumasi gathered in coastal towns where they were allowed to behave like a government-in-exile. By the early 1890s, Asante was well within a British informal empire, and the annexation was made official in 1896, when the British became alarmed about the inland advance of the Germans in Togo to the east and of the French in the Ivory Coast to the west. Annexation by some European power was probably inevitable, as the Asante political system had already failed to respond effectively to the social and economic forces that had been released by the commercial revolution.

THE NIGER DELTA

The Ijo of the Niger Delta were closer still to the impact of the new commerce, and their trading states like Nembe, Bonny, and Kalabari had already passed through one institutional transformation in adjusting to seaborne trade. Rather than being organized by lineages, the fundamental social unit here was the "canoe house," the basic trading organization. In each of these states, the kings were stronger than their eighteenth-century predecessors had been, but they still ruled with the sanction of a council made up of the heads of the individual houses. Each state controlled its own trade zone and the water routes to the interior, with a more informal influence stretching into the hinterland that furnished the slaves for export. As it turned out, this hinterland was also a place where oil palms grew naturally in the forest, so the first adjustment was simply that of adding a new product to the continued movement of slaves toward the sea.

But the end of the slave trade and the growth of the palm oil trade brought changes too. British antislave-trade patrols used Fernando Po (now Isle Macias Nquema) as a base, which gave them the power to intervene forcefully anywhere within reach of their ships' guns. Europeans also came to live on the rivers, to buy palm oil and prepare it for shipment, and their hulks moored offshore became a center of European influence. That influence increased as African suppliers became entangled in a web of credit. The Europeans extended goods on trust, to be paid for in palm oil at a later time. Whereas Africans had supplied their own capital for the slave trade, they now depended on European capital in the oil trade. Credit led to conflict, which in turn led to the establishment of Afro-European "Courts of Equity." These courts, made up of African and European merchants, settled commercial disputes. Their decisions could be enforced through commercial sanctions, but they were also validated in British law through the authority of the British consul assigned to the Bights of Benin and Biafra. Here, as in Egypt or the Gold Coast, informal empire began with European judicial institutions that gave no special advantage to either side in the beginning, but were over time to shift in the Europeans' favor.

At mid-century, however, the delta states were still clear of informal empire; they had switched successfully to legitimate trade. The profits of the oil trade seemed an adequate replacement for the old source of income, and they were earned by much the same people in the same way. But then trouble began. Steamboats began to be used regularly on the lower Niger in the 1850s, trading up to the junction with the Benue and on up both rivers. This carried the riverside trade well into the savanna belt, but it also opened new points of trade on the lower river, in effect giving access to the palm-producing regions previously served by the Ijo canoe routes. The delta states thus found their trade reduced and their future expansion limited. To make matters worse, substitutes for palm oil began to come on the European market at lower prices — peanut oil for some purposes, petroleum for others. The price of palm oil had risen steadily until the late 1850s, but in 1862 it began to decline, and it declined so rapidly that the delta states could not sustain the total value of their exports by shipping larger quantities.

Social unrest also spread, as ex-slaves who had begun as canoe paddlers worked their way into the ranks of the merchants. They were unhappy at being denied power and prestige to match their wealth. Revolts broke out in all the delta states from the 1850s onward, with the British navy called in from time to time to help shore up the old regime. In 1869, part of the population of Bonny emigrated to found a new state, Opobo, under an ex-slave named Ja-Ja, who soon established his control over most of the markets Bonny had once dominated.

Through all of this, the British consuls continued to increase their influence over Ijo affairs. By the mid-1870s, the delta could be counted as part of the informal British empire. By the end of the decade, informal British control stretched up the Niger as well, where the National African Company had scores of trading posts along the rivers. In 1884–85, the British became concerned about French and German annexations elsewhere in Africa. They therefore formalized their hold on the Niger by asking the rulers of the Niger coast and riverside to sign "voluntary" treaties placing themselves under British protection — the first major step toward creating the territorial unit that was to be Nigeria.

SHAYKH UMAR TAAL
AND THE FUTAANKE EMPIRE

By the 1830s, religious revolutions in the western Sudan were markedly less revolutionary. Abdul Kader's reform movement in Fuuta Tooro had been secularized and stabilized since the early century. In the Caliphate of Sokoto and in Borno, the new political structures were in place, and the demand for further change was muted, if not silent. On the Niger bend and in Maasina, the descendents of earlier reformers were fighting one another, as the Kunta shaykhs set themselves up as leaders of dissident Fulbe and Tuareg trying to separate Timbuktu and the Niger bend from the Caliphate of Hamdallahi. Within that caliphate, reform had also lost some of its appeal. In the 1840s, a new group of military men came to power, men who had been too young for the earlier revolution and depended on power politics, not religious fervor, to secure the place of the caliphate in the Niger valley.

At the same time, the earlier reformers had been able to stir men with their demands for a just and godly society, and that demand was clearly not satisfied. As at the height of the earlier movements, people were resentful of their treatment by society for many different reasons, and the idiom of religion could still appeal to people and unite them behind a leader. Flurries of reform preaching and organization were continuous all through the first half of the century. Several broke into open rebellion, but the existing governments were able to suppress them with apparent ease. It was only with the 1850s that a new and somewhat different kind of movement arose under Shaykh Umar Taal, a cleric from western Fuuta Tooro. He built an empire that was larger and more centralized than Hamdallahi or Sokoto had been, and he carved it out of territory that had not been heavily Islamic in the past — rather than attacking existing Muslim rulers for their laxity.

Umar also preached a new religious doctrine, different from the Qādirīya that had served other reformers. His message was that of the Tijānīya, a comparatively new religious brotherhood founded in Fez in the 1780s by Ahmad al-Tijāni. The Tijāni doctrine was more exclusive and rigid than was common to sufi orders. Compared to the Qādirīya, it was also more mystical and concerned with the correct ritual practices to bring a sense of direct contact with God. At the same time, it had a weaker tradition of asceticism than did other sufi orders (or such antisufi reform movements as the Wahabi of eighteenth-century Arabia). Ahmad al-Tijāni's claim to be the "seal" of the saints was also exceptional; it asserted that he was the final Muslim saint in the same sense that Muhammad was the seal of the prophets. This implied that the Tijānīya was different from

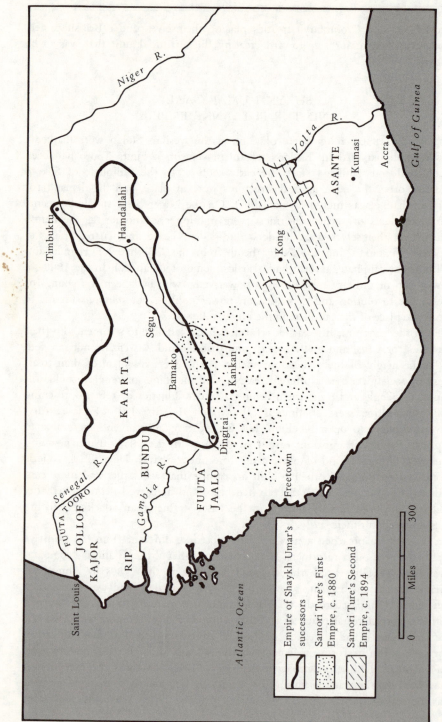

Niger R.

Volta R.

Gulf of Guinea

ASANTE
• Kumasi
Accra •

Timbuktu

Hamdallahi

• Kong

Segu

KAARTA

Bamako •

• Kankan

Dingirai

Senegal R.

FUUTA TOORO

JOLLOF

Saint Louis

KAJOR

RIP

BUNDU

Gambia R.

FUUTÁ
JAALO

Freetown

Atlantic Ocean

The Last Sudanic Empires

Empire of Shaykh Umar's
successors

Samori Ture's First
Empire, c. 1880

Samori Ture's Second
Empire, c. 1894

0   300
Miles

the other sufi orders in offering not merely *a* way to God, but perhaps the only correct way. Some later Tijāni clerics have pushed the claim of exclusivity to the point of making the order appear more a separate sect than a *tarīqa*.

By the 1830s, the Tijāniya was widely followed in the Maghrib and out into the desert, but the main line of transmission to the western Sudan was to come by way of Umar Taal's pilgrimage to Mecca in about 1830. There, the order's khalifa for the cities of Arabia appointed Umar head of the order in the western Sudan. With that authority, he made a slow return toward Senegambia with prolonged stops in Borno, Sokoto, Timbuktu, and Hamdallahi before settling down to preach and build up his own following. The base he chose was not his home country but Dingirai, on the frontiers of the Almaamate of Fuuta Jaalo far to the south.

Umar's early appeal was peaceful and widespread. In 1846–47, for example, he traveled with a group of followers from Fuuta Jaalo down the Gambia valley to the Atlantic, then north through the Serer and Wolof kingdoms, and finally up the Senegal valley through Fuuta Tooro and on south to his base at Dingirai. During the next two years, he began military operations that slowly turned his capital into the center of a small state incorporating several of the smaller kingdoms in the upper Niger valley. Toward the end of 1852–53, he declared a holy war and began still more extensive conquests from Dingirai north toward the upper Senegal through a region mainly Malinke-speaking and non-Muslim.

Umar's jihad was different from those of earlier reformers in that he tried mainly to conquer new territory for Islam, rather than purifying the practices of Muslim governments. He called for no jihad against the existing almaamates of Fuuta Tooro, Fuuta Jaalo, or Bundu, and he was less doctrinaire than most earlier reformers. He played lightly on the differences between his own Tijāni way and that of the Qādirīya. His main interest in the Muslim territories of Senegambia was their support against "pagans" further east. He called for a great *fergo,* or voluntary withdrawal with wives and cattle, from Fulbe Fuuta Tooro and Bundu to follow him eastward. In Bundu, he played dynastic politics so as to establish an Almaami favorable to his interests, but neither there nor in Fuuta Tooro did he try to establish his direct rule. But over the next few years, he drew off as much as 25 percent of the Futaanke population, and half that of Bundu. By 1854, he controlled parts of Kaarta from a new capital at Nioro, in the sahel between the Niger and the Senegal, as the base for a Futaanke empire, sometimes called the Tukolor empire from the name of the sedentary farming class in Fuuta Tooro.

During the rest of the 1850s, his main concern was to continue the fergo from Fuuta in order to build up the new base at Nioro. This inevitably involved a confrontation with the French, who were simultaneously trying to establish their absolute control over Senegal River trade and their informal empire over riverside kingdoms. The Franco-Umarian military confrontation came in 1857, when Umar tried to capture Médine, the French post near the head of Senegal navigation. But the post held out under an Afro-French commander long enough to be relieved by a new force sent upriver by steamboat. The result was not so much a French victory as a standoff, leaving the French in unquestioned mastery of Senegal navigation, while Umar kept his conquests between Dingirai and the Senegal and eastward into the sahel. He continued to visit Fuuta for recruiting purposes, though he never claimed authority there.

Shaykh Umar's next objectives were still further east. In 1860, he began a new series of campaigns for control of the Niger valley from the kingdom of Segu northeast to Timbuktu on the desert's edge. Segu had a Muslim minority, but it was culturally and linguistically Malinke or Bambara and safely "pagan" in religion. Further downstream, however, both Timbuktu and the Caliphate of Hamdallahi were already reformed Muslim, though Qādiri in their version of sufism. Umar first captured Segu, then moved ahead in 1863 to take Hamdallahi and Timbuktu — his first major capture of already-Muslim territory. The military operation was successful; but Umar was killed in 1864 during a counterattack, and his successors were unable to hold Timbuktu.

Umar's death ended the expansive phase of the Futaanke empire. During the next three decades, it settled down to the usual life of a large Sudanese state. Some historians have suggested that if Umar had lived, he might have gone on to conquer Sokoto as well and thus to unify the whole of the western Sudan; but it seems more likely that the empire had already reached its practical limits. It was already too big for continuous central control, so that large provinces were allotted to one or another of Umar's family or followers, though these provinces were larger and fewer than the emirates under Sokoto. Umar's son, Ahmadu Seku, took over the central power under the title *Lamido Juulbe* (commander of the faithful), which was preferred to the older title of Almaami. Trusted followers were given regional command at Dingirai for the southwest, Nioro for the sahel, Hamdallahi and Segu for the Niger valley, and Kuniakari just east of the upper Senegal.

Such a large empire tempted French strategists to make a new set of plans for informal penetration under the Lamido Juulbe's shield, but the local French military commanders preferred to try for outright conquest, which they carried through in a series of campaigns beginning in the late 1800s and ending in 1893.

NEW RULERS FOR SENEGAMBIA

Senegambia's experience with religious reform went back at least as far as Nasīr al-Dīn's jihad in the 1670s, but the Wolof, Serer, and Malinke states near the Atlantic coast and along the Gambia remained unreformed until the 1860s. Then, in a short space of only three decades, the old secular dynasties were overthrown by new clerical leaders preaching a purified Islamic state. Finally, in an even shorter space of time, French and British arms prevailed and established another and still newer set of rulers from Europe.

Most of the old guard of secular-minded, though normally Muslim, rulers worked within a political framework consisting of one or more royal lineages that supplied rulers in turn, and of a council that represented the other important free lineages in that society — balancing, in effect, the royal lineages and one another. Because the lineages themselves were to some extent autonomous units, it was easy for this kind of state to grant autonomy to other groups who might demand it. Over recent centuries, clerics, often with a mercantile background, had asked for and obtained permission to form small autonomous enclaves — often no more than a village and its surrounding agricultural land. There, the clerics and their followers could practice Islam as they wished, free from secular interference. By the early nineteenth century, the kings had created scores of such enclaves, and they were already a source of potential opposition and even an alternate source of authority, should the secular state weaken.

And the secular states of the nineteenth century *had* become weak. The constitutional checks and balances worked so strongly against the monarch that few could maintain effective control, either against important lineage heads or even against their own standing armies of slave-soldiers. These slave-soldiers, or *ceddo* (*thiedo* in French), were an especially serious cause of disorder in the countryside, raiding the peasants in their own territory or across nearby frontiers. Beginning in the 1840s, peanut cultivation began to extend inland from the Gambia River and from the coast. The end of the slave trade may have deprived the rulers and ceddo of some income. It certainly diverted income to the peasants who grew peanuts for export, and to the merchants involved in bulking and transporting the peanuts to navigable water. Disorder, in short, gave the peasantry a grievance against authority, while the clerical-mercantile group could provide leadership for a series of revolts that struck almost everywhere in Senegambia, but with great local variation and complexity.

The central role in this series of revolts belonged to Mamadu Ba, commonly called Ma Ba. He was originally from Fuuta, like Shaykh Umar, but he lived in the tiny riverside state of Baddibu, or Rip, on the north bank of the Gambia. In 1862, he won control of Baddibu and moved on to conquer Saalum as well, with occasional interventions further afield eastward up the Gambia or across to the south bank. But Ma Ba was essentially a religious leader, not a military man, so that his wider influence came indirectly through his followers. Among these were Lat Joor (Dior), who seized power in Kajor, and Alburi Njai (N'Diayi), the ruler of Jollof. Or, coming down through time, Momar Anta Mbake was Ma Ba's friend, the tutor of his son, and the father of Amadu Bamba, who in turn founded the Mourid brotherhood and went on to become one of the most important religious leaders in twentieth-century Senegal. Other revolts continued to the eve of the European conquest. Another cleric, Fode Kaba, established still another new religious state south of the Gambia mouth, while Muslim Fulbe from Fuuta Jaalo overturned a series of older Malinke states further east, though without clerical leadership in that case.

The British and French in the trade enclaves generally tried to support the old rulers in this series of wars, but the secular side gradually lost power in spite of foreign support. The last act was played out in the late 1880s. It began in 1885 with a last religious revolt on the upper Senegal, led by Mamadu Lamin Drame against the secular rulers of Gajaaga and Bundu. Since these states were already solidly within the sphere of informal French control, France entered as well and pursued Mamadu Lamin to his death on the middle Gambia. French forces had already defeated and killed Lat Jor of Kajor in 1886. They drove out Alburi Njai of Jollof in 1890, and they completed their conquest of Fuuta Tooro in 1891, thereby introducing the colonial period to most of Senegambia.

SAMORI TURE AND THE JUULA REVOLUTION

Almost all the religious revolutions sketched so far took place in the northern half of the savanna belt. In the southern half of the savanna (the "middle belt" as the Nigerians call it, sometimes called the preforest zone further west), the socioreligious setting was different. There, Muslims were only a small minority, and Muslim penetration had only recently been carried by the *juula,* or merchants. Islam was therefore identified with the merchant community even more closely than it was further north. Almost all juula were Muslim, though not all Muslims were juula. Before the eighteenth century, the juula communities scattered along the trade routes had a tacit understanding with the local rulers: if the juula stayed out of politics, the rulers would stay out of commerce.

This understanding was broken by such events as the Fulbe jihad of the 1720s in Fuuta Jaalo, which opened access to the coast through a single Muslim state. The first juula revolution broke the tradition again further east by creating another Muslim commercial state at Kankan. Then, from the coastal side, the Sierra Leoneans began to penetrate as merchants by many different routes through and around Fuuta Jaalo. People in Kankan still remember the middle decades of the nineteenth century as a time of special prosperity for their trade.

The religious reform movement in the northern savannas had repercussions in the south as well, if only by encouraging rebels to follow the fashion of stating their objectives in religious terms. The Tijānīya made steady gains after the arrival of Shaykh Umar in the 1840s. Within a decade or so, most of Fuuta Jaalo had joined the new tarīqa. But here the more serious call for religious reform came from a Qādiri leader, Modi Mamadu Jue, who organized a rebellion in the late 1840s. His followers were called Hubu from a term meaning "those who love God." They failed to overturn the almaamate, but they remained an effective rebel military force-in-being into the 1880s.

In the middle decades of the century, another group of rebellions with religious overtones occurred in the region south and east of Kankan. These were, in effect, a new installment of the earlier juula revolution. Some juula leaders founded new states, but none survived very long until, in the 1870s, Samori Ture emerged as a juula leader with remarkable military talents. With his conquest of Kankan in 1880, he became the most important force in the region. By the early eighties, his control stretched from the forest edge northward to include the Buré goldfields and the upper Niger as far downstream as Bamako. But Samori's empire was clearly less Islamic than those created by the early jihads. He was Muslim, but he had joined some of the earlier fighting on the non-Muslim side of things. For a time he adopted a strongly pro-Islamic policy, taking the title of almaami in 1886 and using state power to force conversion. But he later dropped the religious emphasis, and it appears in retrospect that Samori was moved in the first place by the hope that Islam could help to unify the diverse people he happened to control.

Until the 1880s, Samori built his empire without concern for a European threat. The British in Sierra Leone were nonexpansive and served as a convenient outlet for gold and other exports. The French on the Senegal were far away until they began their military advance to the east in 1879. That move was so nearly simultaneous with Samori's own drive down the Niger valley that both arrived before Bamako in 1883. After some initial brushes with French forces, Samori was able to arrange a truce in 1886–87. That left him free to pursue territorial expansion eastward into the present-day Ivory Coast. The French meanwhile were tied up with their wars against the Futaanke empire to the north.

It seems likely that, about the mid-1880s, Samori had reached something like the limits of territory he could conquer with his original resources and support. His empire was ethnically homogeneous, but it had no earlier experience of political unification over such a large territory, and without even the self-interest of its citizens to justify the material cost of still more territorial expansion. In 1888–89, a major revolt broke out throughout the western part of the empire, which the almaami suppressed only with great difficulty.

Then, in the early 1890s, the entire scene changed. The French had finished with the Lamido Juulbe in 1891, and this freed them to concentrate on Samori. Samori, in turn, had begun to acquire late-model rifles through his trade with the English in Sierra Leone. He might have used them in a last-ditch stand against the French, but instead he chose to conquer a new secondary empire to the east of his original holdings, meanwhile fighting a series of rearguard actions against the French. Between 1891 and the beginning of 1894, the French conquered the whole of Samori's original empire, though at great cost in the face of a scorched-earth policy that left them little of value. In those same years, Samori's forces conquered a new empire. At its peak in mid-1896, it took in approximately the northern half of the present-day Ivory Coast and extended eastward halfway across northern Ghana.

In abandoning his original empire, in short, Samori abandoned the objectives of the juula revolution, abandoned the goal of creating a Muslim state, and turned his army into a weapon with which to exact tribute from the conquered people of a secondary empire. It was the clearest case of secondary empire in West Africa, with many resemblances to Rabih's path of conquest across the central Sudan to Bǫrno in that same decade. His end was also the same. It was impossible to hold out against Europeans who had even more and better weapons. His second empire fell in two years. He was captured by a French column in 1898 and exiled to Gabon, where he died two years later.

SUGGESTIONS FOR FURTHER READING

Adeleye, R. A. *Power and Diplomacy in Northern Nigeria, 1804–1906.* London: Longman, 1971.

Ajayi, J. F. A., and Crowder, Michael. *History of West Africa,* vol. 2. London: Longman, 1974.

Akintoye, S. A. *Revolution and Power Politics in Yorubaland, 1840–1893.* London: Longman, 1971.

Brenner, Louis. *The Shehus of Kukawa: A History of the Al-Kenemi Dynasty of Bornu.* London: Oxford University Press, 1973.

Curtin, Philip D. *The Image of Africa.* Madison: University of Wisconsin Press, 1964.

Dike, K. O. *Trade and Politics in the Niger Delta.* London: Oxford University Press, 1954.

Flint, John E., ed. *From c. 1790 to c. 1870. Cambridge History of Africa.* edited by J. D. Fage and Roland Oliver, vol. 5. Cambridge: Cambridge University Press, 1976.

Johnston, H. A. S. *The Fulani Empire of Sokoto.* London: Oxford University Press, 1967.

July, Robert W. *The Origins of Modern African Thought.* London: Faber, 1967.

Last, D. M. *The Sokoto Caliphate.* London: Longman, 1967.

Martin, B. G. *Muslim Brotherhoods in Nineteenth-Century Africa.* Cambridge: Cambridge University Press, 1976.

Munro, J. Forbes. *Africa and the International Economy, 1800–1960.* London: J. M. Dent, 1976.

Person, Yves. "Samori and Resistance to the France." In *Protest and Power in Black Africa,* by R. I. Rotberg and A. Mazrui. New York: Oxford University Press, 1970.

Quinn, Charlotte A. *Mandingo Kingdoms of the Senegambia: Traditionalism, Islam, and European Expansion.* London: Longman, 1972.

Reynolds, Edward. *Trade and Economic Change on the Gold Coast, 1807–1874.* London: Longman, 1974.

Rotberg, Robert I., and Mazrui, Ali. *Protest and Power in Black Africa.* New York: Oxford University Press, 1970.

Wilks, Ivor. *Asante in the Nineteenth Century.* Cambridge: Cambridge University Press, 1975.

Chapter 13

A Century of
Ironies in East Africa

(c. 1780-1890)

THE SUCCESSIVE SOCIAL and economic revolutions that accompanied Africa's increasing involvement in international trade were compressed, in East Africa, into a much briefer time period than on the western side of the continent. The slave trade on the Atlantic coast had grown from minute beginnings in the fifteenth century to a peak in the eighteenth, then changed again in the early nineteenth with the further growth of the Angolan slave trade and the shift along the Guinea coast to ever larger trade in the products of African soil and labor. In eastern Africa, however, from Mozambique in the south to Ethiopia in the north, the slave trade had been insignificant before the late eighteenth century. The rise of a major slave trade, the attempts to abolish it, and the increasing trade in commodities produced within Africa therefore came simultaneously in this region, with drastic consequences for its history.

In one sense, the lateness of these developments made the East· African historian's task easy. Here, the tellers of oral traditions are not forced to reach far back into the memories of their ancestors in order to describe the transformation. In most places, it is still possible to reconstruct from oral sources a picture of society as it was before the start of the slave and ivory trades, and then to see what happened after the trade began. This experiment in historical perception is especially valuable whenever the full impact of the slave trade was delayed until the second half of the nineteenth century. The fathers of today's old men were then alive, and their son's evidence can be taken as a picture of what probably happened earlier in other places, because the changes that were well under way in northern Mozambique by the early eighteenth century, for example, affected some isolated societies only in the 1880s, and, in still other places, had not yet occurred at the time of the colonial conquest.

Slave trading was stimulated in East Africa by two major economic developments. First, the slave-plantation complex, involving imported capital and managers, tropical land, and African slave labor, expanded to the Indian Ocean.

In the eighteenth century, the French brought this system to the Mascarene Islands, including Mauritius and Réunion, 800 miles east of Madagascar. They experimented with a number of crops, but, by century's end, sugar had become the basis of the economy. By the final quarter of the eighteenth century, the French demand for slaves had a substantial effect on the East African coast. Whereas the economy of the Mascarenes was simply the Caribbean sugar economy transplanted to the other side of the world, on Zanzibar the plantation idea was applied to a totally different crop — cloves — and involved a different set of entrepreneurs — Omani Arabs from the Persian Gulf. They too wanted slaves from the mainland. The Omanis who remained at the Persian Gulf used slaves as domestics, on date plantations, and as sailors.

The second major stimulus to the slave trade in East Africa was, paradoxically, the British abolitionist campaign. Between 1815 and 1831, the Anglo-Portuguese antislave-trade treaties outlawed the Portuguese slave trade north of the equator, thus increasing procurement in the south, in both Angola on the west side of the continent and Mozambique on the east. At the same time, the British negotiated the first of a series of abolition treaties with the authorities in control of the East African trading island of Zanzibar. Again the consequences were paradoxical, for the treaties reduced the price asked for slaves, thereby encouraging people to find new local uses for slave labor, so that in the end, the total number of slaves captured each year within East Africa actually increased.

It was thus one of the great ironies of nineteenth-century East African history that the legal abolition of the slave trade in the region led in fact to its extension into new areas. This was true not only of the revived Mozambique trade to Brazil early in the century, but also further up the coast, where the most rapid growth of slave imports to Zanzibar, in the late 1840s, came at a time when increasing restrictions were being placed on the trade. The end of the slave trade by sea from the southern port of Kilwa in 1873 set off a whole new round of trade on the mainland nearer to Zanzibar. Much the same thing happened in Ethiopia, where the slave trade to the Persian Gulf by way of southern Arabia became economic once the British patrols cut off the direct sea route from East Africa.

The extension of the slave trade as a result of abolition is an irony in two senses: as the Oxford English Dictionary defines it, *irony* is "a contradictory outcome of events as if in mockery of the promise and fitness of things"; it is also a drama whose inner meaning — for those who look back on the events — is quite different from the outer meaning it had for those who were immediately concerned. We have not yet reached the bottom of the irony, in either sense of the term, because the "legitimate trade" that abolitionists wanted to substitute for the slave trade was usually a commerce in the products of slave labor. For instance, cloves were considered "legitimate" even though grown and picked by slaves. Rubber and copal (for varnish) collected by slaves on the mainland were also "legitimate," as was grain grown by slaves on the East

African coast. Many prominent abolitionists were quite conscious that they were asking for the local use of slaves who had previously been exported.

On the Indian Ocean sugar islands themselves, abolition led to a labor importation that the major historian of the phenomenon has called "a new system of slavery." The British took the island of Mauritius in the Napoleonic wars and continued sugar production using indentured laborers, whose contracts were enforced by penal sanctions. They were taken from India either by force or in conditions of extreme distress, and given little real chance of returning to India. Conditions for the new laborers on the sugar plantations were nearly identical to the earlier conditions of slave labor.

Along with the new demand for plantation products came an enormous increase in Europe's demand for ivory. Here was another irony of East African history, that the unequal development of the African and European economies should have gone so far that a trivial demand for combs and billiard balls could revolutionize the economy of the entire region. Ivory had been exported to India for at least a thousand years, and this age-old trade continued in the nineteenth century. But in addition, Europe and America began to find new uses for the soft ivory of east Africa. Hard ivory from West Africa had been used for knife handles. Now the softer varieties from the east were used for combs, piano keys, and billiard balls. Others sources of soft ivory were southern Africa and the Nilotic Sudan, but in East Africa demand outstripped supply throughout the nineteenth century, and the price rose continuously.

It rose even more steeply in real terms than it did in monetary value, for the prices of European and American goods were declining at the same time the price for ivory was rising. This was, of course, a consequence of the industrialization of cloth production in the West. Here is another irony, for the terms of trade with the Euro-American world were clearly shifting in East Africa's favor throughout the nineteenth century: Africans had to exchange less and less ivory to acquire more and more cloth. Yet by the end of a century of "improvement," the East African economy was a shambles. The point here is simple. When Africans hunted elephants, they were not building an industry that could lead to further economic growth; they were simply depleting a limited resource. In return, they received cloth, but they also received guns and powder with which to kill more animals, make war, and enslave one another. Some of these activities were uneconomic in themselves, at least in the social cost to East African society. But dependence on a single major export leads to a fragile economy in any case, and heavy dependence on the export of a nonrenewable resource was especially serious in distorting the economy toward activities that would inevitably end after a fairly short period.

MOZAMBIQUE AND KILWA

In the eighteenth century, Portuguese and Indian traders in Mozambique supplied India with ivory, but then, in the early nineteenth century, the ivory trade shifted north beyond the zone of Portuguese control, and Mozambique turned increasingly to the slave trade. It had not been especially large or profitable in the eighteenth century until the French from the Mascarene Islands shifted to Mozambique as a source of supply. They had begun buying slaves mainly in Madagascar in the late 1730s, but when these slaves acquired a fortunate reputation for "insolence," the French switched gradually to Mozambique.

After the turn of the century, New World demand became more important, with Mozambique figuring as a major source of slaves for Brazil. Through

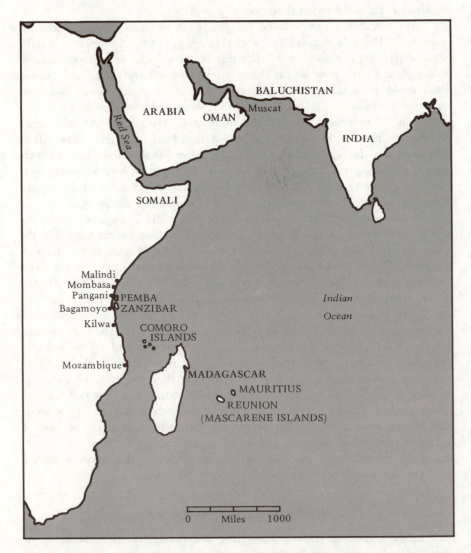

The Indian Ocean in the Nineteenth Century

the 1820s and 1830s, according to recent careful estimates, more than 15,000 slaves were exported each year from the single port at Mozambique Island. The Portuguese also opened many subsidiary ports up and down the coast for direct trade with the Brazilians. Trade to the French islands continued, carried in Arab boats as far as the Comoro Islands north of Madagascar, then onward by the French. Spanish vessels also called for slaves to Cuba, and even a few United States vessels took on slave cargoes for the Americas.

In the last quarter of the eighteenth century, the coastal trade north of the Portuguese sphere also began to grow, first in slaves, then in ivory. This process began in Kilwa though it ended in Zanzibar. In the late eighteenth century, Kilwa was the center of a rivalry among three major outside powers. For the Portuguese, the island port was a difficult competitor, just beyond the range of their control and able to draw on the same hinterland. The Yao traders who supplied Mozambique with ivory could also choose to deal with its competitors at Kilwa. A second power, the Omani Arabs, had been pushing south since the seventeenth century, when Portuguese strength in the northern Indian Ocean began to break up. They drove Portugal out of the Persian Gulf by 1650, then from Mombasa by the end of the seventeenth century. The island of Zanzibar, across a narrow channel from the coast, then became the center of Omani influence on the coast and a major trade link between East Africa and the Persian Gulf. The Omanis also had intermittent control over Kilwa's ivory trade. The French from the Mascarenes were the third power drawn to Kilwa; they were not getting all the slaves they wanted from the Portuguese zone, and they too had had the hope of reaching the southern hinterland through Kilwa.

Kilwa's trade had two special bursts of activity in the late eighteenth and early nineteenth centuries. First, in the late 1770s, the French began to export great numbers of slaves from Kilwa to the Mascarenes, but this phase was brief, first because of Omani opposition, then because of the Napoleonic wars. The second great jump came with the northward shift of the Yao ivory traders to Kilwa after the turn of the nineteenth century; it became increasingly dangerous for them to pass through the slave-trading zones on the way to Mozambique's coast, and the Portuguese raised the duties on Yao trade when demand for ivory was rising dramatically on the world market. This expansion in the ivory trade not only led to the growth of Kilwa's commerce; it was the basis of Zanzibar's commercial empire in the nineteenth century, and ivory became the major commodity in an expanding trade throughout the East African interior far to the north of Kilwa.

ZANZIBAR AND THE EAST AFRICAN ECONOMY [1]

The town of Zanzibar on Zanzibar Island grew from little more than a fishing village in 1710 to a fine trading center dotted with merchants' stone

---

[1] Anyone who writes on this topic is indebted to Abdul Sheriff, whose major work is still unpublished, and to Frederick Cooper, *Plantation Slavery on the East Coast of Africa* (New Haven: Yale University Press, 1977).

houses in 1800; in the nineteenth century, it became a capital city, graced by the palace of the sultans of the Omani dynasty. It also controlled the great trade of the East African coast, and therefore attracted American and European traders. Although a solid base for future growth had been built by 1800, Zanzibar's rise as a commercial center was most dramatic in the nineteenth century. Revenues doubled between 1804 and 1819, and continued to grow afterward. Indian traders who had come for brief visits in the eighteenth century established themselves permanently in ever increasing numbers at the same time Omani Arab plantation owners and caravan traders came down from their homeland in the north. Sultan Seyyid Said of Oman paid his first visit in 1828, but he ended by establishing his dynasty on Zanzibar, which to his predecessors had been only a minor and distant colony.

The Indians, Arabs, English, Americans, French, and Germans who came to Zanzibar traded in one or more of the islands' three major exports. The ivory of the interior was the first, with Zanzibar a major entrepôt for its shipment overseas. The second major export product was slaves, also drawn from the mainland, shipped early in the century to the French islands, but throughout the century to the Persian Gulf and beyond. Zanzibar was also a major destination of slaves for the clove plantations, the third pillar of its economy.

Early in the nineteenth century, a rough division of the export trade developed, with Arabs shipping slaves while the Indians exported ivory. The Indian traders had a competitive advantage because they had information about the Bombay ivory market, where most East African tusks were taken. Some Omani Arabs exported ivory, but they were increasingly marginal traders. In 1800, most Indians on Zanzibar had come for brief visits; a decade later, several were in permanent residence, and their numbers grew along with the value of the island's commerce. Many Omanis also came to settle and enjoyed their own competitive advantage in the slave trade, since many slaves were sold for domestic use on the date plantations in the Persian Gulf.

Of these three products, only ivory rose continuously in profitability throughout the century, to become the main engine of the island's economic expansion. As we have seen, the first boost came from the rise in Portuguese duties at Mozambique, previously India's main supplier. Prices in the rest of East Africa immediately jumped, bringing rapid growth in ivory exports between 1800 and 1820. By this time, when the demands of the Indian market had been met, European and American demand began to grow. Traders from Salem, Massachusetts, played a considerable role in direct trade with East Africa, but most ivory went to Bombay, where part of it was reexported to England. The price of ivory rose continuously from $22 a *frasila* (35 lb.) in 1823 to $89 a frasila in 1873. Before the American Civil War, when the United States was still Zanzibar's main non-Asian trading partner, ivory produced in the slave-trading economy of Zanzibar was exchanged for cotton grown on the slave plantations of the American South. These same Salem traders carried cured beef from Madagascar for the consumption of Cuba's slaves. Whether the ivory was carried to India, to Britain, or to the United States, it was the one product of East Africa that gave sure profits throughout the century, providing capital for other sorts of ventures and leaving a cushion when those ventures faltered.

Ivory had long been passed from hand to hand from the interior to the coast, or brought by hunting bands who ranged up to a couple of hundred miles into the interior. The ivory trade of the nineteenth century, however, provided incentives for the development of caravans that traveled a thousand miles or more, some beginning in the interior and making their way to the coast, others marching up-country from the ocean. The dates of the first caravans are uncertain, but it is clear that caravans were making their way from the coast into the interior of central Tanzania by 1811, and by the 1820s the Arabs appear to have gone beyond Lake Tanganyika into what is now Zaïre. Caravans organized by Nyamwezi from western Tanzania must have begun even earlier. Whether the caravans were led by Nyamwezi, or Arabs, or coastal Swahili-speakers, they all tended by the 1850s to make their way to the land of the Nyamwezi as the main trade center, then to branch northwest around Lake Victoria into Uganda, southwest around the southern end of Lake Tanganyika, or directly west to Ujiji on the lake shore.

The caravans varied enormously in size, ranging from a mere handful of porters to a line of thousands snaking its way across the landscape. At dangerous spots the traders would wait until several caravans had gathered so as to mobilize greater strength in defense. Larger caravans were better able to bargain with powerful local chiefs about the exact amount to be paid in tolls. Such caravans very early developed their own sets of specialists: the *kiongozi* led the way wearing a long bright red gown and other adornments — often the black and white skin of a colobus monkey and a headdress made from the feathers of a crested crane; a medicine man went along to read omens and to make magical charms for the caravan's protection; tent men, cooks, armed guards, and, of course, porters all went along. In the caravans described by the explorer Richard Burton after his 1857 trip, the kiongozi was followed by the bearers of ivory, with cowbells attached to the points of especially large tusks sounding as the caravan made its way. After the ivory came beads and cloth wrapped in large bolsters. Then came the men carrying rhino teeth, hides, salt cones, tobacco, brass wire, iron hoes, supplies and stores, beds and tents.

The trips were long and difficult, beset by the dangers of thieves and at the mercy of powerful authorities along the way. The many caravans that passed through the same few supply stations were perfectly suited to transmitting infectious diseases. The diaries of the nineteenth-century European travelers who followed the caravan routes are filled with frequent casual references to smallpox, "seasoning fever," and numerous other diseases that gave caravan porters a high rate of mortality. The difficulties of the trip, and the unusually labor-intensive means of transport, with one man carrying seventy pounds at the very most, made caravans an enormously expensive way of moving goods.

It paid to carry ivory, which had a very high value per pound, and cloth or beads with which to purchase ivory, but many of the potential export products and consumer needs of the interior were simply not worth the high cost of carrying. Slaves, of course, had the advantage of being able to walk, though the mortality and morbidity rates for slaves moving into unfamiliar disease environments were high, as they were also for porters. The merchants could sustain a moderate loss of life among their human chattel if the price paid for slaves was high enough, but for the slave who lost his life, death was final.

Ivory was the kind of product that led to a moving traders' frontier. The richest area for great herds of elephants and for their valuable large tusks was always further into the interior, beyond the region where the hunters had already taken their first harvest. By the second half of the nineteenth century, many of the most enterprising traders were pushing into the eastern half of present-day Zaïre. Warfare and slave raiding tended to move with the traders' frontier not only because the caravans traded in slaves as well as in ivory, but also because the skills needed for elephant hunting were the same as those for making war and capturing men. In the days of the spear, elephant hunters were highly skilled indeed, although the rapid improvement of imported fire-arms in the 1870s and 1880s made it possible for even the relatively unskilled to hunt elephants.

The onward passage of the frontier often left economic collapse in its wake. On top of the ravages of warfare and slave raiding, the best of the elephant herds were gone. The only good possibility was to exploit the caravans going further into the interior, and some chiefs were able to collect tolls if they controlled an important river crossing or source of water in an arid region. A few people were able to continue elephant hunting on a smaller scale, as the Gogo did just to the east of the Nyamwezi, and a few points grew into important way stations as the frontier moved westward and it became difficult for coastal traders to make the entire trip without an intermediary supply base.

By the 1850s, the Arabs had founded the town of Unyanyembe in Nyam-wezi country. Individual traders maintained storehouses; a general agent was able to dispose of excess cloth, to find porters for caravans, and to supply trading parties with goods. Slaves at Unyanyembe produced food to provision the trading parties, and the town had gunsmiths, carpenters, masons, and other artisans. Many Arabs based themselves at Unyanyembe for years, sending agents or going themselves on trading parties along one of several routes further to the west. Local populations in very fertile areas, both near Unyanyembe and elsewhere along trade routes, went into the provisioning business, founding major rest stops for caravans in order to sell their surplus crops. Other farmers sometimes moved their homesteads to isolated wet spots in the middle of very barren areas, where they could then charge very high prices for provisioning caravans.

One puzzling question about the caravan system is why the Arabs partici-pated in it at all. They were not the originators of the caravans, nor were they the first businessmen to respond to the expanded demand. Although the evidence is shadowy, all the major caravan routes into the interior appear to have been pioneered by the interior peoples themselves. In the Kilwa hinterland, the Yao were carrying on trade before the first coastal traders pushed on into the interior. In southern Kenya, Kamba traders, from the area southeast of

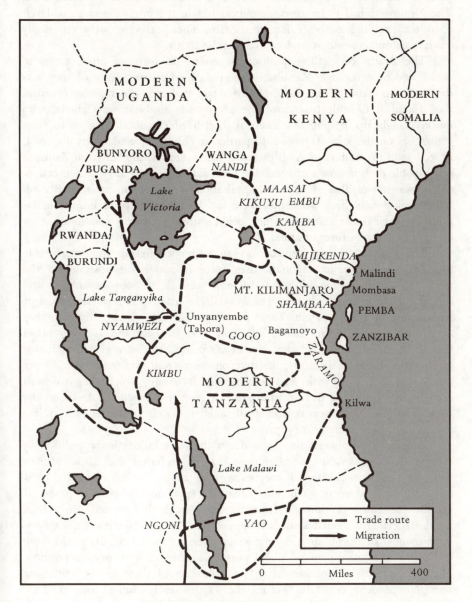

Trade in Nineteenth-Century East Africa

Mount Kenya, traded successfully in ivory before the mid-nineteenth-century period when coastal merchants deprived them of the route they had pioneered. On the Nyamwezi route, trade goods had reached both Uganda and Rwanda in the eighteenth century, and Nyamwezi traders were at the coast by about 1800, perhaps earlier. Nyamwezi caravans also appear to have traveled more austerely than those of the Arabs, and as a result had lower overhead costs. The Nyamwezi had the necessary political ties in the interior and even developed trade-raiding outposts far into Zaïre. Their caravans were reportedly much more numerous than Arab caravans in the 1850s.

The Arabs' competitive position depended on force of arms, access to credit, and influence over Zanzibari trade policies. Of these, force of arms was the least important. While the Zanzibari Arabs had access to superior firearms, they found it difficult to control the arms trade to Nyamwezi chiefs, who quickly caught up in spite of occasional short-lived Zanzibari attempts to place embargoes on the sale of powder to particular chiefs. Up and down the coast, as well as in the centers of Arab presence in the interior, the Sultan of Zanzibar was capable of bringing a considerable force into action on any given occasion, but he was not capable of sustained application of force. This meant that Arab traders could fight back when they were faced with arbitrary or hostile limitations on their trade; although they could improve trading conditions, they could not govern by force of arms.

The crucial role of Zanzibar as an entrepôt offering important trade facilities was far more important than force in making it possible for the island to dominate the hinterland. Credit was an obvious advantage, and capital for the inland trade was readily available from local financiers, most of whom were of Indian origin. These merchants not only charged interest; they also insisted that caravan leaders sell ivory only to them and at lower prices than those prevailing on the open market. Zanzibar also discriminated by means of its tariff structure. In 1864, the duty on ivory from Nyamwezi was $9 per frasila (35 lb.) if the tusks had been brought by Arabs, $15 if they had been brought by Nyamwezi traders, and $12 for ivory purchased by Arabs on the coast. That the Nyamwezi traded at all under these circumstances was a clear indication of their competitive superiority.

Zanzibar's advantage also grew from the island's dominant position in oceanic trade. American and European traders preferred the island because there they could purchase full cargoes without having to sail along the coast collecting cargo at every small port. Zanzibar's trade atmosphere was congenial because the duties on imports from Europe were both low and predictable. Local traders also gained some advantage from price competition among the large number of European and American traders on the island. By establishing and using its control over mainland ports, Zanzibar strengthened its position. Muslims had resided for generations in a number of these towns, and many were independent city-states before the Omani encroachment of the early nineteenth century. The local merchant class had not been active in the caravan trade, but had worked instead through inland traders and powers in the hinterland. The Omani took over the towns, established garrisons in some, began collecting duties, and tried to open the trade routes to the interior as much as possible. Bagamoyo, for example, was the coastal terminus of the Nyamwezi route, and the local Muslims (called Shomvi) had traditionally paid their Zaramo neighbors in the interior for the right to trade through their country. In the 1840s, however, the Zanzibari garrison used force to reduce the tolls, and later the payments to the Zaramo ended altogether.

Although Omani control of the coast was limited, it was adequate at most places for regulating trade. At Kilwa, for example, direct foreign trade in ivory and copal was barred by the second decade of the nineteenth century. The island town of Kilwa with its ocean port declined even as trade prospered. The neighboring small towns on the mainland had adequate harbors for the coastal dhows that carried goods to Zanzibar for transshipment. The greater part of the Tanganyika coast, both north and south of Bagamoyo, was off limits to foreign traders, who were required by treaty to pick up African goods in Zanzibar, and Zanzibar in any case was a natural entrepôt for the trade south of Bagamoyo, because Indian Ocean sailing ships going further down the coast risked being stranded by the seasonal change of wind. Not surprisingly, Zanzibar collected higher duties on the Tanganyika coast, where its control was tightest, than it did in present-day Kenya. There, Mombasa continued to have a little direct foreign trade, even though it was conquered by the sultan's forces in 1837.

THE ZANZIBARI PLANTATION ECONOMY

Zanzibar's position at the division point between trade networks also helped the growth of slave-manned clove plantations on Zanzibar itself and on the neighboring island of Pemba. The Arab planters were able to take advantage of periods when slave prices were low to try out cloves and to staff their own plantations. The caravan trade in ivory provided the poorer Arabs with a chance to accumulate enough wealth to buy a plantation, and some ivory caravans also brought down slaves on the march to the coast.

Clove plantations were tied to the slave trade, and, in a peculiarly inverted way, to the British abolition campaign. Between 1822 and 1876 the British signed a series of treaties with Sultan Seyyid Said and his successors. Each new treaty imposed stricter legal limits on the trade in slaves, yet each was followed by ever higher levels of slave trading. During the first decades of the century, before any treaties were in force, about 10,000 to 15,000 slaves a year were exported from the East African mainland. By the 1860s, when the British were patrolling the sea off the East African coast, the numbers were up to at least 20,000 a year, probably higher. Accurate figures are even harder to find for the period after 1873, when all shipments by sea were made illegal, but the qualitative evidence from across East Africa indicates that slave trading within the region reached new high levels in the 1870s and 1880s.

Rather surprisingly, the price of slaves was either stable or declining during many of the years of most rapid growth in the numbers traded. The contrast with West Africa is especially striking, because there slave prices rose very steeply from the seventeenth century onward and reached a peak at the very end of the illegal slave trade in the mid-nineteenth century. In that case, apparently, rising prices prompted slave traders to go further and further inland in search of slaves for sale. In economic terms, the price elasticity of the supply of slaves was high.

In East Africa also, price elasticity was high when prices were rising. The record of this region makes it clear, however, that the supply of slaves was not elastic when prices declined. Once societies had transformed themselves in order to produce slaves for sale, it was hard to return to the old social order, so they continued to produce slaves, even at lower prices. High slave prices that came with the rare boom periods in the coastal plantation economy caused slave-catchers to penetrate ever further into the interior — and the process could not be reversed when the prices dropped again.

However inelastic the *supply* of slaves when prices declined, the *demand* was elastic in the sense that lowering prices prompted planters and traders on the coast, the clove islands, and in the East African interior to find new uses for slave labor. The long-term effect of this pattern was to substitute a slave-using economy within the region for one that exported slaves to the French islands or the Persian Gulf. Abolition thus did not mean the elimination of the slave trade at least in the short run, but rather the substitution of internal for overseas trade.

Cloves originated in the Moluccas of eastern Indonesia and for centuries grew nowhere else. Seeds were carried to the Mascarene Islands by about 1770. In the opening decades of the nineteenth century, they came to Zanzibar, probably brought by a French-speaking Arab. The first great expansion of clove production on Zanzibar took place after the treaty of 1822 had abolished the trade in slaves to all Christian countries, including the French plantation islands and British-governed India. Cloves would probably have caught on even without the treaty, but the drop in the price of slaves from about $40 in the 1780s to $25 in the 1810s and finally to $20 in the 1820s certainly made the clove plantations far more attractive.

The boom prices for cloves and the enormous expansion in planting came between 1835 and 1845, after which prices declined through the century, except for one brief period. Because it takes six years for clove trees to bear the aromatic flower buds, and longer still to reach full production, the greatest need for slaves to pick cloves came in the 1850s, when clove prices began to drop. Fortunately for the Zanzibari Arabs, the sultan had signed another slave-trade treaty in 1847, this time prohibiting the overseas export of slaves. Slave prices dropped 25 percent immediately after the signing and the Zanzibari filled their plantations with slaves, while other Arabs on the East African coast expanded grain production. The grain plantations, which exported food to Zanzibar, Somalia, and Arabia, continued to grow right up to the colonial conquest — and more profitably in most years than cloves.

Zanzibar and Pemba quickly became the world's most important clove producers, so much so that clove plantations in the Moluccas were driven out of business, but the two islands also found themselves utterly dependent on a single crop with sharply fluctuating prices. In this respect, they went even further than Egypt with its overdependence on cotton. Cloves sold for $10 a frasila (35 lb.) in 1830, $2-$3 in 1856, then went down to less than $1.50 in the 1860s. The plantation owners responded to the falling prices by diversifying production, especially by getting slaves to produce their own food, thus lowering overhead, but they probably also worked the slaves harder in the crisis conditions. One slave could pick the cloves of anywhere from 10 to 20 trees; quite probably, the number of trees increased as clove prices declined, with losses and mortgages mounting. The primary-products trap thus harmed the slave as well as the slave owner.

In 1873, all slave shipments by sea were legally ended, and Zanzibar's slave market closed; in 1876, Zanzibar prohibited slave caravans on land as well. These well-meaning actions led to the final steps naturalizing slavery in East Africa. Grain production on the Kenya coast grew enormously. By a conservative estimate, the plantations around the town of Malindi alone absorbed a thousand slaves in 1874. Many of Zanzibar's clove trees had been destroyed in the hurricane of 1872, which led to a shortage of cloves and a spectacular rise in prices back to the levels of the 1830s. Slaves were smuggled to Pemba by the thousands from the nearby Pangani valley, on the mainland, which had never before been a major slave-producing region.

The difficulties of the slave trade in the years of abolition led many East African peoples to find local uses for slave labor. The Nyamwezi increasingly used slaves for farm labor, while the free men went off to trade ivory. The Gogo and some Kimbu sold ivory for slaves. Kamba traders of Kenya had been buying slaves since the 1840s. In the big grain-producing areas of the Kenya coast, the Mijikenda, the original inhabitants of the coastal hinterland, extended their farms, purchased slaves, and expanded their role in the export business. The Makonde of the Kilwa hinterland used slaves to farm so that freemen could collect wild rubber. None of these were "traditional" uses for low-status labor in East Africa, but in the economic conditions of the 1880s some Africans behaved in much the same way as the alien plantation owners. The lesson is that economics had greater power to shape East African society than did the well-meaning governmental policies on slavery, when slavery was defined as an institution apart from its economic context.

OPPORTUNITY AND INSECURITY
IN THE SLAVE TRADE

The new trade opportunities, and the new dangers, had profound effects on the lives of East Africa's ordinary people. In some places, young men were able to rise rapidly to positions of control; in others, the need for security made individuals more dependent on their clans and lineages than they had been before. Insecurity led the residents of some areas to cluster in fortified villages larger than the previous norm, while in others nucleated villages broke up as commercial farmers expanded the area under cultivation. Opportunistic men built themselves new chiefdoms at the same time that old political units were being torn apart by the slave trade, by Arabs, or by powerful local rebels. Some chiefs traded their own subjects into slavery, while others built defensive armies and refused to deal with outside traders. The local initiatives were as diverse as East Africa's societies — or as the personalities of their leaders.

Any understanding of the choices that Africans faced must begin with the opportunities offered by the new kinds of wealth, and with a recognition that one person's opportunity may be another's tragedy. In Chapter 5, we saw that bridewealth in cattle, or goats, or other high-value goods had always been at the heart of the control exercised by old men over young men. The lineage's control over similar prestige goods for relief in famine, ransom in warfare, and the payment of indemnities gave the group as a whole control over its members. And the king's prestige goods, received as tribute, were essential to his authority. In situations where trade was unimportant, the goods that bestowed control over dependents were procured locally: a man who inherited cattle also inherited control over the young men who needed bridewealth to marry; a king with numerous subjects collected tribute to reward loyal followers. But if cattle, or cloth, or other high-value goods could be obtained through trade, then those with the best trade connections might wrest control from those with tribute-paying subjects or inherited wealth. New sources of wealth meant new possibilities for acquiring power. These were at the heart of East Africa's diverse responses in the nineteenth century. Other factors, such as the arrival of firearms and of meddling coastal traders, or the special political impact of the trade in slaves, also produced changes, but the possibilities offered by new wealth were always central.

For young men within a lineage the new trade conditions operated in two contradictory ways. The possibilities of acquiring wealth on one's own through trade should have made young men more independent of their elders, but the breakdown of lineage authority, which has been spectacular in the twentieth century, was rare in the nineteenth. The insecurities of the slave-trading era made the lineage indispensible as a guardian of the individual's welfare, for lineage wealth could buy back a member captured by kidnappers or pay the indemnity for a person who otherwise would have been sold into slavery after committing a crime. In some places, a young man or woman who showed no respect or who had a difficult personality might even be sold into slavery by close relatives — in an African recapitulation of the Biblical story of Joseph.

An individual was thus offered opportunities for independence while independence was becoming more dangerous by virtue of slave trade. Individuals responded differently to the opportunities and dangers, and widely different social patterns emerged from region to region within East Africa. One possibility was to minimize the dangers (and the individual opportunities) by using wealth from trade to support the preexisting pattern of authority. This is illustrated in the oral traditions of the Embu, of the southeastern slopes of Mount Kenya. Elephant hunters would take their relatives along to bargain with the coastal ivory traders. In the final stages of bargaining, each relative would sit on the ivory in sorrow at its loss. The trader could take the ivory only after paying each one to agree to the trade. The hunter's important relatives were paid more, minor ones less. This practice reinforced the relationships and gave them special recognition.

For traders who wanted to rise, the combination of opportunity and insecurity served as a kind of threshold mechanism. An individual could only afford the insecurity that went with personal independence, leadership, and display if his wealth was very substantial indeed. The result was a combination of strong lineages and dependent, insecure individuals on the one hand, but, alongside, emerging big men, or notables — men who were not chiefs, but who exerted local influence because of their success as traders. A fine line separated the trade notables from the chiefs: for the most part, chiefs could impose their judgments on subject lineages, while big men used the power of persuasion; chiefs could require payment of tribute, while big men gave and received gifts or struck bargains; a chief could pass on his office to his heir, while a notable's goods were divided among his heirs, and his influence was dissipated after his death.

Kennell Jackson's research on Kamba traditions in Kenya has given a magnificent picture of the notables who emerged during the first half of the nineteenth century, the period of the Kamba-dominated ivory trade. Some important Kamba traders used their wealth to achieve prestige and influence by enlarging their lineages through marriage and by adopting dependents whose lineages could not support them in time of famine. These notables distributed their trade goods to local men of influence who could help in recruiting caravan porters. In other societies, chiefs *required* hunters to bring the tusks to the ruler's court, but the Kamba notables had no such authority. Instead, they took wives from elephant hunters' lineages to ensure the flow of ivory from their in-laws. Nor was wealth alone enough to make one an important notable; personal flair and style were also essential. The great Kamba ivory trader Kivui is remembered for his oratory, his puns and use of onomatopoeia, his great storytelling. Ndumbu, another trader, commissioned spectacular lattice copper necklaces for himself and his hunters. Other notables gave feasts.

The spread of slavery together with the periodic abundance of slaves were used by big men to build their followings. Some Giriama notables in the hinterland of the Kenya coast created extensive grain farms for the oceanborne export trade, building their enterprises by adopting dependents who needed food in time of famine, by marrying many wives, by buying slaves for wives when slave prices were low, and by purchasing some male slaves. In patrilineal areas, like Kamba or Giriama, a man's adopted dependents or slave wives were only marginally different from his ordinary wives or dependents; the new conditions simply offered more rapid ways to build a lineage. But in matrilineal settings, a man could not build a following through normal marriage, because his children would ultimately belong to their mother's lineage. A slave wife had no lineage, however, so that a man who married slaves could claim the children as his own in order to build a band of personal supporters.

For a person whose lineage was too weak to provide security, or who wanted to escape lineage restrictions, the household of a notable or the court of a chief were places of refuge. A young man could serve as a soldier, hunter, or porter, a young woman as a wife or soldier's wife, in return for which they enjoyed the protection of their patron. Many of those who ultimately joined a large retinue had first endured enslavement, although others sought a protector when they found themselves at the very margin of survival as free persons.

The need for security and the frequent armed conflict associated with the nineteenth century made it a century of personal armies and standing armies. The fighting forces of most eighteenth-century chiefs and kings had been "countrymen's armies" — fighting forces of ordinary farmers who could be called up at a time of crisis. Nineteenth-century conditions, however, favored standing armies, partly because firearms made it possible for a small force of well-armed men to achieve greater striking power than a large force of poorly armed peasants. The fighters could also be paid in trade wealth or booty; a paid army of strangers had fewer compunctions about slave raiding than a countrymen's army had. Standing and hired armies were spread all across the region. Arab trading caravans were essentially private armies on the move, like those of the jallaba in the Nilotic Sudan. Through the whole of western Tanzania, standing armies carried on raids and fought one another. In Uganda, the king of Bunyoro created a standing army of northerners, from beyond the borders of his kingdom. Even among the chiefless Kikuyu of Kenya, brigand bands called thabari (from the Swahili word safari, for a caravan or a journey) marauded, stole livestock, and burned houses. The Sultan of Zanzibar used a mercenary army drawn from far-away Baluchistan, on the border between present-day Pakistan and Iran.

CENTRALIZED AUTHORITY AND SLAVERY
IN NINETEENTH-CENTURY TRADE

The arms trade, the demand for slaves and ivory, the presence of caravans and Baluchi soldiers, the development of notables and standing armies, all had an enormous impact on the political fortunes of East Africa's chiefs and kings, but the effect on centralized authority was not uniform. In some places, powerful chiefs fell; in others, centralized rule emerged stronger than ever before. In the Shambaa kingdom, about halfway between Mount Kilimanjaro and the Indian Ocean, the royal capital and most of the populated areas were located in a mountain area that was difficult for caravans. Trade routes passed through the plains below, shifting the entire balance of power away from the king in favor of a minor territorial governor named Semboja, who took control of an essential stopping place for caravans and assembled his own corps of elephant hunters. In the 1860s, Semboja made war on the king with arms acquired through trade and the assistance of his trading allies. First, the king's power to maintain order was destroyed; then the 1870s saw a rapid increase in the demand for slaves to work on the clove plantations of Pemba. By the mid-1870s, it had become profitable for local governors both to prey on their own subjects and to make war against their neighbors for the capture of slaves. What had been an orderly, prosperous, and peaceful kingdom during the first half of the century thus broke up into a great many embattled chiefdoms, each seeking its own ties with traders, and each selling slaves.

Some elements in the Shambaa disaster were unique: its mountain location and the sudden growth of the Pemba slave trade at an already difficult moment, for example, were not reproduced in exactly the same form in other societies. Three other elements, however, recurred across East and Central Africa. First, Semboja used mercenary armies. Second, the change followed a shift in the sources of a chief's or king's wealth. Before the expansion of trade, a chief depended on tribute from his subjects with which to reward his followers; the chief or king who had the most subjects was also the most powerful. After the change, a clever trading chief, or one with access to ivory, relied less on his own subjects, and high slave prices sometimes made the sale of subjects profitable. This would have been unthinkable in a period when the chief's main support derived from the farm work of his people. Third, outside trade and raiding allies became involved in internal disputes all across East Africa, although the outsiders in some cases were other trading chiefs of the interior, coastal traders, or a combination of the two.

The characteristic form of Arab or Swahili interference in local affairs was not a frontal assault on an established ruler. The traders were not powerful enough for that. Instead, individual traders or groups of traders made alliances with particular local leaders. Sometimes two Arab traders competing with one another would make alliances with competing local chiefs, thus raising the overall level of violence, possibly by encouraging a weak local contender to carry on the fight when he would have quit in the absence of outside help. In the chiefdom of Unyanyembe, where the most important Arab trading town of Nyamwezi country was located, three chiefly factions competed for control. The Arab traders were deeply involved in the area's politics; one married a daughter of Fundikira, the chief in the 1840s and early 1850s, and renewed the alliance when his wife died by marrying her sister. After Fundikira died in 1858, the Arabs took sides in the succession wars until they got a chief friendly to their interests.

The parallels between the politics of that period and the seamier side of postcolonial politics in Africa are startling. In the 1970s (in Angola, for example, or earlier in the Congo) as in the 1870s, outside forces did not enter the field of battle on their own; rather, they made alliances with local groups who were already fighting one another and who needed help. Mercenary armies took part in a kind of politics of diminished responsibility — soldiers who fight for pay ask fewer questions about the consequences than soldiers do who fight for their king and country. The arms trade offers yet another parallel: every time nineteenth-century European armies developed new weapons and discarded the old ones as obsolete, the castoffs entered the East African trade. The parallels are not accidental. They result from the unequal distribution of political and economic power between Africans and outsiders, combined with formal African political independence — now as then.

The great variety of paths to increased centralization in the nineteenth century are illustrated by two neighboring societies in western Kenya: the Nandi and the kingdom of Wanga. The Nandi, who combined herding and agriculture, occupied a plateau area immediately adjacent to the westernmost groups of cattle-keeping Maasai. The dangers of Maasai cattle raiding in the eighteenth and early nineteenth centuries limited the border Nandi to easily defended forest areas. Then, at some point before 1850, the Maasai were weakened by fighting among their subgroups, and the Nandi, at the same time, gave refuge to a Maasai ritual leader who became the first Nandi *orkoiyot*. It was the orkoiyot's job to predict coming events, to understand the omens favorable or unfavorable to action, and therefore to advise about war and peace. The combination of Maasai decline and increased coordination through the orkoiyot's leadership enabled the Nandi to expand beyond the forest edge at the expense of the Maasai. When, a brief time later, the first trading expeditions appeared, the Nandi were confident that they could control threats from the outside — had they not defeated the former masters of the grasslands? The first Arabs and Swahili (who probably came in the 1850s) were therefore allowed to establish fortified outposts, but then they began to mistreat the Nandi. Local people remember an incident in which young men were imprisoned by the traders, another in which young women were treated disrespectfully, still another in which the traders dumped a bowl of hot porridge over a young man's head. When the Nandi objected, the traders responded with a demonstration quite common in these situations. They placed a shield against a tree, invited the Nandi to shoot arrows, which did not penetrate, and then fired through the shields with muzzle loaders. The Nandi went away, but they returned in an attack that drove the traders from the country; and caravans avoided Nandi country from then on. The Nandi succeeded in avoiding the slave-ivory trade almost completely. They were uninterested in arms, having discovered that they could defeat a force armed with muzzle loaders by charging openly, falling down for the brief period of shooting, and then attacking before the enemy could reload.

Earlier in the century, the small kingdom of Wanga, just to the west of Nandi country, had also been visited by Maasai refugees, who served as mercenaries in disputes among local political leaders. When the coastal traders arrived, they too were drawn into local politics. The king of Wanga made his capital a major stopping place for caravans and gained the traders' assistance in defeating his enemies. His power grew throughout the period. One fascinating continuity emerges in the history of both the Wanga and Nandi. When the British appeared late in the century and began to carry out their conquest, the king of Wanga, who had depended for his power on outside allies, ingratiated himself with the British and began to conquer large sections of the region for them. The Nandi, who had reorganized internally to deal with the external threats of Maasai and traders, fought a series of British expeditions over a period of ten years before finally submitting.

The slave trade also altered the nature of slavery itself. The word *slavery* is dangerous to use, because it means such different things at different times and places. Some sort of servile status existed almost everywhere in Africa before the growth of the slave trade, but its East African form changed dramatically during the nineteenth century. We have already seen that wealth was necessary for increasing the strength of a lineage and its ability to reproduce, whether the wealth was used to pay for wives in the form of bridewealth, or for famine food, or for medicines when someone was ill. When a member of one lineage harmed an individual from another, the balance was redressed by the payment of an indemnity. The indemnity was a transfer of wealth that could be regarded as reproductive capacity. The problem with this system was that, if it went no further, a poor lineage would be able to act irresponsibly, accumulating debts and harming others, yet unable to pay. The solution was to transfer one or more individuals, which thus shifted reproductive capacity directly through people rather than through wealth. Nineteenth-century slavery grew out of this institution, as well as from several other related ways of dealing with individuals who had no lineages — war captives, for example, or people who had been driven out of their lineages for incurring too many indemnities.

The growing demand for slaves in the nineteenth century led to the transformation, in many places, of this relatively benign institution, although slave procurement was by no means uniform across East Africa. In some areas, predatory groups, like the Chikunda elephant hunters of Malawi and Zambia, simply raided their neighbors. In other areas, small-scale kidnapping by aspiring notables was common. Both slave raiding and kidnapping seem to have occurred in places bypassed by the ivory trade, or where the ivory trade stimulated demand for imported goods but then declined. Among the Kamba of Kenya, for example, the period of slave trading came after the decline of the

Kamba ivory trade. Some of the southern neighbors of the Nyamwezi, who had dominated the ivory trade before it shifted to Nyamwezi territory, engaged in slave raiding. In other areas, normal judicial processes were subverted in order to produce slaves. Chiefs would impose huge fines for small crimes knowing the fines could not be paid and slaves would be offered instead.

The uses to which slaves were put also changed. Among the Yao, at least some of the slaves were still assimilated to the new master's lineage as adopted kin. In other places, they were incorporated in the standing armies of chiefs. But some also became a separate agricultural labor force, and this appears to have been new in the nineteenth century, not only for the Arabs on grain or clove plantations, but also for Africans who had never before used slave labor. They produced export crops for the Zaramo in the hinterland of the Tanzania coast and food crops for the Nyamwezi. Among some trading, rubber-gathering, or ivory-hunting populations, they began to work the farms at home while their masters occupied themselves with more lucrative activities further afield.

Where East Africa experienced one form of secondary empire in myriad variants following the introduction of firearms, it also felt the impact of the great mfecane and the furthest reaches of the military innovation based on the *impi* formation and of military organization by age-grades. Although the empire builders from the south were not all Nguni from the coastal plains of Natal, they usually figure in East African history as Angoni or Ngoni. The largest group crossed the Zambezi in 1835 under the leadership of a single chief named Zwangendaba, and they were known as Zwangendaba's Ngoni until their leader died in the late 1840s, when they split up into a number of smaller states. When they had first started their 2,000-mile migration, Zwangendaba's Ngoni totaled only a few hundred people. But their mastery of Zulu military tactics enabled them to conquer along their way. They took many war prisoners, incorporating male captives in servile positions at first, so that each had to obey his Ngoni "father." A captive could become a full member of Ngoni society, however, by founding his own lineage through the capture of wealth or women in warfare. Any age-regiment therefore included not only original Ngoni, but also captives who were in the process of becoming Ngoni in what has been described as a snowball state. From the 1840s on, separate groups of Ngoni stopped migrating and settled down in Malawi, eastern Zambia, and southern Tanzania, where they created new social forms combining local and Ngoni elements.

Southwestern Tanzania, which was already undergoing transformation as the result of the coastal trade, also had to deal with the Ngoni threat. In the process, a number of local armies adopted Ngoni military tactics, and some Nyamwezi chiefs hired roving bands of Ngoni mercenaries. Mirambo, the greatest of the Nyamwezi chiefs, spoke the Ngoni language and (like others among his neighbors) assembled a wild and rootless band of armed followers called *ruga-ruga*, who were modeled at least in part on Ngoni age-regiments.

Among the ruga-ruga were war captives, escaped slaves, deserters, runaways, and all sorts of desperate characters who had been cut loose from their lineage ties. Their tactics were to strike terror among their enemies: they would wear red cloths, to which they would point at the start of a battle, saying, "This is your blood." They intentionally did horrible things on the battlefield in order to shock the opposing army into submission. Mirambo and other chiefs rewarded them with slaves and land, so they could start their own lineages. The age-regiment pattern thus had an origin independent of the coastal trade, yet it fitted in perfectly with politics and warfare in the age of slave and mercenary armies. In one sense, the two varieties of secondary empire met and combined here in central Tanzania.

Alongside the insecurity, disorder, and ruga-rugas, some benefits grew out of the nineteenth-century economic changes, one of them being the expansion of regional trade. Neighbors who traded ivory with one another often expanded their mutual trade in commodities for local consumption rather than export, along routes which ran in every direction, as opposed to the overseas routes which simply ran from the interior to the ocean. Lake Victoria, for example, was crisscrossed by a network of trade ties among lakeshore populations. The islands of the southeastern corner provided dried fish, grain in times of drought, and timber for boat building; the northeast provided salt, while Buganda in the northwest supplied barkcloth; other lake regions sold tobacco and coffee beans. Similar local trade networks developed all across East Africa.

INSULATION AND CENTRALIZATION

Contact between Africans and Europeans in the nineteenth century led to scattered instances of intellectual, religious, economic, and military change. On some parts of the Guinea coast, we have seen that intellectual and political leaders literate in European languages emerged at just the time the political independence of their homelands was being eroded. Other leaders sought firearms or other aspects of Western technology, but those who succeeded best in preserving their political autonomy, before the full European invasions of the 1800s and after, were those who best insulated themselves against disruptive foreigners bearing guns. Success came from the care with which they controlled outside influences, often combined with an advantageous location far from seaports and other centers of alien presence.

This pattern is strikingly illustrated by highland Ethiopia, which began the nineteenth century as a region of numerous princes, most of them adhering to the country's ancient Christianity, each ruling a small territory and squabbling for control over a larger one. Many of the Christian highland princes were dependent on mobile armies of neighboring lowland Muslims. Those nearest the coast had the best opportunity to obtain arms from Europe, but the highlands were to be unified most effectively by Menelik of Showa, whose kingdom, centered on the present city of Addis Ababa, was to the far south of the Christian zone.

The economic setting of Menelik's rise to power was one of increasing demand for slaves from the Ethiopian region. That demand first increased early in the century, when Russia conquered the Caucasus, cutting off that source of slaves for the Ottoman Empire. Then, after 1847, when the British treaty with Zanzibar prohibited the export of slaves from the Zanzibari sphere, Ethiopia became an alternate source. Slaves could be carried across the Red Sea to Arabia and on to the Persian Gulf and Iraq, in spite of British attempts to halt the trade by naval action on the Red Sea. Menelik and other Ethiopian leaders relied

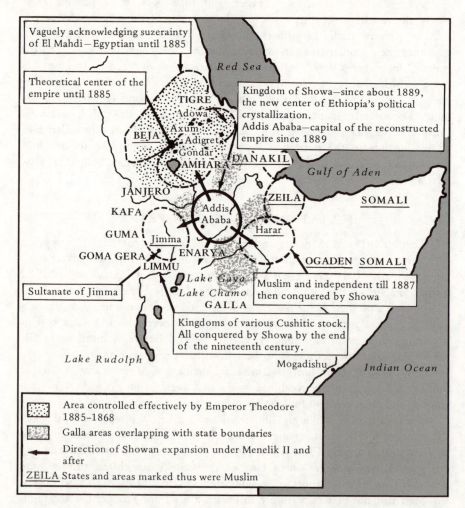

Ethiopia in the Nineteenth Century

on tolls from trade, and especially the slave trade, to buy arms for their empire-building wars. Menelik's kingdom of Showa had the best of both worlds; its subjects were neither slave traders nor enslaved. They merely charged tolls, taking care to expand through the 1870s and 1880s in directions that enabled them to control increasing quantities of trade.

Menelik's main competitor was Yohannes IV, who had more arms and military power, and the ancient title of emperor. Yohannes also had his territorial base near the sea, where he was threatened from two fronts — by the Egyptians and later the forces of the Mahdi in the Sudan, and by the Egyptians and later the Italians operating from the Red Sea coast. And, of course, he still had the rivalry of Menelik at the south. Yohannes defeated Showa in 1875, but he was then forced to accept a weak truce because of the Egyptian presence in the north, and he died in battle against the Mahdist forces from the Sudan.

Menelik had meanwhile taken advantage of his kingdom's secure position to continue the expansion of his Showan base. He made himself emperor in 1889, thus uniting two of the three centers of power in Christian Ethiopia. The third, a mainly Tigriña-speaking highland area in the hinterland of the Red Sea coast, had already been taken over by Italy and incorporated in the colony of Eritrea. By the 1880s, it was essential to have a large supply of modern arms, and Menelik was fortunate in being able to secure them in time to defeat an Italian invasion in 1896. He also used them to build a secondary empire that was to survive as the independent state of Ethiopia.

On the great island of Madagascar, as well as in the large and prosperous kingdom of Buganda in the southern part of present-day Uganda, efforts to keep foreigners under control were combined with spectacular movements toward literacy and the adoption of European religion and ways of life. In Madagascar the process began, characteristically, with the slave trade and its abolition, although (as in the other cases) trade provided only the setting, determining some of the basic resources local innovators might use. In the eighteenth century, Madagascar had been divided among a number of separate and competing political units of varying composition. A whole series of new forces influenced the movement toward consolidation. European pirates driven out of the Atlantic settled on the island's east coast; the demand for slaves in the Mascarenes led to increased exports; and imported firearms helped shift the balance of power among the island's local groups. The Merina kingdom of the highlands near the island's center was one of those which emerged stronger in the process. It grew in power not only because of the profits of the slave trade; King Nampoina (short for Andrianampoinimerina, ruled 1782–1810) also followed an enlightened agricultural policy. He redistributed land, encouraged the production of food crops, and saw to the construction of drainage systems.

Up until the second decade of the nineteenth century, the Merina kingdom was no greater than other states on the island. The main breakthrough came as a result of abolitionist efforts following the British acquisition of Mauritius in the Napoleonic wars. The new governor agreed to provide Nampoina's successor with military instructors and superior firearms in return for the abolition of the slave trade from Madagascar; no mention was made of slavery within Madagascar itself. The treaty of 1817, in fact, punished those who traded in slaves with their own enslavement! The improvements in army organization, and the new weapons superior to trade guns, enabled the central kingdom to dominate all its rivals in a long process involving negotiation, temporary alliances, and limited use of force. Although some areas retained independent or quasi-independent status, Madagascar was now dominated by its central kingdom, whose ruler was thought of as sovereign over the entire island.

Missionaries, European teachers, and artisans were present in the central kingdom through the nineteenth century, with intervals of expulsion, and the Malagasy[2] people were both avid and selective in their adoption of European technology and learning. By 1835, the London Missionary Society claimed to have 4,000 children in its schools. In 1894, the Merina highlands were estimated to have a population of 850,000, of whom 137,000 were registered in Protestant schools, and at least 50,000 actually attended. The total proportion of young people in the highlands attending school was similar to that of western Europe at the same time. In the second half of the century, the kingdom adopted a written legal code. Malagasy doctors were coming out of the local medical school in increasing numbers, and, by 1880, the first European-trained Malagasy doctors returned from Edinburgh.

The achievements of the kingdom, however, were built on a system of slavery. The Merina conquests on the island created a supply of prisoners of war at exactly the time the slave trade was outlawed. The slaves were then used to produce food so that the wealthy and free people of the highlands could enjoy conspicuous consumption, follow new fashions, and learn what was going on in the outside world. In a sense, then, abolition in Madagascar, as in other portions of East Africa, led to the indigenization of slavery — though here it was less to feed the export trade than to produce a graceful style of life. Slaves were the productive force behind the creative outburst in highlands society, where dress, architecture, and the regulations governing marriage were all being recreated.

The same excitement surrounding literacy, new technology, and alien religions swept Buganda in the second half of the nineteenth century, except that here Islam was introduced first, followed by Protestant and Catholic Christianity. The changes came, as in Madagascar, at a time when Buganda had been expanding and when its *kabaka* (or king) had been gaining power at the expense of his neighbors and of local leaders within the kingdom. Over several decades each successive kabaka had made a greater proportion of the admin-

---

[2] Malagasy is an adjective referring to people or things characteristic of Madagascar. Today the country is still named Madagascar, and is also referred to as the Malagasy Republic, but never simply as Malagasy.

istrative positions appointive, rather than hereditary. Buganda had also gained
control of the trade route around the western side of Lake Victoria. Mutesa, who
was kabaka from the late 1850s until 1884, was intensely interested early in his
reign in the culture, religion, and technology of the Zanzibari traders who
came to his court. He was eager for increased numbers of firearms, especially

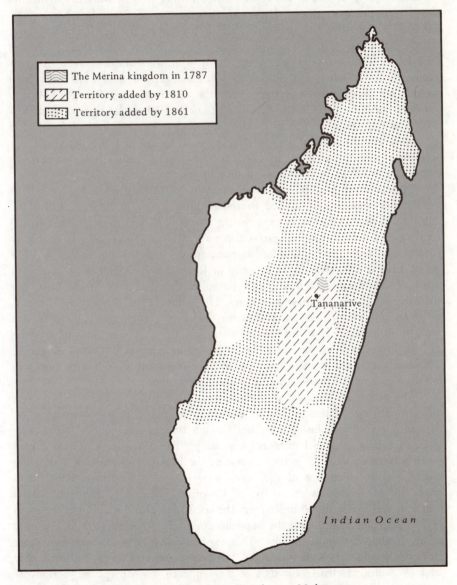

Expansion of the Merina Kingdom on Madagascar

the advanced weapons that were more effective than the usual trade guns, and along with the guns came incidentals such as Zanzibari-style soap, clothing, and bed frames.

Mutesa was also fascinated by theology. In the late 1860s his court adopted the Islamic calendar, fasting, and the reading of the Koran. Those who adopted new religions most easily were the teenage pages who had come from all parts of the kingdom to live at the royal court, in order to seek Mutesa's favor and win advancement as chiefs. They were largely cut off from their local roots, intensely competitive and pragmatic, and impressed by the new technology and culture from the coast. For a while, those who were best at the study of Arabic and Islam were the ones who most easily won the kabaka's favor. A crisis came, however, when the Sultan of Zanzibar proved unable to send help against the threatening Egyptians from the north. New and stricter Muslim teachers began to ridicule the kabaka's practice of Islam, leading to insubordination among the most devout of the royal pages. The kabaka had found that he could not do without the foreigners; now he learned that he could not tolerate having them either. In 1876, the first of Buganda's religious persecutions began with the execution of Islamic martyrs.

Mutesa tried to cope with the situation by playing off religious groups against one another. He invited Protestant missionaries to balance against the Muslims, Catholics to balance against the Protestants, and then returned to the local spirit cults, to balance against them all. Mutesa's successor was unable to control all these forces. Out of desperation, he ordered the execution of a set of Christian martyrs in 1886, only to lose control altogether. A combined army of Muslims, Protestants, and Catholics defeated him in the field but then reinstated him on their own terms. Up to the 1890s, conversions, literacy, religious enthusiasm were all matters for the court — for pages and chiefs. But with the kabaka's defeat, the arrival of the first British forces, and the triumph of the Protestants in the early 1890s, religious enthusiasm swept Buganda. Thousands attended services; new converts besieged the missionaries, books in hand, seeking to clarify the meaning of obscure passages.

The people of Buganda and Madagascar passionately embraced alien ideas and customs, but in these places as elsewhere success in political centralization depended on relative insulation from foreign traders and political representatives, especially at crucial moments of change. The Malagasy kingdom gained security from its location in the interior of the island. The chaos of competing traders and the disruption of alien raids were felt in coastal towns. King Nampoina did not allow traders to live at his capital. Mutesa of Buganda, whose kingdom was five hundred miles from the coast, and also distant from the main Nyamwezi trade route, took the opposite approach: foreigners could live only at his capital, and nowhere else. This explains why Buganda was torn apart from the inside out, with intensified factional conflict at court, followed only later by profound change throughout the kingdom. In both places, periods of interest in alien forces alternated with times of xenophobia, when foreigners were banished. Madagascar had its equivalent of Buganda's religious persecutions during the time of Queen Ranavalona, who reigned from 1828 to 1861; she expelled missionaries, excluded foreign traders, and persecuted local Christians. After her death, when Europeans were admitted to the country, a dancing disease broke out. People were suddenly seized by the illness, which was thought to have come as a message from the ancestors, angry at the abandonment of tradition.

The religious and cultural transformations of Madagascar and Buganda, like the economic changes emerging from the abolition campaign, foreshadowed patterns of collective behavior characteristic of the twentieth century. In abolition, the European insistence on "legitimate" trade showed the first clear preference for using Africans as exporters of primary products, and consumers of European-made industrial goods, in place of the earlier use of African labor exported in the slave trade. In the cultural realm, the characteristic ambivalence toward European culture, combining great admiration and great distaste, was already emerging in the two kingdoms. Factions formed for and against the foreigners in favor of Islam, Protestantism or Catholicism, or traditional religion. All of these divisions were to continue in different form during the colonial period. Perhaps the most profound continuity of all came in the division between the administrative elites with leisure to debate these questions, and the slaves of Madagascar in the nineteenth century — or peasant farmers everywhere in the twentieth — who were just as avid in their search for answers but less comfortable.

SUGGESTIONS FOR FURTHER READING

Alpers, Edward A. *Ivory and Slaves: Changing Patterns of International Trade in East Central Africa to the Later Nineteenth Century.* London: Heinemann, 1975.
————. "Trade, State, and Society among the Yao in the Nineteenth Century." *Journal of African History* 10 (1969): 405–420.
Bennett, Norman R. *Mirambo of Tanzania.* New York: Oxford University Press, 1971.
Burton, Richard F. *The Lake Regions of Central Africa.* 1860. Reprint. St. Clair Shores, Michigan: Scholarly Press, 1976.
Cooper, Frederick. *Plantation Slavery on the East Coast of Africa.* Yale Historical Publications, Miscellany, 113. New Haven and London: Yale University Press, 1977.
Darkwah, R. H. Kofi. *Shewa, Menilek, and the Ethiopian Empire: 1813–1889.* London: Heinemann, 1975.
Deschamps, Hubert. *Histoire de Madagascar.* 4th rev. ed. Paris: Editions Berger-Levrault, 1972.
Feierman, Steven. *The Shambaa Kingdom: A History.* Madison: University of Wisconsin Press, 1974.
Gabre-Sellassie, Zewde. *Yohannes IV of Ethiopia: A Political Biography.* Oxford: Oxford University Press, Clarendon Press, 1975.

Kimambo, I. N., and Temu, A. J. *A History of Tanzania.* Nairobi: East African Publishing House, 1969.

Kiwanuka, M. S. M. Semakula. *A History of Buganda: From the Foundation of the Kingdom to 1900.* London: Longman, 1971.

Low, D. A. *Buganda in Modern History.* London: Weidenfeld and Nicolson, 1971.

Muriuki, Godfrey. *A History of the Kikuyu: 1500–1900.* Nairobi: Oxford University Press, 1974.

Nicholls, C. S. *The Swahili Coast: Politics, Diplomacy, and Trade on the East African Littoral, 1798–1856.* London: George Allen & Unwin, 1971.

Roberts, Andrew, ed. *Tanzania before 1900.* Nairobi: East African Publishing House, 1968.

Shorter, Ayward. *Chiefship in Western Tanzania.* Oxford: Oxford University Press, Clarendon Press, 1972.

Tippu Tip. *Maisha ya Hamed bin Muhammed el Murjebi, yaani Tippu Tip.* Swahili text with translation by W. H. Whiteley. Nairobi: East African Literature Bureau, 1966.

Chapter 14

A Trade Revolution
in Equatorial Africa
(c. 1780-1890)

TRADE HAD PENETRATED more and more deeply into Central Africa during the
eighteenth century, but the increasing flood of trade in the next century was of
an altogether different order of magnitude. Far more than anything that had
happened up to that time, it shattered the relative shelter of the whole equatorial belt. Traders had formerly penetrated from the coasts; now they crossed
the continent — the first recorded trip being that of two Angolan traders in
the first decade of the nineteenth century. By mid-century, Arab and European
travelers followed, among them David Livingstone. The impact of the European explorers, however, was more important for Europe's knowledge of Africa
— hence for future European activity *in* Africa — than it was in the immediate
situation. The expansion of trade networks in African hands came first.

Three systems of trade were involved, and all three were but segments
themselves of the expanding world trading network. The three were based on
the Atlantic, Mediterranean, and Indian Ocean coasts respectively. Coastal aspects and some of the internal operations of the Mediterranean penetration by
way of the Egyptian secondary empire, as well as the penetration from the Indian Ocean, have already been treated in earlier chapters. We will here treat
only the interior aspects of that penetration.

The Atlantic network also had a coastal and an internal aspect. On the
coast, it included both the coast north of the Dande River, which was not under Portuguese control, and the part to the south, which was. In the interior,
however, the Atlantic network broke into two separate segments, though they
were closely linked economically at their base. One segment, called "the great
river network," extended up the line of the Congo/Zaïre and its tributaries
above Stanley Pool (Pool Malebo). The second was the "Luso-African network" running eastward overland, across the Kwango River and beyond, on
through the Ovimbundu highlands. In its furthest reaches, it merged with the
segment of the Indian Ocean network that led from Lake Tanganyika to Ka-

zembe's kingdom, but not until the last third of the nineteenth century. In much the same way, the great river network, through its extensions up the Ubangi and Mbomu rivers, touched the southernmost extensions of the network leading south up the Nile, but that took place only after mid-century.

Long-distance trade in general benefited from the many local trade networks already in existence and sketchily touching one another. The new long-distance networks unified these, promoted spatial specialization, and helped to give greater elasticity to commercial relations over vast stretches of territory.

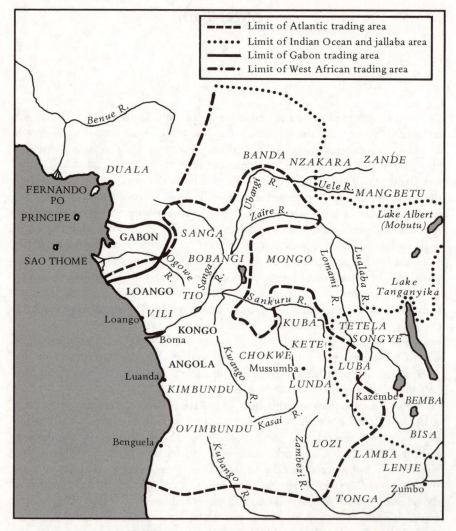

Trading Systems in Central Africa, c. 1875

Up to 1800, most inland trade — certainly in the Luso-African sphere and in Angola — had been "administrative trade." Rulers were in the main traders; they laid down the rules concerning marketing places and were the first to benefit from the profits. This applies just as much to the ruling Council of Luanda as it does to the Lunda king, and the "fairs" regulated by the administration in Angola correspond to the enforced camping sites for caravans in Luanda. But this was not the case north of the Dande or for the great river network. In the east, administrative trade existed by 1800 between Kazembe and the Indian Ocean. But here and elsewhere — even in Darfur far to the north — the system disappeared during the century. No force was strong enough to contain the modest entrepreneur living on little but hope and traveling far and wide. At the end of the period, no administrative trade at all survived. And this meant a social revolution.

MOUNT CAMEROON TO CAPE LOPEZ: THE CAMEROON AND GABON COASTS AND THEIR HINTERLAND

The north-south coast to the north of Cape Lopez had been a backwater in earlier Euro-African trade. The combined volume of the slave trade from this whole coast had been only a fraction — perhaps a tenth — of the exports from either the Congo mouth or the Niger Delta. The dominant political pattern was the lineage, and major lineage heads dealt with the Europeans (who called them "kings") on behalf of the lineage as a whole, though a single ethnic group was dominant on each section of the coast. On the estuary of the Wuri (where Douala now stands), it was the Duala. On the Gabon estuary, the Mpongwe held the equivalent position, and the same was true of smaller peoples in command of the minor markets around Cape Lopez.

Whatever the area or ethnic group, some lineages managed to rise in competition with the rest. On the Gabon, "King Denis" capitalized on his village's position to receive incoming goods from the coast and the Ogowe delta, while "King Georges" dominated the route to the middle Ogowe. There was no higher authority to displace, as there was near the Congo mouth, but the rise of particular lineages forced a rearrangement of the lineage system. The wealthiest lineages now displaced the oldest in prestige and authority, and the shift was a source of disorder. New wealth was attributed to witchcraft, and witchcraft accusations in turn led to poison ordeals and fights. By 1840, election replaced inheritance in the selection of lineage chiefs. People all along the coast became more obsessed with rank and social differentiation. Among the Duala, for example, it was the fashion by 1800 to distinguish six different ranks of slaves. On the Gabon, people laid a special emphasis on "purity" of descent.

The newly rich adopted European goods and some European habits as a sign of their position. In 1826, "King Bell" of the Duala lived in a two-storied wooden house with windows and European furniture. He and other coastal lineage heads used European crockery and eating utensils and sometimes wore European clothes. Many knew how to speak European languages. In time, these differences between the education and style of life available to the wealthy differed so much from the pattern of the common people that true social classes can be said to have existed.

Trade to the interior was mainly peaceful, depending on cooperation rather than force. In general, the people living across the trade routes tried to bar those in the deeper interior from trading to the coast, thus increasing their own profits as middlemen. At the beginning of the nineteenth century, for example, the Mpongwe found themselves surrounded on the land side by Seke, who bought ivory from dispersed Kele hunters further in the interior. The Mpongwe solution was to intermarry with the Seke, to pay well in imported goods, and to depend on the protection of their in-laws to keep trade moving. These same techniques had long been used among the Duala and Mpongwe lineages to assure the cooperation of other coastal peoples.

The slave trade in this region was too insignificant to attract much attention in the earliest decades of the nineteenth century. Ivory was the most important export; but redwood, ebony, wax, and gum copal also figured along with slaves — and rubber began to be added after about 1870. In 1800, the principal maritime traders were British, but increasing numbers of Spanish arrived after 1820, once they had been driven away from other regions by the British antislave-trade blockade. Spaniards also established shore stations and built barracoons, or barracks, to hold slaves awaiting shipping. A typical establishment about 1842 would be a palisaded area of about an acre, with sheds along the wall on two sides, one side for sleeping and the other for daytime use. A barracoon of this size could hold several hundred slaves at a time, or a flow of about one hundred a month. Slaves arrived in dugouts, which could hug the shores of the estuaries to escape cruisers. They departed in oceangoing ships, or sometimes in small schooners headed for the island of São Thomé, whence they were transshipped to Cuba or Brazil.

In time, British naval pressure against the slave trade followed, most effectively in the northern region, where British naval officers signed antislave treaties with the Duala. From the 1840s, the British consul at Fernando Po made regular visits to the Wuri estuary. The slave trade ended by about 1850, and the Duala themselves gradually perfected their dominance over a rich trade in palm oil and ivory along the whole stretch of coast from the Cross River estuary in present-day Nigeria to their own homeland on the Wuri. A vague but effective British informal empire lasted here until the 1880s, when the Germans persuaded Duala chiefs to sign treaties of annexation. In this way, the region of Duala commercial dominance turned into the coastal base for a German conquest of the interior, which ultimately gave territorial shape to the present Republic of Cameroon.

On the Gabon estuary, maritime predominance passed to France in the

1830s. The French navy set up a shore establishment in 1839 with the avowed aim of suppressing the slave trade and furthering commerce, though their true goal was to gain supremacy over British interests in the region. In 1849, they founded Libreville as a French "Freetown" and began the settlement with fifty-two freed slaves brought down from Dakar. This move drove the slave trade from the Gabon estuary itself, but the slave traders simply moved to Sanga-tanga, a site inaccessible to French or British ships about halfway between the Gabon and the mouth of the Ogowe River. At least a trickle of slaves was still being exported from there into the 1880s. Meanwhile, the Libreville post became a base for French exploration into the immediate hinterland. With the European conquests of the 1880s and later, these explorations led to French claims and annexations eastward to the Congo (Zaïre) River and northward to the edge of the Sahara — in effect to the acquisition of French Equatorial Africa, which later became the independent states of Congo-Brazzaville, Gabon, Chad, and the Central African Empire.

During these same decades of European establishment on the coast, an equally important movement was taking place in the interior. This was the great migration of the Fang and their relatives the Bulu, Beti, and Pahouin. In the middle of the eighteenth century, these people lived north of the forest in the southern part of present-day Cameroon, north of the Sanaga-Lom River. With the growth of wars and unrest emanating from the Adamawa grasslands further north and west, they first began retreating southward into the forest. By about 1800, they had become forest dwellers, having adapted very quickly to the new environment. Fang traditions tell symbolically of a compact with the Pygmies who taught them to survive and thrive by hunting, and elephant hunting became a staple of the export trade. But the Fang also brought with them such crops as peanuts, gourds, and tobacco and a superior technology for working with iron; and they quickly took entirely to forest crops like cassava, bananas, plantains, and oil palms.

Once adapted to the forest, they advanced very rapidly, arriving in the hinterland of Gabon, where they scattered or absorbed the sparsely settled Kele hunters and began a movement toward the coast in order to eliminate the middlemen between themselves and the maritime trade. In the south, they reached the middle Ogowe River and the shores north and south of the Gabon estuary by the early 1870s. Further north, Fang who had remained near their original homeland began moving toward the Cameroon coast, only to be stopped by the German advance about 1895. In the longer run, they introduced a single culture to most of northern and central Gabon, to the present-day Republic of Equatorial Guinea, and to much of southern Cameroon, an area including more than a million people by the middle of the twentieth century.

Much of this spectacular success was owing to Fang social organization. It was based on deep patrilineal segmentary lineages, which were joined together in turn through marriage alliances. Marriage rules forced each lineage to take wives from a great variety of other groups. This made for interlineage co-

operation against foreigners and tended to reduce fighting among Fang lineages. Villages were large and stockaded during the migrations, and each was
settled by a lineage segment. Village heads, however, were not the oldest men
of the lineage, but rather the most respected, which in practice meant the
wealthiest. Villages were joined together in turn as part of the larger lineage,
and the leader of a territorial and kinship cluster was again the wealthiest, not
the oldest. These village groups were given further cohesion with the Fang as
a whole through honorary associations, one for men and one for women.
Though these associations were open to all, they were expensive to join, so
that here again, wealth was a source of power. The men's association dealt
with a broad range of political problems and carried out police functions for
the whole region.

The importance of wealth is again illustrated by other aspects of Fang
culture. Bridewealth payments were huge. Political rivalry could be expressed
by a kind of competition, called *bilaba,* where rich men would challenge one
another to match gift for gift until one of them ran out of goods. This mutual
gift giving was also a form of trade, since those nearer the coast would include
more maritime imports in their gifts while those further inland would give
more ivory or other Fang products. The relationship between wealth and power
was so strong that the Fang word *nkukuma,* meaning "leader" or "notable,"
was simply the absolute form of *nkukum,* meaning "wealthy person."

The new territory occupied by the Fang in this great migration was inhabited, but only very sparsely, by people who generally fled. The Fang did
not sell slaves, but neither did they incorporate large numbers of foreigners.
At most, they married a few women captives, but the children of these women
were not considered to be "true" Fang. Once in the forest, the dynamic of
further expansions was exhaustion of the elephant herds and of the soil around
their villages. Villages seemed to uproot themselves quite regularly at ten- to
fifteen-year intervals, each one moving into "empty" country beyond the last
previous Fang settlement. In the process, lineages leapfrogged one another; in
time, any single kinship unit came to be widely scattered through the whole of
Fang territory. As a result, leadership built on wealth, not kinship, became
increasingly important, and the whole process of movement tended to create
a homogeneous culture area stretching over a large territory. But the Fang
way of doing this was only one of several means to a similar end in Equatorial
Africa during the precolonial century.

THE GREAT CONGO COMMERCE

The Congo and Angola together supplied about 60 percent of all slaves
entering the trans-Atlantic trade in the first half of the nineteenth century.
Perhaps a quarter of the grand total came from the ports on either side of the
Congo mouth. When slave exports diminished sharply after the 1850s, ivory
became increasingly important. By the 1860s, ivory moving down the Congo,

or Zaïre, by way of Stanley Pool amounted to a sixth of all the ivory that was marketed in London, and the new trade brought increasing quantities of tobacco, palm oil, and peanuts. By the early 1880s, the annual value of trade at the Congo mouth was about £3 million sterling, somewhat more than the value of trade at the mouth of the Niger.

The heart of the Congo River trade was the market at Stanley Pool, the crucial transit point where boat transportation toward the coast was blocked by the long stretch of the Congo Rapids. The rapids divided the Congo trade into an upper or waterborne segment and a lower or overland segment linking the Pool with a series of ports along the coast both north and south of the estuary itself. Between the ports and the Pool, a series of subsidiary inland markets were also important as transit points for a change of bearers, and each of these had its own middlemen serving the larger trade. These included San Salvador and Kimbalambala still further south, plus towns in Manianga and the copper- and iron-mining district still further north. Most of these markets drew on the caravan trade to the pool, but the southernmost also traded overland to the Yaka capital on the Kwango, while the northern middlemen also sent some trade north into eastern Gabon almost as far as the equator. In either case, the actual bearers were often slaves. The specialists in caravan operations north of the Congo were the Vili of Loango, while the Soso or Zombo were important south of the river.

Within this lower segment of the Congo trade, much of the political authority belonged to men grown wealthy in trade, who had usurped power simply because they had more slaves and more guns than their predecessors. But some of the older authorities still held on to a measure of power. The king of Loango held on more effectively than most, and the king of Kongo could exert some influence from his capital at San Salvador as far as the coast north of Ambriz. These kings, it was thought, had magical powers they could use to block all trade. Perhaps more effective, the merchants of any market town in Kongo who disobeyed an embargo could be looted with impunity by those who remained loyal to the crown.

The lords of the Tio plains monopolized the trade of the region. Around 1800, they had invented a new justification for their authority which sidestepped the older view that it was delegated by the Tio king. Here, in short, the traditional authorities themselves became "big men" through their dominance over trade, and much the same thing happened in the kingdom of Kasanje in the hinterland of Luanda. After 1860, the lords of that kingdom took over real power and reduced the king to a mere cipher.

The main goods moving inland over this lower segment were salt from the coast and a mix of three European products: guns, gunpowder, and cloth. All three had to be present in any transition that involved ivory or slaves. The currency, however, was cloth, designated in "fathoms," though the actual length of the fathom differed from time to time and market to market. On the coast, the Europeans kept their own accounts in other terms, while markets at the

Pool or further inland used still other standards of value that passed as mere goods-in-transit closer to the coast. Strings of blue beads, *nzimbu* shells, cowrie shells, and a variety of metal currencies had to be taken into account. A smart trader could make his profit not merely on moving goods from place to place but by arbitrage operations, speculating on the value of particular currencies in these various markets.

By 1855, Ambriz became such an active trading town that Portugal annexed the place, but the other European traders simply relocated a little further up the coast under British protection. The Portuguese also tried to intervene in Kongo politics by backing a candidate for the throne. When their candidate won and became Pedro V in 1860, he recognized Portuguese overlordship. This situation continued until 1866 in spite of British protests, but then Portugal withdrew following an economic slump in Angola.

The market at Stanley Pool was controlled by Tio middlemen, settled in four sizable towns on the present sites of Kinshasa and Brazzaville. The total trade here was far more valuable than the ivory and slaves that passed on through by caravan to the coast, because river transportation was far cheaper per ton-mile, and bulkier goods could beat the cost of transport. The Pool markets received at least a ton of waterborne goods each day, even in the slack season. During peak seasons, the incoming river traffic would rise to an order of twenty-five to forty tons per day, with redwood, pottery, smoked fish, and beer coming downstream along with the ivory and slaves, while copper and lead from the mines at Manianga, copper jewelry, smoked meat, cassava, and other foodstuffs passed through the Tio markets headed upriver along with the European imports.

The Tio townspeople lived from trade, the manufacture of jewelry, and tobacco growing to supply caravans bound for the coast; they imported most of their food from the surrounding region. The financial structure of exchange was extremely complex, with several currencies in simultaneous use, though particular currencies rose and fell in popularity over time. They were mainly some form of metal bar or rod, with lead from Mindouli prominent at first; this was replaced by copper and then, after 1870, by brass rods imported from Europe. But many operations were carried on credit; the river traders passed their goods to the Tio on credit, receiving their return cargoes only after the Tio had completed the exchange with coastal caravans. Tio society in these towns had been completely transformed by the adaptation to trade on this scale. Each town contained hundreds of slaves and many women, all dependent on one free man. One emporium of perhaps five thousand people would have only five chiefs and their close relatives who could be counted as genuinely free. It goes without saying that all these chiefs were traders, though they also had some other claim to chieftancy as well. The one exception was the wealthiest of all, a certain Ngaliema. He began as the son of a slave who inherited his master's wealth and rose to prominence very rapidly in the 1870s. By 1900, he dominated one of the towns, and his capital in marketable goods was estimated at more than £3,000 sterling, aside even from his important investment in slaves and armaments.

The upper Congo trade was fed by two somewhat different sectors. One consisted of goods that flowed from the east, from the Kasai, Mfimi, and their tributaries, to reach the main Congo by way of the Kwa about 130 miles north of the Pool. The Nunu rivermen dominated this sector from their capital and major market at the confluence of the Kasai and the Mfimi, but their trade further inland was fed by other carriers. The Ntomba of Lake Mayi Ndombe (Lake Leopold II) had been importing European goods since the eighteenth century, in return for redwood, ivory, copal, and pottery. Here too the trade had disrupted lineage structure so that the wealthiest entrepreneurs outshone the elders. Salt was also manufactured on the Mfimi for sale up the Congo or across to the Teke plateau west of the river. The Nunu themselves also made sugarcane wine, which they sold by the boatload both up and down the Congo and also across to the Teke.

The main branch of the upper Congo network was the northern sector following the main river nearly a thousand miles from Stanley Pool to Stanley Falls above Kisangani. From the Pool to the vicinity of the Ikelembe, the Bobangi held the river. Upstream, the Ngala and others were further intermediaries, but the Bobangi and the Ngala were alone in having their corporate life geared entirely to trade and fishing. They had *some* agriculture, of course, and the Bobangi established cassava plantations on the Alima River and elsewhere, specifically to serve trade. The dry-season harvest was prepared in large loaves that could last several months without danger of spoilage — long enough to allow a boat's crew to reach the Pool, perhaps to return as well, without having to buy provisions. Both river peoples traded in everything they could find, exploiting the trade of the Congo tributaries, including trade running down one tributary and up another. The bulk of the trade was not the exchange of ivory or slaves for cloth, gunpowder, and guns, though this indirect trade with Europe was nevertheless the mainstay of the system.

The Bobangi trade system, dating back well before 1800, owed its strength to the fact that many of the major affluents of the Congo emptied into the section of the main river that constituted their homeland. Before 1850, the now-familiar pattern of rich traders replacing chiefs or of chiefs moving into trade on their own was already well developed. Bobangi institutions to cope with their trade network were efficient and simple. The practice of blood brotherhood made it possible to acquire artificial kin in foreign parts. The Bobangi traders also often left off slaves at riverside villages, in part to produce food for sale to passing canoes and to act as local agents. To the local people, these slaves constituted hostages whose presence was a form of guarantee that Bobangi traders would come and go in peace.

Bobangi boats nevertheless traveled armed and often in sizable flotillas for greater security, and the Bobangi had further security in the form of colonies of their own people settled in villages along both banks of the Congo from the mouth of the Ubangi to the Pool. But they were not immune to trade wars. One took place, for example, against the Tio for control of the river between the mouth of the Kwa and the Pool. It was a draw; the Bobangi kept the right to go to the Pool, but they agreed not to settle on the west bank below the Kwa and they had to sell to the Tio once they reached the Pool.

They were limited in a similar way in their passage up the main Congo and up the Ubangi itself. The Ngala took over east of Makandza (Nouvelle Anvers), with clear control over a stretch of the main Congo as far as Bumba, where still others began to dominate. On the Ubangi, the Loi water people took over near the confluence with the main river and sent goods upstream through a number of middle groups, each of which controlled a small section of the Ubangi, as well as the Uele and Mbomu rivers beyond. The Bobangi were freer of competition, however, on the affluents that emptied into their own home stretch of the river. Their major settlements along these reaches had 10,000 people or more and each one tended to be located opposite a major affluent — Bolobo for the Nkeni, Likuba ("the Venice of the north") for the Alima, Bonga for the Sanga, Irebu for the Likouala and the exit from Lake Tumba. On these tributaries, the Bobangi traded over the entire navigable length; some of their trips on the Sanga took them right across the forest to the eastern Adamawa grasslands, where they may well have met Hausa traders from northern Nigeria.

The Ngala and Bobangi had similar customs to begin with, and the growth of their trade with each other brought their customs even closer together. A common pidgin language, Lingala, had already become the trade language for the Bobangi, Ngala, and many others. Along with Lingala came a common culture. Commerce on the main river carried scores of cultural features from one place to another. The knives of office from the bend of the Ubangi became prized insignia among the Tio. House shapes became standardized. Fishing techniques, procedures for creating blood brotherhood, new crops like cassava, lemons, oranges, tobacco, and maize — all these things were broadly accepted along with aspects of social structure, religion, or the kind of talisman used to make rain. The institution of slavery was gradually modified so that settlements up and down the river were reorganized along Tio or Bobangi lines. All this was so well advanced by the end of the century that European visitors thought they recognized a single "tribe," the Bangala, speaking its own language, Lingala, and having its own distinct culture. The traders, in short, had created a single culture over a huge area of Equatorial Africa — similar to the spread of the Fang but created in a different way — first in the towns along the rivers, then spreading inland as well.

Later still, colonial penetration was to follow the trade routes, which intensified the interculturation of African peoples along these routes until it welded the whole northwest of the Belgian Congo and French Middle Congo into a single civilization. In the colonial period, the interchange continued, first under the Congo Independent State, then by the colonial companies acting under Belgian or French authority. For a time, peoples like the Bobangi and Ngala lost and were forced to turn to fishing or to take subordinate jobs as sailors on the European rivercraft. Only in the postcolonial era did they reemerge in positions of command.

ANGOLA AND ITS HINTERLAND

At the beginning of the nineteenth century, the Portuguese posts on the Angola coast lived almost entirely from the slave trade; 85 percent of government revenue and most of the income of the private settlers came directly from that source. A few farsighted governors in previous decades had tried to diversify the economy, even before the slave trade came under serious attack in Europe, but the heavy investment and risk of plantation enterprise were not attractive. As a result, the official abolition of the Portuguese slave trade in 1834 introduced only a gradual change in economic forms and interests that paralleled the similar but earlier commercial revolution in West Africa.

At first, the decree of 1834 was unenforced beyond its provisions turning the ivory trade into a government monopoly. Instead, the main period of transition began about 1845, when Portugal installed a prize court at Luanda, and Great Britain made a unilateral decision to suppress the trade south of the equator, by force if necessary. In 1850, the Brazilian decision to enforce its own antislave-trade legislation was still more serious, though Angolan governors are known to have sent off cargoes of slaves to be smuggled into Brazil as late as the mid-1850s. The final blows to the remaining blockade-runners came in the course of the 1860s, though a few may have sailed even later. Meanwhile, in 1858, Portuguese legislation made it illegal to acquire more slaves within Angola and set up a timetable for the legal abolition of slavery, which occurred in 1875. The real transition therefore came quite rapidly in a period of hardly more than two decades.

The town of Luanda was in decline during the first half of the century. The Portuguese community was smaller than it had been, and parts of the old city had fallen into ruin. The major local traders were heavily indebted to their Brazilian creditors and could no longer easily collect the money they advanced to their own agents in the interior. Culturally, the town showed signs of its already long history as a melting pot. A Luso-African culture was arising. Most of the Portuguese were heavily influenced by their Mbundu neighbors in such matters as medicine, witchcraft, and religion, while the Mbundu had taken over many Portuguese practices along with writing and Portuguese as a lingua franca.

Socially and politically, the Luanda city council, made up of the governor, a few officials, and the major merchants, saw its influence wane in the interior. A genuine social revolution was under way in that a new class had emancipated itself. It consisted of long-distance traders from the interior, whether Mbundu (the *Ambaquista* or *Quimbares*), Portuguese (the *sertanejos*), or others —

including lower-rank Imbangala and Ovimbundu. All these resented the military posts that were still the centers for administration in the interior, and whose commanders tried to enforce the official trade regulations from which the Portuguese of Luanda profited most. The Luanda oligarchy lost its hold just as the Jaga of Cassange or the king of Kongo had done.

The military commanders of the *presidios* continued to levy tribute, to dispense justice to traders, and sometimes to carry out orders from Luanda. The actual agents of local government were the official local chiefs, the *soba*. The sobas levied taxes in slaves for the presidio commanders. And by the 1850s the practice began of forcing farmers to work on European plantations as indentured laborers. In the heartland behind Luanda, many communities had sprung up that were no longer under any chief. They were inhabited by Luso-African traders. By mid-century, this new class was completely out of Portuguese control.

The abolition of the slave trade had mixed economic consequences. Illegal traders were forced to move outside the city to barracoons scattered along the coast between Ambriz and Mossamedes, and the Brazilian capital that supported the trade followed them. As "legitimate" exports like wax and ivory began to replace the dying slave trade, the new trade followed the new paths and hence avoided Luanda. People in Luanda after the 1840s talked about the "economic disintegration of Angola," but especially in Benguela and elsewhere along the coast, times were better after 1840 than before. Settlers in the hinterland tried all sorts of schemes, such as coffee and cotton plantations, but with small success until the American Civil War brought a brief period of high cotton prices. The real gains were in wax and ivory. By the late 1850s, these two products accounted for more than 80 percent of the value of all exports, and that value was considerably higher than the annual value of exports had been in the 1820s when the slave trade still ran strong. Especially in the 1850s and 1860s, the government was able to use its new revenue to expand its territorial control to the east and south in order to capture more trade routes, but the move produced little result outside of Huila, where it brought the Portuguese in close touch with Ovimbundu traders, whose routes by this time reached into the heart of Africa.

The Ovimbundu and Chokwe were, in fact, the main suppliers of ivory, and the abolition of the slave trade brought them a bonanza. The Ovimbundu had developed a series of sturdy kingdoms in the central highlands of Angola during the early eighteenth century and defeated all Portuguese attempts to annex them. By 1800, they raided widely for cattle and slaves, but even then the key states like Bihé and Mbailundu sent caravans to buy slaves and ivory further inland, reaching the Lozi state on the Zambezi. In the 1840s, they broke the Imbangala monopoly at the Lunda capital. By the 1850s, Ovimbundu traders reached Katanga and even crossed Africa. A decade later they reached into central Kasai, in competition with Chokwe and Imbangala.

An Ovimbundu caravan was a large and well-armed body of men often combining the investment of several entrepreneurs, including some Portuguese sertanejos, though a few Portuguese like Silva Porto started caravans on their own. The entrepreneurs usually went along, though kings could and did fit out large caravans on their own. What set them apart from the competition was size and firepower, as more guns flowed inland through Benguela than were available to people like the Imbangala in the hinterland of Luanda or Ambriz.

Chokwe expansion was also triggered by the abolition of the slave trade. In their homeland, the Chokwe had been a little-known but highly skilled group of hunters, gatherers, and ironworkers. Their social organization reconciled the institution of chiefdom on the Lunda pattern with a flexible kinship organization that allowed tiny groups of relatives to hive off for hunting or wax gathering, and incidentally made it easy to incorporate foreign women. Their culture and society were adapted to an agriculturally poor environment and a low density of population. Then came the boom in ivory and wax, and the Chokwe suddenly became wealthy. They exported ivory and wax toward the coast in return for guns and other goods they could sell further inland to buy women slaves, but the women were assimilated into their own society — not exported — and they never sold their own people.

Whether it was overpopulation or the lure of richer hunting grounds that pushed them is unclear; but within a quarter of a century, groups of hunters began to emigrate, following the known trails, mainly toward the north, often under the leadership of junior aristocrats who had no hope of succession in the homeland. Many were able to settle peacefully in a new, sparsely settled region, but the Chokwe pattern of rapid growth combined with their superior weapons soon made them masters of the new country. In a short while, they were able to incorporate whole groups of local people, simultaneously with the piecemeal acquisition of local women through marriage and of young boys and girls as "pawns" for debts and fines.

The Chokwe dispersion began a little before 1850. By about 1865, they were trading into the country between the Kasai and Lulua rivers. Before 1880, they had occupied most of what was to become northern and eastern Angola. After 1874, the demand for rubber entered the picture. At first, most rubber was collected in the gallery forests along the river banks, which were not cultivated but left to the Chokwe hunters. Because women did the tapping and gathering, it was easy for them to go along with their menfolk on hunting expeditions, occupying an empty ecological niche. After about 1886, however, the dominant species of rubber plant was to be found in the higher grasslands, and here rubber gathering was competitive with existing, non-Chokwe agriculture. With that, the Chokwe expansion became less peaceful, but their superior arms gave them easy victories at first. During the 1880s, they overran all of the Lunda country, including the capital, and they were to be effectively stopped and rolled back only in the late 1890s. By that time, they were chronically fighting the forces of the Congo Independent State as well as their older Lunda and Pende enemies. The colonial administration of Angola, however, failed to subdue them until the 1920s, and even after that their peaceful spread by emigration into Zaïre and Zambia continued to the present.

Like the Fang, the Chokwe covered a great area and contributed to its cultural homogenization, but their total cultural impact was less than that of the Fang. They assimilated other people more easily, but the people they assimilated were already under varying degrees of Lunda influence, as were the Chokwe themselves. The particular Chokwe contribution — hunting and smithing skills and the sculptor's art — was comparatively minor. It might have been more significant if their area had not been divided during the colonial period between the Belgian Congo and Portuguese Angola.

Other peoples in the Angola hinterland were affected adversely by the end of the slave trade, notably the old middlemen groups in Luanda's immediate hinterland, and especially Matamba and the kingdom of Kasanje. Matamba went the way of the kingdoms north of the Congo. Its king gradually lost power to the chiefs, who had gone into partnership with Portuguese bush traders and built up enough power to become virtually independent. In 1836, the Portuguese turned it into a presidio. Kasanje held out longer. As long as a market for slaves existed, the king could keep his authority by raiding recalcitrant villages and selling their people through the central market, which he controlled. But the end of the slave trade weakened his position, and a long war with Portugal, centered on the 1850s, left the country barely independent, but no longer a barrier to Portuguese commercial penetration. This meant that Imbangala traders from Kasanje now dealt independently with smaller caravans, competing against the new Ovimbundu operations between themselves and the Lunda, but maintaining and expanding north into present-day Zaïre between the Kwango and the Kasai rivers.

Of the old middleman states, only the Yaka kingdom continued to flourish along the Kwango in reaches where today it forms the frontier between Angola and Zaïre. The key to Yaka success was their extraordinary control over the trade routes leading further east, routes protected by a series of fortified posts that ultimately led to the Kasai.

By the 1870s, the elephant herds had retreated into the wide gallery forests of the Kasai, Lulua, and Sankuru rivers in what is now south-central Zaïre. Here, the animals were pursued with remarkable efficiency by the Lulua, the Kuba, and the Luba Kasai. Among the Lulua, a state was created by two rulers who were successful in putting themselves in touch with coastal traders (later with European explorers and the government of the Congo Independent State) as a means of assuring their supply of arms and the security of the country. The Kuba state was also successful; it invested the proceeds from its ivory sales mainly in slaves captured further east, to such an extent that about 6 percent of the Kuba population in the 1950s was still of slave origin.

The Luba further south were more unfortunate in the first instance. They were raided so heavily by the Chokwe from the west and by the Songye and Tetela from the east that many of them broke and fled to Kalamba's Lulua state or later to the posts of the Congo Independent State. In their new homes, they came to be known as the Luba Kasai. As displaced persons, they had little alternative but to take as much advantage as they could from the educational opportunities offered by the colonial regime. As a result, they came in the long run to monopolize the most desirable clerical jobs in Kasai and much of Katanga. The final act was played out much later, in 1959, when the old rivalry between the displaced Luba Kasai and their Lulua hosts broke out into civil war. The Lulua won, and most of the Luba Kasai were forced to return to their ancestral homeland.

TRADERS FROM THE INDIAN OCEAN

As on the west coast and its hinterland, the penetration of trade from the east coast helped to provoke important economic and political changes in the heart of Africa. It was not, of course, the only source of change, but its influence became more and more important in the course of the nineteenth century. For example, the Kazembe, the king of the easternmost Lunda state on the Luapula, began the century rich from trade, but was supplanted in the 1880s by a new secondary empire, founded by men whose origins and sources of power lay down the trade route to Zanzibar.

By about 1800, the Kazembe had reached the zenith of his power. His was the best organized state among the Lunda kingdoms, his capital wealthy from the flow of tribute and the influx of traders from Tete in the lower Zambezi valley. The flow of goods intensified again in the 1830s, as the "Arab" or Swahili traders opened up the route from coastal Tanzania, and Kazembe's capital became a way station on a route that went on to the capital of the Mwaant Yaav, the emperor of the Lunda. The kingdom was secure from foreign enemies, which induced people to travel and increased cultural interaction. But the pomp and glitter of court life were paid for by the heavy taxes the Lunda lords imposed on the villages. Political stability and security were in fact bought at the price of systematic terror and coercion. Generalized discontent among the people was finally to help outsiders wreck the kingdom.

The Kazembe's nemesis was a Nyamwezi adventurer and trader named Msiri. He arrived about 1860, having followed his father and the spread of trade through central Tanganyika and past the lakes into the Congo basin at a time when Kazembe's kingdom was passing through a terrible smallpox epidemic. Tradition holds that he gained permission to trade in Katanga in return for the secret of innoculation. In any event, he married and settled down in Katanga, gradually becoming involved in local politics. He gathered other Nyamwezi around him, and with their guns he made himself a force in the region. He finally supplanted a local chief and made himself the head of a new secondary empire, though one that had support from the people at large because Msiri's guns defended them from Luba raids. Theoretically, he was still under the Kazembe's overrule, but he intervened militarily in Kazembe's family quarrels. That provoked the Kazembe's anger so much that he ordered the execution of all Nyamwezi and other eastern traders who happened to be at his capital.

This act immediately lost him the support of the Swahili, "Arabs," and others who could have kept him supplied with guns. They counterattacked and killed the king in 1872. That left Msiri in personal control of Katanga, and for a time no Kazembe could keep the throne without either the support of the "Arab" traders or of Msiri's men, now known as the Yeke. Through the 1880s, the Yeke dominated the old heartland, but a new Kazembe recovered part of the Luapula valley in 1892 and turned it into a haven for the many refugees who were then fleeing from the Swahili slave traders. That situation continued until the final Kazembe surrendered to British rule in 1899.

Msiri's secondary empire in Katanga had meanwhile grown even stronger through trade in locally produced copper, salt, and ivory, as well as through advantageous marriages with, among others, the daughters of a Portuguese trader from the Atlantic and an Arab trader from the Indian Ocean. In 1880, his father died and he took the title of *mwami,* or king. During the next decade, his kingdom reached its peak of affluence and power. Msiri's caravans reached both Benguela on the Atlantic and the Indian Ocean opposite Zanzibar. He raided deep into central Zambia and dominated the wreck of Kazembe's territory. His capital was possibly the largest city in Central Africa, but then he began to alienate his subjects just as Kazembe had done. The Sanga people, who had helped Msiri rise from trader to king, rebelled in 1886, and the rebellion dragged on into chronic guerrilla warfare.

After 1886, the European factor also made its appearance in Central Africa, with missionaries resident at Msiri's court. Both the Congo Independent State and the British South Africa Company offered him protectorate status, but he refused. Finally in 1891, an official of the Independent State killed him during a quarrel. The Yeke state disintegrated, and the Sanga rebellion spread everywhere. Ironically enough, Msiri's successor was able to pretend to his old power only by becoming an ally of the Congo Independent State against his former subjects, and that war ended with a Congolese victory only in 1900 — just a decade before the first industrial copper smelter began to operate near the first European colonial town.

Though Msiri's power derived ultimately from the military technology of industrial Europe, its actual cultural consequence in Central Africa was an interchange between different African societies with very little input from European culture. An increased pace of culture change had indeed begun during the heyday of the Kazembe state, but Msiri carried it much further with the introduction of new types of copper mining and especially with a flood of new orders and laws designed to reconcile Nyamwezi customs with those of the local people. Earlier Lundaization had no doubt prepared the way for further change, but the new regulations covered the whole gamut of social relations from bridewealth to the proper composition of social groups. Political ideology, kingship, and the symbols of office were imported wholesale from Nyamwezi country and were thus linked to those of the lake region of East Africa. The Yeke introduced new religious beliefs as well, but they also accepted some cultural features from the conquered people, including the use of the Sanga language.

The Luba kingdom, for its part, began to expand in the late eighteenth century, especially toward the north and toward Lake Tanganyika, but the new vigor was only temporary. Harsh rule sent many of the common people fleeing to the Kasai or to the Songye in the north. Civil wars between contenders for the throne broke out after 1830; by 1860, the kingdom was again reduced to the size it had been in 1750.

Traders from the two coasts entered this drama fairly early. The first traders from the Indian Ocean arrived about 1825, though they became common only after 1850, when they began to encounter Ovimbundu traders from the other coast. Here, it was the Ovimbundu who played the more active role in politics. Their caravans were sometimes directed to plunder villages that incurred the displeasure of the king, and they were sometimes directed against foreign enemies. But the Luba-Ovimbundu alliance only led to popular insurrection from the Luba themselves. From the mid-1880s to 1917, Luba politics degenerated into a series of succession struggles in which Msiri, the Ovimbundu, the Congo Independent State, and even mutinous troops previously serving the Independent State all took different sides. In 1917, Belgium established colonial control over the whole area.

Traders from the east coast were far more damaging to other African societies, especially those to the south of Lake Tanganyika, through eastern Katanga (later Shaba), and up to the northern rim of the plateau country in northeast Zambia. Caravans from the Swahili coast began to appear here in the 1830s and 1840s; they were small at first and engaged mainly in trade rather than raiding. With time, however, as the caravans became bigger, the traders came to recognize their potential. They could make temporary alliances with local rulers to attack others, and then carry off valuable booty in slaves and ivory. By the 1860s, to avoid having to return frequently to central Tanganyika, they began to set up fortified bases in eastern Katanga. This new system wrecked even the power of the chiefs who first allied with the traders, since their allies often turned against them. The smaller states were thus completely destroyed, and the situation remained fluid, not to say anarchic, until the colonial period.

The Bemba chiefdoms of northeast Zambia escaped this fate. About 1800, there were several antagonistic chiefdoms, though all Bemba chiefs were members of a single clan and had close relations in other respects. But after 1835, the most important of these chiefs gradually began to bring others into their orbit. This process continued into the 1860s. By 1870, the Bemba had driven off the Ngoni, and internal unification was moving forward, though not to the point of forming a single unified state. They no longer attacked one another. Instead, they raided their neighbors and carried the slaves and ivory to the East African traders working the routes that passed around Bemba territory. Since *they* went to the traders, the traders had no occasion to visit them; and the

Bemba remained relatively secure from raids. But later, as they came to depend more and more on the guns and ammunition from the east coast, they too became a kind of confederated secondary empire. Like others of the type, it needed external trade to keep going. The Bemba polity therefore collapsed quickly in 1898 when the British cut off their supplies of arms and ammunition. But their relative unity and relative isolation preserved the Bemba plateau as a region free from the impact of Swahili culture and language as it diffused through the whole of eastern Zaïre and as far as the copper belt of present-day Zambia.

The carriers of this massive culture change were, of course, the Swahili traders from the east coast and other traders like the Nyamwezi of central Tanganyika who joined them on the way. In Maniema and eastward to the shores of Lake Tanganyika, the "Arabs" found mainly stateless societies. They turned immediately from trading to raiding, perhaps because of the weakness of the local African political organization, perhaps because the country lacked large markets where alien merchants could deal. By 1870, they had founded a market of their own near the salt springs at Nyangwe on the Lualaba, and it soon attracted the riverain peoples of the Lualaba as well as traders from the east coast. Meanwhile, the caravans roamed and raided all through the open country east of Nyangwe, though they were unable to penetrate the forested region to the north — partly because the forest people were better organized and partly because guns lost some of their advantage in that environment.

The 1870s found the whole country between the forest and the Bemba plateau, from Lake Tanganyika to the Lualaba River, under "Arab" domination, but that domination was merely the freedom of anyone with modern guns to exercise power; it had no political character till Tippu Tib appeared in the mid-1870s. In a sense, it was a part of Zanzibar's secondary empire, though it was far from the center for genuine Zanzibari government. Tippu Tib's contribution was to organize the ingredients of secondary empire that were already present. He began by allying himself with an African chief. When the chief died, Tippu Tib claimed to be a kinsman and the legitimate successor, and he made the claim good within a small area just short of the forest. Soon, other Songye rulers offered alliance, and Tippu Tib was able to line up some of the Swahili traders in Nyangwe as well. Having put together an alliance of local Africans and alien merchants, he moved his headquarters to Kasongo and began to organize a real state. He built roads, laid out plantations, imposed a royal monopoly on the sale of ivory, and appointed his own agents to administer, "speak justice," and collect tribute. He stopped raiding within his own lands, though his people continued to raid abroad for slaves to work the plantations and for ivory to export eastward. In time, his realm even began to spawn subsidiary secondary empires, like one based on Kabinda and organized by a Songye lord, Lumpungu. He became an ally of Tippu Tib, who supplied him with guns so that Lumpungu was able, in his turn, to dominate the whole area south of the forest between the Sankuru and Lomani rivers.

Tippu Tib was barely established when European explorers began to appear in the 1870s. H. M. Stanley passed through Kasongo on his way from Zanzibar down the Congo to the Atlantic. Tippu Tib used the occasion to begin moving down the Luapula River into the forest. By 1882, he reached Stanley Falls. A race for control of eastern Zaïre then developed between Tippu Tib, representing an offshoot secondary empire of Zanzibari origin, and the Congo Independent State, a secondary empire under European control. For this effort, Tippu Tib not only used his own power; he also became an agent for the combined force of the Swahili traders then resident in Maniema. In the short run, he won, forcing the Independent State to evacuate its post at Stanley Falls in 1884. In 1887, the Independent State recognized this victory by appointing him governor of the eastern Congo, but its retreat was only a tactical maneuver. It reproached Tippu Tib for his failure to suppress raiding by others, but simultaneously denied him the arms he needed to police the region. It was officially opposed to slavery; yet its own officials were competing and even fighting the Swahili traders for stocks of ivory in the eastern Congo. Tippu Tib himself retired to the coast in 1890, a wealthy man but convinced that he could not hold out against the Europeans over the long run. Soon, parts of formerly subordinate secondary empires defected, and from 1892 to 1894 the Congo Independent State fought a general and successful war for the conquest of what is now eastern Zaïre.

The political consequences of Tippu Tib's empire were short-lived, but the cultural consequences were profound. In the beginning, he attracted large numbers of Tetela from the core area of his state. These people adopted Swahili culture and a form of Islam, and they spread it along the Lualaba River to Stanley Falls and beyond into the forests of northeastern Zaïre as far as Lake Albert (Lake Mobutu). These men were called "Arabized" somewhat inaccurately, since their culture was a reflection of Swahili coastal culture with a special inflection from the culture of their Tetela homeland, but they brought the first elements of a new cultural cohesion into this vast area of the eastern Zaïre, and in this sense contributed to building a Zaïrois nation for the distant future. This included, in time, an extensive penetration of Islam on the west coast of Lake Tanganyika, in the old Tetela core area, and Stanley Falls. Otherwise, Islam tended to drop out, but Swahili remained as a lingua franca along with many aspects of the Tetela way of life.

THE NORTHERN SAVANNA
AND TRADERS FROM THE NILE

The northern savannas of Central Africa were also dominated by intrusive merchants in this period, but here the demand for ivory and wax are inconsequential. Slaves for Egypt and North Africa were the chief objectives of the alien traders, and the combination of slave raids with the rapid rise and fall of secondary empires was even more disastrous here than a similar pattern of events had been to the south of the forest. As of 1800, the beginnings of these revolutionary changes were barely visible. The political structure of the area was still what it had been for several centuries — a tier of states along the desert edge from Lake Chad to the Red Sea including Bagirmi, Wadai, Darfur, the region of Kordofan normally in contest between Darfur and the Funj sultanate at Sennar, and finally Sennar itself controlling the Nilotic Sudan. The principal trade routes were the north-south axis following the valley of the Nile from Sennar to Aswan and beyond, and an east-west axis staying close to the desert along the whole of the savanna belt. In the early nineteenth century, however, the flow of through traffic along this route was heaviest over the section from Darfur to Suakin on the Red Sea, though a few pilgrims bound for Mecca came through from the far west. Other traffic passing the region of Lake Chad reached only as far as Wadai or Darfur.

The principal traders over these routes were the *jallaba* of the Nile valley. By the end of the eighteenth century, large numbers of Ja'ali, or Nubian, jallaba were operating in trade all along the southern fringe of the major sahelian states, from southern Darfur east to Bahr al-Ghazal and the White Nile south of Sennar, among Nilotic peoples like the Shilluk and Dinka.

Political history in the *sahel* during the early nineteenth century turned on an intricate pattern of relations among the sahelian states themselves, and between them and North Africa. The jallaba were meanwhile aggressively pushing their trade to the south. The political and military reaction on the desert edge was to come only after mid-century. Of the three sahelian states, Darfur was clearly the strongest, with overlordship covering both Wadai and the region of Kordofan, and with easy trade links to Egypt, northeast along the "forty-day road" to the desert bend of the Nile.

Though Darfur remained strong until after 1850, its competitive position weakened on both flanks. In 1821, the Egyptian conquest of Sennar and the establishment of the Egyptian secondary empire in the Nilotic Sudan substituted a strong neighbor with modern weapons for a declining state that had posed no threat. In a short while, Egypt had captured Kordofan and pulled it into the orbit of the Nile valley.

The Sultanate of Wadai, on Darfur's western flank, was a potential threat when it was strong, and it was strong during the reign of Sabun, centering about 1800. Conscious of the power that trade could bring, Sabun sponsored a settlement of jallaba near his capital. He also imported chain mail, firearms, and military advisers from North Africa and minted his own coinage. By pure chance, a route to the north by way of Ennedi and Kufra to Benghazi in Cyrenaica was discovered during his reign, which removed Wadai's previous dependence on transit to North Africa through either Fezzan or Darfur, and Sabun fitted out royal caravans to take advantage of the new route. But Sabun's successors were less able, and the Sultan of Darfur took advantage of a disputed succession in 1838 to put his own candidate into office as the Sultan of Wadai. That, ironically, restored Wadai's power. The new sultan, Muhammad Sharif, quickly made himself acceptable to various factions in Wadai and went on to become his own man and perhaps the ablest ruler that country ever had. He had made the pilgrimage to Mecca, where he met Muhammad ibn 'Ali al-Sanūsi, later founder of the Sanūsīya, a new brotherhood with a strong bias against sufism and toward a return to the purity of primitive Islam.

Al-Sanūsi was originally from Algeria, but he settled, and his order centered, in the steppe hinterland of Cyrenaica and the oases still further south on the way to Wadai. The order soon became an incipient state ruling over the steppe and desert, and it later served to focus resistance, first to the Turks and then to the Italian invaders of Libya after 1911. Meanwhile, it dominated the caravan trade to the south. An alliance between Wadai and the Sanūsīya developed in the 1840s and lasted for the rest of the century, though the sultans of Wadai apparently were not themselves members of the order. This North African connection was one basis for Wadai's new rise to power from the mid-century onward. Muhammad Sharif waged war as far west as Borno, establishing Wadai's hegemony over Bagirmi and its predominance over other territories as far as the Shari River, with some states even west of the Shari paying him tribute.

The states on the desert edge responded in different ways to the new trade opportunities as well as to the potential threat that the traders posed to their political stability. In the first half of the century, the center of jallaba operations was Darfur, which exported slaves, ivory, ostrich feathers, copper, tamarind, gum arabic, and camels to Egypt in return for natron, salt, various metals in bar form, and European manufactured goods and firearms. Some of these goods were reexported east or west along the northern fringe of the savanna. The main imports from the south were copper from the mines at Hofrat en Nahas and slaves captured from among a variety of less organized peoples in the southern part of the savanna.

By 1800, jallaba parties and caravans were already penetrating well to the south of Hofrat en Nahas and into the western half of the present-day Bahr al-Ghazal province, a region that was soon known as Dar Fertit ("land of slaves"). In the desert-edge states, the jallaba had permanent trade settlements called *dehm,* usually located at the capital of the sultan or some important provincial ruler. Darfur made no objection to these settlements, and the number of jallaba there increased tenfold between 1796 and 1870 from about five hundred to five thousand. Further south, the heavily armed caravans set up a series of fortified camps called *zariba*. First developed by jallaba operating from Darfur, these served as bases for the raids and as places to keep booty before it was shipped north.

The Sultan of Darfur regulated these raiding expeditions by granting a permit for each in return for a substantial fee. The policy in Wadai was somewhat different. There, the sultans allowed only one dehm, and that was closely watched. Instead of licensing private raiding expeditions to the south, Wadai used the royal army to conduct annual raids, and managed the slaves as a state enterprise. Some of these practices would be relaxed later in the century, but Wadai remained conscious that the jallaba were not only a source of wealth; they also constituted a danger to public safety.

About mid-century, the jallaba operating southward from Darfur were joined by competitors based on Khartoum. These were European slave traders at first, but, in the 1860s and 1870s, Coptic Egyptians took over from them. The Khartoumers controlled the Nile route, while the jallaba mostly went overland, across Kordofan to Egypt well west of the Nile. One jallaba named al-Zubayr Rahma Mansur, found support in Khartoum which allowed him to eclipse the others and to end by wresting control of all jallaba trade. He turned the former armed caravans into a private standing army and established his headquarters well south of the Bahr al-Ghazal. He overcame other would-be founders of trading territories in this area, presumably because the others were not jallaba (one indeed was a Moroccan). As a result he was recognized by Egypt as governor of Bahr al-Ghazal, which formalized his creation of a secondary empire within a secondary empire. On his own in 1874, he then conquered Darfur in Egypt's name, claiming that *baqarra* cattle nomads in southern Darfur were a danger to the jallaba caravans. Egypt, which had attached special importance to Darfur, hurriedly sent a regular army unit to occupy the country, while Zubayr went to Cairo to plead his case. The Egyptian government kept him there, but his son continued to manage his holdings until the Khartoum government finally sent troops in 1878, at which time Zubayr's secondary empire was absorbed by the larger Egyptian one.

One unit of Zubayr's forces, however, chose to move out to the west under the command of one of his old subordinates named Rābih Fadlallāh or Rābih Zubayr. By 1879, Rābih, with an army mainly recruited by capture or purchase but nevertheless armed with breech-loading rifles, had moved westward into the old slave-raiding territory south of Wadai. Wadai then had to meet a jallaba challenge in spite of its own careful policies designed to keep them in check. Rābih and his force stayed on the southern fringe of Wadai until 1893, building up strength enough to conquer Bagirmi and to defeat the Wadai army sent against them. At this phase, the Kufra route to the north was invaluable, since it brought arms to Wadai while allowing Wadai to cut Rābih off from one route of access to modern weapons. In 1894, however, Rābih conquered Borno and moved his field of operations further west.

Rābih's new empire fell before a French attack in 1900, but the Sanūsīya, Wadai, and Darfur (which had again become independent in 1898) were among the last African states to succumb to European conquest. The French began to conquer what was to be the Republic of Chad only in 1902, and that conquest was completed only in 1913 using three full battalions of French troops, the strongest force ever used in Central Africa. Darfur fell to the English from the Nilotic Sudan only in 1916, while Sanusi resistance to the Italians carried on into the early 1930s.

Meanwhile, the jallaba and the Khartoumers had encroached continuously on the stateless peoples to the south of the sahelian row of large political entities. By 1850, some jallaba had reached the Mbomu River, on the present frontier between Zaïre and the Central African Republic, and even further south to the Uele River and beyond into Mangbetu country. These incursions were disastrous for the stateless societies in the Dar Fertit, where whole ethnic groups were wiped out. Others were forced to emigrate. Most of the Banda peoples were pushed westward progressively throughout the century. This, in turn, put extraordinary pressure on the populations of the western part of the present-day Central African Empire; hemmed in by the southward pressure of Bagirmi from the north, and the eastward pressure from the Fulbe of Adamawa to the west, they had nowhere to go. By the 1880s, however, they achieved a degree of political cohesion and managed to combine forces and to defeat Rābih's attacks.

The Zande and Mangbetu also managed to stand against the traders' attacks, but with heavy damage. Though the Zande along the Congo-Nile divide were fragmented politically into a number of states, they found initially that they could defy both the Khartoum-based traders and the smaller jallaba operating out of zaribas to their north. At first, the traders would ally themselves with a particular chiefdom, helping it to overcome its enemies so as to get the ivory and slaves they wanted. The intensity, if not the frequency, of warfare increased. And in the early 1860s, most Zande states began to attract zaribas from competing Khartoumers. A few years later, the states began to crumble. Zubayr occupied one western state after another, establishing agents to collect tribute and supporting their activities by building fortifications inside the chiefdoms. In the far east, chiefdoms crumbled before the Coptic traders. Only a block in the center was left, and that block was soon beset from all sides. The Egyptians first tried to annex it after 1878, but that attack was cut off by the rise of the Mahdi. The Mahdi's successor then tried, but the Zande defended themselves with guns they had begun to receive by way of the Congo River route through territory now falling to the French north of the Ubangi and to the Congo Independent State to the south. By the 1880s, the danger shifted to slave traders from the east coast, so that Zande country became the place where all three trade networks finally met. In the end, the Europeans divided Zande territory among the Sudan, Ubangi-Shari (later the Central African Empire), and the Congo Independent State. The last Zande state surrendered in 1905.

The Mangbetu reaction in the region of the Ituri forest was somewhat different. There, a state was only just beginning to be formed in the first decades of the nineteenth century. The Sudanic-speaking Mangbetu had been forest people, but a leader united a number of clans and marched north, inviting the submission of the stateless people already there. About 1830, Nabiembali, son of the original leader, became king, and it was he who welded this aggregation of diverse populations into a state. At first, he left the various original headmen and chiefs in their former offices, but he then began a general reorganization, blending some aspects of the Zande political order with the patterns more common among Bantu-speaking people. At the same time, Nabiembali continued the state's eastward expansion, assimilating still more people and simultaneously warding off three major attacks by the Zande. By the time of his death in about 1860, the subordinate chiefs were all his own sons, but they were also sons of the sisters of the formerly independent chiefs because Nabiembali had systematically taken them as wives. Following Zande practice, he also had the chiefs send their sons to his court as pages, so that they would be Mangbetuized and would meanwhile serve as hostages against possible revolt. As they grew up, they were also possible candidates for office.

But this organization did not escape the flaws of the Zande system, and it developed some weaknesses of its own. Nabiembali's sons quarreled among themselves and took on the particular interests of the chiefdoms each had inherited. The Mangbetu state first broke into two, just as the traders appeared, so that one branch allied itself to the newcomers against the other. It gradually began to break into smaller and smaller units, until the whole Mangbetu area became little more than a welter of microstates; yet the Mangbetu culture kept expanding and gaining new territory and people.

Divided as they were in the face of the traders' threat, the Zande and Mangbetu were nevertheless strong enough to prevent the kind of annihilation that overtook Dar Fertit. Their own expansion also united more than fifty different populations of the Uele-Mbomu region and created a rich new texture out of the original cultures. But the process of assimilation was somewhat different in the two cases. The Zande tended to absorb practical techniques like new crops, building styles, or legal customs. They had strong ideas about their own cultural superiority to the conquered. The Mangbetu, on the other hand, assimilated more of the art and ideology of the people they absorbed. They intermarried more easily and produced a new generation that combined both old and new cultural features. Mangbetu country was also richer than the more arid Zande territory. The Zande impressed early European visitors with their power, while the Mangbetu were noted for the richness of their art, the architecture of their royal hall, the splendor of their processions and court life. In either case, the Zande and Mangbetu homogenized the cultures of many peoples over a wide area, and, once again as in other parts of Central Africa, the scale of society expanded dramatically.

At the beginning of the nineteenth century, comparatively small states were still the single most important and dynamic institution among Central African societies. By 1890, the effective regions had increased greatly in scale, but the dynamic and unifying force was no longer political; it was economic. Long-distance trade had completely reorganized the social landscape, with virtually all of equatorial Africa falling within the scope of one of the three great trade networks.

Nor was the reorganization limited to long-distance trade. Local trade networks consolidated and changed the patterns of production so as to create a new spatial specialization and division of labor. All this brought into existence new cultural patterns, marked most forcefully by the spread of linguae francae. Above all, the reorganization of trade created new social patterns. Everywhere, the old aristocracies (both in states and in lineage systems) gave way. Everywhere, achieved status replaced ascribed status, with wealth becoming the prime criterion marking achievement. Everywhere, social stratification increased at the same time social rigidity gave way to a "frontier spirit." This was the century of new men who shied away from established authority to make good on their own. They were also more numerous than the old aristocrats, and the new class of traders became the new elite.

Without the colonial intrusion, the situation would doubtless have stabilized. Secondary empires like Rābih's, Tippu Tib's, and Msiri's would have been consolidated into stable states and would either have moved on to enlarge their territories or else would have been swallowed up by the others, just as Zubayr's had been. Elsewhere, the political vacuum created by long-distance trade would have been filled by territorial units corresponding to segments of commercially organized territory — or to multiples of such segments. Given the origin of this trade in industrial Europe, it comes as no surprise that this did not happen, that instead the territorial outcome of the nineteenth century was the creation of European empires.

SUGGESTIONS FOR FURTHER READING

Birmingham, David. "The Forest and the Savanna of Central Africa." In *Cambridge History of Africa,* edited by John E. Flint, vol. 5. Cambridge: Cambridge University Press, 1976.

Miller, Joseph C. "Cokwe Trade and Conquest in the Nineteenth Century." In *Pre-colonial African Trade,* by R. Gray and D. Birmingham. London: Oxford University Press, 1970.

————. "Kasanje." In *Social Change in Angola,* by F. W. Heimer. New York: Humanities Press, 1974.

Patterson, K. D. *The Northern Gabon Coast to 1875.* London: Oxford University Press, 1975.

Roberts, Andrew D. *A History of the Bemba: Political Growth and Change in Northeastern Zambia before 1900.* London: Longman, 1973.

————. *A History of Zambia.* London: Heinemann, 1977.

Tippu Tib. *Maisha ya Hamed bin Muhammed el Murjebi, yaani Tippu Tib.* Swahili text with translation by W. H. Whiteley. Nairobi: East African Literature Bureau, 1966.

Vansina, Jan. *Kingdoms of the Savanna.* Madison: University of Wisconsin Press, 1966.

————. *The Tio Kingdom of the Middle Congo, 1880–1892.* London: Oxford University Press, 1973.

Vellut, Jean-Luc. "Notes sur le Lunda et la frontière luso-africaine (1700–1900)." *Etudes d'histoire africaine* 3 (1972): 61–166.

Plate 13. The escarpment protecting Thaba Bosiu, the natural
fortification that provided a sanctuary and citadel for Moshweshwe,
the Sotho leader in the nineteenth century. (P. D. Curtin)

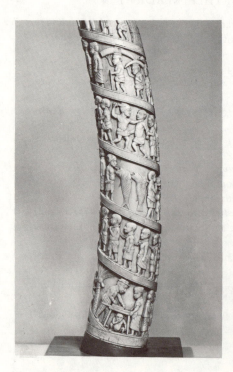

Plate 14. Vili ivory. The scenes represent a
European trader dealing with an African
trader, a caravan of slaves, fishermen bringing home their catch, the executioner
grabbing a criminal, and a caravan of ivory.
The scenes continue all around the tusk to
its very top, showing life as it was seen by
the Vili of Kabinda, Malemba, or Loango.
(Walters Art Gallery, Baltimore)

Plate 15. Prow of a Duala canoe, Cameroon. The prows of nineteenth-century Duala canoes were elaborately carved as a sign of prestige and wealth. (Collection Musée de l'Homme)

Plate 16. Munza, king of the Mangbetu, holding a stylized throwing knife, an emblem of prestige. Munza was the last king. Soon after his death the state fell apart into warring factions. (Lilly Library of Indiana University, Bloomington)

Plate 17. Repairing sails in the shadow of Fort Jesus, Mombasa, built by the Portuguese at the end of the sixteenth century. (P. D. Curtin)

Plate 18. Ethiopian painting of the battle at Adowa in 1896, in which the Italians were defeated. (Courtesy of the American Museum of Natural History)

Plate 19. The chief alkali or Islamic judge of Kano, holding court toward the end of the colonial period under the system of Indirect Rule then in effect in Nigeria. (P. D. Curtin)

Plate 20. An African brass-worker decorating a tray in Bida, Nigeria. Africa craftwork continued into the colonial period and beyond. (P. D. Curtin)

Plate 21. Statue of a missionary (probably a Spiritan Father) from Kongo, late nineteenth century. The statue is not intended as a caricature. It shows how the people of Kongo saw missionaries. (Musée Royal de l'Afrique Centrale)

Plate 22. Harrist church at Bregbo (Ivory Coast). The façade recalls both a common mission church and the carved stools characteristic of the area. Notice the statue on top of the façade, an innovation, and the Calvary on the side, a retention from Catholic practice. (Jacques Maquet)

Plate 23. Ancestor shrine or funerary monument, Ijo, Nigeria, nineteenth century. The shrine represents the head of a house in the Niger Delta and his followers. (Trustees of the British Museum)

Plate 24 (*below*). Doors for the king's palace at Ikere, Yoruba, Nigeria, carved by Olowe around 1910. The scenes represent a meeting between a British District Commissioner, Captain Ambrose, and the king of Ikere. (Trustees of the British Museum)

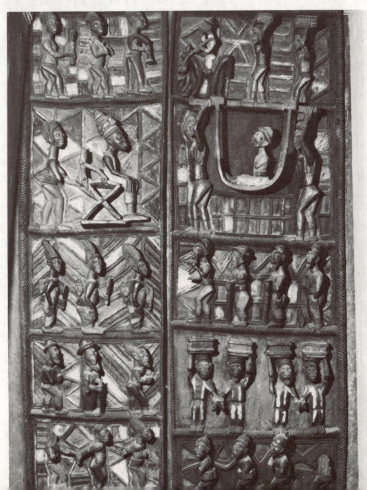

Chapter 15

The European Conquest

IN RETROSPECT, the decade of the 1880s was a major turning point in African history. Until then, the European impact on much of the continent had been made through gradual encroachment, economic penetration, or religious missions. It now assumed the shape of overt annexation, with half a dozen European powers moving rapidly from one conquest to the next, often without waiting long enough to establish a firm administration over territory first acquired. Europeans, then and later, wrote of these events as the "scramble" for Africa that brought most of the continent rapidly and brutally into the colonial period.

European conquest had already come to much of southern Africa, to Algeria in North Africa, even here and there in tropical Africa, as with the British march on Asante in 1874 or the French military push to the upper Senegal in the 1850s. But the empire-building of the precolonial century had been mainly African — Shaykh Umar in the western Sudan, the caliphate of Sokoto in northern Nigeria, the Zulu and other offshoots of the *mfecane* in southeastern Africa, the secondary empire of the Egyptian Sudan, or southward through a congeries of secondary empires on the fringes of the Zanzibari sphere in East Africa.

Some of this empire-building had involved European mercenaries; some, European weapons in African hands; some, a degree of informal control from Europe; but the prevailing European mode of dealing with the less-developed world in the first eight decades of the nineteenth century had been to avoid direct government over large and populous alien territories. The industrial revolution not only revolutionized the European mode of production; it revolutionized Europe's relations with the non-Western world, but its influence was felt first through the new currents of trade, second through the European weapons that created disequilibria of power on the local scene, and only third through the direct use of those weapons under European control.

THE EUROPEAN BACKGROUND: TECHNOLOGICAL FACTORS

The new phase that began in the 1880s owed something to the earlier impact of Europe on Africa. The rise of secondary empires and their inherent instability would be a case in point, because these were a constant and gnawing temptation to European strategists, seeming almost to call out for more direct intervention so that stable conditions for trade or investment could be assured. Other factors making for conquest, however, were implicit in the changing industrial technology.

Some of these changes profoundly altered the way in which the worldwide distribution of resources affected international relations. Just as the search for grain and meat helped spark European expansion across the temperate plains of North America, the Ukraine, or Argentina somewhat earlier in the century, the decades after 1880 were the prime period for Europe's conquest of the wet tropics. This was as true for Southeast Asia and the Amazon basin as it was for Africa, in part because tropical products like vegetable oils or rubber were then increasingly important for European industry. More important, advances in European medical technology in the second half of the century made the wet tropics less inhospitable to alien visitors. Military and industrial technology made the conquest of any non-Western region far cheaper than ever before. As a result, it became tempting to pick up territory whose potential value was doubtful or unknown.

Until the middle of the nineteenth century, people who had been brought up in Europe died in tropical Africa at appalling rates. That loss of life was part of the social cost of any European activity, whether commercial, missionary, or military. In early nineteenth-century West Africa, the annual mortality of newly arrived Europeans varied between 250 and 750 per thousand. The first breakthrough toward greater safety came with the 1840s. Even though the true cause of malaria remained unknown and the germ theory of disease still awaited discovery, European practitioners discovered that the regular administration of quinine, extracted from the bark of the chinchona tree of South America, could serve effectively as a prophylactic; this placed an antimalarial agent in the bloodstream even before the parasites entered through an infective mosquito bite. About the same time, other and harmful ways of treating fevers by means of mercury and extensive bleeding were abolished; those who came down with fever now had a better chance to recover.

As a result, although newcomers still died more frequently than their compatriots in Europe did, the mortality rate dropped to less than a fifth of what it had been — about 50–100 per thousand per annum, as compared with less than 10 per thousand for men in the same age bracket in Europe. Nor was this lesson lost on Europeans of the time. It was strikingly demonstrated to the British public by the contrast between two well-publicized expeditions. On the Niger River expedition of 1841, 28 percent of the European personnel died of disease after an average of less than two months up the river. Only thirty-four years later, in 1874, the British sent a military force of some 2,500 European soldiers on a punitive expedition to sack Kumasi, the capital of Asante. That force also stayed in Africa about two months, but its mortality from disease was only 2 percent. The British never again used European troops on that scale for the conquest of tropical Africa, but they did prove to their own satisfaction that the loss from disease could be kept to levels considered tolerable by the standards of the day.

But it has to be kept in mind that the earlier bad health conditions for Europeans applied only to tropical Africa. The disease environment in the Mediterranean was virtually the same on either side of the sea. Studies of British military mortality over the period 1818–1836 (before tropical medicine became an effective tool) show very different death rates for British troops serving in different parts of the world. Measured in deaths from disease per thousand mean strength of military units, they showed 10 per year for the Cape of Good Hope, 13 for Gibraltar or England itself, 75 to 85 for India or the West Indies, but 480 for Sierra Leone. The danger to newly arrived Europeans, in short, was significantly greater in any part of the tropics, but in the tropical world, Africa was by far the most dangerous.

In 1901–02 came a second breakthrough with the discovery that mosquitoes were the infective vector for both malaria and yellow fever. Antimosquito measures could then be used along with the prophylactic drugs, and the foundation of modern medicine during the intervening decades brought down the death rate from other causes as well. On the Gold Coast, the death rate for European officials dropped by half immediately after 1902, fluctuating between 13 and 28 per thousand per annum until World War I. After 1922, it dropped to less than 10 per thousand. During the high noon of the colonial period, in short, health conditions in Africa were far better for Europeans than they were for Africans and were only marginally worse than those prevailing in Europe.

Iron metallurgy also made revolutionary strides during the second half of the nineteenth century. Broadly speaking, iron products available in Europe or Africa before that time could be divided into three categories according to their carbon content. The earliest form of usable iron was wrought iron, with less than 0.1 percent carbon. It was relatively soft, malleable, easily shaped for a variety of uses, but also relatively expensive to make. More carbon, in the range of 0.1 to 2 percent, yielded steel that was less malleable but harder and far better at holding an edge. Still higher carbon content, in the range of 2.5 to 4 percent, yielded cast iron or pig iron. It was cheap to produce in the nineteenth century, but it was brittle, inelastic, and relatively incapable of withstanding stress. Up to the eighteenth century, the conversion of pig iron into wrought iron cost far more than the initial smelting of the pig iron. Steel remained expensive and limited to such specialized uses as edged tools and weapons.

Iron metallurgy then began to change more rapidly as new and cheaper ways of producing pig iron and converting it into wrought iron or steel came into play. But the most dramatic breakthrough came in the 1860s and 1870s. A series of new inventions included the Bessemer converter for changing pig into wrought iron more cheaply than ever before, the Siemens-Martin process to do the job at much lower fuel costs, and the "basic" process to use cheaper and more easily available phosphoric ores. As a result, the cost of crude steel dropped by 80 to 90 percent between the mid-1860s and the mid-1890s. The combined steel production of France, Belgium, Germany, and Britain rose 83-fold between 1861 and 1913, a continuous rate of gain of more than 10 percent per year. Steel took the place of iron in railways, buildings, ship construction, and a thousand other uses.

Africa felt the impact as a new supply of better and cheaper weapons became available to the Europeans and their African allies. Firearms technology had been comparatively stable during the eighteenth century. The standard infantry weapon from the late seventeenth century nearly to the middle of the nineteenth was the flintlock musket with a smooth, wrought-iron barrel. It took up to a minute to reload and was extremely inaccurate at ranges beyond fifty yards. This was the weapon that spread so widely through tropical Africa in the era of the slave trade. Finer and more accurate weapons were known in Europe from the early eighteenth century — rifles, for instance, with spiral grooves inside the barrel to spin the projectile and thus improve its accuracy — but they had only limited military usefulness, mainly because the bullet had to be tapped down the muzzle, turning with the rifling as it went. It therefore took up to four minutes to load and fire, but an early nineteenth-century rifle was more accurate at three hundred yards than the smoothbore musket at fifty.

Two inventions brought rifles into general use. One was a bullet with a hollow base, which expanded against the sides of the barrel on being fired, so as to catch the rifling. This made a rifle as easy to load as a musket, and the new rifles were first used in South Africa against the Xhosa in 1851. The second invention was the percussion cap, replacing the flintlock, and opening the way to breech loading. Breech-loading rifles were first used on a large scale in the American Civil War, then adopted by European armies in the 1870s. For Africans who depended on the common muzzle-loading musket, the change was catastrophic, because they now had to confront European-style troops with something like ten times the rate of fire at six times the range.

From then onward to the First World War, the Europeans kept developing new guns faster than African states could arm themselves with the last model but one. It was this pace of continuous innovation rather than the mere introduction of breech-loading rifles that created the enormous European advantage. The breechloaders of the seventies were replaced in the eighties by magazine rifles like the Winchester repeater. Early machine guns had meanwhile been invented in the 1860s, though they were not used extensively until the 1880s. Their first use in Africa was during the British conquest of Egypt in 1882, and from then on the Maxim gun became a standard weapon for European-style armies. Light "mountain guns" firing explosive shells and capable of transport on the backs of donkeys made their appearance even earlier, in the 1840s, though artillery was less important in tropical Africa than elsewhere because tsetse flies limited the use of animal power to move heavy guns.

The differential in military power between the Africans and Europeans would never again be so great as it was between about 1880 and 1920. Rifles or, later on, automatic rifles were few indeed under African control. Even fewer machine guns or mountain guns fell into African hands before the First World War. Up to that time, therefore, conquest in Africa was not only far cheaper than it had ever been in the past; it was also far cheaper in lives and money than equivalent operations would ever be again.

In 1896, Ethiopians armed with modern weapons defeated the Italians at Adowa, an event unique for its time but foreshadowing a shift that was to become general. The final conquests of the interwar period were no longer cheap, as the Spanish and French found from their operations against the Riffian Republic of northern Morocco in the early 1920s, or as the Italians found in their conquest of Libya in the 1920s and of Ethiopia in the 1930s. The Africans were still outgunned, but they now had machine guns and up-to-date rifles. But even this shift in the military balance was only a step toward an even greater shift. By the 1950s, African rebels could count on European or Asian friends to supply them with arms, and new guerilla tactics meant that comparatively small numbers of insurgents could tie down much larger numbers of foreign soldiers. Territory that had been comparatively cheap to conquer became infinitely expensive to hold — as the French were to discover in Algeria of the 1950s and the Portuguese in Mozambique and Angola of the sixties and early seventies.

PERMISSIVE FACTORS:
POLITICAL AND INTELLECTUAL

The technology of government administration was still another factor that made the conquest of Africa possible. We often think of technology in purely material terms, though the techniques for ruling an empire can be just as important as the techniques for arming its soldiers, and the ability to exercise close control over a subject population is comparatively recent in world history. Great empires of the past had great difficulty in maintaining continuous knowledge of and control over the actions of their agents. It was in fact rare for the central government even to be able to appoint and remove officials at will.

European countries had been strengthening their administrative powers since the fifteenth century, but even in the most centralized states, such as France or England in the eighteenth century, there remained areas of public power in private hands. Men acted for the government who had not been chosen for their diligence or loyalty and who could not easily be removed if they failed to carry out orders. Some were officials who had bought their offices; some were guild or other corporate officials with the right to govern within their own spheres; still others were rural gentry and nobility with customary jurisdiction over those who worked the land. Governing at a distance posed special problems; provinces tended to become autonomous, while overseas colonies like those in the Americas often became independent states.

European administration was most effectively reformed during the century between the 1780s and the 1880s. Reform began on the Continent with the French Revolution and its Napoleonic aftermath. In Britain, it followed the Napoleonic wars and continued through the mid-century, as successive administrative reforms captured local power from the justices of the peace, made local government and Parliament alike more responsive to the opinion of middle-class voters, and created a bureaucratic civil service capable of providing relief to the poor, police services to the towns, factory inspection, and ultimately municipal services to supply gas, water, sewage, streetcars, and even education for the mass of the population. The innovation was more welcome at first, however, than it was to be in the long run. By the twentieth century, bureaucracy could all too easily become an instrument of oppression — or, at best, a somewhat impersonal institution primarily concerned with its own aggrandizement.

In any event, nineteenth-century Europeans were better able to administer their overseas empires efficiently. The Dutch regime on Java or the British *raj* in India adapted the new government practices in Europe to different conditions. The professionalization of the European officer corps was felt immediately overseas, where army officers often served as administrators. In time, imperial administration itself became a recognized profession with its own special training, a movement that began in 1806, when the British set up the first training school for the future rulers of India. In 1887, France too began a systematic program of training for the professional administrators expected to govern Africa and Indochina.

By the 1880s and 1890s, the sum of a thousand minor changes meant that Europeans could plan and set up colonial governments that could actually govern with fair efficiency. Planners could then look overseas with confidence — sometimes overconfidence, as it turned out — that they could actually carry out a series of policies decided in advance. Imperial governments might now contemplate goals that were far beyond the capability of any government a century or so earlier.

This confidence was one facet of a much broader pattern of European attitudes in the late nineteenth century. Europeans saw around them the material products of the industrial age — railways, telegraphs, cheap cotton textiles, and a rising gross national product. It was only natural to reassess their own position in the world, to increase the value set on their own culture while simultaneously lowering their estimation of others. For centuries, Europeans had had a certain xenophobic dislike of others. Amerindians were considered mere savages. Africans were perhaps "lower" still, since they had long since entered the fringes of European society overseas through the slave trade. Asians, from Turkey to Japan, were thought of as barbarous heathen, though here dislike was sometimes mingled with respect for Asian power or admiration for Asian products such as Chinese porcelain and Indian fabrics. But even that respect tended to diminish in the nineteenth century, as the Europeans saw themselves far ahead and increasing their lead in all things technological.

The Europeans' reevaluation of themselves was reinforced in the early nineteenth century by new currents in biology. European thought in many fields was strongly influenced by the assumption that the natural order of the universe was a "great chain of being," an assumption whose intellectual roots went all the way back to Plato. It implied that all created things would fit into hierarchies of value — in biology, for example, into phyla ranging from the higher animals to the lower, a classificatory system still used today. As biologists of the late eighteenth century became concerned with the place of humankind, it seemed natural to classify *Homo sapiens* as the highest animal. It was also natural to expect the varieties of mankind to fit into a similar hierarchy from highest to lowest. Because the classifiers were European, it was equally natural to place the European variety at the top, and to grade others downward from there. Skin color is the most obvious physical difference. Since the biologists automatically placed the people with pinkish-yellow skins like their own at the top, they found it easy to place the tropical Africans with their dark brown skins near the bottom — and this arrangement had the virtue of conforming to the existing social status of "blacks" and "whites" on the American plantations. It also followed, in the eyes of these biologists, that the superiority of the "higher races" was part of the natural order of things, that it governed their intelligence, their aptitudes and capabilities, hence their "natural" role in history; and the same was true of the "lower races."

It goes without saying that these "scientific" doctrines of racial inequality have long since been found to be completely wrong. But before they were abandoned, the new biology of the nineteenth century enjoyed widespread respect as part of Europe's "scientific" triumph. Many detailed and explicit theories based on pseudoscientific racism were put forward in the 1840s and 1850s, and they gained prestige by association when Darwinian evolution became popular after the 1860s. By the 1880s, learned circles in Europe took it for granted that physical appearance was indeed a mark of the deepest significance in determining culture and the course of history. From then to the first decade of the new century, racism flourished virtually unopposed. About 1910, a few scientists began to point out that culture was learned, not inherited, but their impact on the scientific community was not widespread until after 1920. "Scientific" support for popular xenophobic racism was important even later — witness its place in the ideology of National Socialist Germany to the end of the Second World War — and it can still be found to reinforce racial prejudice, although its support from the scientific community is negligible.

The high tide of pseudoscientific racism thus came between 1880 and 1920. This was, incidentally, the period of the greatest differential in military power between Africa and Europe, and it was also the period when Europe conquered most of Africa. The fact that conquest took place at the relative peak of European power was not simply fortuitous, though the mere coincidence in time is not

enough in itself to establish the power differential as either a necessary or sufficient cause of the conquests. Pseudoscientific racism also entered this picture; it
was reinforced by the fact of European power, which could all too easily be read
as European superiority in other fields as well. Though racism did not cause the
European invasions in any obvious way, it nevertheless had a profound influence
on the way the colonial regimes were organized, simply because it was the popular
philosophy-in-office when they were set up.

THE CONQUEST: EUROPEAN ASPECTS

These permissive factors were only predisposing conditions that made it
easier to promote or organize or justify a specific act of aggression once it
appeared to be desirable. Two conditions peculiar to late nineteenth-century
Europe, however, have been alleged as more immediate causes of empire-building
in Africa. One was the nature of international competition within the European
state system. The other had to do with economic competition at that particular
stage in the growth of European capitalism.

During the mid-century decades, competition between European powers had
been relatively loose. The long years of peace following Waterloo had been
seriously interrupted only by Russian pressure on Turkey and by the rise of
unified monarchies in Italy and Germany. Then international competition became
notably tighter with the outbreak of the Franco-Prussian War in 1870. When
Germany demonstrated that it was not only united but had also advanced rapidly
on the road to industrialization, the victorious German Empire had to be
reckoned with, while the French loss of Alsace and Lorraine helped to feed
French nationalist sentiment and a French demand for countervailing gains
elsewhere. If the European balance of power can be imagined figuratively as a
kind of seesaw, before 1870 the fulcrum was relatively wide. Small realignments
to prevent one end or the other overbalancing the whole were no threat to the
general equilibrium. But after 1870 and up to the First World War, it was as
though the fulcrum had been narrowed — not, perhaps, to a knife edge, but
nevertheless narrow enough to require a response to comparatively small changes
on the other side. This meant that any change in relative advantage overseas,
such as the acquisition of a new segment of African territory, was likely to elicit
a counteraction from other powers. This tight balance could hardly initiate
African conquest, but it was a powerful factor accelerating the process once
African conquest had become an area of international competition among the
European states.

A second alleged cause of European conquest in Africa had to do with the
rise of industrial capitalism as a source of funds for investment. The European
need to invest excess capital once loomed large among the hypotheses put forth
to account for European imperialism; it has fallen by the wayside in recent years,
mainly because European capital investment in Africa was insignificant outside
Egypt and South Africa. We have already seen that European investment in

Egypt was one of the reasons why Egypt fell first into the Franco-British informal empire and then into the real, if disguised, position of a direct British protectorate. In South Africa, it was discovered in the 1870s that the diamond deposits at Kimberley in Griqualand West were immensely rich — and, in time, it turned out that they were the greatest concentration of diamonds in the world. In 1885, European prospectors discovered the goldbearing reef of the Witwatersrand, and that discovery too led on to the final uncovering of a complex of gold-bearing ores that was the largest accumulation of gold in the world.

Trade competition was a more important economic incentive to empire-building, but even here Africa had little to offer as an outlet for European manufactures, and hardly more as a source of strategic raw materials. Great Britain was the most important European state in African trade, yet British exports to Africa in the early 1880s rarely amounted to more than 5 or 6 percent of all British exports, and British imports from Africa constituted less than 5 percent of all imports. Nor were the 1880s an important decade for British African trade. The peak decade of the recent past was 1860–1870, and the total value of British African trade in the eighties was lower than that of any decade since the forties. Economic incentives operated because traders to Africa feared that European competitors might cut off their access after annexing a section of the African coast, not because the total value of African trade was enough to make it a matter of national concern. They therefore responded by asking their home governments to annex, so as to have a protected trade zone of their own. The role of trade competition was therefore like that of international competition in general — a force to accelerate, but not to initiate competitive annexation.

The combination of permissive factors with others that would accelerate the scramble, once started, was nevertheless an explosive mixture. The only thing missing was the trigger or the lighted fuse to set it off. For the years 1879–1882, a number of different triggers have been isolated by diplomatic historians. One can argue over which was first or most important, but in fact a number of triggers were pulled nearly simultaneously in different parts of the continent. If one or another of these had never existed, the others would have done the job. It is more important to understand some of the general psychological factors and the social and political process that induced some Europeans to advocate expansion into Africa — and then allowed that advocacy to prevail over alternative policies.

One part of the pattern was a certain tension between officials on the periphery of European control, who normally wanted to expand the sphere of their control, and other officials at the center of European affairs, who normally opposed expansion. In this instance, we have to do with one of those uniformities in human behavior that occur often enough to be a recognizable pattern, but not often enough to be predictable in each similar case.

The man on the spot at the fringes of a European empire was in a particular political and psychological position. He was the representative of a European power, technologically and militarily more powerful in most cases than his independent Asian or African neighbors. Especially in late nineteenth-century Africa, his available military forces were usually far superior to those of the Africans. This disparity in forces, combined with the cultural chauvinism and racism of the period, tended to make the men on the spot less willing than they might have been to compromise in conflicts with their African neighbors. This tendency was all the more serious in that men on the spot were separated from their own societies and therefore from social controls over conduct. Their local circle of vision was limited to a narrow, cross-cultural situation; and cross-cultural tensions are especially hard to resolve, because different cultures live by different rules for conflict resolution just as they do in other spheres of human relations. The result for the European man on the spot was likely to be an annoying series of frustrations, experienced along with "the flies and the heat" and all the other disturbing aspects of an alien setting. Given the power to do so, the tempting solution was simply to take over the alien society across the frontier, moving from a diplomatic to a colonial situation. Then the European rules could prevail. At the periphery, annexation was the sovereign solution to diplomatic or military conflict.

The central governments, however, had quite a different circle of vision. The realities for central officials were the realities of metropolitan politics — including the politics of personal advancement within the government service. Demands for a forward movement of the frontiers were recurrent from a multitude of men on the spot who could not be satisfied simultaneously. Central officials were under a number of special constraints: taxpayer resistance, even to cheap conquests overseas; the danger that each confrontation settled by force would lead to another in a continuous escalation; the danger of needlessly offending other European powers over inconsequential slices of distant territory.

In most circumstances before the 1880s, these tensions were settled in favor of the center, simply because the central governments appointed men on the spot, gave them orders, and removed them from office when necessary. But central officials might also be caught napping or be manipulated by political circumstances. In that case a man on the spot like McClean on the Gold Coast of the 1840s, or Harry Smith in South Africa, or Faidherbe on the Senegal in the 1850s, might be able to move forward because of central apathy or ignorance of what was going on. But neither McClean nor Smith nor Faidherbe triggered competitive annexation. The level of international tension was still too low; no other European powers felt threatened enough to act in response to first moves. As a result, for most of tropical Africa before the 1880s, though European authority increased spasmodically around the coastal posts, the general rate of expansion was slow.

From the 1880s onward, combinations of circumstances that freed men on the spot from central constraints became more common. In general, the rise of competitive tensions in Europe caused a relaxed vigilance against expansion in Africa. In Africa itself, the rise and spread of secondary empires during the middle decades of the century was a source of instability; and instability beyond the European frontiers was not only bad for trade; it also created a possible foothold for European rivals.

The instability of secondary empires came from their source of power, a quasi monopoly over European arms constituting a kind of windfall gain that was easily lost. It could be lost to neighbors who had found their own source of modern arms, or to subordinates who took the arms consigned to them and hived off on their own course of empire-building. The Zanzibari trading-post domination of East Africa was fundamentally unstable because nothing prevented the political authorities of the interior — whether Zanzibari or local — from setting up their own spheres of control, as Msiri and Tippu Tib did. After the 1880s, the interior of East Africa as far as the Zaïre River basin tended to break down into a series of smaller but tighter secondary empires. The Egyptian secondary empire in the Sudan broke down initially because the Mahdi captured its sub-Saharan center at Omdurman, but the Mahdi was not able to hold onto his own peripheral areas. One section, the Equatorial Province on the upper Nile, held on as an independent state under a European mercenary for nearly ten years. Rābih Zubayr organized another offshoot to the southwest until he ended by capturing Borno and establishing a new dynasty. The Boer republics in South Africa were also secondary empires, which had originally split off from Cape Colony; as time passed, they tended to send out their own offshoots of independent Afrikaner settlers. Some made their way overland as far as present-day Angola, where their descendants lived until the 1970s. Others formed independent republics like the evanescent Stellaland and Goshen. Even the Boer republics themselves seemed stamped with instability in the eyes of British officials in Natal or the Cape.

The frontiers of territory settled by overseas Europeans domiciled in Africa were, in any case, a special situation, in which the balance between aggressive men on the spot and central constraint was harder to maintain, and peripheral aggression became common even before the 1880s. The combination of settlers, military officers, and local government officials tended to prevail in Algeria and South Africa. Expansion in Algeria had gone on steadily after the capture of Algiers in 1830, whether intended by the government in Paris or not. By the time of the great Algerian rebellion of 1871–72, it had given France control of the *tell* and the high plateaus. Similar expansion had been continuous in South Africa, both by the British colonies and the Boer republics, ever since the end run of the Great Trek had turned the flank of the Bantu-speakers' frontier.

In southern Africa, however, the situation was accompanied by tensions among different groups of Europeans. Some were recent settlers who regarded themselves as metropolitan Europeans and who felt a primary allegiance to Great Britain, but the majority, even within the British sphere, belonged to the Afrikaner "European" community. Beyond the British frontiers, similar people felt a primary loyalty to the relatively new Boer republics. In time, Britons, republican Afrikaners, and colonial Afrikaners were to compete for the diamond-bearing regions around Kimberley, for Zimbabwe (Rhodesia), and for almost all the remaining fringe areas to the east and west of the Boer republics. The only non-British intervention south of Angola and Mozambique was the German push into Namibia (which became German South West Africa).

One episode in these rivalries served as a potential trigger for the scramble throughout tropical Africa. It began with a British effort to bring order to the turbulent transfrontier region surrounding the Boer republics. Under settler control, the republics were aggressive against their African neighbors, and from time to time threatened to provoke a general frontier war. A prelude to the crisis came in 1871, when Britain annexed the diamond fields around Kimberley, a territory also claimed by the Orange Free State and the South African Republic (Transvaal). Then, in 1877, Britain annexed the South African Republic itself, with the apparent acquiescence of most of the Transvaal settlers. In 1879, local British officials followed this up with a move against the Zulu state — a typical petty aggression based on the initiative of the local man on the spot, which had not been cleared with London. In the first instance, the Zulu defeated part of the British force, but Britain sent reinforcements, won in the field, and established a quasi protectorate over Zululand. This action removed the Zulu threat to the Transvaal as well, making it safe for the Transvaal Boers to break once more with Britain and to redeclare their independence. They defeated a British force in 1881. This time, Britain recognized the facts as they were and let the Boer republics remain independent until the Anglo-Boer War at the end of the century.

In this case, however, the failure to escalate and to gain a military victory led Britain to treat the Transvaal as a potential rival, and the Transvaal became increasingly formidable after the discovery of gold there in 1885. Up to that point, the British had tried to avoid extensive annexation in southern Africa; now, to shore up their international legal position, they annexed or declared protectorates over whatever African territory remained to the immediate west of Transvaal, claiming all of the unannexed coastline between the Portuguese post at Delagoa Bay and the Cape of Good Hope. The men on the spot, in short, had provoked a crisis over Zululand alone, but the associated problems of dealing with a secondary empire, plus the new significance of the goldfields, led to the paper annexation of virtually all the remaining independent African states south of the Limpopo River. These annexations in turn alarmed other Europeans and helped push them into the scramble for territory elsewhere on the continent.

In other parts of Africa and nearly simultaneously, other kinds of special situations freed men on the spot from the earlier constraints. French military officers in West Africa, for example, had the usual attitudes of men on the spot, but they gained a special freedom from central control following France's defeat by Prussia. A segment of the French public, especially sensitive to the loss of national honor, welcomed military victories almost anywhere. When, in 1879, the French government projected a railway eastward from the upper Senegal, the French military in Senegal were able to turn the operation into a war of conquest against the Umarian Empire, contrary to the intentions of the Paris government. At times, their political allies in France could apply pressure to the central government; at other times, they simply disobeyed or misrepresented the orders they received, secure in the knowledge that victory would bring advancement in rank and protection from civilian superiors in the court of French opinion.

Once started, this process was to continue for more than twenty years as the French moved from the Umarian Empire to a prolonged series of wars with the equally large secondary empire created by Samori Ture from upper Guinea-Conakry eastward to the northern Gold Coast. In time, the west-to-east progress from Senegal was joined by incursions from coastal posts like the Ivory Coast and Dahomey.

Both the French initiative and the west-east direction of conquest are symbolically portrayed on the present-day map of West Africa. The British colonies in the far west —Gambia and Sierra Leone — were prevented by British central authority from making a quick response. They therefore lost most of the hinterland trade area they had once served. Because there was more time for the French push to alarm British authorities at the center, Liberia and British coastal posts further east had more time to protect themselves. As a result, each non-French enclave in West Africa kept a larger hinterland in proportion to its distance from the west; thus, Sierra Leone's was larger than Gambia's, Liberia's larger than Sierra Leone's, the Gold Coast's larger still, and Nigeria's largest of all.

The missionary factor also occasionally served as an inducement to European conquest. Missionaries experienced much the same cross-cultural frustrations that civil and military personnel did, but they were not government officials. They might prefer working under a colonial government to working under African authorities, but they were rarely able to trigger annexation by themselves. In some circumstances, however, their pressure on the home government could swing the balance. A case in point involved the kingdom of Buganda in the early 1890s. British military men there urged the annexation of Buganda, to the north of Lake Victoria, for the usual reasons of forestalling other powers and to protect the sources of the Nile, but the home government was still reluctant. The cost of administering a country five hundred miles from the coast would have been prohibitive without a railroad, and the existing traffic did not justify the building of a railroad on economic grounds alone. The British missionary movement saw to it, however, that the choice presented to the public in 1893 and 1894 was either annexation regardless of cost, or else a withdrawal that would risk the martyrdom of an Anglican bishop and hundreds of African converts. Thus, in spite of its reluctance, the government allowed the annexation of Buganda and surrounding territory that was incorporated in the Uganda Protectorate.

Still another factor that helped weaken central constraints was the felt need to protect existing strategic interests. The British government about 1880, for example, was not interested in acquiring new territory in Africa, but it was very much interested in protecting the empire it already ruled in India. One route to India passed the Cape of Good Hope, while another went through the Suez

Canal and the Red Sea. A weak Egypt controlling Suez, or a weak Turkey controlling the Arabian side of the Red Sea was no threat to the imperial lifeline, as it was called, but a strong European power capable of cutting the route through the Mediterranean and the Red Sea would have been seen as a definite threat to vital British interests. Where vital interests of this kind were concerned, it was no longer a matter of restraining men on the spot. In this situation, diplomatic and even military initiatives might come from the central government itself.

This is why Britain acted so forcefully from 1878 to 1882, first in defending Turkey against Russia and then in pressing its own intervention on Egypt. Egypt's debt was a factor as well, but it was mostly owed to continental European banks. In effect, Britain acted for these banks as a way of preventing their own governments, especially France, from acting more directly on their behalf. But the end result was to leave British officials running an Egyptian government — and hence caught up in a whole new set of circumstances where new men on the ground in northeast Africa had to confront a new set of temptations that would lure them on into the Sudan.

Meanwhile, still another train of events, beginning in the mid-1870s in the Congo basin, led through another route to the scramble for that part of Africa. For more than a decade, King Leopold of the Belgians had been fascinated by the possibility of glory and profit to be derived from the creation of a Belgian overseas empire. From the mid-1870s, his attention centered more and more on the Congo basin; but he was only a constitutional monarch, and the Belgian government and parliament refused to accept his views. Leopold got around this impasse by forming a series of private corporations that were ostensibly geared to scientific and humanitarian aims and that enjoyed international support. These companies masked Leopold's personal control and financial interest in the creation of a private empire — of what was, in effect, a secondary empire run from Europe, though not by a European government. It was an important practical difference, because his men on the spot were not restricted or controlled by a strong central government.

In 1879, even before the full nature of Leopold's project became apparent, and before he had claimed international recognition for the Congo Independent State he was trying to create, pressures of competitive annexation elsewhere in Africa reached Central Africa. A traveler on leave from the French navy appeared on the coast near the Congo with a series of treaties with African authorities; these claimed to give France sovereignty over the region westward from Stanley Pool (Pool Malebo) to the Atlantic. In most circumstances, the French government would not have recognized unofficial treaties of this kind, but this time the French Assembly was piqued by recent British acquisitions, including Britain's unilateral seizure of Egypt. It therefore accepted the treaties as official. They served as the legal pretext for annexing the territory that became the colony of Middle Congo, later the Congolese Republic or Congo-Brazzaville.

By the end of 1882, the new annexations in South Africa, Egypt, the western Sudan, and Central Africa had attained the critical mass needed to alarm

European governments in general. At this point, competitive annexation began in earnest. From 1883 to 1885, Portugal tried to make good its claims to the coast in its old trading zone on either side of the Congo mouth, and it began shoring up its claims to the hinterland of its other coastal holdings. Germany seized coastal enclaves that were later to form the basis of its claims to Togoland, Cameroon, Tanganyika, and South West Africa (now Namibia). Britain hastened to formalize its existing informal relations with African rulers all along the coast, especially near the mouth of the Niger. France took advantage of these British preoccupations to begin an attack on Imerina, the most important state in Madagascar.

By 1884, the rapid pace of competitive annexation threatened to bring about an armed clash between European rivals, and that threat led to a Berlin West African Conference in 1884–85. This dealt mainly with the Congo and Niger basins, but separate, often informal, agreements also served to lay down the ground rules for the rest of the European conquest. An intricate diplomatic charade emerged, in which European powers marked off the African map and agreed among themselves which should be allowed to claim and then to conquer various parts of Africa. This paper division of Africa was virtually completed by about 1900, with lines on the map that looked very much as they were to look in 1914 — or in 1945, allowing for the fact that German Africa was redistributed to the victorious allies in 1919. Paper annexation, however, was only the framework for colonial Africa. The reality drew far more heavily on the actual process of conquest taking place in Africa itself.

THE CONQUEST: AFRICAN ASPECTS

Actual conquest followed the treaty making with a delay of up to twenty years. Most of Africa was under some form of European administration by 1920, though a few territories on the fringes of the Sahara had still to be conquered in the twenties and thirties. These military operations were different from European wars, in which the destruction of an enemy army and the temporary occupation of its territory were the main objectives. Here, the objective was to put Europeans into permanent command over African societies. The possible ways of doing this were as variable as the African political structures themselves. What was appropriate for a microstate or a stateless society would not work in a great empire like the Caliphate of Sokoto. What might work in Rwanda, where the population was as dense as that of western Europe, would not work with Saharan nomads.

The Europeans almost always had the physical ability to win each campaign, but military victory alone was no guarantee that they could then govern indefinitely without imposing a continuing drain on the taxpayers at home. African leaders therefore had a far better bargaining position than their military weakness implied. They could not prevent military defeat, but they could help determine the forms and conditions of colonial rule that followed.

One part of their bargaining advantage was the existence of allies in Europe. The same segment of European opinion that initially opposed expansion overseas tended to keep a watching brief on empire in Africa, and it had significant weight, even at the height of the scramble. France, in many ways the most aggressive of the European powers, normally had a large parliamentary bloc opposed to empire, and that bloc brought down several governments even after the fiasco of the Egyptian expedition of 1881–82. In Britain, Liberals were normally antiexpansionist, and official policy only reluctantly supported expansion during most of the years between 1880 and 1914. In Belgium, parliamentary opposition to empire-building overseas had forced Leopold to go it alone in the first place. German expansionism in Africa grew out of a special configuration of domestic politics in the mid-1880s, and the colonial reform movement became a political force after about 1900.

The antiimperialist sentiment in Europe helped African leaders because the colonial administrators and military officers knew they faced opposition at home. An African rebellion would provoke that opposition, and expensive military operations were unpopular with an even wider public. Though European officials had overwhelming force, concessions to avoid rebellion were worthwhile. It was better to accept African surrender on conditional terms than to face the criticism that was bound to follow expensive military operations. This is not to say that all African leaders enjoyed an equal bargaining position. In many cases, they could do nothing to stave off defeat and annexation on the victors' terms. In others, chance or accidental factors gave some African rulers more power under colonial rule than they had ever enjoyed before.

In their confrontation with Europe, Africans had two separate kinds of choice to make in deciding how to meet the Western challenge. To begin with, they had to react in some way to the fact of Western power — either the threat of conquest or the actual governing power of a colonial regime. They could collaborate and try to seek the favor of the new masters, resist to the end, surrender when defeat was imminent, or attempt to bargain for advantage. The choice was very broad, with many subtle variations. They also had a similar but independent set of choices to make in response to Western culture, including under that head the whole range from firearms and literacy to religion, language, and dress. The choice was not usually a simple "for" or "against," as in the South African dichotomy between "school people" and "red." An African could choose Western weapons and reject Christianity, or the other way round. Nor was his response to Western power necessarily related to his response to Western culture. He could accept Christianity, yet fight to the end against Western rule; just as he could accept Western rule as inevitable and collaborate with the colonial government, yet remain all the more faithful to Islam.

Defensive Westernization had begun in some parts of West Africa even before the period of colonial conquest. The Fante Confederacy, the Republic of Accra, and the Egba United Board of Management in Abeokuta were all attempts to graft Western methods in politics and government onto the older political forms. All three failed in the short run, largely through British opposition, but the effort continued in Abeokuta. About 1904, for example, the Egba United Government was planning to introduce a written criminal code on the Western model and to carry out other administrative reforms. These efforts were never fully implemented, but the Egba United Government ruled Abeokuta as an independent state down to 1914. Though informally a British protectorate, it was nevertheless the last major state in West Africa to lose its independence. With better luck or a more fortunate geographical position than the one it had astride the railway line to northern Nigeria, it might even have survived without formal colonization, much as Liberia did.

In Buganda by 1900, the Christian chiefs had made themselves into a new oligarchy which had won power for itself against the *kabaka* and other chiefs. The oligarchs were very quick to see the advantages of literacy and of European weapons. They also saw the weakness of their military position and did nothing to oppose the British annexation of the country. Many of them, indeed, helped serve the British as subordinate officials administering other sections of the Uganda Protectorate. Nevertheless, they retained a latent power to make British overrule either cheap and comparatively easy or extremely difficult.

Their great success was to translate their bargaining position into a written agreement, the Uganda Agreement of 1900, by which the British government spelled out the concessions it would make in return for Ganda acquiescence in British overrule. The political effect was to keep the title and office of kabaka intact but to assign real power to the *Lukiiko,* a representative body with some of the characteristics of a parliament and others of an oligarchic council. The agreement also assigned ownership of the best land in fee simple to the individual members of the new Christian oligarchy. As a basis for dividing power between the British and a local aristocracy, the agreement worked with remarkably little friction for half a century. The interests it protected, however, were mainly those of a single social class. By the time of independence, a new generation of nationalist leaders had come to see the kabaka and his government as part of the apparatus they hoped to replace by a new and independent government for the whole of Uganda.

Most African kingdoms were merged into new colonial units, as Buganda was made part of the Uganda Protectorate, but a few managed to come through the colonial period with their territorial integrity virtually intact — Tunisia, Egypt, and Morocco in North Africa; Zanzibar, Rwanda, and Burundi in East Africa; Lesotho and Swaziland in the south. In each of these cases, not only the kingdom but the kingship survived under some form of European protectorate, though the amount of actual power in the hands of the king varied greatly. Some were mere figureheads, while others enjoyed more real power in domestic affairs than a constitutional monarch in Europe did.

These precolonial polities survived into the colonial period for different reasons. Zanzibar and the Muslim states of North Africa had a special position in European eyes. Most of them had been recognized for centuries as political entities in European international law. Most of the states in tropical Africa were not so recognized, as might be expected at the nineteenth-century peak of cultural chauvinism. Zanzibar and most of the North African states had also fallen deeply into the web of European credit, financial manipulation, and informal control well before the 1880s. When that control was formalized, it eased intra-European diplomatic tensions somewhat to preserve at least the fiction of a "protectorate" status rather than to demand outright annexation.

A protectorate in European international law could be many things, but the protecting power usually took over some, but not all, of the attributes of sovereignty — say, control of financial and foreign affairs — leaving the rest to the protected government. In fact, the protectorates that France established over Tunisia in 1881 and Morocco in 1910 were more substantial than that. The French set up a regular European bureaucracy in place of the sultan or bey's own administration, but they left the sultan and bey as figureheads. The British protectorate over Egypt from 1882 onward was even more fictitious, in that Turkey was still recognized as the distant suzerain. British control was as real and thorough as was French control over Tunisia, but it remained informal until Turkey entered the First World War in 1914. Zanzibar was in the British informal empire even before 1880, so that the protectorate of 1890 merely tidied up the situation by formalizing the reality.

Rwanda and Burundi kept their identity for very different reasons. They were in the heart of Africa, nearly the last region to be occupied by the Germans during the decade before 1914. By then, the Germans had had some experience with the problems of colonial rule. They found a dense population ruled with apparent stability by a king and aristocracy. Class relations between the Tutsi overlords and the Hutu peasantry were congenial to the social attitudes the administrators had brought with them from Europe. Hence the decision in favor of the least expensive alternative, that is, to let the Tutsi keep the forms and much of the reality of power, though the Germans meant to shift slowly toward European norms over the coming decades.

Lesotho and Swaziland were again different. They kept their identity through skill and luck in manipulating the rivalry between Britain and the Boer republics. Lesotho's experience came first in time and served as a precedent for the other. Moshweshwe, the aging king, was under strong pressure from the Orange Free State in the 1860s. He repeatedly asked for and eventually received annexation by Great Britain as the lesser of the two evils. Britain in turn passed on Basutoland (as it was then called) to the self-governing Cape Colony for administration. In 1880, however, Cape politicians bungled the job by trying to disarm the Sotho. The attempt provoked a widespread Sotho rebellion that was nearly simultaneous with the Anglo-Zulu and Anglo-Transvaal wars. The rebellion was both annoying and expensive, and it gave force to the Sotho request for direct control from London rather than from Cape Town. London agreed, appointing a Resident to advise the Sotho king, and future residents tended to rule through diplomacy and the manipulating of Sotho politics, not by the overt use of force.

The Sotho example was important again after the Anglo-Boer War, when the British wanted to diminish the authority the Transvaal had gained over the Swazi kingdom on the eve of the war, but without offending the Transvaal Europeans any more than was necessary. Their solution was to separate it from the Transvaal and to allow the Swazi king a considerable degree of autonomy under British overrule. Here, as in Lesotho and also in the Bechuanaland Protectorate (Botswana), that solution left the African rulers with far more authority than African rulers managed to keep elsewhere in southern Africa.

Some African rulers also managed to hold on to their power by timely surrender and collaboration, even when European rivalries were not in the picture. Many of the Fulbe emirs of northern Nigeria retained a great deal of power by cooperating at the right time with the earliest British officials. By late precolonial times, they were governors over the provinces of the Caliphate of Sokoto, which had settled down by the late nineteenth century as an incorporative empire, no longer actively expansive, with ultimate control in the hands of the caliph but with most day-to-day command in the hands of the emirs of a dozen or so provinces. The first European incursions from 1887 onward came from officials of the Royal Niger Company, who gradually established authority in the name of Great Britain over any African territory within convenient reach of the navigable waters of the Benue and the lower Niger. In the late 1890s, the company began to impinge on Sokoto's outlying emirates: Ilorin, south of the Niger in Yoruba country, and Nupe, just to the north of the river. In 1897, the company's small force of about five hundred African soldiers made separate attacks on both Ilorin and Nupe. The company then made itself suzerain of Ilorin and replaced the emir of Nupe with one more favorable to its interests, all without raising a unified resistance from the caliphate as a whole, largely because the caliph was equally fearful of the French advance from the west, German feelers sent north from Togoland, and the presence of Rābih's force from the Nilotic Sudan in Borno to the east. As a result, each emirate had to meet the European-commanded forces on its own.

This combination of strong provincial government with the lack of a common military effort from the caliphate as a whole was almost ideal for conquest by very small forces under European leadership. Each emirate could be forced to surrender after one or two sharp engagements. In the years 1902 to 1906, a British force barely exceeding a thousand men advanced in a series of brief campaigns to conquer the emirates one by one. Some emirs surrendered and were confirmed in office. Others resisted briefly and were deposed. Some tried to flee toward the eastern Sudan and to find refuge from infidel rule, but many of the most important refugees were caught and killed at the battle of Burmi in 1903.

Whenever an emir fled or was deposed, however, the British usually had

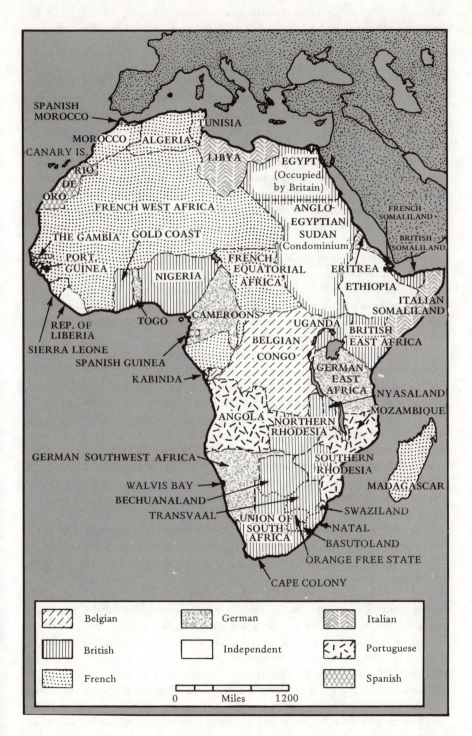

SPANISH
MOROCCO
MOROCCO ALGERIA TUNISIA
CANARY IS.
RIO
DE
ORO
FRENCH WEST AFRICA
THE GAMBIA GOLD COAST
PORT.
GUINEA
NIGERIA
REP. OF
LIBERIA
SIERRA LEONE
SPANISH GUINEA
KABINDA
ANGOLA
GERMAN SOUTHWEST AFRICA
WALVIS BAY
BECHUANALAND
TRANSVAAL
CAPE COLONY

LIBYA
EGYPT
(Occupied
by Britain)
ANGLO-
EGYPTIAN
SUDAN
(Condominium)
FRENCH
EQUATORIAL
AFRICA
ERITREA
ETHIOPIA
ITALIAN
SOMALILAND
TOGO
CAMEROONS
UGANDA
BELGIAN
CONGO
FRENCH
SOMALILAND
BRITISH
SOMALILAND

BRITISH
EAST AFRICA
GERMAN
EAST
AFRICA
NYASALAND
MOZAMBIQUE
NORTHERN
RHODESIA
SOUTHERN
RHODESIA
MADAGASCAR
SWAZILAND
UNION OF
SOUTH
AFRICA
NATAL
BASUTOLAND
ORANGE FREE STATE

	Belgian		German		Italian
	British		Independent		Portuguese
	French		Spanish	

0   Miles   1200

Africa Partitioned, 1914

a choice of legitimate candidates from other branches of the ruling family. As a result, the governor slipped into the position formerly held by the caliph. He confirmed and removed emirs. He appointed a Resident for each of the major emirates, and the Resident's advice was binding. In theory, British control was complete, but the situation was nevertheless precarious. The total military force was tiny for the size of the country. The number of civilian administrators was smaller still. The result was not simply indirect rule through African authorities. It included a conscious policy of leaving considerable latitude to the local ruler, as well as a conscious decision not to press for rapid Westernization. The British not only refrained from all interference with Islam where it was dominant; they even discouraged Christian missions and Western-style education out of deference to local wishes. In this case, conservative African opinion prevailed with the colonial rulers, so that change toward Western norms was far less than it was elsewhere in colonial Nigeria. The social and political order of the pre-colonial period was also preserved to a much greater extent than it was in most parts of colonial Africa. In spite of territorial incorporation in Nigeria, the old ruling class remained in power as effectively as it did in Rwanda or Burundi — and far more effectively than equivalent groups did in North African protector-ates like Morocco or Tunisia.

The Ethiopian experience was a nearly opposite reaction to European power. In contrast to the northern emirs' success in following a policy of sur-render and survival, Ethiopia found it possible to fight and survive. In escaping colonial rule altogether (apart from the brief Italian occupation of 1935–1941), Ethiopia was nearly unique on the African continent. (Liberia was the only other exception, and Liberia's rulers were Afro-Americans, who were Western, not African, in their way of life.) Yet the northern Nigerian emirs and the Ethiopian aristocracy reacted similarly to Western culture. Both sought Westernization for defensive purposes only, and both defended their power and culture with remarkable success until they were overthrown by military coups in the 1960s and 1970s.

In other respects as well, Ethiopia in the twentieth century was not so much an exception to the normal pattern of African history as it was a country where historical trends found elsewhere combined in a particular way. The fact that the Ethiopian monarchy was the only long-standing Christian state in Africa was, of course, a unique element, and one that tended to give Ethiopia a superficially favorable image in Europe. But Ethiopia's success in keeping out the Europeans depended far more on the fact that the small Christian kingdom became the nucleus of a secondary empire. It achieved a stability unusual for secondary empires by drawing on older sources of loyalty, and the emperor's supply of modern rifles and artillery came from a combination of skill, luck, and the configuration of European strategic interests centering on the upper Nile and the mouth of the Red Sea.

The empire Menelik built had a Christian core area whose people spoke Semitic languages like Tigriña or Amharic; but it did not include all such

populations, and the majority came to be non-Christian and non-Semitic. Menelik's capital at Addis Ababa had originally been near the southern frontiers of
Christian Ethiopia. Now it became the center of a much larger secondary empire.
Menelik's conquests included a fringe of Nilotic peoples to the west, the Sidamo
states to the south, the Muslims of the eastern highlands centering on the city-
state of Harar, the vast Somali-speaking semidesert of Ogaden stretching still
further east, and finally the nomadic peoples of the Danakil lowlands, who
were not actually brought under effective administration until the very eve of
the Italian invasion in 1935.

The fact that Menelik and his successors were able to create an empire that
was larger than most European colonies was important for Ethiopia's future.
The scale of political organization in most of precolonial Africa was far smaller
than that, and far smaller than optimum size for political or economic development in the technological conditions of postcolonial Africa. Even at the time
of the conquest, large states like Ethiopia had options that were simply not
open to small states — and still less to the thousands of village-sized microstates
or to the peoples of stateless societies. Most obviously, small states had no real
chance of resisting successfully.

Stateless societies, on the other hand, created special problems for the invaders as well. Because there was no one to make a formal surrender, there was
also no one to survive in office; but in this situation, the Europeans also lost their
chance for the kind of cheap conquest and cheap administration the British
imposed on the Sokoto caliphate. The Ibo, or the Tiv of the Benue valley were
far more expensive to conquer, and such conquests took much longer. The
Europeans could try to accept the "surrender" of important people, but in fact
no one had the power to make more than a personal decision to cooperate with
the new rulers. Effective colonial rule could begin only when a large majority
had made a similar decision. The conquest of Tiv or Ibo country began with
military expeditions marching through in demonstration of British power. Administrative posts were then set up at selected sites, and officials gradually began
to collect taxes and enforce a new kind of law. Missionaries with schools and
some rudimentary health services also helped to show the advantages of peaceful
compliance. In this setting, separate reactions to European power and European
culture had to be made by individual men and women, a process that is better
illustrated for Ibo country by Chinua Achebe's novel, *Things Fall Apart,* than
by any formal works of history.

African as well as European empires had tried in the past to rule over
stateless societies. The Moroccan *makhzen* had problems with the stateless Berber
polities of the Atlas and the desert, and these problems the French inherited
in turn. Adopting the strategies of the makhzen, the French sometimes made
alliances with the great *caïds* of the Atlas, whose power had already spread across
the previous web of kin relations. Or they tried working, as successive Moroccan
governments had done for centuries, with the leaders of the great Muslim *turuq,*
or brotherhoods. Like their predecessors, the great "marabouts" of the twentieth

century were sometimes willing to help preserve order in the countryside in return for government favor. Like the British in northern Nigeria, the French in Morocco found themselves slipping consciously or not, into the former role of the sultan.

Insufficient scale in political organization was also a recurrent problem for leaders of the African resistance to conquest. One response was to create new states as a direct response to the European threat. It was especially common in Muslim North Africa, with precedents going back to the example of 'Abd al-Qādir in western Algeria in the 1840s. Many of these new states were based on the existing institution of the Muslim *tarīqa* in the same way that 'Abd al-Qādir had used the Qādirīya in Algeria. The role of a brotherhood could be especially important among nomads because kinship-based political organization was often ineffective in the face of a foreign threat. The Sanūsīya was one of the most durable and effective brotherhoods in this respect. Its membership stretched from the Nile valley to Lake Chad to the Mediterranean, but its range of effective political authority was much smaller. It nevertheless fought an attempted Turkish reconquest of Libya up to 1911, and after the Italians replaced the Turks in control of the ports, it fought them too. Nevertheless, Italy established effective control by 1932; but the Sanūsīya remained in opposition and took the field again on the Allied side during World War II. At the end of the war, the United Nations recognized the head of the order as king of all Libya, and his successors remained in control of the country until the last was removed by a military coup in 1969.

About 1900, Muhammad Abdille Hassan created a similar state among the Somali herdsmen on the borderland where Italian and British Somaliland joined Ethiopia. Again, the organizational base was a tarīqa and Muhammad succeeded in defying the Europeans until 1920. His movement was like the Sanūsīya in that he favored Westernization for defense only, but otherwise held to the most conservative forms of Islam.

Similar movements could, however, follow the current of Islamic modernism. One of the most important of these staged a rebellion in the Rif mountains between the Spanish and French zones of Morocco. It began about 1920 under the leadership of Muhammad 'Abd al-Krīm, and this time the nuclear tarīqa was not one of the ancient *sufi* orders, but the Salafīya, an order recently founded to combat sufism and to reform Islam. 'Abd al-Krīm called his state the Republic of the Rif, and he tried to obtain international recognition from the European powers. He failed in the long run, but resistance to the Spanish occupation continued from 1921 to 1927.

Although they were only successful as holding operations, these twentieth-century resistance movements exemplify the changed military balance. Italy's campaigns against the Sanūsīya were extremely expensive, given the small number of opponents. It took a Franco-Spanish force of some 250,000 European troops finally to subdue 'Abd al-Krīm, who had managed to acquire about two hundred machine guns — compared with none at all in African hands during the conquest of tropical Africa three or four decades earlier. Muhammed Abdille Hassan was less significant as a resistance figure, but, for all their disdain, the British gave back-handed credit to his stand when they sent aircraft from the *Ark Royal* to bomb and destroy his last headquarters. The final act was most expensive of all, with nearly half a million Italian troops involved in the conquest of Ethiopia in 1935–36.

State-building resistance movements were also common, if less spectacular, in sub-Saharan Africa. Moshweshwe's foundation of Lesotho in the mid-nineteenth century is a case in point, as is Almaami Samori Ture's success in conquering a new empire to the east even as he lost his original base to French conquest. Elsewhere during those decades, however, the pace of conquest was often too rapid to allow time for political reorganization. One result was a pattern of initial and ineffectual resistance by existing, small political units, followed, up to a decade later, by a second and more effective resistance movement having a wider territorial base. The nature of and connection between the two movements is sometimes obscured by the tendency of European historians to label the second and broader war of resistance mere "rebellion," since by then the Europeans had acquired sovereignty over Africa in European international law.

The conquest of Rhodesia is a classic case in point. It began in 1890, when the British South African Company sent a military force into Shona territory, which it occupied without serious fighting. The Shona had no strong central kingdom in any event, and little previous warning of the European threat. Serious military resistance was offered only in 1893–94 by the Ndebele kingdom (an offshoot of the wars of the *mfecane*), which still used the impi formation. The British South African Company's troops defeated those units without difficulty, and the Ndebele kingdom disappeared. In the years that followed, Shona and Ndebele alike were dissatisfied with British occupation, with the loss of their land and cattle, with forced labor, and with other abuses that followed European domination. The old political structures were gone, but the religious authority of a spirit called Mlimo stepped in, speaking through a human medium to urge a mass uprising by both peoples. The revolt came in 1896–97, first among the Ndebele, then among the Shona — who this time used guerrilla tactics rather than engage in open, set-piece battles. It was no mere war between soldiers; the initial rising managed to kill about 10 percent of all the Europeans in the Ndebele kingdom, and the repression was even more bloody in its destruction of African lives.

Another source of resistance could be found in the web of economic interests and informal alliances that were incorporated in the major trade networks. This appeared in a spectacular, if ineffective, manner in the initial resistance of the Tanzanian coastal peoples to the German advance. In 1888, Sultan Khalifa of Zanzibar leased the coast to the German East African Company for fifty years. When the Germans first began to set up coastal trading stations, however, they met with armed resistance drawn from a wide area and organized by

Bushiri bin Salim, a coastal "Arab." The German forces turned out to be unbeatable, and the whole affair ended with Bushiri's defeat and death at the end of 1889. But at least 100,000 men had come to the coast to fight and these represented a wide array of different ethnic groups — Shambaa, Zaramo, Zigula, Yao, Ngoni, Ngulu, Kwere, Hehe, Kami, Sagara, Makonde, Mbugu, Arab, and Swahili. It is worth noting in this case that the economic interests opposed to this grouping — among others, the Nyamwezi and some of the wealthiest of the Arab plantation owners — allied themselves with the Germans.

The so-called Maji-Maji revolt in German East Africa a few years later was similar in scale, though its organizational base was closer to that of the Ndebele and Shona than it was to that of the coastal Arabs. Once Bushiri's revolt had ended, the interior conquest of southeastern Tanzania was carried out over a politically fragmented region that was easily penetrated by moving military columns sent in to overawe the rulers. The Germans were not always successful in avoiding war but many rulers surrendered, and those who chose to fight did so alone and went down to rapid defeat. By 1905, the country was considered sufficiently "pacified" to be held only lightly from a series of semifortified military posts. Then revolt broke out nearly simultaneously throughout all of southeastern German East Africa, a region that was politically and ethnically very diverse. Its suppression turned out to be far more expensive to Germany than the initial conquest had been, and the last of the fighting continued into the latter part of 1907. Here, as in Rhodesia, the wider scale of the revolt derived from its religious base. The name Maji-Maji came from the Swahili word for water, and the revolt spread as far and as rapidly as it did through water magic associated with the cult of Kolelo.

The Maji-Maji and the Rhodesian rebellions had other points in common. Both were mass movements, not the actions of a few armed dissidents. Both were brutally suppressed, and with similar consequences. On the face of it, suppression left the Africans no residual powers, no bargaining position of the kind some had managed to secure in other circumstances. In that sense, the revolts appear completely futile, but in fact they left a mark on the administrations that followed. Both the Germans and the British South African Company were impressed by the seriousness of the revolts and the costs of suppression; both also recognized that their own administrative abuses had in part been at fault. Both tried to reform their methods, and future administrators were sensitized to the fact that their power over African societies was limited. In the much longer run, these early revolts also served as examples of broad-based resistance — examples that were to be followed effectively by the leaders of independence movements some fifty years later.

THE ANGLO-BOER WAR AND ITS AFTERMATH

Of all the wars of conquest the Europeans waged in Africa between 1880 and the First World War, the most anomalous of all was the British conquest of the two Boer republics between 1899 and 1902. It was the only war of that period that employed considerable numbers of troops from Europe or that seriously strained the resources of a European power. Its underlying cause was the South African Republic's difficulty in managing the development of the new gold-mining industry when there were no local resources in trained personnel or in political power to manage the flood of British capital investment. The republican Afrikaners were essentially pastoral farmers with no industrial experience. The mines were therefore developed and operated by foreign (largely British) capital, technicians, and skilled workmen, with Africans providing the manual laborers. By 1899, there were probably more foreigners than Afrikaners in the European male population of the South African Republic (SAR). Trying to cope with this burgeoning mining industry and its utterly alien urban population, President Paul Kruger and the members of the *volksraad* (legislature) refused to give full voting rights to the *uitlanders* (foreigners), fearing that they would subvert the state. The problem was intensified by the determination of several key British and colonial officeholders to bring the SAR back into the British Empire. These were Cecil John Rhodes, a British-born Oxford graduate and one of the most successful mining magnates both in Kimberley and on the Witwatersrand, who became prime minister of the Cape Colony in 1890; Joseph Chamberlain, a Birmingham businessman who was Colonial Secretary in the British cabinet during the crucial years 1895–1902; and Alfred Milner, Chamberlain's choice as British High Commissioner in South Africa from 1897 to 1905.

In 1895 Rhodes concocted an "unofficial" plot to overthrow Kruger's government through a combined invasion and rebellion; but the Jameson Raid — named for the Rhodes lieutenant who led the filibustering expedition into the SAR from the west — miscarried because the uitlanders failed to rise. Although Rhodes was discredited by this fiasco, Chamberlain and Milner proceeded to make a series of demands in the name of the British government, aimed primarily at opening up the franchise to the mass of uitlanders, despite the fact that most of them had no intention of renouncing their foreign citizenship.

In 1899, having imported large supplies of modern weapons from Europe by way of Delagoa Bay and being encouraged by the sympathetic attitude of American and Continental governments, the SAR and its ally the Orange Free State declared war on Britain, in the hope of repeating the performance of 1881. Foreign governments, however, provided no substantial aid; nor did the British government yield when Boer commandos invaded the Cape Colony and Natal and won several quick victories. Instead, the British built up a vast military machine in South Africa that eventually numbered nearly 450,000 men in uniform, whereas no more than about 88,000 men, including volunteers from the Cape Colony, were available to serve in the republican commandos. The British forces soon gained control of the vital railroads and occupied the Witwatersrand and the republics' capital cities; and although the commandos then resorted to guerrilla tactics, the British gradually wore down their resistance, destroying their sources of supply in a series of raids that included the burning of farm buildings and the removal of many civilians to "concentration camps." In May 1902, the commandos laid down their arms and representatives of the republican governments submitted to British rule.

Milner, Chamberlain, and most British Conservatives — especially those with investments in the gold-mining industry — supported the war in the expectation that victory would be followed by a British migration on a large enough scale to "modernize" and "anglicize" the Afrikaners and reduce them to a minority in the European population of southern Africa. They hoped and expected that the entire region would become a wealthy, powerful, and loyal bastion of the British Empire. But, as so often happens, the calculations of the war-makers were not fulfilled. There was no large-scale British migration to postwar southern Africa; the Afrikaners continued to form a secure majority in the European population; and the long and arduous war only accentuated anglophobic emotions and inspired cultural resistance among the *predikants* (clergy) and a vigorous outpouring of protest literature in Afrikaans.

.In Britain, moreover, the length of the war and its cost in men and money created widespread revulsion against the militarists. In the general election of 1906, the Unionist (Conservative) party responsible for the war was overwhelmingly defeated by the Liberal party, most of whose leaders had opposed at least some of their predecessors' decisions. The policy of the new government differed from the old in its means rather than its ends. The Liberals, too, desired to foster the creation of a loyal and powerful southern Africa; but they considered that the way to do so was by making concessions to the Afrikaners rather than by continuing to try to coerce them. Accordingly, they gave both the former republics responsible government, with the franchise restricted to men of European extraction, in the hope that this would win the support of the Afrikaner elite and repair the psychological damage done by the war.

Thus, from one point of view, the Afrikaner republics were like other secondary empires that collapsed or fell under the control of a European power during the period of the scramble. From another point of view, however, the British won the war but gave the Afrikaners the reality of victory in the form of a broad measure of self-government. In this sense, the Afrikaner leaders gained more after their defeat than any other local authorities in Africa were able to gain from their confrontation with Europe, and this victory was very much the result of pseudoscientific racism. The British in London were willing to assume that appropriate concessions would ultimately bring the defeated Afrikaners into the family of self-governing settler territories — those that would later become the independent members of the Commonwealth of Nations — if only because these "European" Africans were "white," while the other defeated secondary empires were ruled by "blacks." But the end result was not a genuine grant of popular self-government — only self-government for the minority of European descent. The interests of the majority of South Africans were sacrificed in order to conciliate this European minority. The position of "nonwhites" within South Africa was to deteriorate during the next half century at the same time that the local European minority acquired greater domination within South Africa and greater independence from Britain.

SUGGESTIONS FOR FURTHER READING

Crowder, Michael. *West Africa under Colonial Rule*. London: Hutchinson, 1967.

Gann, L. H., and Duignan, Peter. *Colonialism in Africa, 1870–1960*. 5 vols. Cambridge: Cambridge University Press, 1969–75.

Hargreaves, John D. *West Africa Partitioned*. London: Macmillan, 1974.

Iliffe, John. *Tanganyika under German Rule, 1905–1912*. Cambridge: Cambridge University Press, 1969.

Landes, David. *Bankers and Pashas*. London: Heinemann, 1958.

Low, D. Anthony, and Pratt, R. Cranford. *Buganda and British Overrule, 1900–1955*. London: Oxford University Press, 1960.

Marais, J. S. *The Fall of Kruger's Republic*. Oxford: Oxford University Press, Clarendon Press, 1961.

Ranger, Terence O. *Revolt of Southern Rhodesia, 1896–97*. London: Heinemann, 1967.

Robinson, Ronald, and Gallasher, John, with Denny, Alice. *Africa and the Victorians: The Official Mind of Imperialism*. London: Macmillan, 1961.

Wrigley, C. C. "The Christian Revolution in Buganda." *Comparative Studies in Society and History* 2 (1959): 33–48.

Chapter 16
The Impact of Europe

JUST AS THE EUROPEAN CONQUEST assumed many different forms, the colonial occupation that followed was equally diverse, though regional similarities also existed. Areas conquered in the great burst of imperialist activity from 1880 to 1905 tended to have one kind of experience. Other regions with an early and significant population of European settlers, like Algeria and South Africa, tended to have another. Territories maintained as "protectorates" with a semblance of Western-style institutions and political life, like Egypt and, to a lesser extent, Tunisia, had still a third. But even such generalizations as can be made for large regions and aggregates of regions will be inaccurate for the smaller entities included in any of them. In the last analysis, we are drawn further and further toward the particular experiences of individual men and women, individual families, individual villages. The plain fact is that the colonial conquests introduced myriad changes into almost every aspect of African life. Even when the fundamental matrix of African culture remained intact, a continuous process of adjustment and readjustment from within was still required to absorb the impact of the West. It may not be possible to do justice to such a complex set of circumstances for the whole of a continent, at least within the space available in a general history of Africa; but in the chapters that follow we shall try to do so, first by looking at the European factor as a common denominator, even though it varied from region to region, then, from a more African perspective, by examining one by one the economic, intellectual, and social aspects of change. In a final chapter, we shall deal with the end of colonial rule throughout much of the continent, as well as with the continuance of European domination in the far south.

THE AIMS OF ADMINISTRATION

When the European powers had finished conquering their new African territories, they had few specific plans or ideas about what to do with them.

Much had been acquired simply for the purpose of keeping other powers out. Specific possibilities suggested the development of gold mining here, cotton growing there, or the building of railways to drain particular exports needed in Europe; but long-range plans for economic, social, or political change were very few indeed.

At another level, however, the Europeans shared some presuppositions and rudimentary aims, even though these stopped short of systematic planning. For instance, all believed that they had come to Africa to keep the peace. They intended to stop intra-African warfare and to suppress those African customs they regarded as repulsive. For whatever reason, they all meant to establish administrations that could control the African populations, either directly through their appointed officials or indirectly through the existing African authorities. This rudimentary goal was bound to cost money, because it required a level of government separate from and superior to the existing African governments. This meant that revenue above and beyond what had previously gone to the African governments had to be found. It might have come from Europe, but European taxpayers expected the colonies to pay their own way, at the very least. Colonial governments therefore acquired a second common goal; they needed to promote some form of economic development to produce taxable income.

As a guide to the way these goals might be achieved, Europeans also brought with them a heritage of ideas about overseas empire. This body of ideas took into account such considerations as the best kind of relationship between the colony and the metropolis, and between colonizers and colonized, as well as a wealth of ideas about projects to accomplish many specific purposes. It was a kind of dialogue running through Western history from the sixteenth century onward, one that was given new emphasis in the nineteenth century, as Europeans reexamined their place in the world in the light of their new industrial achievements at home and new empires abroad.

Some of these ideas, like pseudoscientific racism or the new administrative techniques, had, of course, played a role in encouraging Europeans to acquire overseas empires to begin with. They came on the scene again as background for the policies that were followed once the conquest was completed. Racism contributed to the European view of non-Western peoples, and that view had shifted during the second half of the nineteenth century in important ways. Earlier, from about the time of the French Revolution to the 1850s, the dominant view was one that could be labeled "conversionist." Europeans "knew" that they possessed the one true religion and that their way of life was superior to all others. They took for granted their own duty to spread Christianity throughout the world. They assumed that others would heed the message when they heard it, recognize the superiority of Western culture as a whole, and want it for themselves. They also assumed that culture change would be fairly easy, an assumption that rested in part on the success mass education was enjoying in Europe. Conversionism carried the unstated assumption that cultures might be unequal at a particular point in time, but that all men were made in the image of God, with the ability to reason and the capacity to recognize the best. It was, in short, cultural chauvinism of an extreme kind, but it was not racist.

Then, with the rise of pseudoscientific racism in the second half of the century, conversionism became badly eroded. Racists argued that non-Europeans were inherently and permanently inferior; their culture was part of their inherited racial status and could not be changed. Christians still argued that all men were spiritually equal before God, but even they often admitted that the capacity for salvation in the next life might not imply a capacity for high achievement in this one. If Africans were racially incapable of Westernization, they rationalized, then it might be better for them to develop "in their own way." As conversionism faded out, the doctrine of trusteeship took its place. If Europeans were indeed superior, it was argued, they had special obligations toward the Africans — obligations equivalent to those of fathers to minor children, of men to women, of the strong to the weak. These obligations were increasingly seen as the source of Europe's moral right and even moral duty to establish colonial rule in Africa.

By the end of the nineteenth century, the idea of trusteeship had overwhelmed the conversionist faith, but many different versions of trusteeship were put forward. Much depended on the supposed extent of African incapacity. Those who thought best of African abilities argued that the period of trusteeship would be limited; in time, African colonies would develop enough to emerge as independent states, though still inferior to the West. At the opposite extreme, other Europeans believed that Africans on their own could never achieve anything of consequence. The best they could gain would be acceptance within an overseas European society as a permanent caste of servants. That view was most common among settlers in southern Africa, but it was held by a substantial minority among Europeans in Europe, too. With appropriate alterations, it was also applied by the settlers in the Maghrib to Muslim North Africans. But the dominant position lay somewhere between these extremes, with an emphasis on European obligations as well as African duties. There was nevertheless an expectation that the relationship of trustee and ward would be very long, if not permanent, just as the qualities supposedly passed down through racial inheritance were claimed to be permanent.

THE MEANS OF ADMINISTRATION:
FIRST STAGES IN TROPICAL AFRICA

The first stages of colonial rule, to about 1920, were marked by a great variety of administrative expedients. Some were conceived in the spirit of the new racism. Others were mere stopgap measures that took on a life of their own. Still others were carry-overs from the more egalitarian practices of the earlier nineteenth century.

In the very earliest phase, many African rulers were merely asked to sign a paper and to fly the appropriate European flag. It was only later that the Europeans came back in force, to stay, and to give day-to-day orders. But they rarely came in sufficient numbers to see those orders carried down to the level of the ordinary subject. African intermediaries had to be called upon. Theorists of administration constructed elaborate frameworks on paper in which they argued the advantages of "direct" or "indirect" rule. Under direct rule, the chain of command ran through echelons of European officials as far as possible. By contrast, Indirect Rule stressed the desirability of ruling through African authorities like the emirs of northern Nigeria. In fact, all administrative systems gave orders through *some* African intermediaries. The crucial question revolved around the identity of those intermediaries and the degree of formal or informal authority they could exercise.

The range of choice was very wide indeed. In many cases where the African ruler retained some bargaining power, his authority over local affairs was left intact. It might even increase, because if he could depend on European support, he might gain a freer hand against political rivals within his kingdom. In other places, where the African kingdoms were swept away, colonial rulers made contact with their African subordinates only at the level of the village head. Authorities at that level lacked the prestige and traditional power of kingship; but they were so numerous, and the colonial officials so few, that they could often usurp power informally without fear of being caught.

Sometimes the Europeans tried to recruit their African subordinates without regard to past authority. The Germans in East Africa, for example, began on the coast by simply taking over the Zanzibari administration, which placed a *liwali* in charge of each town, with *akida* serving as his assistants for surrounding rural areas. But then they transformed the office of akida into one mainly concerned with revenue collection, and they greatly increased the number of officials in that rank. As a result, the akida became the principal intermediaries between the German district officers and the village headmen. Instead of being recruited from the local ruling class of the district, the first akida came from the coastal aristocracy of traders, later on from among the graduates of the earliest German schools set up in the coastal towns. The result was a very important though unintended shift in political power away from one segment of the Tanganyikan population to another. Or, as in the Congo Independent State, petty officials might be recruited far more carelessly from the ranks of African soldiers in the state service. There, in their role as the principal agents enforcing the state demands for wild rubber collections, they became petty tyrants with the right to punish anyone at all on the spot by whipping. For collective resistance, or simply for failure to meet their demands, they could call down a punitive expedition to destroy a village or punish a whole district.

Whoever may have been chosen to exercise authority for the Europeans, it was rarely possible to impose European government as it was understood in Europe. African subordinates did not fit into the Western administrative structure at first but rather into a relationship with the European officials that was much closer to the kind anthropologists call patron-client. The first administrators lacked the manpower and the knowledge to rule on their own. In effect, the chosen African leaders became tributary in the same sense that great African kingdoms had ruled through tributaries. The subordinate was allowed to rule, though with some rough guidelines about the kind of rule he was to provide. He entered into a revenue system that was characteristically tributary. That is, he collected taxes from his subjects and passed some part of them on to the Europeans. So long as he could maintain this relationship, the African ruler was free to order his subordinates in his own way, and the patron-client, or tributary, relationship lasted until the Europeans secured enough control to place all subordinates on salary, with the power subsequently to remove them. The chiefs understood this distinction. As a group of headmen in Uganda argued: "If you pay me to wash my table, it will then become your table." But the patron-client relationship gradually evolved toward more systematic administration.

European governments sometimes ruled indirectly through another kind of tributary by subcontracting colonial government to private companies. From the early stages of European expansion overseas, joint-stock companies had occasionally been endowed with the power to govern, to maintain armies and navies, to fight wars, and generally to do all that the granting government itself might have done. The merit of the device was supposed to be its low cost to the home government. The company usually received commercial monopolies or other privileges designed to yield a profit, which could then be used to pay the cost of fighting wars and ruling the colonies.

But profits rarely matched the costs of colonial rule very closely — being sometimes much higher, sometimes much lower — though company rule had the further advantage of disguising the government's actual role in matters likely to arouse criticism. Germany began its conquest of East Africa by chartering a German East African Company, giving it full control of the Tanganyikan territories it might acquire after 1885, though its charter was revoked in 1889. Britain chartered a Royal Niger Company for the period 1885–1900, an Imperial British East African Company (IBEA) for the occupation of Kenya (1888–1893), and Cecil Rhodes's British South African Company (BSA Co.) for the conquest and administration (1889–1930) of what was to be the Rhodesias (later Zambia and Zimbabwe). All these companies except the BSA Company lost their government functions within a few years. In practice, they were either too weak or too strong. IBEA failed financially, and the German East African Company was unable to handle Bushiri's revolt in coastal Tanganyika without calling for imperial troops. The Royal Niger Company had begun as a successful commercial company, but it had to be pushed aside so that African troops under imperial control could oppose French rivals and conquer the Caliphate of Sokoto. On the other hand, although the BSA Company was implicated in the Jameson raid, it was allowed to keep its charter and its administrative powers until 1923.

Leopold of Belgium's private Congo Independent State was a form of company government, with an interlocked nest of different corporate structures, and its governing power was used more drastically than was the case elsewhere in Africa. After 1892, it claimed a monopoly over the entire rubber production of the colony, paying the gatherers a very low price and using the armed power of the state to force villages and individuals to deliver quotas. Force was used to back up a system of forced labor and labor taxation. From all this, the Congo State not only made a magnificent private profit for the king and his friends; it also transferred part of its profits to the Belgian government, the only colony in Africa that paid off directly to a European government.

In addition to these companies that governed whole colonies, other European corporations operated at a more local level — in effect, subcontracting the control and exploitation of a single region or a single product. The government of the Congo Independent State allocated spheres of this kind for mining, railway building, and rubber collection, and some of the subcontractors made fabulous profits — as high as twentyfold within less than a decade for some rubber companies. But these high profits were not universal; the French companies chartered for the colony of the Middle Congo and the Portuguese companies chartered for Mozambique were far less successful. Some made a little profit, but on balance they seem to have shown a net loss, even though their methods were no less brutal than those of their Belgian counterparts.

Elsewhere, comparatively liberal administrative expedients survived from the conversionist phase of European thought. Before the scramble began in earnest, Britain held only a few coastal enclaves in West Africa, and some at least of the British officials accepted the idea that these towns should be governed in the best possible way — which, to their view, was the way towns in Britain were governed, with elected town councils and a mayor. Some precedents went back to the eighteenth century. From the mid-eighteenth century British and French officials of the Senegambian trading enclaves began to recognize the most prominent and influential citizen as "mayor." In 1800, the British also appointed a mayor and aldermen for the municipality of Freetown in Sierra Leone. Though the institution died out for a time, it was refounded in the 1890s. Similar municipal governments were set up in the 1850s for Accra and Cape Coast on the Gold Coast, later on for Sekondi as well, and for Lagos and Calabar in Nigeria. But the rise of the ideology of trusteeship cut off the development of town government at that point. No town annexed by Britain after 1900 achieved an elected city government until the 1950s.

The political pattern was similar in French West Africa. The ancient appointed mayoralties for Saint Louis and Gorée changed in 1848 into elected municipal councils, with the additional right to send representatives to the National Assembly in Paris. That was a one-shot affair, since the Second French Empire of the 1850s and 1860s was not very democratic, even in its government of France. With the foundation of the Third French Republic in 1870, however, both the elected city governments and the elected deputies to the Paris Assembly were renewed. The deputies were usually French or Afro-French at first, but the African inhabitants of the four coastal towns or communes that made up Senegal at that time were entitled to vote on the same basis as the rest. As in British West Africa, however, the spread of constitutional liberalism stopped there. None of the territory France gained after 1880 was brought within the charmed circle of electoral politics until after the Second World War.

That pattern of early political gains, reversed sometime between 1880 and 1900, was true of South Africa too. The Cape Colony and Natal achieved representative government in 1853 and 1856 respectively. The right to vote depended on the ownership of property, but the franchise, at least in theory, was color-blind. In practice, Natal restricted African suffrage by a series of measures that began as early as 1865, so there were never more than a handful of African voters in Natal. Africans held on better in the Cape, however, becoming a majority in a few constituencies by the 1880s, but then special restrictions came in that colony as well. The decade of the 1910s marked the peak period for African electoral achievement before the Second World War: the Reverend Walter Rubusana became the first African member elected to the Cape Provincial Council and Blaise Diagne became the first African Senegalese elected to the French National Assembly. In Senegal, the Africans managed to hang on, and Diagne had a series of elected successors. Not so in South Africa, where Africans, Asians, and Coloured people were specifically ineligible to sit in the central parliament of the Union of South Africa from its foundation in 1910 and were ultimately excluded from the Cape Provincial Council as well. Their right to vote, even in the Cape, was gradually restricted until it was removed altogether in the 1950s, just when colonial constitutions in tropical Africa were again moving in a liberal direction.

THE HIGH NOON OF COLONIAL RULE
IN TROPICAL AFRICA

A new phase in European colonial administration began with the interwar decades. This was marked principally by the dominance of some form of the doctrine of trusteeship reinforced by the lessons of experience, or what were taken to be the lessons of experience during the first phase of colonization. The general result was a more homogeneous administration of the continent, which replaced the most brutal forms of exploitation but also played down the few liberal exceptions that had come down from the past.

In the first decade of the twentieth century, events in Africa tended to strengthen the antiimperialist faction that already existed in most European countries. In Britain, the Anglo-Boer War of 1899–1902 was the most important catalyst of that opinion, though British antiimperialists were curiously blind to some important distinctions. They often failed to see the difference between the Boer effort to stave off imperial control — while simultaneously maintaining racial dominance in southern Africa — and the African resistance movements against any kind of European rule. British antiimperialists were active in exposing colonial scandals in non-British Africa, but remarkably quiet when Britain allowed European settlers to suppress African civil and political rights in the Union of South Africa. German opinion was especially moved by the atrocities committed by their forces during the suppression of the Herero rebellion (1903–1907) in South West Africa (Namibia), and these feelings were reinforced by the impact of the Maji-Maji rebellion in Tanganyika (1905–1907). The Belgian public began to hear murmurs of scandal from the Congo as early as the 1890s, especially those dealing with unbridled exactions of forced labor and forced deliveries of wild rubber. In 1908, the Belgian parliament responded by annexing the Congo Independent State and bringing it under state control. Similar events in Angola, Mozambique, and the French colony of Middle Congo raised a similar outcry for more efficient and humane central control and an end to concessionary companies. Reforms were not immediate, nor effective in every case, but the European governments learned something from the public furor and international opprobrium.

About the same period, it was brought home that African resources were not the boundless treasure some imperialists had claimed during the height of expansionism in the 1890s. Wild rubber had produced great wealth for a few, but at great cost to the Africans. By 1910, the rubber boom was gone forever; plantation-grown rubber from Southeast Asia replaced wild rubber in the world market. Other tropical products such as peanuts from West Africa, sisal and coffee from Tanganyika, cloves from Zanzibar, and cotton from Uganda or the Sudan were exported profitably enough, but only in limited circumstances. The perceived lesson about economic development was that private investment in Africa outside the field of commerce could only pay when it concentrated on directly exploitable resources such as mineral wealth in copper, gold, or diamonds. Outside of North and South Africa, very little private investment went for any other purposes.

Still another "lesson of experience" had to do with education. Conversionists in the mid-nineteenth century had trusted to the "civilizing" value of Christian education. The missions and the colonial governments still offered education on the Western model, if only to fill the demand for clerks and catechists. But the result was not a new generation of submissive clerks who "knew their place" in the colonial order of things. The Western-educated Africans were often discontented with the role assigned them, more argumentative and troublesome by European standards than the "unspoiled, bush African." Many officials began to prefer by far to deal with the traditional African authorities than to suffer the "insolence" of the journalists, lawyers, and other intellectuals who were beginning to emerge as a new elite around the West African port towns or from South African centers of missionary education such as Lovedale in the eastern Cape and Adama College in Natal — or even from the more recently established centers in East Africa or Malawi.

These lessons of experience blended with other tendencies of thought like pseudoscientific racism, which was still triumphant in the 1920s and into the

1930s. Administrative theory and practice were also affected by European influences having nothing to do with Africa. The First World War was crucial; France, Belgium, and Britain all lost a very high proportion of their most able young men of that generation. Even in Europe the result was a kind of historical hiatus, where many trends and developments that seemed imminent as of 1914 simply failed to take place until after 1945, and the Great Depression of the 1930s was a further damper on innovation on European initiative.

Specific theories of administration helped to mediate between these general conditions and the policies that were put into effect. One school of thought, called *associationist,* was especially important in France. It looked back with horror to nineteenth-century conversionism, which in French was called the theory of *assimilation,* in the sense that the colonized were expected to assimilate French culture. Associationists held that such assimilation might be desirable, but it was not possible in practice because non-Western people were racially inferior. It was better, therefore, to aim for mere "association" between the subject peoples and France, so that the colonial subjects could develop within their own, more limited capabilities. The expectation of a permanent relationship between superiors and inferiors was, of course, part of the general idea of trusteeship, of which associationism formed one strand.

The equivalent school of thought in Britain was identified with the idea of Indirect Rule, usually written with initial capitals to distinguish it from the less specific idea of ruling through the existing African authorities. The adherents of Indirect Rule attached a whole body of justification and additional corollaries. They played down the conversionist role of Christian missions and Western-style education and instead encouraged Africans to develop in an "African" way by using Hausa or Swahili as the language of administration in place of English, by establishing strict social segregation between Africans and Europeans, and sometimes by restricting European immigration to a colony. But the expectation was again a long period of trusteeship, or association between colonizers and colonized, without basic changes in the way of life of either.

These theories were hard to apply, however, if only because most administrators had contradictory attitudes. They genuinely believed that Africans and African cultures were inferior, and they genuinely believed that their own way of life was the best the world had known. It was therefore very hard to use any other standards of judgment, even when they conceded in theory that Africa had to develop in its own way. They wanted to rule through indigenous authorities, but they tended to push those authorities into the use of Western techniques of government, with typewriters, mimeograph machines, and the rest. This meant a need for typists, secretaries, and clerks who could do double-entry bookkeeping. Those who worked for European administrators also had to function in French or English or Portuguese. Colonial governments therefore continued to make Western-style education available. They might try to limit the content of that education, as the Belgian Congo did by creating a broad base to the equivalent of high school, then virtually prohibiting education for Africans at the university level. But such limitations rarely worked; it was simply impossible to give people access to education in the language of a technological society and still expect them to remain "unspoiled, bush Africans." Africans educated in Western schools rarely converted completely to Western culture, but they did begin to learn how Western culture worked, and they could borrow what they felt would help them to achieve their own goals for their own societies.

The conversionist faith had few vocal supporters during the 1920s and 1930s, but several colonial measures suggest that it still had a following of sorts — and it was to emerge strongly after the Second World War. Meanwhile, French policy made it possible for an African meeting certain educational and cultural standards to advance from the status of a French subject to that of a French citizen on a footing of full legal equality with Frenchmen from France. Portuguese authorities made a similar concession. Though the numbers of these *assimilados* (in Portuguese Africa) or *évoloués* (in French) were a tiny part of the whole, these men and women were a significant factor in social and political life. In less formal ways, British officials in West Africa, more than elsewhere, were able to make appropriate allowances for the English-trained lawyers, medical men, and others who could pass as "gentlemen."

Beyond these practical "lessons" and common theory, a great deal was borrowed back and forth among European administrations, so that they all came to share a family resemblance — from Morocco and Egypt down to the Cape of Good Hope. The private companies were phased out. African authorities who had begun with unusual latitude or unusual power over local affairs gradually found their power reduced. Colonies that began without institutions for consulting African opinion developed systematic ways to work with African intermediaries, if only at the lowest level. In the British colonies, the example of northern Nigeria under the governorship of Frederick Lugard before the First World War became the model of Indirect Rule, urged on other governors all over British Africa and very widely imitated. In some cases, where no chiefs or other traditional authorities were visible, as among the stateless Ibo, the British created "warrant chiefs" on the rationale that this was an "African" way of governing and therefore preferable to Western institutions such as elected councils for local government.

But colonial powers that tried to preserve African institutions sometimes found them breaking down under the demand for efficiency in government or the impact of social and economic change. After 1906, for example, the Belgian administration in the Congo decided to rule through the chiefs. At the first stage, local administrators were ordered to discover and recognize existing chiefdoms. By 1917, they had discovered about 6,000, which was far too many for efficient government. In line with the idea of "improving" African institutions rather than borrowing from Europe, they grouped smaller chiefdoms, calling each group a sector. As a result, by 1953, they had pared down the 6,000 chiefdoms into 460 chiefdoms and 519 sectors as the recognized units of "native local government." Each of these units was supposed to enforce local African law. But local African law was truly local, and many Africans actually lived in towns and mining camps with ethnically mixed populations. By 1931, the administration had to make an exception for these population centers, recognizing them as exempt from customary law (*centres extra-coutumiers*), though a kind of African common law came into being, especially in Kinshasa. These centers then grew so rapidly that, by 1960, a quarter of the Congolese population lived in them. Much the same happened elsewhere in Africa, wherever urbanization brought people together. The only choice was to impose some form of common law, and the choice usually went to some modification of a Western legal code.

Above the level of African intermediaries, colonial government was remarkably uniform, regardless of the European power in charge. The key administrative unit was a territory variously called a district, *cercle, territoire,* or the like. The head of each district — who might be called a *commandant de cercle,* commissioner, or District Officer — was in charge of all aspects of district administration, from judicial appeals to tax collection, road building, and schools, usually with one or two assistants plus specialized personnel for engineering, medicine, or education. The general administrative officers were recruited with care, and they had to pass through a period of special training.

They were also amazingly few for the extent of territory they governed. The whole of French Equatorial Africa in the mid-1930s was run by only 206 administrative officers, with 400 specialists and technical officers to assist. The whole of British tropical Africa at the same period (leaving aside Egypt, the Sudan, and southern Africa) was governed by about 1,000 general administrative officers, plus another four or five thousand European specialists, while the Belgians ruled the Congo in 1936 with 728 officers in charge of the 104 territories. In Rwanda and Burundi, however, they ruled with an administrative staff of less than 50 Europeans, because African kingship had been preserved there. The ratio of subjects to administrators thus varied from the neighborhood of 1,500 to one in the heavily administered Belgian Congo, to 70,000 to one in the lightly administered Rwanda and Burundi. This range of difference in Belgian Africa alone also appears to represent the range for tropical Africa in general, though these figures cannot be very precise because of incomplete population data. It is clear, in any event, that most day-to-day governing had to be done by African intermediaries.

Above the level of the district, the larger colonies had an intermediary level of provinces, grouping several districts. Then, at the center, sat the governor assisted by his staff and usually sharing power with some form of administrative or legislative council. These councils might consist only of the heads of government departments, sitting as a kind of advisory cabinet, but they usually also tried to represent important interests in the colony such as a few traditional rulers, the chambers of commerce or agriculture, or key trading firms. The Nigerian constitution that lasted from 1922 to 1946 can serve as an example. The governor had a legislative council of forty-five members, and he was obliged to consult it concerning new legislation or other important matters. Two-thirds were officials from the governor's staff, however, which meant that he could order them to vote as he saw fit. The other third were partly appointed by the governor to represent banking, trading, shipping, and the interests of African traders, but four members were elected from the coastal towns that had been allowed to keep municipal freedom: three from Lagos and one from Calabar. Similar constitutions with appropriate local variations were in effect elsewhere in British tropical Africa. In East Africa, for example, governors usually appointed a representative of the Indian minority, and sometimes a single European missionary represented African interests.

African colonial constitutions of the interwar period were peculiarly stable, not because they bred general satisfaction with the colonial order, but because governments were unresponsive to African views. Some protest was heard in council meetings, but most took place outside the political arena, expressed through religious movements, strikes, riots, or the organized refusal of farmers to sell their crops at the prices offered. Toward the end of the 1930s, these protests combined with reformist pressures within Europe itself to produce signs of change, but these projected reforms were overtaken by the impact of the Second World War.

ALIEN COMMUNITIES IN AFRICA: THE PROBLEM OF PLURAL SOCIETIES

From the broadest perspective of world history over the past three centuries, the Europeans conquered most of the world; and their impact on the conquered countries fell into one of three highly significant categories, depending on the demographic mixture of Europeans and local people. In one kind of case, exemplified by the United States or Australia, the Europeans were so numerous and the local inhabitants so few that blanket migration brought Western culture to a whole continent, leaving only small enclaves of unassimilated "Indians" or "Aborigines" to preserve their original way of life. By contrast, in British India or the Dutch East Indies — and in most of tropical Africa — the European administrators, businessmen, missionaries, or others acting for European interests were only a few temporary residents. If a self-sustaining European community of permanent residents spanning several generations ever came into existence, it remained a tiny enclave.

Between these extremes lay a third possibility, the cases in which the permanent community of overseas Europeans became a significant factor in colonial society and politics. When this happened, the local society was divided into two or more separate communities, each with its own way of life, yet living side by side and mutually engaged in that society's affairs. Culturally plural societies of this kind came in many variants. Some had a nearly equal balance between two cultures, as in Malaysia where the number of Chinese and Malays was nearly equal during the colonial period, while the dominant European community was very small. Others were numerically unbalanced toward one culture. Some plural societies integrated rapidly, merging to form a common culture, even though individuals might also retain important aspects of their ancestors' way of life. That happened notably in Hawaii, where people of many different Asian cultures, local Polynesians, and Western settlers assimilated a local variant of the European way of life — and in little more time than the African colonial period. Elsewhere, as in the Andean countries of Peru and Bolivia, Spanish and American Indian cultures lived side by side in the same society for nearly four hundred years without producing much cultural integration outside the field of religion or beyond the social group of mixed Indian and Spanish descent. The amount of political or economic power a community could command was a significant variable. Where overseas Europeans had the support of the colonial government, a comparatively small number could exercise an enormous influence on the country's affairs. The European minority in Kenya toward the end of the colonial period was only about 1 percent of the whole Kenya population, but its influence was immense. The East Indian minority at the same time was about 3 percent. It too had inordinate power because its per capita wealth was greater than that of the African majority, but it had nothing like the weight of European influence.

The African examples of cultural pluralism in the nineteenth and twentieth centuries fit into a special sector of the whole category. The intrusive aliens were always less than a quarter of the whole population, and less than 10 percent everywhere except Algeria and South Africa. They came mainly from India to East and southeast Africa and from Europe to northern and southern Africa and scattered areas between — with smaller numbers of Lebanese traders dispersed through West Africa joining the small communities of Afro-Americans in Liberia, Indonesians and Malays at the Cape, and Arabs already settled in the East African port towns well before the colonial period.

The European movement into Africa coincided with the nineteenth- and twentieth-century peak of racism and cultural chauvinism in Europe itself. These attitudes were extremely important to the settlers' feelings of self-confidence and their ability to justify their dominant position, to claim a monopoly over political power or a right to exploit the local people economically. They were also important to maintaining the European sense of community and solidarity with others of their kind. Almost everywhere, this led to patterns of residential segregation in urban housing, to social segregation in public facilities, and to overt legal inequality before the law. In less official ways, it led to sharp community resistance to culture change, especially to change that seemed to veer toward the African way of life. "Going native" was seldom illegal, but it brought down on the individual the most severe social and economic and even official government pressure. As a result, culture change in the African plural societies almost always meant assimilation of European culture by Africans, very rarely the assimilation of African culture by Europeans. This in itself was a sharp departure from the kind of Afro-European relations that had once prevailed in coastal trading ports, where many Europeans learned African languages, married African women, and left Afro-European families who became prominent in local society. The whole settler community of the *prazeros* in the Zambezi valley from the seventeenth to the nineteenth century Africanized their culture. Before 1750 or so, the Dutch community at the Cape mixed biologically with the local Khoikhoi far more easily than their descendants were to do with Africans in later centuries. European cultural attitudes, in short, began to harden even before the dawn of the colonial era itself.

Table 1 is a rough measure of the seriousness of the settler problem in colonial Africa. Before 1880, Europeans were a significant factor among African populations only in Algeria and South Africa, but they grew to be a severe problem for African societies by the end of the colonial period, even though their demographic weight was highly variable. The various political units fall into four different groups. South Africa is in a class by itself, with the culturally European population constituting 30.1 percent, even though the racially "pure" Europeans came to only 20.8 percent (and that itself was a peak figure; by the mid-1970s, they were less than 17 percent). If Indians and others permanently domiciled in South Africa are added, the total population of non-Bantu-speaking African origin as of the late 1950s would have been nearly a third of the whole. Only an insignificant percentage of any racial or national grouping had migrated to South Africa since 1930, and the vast majority were born in South Africa. Their integration into a broader South African society — culturally plural though it was — made South Africa significantly different from any other country. Even Algeria, whose European population was nearly 11 percent on the eve of independence, represented another order of magnitude, and, indeed, the great majority of the *colons* left voluntarily for France as political refugees when Algeria became independent in 1962 — as the Portuguese of Angola and Mozambique would do in 1974 and 1975.

The problem was less severe in the other territories, and the nature of the European settler population was somewhat different in each case. In Tunisia, for example, the settlers arrived in large numbers early in the colonial period. By 1921, they were already thought to be more than 7 percent of the population — higher than their proportion some thirty-five years later. In Algeria as in South Africa, the "European" population at the time of independence was predominantly African-born. The movement into Angola, Mozambique, Kenya, and Rhodesia, on the other hand, came largely after the Second World War; the European population of Rhodesia and Kenya, for instance, more than doubled between 1946 and 1955, while the settler population of Angola and Mozambique increased nearly as fast as in the postwar decade and kept on increasing when the rate of migration into South Africa and the British territories slowed down after the late 1950s. As a result, the "European" populations of these tropical African territories were genuine Europeans from Europe in much higher proportions than was true for either South Africa or the Maghrib, with obvious and serious consequences for the way these people regarded the permanency of their position in Africa.

TABLE 1 *"Europeans" Resident in Africa toward the End of the Colonial Period*

Country (present-day names)	Percentage of Total Population Classified as "European" (1956)
Union of South Africa	30.1*
Algeria	10.9
Rhodesia (Zimbabwe)	7.2
Tunisia	6.7
Former French Morocco	5.4
Zambia	3.0
Malawi	2.7
Angola	2.5
Mozambique	1.0
Kenya	0.9
Zaïre	0.8

SOURCE: United Nations, *Economic Survey of Africa since 1950* (New York, 1959), pp. 13, 15.
* Counts the "coloured" population as culturally Western. On a racial basis alone, the "European" percentage would be 20.8. Egypt is omitted for lack of equivalent data.

Another important consideration was the relationship of the European community to the land. In Morocco, settlers came to own about 8 percent of the land under cultivation; in Tunisia, as much as 40 to 45 percent in the rich plains south and west of Tunis; and in Algeria, nearly a third of the cultivated land. But most of the best land was managed in large units, and the bulk of agricultural labor was performed by Muslim North Africans. At the end of the colonial period, only about 5 percent of the European population of Algeria was actually settled on the land. Settler farm managers were also common in tropical Africa, but in South Africa, "European" farmers owned virtually all the productive land outside the African reserves which amounted to less than one eighth of the total area; and in the western Cape Province around Cape Town, virtually all the rural population were Afrikaans-speaking "Europeans" or Coloured, while the Bantu-speaking Africans lived in special locations near the principal towns and worked mainly in urban employment.

Land ownership, in turn, was related to the settler community's sense of permanency. In Kenya, for example, most of the European community were not engaged in agriculture; but many important settlers were landowners, and a high proportion regarded themselves as permanent residents who had come with the intention of raising their families and ultimately retiring there when their period of active employment was over. On the opposite side of Africa, the city of Dakar in Senegal had about the same proportion of Europeans as the city of Nairobi had in Kenya, but virtually all of the French Dakarois considered themselves temporary residents. Some intended to stay for a period of years, others for the remainder of their working lives, but both groups meant in the end to return to France and to educate their children for careers in France.

The type and extent of political power available to the settler communities varied greatly between northern and tropical Africa — with South Africa and Rhodesia being in a class by themselves. In the two French protectorates, Morocco and Tunisia, the settlers' most effective political voice was exercised directly on the Ministry of Foreign Affairs in Paris, especially by the large companies and other important interests. In Tunisia, however, the settlers themselves helped to elect a local council with limited powers over the protectorate's budget. Algeria was similar, with local Europeans controlling two-thirds of a representative body called the Financial Delegations, while local Muslims controlled the other third. But neither group was satisfied. The settlers tended to want Algeria's full integration with France — political assimilation as it was sometimes called — but they wanted this in a way that would exclude Muslim Algerians from power and from equality before the law. Some French liberals in the mid-1930s and later tried to push the government toward a policy of political assimilation that would include full civil and political rights for the Muslim majority. They failed in the face of settler opposition; the political reality in Algiers was that the settlers and the French army exercised even greater power in practice than the political institutions gave them formally on paper.

Much the same thing happened in other colonies run mainly from the imperial center in Europe. The Portuguese and Belgian colonial governments were theoretically autocratic, but the local Europeans had their say informally. In most of the French and English colonies in West and Central Africa, the settlers had formal representation, either through appointment to bodies like the Nigerian legislative council (following the constitution of 1922) or, in most French territories, through the Europeans' right to elect representatives to colonial councils. These colonial councils, however, also contained the appointed representatives of other interests, including those of important African authorities or chiefs, and their powers were mainly limited to the approval of the colonial budget. In British East Africa, especially Kenya, the settlers gained a more effective miniparliament that functioned as a legislative council, but they failed in the long run to make their interests dominant, as the settlers in South Africa and Rhodesia had already done.

THE PATTERN OF POLITICS
IN SOUTHERN AFRICA

The striking difference between the settler problem in South Africa and elsewhere was not merely the size of the "European" community; it derived even more from the fact that here the "European" community simultaneously made itself dominant over the Africans *and* independent of Europe. This dual victory in the first third of the twentieth century set a pattern for southern African political and social life that survived beyond the mid-1970s, in spite of the "winds of change" that brought independence under African control to every other part of the continent.

The victory of the Europeans in the far south began in the aftermath of the Anglo-Boer War. The British were conciliatory to the defeated; the Boers of the Transvaal were allowed local self-government, and their first elected leaders were Louis Botha and Jan Smuts, former Republican generals who nevertheless pursued a moderate policy — partly because they realized it was expedient to conciliate the mining industry, but also because they were impressed by the genuine good will behind the British olive branch. Then, in 1910, the Cape Colony, the Transvaal, Natal, and the Orange Free State amalgamated to form the Union of South Africa, under a constitution worked out by the South African politicians. It was a variant of the British model: a formal head of state represented the British monarch, but real executive power was vested in a cabinet responsible to the directly elected house in a bicameral legislature. Four aspects of this arrangement were of lasting significance. First, South Africa became a unitary rather than a federal state: the central government could override all local institutions, including the institutions of the provinces (the former colonies). Second, only "European" men could become members of parliament. Third, the electorate in the Transvaal, the Orange Free State, and Natal consisted exclusively, or almost so, of European men, though the laws of the Cape Province gave Coloured and African voters about 15 percent of the total vote. Fourth, the entire constitution could be altered by a bare majority in both houses of parliament, except for the clause that made Dutch (Afrikaans) an official language together with English — a concession to Afrikaner sentiment — and the clause that upheld the franchise rights of African and Coloured men in the Cape Colony. These clauses could only be amended by a two-thirds majority of both houses.

Since the parliamentary electorate was overwhelmingly "European" from the start, South African political divisions were based mainly on the historic and cultural cleavage between Afrikaners and those of British descent. Some political parties were led by Afrikaners, and dedicated first and foremost to the promotion of Afrikaner interests. Other parties were led by British South Africans, and were dedicated to the promotion of *their* interests. Still others were middle parties, comprising both Afrikaners and British South Africans, dedicated to the reduction of the historic tensions between the two groups. Because the British South Africans were a minority, even of the European population, no British party has ever looked as though it could obtain a parliamentary majority. The main struggle therefore was played out between the Afrikaner and middle parties, with the outcome determined primarily by the conduct of Afrikaner voters.

The political history of South Africa since 1910 falls into two periods, each of which started with middle-party government and developed into Afrikaner government. From 1910 to 1924, the dominant party was a middle party led by Botha and Smuts; this aimed at the gradual fusion of the two European stocks and at cooperation with Britain in international affairs. Then, from 1924 to 1933, the dominant party was an Afrikaner party, which promoted economic nationalism as well as detachment from Britain. This cycle ended during the Great Depression, which drew the two main parties together to form a new middle party, the United Party. In 1948, however, a new and more radical Afrikaner party came into power and has held it ever since.

Meanwhile, independence from Britain became a fact. Initially, the Union of South Africa had the status of a "self-governing colony," just as Canada, New Zealand, or Australia did at that period. Over the next decades, all these territories — with British acquiescence — became gradually more and more self-governing, even to the extent of enjoying a measure of independence in foreign policy by the 1920s. The formal passage of the British Statute of Westminster in 1931 then made them juridically independent if they chose to exercise that option. South Africa did so in 1934, though it remained a monarchy, with the king of Great Britain recognized separately as king of South Africa as well. Republican sentiment, however, was still strong among Afrikaner nationalists, who were dismayed when middle-party governments participated alongside Britain in both world wars — though the declaration of war against Germany in 1939 passed the South African parliament by only a small majority. In 1961, following a referendum of the "European" electorate, South Africa abandoned the monarchy and became the Republic of South Africa. It also dropped out of the Commonwealth, whose new Asian and African members were increasingly critical of its racial policies.

By that time, successive South African governments had whittled away the limited franchise rights originally enjoyed by the African and Coloured inhabitants of the Cape Province, rights that had been entrenched in the constitution. In 1936, African voters were removed from the common electoral rolls and given the right to elect three Europeans to represent them in parliament, and, in 1957, after a long constitutional struggle, the Coloured voters were given four such European representatives as well. But even these seats were abolished in 1960 and 1968 respectively. Since then, only Europeans (including women, who were enfranchised in 1930) have been permitted to vote for members of the South African parliament.

Meanwhile, African resistance and African political activity on the fringes of the constitutional, European-dominated forum had long since made their appearance. One of the ironies of modern Africa is the fact that indigenous Africans in the far south were more exposed to Western cultural influences and more involved in modern industrial life than those further north, yet they were to be under European domination longer. As early as 1900, most South Africans had been influenced by Christian missions. By 1960, nearly 60 percent were Christian. Most had been to some kind of Western-style school, however briefly.

Like subject peoples in other countries and in other periods, modern South Africans developed methods of compensating for their economic and political deprivations. Most learned to appear deferential in the presence of "Europeans," but without surrendering their integrity as human beings. Many transformed the religion of their masters to make it fulfill their own social, aesthetic, and psychic needs. And, despite the fact that the migrant labor system broke up vast numbers of families, Africans established strong community ties even in the segregated city locations. Indeed, the growing point in South African culture was a proletarian ebullience, a spirit that was well portrayed by Ezekiel Mphahlele in *Down Second Avenue*.

In South Africa, political organization among the subject races — as distinct from resistance to conquest — began toward the end of the nineteenth century. The principal organizations were the African National Congress (founded in 1912), the South African Indian Congress (founded in 1920 as an amalgamation of preexisting Natal and Transvaal organizations), and the African Political Organization (whose members were in fact Coloured people). All three bodies were initially fairly small, Western-oriented elite groups, lacking mass support. Their purpose was to realize the promise inherent in the Cape colonial system, first by gaining full equality for the well-educated members of their own communities, later by progressively educating and incorporating the masses. The precedent they had in mind was the step-by-step extension of the parliamentary franchise to all classes and both sexes in Britain. By rational argument and peaceful pressure within the framework of the law, they sought to persuade the existing electorate to reverse the segregationist tide.

For many years, the African National Congress (ANC) remained under the control of lawyers, clergy, and journalists, their professed objectives being to inform the electorate about "the requirements and aspirations of the Native people," to enlist the support of sympathetic Europeans, to promote unity among the African peoples, and, above all, to redress African grievances "by constitutional means." The ANC protested each installment of segregationist legislation from the Land Act of 1913 through the Parliamentary Representation Act of 1936, usually making its protests inside South Africa but sometimes sending delegations overseas — to England in 1913 and to Versailles in 1919. Though the ANC usually acted alone, its leaders were as a rule in close touch with liberal Europeans, and on occasion they sponsored multiracial conferences. By 1948, it was clear that this type of opposition was barren. Instead of being admitted to equality, Africans were being subjected to additional forms of discrimination. All the reformist opposition had achieved in forty years was a succession of rearguard actions, each ending in defeat.

Some Africans also tried before 1948 to create revolutionary movements. The most spectacular was founded by Clements Kadalie, an African from Nyasaland (later Malawi), who created an Industrial and Commercial Workers Union (ICU) with the help of a small group of European socialists and organized a series of industrial strikes starting in 1919. Like its contemporary, the Universal Negro Improvement Association of Marcus Garvey in the United States, the ICU was poorly organized and it disintegrated in the late 1920s, partly from internal weaknesses and partly in consequence of official suppression.

The Communist Party of South Africa was founded in 1921 by Europeans. It was the only political organization in South Africa that recruited members from all racial groups and that had a multiracial executive. But it suffered from ill-judged directives from Moscow, like other Communist parties outside the Soviet Union in that period, and from a series of internal schisms. It never gained a wide following, and it was banned in 1950. Nevertheless, it exerted considerable influence on the ICU, and, by 1948, socialist ideas were attracting the younger and more frustrated members of the ANC and the Asian and Coloured organizations.

Meanwhile the South African government had established control over German South West Africa (Namibia) during the First World War and retained it in the peace settlement under a mandate from the League of Nations. After the Second World War, South Africa, unlike all other holders of mandates, refused to make South West Africa a trust territory under the United Nations, because this would have committed South Africa to preparing it for independence. When South Africa's right to the territory was challenged in the international Court of Justice, it won the case on a legal technicality, but serious opposition from most UN members continued. By the 1960s, the territory had been closely integrated into the South African political and economic system. The majority of its European population was of Afrikaner descent and the territory was in most respects equivalent to a province of the Republic, with representation in the parliament in Cape Town.

When the four colonies united in 1910, politicians in Britain as well as in southern Africa generally assumed that sooner or later the Union would incorporate Rhodesia, Basutoland, Bechuanaland, and Swaziland, which remained under British control. In 1922, the British government decided to terminate the administrative powers of the British South African Company in Rhodesia, and it gave the local electorate, most of whom were European settlers of British origin, a choice: Rhodesia could either join South Africa or become a separate self-governing colony, in which case Britain would retain ultimate responsibility for the territory. To avoid Afrikaner domination, the voters opted for colonial self-government, but Britain refused them full independence under the Statute of Westminster. Nevertheless, the Rhodesian government's racial policies closely resembled those of South Africa, even though the local "white" population was outnumbered by twenty to one. But Britain also listened to African opinion in the other three territories and kept them under direct rule from London, because their people feared the patterns of racial oppression they had experienced in nearby South Africa, where many had worked as migrant laborers.

EUROPEAN "TUTELAGE" IN EGYPT

Europe's impact on Egypt during the colonial period was very different from what it was on the great and diverse mass of tropical Africa, or even on the culturally similar Arabic-speaking and Muslim Maghrib. The French invasion at the end of the eighteenth century, the modernizing policies of Muhammad 'Ali, and the unrestrained Westernization of Khedive Ismaïl in the 1870s had brought Egypt into the penumbra of Western-style politics. From 1866 to 1879, the khedive had permitted an elected representative assembly to function, though the only people it represented were the old aristocracy and the new class of Western-educated officers and officials, plus some of the tiny Egyptian middle class. Effective representation of the whole population was not intended. The assembly was nevertheless a forum in which various shades of opposition to the khedive could be expressed. It was these threads of disaffection that Colonel Urabi Pasha pulled together in 1881–82, along with a demand for independence from the European threat.

His rebellion was at first successful against the khedive, but then he lost to the British invasion. The result was a barely disguised British protectorate, though British control over Egypt was different from other protectorates of the period — for example, from those France established over Tunisia and Morocco. Britain was not interested in establishing lasting control over Egypt. It was interested in the security of the Suez Canal. It therefore chose to avoid offending other European powers, as it would surely have done by simply taking Egypt by outright conquest. The result was mixed. The Ottomans were still theoretically sovereign, but a series of local monarchs of Muhammad 'Ali's dynasty reigned until 1952 under the successive titles of khedive, sultan, and finally king. To keep the office of khedive seemed an easy way of conciliating important people in Egypt, hence of decreasing opposition to British overrule. On the other hand, the Urabi rebellion expressed an opposition to a discredited khedival regime. By returning the khedive to power, the British reintroduced a corrupt ruler and, through his influence, allowed the return of a political class that was to be equally corruptible in its turn.

Other Europeans continued to exercise certain rights acquired in the days of international informal empire. The international body charged with the liquidation of the Egyptian foreign debt still operated, which meant that the British-controlled government had to continue repayment to Egypt's mainly continental European creditors. The British were also limited by the Capitulations, which had already given away some of Egypt's sovereignty respecting resident foreigners. They not only had the right to be tried by consular courts; they were also exempt from certain taxes imposed on Egyptian subjects. Britain might modify these rights, but only with international agreement. In fact, many of the rights enjoyed by foreigners lasted until 1949.

With these advantages, foreigners continued to stream into the country, attracted by a new spurt of economic growth. They remained at 1 to 2 percent of the Egyptian population in spite of enormous local population growth. By 1897, there were 100,000 resident subjects of European powers, plus another 40,000 who had been born in some other part of the Ottoman Empire — mainly Syrians, Turks, and Circassians. These "European settlers" were principally city people and they remained city people, concentrated in the skilled trades and commerce. They were also mainly from the eastern Mediterranean, not from Britain or even Western Europe. The British officials who came to take high administrative posts or top positions in British firms were comparatively few. Alexandria was the "settlers' " city, and it became a "European city" on the African continent in the same way that Nairobi or Dakar were to be European cities, even though most inhabitants were African.

In spite of urban concentrations, foreigners also penetrated far into the agricultural economy. The government sponsored irrigation works to increase agricultural production, especially of cotton for the British textile industry. These works were built under foreign technicians. The land was often distributed by large land companies that built subsidiary irrigation works and then sold off the land in smaller units to the Egyptians who would actually manage production. Some large farms, however, remained under foreign control and management — some 13 percent of the arable land in 1900, increasing to 15 percent by 1913 — while Egyptian agriculture moved toward a dangerous dependence on cotton, rising from 12 percent of the total value of agricultural production in 1879 to 22 percent by 1913.

The decision to retain khedival government meant that British officials had to use a form of "indirect rule," and a form in which theory and practice were often quite distinct. The principal official bore the unlikely title of British Agent and Consul-General. In theory, he was only an adviser to the khedive, but the Anglo-Egyptian agreement provided that his advice had to be taken and acted upon. In effect, this meant that the consul-general had the power to order the appointment or dismissal of ministers of the Egyptian government, including the prime minister. He could also see to it that British "advisers" were appointed to help out the heads of various government departments and bureaus; and their advice also had to be taken, so that they became the effective department heads. The commander-in-chief, or *sirdar,* of the Egyptian army was a directly appointed British official, who also functioned as governor-general of the Sudan after its reconquest from the Mahdi. Britain had, in short, the opportunity to run the government of Egypt in any way it chose, but it chose not to run it quite so intensively as its theoretical power allowed. The consul-general had a kind of veto power over the khedive's acts, but he used it sparingly. The khedive retained enormous power — far more than remained to the king or queen of England at that time. The British also refrained from detailed interference in certain spheres of government, such as the Egyptian court system, local government, and the police. Their intervention was most intense, in short, in foreign and military affairs, fiscal administration, and economic development of the agricultural sector.

The political balance that emerged in Cairo was a shifting equilibrium between the consul-general, the khedive, and the representative council that developed over the decades into a kind of Egyptian parliament, though one with a restricted electorate. This body began in 1883 as a thirty-man legislative council, a bare majority being elected, the rest appointed by the khedive. During the decade before the First World War, the elected element increased and political parties began to function. Saad Zaghlul then emerged as a parliamentary spokes-

man for Egyptian independence. In 1918, he began the Wafd party, which was
to be the dominant nationalist party until 1952, first under his own leadership
and then, after 1927, under Mustapha el-Nahas Pasha. Meanwhile, Britain formally annexed Egypt when Turkey entered World War I on the opposite side,
then "liberated" Egypt once more in 1923 under a constitution that increased the
powers of the khedive and the parliament alike. But Britain also retained effective control over the Suez Canal, over the Sudan, and a strong influence in
Egyptian affairs generally. Egypt was independent in name only, but the relax-
ation of British control made it possible for Nahas Pasha and (after 1937)
King Farouk to build their personal fortunes and the power of their followings.

After the Second World War, political protest from the mass of the Egyptian population became important for the first time. A Communist party became
active. On the right, the Muslim Brotherhood became a significant mass movement. Founded as far back as 1929, it now combined Islamic conservatism with
other elements suggesting European fascism. The power of the brotherhood
peaked in the years 1947–49, nearly simultaneously with the Egyptian defeat by
Israel in the struggle over Palestine in 1948–49. The lost war discredited both
the king and Nahas Pasha, leaving an opening for new leadership of some kind.
In July 1952, the army staged a coup d'etat that marked the beginning of the
Egyptian revolution. Colonel Gamal Abd al-Nasser emerged as the most important leader in a movement that was simultaneously opposed to the monarchy
and the old regime within Egypt, opposed to the continued British military
presence in Egypt and the Suez Canal zone, and in favor of social and economic
justice for the Egyptian population.

The Nilotic Sudan was a further issue in Anglo-Egyptian relations until the
mid-1950s. When the British led the reconquest of Egypt's empire against the
Mahdi's successor in 1898–99, they had done so in Egypt's name and with many
Egyptian troops. At the same time, they resisted the idea of recreating a secondary empire under the control of their Egyptian protectorate. The result was to
make the Sudan a condominium, theoretically shared between Egypt and Britain.
In fact, the British were the dominant partner in the beginning and remained
so to the end. They governed the Sudan more systematically than they governed
Egypt, with a regular system of district administration, similar to that used in
other parts of Africa. A special elite corps of administrative officers — the
Sudan Service — was recruited for the purpose. They also carried policies of
social and legal change further than they bothered to do in Egypt, bringing in
English as the language of administration, and as the language of education in
the southern Sudan, beyond the region of previous Muslim dominance. They
introduced European codes of civil and criminal law as modified by previous
experience in British India, with increasing dependence after the mid-1920s on
Indirect Rule through existing Sudanese authorities, rather than on the previous
kind of indirect rule through Egyptian subordinate personnel. As a result, the
Sudan and Egypt tended to grow apart rather than closer together. Many Egyptians looked on the Sudan as a region for future colonization by excess Egyptian

population, but a new generation of Sudanese looked with foreboding on the possible consequence of British withdrawal and Egyptian dominance. As a result, Sudanese independence was thrown into the hat along with other issues to be worked out between Egypt and Britain in the wake of the Egyptian revolution.

AFRICA IN TWO WORLD WARS

By 1914–18, the main phase of colonial conquest in tropical Africa had barely been completed; in some places it had to be postponed until the end of European hostilities. African participation was inevitable, if only because Africa was the most important region outside Europe where "German" and "Allied" territory had common frontiers. With command of the seas from the beginning of the war, the Allies had no practical difficulty walking over the Germans occupying Togo, Cameroon, or German South West Africa. And most of the fighting there, as in the original conquest of Africa, was done by African troops serving under European command. In addition, thousands of Africans were recruited in the French colonies to serve on the European western front. The most important fighting in Africa was in the east, where the German governor of Tanganyika organized an African military force strong enough to occupy thousands of "European" South Africans, Indians, and East African troops nearly to the end of the war, fighting a long campaign of movement that reached southward into Mozambique and ended with his surrender in northern Zambia. In the process, Kenya alone lost tens of thousands of men who died, mainly of disease, after being forcibly recruited into the carrier corps.

The Second World War was far more significant for Africa as an important catalyst of the liquidation of colonial rule, though in ways that were far from obvious at the time. The second war may be seen as having begun in Africa long before it broke out in Europe — not with the German invasion of Poland in September 1939, but with the Italian invasion of Ethiopia in 1935. From one point of view, this campaign can be regarded as the last in the conquest of Africa, which had been continuing at a low rate in marginal parts of the continent ever since the main show was finished about 1905. But the new Italian campaign was different from the main conquest of Africa. Its cause was very much tied up with Italy's — and Mussolini's — position in Europe. Far from being a cheap little war, like the one in which Britain conquered the vastly more populous emirates of northern Nigeria with less than 2,000 African troops, the Italians deployed more than 120,000 Italian soldiers at the beginning of the campaign and would use nearly half a million Africans and Italians before it was finished. They also employed air cover, poison gas, and other military developments of the previous three decades.

The main phase of the war was finished within a year, in spite of some continuing guerrilla resistance. Emperor Haile Selassie fled to England, to create what amounted to an unofficial government-in-exile until he could secure foreign help to regain his position — an option simply not available to African rulers at the height of the scramble. Help came in due course. When Italy entered the European war in 1940 on the side of Germany, the Italian forces in Ethiopia, Somalia, and Eritrea were cut off and caught between British, Indian, and African forces in the Sudan and Kenya. The result was a rapid and comparatively easy conquest leading to Haile Selassie's return in 1941, after only five years of Italian occupation.

The war in North Africa was more seriously contested. Italian control of Libya opened the way for a British attack westward from Egypt beginning late in 1940, in the wake of the fall of France. But the Germans and Italians drove southeast through the Balkans in the spring of 1941 and simultaneously pushed the British from Libya far back into Egypt. After a seesaw in the western desert, the British barely held at El Alamein in the early summer of 1942, when the Germans were only 70 miles from Alexandria. By November, a seaborne Anglo-American force attacked Morocco and Algeria, and the Allies once more moved west from Egypt, meeting in Tunisia in May 1943 to complete their control of North Africa as a springboard for further advances on Sicily, Italy, and finally France.

While these battles in North Africa were essentially a sideshow, the Axis lost there nearly a million men killed or captured. The North African campaigns of 1943 were also the turning point in the European war in the west, but that merely highlights the fact that it *was* a European war, in which the Europeans did the bulk of the fighting over European issues, even though they fought on African soil. African troops participated, like those from British East Africa who helped secure Madagascar for the Free French, as they had earlier fought in Ethiopia; and African troops participated in the mopping-up operations, as in the French reconquest of Indochina after the Japanese surrender.

But the main influence of the war on Africa came in other ways. People of the African colonies were required to make a substantial effort that included real sacrifices in living standards, conscription of young men, and the same range of wartime shortages experienced elsewhere in those years. Out of this experience came a new sense of frustration with colonial rule. For some it also brought a broadening of horizons. The servicemen returning from distant theaters of war had a new and more intimate sense of what the rest of the world was like. The seriousness of the wartime pressures brought a more realistic understanding of the power position of the colonial masters, especially in places like Morocco and Algeria where the fighting had actually taken place. The postwar move to independence on the part of Pakistan and India and Ceylon was still another piece of evidence that worldwide colonial regimes were neither monolithic nor unbeatable. In all these ways, the Second World War ended the high noon of colonialism in Africa. After that, pressures for independence were to increase and build on their earlier beginnings, while the colonial powers on their own began to move in new directions that were themselves a response to the new conditions of the postwar world. But these postwar conditions were not a result of the war alone. In Africa in particular, they had been formed over decades of fundamental change in the basic conditions of life.

SUGGESTIONS FOR FURTHER READING

Ahmed, J. A. *The Intellectual Origins of Egyptian Nationalism*. London: Oxford University Press, 1961.

Austen, Ralph A. *Northwest Tanzania under German and British Rule*. London and New Haven: Yale University Press, 1968.

Berque, Jacques. *French North Africa: The Maghrib between Two World Wars*. London: Faber, 1967.

Bourdieu, Pierre. *The Algerians*. Boston: Beacon Press, 1962.

Gray, Richard. *The Two Nations*. London: Oxford University Press, 1960.

Gulliver, Philip, ed. *Traditions and Transitions in East Africa: Studies of the Tribal Factor in the Modern Era*. London: Routledge and Kegan Paul, 1969.

Hancock, William K. *Smuts*. 4 vols. Cambridge: Cambridge University Press, 1962–68.

Harlow, Vincent, Chilver, E. M., and Smith, Alison, eds. *History of East Africa*. Vol. 2. Oxford: Oxford University Press, Clarendon Press, 1965.

Johnstone, Frederick A. *Class, Race, and Gold: A Study of Class Relations and Racial Discrimination in South Africa*. London: Routledge and Kegan Paul, 1975.

Kuper, Leo. *An African Bourgeoisie*. London and New Haven: Yale University Press, 1965.

Marks, Shula. *Reluctant Rebellion: The 1906–08 Disturbances in Natal*. Oxford: Oxford University Press, Clarendon Press, 1970.

Mason, Philip. *The Birth of a Dilemma*. London: Oxford University Press, 1958.

Mayer, Philip. *Tribesmen or Townsmen*. Cape Town: Oxford University Press, 1961.

Mokgatle, Naboth. *The Autobiography of an Unknown South African*. London: Hurst, 1971.

Moodie, T. Dunbar. *The Rise of Afrikanerdom: Power, Apartheid, and the Afrikaner Civil Religion*. Berkeley: University of California Press, 1975.

Mphahlele, Ezekiel. *The African Image*. London: Faber, 1962.

———. *Down Second Avenue: Growing up in a South African Ghetto*. London: Faber, 1971.

Mungeam, G. H. *British Rule in Kenya, 1895–1912*. London: Oxford University Press, 1966.

Thompson, Leonard. *The Unification of South Africa, 1902–10*. Oxford: Oxford University Press, Clarendon Press, 1960.

Thompson, Leonard, and Butler, Jeffrey, eds. *Change in Contemporary South Africa*. Berkeley: University of California Press, 1975.

(See also the bibliography for Chapter 15.)

Chapter 17

The Colonial Economy

AFRICAN ECONOMIES had been changing over the centuries, long before the European impact was felt. They continued to change during the colonial period, and much of the initiative for this change came from Africans themselves — each responding in his or her own way to the range of options they could invent or discover in the material and technological environment they inhabited. In the colonial period, Africans also met a new set of conditions imposed from the outside. They met, in fact, two different sets of conditions that should be distinguished. One was the consequence of Africa's increasing integration into a worldwide economic order. A world economy had existed before the eighteenth century, but the industrial age brought a far more intense web of interconnection that caught up people everywhere. Africa felt that pull in important ways well before the colonial period began, and the influence of the world economy was stronger than ever after the colonial period had ended. The second set of outside influences came from the fact of colonial rule — from the particular policies of particular governments — and that set ended with the close of colonial dependence.

ECONOMIC POLICIES

Europeans tried to do many different things in Africa, but the range of things tried most frequently was narrow enough to permit generalization. All colonial governments had certain common points of view about economic policy, however much they differed in detail. One of these was the general expectation that African colonies should pay their own way, that they should have a balanced budget. This expectation may seem too obvious for repetition at this point, but it became important because most new colonies could *not* pay their own way. The Europeans insisted on imposing a bureaucratic superstructure on top of whatever government existed in precolonial times. They needed a modern military establishment to hold the country and to guard against rebellion. All this cost money. And in the background were the European taxpayers, who could make their woes felt through the central government in Europe — and the potential African taxpayers, who might be driven (and sometimes were driven) to rebellion by excessive taxation. Rebellion could, of course, be suppressed, but only at a cost far exceeding any additional tax yield involved.

The result was the nearly universal goal of economic development, which individual colonial administrators tried to carry out in the light of local conditions. The kind of development they might plan for depended on a number of crucial variables. One was the type of political control they had already decided on — light administration and indirect rule as in Rwanda or northern Nigeria, more direct administration as in the Belgian Congo or French West Africa, a company regime such as existed in the early decades in Rhodesia, or a parliamentary system with European overrule as in Egypt. Each kind of colonial administration implied a different decision-making process and a different set of possible outcomes, because a different combination of European and African interests was represented.

Still another determinant of economic policy was resource endowment, especially resource endowment against a background of technological change. Changing technology was a crucial factor in causing the shifts in demand that were made on Africa by the world economy. In the early nineteenth century, the increased use of machinery helped create a strong demand for oils and fats. Toward the end of the century, that demand led to the development of petroleum, among other substitutes, so that the tropical vegetable oils were no longer so important. But petroleum led to the internal combustion engine, and light engines made motor cars possible; automobiles, in turn, were among the background causes of a vast new demand for rubber from the 1890s onward. High rubber prices led to the ruthless exploitation of Central Africa through forced gathering, but they also led to more efficient rubber plantations. After 1913 or so, wild rubber virtually disappeared from world markets, which meant that Africa ceased for a time to be a source; and when African rubber revived, it was not until the 1920s and then mainly in Liberia, which in turn developed a deep dependence on that single crop and on the firm that had introduced it.

The world market also wanted minerals from Africa, under conditions in which both demand and supply shifted with changing technology. Gold had been important since the Middle Ages, but the gold exported from Africa in the past was mainly from placer deposits that were easily worked by means of preindustrial technology. The vast South African gold deposits, the largest found anywhere at any time, were unknown to the outside world until the 1880s, but the technology for working them was also unknown until the nineteenth century. The quantity of gold in the South African fields was enormous; but it was found in hard-rock veins that ran very deep, and the gold content per cubic meter of ore was comparatively low. To mine it at all required crushing and hoisting machinery, and to mine it profitably required a complex technology for

underground hard-rock mining and another for the extraction of the gold from
the ore on the surface. Other important minerals of recent decades were known
and worked for centuries — the gold of Zimbabwe or the copper of Katanga
and Zambia, for example. African iron ore, on the other hand, was comparatively unimportant outside Algeria and South Africa until the very end of the
colonial period. African bauxite deposits had no importance at all until aluminum technology developed between the two world wars.

Technology and resource endowment were intimately, if indirectly, related
to a third crucial determinant of economic policy: the size and importance of
the settler community in particular territories. European capital was invested
where exploitable resources promised the most attractive returns. Settlers tended
to follow capital investment in technologically complex enterprises. Egypt, for
example, attracted very large investment — more than £11 sterling per capita
by 1900 in the public sector alone, with nearly £8 sterling per capita added in
the private sector between then and 1914, considerably more per capita than
was invested anywhere else outside South Africa. But most of this investment
went into transportation and irrigation works, which could be handled by
Egyptians without large-scale immigration of skilled workers, and most foreign
immigrants to Egypt went into commerce and services. Agriculture, however,
attracted a larger proportion of European settlers to the Maghrib, East Africa,
and the eastern Congo. But the greatest connection between European settlers
and European capital was in the mineral production of southern Africa from
the Witwatersrand north to Katanga and the Zambian copper belt. On the eve
of the Second World War, outside per capita investment was estimated at £56
sterling in South Africa, £38 in the two Rhodesias (Zimbabwe and Zambia),
and £13 in the Belgian Congo, but not more than £10 anywhere else in tropical
Africa. South Africa and Southern Rhodesia were also the territories that attracted the largest number of settlers and endowed them with the largest measure
of political power.

RACIAL DOMINANCE AND
ECONOMIC GROWTH IN SOUTH AFRICA

South Africa was drawn into the fringes of industrialization faster than
any other part of the continent. The economic impetus went back to the diamond
discoveries of the 1870s, followed by Witwatersrand gold in the 1880s. Both
minerals required very heavy capital investment. This meant an early concentration of ownership and management. By 1899, De Beers Consolidated Mines had
amalgamated and concentrated the diamond industry and possessed a virtual
world monopoly on diamond sales through a London syndicate. Gold mining
came to be organized in a hierarchy of interrelated companies and through an
industrywide Chamber of Mines. Capital and technical personnel flowed in from
Britain, continental Europe, and the United States. "European" farm owners in
South Africa were drawn in as suppliers of food to the mining camps and

cities. The Chamber of Mines organized the recruitment of unskilled African labor from all the colonial territories in southern Africa and Mozambique.

The Anglo-Boer War of 1899–1902 brought a temporary stoppage of mining operations, and it destroyed many farms, but recovery was well under way by 1914, and the First World War stimulated local manufacturing to replace distant sources of supply. A decade of relative stagnation followed in the late 1920s, but after 1933 southern Africa entered a period of economic growth that persisted with only minor setbacks to the mid-1970s. Although mining remained important, the sector with the most rapid growth was manufacturing, which exceeded the total value of mining production by the early 1950s. A similar diversification took place in the sources of capital investment and foreign trade. Where Britain had once been nearly the sole economic partner overseas, the rest of the industrial world, including the United States and Japan, played a larger part after the Second World War.

This growth was remarkable, but it was unevenly divided. It was generated primarily in a few industrial areas: the Witwatersrand, including Johannesburg and Pretoria; the main ports from Cape Town through Port Elizabeth and East London to Durban; and, more recently, the region of Salisbury in Rhodesia. Most of the European farm managers were gradually pulled into the growth sector, with massive supports from their governments, but the rural areas of dense African population tended to become poorer per capita, not richer. Whereas they had once been self-sufficient in food, most became deficit areas to which food had to be imported and paid for by the earnings of migrant labor in the mines, industry, or "European" agriculture. The unequal distribution of wealth within the geographical region increased until, by the late 1960s, the Republic produced 90 percent of the region's gross domestic product, Rhodesia produced 8 percent, Namibia produced 2 percent, and the three territories with African governments — Botswana, Lesotho, and Swaziland — jointly produced only about 1 percent.

The product of economic growth was also distributed unevenly among the various racial groups, following a pattern that emerged at the beginning of the diamond and gold mining era. Skilled workers at first had to be attracted from abroad by the payment of wages competitive with those offered elsewhere in the industrialized world. Unskilled workers could be recruited in the rural African areas to work for a year or so at a time before returning to their homes. They were paid low wages on the assumption that village agriculture provided the main support for their families, and most remained unskilled. The result was a two-tiered labor system — one level of skill and remuneration for Europeans and another for Africans. In the course of time, as local "Europeans" acquired the necessary skills, the mining industry became less dependent on attracting operatives from overseas. But the two-tiered system persisted, and the pay differences increased rather than diminished. Europeans were allowed to organize unions for collective bargaining under the threat of a strike. Africans were excluded from "European" unions, from strike action, and from the bargaining process. The South African government also applied a so-called Civilized Labor Policy, reserving certain jobs for Europeans regardless of their ability, thus providing sheltered, high-wage employment for the least capable in that category.

Mining and industrial employers might seek their own interest by reducing the number of highly paid European employees and increasing that of Africans, upgrading the level of their skills, but the political power of the European workers always loomed in the background. A series of confrontations occurred, culminating in a very serious European miners' strike in 1922 that had enduring consequences. The strike turned violent and was finally suppressed by government troops at the cost of 230 lives. The suppression of the "Rand Rebellion," as it was called, was a short-term victory for the Chamber of Mines, but in the longer run the mine owners never again tried to break the two-tiered labor system. The power of the European working class was also underlined at the next election, and its privileged position became an accepted reality of South African political life. In 1935, the average cash wages paid each European miner were 11 times the wages paid the average African miner. By 1960, the difference had increased to 16 times, and the Europeans also received far more in fringe benefits than the African miners did. Even in industry and the building trades, the differential was 5 to 1.

The "European" South Africans, in short, derived immense material benefit from urbanization and industrialization — as industrial and commercial managers, bureaucrats, skilled workers, and capitalist farmers. Indeed, by the 1960s, their standard of living was among the highest in the world. By contrast, poverty prevailed among the Africans, including those who lived in the three countries under British rule. The lands left to them became overpopulated and remained undeveloped areas, in some cases becoming rural slums. Unable to sustain a modest self-sufficiency there, a high proportion of the adults — especially the men — were obliged to leave their reservations temporarily or permanently to work for "European" farmers or urban employers on conditions over which they had scarcely any control. Data permitting a full picture are not available, but rough estimates for 1954 put the average family income of Coloured and Indians at about 19 percent that of Europeans, of urban Africans at 13 percent, of African farm workers at 7 percent, and of Africans on the reserves at 6 percent. "Europeans" generally enjoyed excellent nutrition and medical services; kwashiorkor and other deficiency diseases were widespread among Africans.

AFRICAN AGRICULTURE AND COLONIAL PLANNING: THE PLANTATION SECTOR

Over most of Africa, the main resource was agriculture. Economic development therefore meant agricultural development, which implied new crops and new techniques to increase total yields. But total yield meant one thing to African farmers and another to colonial administrators. Africans were likely to look at that part of the total production they were allowed to keep for their own use. Planners were likely to look only at the increased yields that could be channeled into exports, because exports alone built up the foreign trade balances they needed to pay the external costs of running the colony. Foreign balances were also needed to pay for imports, and import duties were the easiest forms of taxation to collect.

By the First World War, planners had already come to think in terms of two alternate models for agricultural change. One depended on the individual African farmer's response to the price offered on the market for his produce. The second was to displace Africans from ownership of the land, bring in European enterprise, and set up plantations under European managers using African labor.

In the view of most colonial administrators, peasant agriculture was safer but less likely to produce striking increases in yield. Planners saw the peasants as backward, conservative men who were fearful of abandoning the methods of their forefathers. Recent studies in agricultural history, however, tend to show that African farmers were not unthinking traditionalists. They were usually willing to change, and even anxious to change, if they could see the possibility of substantial profit at small risk. They were unwilling however, to divert their effort when future yields and prices were uncertain. They sometimes lacked the technical knowledge needed for new crops, and they almost always lacked capital for major investment in tractors, fertilizers, irrigation works, or even for a small-scale investment in, say, the planting of tree crops that would not yield for a period of years. Plantations under European control seemed more likely to yield exportable produce, but they involved a greater disruption of African society, creating predictable social and political problems. It was also hard to find capitalists willing to invest at a risk in a new enterprise.

In any event, planners made decisions for or against peasant production, for or against various kinds of plantation or settler agriculture, even though they were not always carefully thought out. Sometimes the decision was not even conscious but was simply made by default, but decision-making was consistent enough to create a degree of uniformity across large regions regardless of colonial boundaries. Throughout West Africa other than Liberia, the final outcome favored peasant agriculture in African hands. European investment was generally limited to government-built infrastructure like roads, railroads, and port works. Private investment was largely by commercial firms dominating the export of the final product and the import of European goods. This West African pattern grew partly from the fact that Europeans had been trading in West Africa for centuries in goods that the Africans produced and delivered to them for export. Africans had shown themselves willing and able to respond to reasonable price incentives, so the precedent held.

A certain amount of conscious decision-making also took place. The British West African officials had adopted Indirect Rule as a relatively cheap way of governing. Land alienation on a large scale would have compromised the chiefs' power to govern for Britain. The most important direct confrontation came in

1907, when the Lever soap interests began asking for a palm oil plantation concession somewhere in British West Africa. The British government turned down the request, largely from political and social considerations. As a result, Lever applied to Belgium, organized a subsidiary, the Huileries du Congo Belge, and got a concession of 1.9 million acres in 1911. And, in terms of exportable product, they may have been proven correct. Between 1909 and 1936, Congolese palm oil production increased tenfold, while Nigerian production merely doubled. But the British decision was not based on the predicted exportable product alone.

In French West Africa, the dominant outcome was peasant production, even though the government leaned toward plantations a good deal of the time. Part of the problem was to make land available to European capitalists without doing great injustice to its African owners. The problem was further complicated by shifting cultivation. Land cropped for a few years would be allowed to grow up as bush to regain its fertility. The land most often belonged to a lineage or a village, which then assigned it to households for temporary use. French officials tried one scheme that involved registering all land under a system of individual ownership, so that individuals could freely sell their share to a plantation; but the scheme turned out to be impractical. For a time after 1935, the French West African government turned more actively to a policy favoring plantation agriculture. A few hundred thousand acres in French Guinea, Dahomey, and the Ivory Coast were granted to Europeans in the late 1930s, but most of these concessions were unused and had lapsed by the time of independence. The most acceptable explanation for this outcome seems to be that plantations might have been successful had the government been willing to intervene really decisively against African interests in favor of the European planters. But that intervention would have required forced labor as well as expropriation of the best African-held land, and the colonial government was not willing to go that far. Without that intervention, plantation agriculture was simply not competitive with African peasant agriculture.

It did become competitive, however, in large parts of East, Central, and southern Africa, where decisive government intervention favored the European planting class. In Kenya, Rhodesia, and parts of Kivu Province in the Belgian Congo, as well as in South Africa, large tracts of the best land were taken from the Africans and reserved for European management and ownership. In Kenya, the result was the "white highlands" policy, by which some 16,000 square miles were reserved for cultivation by European managers on long leases. It was the government intention that European-managed farms should produce most of the export crops, while smaller farms and less heavily capitalized African farms would produce food for local consumption. Certain crops, like coffee, were reserved by law to farms under European ownership. As a result, by the early 1950s, "European" production accounted for 95 percent of Kenya's agricultural exports, though it constituted only about a third of total farm production.

In Rhodesia and South Africa, the territorial division into African and

European sectors went even further. The South African Land Act of 1913 was crucial in creating the pattern that persisted thereafter. It divided the whole country between the "Native Reserves," where land could only be owned by Africans, and the rest of the country, where it could only be owned by people classified as "white" (except for a few places where Coloured or Asians could own land). In theory, Africans could move into the "white" areas only as temporary sojourners, never as permanent residents. This theory was implemented to a considerable extent by rigorous "pass laws." The 1913 act set aside nearly 88 percent of the land in South Africa for only 20 percent of the people. Some "European" South Africans actually worked on their farms, but most of the work on "European" farms was done by Africans — an increasing proportion as time went on. By 1951, some 30 percent of the African population actually lived and worked on European farms. By the 1960s, they outnumbered the Europeans on European farms by a ratio of 10 to 1. But the fact of ownership reserved by law gave the European farmers an immense advantage. Their per capita annual income was many times that of their African employees. But the combination of the best land, the best agricultural education, and the best access to capital meant that European farmers were also the most productive. By the mid-1950s, European farms produced 98 percent of South Africa's marketed wheat, 92 percent of the marketed maize, and 96 percent of the marketed wool.

The agricultural pattern of the Maghrib was similar. Some of the nineteenth-century settlers from Europe had been farmers who worked their own land, but in the interwar years, the Europeans in agriculture tended to be managers of larger and larger units. In 1914, for example, 6 percent of the active agricultural population in Algeria were settlers or their descendants; by 1930, the figure had dropped to 3 percent, though Europeans were more than 10 percent of the whole population. By 1934, the 26,000 European landowners held an average of more than 200 acres each, while more than 400,000 Algerian landowners held an average of only 43 acres each.

In the Maghrib as in South Africa, the combination of capital, technical knowledge, and the best land resulted in high yields on European-managed farms, and low yields where the Africans farmed their own land. Tunisian wheat yields in the early 1950s were three times as high on "European" as on African farms. In Algeria on the eve of the war of independence, European farmers produced 66 percent of all wheat, virtually all wine, and 84 percent of the olive products. As in South Africa, an inordinate share of the gross territorial product was diverted to the European settlers.

One alternative kind of agricultural planning was to combine high capitalization and technical assistance while leaving African farmers in charge of their own land, not simply as day laborers working for a favored community of foreign origin. To do this required government initiative and capital, but it could be attractive where large irrigation projects called for government capital in any case.

One of the most successful projects in interwar Africa was the Gezira scheme between the Blue and White Niles in the Sudan south of Khartoum. It began in 1925 with a dam across the Blue Nile at Sennar. Land lower down could then be irrigated by gravity flow through a series of canals. Rather than simply expropriating the land, the government gave each of the original owners a long-term lease. It then redistributed the land, often to the original owners, in blocs of about forty acres. Each new tenant was instructed in cotton growing and required to plant about a quarter of his holding in cotton. The rest could go into food, fallow, or fodder for animals, as the tenant might choose. During the colonial period, the government allowed a private syndicate to take charge of transportation, ginning, and marketing. When the cotton was exported, the proceeds were divided so that the government got 40 percent to pay for the land, irrigation works, and supervision, the tenant got 40 percent, and the syndicate got 20 percent. The tenant also retained full rights to dispose of the product from the other three-quarters of his holding as he saw fit.

The scheme was a success from the start. Extensions brought the total irrigated area to a half million acres by 1929 and to more than a million acres after the Second World War. At the time of independence in 1955, it supported a half million people and provided nearly half the total value of Sudanese exports. The Sudan paid a price, however, in undue dependence on a single export commodity, just as Egypt did.

Other irrigation schemes of this type were less successful. The French took the Gezira as a model for a similar project in the French Sudan (now Mali). The original project of 1932 called for dams to irrigate some 400,000 acres, or about the extent of the existing Gezira project. Tenants on previously uncultivated land were to grow cotton, and rice as a food crop. The Office du Niger, a public enterprise, was created to build the dams and irrigation canals. By the time of Malian independence in 1962, however, only 18,000 acres were actually irrigated and settled by some 37,000 people. In contrast to the Gezira's success, the Office du Niger could not even repay the cost of the original public investment, and individual settlers were often unhappy with the way in which their lives and work were administered.

AGRICULTURAL CHANGE ON AFRICAN INITIATIVE: SENEGAMBIA PEANUTS, GOLD COAST COCOA, UGANDA COTTON

In spite of administered development schemes and settler and plantation agriculture, most African agriculture and herding, in the colonial period and after, was done by African farmers making their own decisions. Even though their production was not always dominant in the export sector, it was by far the greater part of total agricultural production outside South Africa and the Maghrib. The most important element of agricultural change in the colonial period was therefore the piecemeal adjustments made by individual farmers in response to the opportunities they could discover. These changes are often hard to trace, because they went unnoticed by European observers. Among the most important were changes in the production of food consumed mainly by the producers and their families, like the spread of maize and manioc throughout tropical Africa, a shift that was still going on in the colonial period though it had started in the sixteenth century. The end result, however, was a basic and permanent change in Africa's capacity to support its human population.

Some crops that were later to be important as exports began as food crops for African consumption, even though they may have originated outside Africa. The spread of peanuts is an effective illustration of African initiative. The first peanuts came from America to West Africa in the seventeenth century or earlier. By the early eighteenth, they were cultivated in the northern belt of the savanna from the Atlantic eastward into present-day Mali. By the nineteenth century, they were grown in northern Nigeria as well, though they may have come there a century or two earlier.

The next crucial stage was the commercialization of the crop and the beginnings of overseas export. We have already seen its influence on the course of religious revolution in Senegambia. In the 1830s, merchants in the Senegambian trading posts discovered that peanuts could be sold in Europe and the United States. Production for export began to spread seriously in the 1840s, with France as the most important market overseas. The first regions to develop were northern Kajor and Waalo (where camels brought down from Mauritania provided comparatively cheap transportation to the ports) and the banks of the Gambia and Saalum rivers, where efficient river transportation had existed for centuries. Gambian peanut exports rose to 10,000 metric tons a year in the early 1850s, then more slowly to a range of 15,000 to 20,000 metric tons annually in the final quarter of the nineteenth century.

This increased production called for the diversion of African resources from other activities. The lower Gambia valley was not heavily populated, so that land was available, but labor was not. The African response as early as the 1840s was labor migration, with men and sometimes families moving as much as three or four hundred miles through a dozen political jurisdictions to take up land near the Gambia. Here the workers hired land from the local lineage heads, sometimes paying in labor. They then planted part of the land in peanuts and part in millet, maize, or some other food crop that would carry them through the coming year. These "strange farmers," as they are called in Gambian English, sold the crop at the end of the season and bought an assortment of imported goods for resale on their return home. Their annual pattern of activity thus began with seasonal work in agriculture, from which they earned capital for investment in a single venture in long-distance trade, over routes that could take as long as a month to travel in either direction. As early as 1848, most of the peanuts exported from the Gambia were grown by strange farmers from the interior, though local people who were not landlords also profited from river shipping and bulking the peanuts for sale to the large French firms that came to dominate final export to Europe.

Peanut production in Senegal rose at first a little more slowly than it did on the Gambia, probably because the Senegal River flowed north of the best peanut land, which meant that camel caravans were needed to move the crop to the Senegal River ports or to the coast at Dakar, Rufisque, or Saint Louis. Then, in the 1870s, the government of Senegal built a railroad from Dakar to Saint Louis at the mouth of the river, passing through some of the best peanut-growing territory in the kingdom of Kajor — even though Kajor was only under informal empire, not yet annexed by France. The railroad was a financial failure and had to be subsidized by the French government, but peanut production boomed, reaching 140,000 metric tons exported through French-controlled ports by 1900.

A new phase in Senegalese peanut farming began in the 1890s with the movement of settlers from the old peanut areas eastward into parts of Kajor and Jollof previously used only seasonally by Fulbe herdsmen. Some of this movement took place on the individual initiative of pioneer families, but, after 1912, much of it was organized by the religious brotherhood of the Murīdiya. This new *tarīqa* was an offshoot of the Qādirīya, founded by Amadu Bamba, whose father had been associated with Ma Ba and other *jihad* leaders of the 1860s and 1870s. One of the strongest Mourid principles was the complete submission of the individual member to the authority of his *shaykh,* that is, to the authority of one of the clerical members, who in turn represented the supreme authority of the Amadu Bamba and his successors. One acceptable form of submission was to join a *dara,* or farming group, in effect an economic unit that worked the shaykh's land. These dara became the units of agricultural colonization pushing eastward into new land.

In the early colonial period, the French suspected the Mourids of "religious fanaticism," but they changed their opinion after 1912, and Mourid leaders rose to positions of great political power in colonial and independent Senegal. On the eve of independence, Mourids totaled about 20 percent of the Senegalese population, and the brotherhood controlled about a quarter of Senegal's peanut production. Less fortunately, its agricultural colonization was too intensive for the marginal land it brought under cultivation. Much of it suffered so severely in fact that it may never recover the fertility it had under wiser use before the 1920s.

Gold Coast cocoa was also notable as an export crop developed largely through African initiative. It too was American by origin, but suitable to the forest zone, not the savanna. In recent years, the West African forests from the Ivory Coast through Ghana and western Nigeria have accounted for about two-thirds of world cocoa production entering trade. Cocoa came first from America to Fernando Po (Ile Macias Nguema) as a plantation crop. Seeds may have been introduced to the Gold Coast forest at several different times, but one introduction took place in 1879 by way of a contract laborer who was returning from Fernando Po to the forested Akwapim ridge in the hinterland of the Accra plain. No cocoa exports are recorded before 1891, and the total rose to only 500 metric tons by 1900. By 1911, however, exports were 40,000 tons, and from then onward the Gold Coast was the largest single cocoa producer in the world.

The speed of this development was impressive, and it reflects the organizing activity of African entrepreneurs, at first mainly from the Akwapim ridge. They began with small plots of three to six acres on the ridge itself. Because cocoa trees need shade, cocoa could be underplanted in forest conditions, leaving large trees standing, but suitable land on the ridge soon ran out. Farmers from Akwapim then began to buy or rent land in the lightly inhabited forest country to the west. Most societies on the ridge were accustomed to individual land ownership, but most forest societies further west vested control in the lineage head, who could, however, sell land. One problem for the cocoa entrepreneurs was to get together enough money to purchase a tract as a single transaction. They met this problem by forming buying cooperatives, which could make large purchases and then subdivide them among the individual members. Before 1914, in the single state of Akim Abuakwa, some 800 square miles were sold off to strangers to be turned into cocoa farms.

As the movement continued into the 1920s, other people joined the Akwapim — Fante from the coast, Krobo, Shai, and Ewe from the northeast. Entrepreneurs in southern Ghana used the profits from one farm to recover enough capital to make a second purchase, usually at a distance as the frontier of cocoa planting moved west and north. In this way, the individual farmer might find himself with three or four plots scattered across the southern Gold Coast. Others came into the cocoa industry as middlemen, buying from the farmers, bulking, and reselling to other traders or directly to the European export firms. The Asante were less willing than some to sell off their forest land, but they went into cocoa planting independently, with initial capital often derived from the rubber boom that had just ended about 1913. Others used the proceeds from cocoa farming for investment in other sectors of the economy, most significantly in their children's education, so that Akwapim became famous for its many privately supported schools and its contribution of Western-educated people to the government service and the professions.

The intensity of cocoa development soon caused a labor shortage, especially at harvest time during the dry season. Since that was a period of underemployment in the savanna country, young men began to move south for seasonal work — at first from northern Ghana but then from Upper Volta and other French colonies. By the end of the 1950s, as many as 320,000 non-Ghanaian migrants were crossing the frontier each year. The new agriculture not only moved cocoa farmers out of their relatively isolated ethnic homelands; it also moved immigrants over hundreds of miles into a new socioeconomic setting on a larger scale than that of any precolonial society. This increase in scale, in Ghana and elsewhere, was to be important for its contribution to the sense of solidarity within the new nations that emerged after independence.

Ghanaian entrepreneurship in the cocoa industry was unusual, both in its freedom from government initiative and from that of the traditional political authorities. In the longer run, the cocoa farmers were to work with the chiefs for political and economic ends, especially in 1937–38, when they withheld their cocoa from the market and broke an attempted price-fixing arrangement by the European firms. But the first developments took place largely under local initiative with new leadership and voluntary cooperation. They engaged in such enterprises as joint land purchases and building access trails and bridges — often working through agencies like the Christian churches in further cooperative efforts, such as Akwapim educational development.

Other shifts in cash-crop production by African peasants involved much more initiative from nonpeasant sources, with quite different socioeconomic results. Ugandan cotton is a useful example. The political background was the Christian revolution in Buganda in the 1880s and 1890s. The victors obtained a formal settlement with Britain — the Uganda Agreement of 1900. Its formal terms covered Buganda only, but it set a precedent that was important in the neighboring provinces of Bunyoro and Busoga as well. The crucial fact was that a set of important chiefs emerged with a good deal of authority at a political level intermediary between the British officials of the Uganda Protectorate and the individual peasants.

The world economy affected Uganda suddenly in 1901, when the railroad from Mombasa reached Kisumu on Lake Victoria. Up to that time, head-loading from Lake Victoria to the coast had cost an estimated £200 sterling per ton; on the railroad it cost £2.40 per ton. Peasant initiative might have emerged more rapidly if Uganda peasants had operated for centuries on the fringes of the world market, as the Gold Coast peasants had done. But the initiative came immediately, and from other sources. The British government was anxious to gain traffic for the railroad; the Ugandan government was anxious to have an export so as to create taxable income. The British Cotton Growing Association was anxious to promote cotton growing in the British Empire so as to cut dependence on foreign sources. The Uganda Company, Ltd. was also on the scene. It was partly a commercial firm eager to make a profit from ginning and shipping cotton, but it also had connections with the Church Missionary Society, the most active of the Protestant missions.

The government, the association, the company, and the missions all went to work together. The association provided seeds and technical advice and set up central cotton gins to prepare the crop for shipment. The Uganda Company, the government, and the missions enlisted the help of the chiefs (who were also the landowners in Buganda). The chiefs distributed seed to their tenants and made sure that it was planted and harvested according to instructions. This more or less involuntary first cultivation was a demonstration of its economic and agricultural feasibility, and other farmers began to cultivate it on their own initiative; the Uganda Company, for its part, helped export a crop that soared in value from £43,000 in 1903–04 to £307,000 in 1910–11. By then, it already amounted to more than half of Uganda's total exports; by the early years of World War I, it reached 70 percent.

Concentrated cash-crop production drew migrant labor into Buganda province from other parts of the protectorate even before 1914. During the interwar years, the flow increased, with thousands walking across colonial frontiers from Rwanda, Burundi, western Tanganyika, and Kenya. By 1946, the estimated annual flow had reached 140,000 from Rwanda and Burundi alone. Many of these migrants came for a season only, but many others began to settle down for a period of years. They learned Luganda, assimilated Ganda culture — and the second generation *were* Ganda. The socioeconomic consequences of migration also spread back to the source. In positive ways, Rwanda and Burundi were relieved of overcrowding and starvation in time of famine. But migration had less favorable consequences, leaving families without husbands to subsist, if they could, on remittances and submarginal agriculture.

The social consequences in Uganda were also important, and quite different from those that followed cocoa or peanuts in West Africa. In the Gold Coast, for example, African initiative not only sparked the cocoa industry from the beginning; African entrepreneurs also appeared in specialized activities like commercial seed production and commerce — in many branches, from cocoa buying to distribution and retailing of imports from abroad, to trucking migrant workers from the north. In Uganda, the main African initiative came from the chiefly class, but the chiefs were usually administrators and they stayed in administration. The peasantry grew the cotton, but they remained cotton growers; Europeans stepped in as the main operators of ginneries. East Indians came into the retail trade in large numbers, purchasing cotton and other export crops and supplying imported commodities to the countryside.

One result was that Indians came to dominate petty commerce, and ordinary Ugandans developed a deep resentment. This resentment was one root of the expulsion in 1971 of some 80,000 Indians who carried British passports, and the result was an economic disaster because skilled Africans were not available to fill the gap and to maintain the flow of agricultural exports and retail trade. Cyril Erlich, an economic historian of Uganda, has argued that its pattern of agricultural development was too paternalistic. Peasants learned to respond, but only to incentives laid out for them by others. With the move toward independence, able and intelligent Africans were attracted into the government service rather than to trade, so that African paternalism replaced colonial paternalism; and the country missed the healthy play of individual initiative found in West Africa.

FOREIGN INVESTMENT AND AFRICAN ECONOMIC GROWTH

Most economists looking back to the colonial period agree that a principal brake on African economic development was a lack of capital investment. Some capital might have been generated within Africa by appropriate government policy, but the main problem was lack of capital from overseas. Colonial governments did invest something in infrastructure and even in development (the Gezira project is an example), but the overall rate of investment was low. Private investment from overseas was especially weak. Up to the Second World War, total foreign investment in sub-Saharan Africa has been estimated at about $6 billion at current prices, half of it government and half private. The bulk of private investment was in minerals and mineral-associated subsidiary industry, heavily concentrated in the south. Private foreign investment in agriculture was also concentrated in the far south and in North Africa.

In the postwar decades, the annual rate of foreign investment increased to several times the prewar rate, but private investment continued at less than half the total. With the approach of independence and on into the early 1960s, aid from overseas in the form of free gifts or loans at low rates of interest became increasingly important. In the peak year, 1964, it reached more than one billion dollars from western Europe and North America alone, but total aid then declined in the late 1960s and on into the seventies.

Throughout the colonial period, foreign investors, both private and public, placed their funds overwhelmingly in the export sector. The result was lopsided economic development centered on foreign trade. Part of the cause was government concern to encourage a viable export crop or mineral production, but European officials and investors also looked at Africa from a Europe-centered point of view. They knew about European economic demand, but not about the African economy. They therefore placed investment to meet the demand they knew, for wine from Algeria or cotton from Egypt, for example. In theory, capitalist investment should have been placed so as to give the investors the greatest possible return on their money, but they rarely considered the possibility of investing in an enterprise that served local needs. Thinking instead of European needs, private and public investors alike acted to maximize the security and productivity of the home economy in Europe, rarely to maximize the productivity of the colonial economy, or even to maximize the return on private capital invested overseas. The exception was South Africa, where the inordinate incomes of the European caste helped provide a substantial local market and a local source of capital.

The growth of cotton production in Ubangi-Shari (now the Central African Empire) between the wars is a telling example of uneconomic investment and uneconomic development. Given the colony's great distance from the sea, it might have been rational economically to encourage small-scale industry, drawing on local raw materials and then selling the manufactured product in a local market — say, small textile factories using local cotton to make cloth. The French administration decided instead to push cotton as an export crop. As a result, cotton had to be carried overland to the Ubangi River, down the Ubangi and Congo to Stanley Pool, then by rail to Pointe Noire, and finally by sea to France. Transportation and handling costs were so high that the peasants received only a small fraction of the price paid in France, such a small fraction, in fact, that planting cotton was not worth their while. The colonial government therefore resorted to forced cultivation; each farmer in certain designated regions was required by law to plant a certain area in cotton (about one acre in the 1950s). But forcing the farmers to grow a crop that was uneconomic for them also forced the government into major expenditures for a whole echelon of subadministrators whose job it was to enforce the law at the local level. That too was uneconomic. Successive governments appealed to European enterprise to help with ginning, bulking, and transportation to the coast, but they ended by subsidizing cotton-buying companies, subsidizing river and rail transportation, and paying very heavily indeed to suppress a serious rebellion in the late 1920s — a rebellion that was directly traceable to African resentment over forced labor and forced cultivation.

But the plan succeeded after a fashion. By the late 1950s, French Equatorial Africa (including Ubangi-Shari) was producing about 10 percent of the cotton fiber used in France, which was 80 percent of the cotton reaching France from its overseas empire. By that time, cotton export could pay its own way, but only after having warped the economy toward a form of production that was, for several decades, unprofitable to the peasants, unprofitable to the colonial government, unprofitable to French cotton-buying firms, and probably unprofitable to the French metropolitan government as well.

European investment tended to produce lopsided African economies in another way as well. Wherever European capital was invested, it tended to bring in the latest European technology. This occurred in the new mines of the Witwatersrand of the 1890s, in Katanga in the 1920s, and in the Orange Free State goldfields in the 1950s. It was also the case with agricultural investment in the Maghrib, South Africa, and the settler areas in between. Highly capitalized and technologically advanced enterprises could produce for the world market, but they became one advanced sector in economies that were otherwise far less advanced. As a result, resources and manpower were pulled into the advanced sector, while the less advanced remained technologically backward, starved for capital and government attention.

This tendency was reinforced by the colonial governments' emphasis on production for export. The fact that half the foreign investment in sub-Saharan Africa was government-derived was a major factor. A government could choose to place its investment so as to favor local production for a local market and the long-term goal of maximum gross territorial product. Or, it could go instead for ports, railways, and other facilities to clear the way for exports to the coast and on to Europe.

The continent's general web of transportation and communication facilities was so distorted at the end of the colonial period that a telegram from one colony to its neighbor, only a few hundred miles away, often had to go by way of Europe. Even if private investors had had the information to make possible a careful selection of the most profitable forms of investment for local sale, prior government investment had already set the boundaries of what was and was not profitable. By investing in the export-centered infrastructure, governments attracted what little private investment came to Africa into the same sector. Government investment, in short, was often placed with a mind to other goals than maximizing local productivity, and that fact alone could guide the private sector into an emphasis that was not necessarily the most conducive to long-term economic growth. This was especially true of rail lines; those planned and built in early colonial times did a lot to mold the forms and direction of economic development in the decades to come.

RAILROADS

Africa was a continent badly suited to the early development of a dense railroad network. Population was sparse through most of the savanna country; centers of agricultural production were scattered; and agricultural exports were often seasonal, creating a peak load for a few months and then leaving the railroads underused during the remainder of the year. As a result, most investment in railroads for tropical Africa was unprofitable. Only South Africa developed a linked system comparable to those of Europe or North America, though the French government in the Maghrib built a rudimentary network. The Anglo-Egyptian Sudan and Nigeria also came to have an unusual degree of railroad development compared to the rest of tropical Africa. In general, however, profitable railroads were those that served the major centers of mineral extraction from Katanga southward. Elsewhere in tropical Africa, railroads were either built on the government's clear understanding that it was subsidizing other forms of economic development, or were started by private investors who hoped to make a profit but ended with some form of government subsidy, if not government ownership.

In East Africa, the unprofitability of railroad construction was recognized in advance, but the Uganda Railway built from Mombasa on the Kenya coast to Lake Victoria between 1895 and 1902 is a classic early example of railroad building for political ends — that nevertheless brought important economic consequences in its wake. (And the neighboring line from Dar-es-Salaam to Lake Tanganyika in German East Africa was built with similar motives and results.) The Uganda Railway grew out of the larger strategy of the scramble for Africa. Britain was already in Egypt and concerned about the fate of the Nilotic Sudan. It seemed important to control the outlet of the Nile from Lake Victoria, rather than to let the territory that was to be Uganda fall to Germany or the Congo Independent State. Because no existing traffic could justify the investment and the colonial governments lacked the resources to build a railroad on their own, construction required a separate act of the British Parliament, a conscious subsidy paid for by the British taxpayers and justified to them as a way of combating the slave trade and of cutting the costs of administering Uganda so far from the coast.

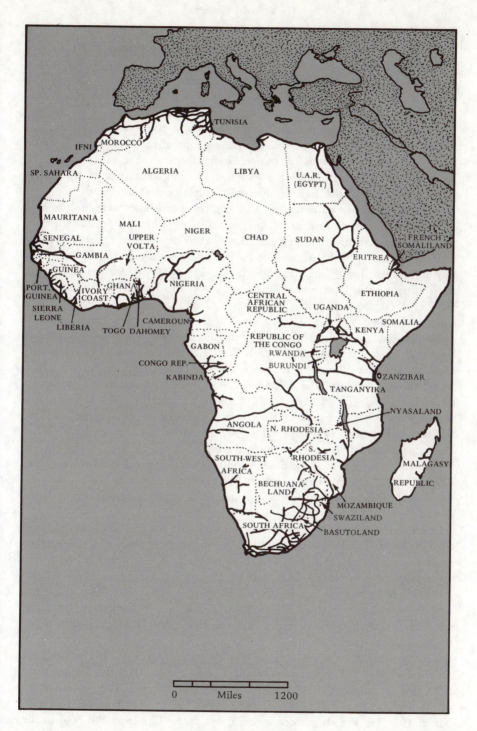

Railways in Africa, 1960

Once the line was built, however, the colonial governments of Kenya and Uganda were anxious to reduce their operating losses by trying to shape economic development so as to create traffic. Because the railroad passed through the relatively cool and well-watered highlands, it was natural to think of agricultural development, and the "white highlands" policy followed as an indirect result of railroad construction for humanitarian and political ends. Further inland, in Uganda, the railroad was the obvious incentive that sparked government sponsorship of cotton cultivation. Indirectly, then, the rail line was an important factor both in creating a settler problem in Kenya and in setting the stage for the paternalistic character of economic development in Uganda.

All rail lines had important political consequences. Many were built to link a particular hinterland to a particular port, usually within the framework of a single colonial territory. The transportation systems thus created a physical reality that gave meaning to the colonial boundaries, however accidental their creation may have been during the scramble. In the French West African territories, feeder lines of this kind brought exportable goods to Dakar from Senegal and the French Sudan, to Conakry from French Guinea, to Abidjan from the Ivory Coast and Upper Volta, to Lomé from Togo, and to Cotonou from Dahomey (now the République du Bénin). But these lines were never given the internal links that might have created a French West African rail network. By contrast, Nigeria, the other colonial federation in West Africa, built a rail network that served the northern hinterland through Lagos in the west and Port Harcourt in the east; this helped to tie the north to the two southern regions and to create interregional interchange during the crucial decades of the colonial period. The fact that francophone (French-speaking) West Africa lacked a similar basis for intercommunication was part of the background for the breakup of the French West African federation at the time of independence. In much the same way, the long period of intercommunication in Nigeria formed part of the background that kept Nigeria a single country in spite of the attempted secession of Biafra during the years 1967–1972.

Though the French failed to link up their rail lines in West Africa, they tried to use rail links to pull together the disparate territories of their other federation of Equatorial Africa. It was no easy task. The closest rail link to the savanna country in central Chad was over Nigerian railroads or those of the Anglo-Egyptian Sudan. Exports from Ubangi-Shari (now the Central African Empire) could have reached the sea most easily through Cameroon. But these alternatives would have required substantial investment in new railways, while the navigable course of the Congo and Ubangi rivers gave a clear run from near Bangui southward to Brazzaville on Stanley Pool. The rapids below the Pool required overland transportation to the Congo estuary, but the Congo State filled that gap during the 1890s with a railway from Matadi to the eastern shore of the Pool. At first, that railroad carried goods for the French colonies as well, but in 1914 the French decided to build a separate line from the Pool to the coast through all-French territory.

The result was the Congo-Océan railroad, only 317 miles long but one of the most notorious errors of the colonial era. It was prompted by French national pride and strategic considerations, but it was completely unjustifiable on economic grounds. It was not started until 1921 and not completed until 1934. Meanwhile, the Belgians across the river rebuilt the line from Matadi to Kinshasa, increasing its capacity tenfold by 1930, so that it could easily have accommodated the traffic of French Equatorial Africa as well as that of the Belgian Congo.

The Congo-Océan also posed special construction problems. It ran through a zone that was very thinly populated, so that workers had to be recruited elsewhere. They were, in fact, recruited by force from all parts of French Equatorial Africa. By the time the line was finished, some 127,000 individuals had worked on it for at least a short period, or more than 1 percent of the male population of the whole federation. Many of these men came from the savanna country in Chad and Ubangi-Shari, north of the forest zone. They were therefore unprepared for the diseases they encountered in the forested Mayombe highlands the railroad had to cross. They were also underfed and ill-housed. As a result, the overall death rate reached 10 dead for every hundred man-years of labor expended on the rail line, as high as 24 dead per hundred man-year at the peak of mortality, or a total of 45 dead workers for each mile of narrow-gauge track.

Even after it was finished, the Congo-Océan ran at a loss, and the loss was passed on as a tax burden falling most heavily on the same peasants whose fathers and grandfathers had built it. Government regulations forced as much traffic as possible to pass down the line of the rivers and by sea to Pointe Noire. Since peanuts from Chad and cotton from Ubangi-Shari were sold at the world market price, French insistence on their being shipped over a high-cost transportation route simply meant that peasants in Chad and Ubangi-Shari received a smaller share of that world price than they might have done if the crop had passed through Nigeria or Cameroon or the Belgian Congo.

The interplay of politics and economics worked somewhat differently in southern Africa. Railroad building there was economically feasible, as it rarely was in tropical Africa, but railroad politics tended to reinforce the rivalries of port towns, with each trying to secure or extend its economic domination over its hinterland. In the 1870s (after the diamond fields had opened at Kimberly) Cape Town, Port Elizabeth, East London, and Durban all began railways aimed at extending their reach to the new mining area. After gold was discovered on the Witwatersrand, these same lines were extended toward Johannesburg, but the South African Republic (Transvaal) was concerned about its own strategic position, which would have been weakened if its only access to the sea had been through British-controlled ports. It preferred to work out its own rail link to Lorenço Marques in Mozambique, which was incidentally the shortest route to salt water. Cape Town interests, though temporarily frustrated in their effort to build a line through to Johannesburg, were already extending the railroad from Kimberly northward, through Botswana and on into Rhodesia, until it finally reached the Zambian copper belt in 1909 and ultimately tied in to the Belgian system serving Katanga. (It was, incidentally, from a base on this rail line that Cecil Rhodes organized the Jameson raid into Transvaal, and the northern sections were initially financed by Rhodes's British South African Company.) But Cape Town in the last analysis was simply too far away to dominate the hinterland north of the Limpopo, much less north of the Zambezi.

Later rail lines reached out from Rhodesia through Mozambique to Beira. Finally, in 1976, the Tanzam railroad was completed from the copper belt to Dar-es-Salaam with aid from the People's Republic of China. Here again, the main objective was not economic but strategic — to free Zambia from dependence on rail lines passing through either Rhodesia, Angola, or Mozambique, all of which were still under European domination when the line was begun.

MIGRATION

Throughout Africa, economic change meant that people had to concentrate where resource endowment made development possible. They moved from a broad distribution based on agriculture largely for their own consumption into new patterns of concentration at railroad junctions, mines, plantations, administrative centers, or the port cities that grew up along the coasts to handle the export trade. The change of residence usually began with a temporary move, often seasonable and undertaken by young males alone. The migrants then returned again and again, brought their families or married in their new homes, and finally stabilized as new residents. This pattern of seasonable migration passing into a definitive change of residence was broadly typical of tropical and North Africa.

In South Africa, however, another form of migration developed that involved a regular and systematic oscillation of workers between nearly self-subsistent farming in the African reserves and wage work for "European" farms, mines, or in the towns. The difference here was that labor was discouraged from becoming stabilized in the new centers. The origins of this system went back to the Afrikaners' eruption onto the high veld and into Natal in the wake of the Zulu mfecane. The European migrants had two different and partly contradictory goals for the Africans they had conquered. They wanted land, and they took possession of the best land available. This implied a need to drive away the original owners. But the European farmers also wanted *some* Africans around — just enough to meet their demand for laborers to work the land. Even before 1900, the South African colonies and republics passed laws designed simultaneously to drive off "excess" labor, to control the African labor force, and to make sure that additional labor could be recruited when needed. One set of laws limited the number of Africans who could remain as "squatters" on "European" land. Vagrancy legislation helped to give the European farmers a measure of control over the workers.

All Africans were meanwhile forced to pay high rates of direct taxation —

hut or poll taxes — the intention being to force them into the wage sector, on the theory that African farmers were underemployed on their own land. Taxation of this kind began in Natal in 1849, and in time it spread to nearly the whole of colonial Africa. At first, the payments were set high enough to pinch — for instance, a month's wages in a single payment, sometimes even more. And the rates could be adjusted to meet specific goals. The Transvaal legislation of 1870, for example, provided that Africans working and living on "European" farms should pay only £.125 sterling each year. Those who worked for Europeans but lived elsewhere paid £.25, while those who lived and worked on their own land had to pay £.50.

After gold mining began on the Witwatersrand, labor recruitment became more systematic. The Chamber of Mines set up a central recruiting organization to serve the whole industry, and it soon reached outside the Transvaal and even beyond the British South African colonies. By 1910, non–South African recruits from Mozambique had become the main source of unskilled labor for the South African mines. During the interwar years, South African practice and theory agreed that African labor *should be* migratory in regular oscillations. The "Europeans'" underlying belief was that Africans should be supported by the land in the reserves unless their labor was needed in "European" South Africa; but then they were to come as temporary sojourners only, never as residents with a right to remain. In fact, the reserves could not support all the people assigned to them; periodic labor in the towns was a necessity, both for the workers and for the industry they served. South African legislation meanwhile tended to limit the period of each visit, and the presence of women and children on the reserves was a pull that made for periodic visits "home." In effect, the low wages paid African labor in the cities and farms were subsidized by the labor of women and children on the reserves.

But oscillating labor was not cheap, even though the wages were low. Short-term migrants were unskilled and inefficient, and it was expensive to train them for the new jobs. Some people in the mining industry came to realize at an early date that the cost per unit of work performed was inordinately high. In the early 1920s, Union Minière, the largest mining company in Katanga (now Shaba), began to stabilize mining labor by encouraging workers to bring their wives and families and settle down as long-term residents of the mining towns. Union Minière's labor turnover thus dropped from 96 percent per year in the early 1920s to less than 7 percent ten years later. In the 1930s, mining companies in northern Rhodesia also shifted to a policy of stabilizing the labor force.

These experiments were known, of course, in South Africa, but there European trade unions and European opinion generally feared that stabilized labor would ultimately mean African competition for the skilled jobs reserved for European workers. Still further in the future, it might threaten to integrate the races. South African mines, and to some extent industry as well, therefore kept to oscillating labor as a matter of policy, though some stabilization took place as a matter of fact. Nevertheless, by about 1950 it was estimated that at any particular time half a million Africans with households in the reserves were absent, at work elsewhere in South Africa. By implication, then, in the early fifties more than two million men spent their lives shifting back and forth between work in the "white" portions of the Union of South Africa and relatively inefficient agriculture in neighboring countries or the South African "native reserves."

For North Africans, industrial Europe was a similar magnet for labor migration, with a similar tendency toward oscillation. Algerians began going to France as temporary migrants during the interwar period, and larger numbers from all three Maghrib territories began to go after the Second World War — rising from 40,000 in 1946, to nearly a quarter of a million on the eve of the Algerian war for independence in 1954, to nearly a million in 1970. The size of the migration, in short, was about the same in the 1960s as the movement of Africans into "white" South Africa, and it was substantially greater than the number of Europeans still resident in the Maghrib. As in South Africa, the North Africans gradually became dependent on wage work in France. As early as 1954, it was estimated that migrants' remittances were equal to the total wages paid by Algerian agriculture, so that work in France directly or indirectly supported about a quarter of the Algerian population. At the same time, the French economy became increasingly dependent on a labor force drawn from North Africa and less developed parts of Europe, such as Spain and southern Italy. As in South Africa, Algerians and other migrant workers were not encouraged to settle down as permanent residents; their lack of skills forced them into the worst-paid jobs; and their legal rights were inferior to those of French citizens; but they were not subject to the full range of overt discrimination Africans had to accept in South Africa.

Migration was equally intense in tropical Africa, but there the population moving to the cities and centers of export agriculture tended to settle permanently after an experimental period of seasonal migration. In West Africa west of Nigeria, the principal flow carried people from the savanna into the forest belt and the coastal cities — in Senegambia, westward to the peanut-growing region or ports like Dakar. Seasonal migration continued even after the Second World War, with about four seasonal migrants for each permanent migrant in a typical year, but the permanent migration was more important over the years and brought about a really significant shift in population. For all West Africa west of Nigeria, the forest and coastal region had about a third of the total population before 1920; by 1970, it had half the total, and this shift implied the permanent displacement of about three million people, who, with their descendants, came to make up about a fifth of the coastal and forest population. Nigeria was a little different from the rest of West Africa in that its growth centers were more evenly distributed between savanna and forest. Some people, especially skilled and clerical workers, moved north from the forest to cities like

Kano or Kaduna, while other, less skilled workers were simultaneously moving south to the coastal towns or the cocoa and kola regions in the forest.

Most East African migration other than the large movements from Rwanda and Burundi to other, less-overpopulated territories also took place within colonial boundaries. The Kenya highlands and cities like Mombasa and Nairobi attracted people from other parts of Kenya. Tanganyikans also moved to the towns, to sisal plantations near the coast, and to the clove plantations of Zanzibar and Pemba offshore; some were even attracted as far away as the gold mines of South Africa.

People also moved for noneconomic reasons, to avoid forced labor, for example — especially from French West Africa to the British colonies, where forced labor was far less extensive in the interwar period. Muslims from all over Africa traveled to Mecca as a religious duty, and many took years, working along the way. Some settled down and never returned home. The Republic of the Sudan in particular attracted a large concentration of pilgrim-settlers. The census of 1955 showed that fully a fifth of the whole Sudanese population came from further west, perhaps a third of these from west of Lake Chad. Migration of political refugees was also common. Some Muslims in the Futaanke empire of the upper Niger valley fled eastward into Nigeria when the French defeated the Lamido Juulbe. Others from Nigeria fled still further east when the British conquered northern Nigeria. After independence, the movement of political refugees again became important. More than 100,000 Tutsi fled from Rwanda when the Hutu peasantry rose against their former masters in 1962 and afterward. Even more Hutu fled from the Tutsi government of Burundi in the late 1960s. Still others were expelled or became involuntary refugees. In 1969–1970, Ghana expelled more than 200,000 foreign-born residents — many of whom had lived there for decades — for reasons of simple xenophobia mixed with fear of economic competition. And in 1971, Uganda expelled the Indians. Ethnic rivalries, indeed, brought major population movements whenever a postcolonial state threatened to break apart, as happened when Katanga tried to secede from Zaïre in the early 1960s, or again when Biafra tried to secede from Nigeria in the late 1960s.

In its broadest setting within the sweep of world history, however, the African migrations of the colonial period and later were part of a much more extensive and worldwide movement from the less industrialized to the more industrialized zones of the world economy. It included the movement of peasants into cities, of Koreans into Japan, of Turks into West Germany, and of Chicanos to California, just as it also included, as part of a broader picture, the South Africans in Soweto and the Algerians in slums outside Paris or in *bidonvilles* on the outskirts of Algiers. In each of these cases, the specific problem has its own particular character — just as South African race relations grew out of the special circumstances of South African history — but they all share other characteristics with Africa. In all these cases and their many equivalents in other countries, the immigrant cultural minority has fewer rights under the law than the old residents. This inequality poses a worldwide series of problems that reaches far afield to touch other aspects of social life, from race relations to educational policy.

Migration, in short, is a secondary offshoot of industrialization, which has the economic power to order a redistribution of resources and people toward the centers of growth. For Africa, migration and culture conflict growing out of migration began before the colonial period, with the first African effort to respond to the industrial demand for its raw materials. They continued during the colonial period, heightened by intentional emphasis on an export economy, and they continue after the colonial period as a fundamental factor behind many of Africa's social and economic problems. But the problem of migration is only one aspect of a broad pattern of intellectual and social change that drew on political and economic bases laid down during the colonial period.

SUGGESTIONS FOR FURTHER READING

Berry, Sata. *Cocoa, Custom, and Socio-Economic Change in Rural Western Nigeria.* London: Oxford University Press, 1975.

Brett, E. A. *Colonialism and Underdevelopment in East Africa: The Politics of Economic Change.* London: Heinemann, 1973.

Cruise O'Brien, Donal. *The Mourides of Senegal: The Political and Economic Organization of an Islamic Brotherhood.* Oxford: Oxford University Press, Clarendon Press, 1971.

Hill, Polly. *Migrant Cocoa Farmers in Ghana.* Cambridge: Cambridge University Press, 1963.

Houghton, D. Hobart. *The South African Economy.* 2nd ed. Cape Town: Oxford University Press, 1967.

Meillassoux, Claude. *The Development of African Markets and Trade in West Africa.* London: Oxford University Press, 1972.

Munro, J. Forbes. *Africa and the International Economy.* London: Dent, 1976.

Van Der Horst, Sheila. *Native Labour in South Africa.* Cape Town: Oxford University Press, 1942.

Van Onselen, Charles. *Chibaro: African Mine Labour in Southern Rhodesia, 1900–33.* London: Pluto, 1976.

Wilson, Francis. *Labour in the South African Gold Mines, 1911–1969.* Cambridge: Cambridge University Press, 1972.

Chapter 18

African Religion, Art, and Thought in the Colonial Era

THE EUROPEAN IMPERIALISTS in Africa justified their presence by a self-imposed task, a civilizing mission, *to civilize* being defined in a standard French encyclopedia of the day as "to improve the moral, intellectual, and industrial condition of a country or people." "To improve" meant, of course, to remake in the European mold, and the colonial impact in that direction was undoubted. The process involved a gigantic clash between African and European values and ideas, a clash that was perhaps subtler and less spectacular than political or economic conflict, but just as significant for the colonial era and the African future. The imperialism of the mind was no less important than political or economic imperialism.

Not all Europeans believed in their own justification, however; many colonial administrators under the influence of pseudoscientific racism regarded the true "civilization" of Africa as an impossible task, better not attempted. But the missionaries had cultural change as their main endeavor, and almost all other Europeans regarded their own culture as vastly superior to anything in Africa. They reflected this attitude in all aspects of their behavior. They were therefore culturally abrasive to Africans, whether consciously or unconsciously. Nor was the clash of cultures muted by the occasional European effort *not* to change African cultures, though such efforts did exist.

CHRISTIAN MISSIONS

Even religions claiming to have the whole and only Truth do not necessarily proselytize. Judaism stopped after the first century A.D., and Islam had no formal missionary organization before this century; but Christianity has a very ancient proselytizing tradition stretching back to Saint Paul. Ethiopia, the Sudan, Egypt, and the Maghrib were all converted to Christianity by missionaries before the rise of Islam, but the missionary tradition could also be quiescent for long periods. Neither the Coptic Church of Egypt nor its Ethiopian offshoot made very significant efforts to convert "pagans" until the twentieth century. European Catholicism made little effort at peaceful conversion in any part of Africa until the late fifteenth century, when the Portuguese first made maritime contact with sub-Saharan Africa. The Catholic Reformation of the mid-sixteenth century stimulated a broad effort both in Europe and overseas, which bore fruit mainly in the kingdom of Kongo and in Angola during the seventeenth century. Christianity survived in Kongo even after the missionaries lost control during the eighteenth and nineteenth centuries, though it became closely integrated with existing Kongo religions. Protestant missionary activity anywhere overseas was quiescent until the late eighteenth-century pietistic revival in Germany and the Evangelical revival in England. Their African missions began in the 1790s and reached a new peak of activity in South, West, and East Africa during the 1840s. The new Protestant effort inspired a competitive response from Catholics, especially after the mid-nineteenth century, with new orders like the White Fathers founded specifically for African missionary work.

Protestant and Catholic goals and doctrines were quite different. Many of the Protestant denominations were deeply influenced by the Evangelicalism that had grown out of the Wesleyan movement and its continental equivalents. For them, salvation came through grace acquired in an intense personal way. They laid great stress on Bible study and moral conduct, which implied a rather drab lower-middle-class existence illuminated by flashes of spiritual insight. Cleanliness and thrift were considered major virtues. Most amusements were condemned as frivolous traps of the Tempter, and these tended to include gambling, alcohol, tobacco, dancing, and drumming. The cardinal sin was the carnal sin — sex. In the spirit of the Victorian age, this prudery implied strong opposition to nakedness and, obviously, to polygyny. Some of the fundamentalists found that faith was more important to religious life than training for the ministry, so that many pastors were not educated to the equivalent of a university degree.

By contrast, Anglican, Lutheran, and Catholic missionaries were better educated and more firmly governed. Among them, ritual was more important; grace came to those who observed the liturgy guided by the clergy. Personal salvation was still stressed, however — a goal that ran counter to the communal ethics of most African societies, though the link between Christian duty and European culture was less strict. Amusements were allowed and lapses were more easily forgiven. The fact that Catholic clergy were celibate, while the Protestant were not, made a big difference. The European pastors' households became a standard for measuring proper conduct, and they made for a greater Westernization of ordinary life than was likely where male missionaries ran a more relaxed bachelor's establishment. The Catholic priesthood was also trained to at least the European university standard; and the possibility of achieving this status was held out to converts, though the commitment to education varied with the order, ranging from the traditional Jesuit emphasis on learning to the Salesians, who recruited missionaries in working-class circles and specialized in technical training. The Protestant emphasis on Scripture automatically called for basic literacy, but not necessarily for much more, and rarely reached beyond the level of European secondary schools even for the "native clergy."

But the ways in which missionaries went about their work were probably more important than their education in determining the missionaries' social or intellectual impact. The first steps usually included building a house or a church on a plot leased from the local authorities or granted by the government. Funds came from Europe at first, though local collections and grants from the colonial government for such activities as education and health became more important during the high noon of colonialism. The first to flock to the mission were usually those who had little to lose. Especially in East and Central Africa, they were often slaves who had been bought and liberated by the missionaries, people displaced by war or disease, the uprooted generally. The crucial fact is that they moved their residences to the mission village. After a few years, converts would appear who were willing to be baptized and identified to all as people of the mission. The growth of mission villages, in short, reproduced here and there throughout Africa a phenomenon very similar to the one that produced rapid assimilation of Western culture among the recaptured slaves settled in Sierra Leone in the early nineteenth century. An alternative missionary approach was to begin by trying to win over an African ruler, in the hope that his subjects would follow. This was not possible once a colonial regime had come into existence, but it was the pattern in Botswana, Madagascar, Buganda, and with Msiri, and its consequences, where it was successful, held over into the colonial period.

At times, this separation of Christian villages under the protection of missions could lead to a clash with colonial authorities, who believed, sometimes quite correctly, that the missionaries had turned themselves into secular rulers. One celebrated case involved the Jesuits' practices in lower Zaïre. Here, they began about 1895 with the resettlement of large numbers of orphan children entrusted to the mission in the wake of sleeping sickness epidemics. They first assigned these orphans to a "chapel farm" directed by a young unmarried man. By 1902, some 250 of these villages had come into existence; they were mostly self-supporting and thriving, but they were under no other authority than that of the missionaries — not even African adults. The mission had its own courts and its own penal system, which made it a state within a state. It had to give up the fullest of these claims in 1914, but other missions could be found protecting "their people" from secular authority until well after the Second World War.

By the 1920s and 1930s, most missions had shifted their emphasis from converting adults to that of enrolling children in schools where Christianity was part of their education. By the time of independence, 50 million Africans had become Christian, roughly half the population outside Muslim areas. The leadership of African Christianity had by that time passed into African hands. The other half of the population was also influenced by Christianity, but African

Christianity was not necessarily identical in doctrine and ritual to the forms the missionaries had brought to the continent, nor were all African Christians equally committed. This Africanization of Christianity does not imply that the religion had become "impure." Rather, it was simply shifted to a new cultural setting, as had often happened before — including the initial shift of Christianity from the Jewish Levant to the Latin West.

Conversion began with the problem of translation. A catechist trying to explain the creed was inevitably inspired to make analogies and parallels with local culture, if only to make sense of the unfamiliar teaching. Some aspects of doctrine were inevitably altered in the process. At the outset, the role of the first converts was of crucial importance, though often hard to document. It was they who informed the missionaries, taught them the local language, helped to translate the Scriptures. In Uganda and elsewhere, the enthusiasm of the catechists dictated a pace of Christian expansion far more rapid than the missionaries themselves planned.

Conversion, even in the beginning, was often a group phenomenon. A local population would see Christianity as a new movement, equivalent to one of the older or classical African religious movements to which they had sometimes rallied in the past in times of stress. The imposition of the colonial order was experienced as a time when evil in the world was on the increase, thus necessitating new measures to deal with it. Joining the church could therefore take place with the usual signs that accompanied the acceptance of a new movement — fervor and enthusiasm, destruction of charms, and so on. Other acts of conversion might be ordered by the ruler and include whole villages. Real conversion by personal decision came only later. Many conversions were also a matter of family decision to place one member of the lineage with a potentially powerful alien leader. At the height of the colonial period, other motives came to the fore, including a need to learn a European language so as to hold a skilled job or become a clerk. People sometimes chose one denomination rather than another on the basis of the type of education it offered. Alternately, the choice of denomination might depend on political motives. A kind of protest could be registered by joining a nonofficial church — the Catholic in Tanzania or Rhodesia, for example, or the Protestant in the Belgian Congo.

Opposition to Christianity on the part of the traditional or classical African religions was surprisingly slight. They tended to stress ritual and communal participation above all else. The participant's belief about the meaning of the ritual was less important. Christian ritual could therefore simply be added on Sunday. Friction became inevitable only when African Christians refused to participate in other rituals; they often had to choose between leaving their African community or becoming "backsliders" in the eyes of the Christian community. The most violent opposition to the new churches was registered in defense of seemingly nonreligious practices. In Kenya, for example, a violent outburst against the Christians came in defense of clitoridectomy, or the removal of part of the female clitoris in an operation parallel to male circumcision. The churches had been neutral about circumcision, but they tried to ban clitoridectomy as a savage practice. What Africans resented most, in short, was not the new doctrines but the attempts to impose a European code of ethics. African resistance was therefore strongest in defense of marriage customs like polygyny or the payment of bridewealth.

The position of the African clergy was an important source of conflict between the converts and the missionaries. In spite of some strong implications in Christian doctrine concerning the equality of all human beings before God, most missionaries of the early twentieth century were deeply influenced by pseudoscientific racism. They preached spiritual equality but they dragged their feet when it came to training an African clergy to replace themselves. Some African priests had been ordained in past centuries, and institutions like Fourah Bay College were founded to help train an African clergy. The first Catholic priest trained in a local seminary in the Belgian Congo was ordained in 1917, and after a time lag, bishops were consecrated and African cardinals were named as well, but more or less overt discrimination against the African clergy continued in the actual administration of the churches until the 1950s. This discrimination aroused African resentment from the early colonial period onward. Especially in the Protestant churches, it led whole congregations to split off from the parent missionary church. The new Africanized churches, which dropped the institutional links but retained doctrinal orthodoxy were sometimes called "Ethiopian" churches, as distinguished from others called "Zionist" that both broke the institutional tie and departed from a strict adherence to missionary teaching.

AFRICAN RELIGIONS

Islam was by far the largest of the precolonial African religions, and it continued to expand during the colonial period. But this expansion was not general or continuous. It was extremely rapid in West Africa, so much so that today most of the northern savanna of West Africa seems well on its way to becoming completely Muslim. The process of conversion there drew on the profoundly African historical roots of Islam, as well as on the heritage of enthusiasm left over from the great nineteenth-century *jihads*. In East and Central Africa, on the other hand, Islam spread less rapidly than Christianity did. It has been argued that West Africans preferred Islam to Christianity as a form of protest against colonial rule, but, if so, this was not the case in East Africa. Nor did the religious frontiers change much in the horn of Africa or the Nilotic Sudan; it was only in the Boran and the Nuba mountains that Islam made any gains at all. All around the fringes of Ethiopia, old religious animosities were so strong that peoples' very identities were expressed in religious terms.

In North Africa, the major question was the relationship between Islam and modernization. A minority of secularized and Western-educated intellectuals rejected religion altogether. At the other extreme, a vocal group of preachers held that everything modern or Western was evil in itself, though their follow-ing dwindled decade by decade. Otherwise, many positions between these extremes were possible, and they were argued most passionately in Egypt, par-ticularly at al-Azhar university. Even before the foundation of the British protectorate, Jamal al-Dīn al-Afghāni had claimed that all modern progress had been revealed in Islam and could be reconciled with that religion; if only Muslims would unite under a single caliph, they would be more than equal to the Christians. This form of Muslim nationalism was an important factor in Urabi Pasha's revolt in 1880–82, and the doctrine of Islamic modernism was further elaborated by Muhammad 'Abdu, who became mufti of Egypt before 1900. By the interwar period, however, the most important split in Egyptian Islam was no longer between the older 'ulamā and the rising modernists. A more intense reaction toward a glorified Muslim past appeared as the goal of a group identified as "new traditionalists," and these men became the core of the Muslim Brotherhood. But it was as much a political as a religious movement, with cells probably copied from Communist practice, schools, a medical service, and a military arm. It became a major force in Egyptian politics in the 1940s and 1950s, with as many as 200,000 members, and it was only suppressed in 1966 after the military coup had oriented the Egyptian revolution in another direction.

Further west in North Africa, the older tendencies of sufi Islam continued and were sometimes strengthened, as for instance, by the continued power of the Sanūsīya in Cyrenaica and its vicinity, or even by the rise and importance of the Tijānīya throughout the Maghrib, though the Tijānīya was apolitical or even pro-French through much of the colonial period. But alongside these older tendencies was the influence of Islamic modernism, frequently traceable to Muhammad 'Abdu and his followers in Egypt and the Levant. As their doctrine would suggest, the modernist opposition to European rule tended to take the form of participation in Western-style political movements like the Destour Party in Tunisia. In Algeria and Morocco as well, they were found alongside secular-minded nationalists in all the protest and opposition movements that were to grow into the political parties that finally won independence in the 1950s.

South of the Sahara and west of Lake Chad, modernism was far weaker. The Tijānīya grew into the most important single order, surpassing the Qādirīya, which nevertheless remained strong. But here too, new religious orders were founded. The Murīdiya in Senegal was one of the most important of these, and for reasons other than its crucial role in agricultural colonization. Just as it had been an offshoot of the Qādirīya, another new order, the Hamaliya, was founded in 1925 near Nioro as an offshoot of the Umarian Tijānīya. Though its followers were far fewer, it was more widespread than Murīdiya; and it was more impor-tant as a continuing source of opposition both to the French and the old African elite. It appealed especially to the downtrodden, admitting both women and slaves into close-knit congregations that had something of the character of a secret society intentionally isolating itself from the rest of the population. Other influences came from Asian Islam, especially through the Ahmadiya whose head-quarters were in Pakistan. It proselytized on the model of Christian missions, having regular outposts to spread its particular version of Muslim doctrine through the agency of paid teachers. Its doctrine also deviated somewhat from Middle Eastern orthodoxy by incorporating Christian, Jewish, Mazdean, and Hindu elements, and holding, among other things, that Muhammad was not the last of the prophets.

Classical African religions also continued and they held the allegiance of half the population outside Muslim Africa. But they also came under the influ-ence of Islam or Christianity. The notion of God in the monotheistic religions influenced their conception of a First Cause, for example. But their most dynamic contribution in the colonial period was the phenomenon of new religious move-ments that spread rapidly, and often over long distances. They had something in common with precolonial "witch-finding" movements, but the term is really no more accurate than it would be to call a Christian revival a "sin-finding" movement. Not many of this new type of movement are reported for the pre-colonial period, but more may well have existed. One such movement, however, the Chwezi or *Mmandwa* cult, spread to the whole of the East African lake region from a source that was probably in Bunyoro.

Such movements began with the visions of a leader. His or her prophetic inspiration, often derived from dreams, became convincing to the local com-munity, usually after several years had elapsed. Once the community accepted the message, it followed new, highly emotional rituals of renewal. The new message embodied in the rituals was usually constructed from well-known symbols in new combinations and invested with a new meaning. The first con-gregation developed internal organization and leadership. The movement would then spread, often irregularly, from one place to another, but often very fast. Its progress would appear more like the outbreak of a rash on the map than an advancing weatherfront. Initiation often assumed a theatrical quality. Because dreams were considered to be significant almost everywhere, secondary leaders could elaborate on the original cult. When it moved into a new culture area (which entailed temporary slowing down of the rate of diffusion), the content could be translated by subsidiary leaders into new sets of symbols familiar to that area. Internal organization could vary; even the name might change while the movement spread.

Most explanations have sought the causes of these movements in social factors: the felt need to protest, or the revolt of the downtrodden in a period of rising expectations — much the same factors, in short, as are used to explain the rise of African Christian churches. Some were clearly a focus for early resistance to colonial rule, just as older cults like the Mwari in Rhodesia or secret associations like the Poro in West Africa were foci of resistance. Examples would include the Dinka and Nuer prophets who opposed the Egyptian second-ary empire, or war-charm movements in Madagascar and the Congo basin. The best known, however, is Maji-Maji in Tanzania during the first decade of this century. Its religious leader was Bokero, a priest of a widely revered nature spirit near Rufiji. At a time of crisis following the imposition of compulsory cotton cultivation, he and other priests began to turn out war medicine in the same way they had once provided fertility medicines dependent on the strength of this same spirit. The word *maji* means "water" in Swahili, and the function of the war charms was to turn bullets into water — a common feature of other movements using war charms. Once the movement had spread beyond its heartland, it went beyond mere protective medicine to take on the characteristics of a full-fledged religious revival, claiming the power to remove two kinds of evil: witches and Europeans. But the movement seems to have died out more quickly than most, perhaps because it retained its focus on the war charms.

Christian Africans had equivalent movements in their secessions from the official churches. The earliest secession, the Ethiopian type, can be traced to Angola in the early seventeenth century, whereas the first of the Zionist type was founded in 1694 by Chimpa Vita Beatrice in the kingdom of Kongo. Such movements flourished even more after the nineteenth century. A recent estimate for independent churches in sub-Saharan Africa puts the number of movements at about 6,000 and the number of people affected at nearly 8 million, or 14 percent of all African Christians. The number of movements is not so important, because it includes small splinter groups along with major movements like the Kimbangist church, with its half million followers, and the widespread Bapostolo movement, which is found from South Africa north to Tanzania and Zaïre. The total numbers nevertheless indicate the extent of schism in African Christianity, a further reminder that schism is a basic tendency in all African religions, especially if the new Islamic brotherhoods are taken into account.

Like its counterparts in the classical African religions, independent Christian movements usually began with a visionary leader, prophecy, an important role for dreams, and the reassessment of existing symbols. A previous connection with an official church was also important, and the majority of leaders seem to have been catechists — hence associated with magisterial authority. This is a major difference from most non-Christian religious movements, because here the organization as well as the doctrine seems to have had Christian roots. Preaching remained central, and baptism was important as a form of initiation into the cult.

A great deal also depended on the prophetic and organizational gifts of the leadership. The African Greek Orthodox Church of Uganda had weak leadership when it emerged in 1929. The leader wanted autonomy, but he also wanted respectability and equality with the other major churches. He therefore joined the general communion of the official Greek Orthodox Church in 1946, but again dropped out in 1966 to form the African Orthodox Autonomous Church after Greek missionaries (technical assistants) were judged to be inadequate. But some independent churches had hardly any visible leadership; the African Independent Pentecostal Church, for instance, was formed in Kenya in 1930 when local outposts simply declared their independence from the central mission station and then loosely "agreed" together.

In most cases, doctrinal elements were stated early and distinctively. Among the most famous prophets of the colonial period were William Wade Harris of Liberia and the Ivory Coast from the 1910s onward, Simon Kimbangu in lower Zaïre in the early 1920s, Maranke, the founder of Bapostolo, in Rhodesia about 1932, and Elliot Kamwana, the founder of Watchtower, in Malawi about 1908. The first three preached a distinct doctrine from the beginning. Kamwana's teaching, however, diverged very little from that of Jehovah's Witnesses, the parent body, though the doctrine altered almost beyond recognition on its spread into Zambia and Zaïre under the name Kitawala. At least a part of this innovative dynamism seems to have come from an absence of church organization.

Many founders of new churches were neither unusual nor impressive personalities; nor were they solitary "voices in the wilderness." Oshitelu, who founded the Nigerian Aladura Church in 1929, was one of several mystics prominent in his time and place. At least one founding figure was a European, a Franciscan priest and mystic, whose followers formed the *jamaa* movement in Zaïre and Tanzania and carried it beyond his control. Founders became prophets because their followers chose to see them as such; the message mattered more than the personality. Fervor mattered more than theology, and fervor continued as the essence of most of these movements for a long time before they became routinized.

No single explanation can cover the great variety of these movements. To call them "religions of the oppressed" or "a retaking of the initiative" is tempting but unprovable. They were not merely expressions of economic unhappiness or collective frustration, or of discontent with European rule. They were deviant movements, but not movements of deviants; they appealed to all levels of the population. Nor was Christianity itself to blame, as most African Christians remained with the ecclesiastical structure imported from Europe. Instead, a mixture of all these factors — and others — may have been present in each case. Perhaps the only thread tying them all together was the fact that these were communal congregations with face-to-face relationships among their members; as such they carried over the institutional forms of precolonial African religions.

One final religious current was prominent in the European world as well. This was the growth of secularization — in the end, of agnosticism. It began first in Egypt and seems associated with Westernization. It was strongest in the cities, among the higher classes, and the best educated, but it was not confined to these groups. Skeptical attitudes existed even within the framework of classical African religions. Given the pragmatic nature of many of these religions, the growth of secularism should be surprising only to those who have accepted the stereotypes of Africans as essentially superstitious. Few agnostics, however, showed much hostility toward religion, and many returned to their church when faced with a crisis. No organized group has yet taken a militant stand against *all* religion, though several African governments, both colonial and independent, have tried to cut back on the influence of particular religious organizations. Variants of Marxism dominate these new ideologies expressing secular sentiments.

EDUCATION

Education takes place in all societies as part of the process of socialization. In precolonial Africa, general education began at home as soon as a child learned his own language. Education beyond that might be quite informal, but apprenticeship at home or in the workshop of a craftsworker was essential for learning technical skills. Reading and writing were taught in Muslim Africa by village Koranic schools, or in Ethiopia by parochial schools. At this elementary level, the first object was to familiarize the students with the Holy Books, often making them learn portions by rote. A real grasp of the three Rs came only at the next level — the highest normally found in an ordinary village. Thus, formal instruction existed wherever literacy was found, but it might not extend very far.

Formal higher education was available only in the *medersa* of North Africa or the higher monastic schools of Ethiopia. Elsewhere, West African 'ulamā or Ethiopian *dabtara* taught higher skills on a more informal basis. These stressed disciplines considered ancillary to religion, such as grammar, literature, music (in Ethiopia), or law (in Muslim Africa generally). Still further advanced were disciplines considered to be culturally valuable, such as medicine, geography, history, and mathematics. Even in formal schools, education was a form of apprenticeship characterized by close personal relations between teachers and pupils; students were often attached to a single master, though they could switch from one to another. Ethiopian teachers usually remained attached to a particular monastery, while Muslim teachers were highly mobile, if not altogether itinerant.

In spite of early rudimentary European schools along the coast, questions of African education in a Western vein were posed seriously only in the nineteenth century. Missionaries were among the first to be concerned, since they too had a Holy Book to teach. They began with the idea that formal schools were essential to education, simply because education worked that way in Europe. For them, schools were places where pupils listened to teachers, took examinations, and received diplomas certifying knowledge. Discipline was important, not only to make children study but also to mold desirable habits. It may have been considered more important than learning itself.

Education was to be a major tool in the cultural conquest of Africa, and the colonial powers recognized that fact at an early date. France established the first government schools in Senegal in 1818 — not missionary this time, but run by laymen "out of respect of the Muslim faith." At first, Wolof was used as the medium of instruction, but later French became the sole teaching language for tropical Africa, even in elementary schools. Vocational training was the main goal of education in colonial Africa throughout the nineteenth century, but conflicting claims soon made their appearance. As early as 1854, the Senegalese government established an *Ecole des otages* (literally school for hostages) in Saint Louis, ostensibly for the education of the sons of hinterland chiefs and kings, who were sent there to reside as evidence of their parents' friendship for France. Here the object was to train an elite that would afterward be attached to

French interests. English-language equivalents later developed in British colonies, the first being a school for the sons and nominees of chiefs at Bo in Sierra Leone in 1905.

On the British side, the earliest schools were the mission schools of Sierra Leone, and the first South African center for instruction in English was founded in Cape Town in 1803. Most education was left to the missionaries, even when it was paid for by the government. The aim was straight conversionism, to make the pupils, in the words of an early report, "English in tastes, in opinions, in morals, in intellect." It consisted of the three Rs, with elements of grammar and geography, and a strong emphasis on religion. Authorities at least paid lip service to the ideals of vocational training for African pupils, but the Sierra Leone curriculum was definitely "clerkly." After 1843, Basel missionaries in Ghana taught more practical subjects and manual training, and they began giving elementary education in the local vernacular. The main line, however, remained an insistence that a knowledge of English was necessary for civilization, so that English and French educational systems in tropical Africa were remarkably alike, especially when mission schools were established in French-speaking territories.

After the European conquest, this pattern was transmitted all over tropical Africa, with small variations. Catholic missions and the Belgian Congolese government stressed early education in the vernacular, while the Portuguese and French insisted on the European language from the beginning. English territories sometimes gave primary education in the vernacular, though northern Nigeria and the Sudan were exceptions in discouraging missionary education for Muslim children. Northern Nigeria also kept Hausa as the language of instruction, stressed practical training more than was done elsewhere, and left free time for Koranic studies.

The contrast between this policy and that begun in Sierra Leone a century earlier represented the shift in European thought from conversionism to trusteeship. Manual and practical training was judged appropriate for students who would rarely rise to posts of command in their own societies. Too much education would only help produce a disgruntled and overambitious element, or so it was thought. And the general precedent of northern Nigeria was adopted as a recommendation by the First World Missionary Conference in 1910. But colonial administrations and missions still needed clerks and clergymen, and these were the occupations that promised upward mobility for educated Africans. Clerkly education therefore continued to be most in demand, while vocational training remained rudimentary.

Language and educational policy was not, in any event, wholly dictated by European wishes. Pressure from the students themselves led to the shift toward academic rather than "practical" subjects. Few pupils wanted to go through the cost and hardship of study, only to be prepared for rural life and a low living standard. They knew that good grades in academic subjects meant an opportunity for employment in the towns.

Though language policy led to a division of the continent into French-speaking, English-speaking, and Portuguese-speaking blocs even before 1914, thus mortgaging for the future ease of communication within Africa, Africans had strong views about the language of instruction and could sometimes make these heard even during the colonial period. In Kenya, for example, it was African opinion that pushed for and got primary instruction in English rather than Swahili, because Kenyans sensed that English was a world language that would open more doors to knowledge. In Tanzania next door, the decision after independence was to make Swahili the primary language of instruction, with the aim of making it the national language. North Africans tended to return to Arabic, for similar reasons, and Somalia substituted the local language for the English and Italian of the colonial period. Ethiopia, on the other hand, changed from the colonial Italian to a system of instruction entirely in English after primary school. The choices between the vernacular and a world language were far from clear in postcolonial Africa. Vernaculars gained a little in francophone territories, except Zaïre, which moved more firmly toward French. Whereas Tanzania might choose the vernacular to foster a sense of nationhood, the Republic of South Africa tried to impose vernacular education on the African majority in the reserves as a way of preserving parochialism and highlighting ethnic divisions. The government attempt to substitute Afrikaans for English in the African locations around Johannesburg was the spark that set off a wave of serious riots there in 1976.

Once a system of primary education had been created (with a somewhat different timetable for different parts of Africa), the colonial governments began moving on, first to teachers' training schools, then to ordinary secondary schools, seminaries, and vocational schools, and last of all to university education on a par with institutions in Europe itself. Two general options were available. One was to develop secondary and higher education fairly rapidly, sending some students to European universities at an early date, at the expense of mass education at a lower level. The second was to build primary education first and more thoroughly, so as to create a shorter and broader educational pyramid. Only the Belgian Congo took this second course. It made decolonization more difficult for lack of an educated elite, but had other advantages; in the early 1970s, the literacy rate in Zaïre was close to 40 percent, as against only about 25 percent in Ghana or Nigeria and 10 percent in Senegal.

In spite of a few pioneering efforts in Sierra Leone during the nineteenth century, secondary education was not considered seriously until after the First World War. Between 1922 and 1925, all the major colonial powers except Portugal published comprehensive policy documents on education. All praised the desirability of suiting secondary schools to African needs, but they also insisted on preserving an equivalence between African and European diplomas, which meant in practice following the standardized curricula of the unitary school systems then the fashion in Europe. The diploma became a passport to European "civilization" — and, far more importantly, a passport to jobs and entry into the new colonial elite.

The practical role of secondary schools was to become the strongest agents of Europeanization. Most were boarding schools, so that pupils were separated from their home environment and placed in another where every aspect of their lives could be molded to fit their teachers' mental image of "civilization." The training also emphasized social ethics and groomed pupils for leadership. This, too, was in line with the contemporaneous European tradition, where, in the 1920s, only a select minority went to high schools. It was also a European tradition to limit female education. Girls were not only a very small part of the total school population at any level; they were also taught domestic rather than academic skills and rarely went on to secondary schools. These policies foresaw a pattern for educated African families that would mirror the European pattern, in which men went to the office and women remained at home.

A specialized type of secondary school had the particular aim of preparing students for the administrative service, and these schools — like Katsina College in Nigeria, Achimota in Ghana, Fourah Bay in Sierra Leone, William Ponty in Dakar, Gordon College in Khartoum, or Kisantu in Zaïre — had an impact that can hardly be overrated. They were sometimes the nurseries of entire national elites — Westernized, alienated from the mass of the population, but fervent nationalists with the intention of exercising the leadership roles for which they had been trained.

The location of these schools was symptomatic of European expectations. Where settlers were few, more secondary schools were set up to train Africans for skilled, clerical jobs. By 1938, for example, Nigeria had forty-two full secondary schools; Uganda had one; but the settler colonies of Kenya, Nyasaland (later Malawi), and Northern Rhodesia (later Zambia) had none at all.

Universities came last. The first full university degrees for "European" South Africans could not be awarded until 1873, and Fort Hare, the first college for Africans, opened in 1916. The first Western-style university in North Africa was opened at Cairo in 1909, and universities elsewhere came only after World War II. Universities, in fact, implied a challenge to the whole colonial structure. But the curricula were not as culture-bound as those of the secondary schools, though they still kept equivalence with European degrees, and each colonial power followed its own university fashions. On the British-run campuses, teachers believed themselves to be more *in loco parentis* than their French colleagues did. French-run universities developed characteristically French bureaucratization, while the Belgian Congo had the most autocratically led university in Africa. But the freedom allowed students was generally sufficient to prevent their being as completely isolated from the rest of society as the secondary-school boarders had been.

Both rulers and ruled saw education as an instrument of power — an instrument to maintain power by transforming Africans into black Europeans, or an instrument to gain power and wealth through "modernization." But both misjudged the consequences and overrated the power of education. Africans did not become loyal Europeans, and degrees failed to solve all problems. Many students nevertheless took on aspects of Western culture, though they were blended with local ways. At times they took on the patterns of particular European subcultures to a remarkable degree, varying from incidentals like preferences in beverages or bread to significant notions about the proper organization of a government or a university. Such differences between elites have sometimes added misunderstandings to the relations between francophone and anglophone Africa.

Education in northern and southern Africa ran a different course, largely because the settler communities there demanded separate education for their own children. The trend had already begun in nineteenth-century South Africa, and segregated education became more rigid over time until the 1950s, when the government assumed complete control of all education for Africans. At the university level, it set up three ethnic colleges for Xhosa, Zulu, and Tswana respectively, as well as separate colleges for the Indians of Natal and the Coloured people of the western Cape. The intention was to isolate all ethnic and racial groups from one another as well as from the outside world.

The problem of separate schools for settlers was compounded in North Africa by the prior existence of a Muslim system for training a literate elite. The Egyptian precedent was crucial, because secular education was not only on a Western model; a specifically French model dated well back into the nineteenth century. Meanwhile, al-Azhar continued to flourish and to go its own way during the whole period of the British protectorate. Secular schools on a Western model were available to some North Africans in the Maghrib — sometimes alongside the settlers' children, but occasionally segregated. The fundamental ambiguity of education in two different cultural traditions continued after independence. The Moroccan Faculty of Letters in 1965, for example, offered three kinds of degree: a Moroccan degree in Arabic, a Moroccan degree in French, and a degree equivalent to the French standard. But the gap between secular and religious education has been narrowed slowly. In 1961, al-Azhar was partly reformed along the lines of a Western university, while Egypt has moved toward massive Arabization and expansion of the elementary school system. The countries of the Maghrib have tended to follow a similar course.

IDEOLOGIES

All collective thought is ideology, and all societies have ideologies covering a great range, including views about the world, the nature of man, the ideal society, or the proper behavior of one individual toward another. These can be called dominant ideologies, because they shape thought on other subjects. Even such subjects as the classification of plants and animals, a universal concern in precolonial Africa, were influenced by the dominant ideologies, because the classification of other living things follows the principles of classification believed to hold for people.

The whole ideology of any precolonial African society has never been recorded, but scholars have tried to explore mores of thought, either directly or through the study of symbols. They have studied the Dogon of Mali especially intensively over almost a generation, and these studies reveal a complex body of general ideas, myths, and classifications, as well as particular speculations by individual Dogon thinkers who began with the collective thought but then used it to deepen their personal understanding of the world.

Dominant ideologies affect everyday life as well as religion. Theory about disease, for example, often depends on ideas about ultimate reality and humanity's place in it. In some parts of Africa, people believed that illness and other misfortunes were the work of personal enemies who had sent them, and no physical cure could succeed unless the witch's curse was first removed. The medicine man therefore had to be a religious specialist as well as a herbalist. When these people heard about the germ theory of disease, they could accept it without giving up their old explanations. They now argued that germs were merely the agents of a witch; they caused the disease, but a witch must have caused them to harm one person instead of another.

Imported Christian religions also carried ideologies, including notions about personal responsibility, faith, the spiritual equality of men, and others that affected and still affect collective thought. Some of the values and ideas that came with Christianity eased the way for other Western ideological constellations like nationalism, a reaction against alienation, and socialism, though our knowledge of the history of ideas in Africa during the colonial period is still in its infancy.

Nationalism was an imported ideology that can be defined in many ways, but most historians would accept the definition of nationalism as "a state of mind, giving *supreme loyalty* among the groups to which a person belongs to his territorial state group." This state of mind became common in Europe only toward the end of the eighteenth century and was linked with other notions about democracy and equality. Its implicit corollary was that a single people should be united in a single independent state. In the context of nineteenth-century Europe, this implied that politically separated peoples with a common language, like the Germans, Italians, or Poles, should be united in a single state. The same word, *nationalism,* was also used in Europe for the movements of peoples who sought to break away from larger, multinational political units — Greeks from the Ottoman Empire, Irish from the United Kingdom.

It was this second kind of nationalism, as justification for an independence movement, that became most prominent in Africa south of the Sahara, but the other idea of unifying like peoples into a single state was already important in late nineteenth-century North Africa. It occurred especially in a pan-Islamic context with Jamal al-Dīn al-Afghāni in Egypt, the distant hope here being that all Muslims could once more be united in a single Islamic empire, as they had once been in the ninth century. But other goals were also available to Egyptians, depending on the way they chose to define the nation. They could see themselves as part of a greater Arabic-speaking world seeking its independence from the

Ottoman Turks, or they could see themselves more narrowly as Egyptians trying merely to protect their autonomous status within the Ottoman Empire and later to free themselves from the British protectorate and its aftermath.

South of the Sahara, the various meanings of nationalism were expressed by members of the Westernized elite even before the European conquests were completed. Edward W. Blyden was one of the earliest to take up these ideas. He was born in the West Indies but became a teacher in Liberia in the 1860s, was active in Sierra Leone from the 1870s, and remained an important intellectual voice for English-speaking West Africa generally until well into the twentieth century. He thought of an African nation, not a Liberian or Sierra Leonean nation, and his main concern was nation-building, though he evoked the names of European nationalists such as Kossuth, Bismarck, and Cavour. His first concern was education, especially higher education that could serve as a medium for integrating and preserving African values. J. E. Casely Hayford carried the ideology further still with his book *Ethiopia Unbound* (1911) and his organization of a National Congress of British West Africa in 1920. His ideal was not so much pan-African as pan-anglophone West African, and he looked to a state that would incorporate all the English-speaking territories from the Gambia to Nigeria, and where the commonalty would be an elite united by an English education and the goal of modernization. Marcus Garvey's appeal in the 1920s for an African homeland also had a strong emotional appeal. He wanted an African state, independent of European rule, that would be a center not merely for Africans but also for the national sentiments of the Afro-Americans of the diaspora.

In the longer run, these various pan-African themes were to be important ideologically as a background for common action through agencies like the Organization of African States, but the successful mass movements and political parties of the 1940s and 1950s opted for another framework — that of the existing colonial boundaries. The final cry was for independence within those boundaries, to be followed by modernization and nation-building, without regard for any preexisting sense of nationality. In the still longer run, a main problem after independence was to instill a sense of nationhood that would unite all citizens in loyalty to the state, a process still under way and rather slow to develop in parts of East Africa, and in some of the French-speaking states of Central and West Africa.

A rather different pattern of ideology emerged in South Africa. The Anglo-Boer War opposed two different European nationalisms, and Afrikaner nationalism grew in strength through the early twentieth century to become a central justification for white supremacy within the South African state — and for that state's independence from Britain. On the African side, an African National Congress was formed in 1909, taking its name from and modeled after the Indian National Congress, but with a program that aimed at equal rights for Africans and Indians within the South African state, not independence or autonomy. By a curious ideological twist, it was the "European" South African government that recalled preexisting African nations in the 1950s when it inaugurated the policy of apartheid or separate development, with the goal of autonomous and separate states for the Xhosa of the Transkei, the Zulu of northern Natal, and others. Most African South Africans through the 1960s still claimed that their goal was one of equal rights within a South African state, though a few radicals began to answer one racial nationalism with another and to look forward to the possibility of their own form of apartheid by expelling the European minority.

Ideology took still another turn in the tropical French colonies. The early phases were similar to those in British West Africa, with Blaise Diagne winning an election as deputy from Senegal to the French National Assembly under the slogan "Senegal for the Senegalese." But his practical thought was closer to that of Casely Hayford. He wanted a united French-speaking West Africa with continued ties to France, but new currents were to develop especially in the 1930s and among the hundreds of African and West Indian students who began to flock to Paris. There, they found themselves in close contact with many Europeans, and, for the first time, with Europeans who knew nothing at all about Africa, though they were thoroughly inbued with the current teachings of pseudoscientific racism with its automatic assumption of African inferiority. They also felt the strains of cultural alienation, as they tried to cross the cultural barriers and to meet the Europeans on their own ground — strains of ambivalence and alienation both from the way of life of their own childhood and from the way of life they were trying to master as a means of dealing with Europe. One result was the ideology of *négritude.*

The first leader was Aimé Césaire, a West Indian of African descent, and the movement's charter was his *Cahiers d'un retour au pays natal* ("Return to My Native Land," 1939). He claimed that European stereotypes about Africans were not necessarily incorrect, merely that what Europeans saw as vices were really virtues. Africans thus had a spiritual mission, in opposition to the cold, cerebral quality of Western civilization. Its essence was *négritude,* the quality of blackness, a warm, human, emotional, ethical, and generous approach. Ideas of an innate national character had been common in Europe for some time and were closely associated with pseudoscientific racism in the late nineteenth century. They also tied in with the combinations of racism and nationalism that emerged in the various European fascist movements of the 1930s, and they drew from strains of South Asian nationalism that tended to set off Asian spirituality against the materialism of the West.

Césaire's achievement, seconded by his fellow poet and onetime fellow student, Léopold Senghor of Senegal, was to turn an inferiority feeling into positive channels. To be "black" was no longer a stigma but a privilege. One result was to build a kind of confidence that was important to the struggle for independence, but the ideology was quite different from the usual Nigerian or East African intellectual response, which stressed the equality and similarity of all human races. The idea of negritude said something more; all were equal, but they were also different. "Black" people had their own peculiar strengths. A variant was to shift from blackness to Africaness — to *africanité*, in Senghor's version, or to the cult of the "African personality" as popularized by President Kwame Nkrumah of Ghana during the 1950s and 1960s.

Africanité, however, remained confined to sub-Saharan Africa and largely to French-speaking Africa. North Africans were already convinced of their own values, as reinforced by the intellectual renaissance of Islam. As far as they were concerned, their own civilization was fully equal to that of the West, if not superior; and it was certainly different. In sub-Saharan Africa, cultural alienation of the new elite had gone furthest in French and Portuguese territories, and it was in French-speaking Africa that the concept of *africanité* had its greatest appeal. The journal *Présence africaine* expounded the doctrine from 1947 onward, with its greatest influence again in French-speaking Africa, not merely because it was written in French but also because it was written in a way that appealed to alumni of the French educational system. After independence, *africanité* shifted slightly to become a search for *authenticité*, a search for the "authentic" and pristine African values of precolonial times. This last development was best expressed in Zaïre, where the Belgians had not sought to impose a homogeneous European national culture to quite the extent that France or Britain had done in their colonies. But, once formulated in Zaïre, the concept swept on to most other French-speaking countries.

The result was not necessarily a reaction, an effort to return to past culture; rather, intellectual innovation had to be legitimized by an appeal to the past. This is what happened with the socialist ideology in an African setting. In the beginning, socialism was intertwined with ideas of equality, "the rights of man." A just distribution of the world's goods seemed to go along with the just distribution of political power that was expected with independence. Many of the early nationalist leaders became familiar with socialism in its European setting. They found the British Labour Party or the Communist and Socialist parties in France and Belgium relatively receptive to their hopes for independence. Especially those who had lived or studied in Paris became familiar with the various strains of doctrinal Marxism. After independence, countries all over the African continent claimed to be socialist, but they rejected doctrinaire Marxism in favor of "African socialism." Many claimed that precolonial African cultures with their emphasis on the communal rights of lineages and other groupings had actually been "socialist." They approved of most of the goals of European socialists, such as the abolition of social classes and state control over production, but they left out the ultimate Communist vision of the withering away of the state.

One of the most persistent and systematic moves toward African socialism came in Tanzania under Julius Nyerere. Its ideology was spelled out in the Arusha Declaration of 1967. The basic tenets were to be equity and self-reliance. Equity was to come through cooperation within the framework of the local community or village, the *ujamaa* (a Swahili word derived from the Arabic word for community). In the ujamaa villages, ordinary farmers were to assume cooperative control over the means of production. The state stood by to provide assistance and to prevent the rise of a separate class of wealthy landowners. Rural development had first priority over urbanization or industrialization. Self-reliance was to be achieved by holding the world economy at arm's length, by avoiding heavy emphasis on the export sector. This angle drew something from contemporaneous Latin American thought concerning the political and economic dominance of the more developed countries over the less developed. The originality of Tanzanian socialism lies in its perception of the individual's role in relation to the community, but it also drew from a great array of socialist thought around the world, including Yugoslav and Chinese ideologies, and it had some faint reflections of *négritude*.

In spite of the common professions of socialism in postcolonial Africa, practical policies differ greatly. Most African governments are in fact military regimes; many others are one-party states with limited participation from the mass of the people. Some are even committed to liberal, nonsocialist ideologies. But in spite of these differences, they share a common aim: a primary emphasis on material progress as the goal, with state action and planning as the means. Along with this comes a general fear of "neocolonialism," meaning slightly different things to different commentators, but including the belief that after independence the industrialized nations still controlled African economic life, if not directly through political intervention, then indirectly through the power of multinational firms and even more indirectly through their control of the world market that sets the prices on goods Africans have to sell and on those they want to buy. An extreme version of this ideology insists that the very prosperity of the industrialized countries had been achieved only at the cost of underdevelopment elsewhere in the world.

VISUAL ARTS

The common stereotype concerning African visual art is that it began to decline on contact with the Western world and died out during the early colonial period. Along with that belief is the common Western view that African art, like African society, had been virtually changeless in precolonial times. But in fact, African art was changing constantly before the colonial impact began, it has changed continuously since, and it may well be that the second half of the twentieth century will be recognized by later generations as a period of important artistic renaissance. Some changes of the colonial period were related to changes in patronage, as the social classes that had once been the main users of art lost wealth and power and new consumers emerged. Others derived from new contacts with the non-African world, which made available new techniques, new materials, and the knowledge of new themes and styles.

To be sure, some of those who had once patronized artistic production now lost the occasion to commission new works, but the old elite did not fall suddenly from power, and it still placed orders. Yoruba chiefs in Nigeria continued to order carved doors for their palaces until the 1940s and kept up the structures almost unchanged in some cases, as at Akure. Artists still made masks for initiations and statues for cults. The local bourgeoisie in North Africa still bought chased brasswork, carpets, and other decorative craft production. Feasts with displays of finery, bodily decorations, dancing, and music still took place from time to time. And new patrons emerged. Even before 1918, African art began to be recognized in Europe, with Paris becoming the capital for the international diffusion of African art works to museums and private collections. Some of this art collected outside Africa was of precolonial origin, either looted from shrines or "bought" in forced sales to European officials, but most was produced by African artists during the colonial period itself.

New patrons emerged in Africa as well. Missionaries who had been destroyers of "fetishes" nevertheless encouraged Christian art and sometimes promoted commercial art through their schools. The first demand for church art was hampered by the insistence on following European canons such as the "golden proportions" of sculpture and painting, but in time African artists broke free, especially in the independent churches. A Harrist church at Bregbo in the Ivory Coast is an especially impressive monument built by Africans for Africans in a style that borrowed much from European church art but assimilated it completely to the older African tradition. A few administrators also patronized African art, and even a few foreign businesses. Examples can be found in the carved doors commissioned for Nigerian banks, and in the sculptures commissioned for an Esso station in Oshogbo, Nigeria.

Nor should tourist and "airport" art be neglected. Some of it had no more significance as original art than the Swiss cuckoo clock, but it provided craftsmen with employment, and here and there a painting or sculpture of real merit emerges. Tourist art first began to be produced in the interwar period, with such products as Buta ebony elephants from the Belgian Congo or Ugandan salad spoons. But increased demand after the Second World War brought some very impressive responses, including some from peoples who lacked a strong craft tradition. The Kamba in Kenya, for example, developed a craft industry specializing in hand-carved but mass-produced Maasai warriors, antelopes, and the like, dating back to about 1914, when Mutsiya Munge, a part-time carver of stools and spoons, went into full-time production. Part of the secret of the Kamba craft industry was the ability to take orders for hundreds of pieces and then to deliver them to the curio wholesalers. By the 1960s, thousands of carvings could be seen lined up in front of the airports and hotels where tourists were likely to stay, not only in Kenya but everywhere from Johannesburg to Dakar, and the naturalistic Kamba style has been widely imitated by others. Other, more recent production of East African carvings has been in the Makonde style, which draws far more on African models, though it too is mass-produced.

Still another kind of tourist art was more individual, some of it coming from the work of European art instructors who taught techniques of painting and sculpture but sought to avoid dictating styles, though their approval or disapproval certainly had an influence, and their workshops often turned out work that was stylistically distinctive. The most famous school of this kind began in the 1950s in Potopoto, a section of Brazzaville, then in the French Congo. The uniform medium was gouache, which was painted on blotting paper in a flowing, dynamic style without perspective. The stick-figure way of depicting people was vaguely reminiscent of doodles or rock paintings, and the paintings were sold by street peddlers all over Africa. Later on, in Kinshasa, this style evolved in the direction of abstract painting. Other paintings done in Lubumbashi recall European tapestries, while sculptures there used a few basic and massive forms covered with decorative patterns. A similar workshop at Salisbury in Zimbabwe evolved another style, in which the stone was carved in such a way as to preserve its original shape.

The subjects portrayed in commissioned art also changed in the colonial period, as they had been changing in the past, even though many of the classical masks and other objects were still carved in an evolved classical style. Europeans, with their pith helmets, hammocks, and carriers, and later on, with their bicycles, cars, trains, sunglasses, and sewing machines, began to be represented in African art even before 1900. As these phenomena were represented in African styles, they often appeared to Europeans as caricatures, though they were not. Other changes in subject were less obviously drawn from European influence. Animals and vegetation began to be shown more frequently, landscapes appeared, and religious iconography responded to the tastes of an urban African clientele, as well as to those of potential European customers.

New trade contacts brought new media for African artists and required new techniques. Oil paints for polychrome sculpture had been adopted in the nineteenth century. Foreign-dyed thread was used in textiles as soon as it became available, as was concrete for sculpture. Aluminum became a favorite medium for sculpture and jewelry about the time of the Second World War. Architectural techniques were revolutionized by modern engineering and its materials, while a great variety of steel tools made carving easier. Joinery in wood had been rare before 1900, but new techniques freed carvers from the constraints of volume imposed by the necessity of carving each piece from a single block of wood.

Styles also evolved, in continuity with the past traditions that were strongest in sculpture and graphic decoration. Local carvers in the classical line, such as Olowe of Ise in Nigeria, did remarkable work. Olowe is probably the greatest virtuoso Yoruba sculptor of this century, and his work bears comparison with the best Yoruba art of the past as well. Some critics have charged that the new work was shoddier, that it lacked the symmetry of the old, or that polychrome paints had had a disastrous effect. But much of this is pure snobbery, or the result of looking only at mass-produced commercial curios instead of at the best of recent art works. Neither new models nor new media destroyed creativity, though they led to variants of the classical style or to altogether new styles.

Objects as diverse as a Bamun aluminum crucifix in Cameroon, a wooden statue of a saint in Senegal, and concrete funerary monuments in lower Zaïre or in southern Nigeria all illustrate this point, though the usual museum collections and reference books on African art concentrate on classical styles and the older products.

Finally, it should not be forgotten that a Western education sometimes included art education, that many prominent artists now practicing in Africa were educated in European art schools, and that they paint or carve in a style that shows local influence but is nevertheless part of the larger ecumenical art tradition of the modern world. A painter like Afewerk Tekle of Ethiopia would be representative of a very diverse group. In response to critics who may say that their work lacks true African *authenticité*, it should be kept in mind that the ecumenical tradition itself owes much to African models and was incorporated in the Western tradition by Picasso and other Western artists earlier in this century.

THE PERFORMING ARTS

No direct records of the performing arts have survived from any date before the late nineteenth century, when the first sound recordings and still photographs of African dance were made. Knowledge of precolonial styles must therefore depend on the assumption that performances observed in this century must certainly reflect earlier traditions. Except for music, the Western challenge to the African tradition was very weak in these fields. Western art dances like ballet were rarely seen in colonial Africa. Western social dancing seemed mere foot shuffling and was of no inspiration to African dancers. Western officials and missionaries for their part, left African dancing alone unless it seemed lewd in their eyes — but even their attempted prohibition of "lewd" dances rarely had any influence. The European musical impact was stronger, coming first through hymn singing, Gregorian church music, and military bands, later on through dance music from radio programs and phonograph records. Only a tiny minority was exposed to Western art music, and very few were ever trained to perform or compose in that style.

Classical African dancing nevertheless changed in the colonial period. Initiation dances borrowed imaginatively from military parades and even gymnastics. Spirit-possession dances sometimes featured European body language, at least when they depicted Europeans. Costumes and body decoration played an important part in African dance, and these "minor arts" also weathered the colonial period, though they changed in response to new ideas about style and modesty in dress.

The bobongo, a completely new form of African ballet with vocal music, arose in Zaïre around 1910. It involved pantomime and song by a succession of figures until the culminating appearance of the prima ballerina, who descended from a kind of pagoda to be carried on the shoulders of her dancers. The bobongo was competitive, like intervillage wrestling elsewhere. It was a mock battle played in dance and song, with the prize going to the most spectacular or imaginative performance. And a single person created the whole form.

The Beni dance was even better known because it spread all over East and Central Africa from its origins in Lamu on the Kenya coast during the 1890s. It began with competing teams representing the antagonistic halves of the town, later adding aspects of military drill and appropriate bugle music. The Beni dancers also developed their own songs, with new variations as the movement spread, as well as new social connotations. In time, however, most Beni troupes disbanded as the older generation died out and the young turned to "jazz" entertainment, including modern songs and social dancing, in preference to the problems of organizing complex performances.

But classical African dance turned "modern" in another way. Folkloric ballet companies first appeared in the 1950s under the auspices of colonial governments. Since the mid-1960s, almost every African country has produced one or more troupes, either performing mainly for an international audience, like the Ballets Africains de Guinée, or else mainly in African cities in competitive situations, like the Nigerian dance festivals. The second of these trends is closer to the classical pattern, while the first is more spectacular, indeed acrobatic. A new style of ballet may well emerge, but it will probably be closer to the Western art of the circus than to the older traditions of African recreational dancing. The older African dancing was essentially a popular form of amusement for the dancers themselves, not a spectator sport. Because most people danced for fun, new ways of having fun, like soccer matches and social dancing, have actually contributed more to the decline of group dancing in African cities than have competing Western dance forms.

In somewhat the same way, African music was rarely performed to be heard by a silent and fully attentive audience. Passive audiences of any kind are comparatively rare in Africa. Classical African styles based more on rhythm than on melody were little affected by Western models, if only because Western music was comparatively weak on rhythm. But Western melodies did influence vocal music, and the guitar became the favorite accompaniment for songs. Church hymns were also an immediate success in many parts of Africa, sung in the fields and pastures as well as in church.

New kinds of urban music also appeared, with varying roots. Some drew something from political songs, which were a feature of party propaganda before independence, but which were now fitted out with new words to suit all occasions. Other songs commemorated the half-remembered events of the colonial past. Other forms grew out of styles of dance music, like the South African pennywhistle (named for the instrument used), the West African "high life," or the "Brazilian" styles of Central Africa. The Brazilian style, like the high life, involved trans-Atlantic exchange. One major input was vocal music of the lower Zaïre valley, accompanied on the pluriarc, a guitarlike instrument. This music went with the slaves to Brazil, where it was then influenced by other

African and Western strains. It then came back as the cha-cha-cha, the samba, and the like, to be played on disks and radio, and was instantly popular. But with urbanization and the multiplication of urban social centers like bars, Zaïrois singers began to modify it in their own way. By the late 1950s, they too were composing and pressing their own records for export, and the Congo Jazz style, as it was called, penetrated into other parts of Central and East Africa, and west to Nigeria and beyond.

By the 1960s, Kinshasa had become a mecca for singers, of whom Franco was the best known. The new styles had great originality and aesthetic value, while some of the lyrics were among the best popular poetry in African languages. Musicologists sometimes deplore the contamination of classical African music in an age when urban music from all over the world is available through cheap transistor radios, but in fact such "corruption," in Africa as elsewhere, constitutes a source of musical innovation and each new style has to be judged on its own merits.

African composers working in the medium of Western art music are more rare than African graphic artists who use Western styles. Until the recent past, such work was limited to a little religious music for the organ or military music for brass bands, though some group vocal music and works like the well-known *Missa Luba* are genuine works of art in any cultural setting. Musical conservatories outside Egypt date mainly from the postcolonial period, and Western music has not yet attracted creative talent. This is especially true of opera, which seems to be as closely tied to European culture as the kabuki theater is to Japanese. The few Nigerian operas of value have achieved distinction mainly by disregarding the European conventions that surround that form of art.

LITERATURE: ORAL AND WRITTEN

Oral art flourished throughout the colonial period, and oral performances still reign supreme with audiences that remain 70 percent illiterate. Only radio broadcasting competes directly with oral performances, and a lot of broadcast time is still given over to classical song texts and other recitations. The wealth of these oral literatures seems inexhaustible, and African performers are still composing and performing new song texts, poetry, and epic stories. The range of types is enormous, from the formal narration of myths to the telling of long stories night after night, from the daily use of maxims and proverbs to artistic recitation that encapsulates song, proverb, and variations on the basic theme so that each performance is a new creation. Poets and oral performers are still found in all parts of Africa. Some, like the Moroccan troubadors, roam from place to place, performing for new audiences, while others, like the Xhosa women storytellers of South Africa, perform for their neighbors. Whether amateur or professional, large-scale or small, oral performance remains art. Like other art, some products are better than others, and there are rules of composition to be adhered to, violated, or overcome. Some of the sentiments expressed may be trivial, whereas others touch lofty universal themes. Some are long narratives of epic breadth, whereas others are microart, like folk sayings. In any event, they continue to live and to evoke responses down to the present.

Scholars have barely begun to record this treasure house of art, though some remarkable collections already exist. But full recordings in both video and audio are sadly lacking, as they are for the older forms of African dance; and video recordings of an African storyteller are necessary for a full understanding of his or her art. Gestures and expressions which are a part of the complete performance, are inevitably missing in written literature.

This great fund of oral art felt the impact of written literature in the colonial period, but less than one might expect. Content was little changed. Form changed somewhat with the introduction of rhyme, which was sometimes tonal, but occasionally syllabic, as in Swahili. Poets also began to allow themselves less freedom in versification, but this was not universal. Modern Mongo poems in Zaïre are freer than the classic Mongo poetry, even though they incorporate tonal rhyme. On the other hand, the impact of oral on written literature was substantial. This was not simply a matter of writing down the oral literature, sometimes with embellishment. Oral literature also had a more subtle influence on the canons of composition or the stock of symbols and metaphors used. Léopold Senghor's poetry in French, for example, owes a heavy debt to oral literature that only a Senegalese could fully appreciate.

Written literature began to appear first in the early centers of Western education, though most of the earliest African authors wrote in African, not Western languages. One of the earliest works, and one that may still be the African masterpiece of this century, was Thomas Mofolo's *Chaka,* dealing with the key figure of the *mfecane* and first written in Sotho about 1910, though it became famous only after its translation into English in 1931. Mofolo may have seen his work as history, but it was also a towering work of art. Many European critics thought the work "must" have been inspired by Shakespeare. It was not, but such a reaction shows the class to which it belongs.

Flourishing written literatures began in some cases in the nineteenth century and continued into the twentieth in languages as diverse as Xhosa, Zulu, and Sotho in the south; Yoruba, Hausa, Igbo, Twi, and Tiv in West Africa; and Luba, Kongo, Mongo, Rwanda, and others in Central and East Africa. New works also appeared in languages long since committed in writing, such as Malagasy, Swahili, and Somali. And it is important not to neglect Afrikaans as an African language. It is not the same as Dutch, nor was it confined to the Europeans in South Africa. It was the home language of the Cape Coloured people as well, and Afrikaans poetry by Coloured authors has been among the most impressive Afrikaans literature of this century.

These vernacular writings drew on forms and ideas from the West as well as on oral literature. Mofolo was only one among many to be influenced by the style of the King James Bible. And Catholic writers were also influenced by religion. Alexis Kagame of Rwanda wrote a long poem about the creation of the world in which he married instruction in Christian doctrine to local imagery and style. But the most important developments in written literature were postponed until after 1945, though African writers were already gaining experience in Western forms such as serial novels, which appeared by installments in newspapers.

Meanwhile, the Arabic literary revival, with its roots in nineteenth-century Egypt, continued and spread, though Arabic differed from other African languages. It was very widely diffused, and, as the language of a holy book, it had a rich and ancient literary heritage that was influential even where Arabic was not the home language. This influence was felt throughout Muslim Africa, where it affected both the verbal and written literature in languages like Swahili. The Egyptian literary revival was especially impressive after the First World War. Novels, dramas, short stories, and new verse forms were all used, while the earlier and flowery Arabic style became more direct. The Arabic press and the spread of popular education were both important here. After the Second World War, major literary figures began to appear, like Najib Mahfuz, and postwar poetry turned to the use of traditional imagery in a fascinating, if somewhat esoteric way.

European languages were taught in schools, and generations of African children became familiar with their themes and styles, if only through being forced to write essays on such subjects as the joys of haymaking in the French countryside or on equivalent British or Portuguese subjects. These models were too alien to have a direct impact, but they could serve as examples of the way in which landscape or psychological description might someday be used with African subject matter. And the literary form most taught was the novel, which in time was to be the most common form of sub-Saharan written literature.

The French policy of education in French from the beginning partly explains why the French novel appeared first. The first prize-winning novel was *Batouala* by Maran in 1921 — a novel of protest by an Afro-West Indian. A more serious beginning dates from the foundation of the journal *L'étudiant noir* in Paris during the mid-1930s. *Présence africaine* followed after the Second World War. The earliest and most outstanding poet was Léopold Senghor, whose *Chants d'ombre* were written in the thirties, though not published until 1945. Others followed, among them, Camara Laye of Guinea-Conakry whose *Enfant noir* (1953) was an autobiographical prose poem projecting his African childhood into a kind of Utopia. Among later outstanding francophone writers was the poet Tchicaya U'Tamsi, whose poetry built on intricate patterns of Christian, Graeco-Roman, and African themes in a surrealistic vein. The meaning of any poem in the collection could only be grasped by reference to the others, because core images were scattered throughout in varying guises.

Francophone African literature was otherwise remarkable for the large number of very competent authors who appeared after 1955, with novels, poetry, and drama set in such refined French that it seemed almost to imply a disdain for oral literature and vernacular languages, even though these were obvious sources of inspiration. Ideas of negritude provided a common theme. Some artists like Ousmane Sembène, however, went further with intense realism in an effort to portray "the people" as accurately and sympathetically as possible; Sembène also expressed this realism in remarkable films like *Mandabi,* as well as in his novels.

Afro-Portuguese literature is old, but its quality is uneven and it is little known. Some poetry from Angola dates to the 1870s, and poetry was generally more important there than it was in anglophone or francophone territories. As in the French colonies, much of the literature turned on protest against the colonial regime, with influences also coming from the local oral literature and from French ideas about negritude. The novel *As serments da libertade* (Seeds of Liberty, 1965) combined resentment of colonialism, folkloric elements, harmony between Africans and their environment, and a defense of Afro-Euro-peans. Measured by the intent and feeling of the authors, lusophone literature can boast a long and respectable tradition, but little aesthetic value. This may be because few Africans had the chance to write or publish in the Portuguese colonies.

The first major work of Anglo-African literature was Amos Tutuola's *The Palm-Wine Drunkard* of 1952. It had no antecedents in Afro-European ideas about negritude, nor pretentions about the use of English. Written for Nigeri-ans, it strung together a sequence of folk tales in much the same way some European composers have strung together a number of folk tunes to make longer orchestral works. But the strength of Tutuola's books was the strength of his own fantasy and the color of his untutored prose, which alternately falls back on African grammatical forms and rises to ebullient and innovative word formation at the same time that it respects English rules governing usage. A critic's argu-ment about the motive behind this eccentric use of language obscured Tutuola's significance at first. It is now recognized, however, that his works not only were the first important novels in English from tropical Africa; they were also rooted in Nigerian verbal art, with printed precursors in the form of the so-called Onitsha chap books — cheap popular novelettes or plays written in local English, but using extremely visual language and bursting with vitality — though in these entertainment clearly outweighed aesthetic considerations.

With Tutuola, we see that the roots of Anglo-African literature were clearly different from those of French-speaking Africa, and later writers confirmed the difference. It was less highbrow and precious, though some of its masters outdid their French-speaking counterparts — like Chinua Achebe, another Nigerian whose trilogy *Things Fall Apart, The Arrow of God,* and *No Longer at Ease* (1958, 1960, and 1964) are at the very summit of African novels produced so far. In contrast to Tutuola, Achebe's mastery of the English language is superb and the influence of English literature profound; yet the wellsprings of his inspiration remain his home environment. He tells of the colonial impact, not by simple denunciation, but through the play of new influences on varied per-sonalities at successive stages of intensifying culture contact.

Among other Nigerians, the poet John Pepper Clark celebrates the landscape, and his interests as a playwright have led him to study Ijo ritual plays and to follow their patterns, on the model of Yoruba folk opera. The foremost Nigerian playwright, however, was Wole Soyinka. His plays, appearing from 1959, combined a tragic sense of the obstacles to human progress with an incisive satirical approach. Each play was a comment on the state of society and its current values. His sense of the most appropriate forms of speech for the theater was most distinctive, but part of his achievement went back to a skillful interweaving of Yoruba and European themes, images, and techniques.

In Bantu-speaking Africa generally, important writing in English appeared first in South Africa, with East and Central Africa lagging far behind the western part of the continent. The South African tradition dates back to the nineteenth century and was mainly in the hands of "European" writers in English or Africans writing in African languages. Later Africans also wrote in English, but their novels, like those of the European South Africans, dealt first and foremost with race relations. Life under apartheid was so harsh that no novel could escape obsession with color and class. Despite such bestsellers outside South Africa as Allen Paton's *Cry, the Beloved Country* or genuine masterpieces like Nadine Gordimer's *The Conservationist,* few of the political novels were really first-rate, however moving they may have been as tracts for their times. One of the most widely praised is Ezekiel Mphalele's autobiography, *Down Second Avenue* (1959), but many of the best literary minds in southern Africa, including Mphalele himself as well as Nadine Gordimer and Doris Lessing of Zimbabwe, have all gone into more or less voluntary exile in Britain or the United States.

Across all these fields of African religion, art, and letters, the impact of Europe has been too profound for an easy assessment to be possible. Moreover, Western influence has been as strong since the end of the colonial regimes as it was at the high noon of colonialism. Indeed, the results of the colonial period generally only began to bear fruit after the Second World War. A consideration of recent intellectual trends or straws in the wind raises more questions than can be conveniently answered. Has Africa lost its soul, as writers on *africanité* claim? Or is the dominant feature today a continuity between the precolonial past and an emerging culture that is both modern and African? Even the question is badly put, implying, as it does, that two ingredients were present — European and African culture — and that they might be expected to react like two chemicals joining to form a new compound. Some concepts from the social sciences, like syncretism or acculturation, suggest some such process, but cultures do not behave like chemicals. Change occurs and would have occurred with or without stimuli from the outside. European cultures changed remarkably during the period of colonialism in Africa. Classical African cultures changed too, faster perhaps than they might have if they had not been reacting to so many different stimuli, or if African societies had not been changing rapidly at the same time.

But, aside from a few individuals, Africans kept their African ways of life and thought. The stress on négritude arose in the West Indies and in Paris, where contact with alien cultures was most intense. The fears of those who lived and wrote about Africa in that setting were never the nightmares of most Africans; to the great majority, in fact, they were never even a serious concern. As the history of religious change or the vitality of oral literature shows most clearly, Africans chose the foreign elements they wanted to adopt, and they translated those elements into terms congenial to their own collective experience.

SUGGESTIONS FOR FURTHER READING

Abernethy, David B. *The Political Dilemma of Popular Education: An African Case.* Stanford, Cal.: Stanford University Press, 1969.

Barrett, David B. *Schism and Renewal in Africa.* Nairobi: Oxford University Press, 1968.

Horton, R. "On the Rationality of Conversion." *Africa* 45 (1975): 219–235, 377–399.

Jahn, Janheinz. *A History of Neo-African Literature.* London: Faber, 1968.

July, Robert W. *The Origins of Modern African Thought: Its Development in West Africa during the Nineteenth and Twentieth Centuries.* New York: Praeger, 1967.

Mitchell, Richard P. *The Society of the Muslim Brothers.* London: Oxford University Press, 1969.

Moore, Gerald, and Beier, Ulli, eds. *Modern Poetry from Africa.* Harmondsworth, Eng.: Penguin, 1963.

Ranger, Terence O. *Dance and Society in Eastern Africa: The Beni Ngoma.* London: Heinemann, 1975.

Ranger, Terence O., and Weller, John. *Themes in the Christian History of Central Africa.* London: Heinemann, 1975.

Rotberg, Robert I., and Mazrui, Ali. *Protest and Power in Black Africa.* New York: Oxford University Press, 1970.

Sundkler, Bengt. *Zulu Zion and Some Swazi Zionists.* London: Oxford University Press, 1976.

Willett, Frank. *African Art.* London: Thames and Hudson, 1971.

Chapter 19
Social Change
in the Colonial Era

THE CENTRAL QUESTION regarding twentieth-century social change in Africa is how European political power was translated into influence over the fate of African society. Conquest was itself a traumatic act of social change, for it destroyed many of Africa's rulers. The conquerors soon made decisions of fundamental importance, such as whether a colony's farmers were to earn their living on their own land or be forced to work on European-owned farms or mines. Early political and economic decisions directly affected everyday African life. Africans in turn moved to preserve control over their own fate by a variety of means: by resisting conquest, forced labor, and agricultural regulation; by making deals to cooperate with Europeans on negotiated terms; and, most frequently, by ignoring or misunderstanding the requirements of the colonizers.

Misunderstanding was by no means one-sided — the relation between colonizer and colonized, European and African, became in time a working misunderstanding. Its practical implications always varied with the relative power of the two sides. When the rulers controlled a dense administrative structure and a large police force, as in South Africa in the 1950s, room for creative misunderstanding on the African side was limited. When administration was weak, as in isolated sectors of most colonies, subjects could afford to misunderstand their rulers' wishes. Fully autonomous African action against the colonizers' wishes was most frequent when colonial power declined, as it did in West Africa in the 1950s. Within the colonial framework, African social groups and strata defined their positions not only in relation to the rulers, but also in relation to one another.

PATTERNS OF DISEASE

One badly misunderstood aspect of the colonial impact was the pattern of disease. The period just before and after the conquest of Africa was one of epidemiological and ecological disaster. Observers at the time estimated that as much as a third of Buganda's population died in the sleeping sickness epidemic that began in 1902. Estimates for mortality run even higher for the sleeping sickness epidemic in the lower Congo region. At about the same time, smallpox epidemics ravaged the population of scattered areas all the way from Kenya to Nigeria. Statistics show large increases in the death rate among those who came from a distance to work in the South African or Southern Rhodesian gold mines. We have already seen that the death rate on the Congo-Océan railroad was 100 per thousand man-years of labor — as against a death rate that should not have been higher than 20 to 40 per thousand for men at the prime of life who were fortunate enough to stay home. Nor was this an unusual pattern. Workers from the Kenya highlands died at rates as high as 145 per thousand in Mombasa and nearby coastal regions on the eve of the First World War.

The history of disease in Africa is only now attracting sustained research, but some of the causes of high levels of mortality are already apparent. People who moved into new and strange disease environments often lacked the inherited or acquired immunities that protected the local population. Workers from the Kenya highlands who moved to the coast, for example, were not protected from malaria by either the sickle-cell trait or by resistance acquired through childhood infection. At the same time, people in motion also carried new diseases or new strains of disease into regions where they were unfamiliar — regions where people lacked the immunities needed for their protection. Then, too, many migratory or forced workers found themselves with appalling working conditions and a very bad diet at the workplace, and this too helped to account for a higher death rate. Also, epidemic diseases tend to break out only when a sufficiently high concentration of nonimmune population is present. Such concentrations were called together for mining, railway construction, or plantation labor where the density of population became an additional factor making for increased death rates.

The enormous increases in the rural death rate that occurred during the sleeping sickness and smallpox epidemics are much more difficult to explain. Neither sleeping sickness nor smallpox was new in Africa in the colonial period, although it is possible that subtle changes in the sleeping sickness parasite gave this disease renewed virulence. Changes in the African disease environment of the 1890s, however, have been much more carefully substantiated by research so far. The first change was the enormous loss of wildlife and cattle as a result of a sweeping plague of rinderpest, perhaps introduced by the Italians in Eritrea, perhaps by the British who imported Russian cattle to feed their troops in the Nilotic Sudan. Whatever the source, the enormous losses of cattle led to outbreaks of disease among the human population as well, for the control of sleeping sickness depends on the maintenance of a delicate balance among wildlife, cattle, and humans. The decline of herds led to the expansion of bush vegetation, leading, in turn, to the spread of tsetse flies carrying sleeping sickness.

Colonial administrators, who misunderstood the pattern, attempted to control the disease by moving people away from the encroaching bush, leading to still further spread of tsetse flies and sleeping sickness.

The movement of peoples obeying the sleeping sickness regulations was only one part of a much more general pattern of increased population movement in the early colonial period, owing partly to urbanization and economic change, but partly also to the arbitrary requirements of colonial administrators. Local authorities in many places insisted on gathering scattered rural people into large villages for greater government control, thus creating a concentrated nonimmune population for epidemic smallpox. Belgian administrators in the northeastern corner of Zaïre forced people who live scattered on the upper hillsides above the Semliki valley to move down to more accessible villages, to make administrative control easier. A large proportion of the valley's population then died of sleeping sickness.

The new prevalence of death from disease reinforced the psychological impact of conquest. When a woman in southeastern Nigeria was asked in 1930 why the women of her region had rioted in protest against British rule, she answered that, "The land is changed — we are all dying." The colonial officers of that period, in the rare cases when they actually heard what was being said about them, took the talk of life and death — like talk of spirits and mediums — as a romantic but misguided harking back to the ideas of a past era. But the more historians learn of the biological history of the early colonial period, the clearer it becomes that the talk of death was a literal description of what was happening.

In scattered instances all across Africa, disease was taken to be the conscious work of Europeans — a kind of planned biological warfare that could not be separated from the military campaigns of conquest. The disruption accompanying the military act of conquest led frequently to famine, the movement of people in search of security and food, then epidemics among the newly concentrated nonimmune population. Epidemics interacted in still other ways with the events of conquest. In Rhodesia, rinderpest may have helped to provoke the Shona and Ndebele resistance of 1896–97, but, after the revolt and defeat, it also left the Africans dependent for employment on European farms. In Kenya, the pastoral Maasai suffered severely from both rinderpest and bovine pleuropneumonia, which prevented their mounting the kind of military resistance they might have done a few decades earlier. In other instances, the Europeans took a temporary population decrease as an incentive for seizing "uncultivated land" from the Africans, as they did from the Kikuyu in the Kenya central highlands. When the population recovered, it found itself with a land shortage and European settlers occupying much of the best land. As far away as the northern Ivory Coast, Samori Ture found his final resistance against the French weakened by rinderpest that swept away his cattle at a crucial moment. Again and again the disruption of warfare against the Europeans brought population movement and deaths from disease that were far more numerous than those caused by the actual military operations themselves. But serious as these population losses were in the early colonial period, they turned out to be a temporary phenomenon. Most African populations had begun to grow again by the middle decades of the colonial period, with increasing rapidity as time went on, so that many parts of present-day Africa face a problem of overpopulation.

FROM SLAVERY TO MIGRATORY LABOR

One of the most significant social changes enforced by the European rulers was the end of African slavery, and here cross-cultural misunderstanding was especially severe. Slavery in precolonial Africa had had two main uses. A political leader could count on his slaves as followers loyal to him alone, hence as men who could be trusted with administrative tasks, or as soldiers on the model of the slave-soldiers so common throughout the Muslim world. In addition, slavery was a key institution for moving people from place to place when workers were needed for an economic enterprise. After the first generation, they were usually allowed to settle down into some form of social subordination that no longer involved the master's right to resell them into the ranks of newly captured or enslaved people.

The colonial rulers themselves needed to recruit secure followers, and especially soldiers. They, too, needed to promote labor migration for the sake of colonial business. In Europe, meanwhile, the abolition of the slave trade and slavery had been one of the chief public justifications for the expense of colonial conquest. The continuance or reimposition of outright slavery were unacceptable to the home electorate. The colonial rulers in Africa therefore maintained various legal fictions in order to avoid public scandal in Europe while meeting their own needs for labor and those of their African friends. They argued that African "domestic slavery" was illegal within a British "colony," for example, but it could be tolerated within a British "protectorate." It was therefore allowed to continue legally and officially as late as the 1920s in some cases, and it continued illegally and unofficially much later than that. The French sometimes recruited men for the famous military units called *tirailleurs Senegalais* by offering a "recruitment bonus" approximately equal to the value of a slave. Chiefs, even beyond the range of current French control, were encouraged to send forward "recruits," in return for the bonus. Some of the concessionary rubber-gathering firms in the Congo Independent State used soldiers recruited through purchase as the military arm enforcing rubber deliveries, so that slave-soldiers were allowed to lord it over the populace that was theoretically free.

In the longer run, the colonial powers accepted the end of slavery as an obligation that they would sooner or later enforce. But they tended to end it slowly among their African friends and vigorously among their enemies. In the French wars of conquest, resisting chiefs lost their slaves, even though African soldiers on the European side were allowed to keep *captifs*, a euphemism for slaves taken from defeated villages. The British also emancipated slaves with greatest vigor among enemies whose power they were eager to destroy. In the late nineteenth century, the kingdom of Benin in southern Nigeria had first refused to trade with the British. In 1897, it killed most of the members of a British expedition that blundered into the midst of a solemn royal ritual. The punitive expedition that finally took Benin, and plundered it of the now-famous Benin bronze statues, found itself in possession of an empty city. To bring the people back, the first British Resident decreed that all slaves who returned before their masters did would be free, and he later arbitrarily freed great numbers of the king's slaves. Where the British had formed alliances with local rulers, however, slavery was allowed to survive for a longer period, as among the emirates of northern Nigeria and on the east coast plantation island of Zanzibar. In both places around the turn of the century, the emancipation decrees were softened by requiring slaves to claim their freedom in courts controlled by the class of slave masters.

Residues of slavery could be found in both regions fifty years later. On the Arab clove plantations of Zanzibar, the former slaves became squatters who acquired the right to farm land for themselves by continuing to work for their former masters. In northern Nigeria, the children and grandchildren of slaves made payments of grain in return for the right to work land owned by their former masters. One member of the slave-owning class explained to an anthropologist: "If you buy a hen and a rooster in the market and they have chickens, to whom do the chickens belong?"

In many places across the continent, local people remembered which of their neighbors stemmed from free and which from slave families. In some cases, ex-slaves could only marry other low-status people; in others, marriage was open. Sometimes descendants of slave families still take seriously obligations of respect and deference to their former masters, asking formal permission to marry, reporting deaths, and giving small customary gifts on important occasions. Over time, many other families have succeeded in their struggle to leave slave status behind. Some voluntarily paid their former masters a sum that would have freed a slave a hundred years ago. Others chose to begin life anew as freemen simply by moving to a place where no one knew of their servile origins. In many places, freed slaves were among the early converts to Christianity, which offered both the security of a mission institution and a culture radically different from the old one. But freedom from slavery did not usually entail outright rejection of the master's culture. On the East African coast, where the slave owners had been Muslims, the freed slaves showed increasing devotion to Islam, joining and sometimes leading movements to restate fundamental religious ideas in egalitarian terms.

Even as they weakened their subjects' power to coerce labor, the colonial governments brought in their own forms of coerced labor, most general and crude in its enforcement in the early decades of colonial rule. Workers were paid something, but they could be assigned to private European firms that needed cheap labor, as well as used for public works projects. In the early twentieth century, the Portuguese sent "contract laborers" in chains from Angola to the island of São Thomé in the Gulf of Guinea, from which comparatively few returned. British local officials often used their informal patronage of African authorities to recruit workers who would not have responded to wage payments alone.

Before 1910, the French created "liberty villages" for the resettlement of ex-slaves, but rather than protecting former slaves from their masters, they were used as a source of forced labor for government projects. An African who escaped was liable to recapture and one month in prison. The institution shows the Europeans' remarkable capacity for euphemisms in the early colonial period. Conquest was called "pacification," slave settlements were "liberty villages," Africans subjected to forced labor by the Portuguese were called *libertos*.

All across the continent, Africans resisted forced labor. Workers who had been rounded up for mines or plantations deserted. Country people hid in the hills when labor gangs came around. Others adopted the classic ruse of the powerless — feigning stupidity. Farm laborers from one isolated part of East Africa escaped compulsion after an initial period of planting banana seedlings upside down, thus convincing European farmers that they were hopelessly stupid. Over time, forced labor decreased because of African resistance, criticism from Europe, and the fact that compulsion could turn out only limited numbers of workers without a large and expensive police force to ensure that thousands would not slip through the net. In the longer run, economic pressures did the same job at lower cost.

COLONIAL LABOR SUPPLIES

The colonial government affected the everyday lives of all its subjects by establishing economic incentives and constraints to bring about a particular pattern of African participation in the labor force. One device was almost universal after the end of forced labor: the imposition of high levels of taxation, to be paid in cash rather than in kind, compelled Africans to give an important share of their labor to the Europe-centered economy. Compulsion through taxes was only part of the driving force behind increased labor participation, however, for African desires for consumption contributed greatly to the growth of labor for cash. The colonial period presented vastly expanded opportunities for ordinary people to purchase imported consumer goods. Even in very isolated parts of the continent imported cloth, kerosene lamps and fuel, soap, and imported cooking pots all became part of everyday life.

A peasant who needed cash could choose among several uses of his labor: he could sell his own cash crops, work for a wealthier African cash-crop farmer, or work for a European. His choice depended on the pay and working conditions in each case and the extent to which each kind of labor interfered with the production of food crops for subsistence. In colonies where they predominated, European settlers, plantations, or mines could recruit numerous African laborers

if the profits of peasant farming were lower than the wages in the European
sector. In Kenya, Nyasaland, Northern Rhodesia, and Angola, the squatting system
provided an alternative nonwage source of African labor. In Kenya just after the
turn of the century, for example, the government gave settlers 1,000-acre tracts
of agricultural land or 5,000 acres of pastureland. The settlers, in turn, gave
part of their land to African squatters in exchange for labor or for a share of
the African farmer's crops. The squatters' position was fundamentally weak, for
they had no rights on the land they farmed. As land became more expensive, as
settler agriculture was able to use an increasing proportion of it, squatters found
their share reduced. By 1918 the government required every man among the
squatters to work 180 days a year for his settler. Then, in the 1930s, settlers
began to limit the number of acres a squatter could hold and insisted on the
removal of African-owned herds of cattle. Many squatters were ultimately driven
off the land completely, often bitterly remembering that their own grandparents
had lived there before the settlers appeared.

A second technique for creating an inexpensive labor supply was to reduce
the earnings of Africans on their own farms. To a certain extent this happened
naturally, because the settlers had better access to resources. Governments in the
Rhodesias and Kenya made it easier for settlers to procure land near the rail
line for the transport of cash crops. Governments gave large tracts to settlers,
small plots or poor land to African farmers. Government control of duties, of
marketing, and of veterinary services was frequently manipulated to deprive
African farmers of cash income. In Kenya they were not permitted to grow
coffee, supposedly because poorly tended African coffee could spread diseases to
settler farms, but quite clearly because peasants who earned money from their
own crops would not work for low wages. Quarantines imposed by the Kenya
Veterinary Department prohibited African herders from taking their cows to
market. And in Southern Rhodesia, a central marketing board paid African
farmers much lower maize prices than were paid to Europeans.

Economic pressures that were intended to force peasants off their farms
to work cheaply in the local wage economy would fail in a territory where
migrant laborers could seek higher wages beyond its borders. Through most of
the period before World War II, the highly profitable South African mines paid
the highest wages in the southern African region. Southern Rhodesian mines, in
their turn, paid higher wages than settlers to the north of them. As a result, each
territory in the region lost labor to its neighbors further south. Nyasaland settlers
convinced their government to raise taxes, only to find workers heading for
Southern Rhodesia and South Africa, while Southern Rhodesia lost its own
labor to South Africa. Back in the early decades of the century, the Southern
Rhodesian mines made up their deficit through labor recruiters who used compulsion in many cases. Nyasalanders worked voluntarily in Rhodesia if they ran
out of money for food and lodging while heading further south. Once they had
taken jobs, however, they could not leave because a Masters and Servants Ordi-
nance made breaking a labor contract a criminal offense. As the Rhodesian mines

became more and more profitable in the 1920s, they shifted to a higher proportion of voluntary labor, while the labor recruiters took their captives to settler farms.

The pattern of mobile labor had important social consequences. Most wage workers were men, and most of them at first left their wives behind. Even when mining companies encouraged "stabilized labor," as they did in the Belgian Congo after the late 1920s, many migrants were still seasonal workers who left their wives behind. Many remained caught in the South African pattern of oscillating migration (see Chapter 17), which discouraged permanent settlement, contributed greatly to rural impoverishment, and also led to the development of men's and women's subcultures, one focused on life in town and wage employment, the other on the relatively isolated (but interdependent) life of the village.

But the new mobilities also offered some a chance to escape rural social constraints. Young Mossi couples who could not win their parents' consent to marry might elope to the Gold Coast, where work could be found. The choice of leaving was obviously more open to men than to women, who could go along only if their husbands were willing to take them, of if they chose to become prostitutes in town. Women's chances for more respectable urban employment increased in successive generations of urban migration. Only a small proportion of the men who left were never seen or heard from again. For most, the farms at home ensured that they would have enough to eat when they became too old or too ill to work. Migrants thought of the money sent to kinfolk back home as a kind of insurance premium that would guarantee their security in old age.

PEASANT PRODUCTION AND RURAL INEQUALITY

In colonies that derived taxes and export earnings from peasant production rather than from settlers or mines, the ordinary cultivator's range of economic choice was wider, government's control more subtle and indirect. It required greater interference to hold down peasant production in white settler colonies than it did to encourage peasant production. In the earliest period, as we have seen, African farmers usually took the initiative in commercialization, with governments intervening briefly to demonstrate new crops. Significant numbers of agricultural officers took up work in most colonies only during the interwar period, and then with little effect. Before the Second World War, the colonial governments limited their interference in farm production to rare cases of the enforced production of particular crops, usually unprofitable ones. Peasant resentment was turned most often against the large European import-export companies, which bore the popular blame for falling world market commodity prices or rising prices of manufactured imports.

The crucial government decisions determined which regions and which crops were to be favored with transportation and other services. The greatest inequalities, greater than those between rich and poor farmers in cash-crop zones, were between regions served by transport and regions isolated from cash markets. The isolated areas were often so unprofitable from a cash-crop point of view that they were driven to export migrant labor. But they were not necessarily poor in resources — even the richest land without a road or a railway could not pay the farmers' taxes.

In the early colonial period, many of the wealthiest farmers had accumulated capital or taken advantage of a favorable location obtained before conquest. Earlier patterns of stratification therefore continued and were reinforced. In Ghana, the entry into cocoa-growing was made by people in Akwapim, whose geographical position near Accra, a main port town with an outlet for surplus agricultural products, had brought them into production for the market at least by the eighteenth century. In Nigeria, on the other hand, the first to introduce cocoa farming were descendants of the recaptives from slave ships, who had settled in Sierra Leone and then returned in the mid-nineteenth century. With their knowledge of English and of commercial conditions abroad, many became successful merchants and moved from that into cocoa farming. James Davies, one of the earliest large-scale cocoa farmers, followed this pattern. In the 1880s, he took up cocoa farming. By 1892, he owned about 10,000 cocoa trees, which produced several tons a year for export. Further west in the Ivory Coast, the initiative in cocoa growing also came from commercial people — this time from Muslims whose main trade lay north toward the savanna country rather than south toward the coast.

In these and many other cases, the important factors seem to have been experience with production for a market (not for one's own consumption), some accumulation of capital, and a network of information from a wider sphere to guide entrepreneurial decisions. Men who were wealthy and powerful in the old ways had the added advantage of being able to dispose of the labor of clients, who were sometimes relatives, sometimes former slaves. In the Nigeria cocoa areas, many of the first farmers to turn to the new crop were past slave owners who used the freedmen on their farms. But the older pattern of stratification could also be reversed, as it was when freed slaves were the first to go to European schools while their former owners resisted European culture. The former slaves could then emerge as a new class of comparatively wealthy men.

The speed with which inequalities developed in rural areas depended in part on the relative abundance of land suited to the dominant cash crop. Where land was plentiful, successive generations of farmers could take up cash-crop production, and all might rise together. But inequalities could still develop. The Nigerian cocoa region was relatively open to enterprising men. Even the ex-slaves who began as laborers often managed to invest their wages in their own cocoa farms and rise in social position; but by the 1950s, even in this relatively egalitarian situation, about 10 percent of the cocoa farmers held 41 percent of the land planted in cocoa trees. Where land was more limited, a large gap quickly opened between the wealth of those who had enough land to grow cash crops on a large scale and those who did not. In the mountains of Tanganyika, for example, relatively small areas had the rainfall, soil, and temperature needed for growing high-priced *arabica* coffee. Because no other crop was as profitable, farmers with coffee land quickly became wealthier than their neighbors who grew no coffee. People without coffee land nevertheless remained as farmers working the inferior land that was still abundant, but their subsistence was more uncertain and they often had to supplement farming with wage labor.

Land scarcity and the changing economy also changed people's rights to the land. Wholesale seizure of the best land was obvious and revolutionary in South Africa, the Maghrib, and other settler regions. Colonial conquest could also bring about redistribution of the land among Africans. In central Uganda, the ruling oligarchy managed, with British cooperation, to transfer the best land to themselves in European fee-simple ownership.

Land tenures also changed in more subtle ways. In precolonial Africa, enough land was usually available to those who needed to farm it. Valuable land that could be sold was distinguished from free land by the labor invested in clearing it, in planting trees or permanent crops. The local chief, ritual leader, or lineage head gave his permission for newcomers to move into a territory, since their arrival would have implications for local political and kinship arrangements. These political rights of admission to unimproved land were quite separate from the right to sell improvements. Even land with trees or some other permanent labor investment was difficult to sell, once the original clearer or planter had died, for his rights were normally passed on to all his heirs as a group. Rights to use the land for a period might be divided among individual heirs, but the right to sell it to an outsider was dependent on the entire group's unanimous permission. In practice this meant that land was not usually sold.

Two major changes came with the colonial period. First, colonial governments worked on the theory that all land had an owner, even when it was unoccupied and unimproved. In many cases the conquest governments laid claim to all land not under cultivation, awarding some of it to settlers, delimiting some of it as forest reserves, and keeping the remainder for government use or sale. This attitude was quite different from the precolonial chief's right to welcome or turn away newcomers, based as it was on the assumption that land was abundant and not to be sold, and that new followers were to be welcomed as contributing to local armed strength and prestige. The idea of owning the right to sell land that neither you nor your ancestors (nor, for that matter, anyone's ancestors) had worked on was completely foreign. The second change resulted from the increasing scarcity of land as a result of population increase, colonial land seizures, and the growth of opportunities for cash-crop farming. The increasing value of such crop land, or even of fertile land for subsistence crops, created pressures for the definition of individual rights. Permanent labor migrants and those squeezed off the land wanted to be able to sell their rights before leaving, contributing in turn to rural inequality between those who assembled large holdings, smaller peasants, and the landless. Private rights to sell land did not develop uniformly across Africa at the same time. In some places it has not yet come about, whereas in others like the Egyptian Nile valley, where commercialization began much earlier, it had been completed before the onset of the African colonial period.

The individualization of land tenures was at times a matter of government policy. The ruling powers found that collectively held land was hard to buy or sell, and they believed that this immobility of a major factor of production slowed down growth in the settler or export sector. In French Algeria, as far back as the 1850s and 1860s, land ownership was individualized so as to make it available for sale to European settlers — and, incidentally, to break the social solidarity of large lineages whose military power threatened French control. By the time of independence, this policy had not only succeeded in transferring two-fifths of all Algerian farmland to foreign owners; most of the land still held by Algerians also changed from collective to individual ownership. This reduced the great majority of Algerian farmers to plots smaller than twenty-five acres, while many others lost their land altogether and became a landless proletariat of agricultural workers on the European farms — or on those of the Algerians who succeeded in putting together sizable holdings under individual control. The French tried this policy south of the Sahara as well, but without insistence. As a result, the actual individualization of land titles was no greater in French-speaking Africa than it was in English-speaking tropical Africa.

URBANIZATION

Urbanization is a major theme in twentieth-century social history all over the world, and Africa is no exception. Africa had its own forms of city life before the colonial conquest. Alexandria, Carthage, Cairo, and Fez come immediately to mind for North Africa, and urban centers south of the Sahara have also had a distinguished past. Desert-edge towns like Timbuktu and Gao or commercial centers of the savanna like Sennar and Jenné attracted merchants and scholars, artisans and nomads. The mosque and the marketplace served as centers of urban life, which had its own characteristic style of architecture built of adobe in desert hues, the horizontal lines of massed flat-roofed houses broken only by the slender round towers of the mosques. Further south, the Yoruba towns of the forest zone, in what is now southwestern Nigeria, held populations in the tens of thousands, most of whom supported themselves through agriculture. The life of these farmer townspeople was a mirror image of commuter life in modern American suburbs. They preferred town life at the expense of commuting to their farms in the countryside. They remained at their farms overnight during the heaviest agricultural seasons, and those with distant farms stayed in the country for weeks; but the city was home.

Some colonial cities grew up around preconquest centers — Ibadan and Lagos in Nigeria, Mombasa in Kenya, Kampala in Uganda. In North Africa, Algiers and Tunis were ancient centers, while Rabat and its twin town Salée were ancient seaports, but other cities had only been tiny villages, even open fields. Casablanca was virtually a new creation of the colonial period, and Oran grew to prominence mainly because the French used it as their main naval base in Algeria. Throughout Africa, many of the new cities were ports or rail junction points. Nairobi began as a shunting point on the rail line from Mombasa to Lake Victoria. Dar-es-Salaam was a convenient but hitherto insignificant seaport on the Tanganyika coast. As often happened, its choice as the railway terminus meant that it gathered in traffic that had previously flowed through more diverse channels. Much the same was the case with Kinshasa, one of many small trading towns on Stanley Pool, which the Congo Independent State happened to choose as an early headquarters. But because of the extractive nature of the colonial economy, these cities in tropical Africa attracted very little industry until the 1950s and 1960s; their main economic function was to serve the export sector.

In mineral regions, the main cities often grew up around the mines, like Lumumbashi in Zaïre, the copper-belt towns in Zambia, or Johannesburg in South Africa. But the choice of a town as colonial capital also made it attractive to industry later on, if only because it already had a variety of urban services and transportation links. Kaduna, a new junction point and regional capital in northern Nigeria, became an industrial center in competition with the old Hausa cities. Pretoria in South Africa became a major steel manufacturing city long after its original choice as capital of the independent South African Republic before the Anglo-Boer War.

Whatever the original reason for being, most African cities grew rather slowly at first, which is an index of the comparatively low level of capital investment. But urban growth rates increased over time, most rapidly after the Second World War when established cities attracted workers in search of jobs and employers in need of established transport, banking, and skilled labor.

Colonial governments followed a great variety of policies toward urbanization, but two principal types can be distinguished — one of tight control, one loose. Tight control tended to be associated with the colonies south of the Sahara where large numbers of European settlers had gone to live. It was epitomized by the policies of South Africa and Zimbabwe (then Rhodesia). There, urban policy was closely related to the prevalence of oscillating migratory labor to the mines, and with government efforts to segregate the different races from one another.

After the Union of South Africa was formed in 1910, a series of laws began to limit Africans' freedom of movement to and within urban areas. Some were like the Jim Crow laws used to enforce Euro-American racial domination in the United States after the Civil War, but the American legislation took it for granted that "whites" and "blacks" were going to live together in the same society, even while taking it for granted that Euro-Americans would be on top and the Afro-Americans on the bottom. This American form is sometimes called *horizontal race segregation.*

Horizontal segregation had a long history in South Africa, too, but the South African government's response to urbanization was to introduce *vertical segregation* as well, on the theory that Africans belonged in the reserves. They could be allowed to live in urban centers, but never as a right and always with the understanding that they were not citizens at all but, rather, foreigners visiting "European" South Africa. Thus, Africans were not allowed to own land outside the proclaimed reservations. Africans in excess of those needed even in the European rural areas were removed to their so-called homelands. Africans who worked in the cities were obliged to live in special "locations" set aside for their temporary residence. Some were specially constructed townships, like the Soweto townships strung out along a commuter railroad leading into Johannesburg. Others were "compounds" maintained by mining companies near the mines, with barracks for single men who came in to work as unskilled labor. Some of the skyscraper apartments in Johannesburg even had a top floor set aside as a legal "location" for the domestic servants who worked for European tenants; this was so that tenants could have servants on call yet still meet the government requirement that "whites" and "blacks" not live under the same roof. An African had to have a passbook, identifying him and, if he was away from his "homeland," showing that he was legally entitled to be there. This applied to women as well as men. In some diamond-mine compounds, indeed, the workers were not allowed to leave at all during the whole period of the labor contract, and then they had to return directly to their "homelands" or to their country of origin.

During the 1940s, Afrikaner intellectuals modified and further developed a theory justifying vertical segregation under the catchword apartheid, or separateness. Each racial group in South Africa was deemed to be a distinct entity with its own unique culture; each group should "develop along its own lines in its own area"; none had any claims on the government for social or economic equality, much less for political rights outside its "homeland." During the 1950s and 1960s, the National Party, which had come to power in 1948, began to implement apartheid as fully as it could. Real separation of the races was, of course, completely impossible because the economy could not function without African labor. But the government formalized the existence of "homelands" created from the existing African reserves — one "homeland" for each of ten different ethnic groups — Xhosa, Zulu, Tswana, and so on.

Initially, the African authorities in these territories were men whom the government recognized as being the traditional chiefs, and their powers were negligible; later, starting in 1963 with the Transkei, the "homelands" were given a form of local self-government with a parliamentary system, in which all adult members of the appropriate ethnic group, whether they lived in the "homeland" or elsewhere in the Republic, were eligible to vote for members of the "homeland" legislature. The government also attempted to reduce the fragmentation of the "homelands," most of which consisted of numerous tracts of land separated by "white" farms, by a process that involved the forced removal of many thousands of Africans, but of very few Europeans, from their homes.

A similar restructuring took place in the educational system. Previously, schools for Africans had been founded and managed by missions, with small government subsidies, and a few Africans had been admitted to some established universities. In the 1950s, the government assumed direct control over all African school education and prohibited private people from running schools without an official license; the government also created three uniethnic colleges for Xhosa, Zulu, and Sotho-Tswana students, and prohibited the established universities from admitting African students unless they had official dispensation in each individual case.

In Rhodesia, segregation was practiced as firmly as it was in many parts of South Africa; and it was vertical as well as horizontal. The countryside was divided, with the best land along the rail lines reserved for European settlers and the more inaccessible districts reserved for African occupation. Elsewhere, where settlers were present in large numbers, as in Kenya around Nairobi, economic as well as political pressures made it difficult for Africans to flock into town unless they were employed, and their movements were somewhat restricted, though in no case as drastically as in South Africa or Rhodesia.

In much of tropical Africa north of the equator, and in the East African territories of Uganda and Tanganyika, country folk were free to come to the city and leave again as they chose. They were not forced to work exclusively for Europeans, which allowed for a richer texture of jobs, and small businesses came into existence under African owners. Africans could generally own real estate (though sometimes a particular part of town was restricted to European ownership), and such ownership gave security and a path for economic advancement to at least a few. Restrictions on African progress were subtle: exclusion from the most remunerative jobs in government and commercial companies, and the unwillingness of European-owned banks to extend credit for African commerce or real estate. Many Africans came into the towns from rural areas near enough to permit them to commute home for weekends. The security of the nearby farm, along with the comparatively high prices of produce sold in town, made it possible to seek increasingly responsible jobs and to invest in business. These advantages did not exist in the settler territories, where most of the land surrounding the cities was owned by Europeans.

In North Africa, controls on urban life were comparatively loose in spite of the large number of settlers in the Maghrib. During the colonial period, the cities of the Maghrib assumed a characteristic regional form that symbolized many of the social changes that had taken place over the past century. In most cities, the old core was a fortress, like the *Kasbah* of Algiers — a center around which merchants and tradesmen first came together. In time, the city surrounding the fortress was itself surrounded by a wall. Then, with the colonial period, the Europeans found no place for themselves in the crowded alleyways of the old city, so they began to build a *ville nouvelle,* a new city alongside the old with wide boulevards, the latest European style of architecture, smart apartment houses and suburban villas for the well-to-do settlers, as well as a European slum area for those who failed to make it into the colonial middle class. Because the settlers in the Maghrib were mainly urban people, in spite of their role as land-owners, North African cities were often more European than African in population. This was the case in Casablanca, Oran, and Algiers, though less so in smaller or provincial cities. With time, however, and especially in the 1950s and 1960s, a third element came to be added to the complex. This was the unregulated growth of slum areas of homemade housing constructed out of used crates, old timbers, and gasoline drums beaten out flat. These shantytowns, or *bidonvilles* (*bidon* being French for gasoline drum), were home to the unemployed who could no longer find support in the countryside.

By the 1960s, almost every African city had its equivalent, though there were regional variations. In tropical Africa, where the Europeans were comparatively few, a special residential quarter was usually set up toward the end of the nineteenth century as a kind of ghetto for Europeans, justified as a device for protecting them from diseases carried by the Africans, especially malaria. But the African town remained the commercial center and it predominated in the modern city. Something of the Maghribine pattern emerged in northern Nigeria, where the old cities were also surrounded by walls. There, a small administrative quarter for Europeans was planned outside the walls, but alongside it was a *sabon gari,* or strangers' quarter for African newcomers who were not Hausa in language and culture. In time, many of the sabon gari assumed the same commercial role played by the *villes nouvelles* of North Africa, but here the settlers were Africans from southern Nigeria who wanted to cash in on the better educational opportunities available in the southern regions through most of the colonial period.

One profound difference between the settler cities of the South African type and the others was in marriage patterns and the place of women. The settler cities excluded most African women, whether by law, because the alien job structure left few places for women, or because the impoverished male migrants could not afford to bring their wives. By the 1950s, Salisbury, in Rhodesia, had seven men for every woman, while the ratio in Nairobi was five to one. Under these circumstances, the few women felt an enormous pressure toward promiscuity. Where housing was controlled, a woman who came to town in search of independence was often forced to live with a man in order to find a home. In the restricted job market, women supported themselves by domestic labor, beer brewing, and the sale of sexual services. Young wives who came to town from the country with their husbands were besieged by potential lovers, so that many men preferred to leave them behind.

Ratios of men to women were much more even in the loosely controlled cities. Because a very high proportion of women there came from the countryside near the town, they could remain in touch with their parents, brothers, and sisters. Many women in the West African forest towns went into business for themselves as traders. This pattern was different from that of East and Central Africa partly because several West African cultures considered trade to be woman's work; but government policy regarding freedom of movement, African ownership of land near town, and the requirements for traders' licenses were additional factors.

One easy way to dramatize the rapidity of social change in Africa would be to contrast rural life as the old way with urban life as the new. But this would be false and misleading for several reasons. Rural life also changed dramatically in the twentieth century: by 1950, life in the Nigerian countryside was no more like rural life there a hundred years before than urban Nigerian life of that period resembled earlier city living. And, as we have already seen, migrants moved back and forth between country and city, participating in the life of both, so that changes in the life of town and country frequently meshed as a single coherent set of changes in the lives of individuals. Finally, people who moved to the city did not simply strip themselves of their former culture, or their sense of what was just and meaningful. The first generation of migrants brought with them old ideas and institutions, which they then modified to fit the urban context. Other institutions they adopted from their neighbors; still others they created afresh.

Instead of setting up a polarity between rural conservatism and urban dynamism, it would be more accurate to imagine people whose heritage was precious to them, facing new problems in an unfamiliar social context. Some of their changes were a response to the new context. In some sparsely settled rural areas, for example, a woman at home was expected to make tea or offer snacks to almost any distant neighbor who happened to pass by. But rural women who moved to town quickly learned to save their offerings for a few close neighbors. Migrants also left behind full, well-defined networks of kinfolk, only to find a few haphazardly selected relatives in town. Quite commonly, they extended intimate kinship terms to the distant or unrelated people they found in town, calling vague connections "brother," or perhaps addressing the landlady as "mother."

To take care of their needs in the city, they often reconstructed a version of their home social organization. In Kampala, for example, Luo migrants from western Kenya founded a Luo Union in 1947 to care for migrants in distress, to found nurseries and schools, and to form soccer teams or hold dances. But as more migrants poured in, the Luo Union became too unwieldy to deal with burials, or to care for the penniless who had no way of getting home. Subdivisions of the Luo Union were then formed, which paralleled the major territorial subdivisions back home in western Kenya, with migrants from Gem in one group, from Ugenya in another, and so forth. Just as each separate home territory held the lands of several major clans, the territorial units of the Luo Union were divided into clan associations. The home organization was reconstituted so precisely because the Luo were relatively insecure, as non-Ugandans in Kampala, and because they still thought of their farms in Kenya as their real homes.

A similar reconstitution of traditional structure took place in Mushin, a sprawling, seemingly chaotic suburb of Lagos. In this case, the migrants who felt most at home were the Yoruba from just north of the city. In the precolonial Yoruba towns, each local section had its own council, made up of free landowning heads of lineages, while strangers and clients were excluded from the political process. Several levels of councils mediated between the ordinary residents and the *oba,* or chief. After the Second World War, when Mushin began to expand rapidly, the owners of houses began to assume the role of landowning lineage heads, with their tenants as clients. A landowner was expected to mediate disputes among his tenants. Before long, local landowners' councils, very much like the councils of precolonial Yoruba towns, began to form, and then groups of councils united under obas. When cholera struck, or the local market was disrupted, the oba was expected to propitiate the appropriate *orisha,* or Yoruba deity. But new social forms also blended with the old. For example, the obas of Mushin sometimes propitiated the old deities, sometimes made Islamic prayers. In Kampala, men who belonged to the Luo Union might also be members of debating societies including other members from all over East Africa. People could meet one day in an ethnic union, the next in the YMCA.

Similar adaptation to new contexts took place in the countryside, though there the casual observer would find it harder to perceive change, because the villages of adobe houses often looked as though they were relics of a former era. Among the Shambaa of northeastern Tanzania, for example, the economic basis of lineage relationships was revolutionized in the twentieth century, without government officials becoming aware that any such thing had happened. In the nineteenth century, criminal acts had been punished by assessing an indemnity against the individual who had committed the crime, and his lineage was expected to contribute. An offender who failed to pay might be enslaved, perhaps with some of his relatives as well. The lineage therefore kept an emergency fund that was, in a sense, corporately owned, to insure lineage members against enslavement and to use in other crises, especially famine and illness. Those who shared in the fund also joined to pay the bridewealth of young men and to consume the bridewealth of young women. But all this changed with colonial rule. Most lineages divided up their funds, and such funds are now almost unknown. Bridewealth in recent years was paid by the young men themselves or by their fathers, not by the whole lineage. A bride's father received the entire bridewealth.

These fundamental changes took place because colonial rule was a new context. Criminals no longer paid indemnities; they were sent to prison instead. Relatives could have used the common fund for other purposes, but they found it difficult to agree. Should it be used for school fees, for rituals, for traditional or modern medicine, for cash-crop farms, or for migrants' bus fares? Elsewhere, too, as inequalities grew between white-collar workers and farm workers, between large and small farmers, the wealthier preferred to break their economic ties with their poorer relatives. Similar but unnoticed lineage fragmentation took place in a thousand different ways all across Africa.

AFRICAN ELITES

If *elite* is taken to mean those in control, those capable of imposing their will on others, then the primary colonial elite was European. The colonial power, sometimes in consultation with its unofficial business or mission sector, decided on the economic and educational framework. Africans could fight to make space for themselves within that framework, but foreigners made the fundamental decisions — including decisions that governed the fortunes of the African elite groups. It was they who decided which religious leaders would be imprisoned, and which should be given a state subsidy. It was they who set the fundamental educational policies that determined whether a particular colony would have a broad base in Western-style primary education, with few or no university graduates, or whether it would educate a few people to a high standard. It was they who encouraged or discouraged Africans from making their way into cash-crop agriculture or from participating in trade. Fundamental decisions like these indirectly set the social patterns that, in the long run, were to determine who remained in control once the Europeans were gone.

Africans educated to a high standard in European languages owed their influence throughout the colonial period to their ability to negotiate and debate in the language of the conqueror; they were unable in most cases to compete successfully for expatriate jobs (except for the brief period before independence) because education without power was not a sufficient qualification. The coastal intelligentsia, which had been influential on the western side of the continent through the decades before conquest, actually declined with the arrival of European rule. With the expansion of Portuguese rule in Angola, assimilated Africans who had held government jobs were dispossessed by job-seekers newly arrived from Portugal. On the Gold Coast, Africans who had been educated in Europe, and who had held influential jobs in the small British enclave, were reduced to lower-level clerks and administrative assistants when full colonial rule was established at the end of the nineteenth century.

Because many of the educated elite worked for the government or for European firms, salary levels were important in molding the future society. European civil servants were normally paid somewhat more than people with the same qualifications doing the same work would earn in Europe, while Africans were paid a small fraction of that wage. This imbalance was the natural outcome of a system in which Europeans made the basic decisions on educational opportunities for Africans, and on job definitions and salaries for both races. In the mid-1950s, the few Africans permitted to become civil servants in Northern Rhodesia received salaries equal to only 3 to 16 percent of the lowest salaries paid to Europeans. But as the "Africanization" of the civil service accelerated in the 1950s in most of tropical Africa, the principle of equal pay for equal work was introduced, so that salaries paid to Africans were brought into line with those paid to the "expatriate" government workers. This often brought the incomes of African civil servants, and university graduates generally, to higher levels than people of equivalent education enjoyed in Europe — to income levels completely out of line with those prevailing in the colony. In southwestern Nigeria just before independence, an unskilled laborer earned about £75 a year; the most skilled craftsmen earned about £300, but government salaries paid to university graduates began at £750 and rose to £3,000.

Education, in short, was a passport to a comfortable life, and it was a way open to talents at first. Many secondary schools charged school fees, but the able son of an illiterate farmer could often make his way through to a university degree by depending on support from the wider lineage. In the next generation, however, the class lines began to solidify, even though school fees generally were lower and entrance into secondary schools and universities were supposedly based on merit as measured by competitive examinations. The educated first generation read books with their children, made sure they attended good schools, and provided tutors to prepare them for entrance examinations. In Ghana, just after independence, the son of a secondary-school graduate had seventeen times the chance of attending secondary school himself, as compared with the son of an illiterate. A university graduate's son found his chances again doubled. The children of the unschooled still get into African secondary schools and universities, but their chances are smaller each year as the class lines of the future harden.

Against the rise of the Western-educated elite was the continuing power and prestige of the traditional elite: the descendants of the precolonial political authorities and important religious leaders like the heads of the Muslim brotherhoods. Though the old and the new elite groups were not necessarily hostile to one another, their fortunes over time in West Africa form a kind of counterpoint. The educated elite rose in power within the European sphere from the middle third of the nineteenth century on to about the 1890s. Meanwhile, those chiefs who found themselves under European rule tended to lose power. Then, with the rise of European empire, the Europeans needed clients, and the traditional authorities were thought to be more trustworthy and to have prestige the Europeans could use. They therefore entered the administrative structure as *chefs de canton* or as "native authorities" just at the time when pseudoscientific racism in Europe combined with improving health conditions for Europeans in tropical Africa to bring about a wholesale dismissal of educated Africans from the higher posts in the civil services.

This pattern, most prevalent in tropical Africa, can also be seen more dimly in the Maghrib, where the French made tacit alliances with the great lords of the Atlas and the heads of some of the important Muslim brotherhoods, while rejecting the claims of those educated in French, as they also rejected those of the urban *'ulamā*. In the Anglo-Egyptian Sudan, the governors-general introduced a form of indirect rule that allowed them to balance increased authority to provincial leaders against the possibility of a renewed bid for power by the followers of the Mahdi. Even in French West Africa, where colonial rule was theoretically direct rather than indirect, the French used traditional leaders to balance the power of elected representatives in Senegal. And similar tendencies could be found in the Belgian Congo, in Uganda and Tanganyika, and on south through Rhodesia to South Africa, where a part of the scheme of apartheid involved devolution of power to rural chiefs as a makeweight against urban and Westernized opposition from organizations like the African National Congress. In Northern Rhodesia, the government even tried to divide the urban working class by setting up "tribal representation," who, it was hoped, would discourage trade unionism.

The rise of independence movements in the years after the Second World War spelled an end to aristocratic power, at least under its old forms. The new nationalist parties were led by Western-educated people who wanted to take over the machinery of colonial government, not to return to the smaller, precolonial states. They soon began to look on the aristocrats as natural enemies because the aristocrats were beholden to the colonial regime for their official authority. Sometimes the aristocracy held on for a time, as the emirs of northern Nigeria did by organizing their own political party, the Northern People's Congress, in competition with other parties under educated leadership. In Kenya, one of the most important symbolic acts leading up to the armed Mau Mau revolt was the assassination in 1952 of Waruhiu, a senior chief.

A third African elite, the commercial people, had also risen rapidly in power and wealth during the nineteenth century. This was especially so in tropical Africa, not only among the *jallaba,* or petty traders, operating from the upper Nile, but also within the Sierra Leonean and Americo-Liberian trade networks spreading inland from the West African coast, and among the Swahili and Nyamwezi traders of East Africa, or the merchants who provided Samori Ture's first power base in the preforest region of West Africa. Like the educated elite, they suffered a relative decline with the establishment of the colonial governments. Though the quantity of goods traded increased enormously with the coming of railroads and roads, African traders were not always allowed to share equally in the new commerce. But there were important differences from one region to another.

In the Belgian Congo and French Equatorial Africa, the colonial state claimed a monopoly over the product of the soil, which it granted on a concessionary basis to favored European companies. The companies in turn carried trade on their own account, and employed Africans, but no longer in their old role of independent entrepreneurs. A few important groups of Africans, like the Bobangi canoemen of the Congo River, carried on a thriving trade in products of local consumption, but the network that fed the export trade passed into European hands. Large firms controlled the final passage through the ports, while more humble settlers, often of Greek or Portuguese origin, tended to control the collection of produce and the retail distribution of European imports. In East Africa, immigrants from India fell into an equivalent position in retail trade, leaving Africans only a tiny share of trade.

In West Africa, on the other hand, the giant European trading firms such as United African Company took over only the final stages of export and import, leaving a very wide area to be occupied by African "middlemen," who were often women, competing in some places with Syrian and Lebanese immigrants who undertook some of the functions performed by Indians in East Africa. Those who worked closely with the great trading firms, however, worked under such limiting conditions that they rarely rose to be truly independent traders. Here as in Equatorial Africa, the most successful African merchants were those who worked on their own, often in the important commercial sector of nonexported commodities like cattle driven south from the savanna to markets near the coast, kola nuts from the forest to the savanna, or salt from the desert or seaside to the heart of the western Sudan. The result was a large and influential commercial class in West Africa, though only a few became really wealthy.

Meanwhile, intentional colonial policy was largely responsible for the virtual disappearance of the commercial elite in East and Central Africa. Banks and trading firms distrusted Africans, partly as a result of pseudoscientific racism, partly because the Africans seemed to lack the kind of capital resources that would make them good credit risks. Indians, on the other hand, had access to Indian money-lenders, as well as to European banks and trading firms, which also supplied credit to the petty Portuguese and Greek traders. Even in West Africa, the Lebanese had much easier access to bank credit than Africans had, which gave them freedom to operate more independently than the bulk of African middlemen, whose main source of credit was a trading firm that could advance European goods against palm oil or cocoa to be delivered at the end of the crop year. But the immigrant merchants were also strong competitors. They were skilled traders with a long commercial tradition in their homelands; they were ready to put off consumption in favor of reinvestment; and they could operate on low profit margins. Unlike the great European firms, which were few enough to be able to fix prices to their own advantage, they operated competitively in most settings.

The long-term problem was not so much economic as social. In a colonial society that defined privilege in racial terms, it was all too easy for the immigrant trading communities to hold themselves aloof from the rest of the population and to seize whatever advantage they could find as members of the ruling race — or, in the case of the Indians, though taking second place to the Europeans, to claim superiority over their African neighbors. In postcolonial East Africa, the problem of Indian integration is still unsolved.

The last important African elite to emerge was the military, and here again colonial policy played an important role, though administrators obviously gave no thought to the possible consequences of their policies for postcolonial Africa. The British, for example, consciously sought to recruit soldiers from particular ethnic groups they thought of as "martial races." These were usually people from the colonial fringes who had a low level of economic opportunity and education. They formed an inordinate proportion of the colonial armies — and, more significantly, of the noncommissioned officers who were to rise to command positions after independence. There is no evidence that such people were really better suited to soldiering than any others, but the policy — and prophecy — tended to be self-fulfilling. Specialized recruiting had the tactical advantage of maintaining an ethnic split between the military and the people of the colonial capital, who were most likely to cause the government trouble. The Kikuyu of central Kenya, for example, had a negligible role in the colonial army that was called on to suppress a Kikuyu-dominated rebellion in the early 1950s. In Uganda, the focus of politics was in the south, while most soldiers were recruited in the north, with the result that General Idi Amin's military regime of the 1970s could in part be characterized as the domination of a fringe region over the center.

The Belgians, on the other hand, followed the opposite policy, mixing men of various ethnic origins in each military unit. But their policy too contained a fatal flaw. Right up to independence, Africans were not allowed to become officers. At independence, only three Africans had risen to the N.C.O. rank eligible for an officer's commission. This was part of the background of the army's mutiny in 1960, which set off a long and difficult series of civil wars.

The French left a different legacy as a result of their policy of conscripting large numbers of African soldiers for service in the French Empire generally, not merely in Africa. When these forces were cut back in the early 1960s, after the end of the Algerian war, the newly independent nations were left with the serious problem of reintegrating the returned soldiers. When the Togolese head of state refused to provide them with jobs, he was quickly overthrown. Other governments, which were not overthrown, faced threats that seemed equally serious on the surface. More fundamentally, it was the military, rather than the Western-educated or the traditional elite, who became politically dominant in most of tropical Africa. But that was much later, after the colonial period had been ended through a process in which the military hardly played a role.

SUGGESTIONS FOR FURTHER READING

Arrighi, Giovanni, and Saul, John. *Essays on the Political Economy of Africa.* New York: Monthly Review Press, 1973.

Berry, Sara. *Cocoa, Custom, and Socio-Economic Change in Rural Western Nigeria.* London: Oxford University Press, 1975.

Clayton, Anthony, and Savage, Donald. *Government and Labour in Kenya, 1895–1963.* London: Frank Cass, 1974.

Crowder, Michael. *West Africa under Colonial Rule.* London: Hutchinson, 1967.

Epstein, A. L. *Politics in an Urban African Community.* Manchester: Manchester University Press for the Rhodes-Livingstone Institute, 1958.

Ford, John. *The Role of Trypanosomiases in African Ecology.* Oxford: Oxford University Press, Clarendon Press, 1971.

Foster, Philip. *Education and Social Change in Ghana.* London: Routledge and Kegan Paul, 1966.

Hafkin, Nancy J., and Bay, Edna, eds. *Women in Africa.* Stanford, Cal.: Stanford University Press, 1977.

Lloyd, Peter, ed. *The New Elites of Tropical Africa.* London: Oxford University Press for the International African Institute, 1966.

Mitchell, J. Clyde. "Theoretical Orientations in African Urban Studies." In *The Social Anthropology of Complex Societies,* edited by Michael Banton. London: Tavistock Publications, 1966.

Parkin, David. *Neighbours and Nationals in an African City Ward.* London: Routledge and Kegan Paul, 1969.

Sandbrook, Richard, and Cohen, Robin, eds. *The Development of an African Working Class.* London: Longman, 1976.

Simons, H. J., and Simons, R. E. *Class and Colour in South Africa, 1850–1950.* Harmondsworth: Penguin, 1969.

Southall, Aidan, ed. *Social Change in Modern Africa.* London: Oxford University Press for the International African Institute, 1961.

Van Onselen, Charles. *Chibaro: African Mine Labour in Southern Rhodesia, 1900–1933.* London: Pluto Press, 1976.

Wilson, Monica, and Thompson, Leonard, eds. *The Oxford History of South Africa.* Vol. 2. London: Oxford University Press, 1971.

Chapter 20
African Resistance and the Liquidation of European Empire

IN THE BROADEST TERMS, African resistance to European rule took three different forms at three different periods of time. The first and third of these are distinguished by their institutional forms of organization. The first was the resistance to conquest — primary resistance, organized through the precolonial government structures. That category also includes a subtype of state-building resistance, in which the resistance leaders had to create a new political structure, and the obvious examples of this subtype are ʿAbd al-Qādir in Algeria, the Maji-Maji revolt in Tanganyika, and later phases of the Shona and Ndebele "rebellions" in Rhodesia. The third category, on the other hand, was modern nationalism, organized so as to take over the colonial state as the appropriate framework for a renewed and independent African political life.

Primary resistance had ended in most of Africa before the First World War, and modern nationalism scored no victories until after the Second. The period between was dominated by an inconvenient second category, so varied that it hardly deserves to be a category at all. Some resistance was organized around elite political parties like the West African National Congress or the African National Congress in South Africa. Other acts of protest were as various as strikes, riots, religious movements, or peaceful opposition to colonial rule expressed through the press or the political process. This great variety is marked off and defined most clearly by what it was not; it was neither primary resistance nor was it modern nationalism.

THE SEARCH FOR AUTONOMY
AND THE BASES OF UNITY

It is neither possible nor appropriate in a book of this scope to wend our way through the myriad events of protest and resistance. But it is worth looking for patterns of organization and ideology that make it possible to see some of the ways Africans worked together to preserve an area of autonomy for themselves in the colonial world and to discover forms of united action.

One of the principal marks of the interwar search for unity on a scale larger than any local social grouping was the effectiveness of religion at uniting people over a large area. This is no doubt one reason why the most successful state-building efforts from 'Abd al-Qādir through the Sanūsīya to Muhammad Abdille Hassan in Somalia were based on a religion with universal claims. This is one reason why the colonial officials paid careful attention to Islam as a potentially unifying force. Especially in North Africa, the French entered actively into religious politics, suppressing some leaders, but subsidizing others who seemed likely to cooperate and support European rule. Appeal to the name of Islam could be a threat even to Muslim governments. The sweep of religious revolt all across the Sudan in the nineteenth century is illustration enough of the ways in which this appeal could unite people with a variety of different grievances and different goals. Similar movements stopped short of full religious revolt during the colonial period, but such movements as the Hamaliya in the French Sudan (later Mali) and the Muslim Brotherhood in Egypt of the 1940s illustrate the incipient force that might have turned into full-scale rebellion, given the right circumstances.

Christian sects of the "Zionist" type, separated from the European missionaries and from European versions of Christian orthodoxy, were also likely to turn against the colonial regimes. Just before the First World War, for example, Elliot Kamwana organized the Watchtower movement, based on the American sect of Jehovah's Witnesses, in his native Nyasaland (later Malawi), after which it spread through the surrounding colonies. Kamwana, like the parent society, preached the second coming of Christ, but it turned anti-European because he predicted it for 1914, at which time he claimed the millennium would bring the departure of the Europeans, the end of taxation, and a return to African self-government. The threat alarmed the Nyasaland government, which sent Kamwana into exile and tried to break up his following. It failed, as we have seen, and the Watchtower was to be preached very widely through Central Africa and to retain a strong anti-European flavor until the end of the colonial period.

Further north, in the lower Congo about 1920, Simon Kimbangu first gained his religious following in a way that was common to many new African sects, by demonstrating a power to heal; but some of his adherents predicted in 1921 that fire from heaven would wipe out the Europeans, others that Afro-Americans would return to liberate their brothers and sisters. As a result, the Belgian authorities put Kimbangu in prison for the rest of his life, though the movement itself went on, with occasional displays of anti-European sentiment. Even the so-called Ethiopian churches could sometimes serve as a basis for resistance. John Chilembwe of Nyasaland was an orthodox Christian minister who in 1915 made his congregation the nucleus of an open revolt, but this was rapidly suppressed.

Of the various solidarity feelings that could bring people together in protest against colonial rule, one of the most unusual was gender. The most famous example, in 1929–1930, was a set of serious riots in southeastern Nigeria, known as the Aba women's war. Many, if not most, women in the region participated separately from the men. Separate women's action was possible in part because society contained separate women's organizations. Some of the women's grievances were also directed at some of their own men, especially at those who accepted office under the British as "warrant chiefs." The women also came to feel threatened *as women,* especially in regard to their fertility and the survival of their children. Finally, they came to believe that the colonial troops would not fire on them — could not, therefore, impose themselves by force as they had done in defeating their menfolk two decades earlier.

The movement drew on grievances dating as far back as the conquest as well as on sharper memories of the terrible mortality suffered during the postwar influenza epidemic. Western cultural penetration together with a new political thrust through the imposition of warrant chiefs were further disturbing signs. The first women's manifestation came in 1925, when groups of women showed up to dance and sing their opposition in front of the warrant chiefs' compounds. They told people to return to the old ways, to reject Western dress and colonial currency, and sometimes promised that rejection of Western culture would force the British to withdraw. Then, in 1928, the British began collecting taxes for the first time. The next year, they began counting the women as well as the men for census purposes. The women took this to mean that they as well as their men were to be taxed. Even more disturbing, local custom allowed the counting of slaves only. To count free people was therefore boastful before the spirits, tempting them to kill off the living. At the very least it implied that both men and women were slaves.

In 1929, the women moved on in a series of riots, destroying Native Courts the British had set up and looting local stores run by British firms. In the largest confrontation, more than 10,000 women converged on an administrative center, their faces covered with blue paint, and fern-covered sticks in their hands symbolizing unity and danger. In this case, the soldiers fired, killing more than fifty women. The government then made an effort to allay some of the grievances, and the movement died down, though the women remained bitter far into the next decade.

Still another basis for solidarity and common action was a shared economic interest. Consumers could unite in opposition to common grievances like high prices or low quality. Producers could unite as a common corporate group — say, all cocoa farmers, farm workers, and middlemen in opposition to low cocoa prices. Or people at a particular status level could unite — for example, wage earners in favor of higher wages. In colonial Africa, united action by workingmen usually involved a small proportion of a colony's population, while brief movements protesting import prices had a larger popular base and did far more to fuel independence movements. They were especially common in the period of high import prices between 1945 and 1950, coming usually in the form of urban riots, with some looting of alien-owned shops and trading-company warehouses. Some, however, were more impressive and sustained. The Anti-Inflation Campaign Committee on the Gold Coast in January 1948 organized consumers, who refused to buy cotton prints, canned meat, flour, and alcoholic beverages for almost a month, a boycott that finally forced the trading companies to cut their profit margins. This movement supported the political parties simultaneously pushing for self-government, the effort that was to bring Kwame Nkrumah into office as premier in 1951.

Common action by producers was even harder to organize, and the most successful interwar example also comes from the Gold Coast. In 1937, world prices for cocoa were low in any event, but the major trading companies agreed to divide the market and thus to lower the price paid producers. The farmers combined under the leadership of the traditional political authorities, with the general support of all people in the cocoa-growing regions, to "hold up" the crop, keeping most Gold Coast cocoa off the market until the big firms consented to raise the price. The effort produced little immediate relief, but it did alarm the government into investigating the monopolistic practices of the trading firms.

Ordinary labor union activity was easier to organize, if only because fewer people had to be reached. African unions were illegal in South Africa, the most industrialized region. After the collapse of Clements Kadalie's ICU in 1920, only the "European" unions had an effective voice, and they were powerful instruments for maintaining the industrial color bar and the great gap between European and African wages. In the Maghrib and in French-controlled Africa generally, such trade unions as existed tended to affiliate with one or the other of the major trade union federations in France. These in turn tended to associate themselves with the division of the French left into Socialists on the one hand and Communists on the other. The earliest impressive strike action was mounted by the building trades and the dockers of Oran and Algiers in the years 1927–29. The most important of the interwar period came in 1936 with the patching up of the Socialist-Communist conflict and the formation of a United Front in France itself. Serious union activity could then move out from the cities into the countryside, not only in Algeria but in Tunisia and Morocco as well. Tropical Africa, on the other hand, had comparatively few wage laborers, but common action in the West African port towns existed from at least the 1890s. Even in Rhodesia, workers' action in 1899 managed to bring about the financial failure of an especially badly managed mine, simply because migrant workers refused to sign up. But union activity between the wars was comparatively unimportant there.

After 1945, unions took on new significance, and many of the prominent union federations were associated with political parties of the independence movement. But the nationalist leaders and the trade unions tended to part company during the 1950s. This was partly because the independence movement now had real strength far beyond the urban working class and wanted to avoid such a narrow focus. In addition, the most powerful unions were often organized government employees, and leaders of the independence movement could already see themselves as a new generation of management. In any event, of the independence leaders, only Sékou Touré of Guinea-Conakry rose to power through the trade union movement.

ETHNICITY AND NATIONALISM

A final basis for united action was a sense of common culture and shared historical experience. These were also the basis for the European sense of nationhood, but, as we have seen, nationalism in Africa, as expressed by the Western-educated elite, had more to do with their common experience *as Africans* than it did with the historical experience of a particular ethnic group. It was, in short, closely related to present-day Pan-Africanism. Interwar movements that called themselves nationalist appealed for better treatment of all Africans by the colonial powers, for the redress of specific grievances, and for independence in conditions of racial equality only at some time in the future.

At another level in colonial Africa, people had another kind of solidarity with those who came from the same place, shared a way of life, and perhaps shared experience of a particular local form of colonial rule — whether intense settler presence or extreme land shortage. In fact, ethnic loyalty of this sort had more in common with the "nationalism" of nineteenth-century Poland or Ireland than it did with the kind of remedial change advocated by the African National Congress in South Africa. In current newspaper language, however, this sense of African ethnic identity tends to be called "tribalism" rather than nationalism, and the usage causes immense confusion. It tends to distort the fundamental similarities among social processes — in other words, to make Africans seem more different from Europeans or Americans than they are in fact. When French-speakers riot against Flemish-speakers in Belgium, the press calls it a language dispute. When an equivalent event takes place in Africa, the press calls it "tribal warfare." And the press makes a similar error in using the term *tribalism* for events as various as the religious struggles in northern Ireland, the movement for an independent Quebec, or tensions between the Jews and the state in the Soviet Union. This is one reason historians today try to avoid *tribe* as a term of analysis; it can mean altogether too many things to be useful.

The usage also suggests that the African sense of ethnic identity has been there from time immemorial, that ethnic differences are immutable and must necessarily intervene in political life. In fact, people in Africa can change their sense of ethnicity quite rapidly. In Zanzibar in 1924, 33,944 individuals identified themselves as Swahili for census purposes. Only seven years later, the number dropped to 2,066. They still spoke Swahili, but it was no longer fashionable to use Swahili for primary self-identification. In the early years of the Belgian Congo, the Belgians recognized the Bangala as one of the great "tribes" along the Congo River. By 1958, Belgian ethnographers decided that no such tribe existed, though Lingala remained an important trade language.

Colonial policy impinged on people's feelings of ethnic identity in many different ways. The South African state made a conscious attempt to create "homelands" for different "tribes" in an effort to reinforce ethnic feelings and hence to reduce the possibility of united action. It followed so closely a similar policy instituted by the Soviet Union in Central Asia that the "homelands" are often called "Bantustans," after Soviet territories like Kazakhstan or Uzbekistan.

The practice of indirect rule in tropical Africa was designed in part to produce the same end, and it may well have reinforced local solidarity like the feeling of being Asante, as against loyalty to the Gold Coast. It certainly did so in Uganda, where the Ganda people were allowed to keep a representative assembly. They therefore expressed their discontents in terms of ancient Ganda rights, rather than as a generalized set of African grievances against the colonial state. At independence, the narrower solidarity of the Ganda was a real block to national unity for the larger Uganda Protectorate.

In the Maghrib, the French tried to use language rivalries in a similar way. They sensed that the Arab-speaking majority was the most important threat to their rule, provided it could unify the country as a whole. They therefore turned to the Berber-speaking minority, especially in Morocco. In 1930, the most decisive impact of this policy came from the issuance of the "Berber Dahir" in the sultan's name — a decree that had the effect of favoring Berber traditional law rather than Muslim *shar'ia* law. It backfired; rather than rallying Berbers to the French cause, it rallied Muslims in opposition to the colonial regime and inspired the first serious organization that would in time turn into an independence movement.

Some instances of increased ethnicity came only directly from government action. Before the colonial impact, the Kikuyu of central Kenya had no deep consciousness of a common identity, probably because they lived on separate mountain ridges, had very local historical traditions, and no unified political leadership. Then came the expropriation of much of their land to form the "white highlands," the building of Nairobi in their midst, and the concentrated assault of mission Christianity. Their most important common institution was the practice of oath-taking to enforce agreement and unity of action, even though they had no centralized political authority. When they finally reacted to the trauma of the colonial experience in the "Mau Mau" rebellion of 1953, the oath emerged to enforce unity, secrecy, and discipline. Kikuyu feelings of ethnicity were created by the colonial experience, reinforced by new intercommunication in the urban setting, and finally forged in battle through their rising against the British.

But a common culture was not necessarily enough to create an ethnic solidarity all by itself. The colonial experience could also split apart people who were culturally similar. That happened to the Luba Kasai and the Lulua in the Belgian Congo. They still speak the same language, and cultural differences in the precolonial period were negligible; yet a violent hostility developed during the colonial era. First, the Luba Kasai were more drastically uprooted in the period of the slave trade and secondary empire after the middle of the nineteenth century. Being shaken out of their local setting, they tended more often than the Lulua to go to the European schools, while the Lulua kept their old pattern of education for farming. As a result, the Luba Kasai got the best jobs at the mines in Katanga. They became more prosperous agriculturally because the rail line crossed their territory and they could sell their food at the mines as a cash crop. By the 1950s, Lulua land began to be scarce and they too had to go to work in the mines, only to find the Luba Kasai already entrenched in the best positions. The Lulua's response, by 1952, was first to unite in an ethnic association dedicated to improving their competitive position. In 1959, the animosity turned into urban guerrilla warfare of the bloodiest kind, in which the Lulua drove the Luba Kasai out of Lubumbashi. Economic rivalry won out over ethnic similarity, and it came to be channeled through solidarities created during the colonial period itself, not inherited from the past.

Nor was ethnic unity limited to Africans of long-term African descent. The linguistic division between English-speaking and Afrikaans-speaking "European" South Africans was just as much an instance of "tribalism" or ethnic politics as any other. In some ways, it was more bitter than most, because it was strengthened by the heritage of the Anglo-Boer War. The victory of the National Party in South Africa in 1948, then, brought in the domination of a "tribal" minority over the South African state during the next quarter century or more. But the Afrikaner ethnicity had a curious feature. Its self-identity was based on language and race simultaneously, even though the boundaries of race and language were not the same. Language was used to exclude the English-speaking, even though they were fellow Europeans in physical type. Race was used to exclude the Coloured people, even though Afrikaans was their mother tongue.

Given the importance of nationality in European politics, it may seem curious that African ethnic feelings were in fact no more divisive than they were as colonial Africa moved toward independence. Only Somalia succeeded in uniting two previous colonies — British and Italian Somaliland — in a common state based on ethnic identity. Throughout the rest of Africa, the boundaries of the independent states recapitulated those of the colonial states, in spite of the fact that those boundaries often divided African ethnic groups. In several instances since independence, a secession movement has developed into a real threat to the unity of a particular state. In the early 1960s, Katanga (now Shaba) threatened to make good its secession from Zaïre, but it failed. Later, the Ibos of eastern Nigeria fought a civil war for the independence of Biafra as an ethnic state, but that failed too. The mainly non-Muslim peoples of the southern part of the Republic of the Sudan also tried for their independence, but they too were reincorporated.

No general explanation quite covers all these failures, but it is certainly important that virtually every African state is vulnerable to ethnic secession movements, and therefore all states tend to unite against them except in rare cases. The independence movement was first of all an effort to remove European rule. A common ethnicity was a force for unity in that struggle up to a point; it could be used with Asante to create a unified opposition to colonialism, but, at the same time, the very fact of Asante unity was likely to prevent a greater unity of all Gold Coast people against the British.

POLITICAL PARTIES
AND INDEPENDENCE MOVEMENTS

Although ethnic, economic, and religious solidarity were all to play a role in the independence movements, the actual organizations that carried Africa to independence were political parties, organized on the European model. Because the party needed to appeal to as many different kinds of people as possible, parties often played down any connection with a particular ethnic group, just as they came to play down their affiliation with an economic force like organized labor. On the other hand, parties sometimes had strong ethnic backgrounds, in fact if not in theory, and they could use ethnicity as a way of building up a quick grass-roots following in rural areas. The three main parties in Nigeria shortly before and after independence were thus not only representative of the three regions into which the country was divided, they also represented the three main language groups — Ibo, Yoruba, and Hausa. Political parties needed not only to be able to respond to grass-roots opinion, but, if necessary, to create grass-roots opinion by channeling people's felt grievances into common action.

Political parties existed in Africa, both north and south of the Sahara, even before the main colonial conquests began in the 1880s. They continued through the colonial period, wherever any kind of representative political institutions made them possible, and sometimes where they had to function as a kind of lobbying group outside formal political life. We have already seen their appearance in Egypt just before the British take-over in 1882, in the privileged *communes* of Senegal, and in the British West African towns that were able to retain municipal governments. Among the active pressure groups were Clements Kadalie's ICU and the African National Congress in South Africa, the West African National Congress, and the Graduates' General Congress founded in the Anglo-Egyptian Sudan in 1938.

By 1940, some kind of political party, pressure group, or informal organization of "nationalists" existed in almost every African colony. But membership was limited in almost every case to Western-educated, middle-class, and urban Africans who were in a position to understand how the colonial state worked — and who recognized that the best way to achieve independence was to work within the state and ultimately to seize control for themselves, either by force or through negotiation. In the political climate before World War II, however, independence seemed so remote that even the request for ultimate independence was often left out of the nationalists' formal demands — in favor of smaller gains like increased powers of self-government.

Then came the Second World War, which in Africa served as a major catalyst of the independence movements. It sometimes hardened attitudes, sometimes modified them, but everywhere it sharpened and brought out into the open the aspirations for further social, economic, and political change — aspirations that had been building since before the First World War. The problem was to find a way to channel and coordinate the demands of so many different groups and ranks within society. In general, the solution was to broaden the existing tiny, middle-class parties so as to reach the urban workers and the rural masses.

The transition came at different times in different colonies. The Algerian experience is indicative for the Maghrib. In Algeria, the first attempt at mass parties began with the Popular Front in France, which allowed relative electoral freedom in Algeria for the first time in 1937, but the real breakthrough was delayed until the end of the war. In 1946, Messali Hadj joined with others to found the Mouvement pour le Triomphe des Libertées Democratiques (MTLD, or Movement for the Triumph of Democratic Liberties). After shifts in leadership and organization, a fraction of the MTLD went on to become the Front National de la Liberation (FLN), which fought the war of independence against France from 1954 to 1962.

Egypt, of course, had a long tradition of political life in which politics spread gradually to broader sectors of the population, but the first mass parties in the Anglo-Egyptian Sudan appeared only in 1943. One, the Ashiqq' (Brothers), reached the masses through an informal alliance with the religious brotherhood of the Khatmiyya, while the other, the Umma (Nation), worked through the posthumous son of the Mahdi himself. These two parties took up the old rivalries between Sudan's most important religious brotherhoods, each looking ahead to the new kind of relationship that the Sudan would have to have with both Britain and Egypt after the war.

South of the Sahara, mass parties came first in West Africa, where the elite parties had also played a greater role. In the Gold Coast, the main postwar nationalist party was the United Gold Coast Convention (UGCC), the voice both of the Western-educated urban elite and of some of the chiefs in the southern part of the country. In 1949, Kwame Nkrumah, a young man returned from his education in America, split off with some of the younger members, formed the Convention People's Party (CPP), and turned it into a mass party. In Nigeria, Nnamdi Azikiwe's National Congress of Nigeria and the Cameroons (NCNC) was founded in 1944, with an Ibo base but an effort to represent all Nigerians. But until after 1952 it lacked the kind of grass-roots support the CPP enjoyed in the Gold Coast.

In French West Africa, the move from relatively elite parties to mass parties came even later. Political activity was possible in all parts of French West Africa only after 1946, and it then included representation in the National Assembly in Paris. The political parties that emerged were actually quasi federations of local parties, of which the Rassemblement Démocratique Africain (RDA) was the strongest and most broadly based. The move toward grass-roots organization emerged unevenly in the different territories. In some, they were barely effective even at the coming of independence, but the general momentum of the independence movement was strong enough to carry whole sets of colonies with it.

Mass parties were even slower to develop in parts of East and Central Africa, though the independence of Ghana in 1957 provided an example and an inspiration, so that mass parties were in the making almost everywhere by 1958.

The significant fact is the very late appearance of mass parties and electoral politics. African resistance was present from the beginning of the colonial period, but the political instrument that was to lead most of North and tropical Africa to independence came into existence only at the very end. Colonial rhetoric made much of the value of European "tutelage" as a preparation for ultimate independence, but this tutelage was quite uneven. Most Africans adjusted to the world economy, as they had to do. Many of them had a fair chance to encounter Western culture and make their own adjustments to the advantages and disadvantages it held out. But the opportunity to practice electoral politics in the democratic tradition was very limited indeed until the 1950s. African leaders learned first of all how to use political organizations so as to gain power; they had almost no opportunity to practice the harder art of peacefully giving up power after an electoral defeat.

In southern Africa, the nationalist movement took a somewhat different direction because of settler control, but it was not completely different. There too, a more militant stand emerged after the Second World War. When the war ended, the African National Congress (ANC) was still in existence, but it had never been very effective. In 1944, a number of young intellectuals, including Walter Sisulu, Anton Lemebede, Oliver Tambo, and Nelson Mandela, formed a new group that gained control of the ANC in 1949. Their new program included strikes, civil disobedience, and noncooperation in order to coerce the government into repealing its discriminatory laws. In 1952, they elected Albert J. Luthuli as president-general of the Congress. Similar shifts toward militancy came from the South African Indian Congress and a Coloured political organization.

Through the 1950s, the ANC, working in concert with the other two groups and often with liberal "European" or multiracial organizations as well, began a series of nonviolent campaigns in which the main tactic was openly to disobey discriminatory laws, thus courting arrest. In the first campaign in 1952, more than 8,000 people were seized. A second campaign in 1955 led to more arrests and more repressive legislation. This time, the leaders of the alliance were jailed and charged with high treason. But although they were subjected to a long treason trial, none were convicted.

By then, some of the more militant Africans doubted the effectiveness of the alliance and came out for a purely African movement dedicated to the emancipation of the African majority by any possible means — violent or other-wise. After failing to gain control of ANC in 1959, they seceded to form a new Pan-Africanist Congress (PAC) under Robert Sobukwe. In 1960, the PAC began a new campaign, during which large numbers of Africans presented themselves at police stations without their passes, inviting arrest. At the police station in Sharpeville near Johannesburg, the police opened fire on the crowd, killing sixty-nine African protesters. The "Sharpeville massacre" evoked sym-pathy demonstrations all over the country and expressions of sympathy from the outside world, but the government struck back with legislation that outlawed the ANC and PAC alike and went on to outlaw the multiracial Liberal party as well. That ended the Africans' opportunity for open, lawful opposition to the South African political system. African politics in South Africa dropped to a low level of activity from the early 1960s until the mid-1970s, when a new international situation began to emerge in southern Africa.

THE LIQUIDATION OF EUROPEAN EMPIRES IN NORTHERN AND CENTRAL AFRICA

Even as the rise of mass political parties was giving African leaders a new kind of voice for protest in the 1950s, the aftermath of the war gave the Euro-pean powers a new perspective on Africa. As the colonial powers emerged to the shock of victory and devastation in 1945, they did so with good will toward the African colonies for their wartime loyalty and contribution to the Allied victory. They tended to count on continued loyalty, as well as on African resources in the "cold war" they were just beginning to wage against the Soviet Union and its friends. At the same time, anti-colonialism was also increasingly popular. Britain moved rapidly to accept the independence of India and Pakistan in 1947, though France and the Netherlands decided to fight for their continued place in Southeast Asia. It was not until the Dutch failure to reconquer Indo-nesia became apparent in 1950, and the French army met its spectacular disaster at Dien Bien Phu in 1954, that the new configuration of power in the world became obvious, even though it had been foreshadowed as far back as the Rif War in the 1920s. (Perhaps even then it was not quite as obvious as it should have been, because the French were to learn the lesson all over again in Algeria in the late 1950s, as the United States was to learn it in Indochina in the 1960s.)

Nevertheless, in the long perspective of history, the European conquest and the decolonization of Africa took place with amazing rapidity. Only four dec-ades, 1880–1920, account for the bulk of the conquest. Only two decades, 1955–1975, account for most of the liquidation of that empire. One part of the explanation is that the factors behind the conquest were now reversed. After 1945, colonial territory was no longer an important aspect of intra-European rivalries; all European powers were overshadowed by the Soviet Union and the United States, and these superpowers had no African colonies. The ideological background had also shifted away from the racism and cultural chauvinism of the late nineteenth century. Empire-building was no longer considered a moral achievement. On the contrary, to hold on to unwilling colonies was a source of international disrepute in a world where each year more members of the General Assembly belonged to the group that would later be called the Third World.

These factors, however, were only incidental compared with the shift in the balance of military cost. In the late nineteenth century, the known benefit of African empire to a European state was not very large, but the cost of conquest was exceedingly small. By the third quarter of the twentieth, the benefit of African empire was better known, and it was still not large; but the cost of holding on against the opposition of an organized local liberation movement had become astronomic. No European country could afford that cost for long, though the recognition of that fact was slow to emerge.

The first breakthrough toward independence came in the north, in precisely those places where Europeans had kept at least the fiction of holding protectorates. Egypt, for that matter, was formally independent before 1914 and again after 1922, though the reality of British rule went back at least to 1882 and continued in some respects till the mid-1950s. For thirty years after formal independence, Britain retained a treaty right to control Egyptian defense, foreign, and Sudanese affairs, as well as the right to international transit through Egypt by way of the Suez Canal. The newspaper phrase for these continued rights following a period of formal colonization is "neocolonialism," but the reality was hardly different from the kind of "informal empire" that so often preceded formal annexation. In Egypt, the parallels between pre-1914 and post-1922 are even more striking. In either period, such parliamentary institutions as existed were ineffective in dealing with the king, who retained substantial power. They were even more ineffective in dealing with the British occupation. The initial "nationalist" opposition to the British occupation in 1882 came from Egyptian army officers who backed Urabi Pasha's coup and tried to make a military stand in spite of Egypt's weakness. That effort failed, but the final phase of opposition to Britain began in 1952, when another group of army officers, this time organized by Gamal 'Abd al-Nasser, seized power in another coup that ended the monarchy. The new Nasser government reopened negotiations with Britain, which led to a new agreement ending British rule over the Sudan, and gave that country a choice between union with Egypt or separate independence. The Sudan chose separate independence and became, in 1956, the first of the newly independent states south of the Sahara. Meanwhile another agreement ended the British military presence in the Suez Canal zone as of 1955, and this marked the final end of British informal empire.

Ethiopia regained full independence with similar timing. At the beginning of the Second World War, the British navy cut off Italian East Africa from its metropolis. In 1941, British armies began moving in from Kenya and the Sudan, leading to an Italian surrender and the return of Emperor Haile Selassie in 1942. But Ethiopia remained under Britain's informal protection until the end of the war and even into the early postwar years. The final steps toward decolonization in the horn of Africa came only in 1949, when the United Nations placed Italian Somaliland under Italian trusteeship for ten more years but allowed a union of Ethiopia and the former Eritrea in 1952. That act completed the decolonization of the Ethiopian highlands — at least as far as European empires were concerned.

The Maghrib's course to independence was more troubled. Independence movements began in the interwar period in all three Maghribine territories, with the best organized in Tunisia under Habib Bourguiba and the weakest in Morocco. Tunisia and Morocco nevertheless came to independence nearly simultaneously, largely because Sultan Muhammad V of Morocco supported the nationalist cause with the power and prestige that remained to his office. French governments tried a variety of maneuvers, such as sending the king into exile for a time and searching for other allies in Moroccan society, but the resistance movements in the countryside continued and grew through the early 1950s. After the beginning of the Algerian war for independence in 1954, France decided to cut her losses in the two protectorates, granting self-government to Tunisia in 1955, followed by independence in 1956, the same year Morocco also became independent under Muhammad V.

The French regarded Algeria differently. It was legally part of France, not a mere protectorate, and it had far more European settlers. The first postwar revolt broke out in the region of Constantine in 1945, but it was local, brief, and easily suppressed — at the loss of several thousand Algerian lives. The final war began in 1954 when the diverse independence movements united to form the FLN (National Liberation Front) and to call for general rebellion. Military operations were modest at first, but after 1958 the French had to keep more than a half million troops in Algeria. As time passed, the war became increasingly unpopular with the French public, but the Paris government gradually lost its control over Algerian operations to an informal but effective alliance between the French military and the European colonists.

Finally, in 1958, the French army in Algeria revolted successfully against the Fourth Republic. The constitution of the new, Fifth Republic provided for a strong president, initially Charles de Gaulle, but he was not the die-hard imperialist settlers had bargained on. Because he had been leader of the Free French in the Second World War, he was a symbol of patriotism; he could therefore give in where others lacked the political courage to do so. He took France out of Algeria by a series of gradual steps, spread over several years, each executed with the danger of renewed military revolt in the background. When independence finally came in 1962, the settlers and extremist military, organized as the Secret Army Organization (OAS), tried one final coup, but it failed. Almost all the settlers fled to France, in fear of reprisals for their final acts of terrorism.

The independence movement south of the Sahara moved in elaborate counterpoint to the independence movements in Egypt and the Maghrib. The first stage, approximately 1951–1960, brought generally peaceful agreement on independence for British West Africa, Madagascar, French Africa south of the Sahara, and the Belgian Congo. The second stage, overlapping slightly and located in the early 1960s, brought independence to British East and Central Africa, to Rwanda and Burundi, and to the three still-British territories in southern Africa — Botswana, Lesotho, and Swaziland. After a hiatus of nearly ten years, the third stage came in a rush in 1974–75, leaving Namibia (formerly German South West Africa), South Africa, and Rhodesia (Zimbabwe) as the only significant remnants of European power.

Because the end of colonial rule came as rapidly and finally as it did, one can easily forget that the outcome was not what everyone had wanted all along. Britain and France in particular were agreed on the need for colonial reform, but they emerged from their wartime experiences with different objectives. The British were used to the idea of colonies moving toward self-government and then independence within the Commonwealth; the recent examples of India and Pakistan were there for all to see. They expected the process to take a long time in the African colonies but they nevertheless expected it to happen. They tended to distinguish, however, between West Africa, with its comparatively few settlers, and other territories like Kenya and Rhodesia, where settlers, and settlers alone, enjoyed political rights. The problems of European settlement, and of the even larger Indian minorities in Kenya and Tanganyika, suggested that independence there could only follow a long period of gradual preparation and tough bargaining.

In France, independence was not accepted so readily. The postwar period brought a return to the conversionist ideal of the nineteenth century and the hope that African colonies could make steady progress toward equality with France in a wider French Union (later called the French Community), which was similar to the British Commonwealth of Nations, but with more formal ties. As a result, the new political constitutions drawn up for Africa in 1946 began by removing the abuses of the past, like forced labor and some forms of legal inequality. They also brought in new parliamentary bodies to function as embryo legislatures in Madagascar and in each of the colonies that made up the two large federations of French West and French Equatorial Africa.

The most impressive forward movement, however, was the widening of African representation in the French National Assembly itself. African representatives in Paris amounted to only a few dozen, but this handful of African politicians gained a sense of power in a larger setting. They sat in French cabinets, helped to make policy for France as well as for the colonies, not by voting as a colonial bloc but in alliance with several different groups in French political life. That participation paid off in the form of greater equality with France, a gradually broadening franchise, spreading self-government at the municipal level, and other specific gains. It also paid off on the French side, as the Africans voted their support for the war in Indochina, and later for the war in Algeria. In the mid-1950s, many French observers looked back with pride on their achievement in taming the forces of "nationalism" that had brought so much apparent disorder to the political life of nearby British colonies.

Disorder was especially apparent in Nigeria and the Gold Coast during the immediate postwar years, partly because of a vigorous local press, partly because of economic discontents, and partly because of the new mass parties. The British were willing, however, to move toward independence, and the existing elite of chiefs in the countryside and Western-educated leaders in the towns were willing to accept a moderate pace. Not so the young men who gathered around the CPP in the Gold Coast, or Azikiwe's NCNC in Nigeria. They were determined to apply pressure, still short of open revolt, in order to force an earlier timetable. The British faced a choice between speeding the march toward independence by giving in gracefully, or facing a period of repression and bitterness. They decided to give in, with an important symbolic gesture in 1951. Kwame Nkrumah was in jail as a political prisoner, but his CPP won the Gold Coast election. The governor allowed him to leave jail in order to take his place as the newly elected premier. A preparatory period of limited self-government followed, and the Gold Coast became independent under the new name of Ghana in 1957. Nigeria, Sierra Leone, and Gambia followed within the next few years.

Meanwhile, in 1956, French tropical Africa moved a step closer to self-government within the French Community with the passage of a new constitutional, or framework, law (*loi cadre*). It brought in a broad new group of reforms, which had the effect of tying each colony directly to France, though increasing its representation in Paris. But African acquiescence in a form of self-government that was less than full independence began to be eroded by the independence granted Morocco and Tunisia in 1956, independence for Ghana in 1957, and the army revolt that brought General de Gaulle to power in 1958. Along with his offer of self-determination to Algeria, de Gaulle offered French tropical Africa a choice between immediate independence — with an immediate cutoff of all French aid — or continued movement toward self-government within the French Community. The decision was made in September 1958 by special referendum in each colony. Only Guinea-Conakry voted for immediate independence, but the apparent success of the idea of an Afro-French Community was short-lived.

By 1960, the independence movement was already a visible success in the British and Belgian territories of West and Central Africa, as it was in Algeria. France then gave up its effort to keep a formal political hold south of the Sahara. In 1960 and 1961, the former French territories became independent one by one, with continued aid and France's blessing — and a French hope that good grace would preserve good will and create an informal sphere of French neo-colonial influence.

The second-stage movement toward independence for East and Central Africa began with protests, which became more and more vociferous through the decade of the 1950s. Britain and Belgium, however, still refused the concessions that Britain and France had made elsewhere. Up to about 1955, the Belgian government tried to isolate the Congo from the winds of change and did little to prepare it for the independence that others thought was bound to come sooner or later. But isolation failed. Protest movements became better organized and more violent in 1958. By early 1959, it was clear that independence would have to come soon, or else Belgium would face a costly war on the Algerian model. The government then advanced the date and gave the Congo immediate independence in mid-1960. Rwanda and Burundi followed in the next two years.

In British East Africa, unrest among the Kikuyu of Kenya in the years 1952–56 turned into a guerrilla movement that reached open revolt, which the British called "Mau Mau." They suppressed Mau Mau, but the revolt helped highlight the problems facing the minority of overseas Europeans who dominated the economy. One solution was to give up and get out, as the Algerian settlers were finally to do in 1962. Another was for Britain to grant independence on the basis of "one man, one vote" and trust that the future African governments would show forbearance in dealing with their European and Indian minorities. British policy in the late 1950s tried to avoid either course, preferring to set up special constitutional provisions to shield the minorities after independence.

In 1960, however, it became clear that the independence movement was very strong, and no constitutional measures passed before independence could be guaranteed once independence was a fact. One by one, the three East African territories became independent on the basis of "one man, one vote," followed by Zambia and Malawi. But that was the end. In 1965, the Rhodesian government, representing only the overseas European minority, made a unilateral declaration of independence (UDI) from Britain and declared its intention of maintaining its racial monopoly over political power. This time Britain, not France, faced a revolt by its settlers in Africa, and the British government caved in where France had fought. It declared its opposition to any Rhodesian independence that was not based on racial equality, but nevertheless refused to use force. The Rhodesian Europeans gained a decade of grace before the crisis faced them once more.

The Rhodesian settlers' unilateral declaration of independence ended the second stage of sub-Saharan decolonization. For the next nine years, until April 1974, the line of advancing African independence stabilized at the northern frontiers of Angola, Mozambique, and Rhodesia. Independence movements were not dead, but neither the Portuguese nor the settler governments of Rhodesia and South Africa would give in without an all-out fight. Guerrilla movements began a long war of liberation in Guinea-Bissau, Mozambique, and Angola. The Organization of African Unity (OAU) tried to organize international pressure. The African members of the United Nations got a UN vote in favor of economic sanctions against Rhodesia; but many members, including the United States, refused to honor their obligation to comply, while South Africa and Portugal supported Rhodesia. The guerrilla movements fared better over the years, with most of Guinea-Bissau and large parts of Mozambique in rebel hands by 1974.

Then, in April 1974, the Portuguese army revolted in Portugal itself, overthrew the ruling dictatorship, and began a series of social and economic reforms — including decolonization. First Guinea-Bissau, then Mozambique, the Cape Verde Islands, São Thomé and Principe, and finally Angola became independent before the end of 1975.

The Portuguese defection left the Rhodesian government in a precarious position. An African National Congress had been founded there in 1934, but it did not become a dynamic movement until after the Second World War. In 1963, it split into two bitterly hostile factions — the Zimbabwe African People's Union (ZAPU) and the Zimbabwe African National Union (ZANU), which were divided by ideological, personal, and some ethnic differences. From their bases in Zambia and Mozambique, both began to send guerrilla units into Rhodesia with increasing strength and frequency from 1975 onward. The Europeans in Rhodesia were more and more dependent on South African support, but South Africa began to doubt the long-term wisdom of propping up a government supported by only 5 percent of its own people and recognized by no other nation in the world. The United States government also became alarmed that racial warfare in Rhodesia might encourage Russian or Chinese intervention on the African side. In 1976, South African and American pressure together persuaded Rhodesia to negotiate with representatives of the African nationalist movements.

The independence of Angola also put pressure on South Africa, particularly in regard to Namibia, which had been assigned in 1919 to South Africa as a mandated territory under the League of Nations. After the Second World War, it should have moved toward independence like the other mandated territories, but South Africa held on. Meanwhile, the South West African People's Organization (SWAPO) received UN recognition as the only legitimate representative of South West Africa, and it began to prepare for possible guerrilla campaigns like those launched into Rhodesia. South Africa planned to grant independence by 1978 under a form of apartheid that would divide South West Africa into eleven states, one controlled by the Europeans and endowed with most of the land and mineral resources, with ten client states representing the ten principal African ethnic groups.

In South Africa home territory, other signs of instability appeared in the mid-1970s, often coming from the very institutions the government had created to defuse and divide resistance to European supremacy. In spite of their weak economic position, the leaders of the eight "homelands" were not the mere clients the government had intended. Gatsha Buthelezi, prime minister of the Zulu, organized his opposite members in the other homelands and declared that Africans should seek fulfillment "not in unreal separate freedoms, but in one South Africa, and in the only seat of power: Parliament." Nor were the Coloured people appeased by their separate Coloured Council. Even the uni-ethnic African university colleges began to generate a vigorous black consciousness movement, denying European cultural superiority, emphasizing the integrity of African culture, not the ethnic divisions, and seeking to politicize the African masses. Moreover, African workers in many of the cities staged a series of strikes in defiance of the law.

The government response was a combination of suppression and reform. It arrested whatever resistance leaders it could locate, reduced freedom of the press, answered force with force in urban riots, and tried to persuade the "homeland" leaders to accept independence, so that many Africans would become "foreigners" without any claim to political rights in the rest of South Africa. The government also opened some previously segregated facilities, and encouraged industry to raise Africans' wages — though not to the point of giving them equal pay for equal work. It managed to break the solidarity of the homelands by persuading Transkei to opt for a separate independence, and it renewed its efforts to establish diplomatic relations with tropical African states and to improve its image abroad. The new wave of decolonization might sweep through Zimbabwe and Namibia, but there was still no secure sign in the mid-1970s that it would end white racial domination over South Africa.

Index

Italics indicate references to maps.